4th Edition

파고다 토익 RC
고득점 완성

4th Edition

파고다 토익 ⓡⓒ 고득점 완성

초 판 1쇄	발행	2016년	4월	29일
개정 2판 1쇄	발행	2016년	12월	26일
개정 3판 1쇄	발행	2019년	1월	5일
개정 4판 1쇄	인쇄	2023년	10월	31일
개정 4판 2쇄	발행	2024년	9월	4일

지 은 이 | 파고다교육그룹 언어교육연구소, 라수진
펴 낸 이 | 박경실
펴 낸 곳 | **PAGODA Books** 파고다북스
출판등록 | 2005년 5월 27일 제 300-2005-90호
주   소 | 06614 서울특별시 서초구 강남대로 419, 19층(서초동, 파고다타워)
전   화 | (02) 6940-4070
팩   스 | (02) 536-0660
홈페이지 | www.pagodabook.com

저작권자 | ⓒ 2023 파고다아카데미, 파고다 에스씨에스

ISBN 978-89-6281-909-0 (13740)

파고다북스	www.pagodabook.com
파고다 어학원	www.pagoda21.com
파고다 인강	www.pagodastar.com
테스트 클리닉	www.testclinic.com

Ⅰ 낙장 및 파본은 구매처에서 교환해 드립니다.

4th Edition
파고다교육그룹 언어교육연구소, 라수진 | 저

파고다 토익 RC

® RC

고득점 완성

PAGODA Books

파고다 토익 프로그램

독학자를 위한 다양하고 풍부한 학습 자료

각종 학습 자료가 쏟아지는

파고다 토익 공식 온라인 카페
http://cafe.naver.com/pagodatoeicbooks

교재 Q&A
교재 학습 자료
나의 학습 코칭
정기 토익 분석 자료
기출 분석 자료
예상 적중 특강
논란 종결 총평

온라인 모의고사 2회분
받아쓰기 훈련 자료
단어 암기장
단어 시험지
MP3 기본 버전
추가 연습 문제 등 각종 추가 자료

파고다 토익 기본 완성 LC/RC
토익 기초 입문서
토익 초보 학습자들이 단기간에 쉽게 접근할 수 있도록 토익의 필수 개념을 집약한 입문서

파고다 토익 실력 완성 LC/RC
토익 개념&실전 종합서
토익의 기본 개념을 확실히 다질 수 있는 풍부한 문제 유형과 실전형 연습 문제를 담은 훈련서

파고다 토익 고득점 완성 LC/RC
최상위권 토익 만점 전략서
기본기를 충분히 다진 토익 중상위권들의 고득점 완성을 위해 핵심 스킬만을 뽑아낸 토익 전략서

600+ 700+ 800+

파고다 토익 입문서 LC/RC
기초와 최신 경향 문제 완벽 적응 입문서
개념-핵심 스킬-집중 훈련의 반복을 통해 기초와 실전에서 유용한 전략을 동시에 익히는 입문서

파고다 토익 종합서 LC/RC
중상위권이 고득점으로 가는 도움닫기 종합서
고득점 도약을 향한 한 끗 차이의 간격을 좁히는 종합서

이제는 인강도 밀착 관리!
체계적인 학습 관리와 목표 달성까지 가능한
파고다 토익 인생 점수반
www.pagodastar.com

최단기간 목표 달성 보장
X10배속 토익
현강으로 직접 듣는 1타 강사의 노하우
파고다 토익 점수 보장반
www.pagoda21.com

파고다 토익 적중 실전 LC/RC
최신 경향 실전 모의고사 10회분
끊임없이 변화하는 토익 트렌드에 대처하기 위해
적중률 높은 문제만을 엄선한 토익 실전서

900+　VOCA+

파고다 토익 실전 1000제 LC/RC
LC/RC 실전 모의고사 10회분(1000제)
문제 구성과 난이도까지 동일한 최신 경향 모의고사
와 200% 이해력 상승시키는 온라인 및 모바일
해설서 구성의 실전서

파고다 토익 VOCA
LC, RC 목표 점수별 필수 어휘 30일 완성
600+, 700+, 800+, 900+ 목표 점수별,
우선순위별 필수 어휘 1500

목차

PART 5 GRAMMAR

PART 5 VOCA

Actual Test 3회분 및 해설은 www.pagodabook.com에서 무료로 다운로드 가능합니다.

이 책의 구성과 특징

>> **PART 5** GRAMMAR 토익 중·고급자들을 위한 토익 핵심 문법과 문제 유형을 학습한다.
VOCA Part 5, 6 필수 동사, 명사, 형용사, 부사 어휘를 핵심 어휘 문제로 정리한다.

>> **PART 6** Part 5에서 학습한 어법 적용 문제, 어휘 문제, 글의 흐름상 빈칸에 알맞은 문장을 고르는 문제에도 충분히 대비한다.

>> **PART 7** 문제 유형별 해결 전략과 지문의 종류 및 주제별 해결 전략을 학습한다.

OVERVIEW

본격적인 학습의 준비 단계로, 각 Part별
출제 경향 및 문제 유형, 그에 따른 접근
전략을 정리하였다.

핵심 문법

UNIT별 기본 개념을 예제과 함께 익히고,
정답에 쉽게 접근할 수 있는 문제 풀이 전
략을 제시하였다.

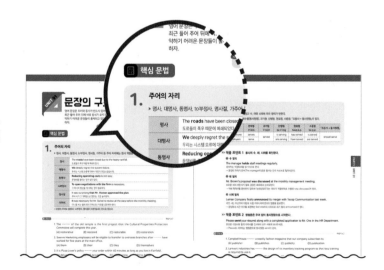

Practice

다양한 토익 실전 문제를 접할 수 있도록 핵심 빈출 유형과 고난이도 문제를 각 Part별로 골고루 구성하였다.

PART 5 GRAMMAR 24~25문항
　　　　　　VOCA 10문항
PART 6 16문항
PART 7 지문 유형별 3~6지문

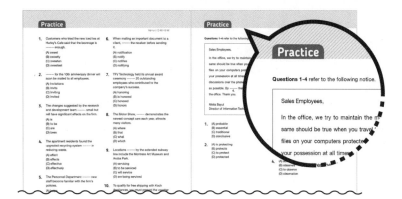

REVIEW TEST

각 Part별 학습한 내용을 마지막으로 체크할 수 있도록 정기 토익 시험과 동일한 유형과 난이도의 단원 복습 문제를 제공하였다.

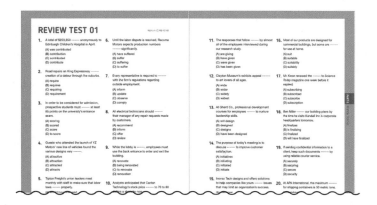

ACTUAL TEST

토익 시험 전 학습한 내용을 점검할 수 있도록 실제 정기 토익과 가장 유사한 형태의 모의고사 3회분을 제공하였다.

(www.pagodabook.com에서 무료로 다운로드 가능)

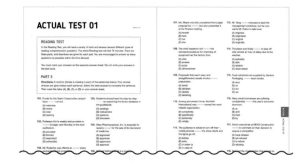

토익이란?

TOEIC(Test of English for International Communication)은 영어가 모국어가 아닌 사람들을 대상으로 일상생활 또는 국제 업무 등에 필요한 실용 영어 능력을 평가하는 시험입니다.

상대방과 '의사소통할 수 있는 능력(Communication ability)'을 평가하는 데 중점을 두고 있으므로 영어에 대한 '지식'이 아니라 영어의 실용적이고 기능적인 '사용법'을 묻는 문항들이 출제됩니다.

TOEIC은 1979년 미국 ETS(Educational Testing Service)에 의해 개발된 이래 전 세계 160개 이상의 국가 14,000여 개의 기관에서 승진 또는 해외 파견 인원 선발 등의 목적으로 널리 활용하고 있으며 우리나라에는 1982년 도입되었습니다. 해마다 전 세계적으로 약 700만 명 이상이 응시하고 있습니다.

≫ 토익 시험의 구성

	파트	시험 형태		문항 수	시간	배점
듣기 (LC)	1	사진 묘사		6	45분	495점
	2	질의응답		25		
	3	짧은 대화		39		
	4	짧은 담화		30		
				100		
읽기 (RC)	5	단문 공란 메우기 (문법/어휘)		30	75분	495점
	6	장문 공란 메우기		16		
	7	독해	단일 지문	29		
			이중 지문	10		
			삼중 지문	15		
				100		
계	7 Parts			200문항	120분	990점

1979 첫 토익

2006 NEW 토익

2016 신 토익

Present

토익 시험 접수와 성적 확인

토익 시험은 TOEIC 위원회 웹사이트(www.toeic.co.kr)에서 접수할 수 있습니다. 본인이 원하는 날짜와 장소를 지정하고 필수 기재 항목을 기재한 후 본인 사진을 업로드하면 간단하게 끝납니다.

보통은 두 달 후에 있는 시험일까지 접수 가능합니다. 각 시험일의 정기 접수는 시험일로부터 2주 전에 마감되지만, 시험일의 3일 전까지 추가 접수할 수 있는 특별 접수 기간이 있습니다. 그러나 특별 추가 접수 기간에는 응시료가 4,800원 더 비싸며, 희망하는 시험장을 선택할 수 없는 경우도 발생할 수 있습니다.

성적은 시험일로부터 12~15일 후에 인터넷이나 ARS(060-800-0515)를 통해 확인할 수 있습니다.

성적표는 우편이나 온라인으로 발급받을 수 있습니다. 우편으로 발급 받을 경우는 성적 발표 후 대략 일주일이 소요되며, 온라인 발급을 선택하면 유효 기간 내에 홈페이지에서 본인이 직접 1회에 한해 무료 출력할 수 있습니다.

시험 당일 준비물

시험 당일 준비물은 규정 신분증, 연필, 지우개입니다. 허용되는 규정 신분증은 토익 공식 웹사이트에서 확인하시기 바랍니다. 필기구는 연필이나 샤프펜만 가능하고 볼펜이나 컴퓨터용 사인펜은 사용할 수 없습니다. 수험표는 출력해 가지 않아도 됩니다.

시험 진행 안내

시험 진행 일정은 시험 당일 고사장 사정에 따라 약간씩 다를 수 있지만 대부분 아래와 같이 진행됩니다.

>> 시험 시간이 오전일 경우

AM 9:30~9:45	AM 9:45~9:50	AM 9:50~10:05	AM 10:05~10:10	AM 10:10~10:55	AM 10:55~12:10
15분	5분	15분	5분	45분	75분
답안지 작성에 관한 Orientation	수험자 휴식 시간	신분증 확인 (감독 교사)	문제지 배부, 파본 확인	듣기 평가(LC)	읽기 평가(RC) 2차 신분증 확인

* 주의: 오전 9시 50분 입실 통제

>> 시험 시간이 오후일 경우

PM 2:30~2:45	PM 2:45~2:50	PM 2:50~3:05	PM 3:05~3:10	PM 3:10~3:55	PM 3:55~5:10
15분	5분	15분	5분	45분	75분
답안지 작성에 관한 Orientation	수험자 휴식 시간	신분증 확인 (감독 교사)	문제지 배부, 파본 확인	듣기 평가(LC)	읽기 평가(RC) 2차 신분증 확인

* 주의: 오후 2시 50분 입실 통제

파트별 토익 소개

PART 5

INCOMPLETE SENTENCES
단문 공란 메우기

PART 5는 빈칸이 포함된 짧은 문장과 4개의 보기를 주고 빈칸에 들어갈 가장 알맞은 보기를 고르는 문제로, 총 30문제가 출제된다. 크게 문장 구조/문법 문제와 어휘 문제로 문제 유형이 나뉜다.

문항 수	30문항(101~130번에 해당합니다.)
문제 유형	- 문장 구조/문법 문제: 빈칸의 자리를 파악하여 보기 중 알맞은 품사나 형태를 고르는 문제와 문장의 구조를 파악하고 구와 절을 구분하여 빈칸에 알맞은 접속사나 전치사, 또는 부사 등을 고르는 문제 - 어휘 문제: 같은 품사의 4개 어휘 중에서 정확한 용례를 파악하여 빈칸에 알맞은 단어를 고르는 문제
보기 구성	4개의 보기

▶▶ 시험지에 인쇄되어 있는 모양

어형 문제
▶▶

101. The final due date for ------- of all budget reports has been pushed back for three days.

(A) complete (B) completing
(C) completion (D) completely

어휘 문제
▶▶

102. After being employed at a Tokyo-based technology firm for two decades, Ms. Mayne ------- to Vancouver to start her own IT company.

(A) visited (B) returned
(C) happened (D) compared

문법 문제
▶▶

103. ------- the demand for the PFS-2x smartphone, production will be tripled next quarter.

(A) Even if (B) Just as
(C) As a result of (D) Moreover

정답 **101.**(C) **102.**(B) **103.**(C)

PART 6

TEXT COMPLETION
장문 공란 메우기

Part 6는 4개의 지문에 각각 4개의 문항이 나와 총 16문제가 출제되며, Part 5와 같은 문제이나, 맥락을 파악해 정답을 골라야 한다. 편지, 이메일 등의 다양한 지문이 출제되며, 크게 문장 구조/문법을 묻는 문제, 어휘 문제, 문장 선택 문제로 문제 유형이 나뉜다.

문항 수	4개 지문, 16문항(131~146번에 해당합니다.)
지문 유형	설명서, 편지, 이메일, 기사, 공지, 지시문, 광고, 회람, 발표문, 정보문 등
문제 유형	- 문장 구조 / 문법 문제: 문장 구조, 문맥상 어울리는 시제 등을 고르는 문제 - 어휘 문제: 같은 품사의 네 개 어휘 중에서 문맥상 알맞은 단어를 고르는 문제 - 문장 선택 문제: 앞, 뒤 문맥을 파악하여 네 개의 문장 중에서 알맞은 문장을 고르는 문제
보기 구성	4개의 보기

▶▶ 시험지에 인쇄되어 있는 모양

Questions 131-134 refer to the following e-mail.

To: sford@etnnet.com
From: customersupprt@interhostptimes.ca
Date: July 1
Subject: Re: Your Subscription

Congratulations on becoming a reader of *International Hospitality Times*. ----131---- the plan you have subscribed to, you will not only have unlimited access to our online content, but you will also receive our hard copy edition each month. If you wish to ----132---- your subscription preferences, contact our Customer Support Center at +28 07896 325422. Most ----133---- may also make updates to their accounts on our website at www.interhosptimes.ca. Please note that due to compatibility issues, it may not be possible for customers in certain countries to access their accounts online. ----134----. Your business is greatly appreciated.

International Hospitality Times

문법 문제
▶▶

131. (A) Besides
(B) As if
(C) Under
(D) Prior to

어휘 문제
▶▶

132. (A) purchase
(B) modify
(C) collect
(D) inform

어형 문제
▶▶

133. (A) read
(B) readable
(C) readers
(D) reading

문장 삽입 문제
▶▶

134. (A) We have branches in over 30 countries around the globe.
(B) We provide online content that includes Web extras and archives.
(C) We are working to make this service available to all readers soon.
(D) We would like to remind you that your contract expires this month.

정답 **131.**(C) **132.**(B) **133.**(C) **134.**(C)

PART 7

READING COMPREHENSION
독해

Part 7은 단일·이중·삼중 지문을 읽고 그에 딸린 2~5개의 문제를 푸는 형태로, 총 15개 지문, 54문제가 출제되어 RC 전체 문항의 절반 이상을 차지한다. 같은 의미의 패러프레이징된 표현에 주의하고, 문맥을 파악하는 연습을 한다. 키워드 파악은 문제 해결의 기본이다.

문항 수	54문항(147~200번에 해당합니다.)
지문 유형	- 단일 지문: 이메일, 편지, 문자 메시지, 온라인 채팅, 광고, 기사, 양식, 회람, 공지, 웹페이지 등 - 이중 지문: 이메일/이메일, 기사/이메일, 웹페이지/이메일 등 - 삼중 지문: 다양한 세 지문들의 조합
문제 유형	- 핵심 정보: 주제 또는 제목과 같이 가장 핵심적인 내용을 파악하는 문제 - 특정 정보: 세부 사항을 묻는 문제로, 모든 질문이 의문사로 시작하며 지문에서 질문의 키워드와 관련된 부분을 읽고 정답을 찾는 문제 - NOT: 지문을 읽는 동안 보기 중에서 지문의 내용과 일치하는 보기를 대조해서 소거하는 문제 - 추론: 지문의 내용을 바탕으로 전체 흐름을 이해하며 지문에 직접 언급되지 않은 사항을 추론하는 문제 - 화자 의도 파악: 화자의 의도를 묻는 문제로, 문자 메시지나 2인 형태의 대화로 출제되며 온라인 채팅은 3인 이상의 대화 형태로 출제 - 동의어: 주어진 단어의 사전적 의미가 아니라 문맥상의 의미와 가장 가까운 단어를 고르는 문제 - 문장 삽입: 지문의 흐름상 주어진 문장이 들어갈 적절한 위치를 고르는 문제로, 세부적인 정보보다 전체적인 문맥 파악이 중요한 문제
보기 구성	4개의 보기

▶▶ 시험지에 인쇄되어 있는 모양

Questions 151-152 refer to the following text message chain.

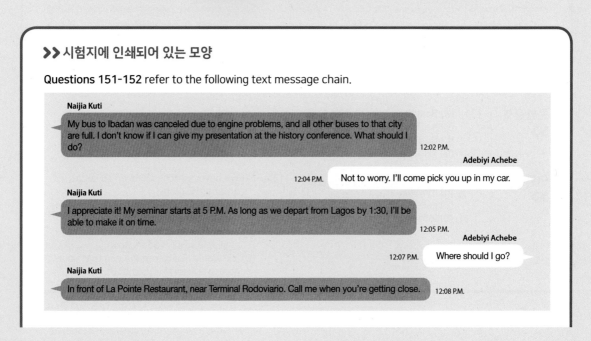

Naijia Kuti

My bus to Ibadan was canceled due to engine problems, and all other buses to that city are full. I don't know if I can give my presentation at the history conference. What should I do?

12:02 P.M.

Adebiyi Achebe

12:04 P.M.   Not to worry. I'll come pick you up in my car.

Naijia Kuti

I appreciate it! My seminar starts at 5 P.M. As long as we depart from Lagos by 1:30, I'll be able to make it on time.

12:05 P.M.

Adebiyi Achebe

12:07 P.M.   Where should I go?

Naijia Kuti

In front of La Pointe Restaurant, near Terminal Rodoviario. Call me when you're getting close.   12:08 P.M.

151. At 12:04 P.M., what does Mr. Achebe most likely mean when he writes, "Not to worry"?
(A) He has a solution to Ms. Kuti's problem.
(B) He can reschedule a presentation.
(C) He knows another bus will arrive soon.
(D) He is happy to cover Ms. Kuti's shift.

152. What is implied about Ms. Kuti?
(A) She has a meeting at a restaurant.
(B) She is going to be late for a seminar.
(C) She plans to pick up a client at 1:30 P.M.
(D) She is within driving distance of a conference.

정답 151.(A) 152.(D)

Questions 158-160 refer to the following Web page.

http://www.sdayrealestate.com/listing18293

Looking for a new home for your family? This house, located on 18293 Winding Grove, was remodeled last month. It features 2,500 square feet of floor space, with 5,000 square feet devoted to a gorgeous backyard. Also included is a 625 square feet garage that can comfortably fit two mid-sized vehicles. —[1]—. Located just a five-minute drive from the Fairweather Metro Station, this property allows for easy access to the downtown area, while providing plenty of room for you and your family. —[2]—. A serene lake is just 100–feet walk away from the house. —[3]—. A 15 percent down payment is required to secure the property. —[4]—. For more detailed information or to arrange a showing, please email Jerry@sdayrealestate.com.

158. How large is the parking space?
(A) 100 square feet
(B) 625 square feet
(C) 2,500 square feet
(D) 5,000 square feet

159. What is NOT stated as an advantage of the property?
(A) It has a spacious design.
(B) It has been recently renovated.
(C) It is in a quiet neighborhood.
(D) It is near public transportation.

160. In which of the positions marked [1], [2], [3], and [4] does the following sentence best belong?

"A smaller amount may be accepted, depending on the buyer's financial circumstances."

(A) [1]
(B) [2]
(C) [3]
(D) [4]

정답 158.(B) 159.(C) 160.(D)

학습 플랜

4주 플랜

DAY 1	DAY 2	DAY 3	DAY 4	DAY 5
[PART 5 GRAMMAR] UNIT 01. 문장의 구조와 　　　　수 일치 UNIT 02. 시제 UNIT 03. 능동태와 수동태 REVIEW TEST 01	UNIT 04. 명사 UNIT 05. 형용사 UNIT 06. 부사	UNIT 07. 대명사 UNIT 08. 전치사 REVIEW TEST 02	UNIT 09. 명사절 접속사 UNIT 10. 형용사절 접속사 UNIT 11. 부사절 접속사 REVIEW TEST 03	UNIT 12. to부정사 UNIT 13. 동명사 UNIT 14. 분사 UNIT 15. 비교·가정법·도치 REVIEW TEST 04

DAY 6	DAY 7	DAY 8	DAY 9	DAY 10
[PART 5 VOCA] UNIT 01. 동사 어휘 1 UNIT 02. 동사 어휘 2 UNIT 03. 동사 어휘 3 REVIEW TEST 01	UNIT 04. 명사 어휘 1 UNIT 05. 명사 어휘 2 UNIT 06. 명사 어휘 3 REVIEW TEST 02	UNIT 07. 형용사 어휘 1 UNIT 08. 형용사 어휘 2 UNIT 09. 형용사 어휘 3 REVIEW TEST 03	UNIT 10. 부사 어휘 1 UNIT 11. 부사 어휘 2 UNIT 12. 부사 어휘 3 REVIEW TEST 04	[PART 6] UNIT 01. 시제 UNIT 02. 대명사

DAY 11	DAY 12	DAY 13	DAY 14	DAY 15
UNIT 03. 연결어 UNIT 04. 어휘 선택	UNIT 05. 문장 선택 REVIEW TEST	[PART 7] UNIT 01. 문자 대화문과 　　　　화자 의도 UNIT 02. 편지·이메일· 　　　　문장 삽입	UNIT 03. 광고 UNIT 04. 공지·회람	UNIT 05. 기사 UNIT 06. 양식

DAY 16	DAY 17	DAY 18	DAY 19	DAY 20
UNIT 07. 이중 지문 UNIT 08. 삼중 지문	REVIEW TEST	ACTUAL TEST 01	ACTUAL TEST 02	ACTUAL TEST 03

8주 플랜

DAY 1	DAY 2	DAY 3	DAY 4	DAY 5
[PART 5 GRAMMAR] UNIT 01. 문장의 구조와 수 일치 UNIT 02. 시제	UNIT 03. 능동태와 수동태 REVIEW TEST 01	UNIT 04. 명사 UNIT 05. 형용사 UNIT 06. 부사	UNIT 07. 대명사 UNIT 08. 전치사 REVIEW TEST 02	REVIEW TEST 01&02 다시보기 - 틀린 문제 다시 풀어보기 - 모르는 단어 체크해서 암기

DAY 6	DAY 7	DAY 8	DAY 9	DAY 10
UNIT 09. 명사절 접속사 UNIT 10. 형용사절 접속사	UNIT 11. 부사절 접속사 REVIEW TEST 03	UNIT 12. to부정사 UNIT 13. 동명사 UNIT 14. 분사	UNIT 15. 비교·가정법·도치 REVIEW TEST 04	REVIEW TEST 03&04 다시보기 - 틀린 문제 다시 풀어보기 - 모르는 단어 체크해서 암기

DAY 11	DAY 12	DAY 13	DAY 14	DAY 15
PART 5 GRAMMAR 복습	**[PART 5 VOCA]** UNIT 01. 동사 어휘 1 UNIT 02. 동사 어휘 2	UNIT 03. 동사 어휘 3 REVIEW TEST 01	UNIT 04. 명사 어휘 1 UNIT 05. 명사 어휘 2	UNIT 06. 명사 어휘 3 REVIEW TEST 02

DAY 16	DAY 17	DAY 18	DAY 19	DAY 20
REVIEW TEST 01&02 다시보기 - 틀린 문제 다시 풀어보기 - 모르는 단어 체크해서 암기	UNIT 07. 형용사 어휘 1 UNIT 08. 형용사 어휘 2	UNIT 09. 형용사 어휘 3 REVIEW TEST 03	UNIT 10. 부사 어휘 1 UNIT 11. 부사 어휘 2	UNIT 12. 부사 어휘 3 REVIEW TEST 04

DAY 21	DAY 22	DAY 23	DAY 24	DAY 25
REVIEW TEST 03&04 다시보기 - 틀린 문제 다시 풀어보기 - 모르는 단어 체크해서 암기	PART 5 VOCA 복습	**[PART 6]** UNIT 01. 시제 UNIT 02. 대명사	UNIT 03. 연결어 UNIT 04. 어휘 선택	UNIT 05. 문장 선택 REVIEW TEST

DAY 26	DAY 27	DAY 28	DAY 29	DAY 30
REVIEW TEST 다시보기 - 틀린 문제 다시 풀어보기 - 모르는 단어 체크해서 암기	PART 6 복습	**[PART 7]** UNIT 01. 문자 대화문과 화자 의도 UNIT 02. 편지·이메일·문장 삽입	UNIT 03. 광고 UNIT 04. 공지·회람	UNIT 05. 기사 UNIT 06. 양식

DAY 31	DAY 32	DAY 33	DAY 34	DAY 35
UNIT 07. 이중 지문 UNIT 08. 삼중 지문	REVIEW TEST	REVIEW TEST 다시보기 - 틀린 문제 다시 풀어보기 - 모르는 단어 체크해서 암기	PART 7 복습	ACTUAL TEST 01

DAY 36	DAY 37	DAY 38	DAY 39	DAY 40
ACTUAL TEST 01 복습	ACTUAL TEST 02	ACTUAL TEST 02 복습	ACTUAL TEST 03	ACTUAL TEST 03 복습

PAR

GRAMMAR

RT5

단문 빈칸
채우기

OVERVIEW

Part 5는 빈칸이 있는 문장이 하나 나오고, 4개의 선택지 중 빈칸에 가장 적절한 단어나 구를 고르는 문제로, 총 30문항이 출제된다.

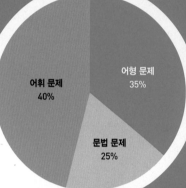

어형 문제
35%

어휘 문제
40%

문법 문제
25%

문제 유형 분석

어형 문제 | 빈칸의 자리를 파악하여 선택지 중 알맞은 품사나 형태를 고르는 문제
어휘 문제 | 같은 품사의 네 개 어휘 중 정확한 용례를 파악하여 알맞은 단어를 고르는 문제
문법 문제 | 문장의 구조 파악과 구와 절을 구분하여 접속사나 전치사, 부사 등을 고르는 문제

최신 출제 경향

- 문법적 지식과 어휘력을 동시에 묻는 문제들이 증가하고 있다.
  ⋯→ 명사 자리인데 선택지에 비슷하게 생긴 명사가 두 개 이상 나오는 문제가 출제된다.
- 두 가지 이상의 문법 포인트를 묻는 문제들이 출제되고 있다.
  ⋯→ 동사의 문장 형식을 이해하고 태를 결정하는 문제가 출제된다.
- 다양한 품사의 선택지로 구성된 문제들이 출제되고 있다.
  ⋯→ 부사 문제이지만 전치사, 접속사, 관용 표현 등으로 선택지가 구성된다.

핵심 학습 전략

- 무조건 해석부터 하지 말고 선택지를 보고 [어형 문제/어휘 문제/문법 문제] 중 어떤 문제인지부터 파악한다. 어형 문제는 해석 없이도 답이 나오는 문제가 대부분이므로 최대한 시간을 절약할 수 있는 방법으로 풀어나가야 한다.

- 고득점을 얻기 위해서는 한 단어를 외우더라도 품사, 파생어, 용법을 함께 암기해야 한다. 예를 들어, announce와 notify를 똑같이 '알리다'라고 외워두면 두 단어가 같이 선택지로 나오는 어휘 문제는 풀 수 없다. notify 뒤에는 사람만이 목적어로 나온다는 사실을 꼭 알아 두어야 한다.

단계별 문법 학습 전략

(1) 문장의 구조를 결정하는 5형식 동사와 품사별 문장 성분의 역할과 문법을 학습한다.
(2) 구와 절을 연결하여 문장을 확장시켜주는 전치사와 접속사의 역할을 학습한다.
(3) 동사의 시제와 태, 가정법, 분사 구문 등의 다소 까다로운 문법 지식을 습득한다.

문제 풀이 전략

1. 어형 문제

아래 문제처럼 한 단어의 네 가지 형태가 선택지로 나오는 문제를 어형 문제 또는 자리 찾기 문제라고 한다. 어형 문제는 빈칸이 [주어, 동사, 목적어, 보어, 수식어] 중에 어떤 자리인지를 파악해서 선택지 중 알맞은 품사나 형태를 고르는 문제이다.

> Our focus group will make direct ------- between several competing brands of carbonated drinks.
>
> (A) comparisons   (B) comparable
> (C) compare   (D) comparing

빈칸은 이 문장의 목적어 자리이며, 보기 중 목적어 자리에 들어갈 수 있는 품사는 명사 (A) 뿐이다.

2. 어휘 문제

아래 문제처럼 같은 품사의 네 가지 다른 단어가 선택지로 나오는 문제를 어휘 문제라고 한다. 어휘 문제는 최소한 빈칸 주변을 해석해야만 풀 수 있고, 어려운 문제의 경우에는 가산/불가산 명사의 구분, 자/타동사의 구분과 같은 문법 사항까지 같이 포함되어 출제되기도 한다.

> I have enclosed a copy of my résumé for your ------- and look forward to hearing from you soon.
>
> (A) explanation   (B) participation
> (C) reference   (D) consideration

빈칸은 전치사 for의 목적어 자리에 어떤 명사 어휘를 넣으면 가장 자연스러운지를 고르는 문제인데 '당신의 고려를 위해 제 이력서를 첨부합니다' 정도는 해석해야만 정답 (D)를 고를 수 있는 문제로 어형 문제보다는 훨씬 난도가 높다.

3. 문법 문제

아래 문제처럼 종속접속사, 등위접속사, 전치사, 부사 등이 선택지에 같이 나오는 문제를 문법 문제라고 한다. 문법 문제는 그 문장의 구조를 파악하여 구와 절을 구분하고 절이라면 여러 가지 절 중 어떤 절인지를 파악해야 하는 어려운 문제들로 대부분 해석까지도 필요하다.

> We need more employees on the production line ------- production has increased by 60 percent.
>
> (A) although   (B) since
> (C) because of   (D) so

빈칸은 두 개의 절을 연결하는 종속접속사 자리이다. 전치사인 (C)와 등위접속사인 (D)는 답이 될 수 없고, 접속사 (A)와 (B) 중에서 '생산이 증가했기 때문에 추가 직원을 고용해야 한다'는 의미에 맞는 (B)를 답으로 고르는 문제이다.

문장의 구조와 수 일치

영어 문장은 주어와 동사가 반드시 있어야 하며, 주어와 동사 찾기는 문장 해석의 가장 기본적인 단계이다. 최근 들어 주어 뒤에 바로 동사가 오지 않고, 주어와 동사 사이에 수식어가 들어가서 문장 구조를 쉽게 파악하기 어려운 문장들이 출제되고 있다. 주어와 동사 사이에 오는 다양한 형태의 수식어구를 익혀 두도록 하자.

> **Tip!**
> 문장의 구조와 수 일치 유형은 매회 0~2문제가 출제되고 있고, 1문제 출제 빈도가 가장 높아!

핵심 문법

1. 주어의 자리

▶ 명사, 대명사, 동명사, to부정사, 명사절, 가주어 등 주어 자리에는 명사 역할을 하는 단어, 구, 절이 온다.

명사	The **roads** have been closed due to the heavy rainfall. 도로들이 폭우 때문에 폐쇄되었다.
대명사	**We** deeply regret the system failure. 우리는 시스템 오류에 대해서 대단히 유감스럽습니다.
동명사	**Reducing operating costs** is not easy. 운영비를 줄이는 것은 쉽지 않다.
to부정사	**To open negotiations with the firm** is necessary. 그 회사와 협상을 개시하는 것이 필요하다.
명사절	It was surprising **that Mr. Hoover approved the plan**. 후버 씨가 그 계획을 승인했다는 것은 놀라웠다.
가주어	**It** was necessary for Mr. Daniel to review all the data before the monthly meeting. 다니엘 씨는 월례 회의 전에 모든 자료를 검토해야 했다.

* 문장의 주어로 동명사, to부정사, 명사절이 오면 동사는 단수로 받는다.

+ check .... 해설서 p.2

1. The ------- of the old temple is the first project that the Cultural Properties Protection Committee will complete this year.

   (A) restorative   (B) restored   (C) restorable   (D) restoration

2. Swerve Marketing employees will be eligible to transfer to overseas branches after ------- have worked for five years at the main office.

   (A) them   (B) their   (C) they   (D) themselves

3. It is Pizza Lover's policy ------- your order within 40 minutes as long as you live in Fairfield.

   (A) deliver   (B) will deliver   (C) is delivering   (D) to deliver

2. 동사의 자리

▶ 동사는 주어의 인칭과 수, 태와 시제에 따라 형태가 변한다.

▶ 3인칭 단수형, 복수형[동사원형], 과거형, 진행형, 완료형, 수동형, 「조동사 + 동사원형」이 있다.

	현재형 V-(e)s	과거형 V-(e)d	진행형 be V-ing	완료형 have p.p.	수동형 be p.p.	「조동사 + 동사원형」
An employee	serves	served	is serving	has served	is served	should serve
Employees	serve		are serving	have served	are served	

>> 적중 포인트 1 동사의 수, 태, 시제를 확인한다.

❶ 수 일치

The manager **holds** staff meetings regularly.
관리자는 직원회의를 정기적으로 연다.
⋯▶ 문장의 주어가 단수(The manager)이므로 동사는 단수 holds로 일치시킨다.

❷ 태 일치

Mr. Brown's proposal **was discussed** at the monthly management meeting.
브라운 씨의 제안서가 월례 경영진 회의에서 논의되었다.
⋯▶ 뒤에 목적어를 동반하지 않으며 '논의되었다'라는 의미가 적합하므로 수동태 was discussed가 된다.

❸ 시제 일치

Leman Company finally **announced** its merger with Tecop Communication last week.
리먼 사는 지난주에 마침내 티콥 커뮤니케이션과의 합병을 발표했다.
⋯▶ 문장에서 시간 어구를 표현하는 last week이 나오므로 과거 동사 announced가 된다.

>> 적중 포인트 2 명령문은 주어 없이 동사원형으로 시작한다.

Please **send** your résumé along with a completed application to Mr. Cho in the HR Department.
완성된 지원서와 함께 이력서를 인사부의 초우 씨에게 보내주세요.
⋯▶ Please로 시작하는 명령문으로 동사원형 send가 된다.

+ check ⋯⋯⋯⋯⋯⋯⋯⋯⋯⋯⋯⋯⋯⋯⋯⋯⋯⋯⋯⋯⋯⋯⋯⋯⋯⋯⋯⋯⋯ 해설서 p.2

1. Campbell House ------- a weekly fashion magazine that our company subscribes to.
   (A) publisher   (B) publishes   (C) publicity   (D) publication

2. Lamvert Industries has ------- the design of its inventory tracking program so that less training is required to use it.
   (A) simplify   (B) simplified   (C) simplifies   (D) simplification

3. To get to Michellan's Cuisine, ------- the stairs at the east end of the building.
   (A) use   (B) used   (C) uses   (D) using

3. 주어 뒤에 오는 수식어

▶ 주어 뒤에 동사가 바로 나오기보다 주어와 동사 사이에 다양한 수식어가 나올 수 있다.

주어	+	형용사구	+	동사
		전치사 + 명사		
		분사구		
		관계대명사절 / 관계부사절		
		to부정사 (형용사적 용법)		
		(that) 주어 + 동사		
		동격		

>> **적중 포인트** 주어 뒤에 오는 수식어구는 문장에서 동사의 수 일치에 영향을 주지 않는다.

❶ 주어 + [형용사구] + 동사

People **unfamiliar with the new software** should consult the manual.
새로운 소프트웨어에 익숙하지 않은 사람들은 설명서를 참조해야 한다.

❷ 주어 + [전치사 + 명사] + 동사

The inspectors **from the company** are planning to visit the factory in Jakarta.
회사의 감독관들이 자카르타에 있는 공장을 방문할 예정이다.
···▸ 주어(inspectors) 뒤에 오는 수식어구 일부(the company)를 주어로 혼동하지 않도록 한다.

❸ 주어 + [분사구] + 동사

Any employee **ordering extra supplies** has to receive approval from the immediate supervisor.
추가 물품을 주문하는 어느 직원이든지 직속상관의 승인을 받아야 한다.
···▸ 주어(Any employee) 뒤에 오는 수식어구 일부(supplies)를 주어로 혼동하지 않도록 한다.

Those **interested in organizing the upcoming party** should contact Mr. Kim as soon as possible.
다가오는 파티를 준비하는 데 관심 있는 사람들은 가능한 한 빨리 김 씨에게 연락해야 한다.

❹ 주어 + [관계대명사절 / 관계부사절] + 동사

The man **who is sitting next to Ms. Lie** is my boss.
라이 씨 옆에 앉아 있는 남자는 내 상사이다.

❺ 주어 + [to부정사] + 동사

The books **to be displayed at the Seoul Book Fair** will be ready by Wednesday.
서울 도서전에 진열될 책들은 수요일까지 준비될 것이다.
···▸ 주어(books) 뒤에 오는 수식어구 일부(Seoul Book Fair)를 주어로 혼동하지 않도록 한다.

❻ 주어 + [(that) 주어 + 동사] + 동사

The documents **(that) you requested** have been already sent to Mr. Kim.
당신이 요청했던 서류들이 김 씨에게 이미 발송되었다.

❼ 주어, [동격], 동사

Avery Moore, **the well-known novelist**, will visit Japan next month.
유명한 소설가인 에이버리 무어는 다음 달 일본을 방문할 것이다.

1. Those employees ------- in participating in the photography competition are requested to submit their entries by March 23.

   (A) interest   (B) interesting   (C) interested   (D) interests

2. The safety procedures for the laboratory ------- in Section 9-D of the staff handbook.

   (A) will outline   (B) is outlined   (C) to outline   (D) are outlined

3. Although the camera ------- selected is currently unavailable in your desired color, we have the same model in metallic blue.

   (A) you   (B) that   (C) was   (D) have

4. 동사의 종류와 문장의 형식

▶ 문장은 최소 주어와 동사로 이루어지지만, 동사의 의미에 따라 목적어나 보어가 필요하다.

▶ 동사 뒤에 오는 목적어나 보어의 유무와 종류에 따라 5가지 문형으로 나뉜다.

자동사	1형식(완전 자동사)	「주어 + 동사」
	2형식(불완전 자동사)	「주어 + 동사 + 주격 보어」
타동사	3형식(완전 타동사)	「주어 + 동사 + 목적어」
	4형식(수여동사)	「주어 + 동사 + 간접목적어 + 직접목적어」
	5형식(불완전 타동사)	「주어 + 동사 + 목적어 + 목적격 보어」

>> 적중 포인트 1 1형식 문장: 「주어 + 동사」

China's exports and imports **fell** sharply in December.

중국의 수출입 물량이 12월 들어 급격히 떨어졌다.

⋯→ 동사 fell(fall의 과거형)은 '떨어지다'라는 의미로 어떻게[→ 급격히], 언제[→ 12월에]를 나타내는 부사와 전치사구의 수식을 받고 있다.

There **are** many **suggestions** to improve employee productivity.

직원 생산성을 개선하기 위한 많은 제안이 있다.

⋯→ 「There + be동사」는 뒤에 오는 주어의 수와 일치시킨다.

관용적인 「자동사 + 부사」 표현	
arrive late	늦게 도착하다
function[work] properly	제대로 작동하다
proceed steadily	꾸준히 나아가다
start immediately	즉시 시작하다
begin promptly	신속하게 시작하다
grow rapidly / steadily	빠르게 / 꾸준히 성장하다
speak eloquently	유창하게 말하다
travel extensively	널리 여행하다
work together[collaboratively / jointly]	협력해서 일하다
work closely	긴밀하게 일하다
increase / decrease dramatically	급격하게 증가하다 / 감소하다
increase significantly[considerably / substantially]	상당히 증가하다
decrease significantly[considerably / substantially]	상당히 감소하다

관용적인 「자동사 + 전치사(구)」 표현			
account for	~을 설명하다[차지하다]	agree to[with/on/upon]	~에 동의하다
appeal to	~에 호소하다	apply to/for	~을 적용하다/신청하다
benefit from	~으로부터 이익을 얻다	compensate for	~에 대해 보상하다
comply with, adhere[conform] to	~을 지키다[준수하다]	concentrate[focus] on	~에 집중하다
collaborate on[with]	~과[~와] 협력하다	contribute to	~에 기여하다
enroll in	~에 등록하다	deal with	~을 처리하다
insist on[upon]	~을 고집하다	inquire about	~에 관해 문의하다
object to	~에 반대하다	interfere with	~에 지장을 주다
proceed to/with	~로 나아가다/계속하다	participate in	~에 참여하다
refrain from	~을 삼가다[자제하다]	refer to	~을 참고하다
rely[depend/count] on	~에 의지하다[의존하다]	register for	~을 등록하다
respond[reply] to	~에 답하다	remark[comment] on	~을 말하다
specialize in	~을 전문으로 하다	search for	~을 찾다

>> 적중 포인트 2 2형식 문장: 「주어 + 동사 + 주격 보어」

A newly developed computer **became** available.
새로 개발된 컴퓨터가 출시되었다.

become, grow, turn, get	~이 되다
be, remain, prove, seem, appear, stay	~이다

>> 적중 포인트 3 3형식 문장: 「주어 + 동사 + 목적어」

❶ 자동사로 착각하기 쉬운 타동사

At the meeting, we will **discuss** the problem concerning the misuse of company telephone.
회의에서, 우리는 회사 전화의 남용에 대한 문제에 관해 논의할 것입니다.

⋯▸ '~에 관해 논의하다'로 해석된다고 자동사로 착각하여 뒤에 about을 쓰지 않도록 유의한다. (discuss about X)

access	~에 접근하다	accompany	~와 동반하다	contact	~에게 연락하다
discuss	~에 관해 논의하다	explain	~을 설명하다	reach	~에 이르다

❷ that절을 목적어로 취하는 3형식 동사: 「동사 + (to 사람) + that절」

The readers **mentioned** (to us) that the source for the story was unreliable.
독자들은 이야기의 소재가 믿을 수 없었다고 (우리에게) 이야기했다.

say	말하다	mention	언급하다	announce	발표하다
suggest	제안하다	recommend	추천하다	indicate	가리키다
explain	설명하다				

>> 적중 포인트 4 4형식 문장: 「주어 + 동사 + 간접목적어 + 직접목적어」

The judges **gave** Mr. Simpson an award.
심사위원들은 심슨 씨에게 상을 주었다.

give	주다	send	보내다	offer	제공하다
grant	수여하다	award	수여하다	win	얻게 해주다
assign	할당하다	show	보여주다		

☑ that절을 직접목적어로 취하는 4형식 동사: 「동사 + 사람(간접목적어) + that절(직접목적어)」

Personnel Office will **inform** all applicants that there is a delay in the selection process.
인사과는 모든 지원자에게 선별 과정에 지연이 있다는 것을 알려줄 것이다.

inform	알리다	notify	통지하다	remind	상기시키다
assure	확언하다	convince	확신시키다		

>> 적중 포인트 5 5형식 문장: 「주어 + 동사 + 목적어 + 목적격 보어」

❶ 「주어 + 동사 + 목적어 + 형용사」

I **found** it important to protect my personal information.
나는 내 개인 정보를 보호하는 것이 중요하다는 것을 알게 되었다.

make	~을 …하게 만들다	find	~이 …한 것을 알게 되다/~을 …하다고 여기다
leave	~을 …한 채로 두다	consider	~을 …하다고 여기다
keep	~을 …하도록 유지하다	deem	~을 …로 여기다

❷ 「주어 + 동사 + 목적어 + to부정사」

Ms. Terry **asked** her assistant **to** fax the contracts.
테리 씨는 그녀의 비서에게 계약서를 팩스로 보내달라고 요청했다.

ask/urge/request/require, want	요구하다, 원하다
encourage	장려하다
allow/permit, enable	허락하다, 가능하게 하다
cause, advise, expect	야기시키다, 조언하다, 기대하다

+ check ·········· 해설서 p.2

1. Due to limited spots, please let Mr. Matthews know as soon as possible if you can ------- the seminar tomorrow.

   (A) reply　　　　　(B) send　　　　　(C) go　　　　　(D) attend

2. Merris Inc. staff should visit the company's online bulletin board to become ------- with the recently revised security policies.

   (A) familiarize　　　(B) familiar　　　(C) familiarly　　　(D) familiarity

3. Ms. Yen is organizing the company's anniversary party, so please let ------- know whether you will bring a guest.

   (A) hers　　　　　(B) herself　　　　(C) she　　　　　(D) her

Practice

1. Customers who tried the new iced tea at Hurley's Cafe said that the beverage is ------- enough.

(A) sweet
(B) sweetly
(C) sweeten
(D) sweetest

2. ------- for the 10th anniversary dinner will soon be mailed to all employees.

(A) Invitations
(B) Invite
(C) Inviting
(D) Invited

3. The changes suggested by the research and development team ------- small but will have significant effects on the firm.

(A) is
(B) to be
(C) are
(D) been

4. The apartment residents found the upgraded recycling system ------- in reducing waste.

(A) effect
(B) effects
(C) effective
(D) effectively

5. The Personnel Department ------- new staff become familiar with the firm's policies.

(A) helps
(B) helping
(C) help
(D) to help

6. When mailing an important document to a client, ------- the receiver before sending it.

(A) notification
(B) notify
(C) notifies
(D) notifying

7. TFV Technology held its annual award ceremony ------- 20 outstanding employees who contributed to the company's success.

(A) honoring
(B) is honored
(C) honored
(D) honors

8. The Motor Show, ------- demonstrates the newest concept cars each year, attracts many visitors.

(A) where
(B) that
(C) what
(D) which

9. Locations ------- by the extended subway line include the Montress Art Museum and Aruba Park.

(A) servicing
(B) to be serviced
(C) will service
(D) are being serviced

10. To qualify for free shipping with Koch Appliances, you must present the voucher ------- in the mail.

(A) that was sent
(B) for sending
(C) have to send
(D) has sent

11. Please ------- Ms. Kim's e-mail sent on February 4 if you have any further questions about the procedure.

(A) look
(B) inquire
(C) appeal
(D) consult

12. The anticipated arrival time for the package ------- on the number of deliveries the driver must make tomorrow.

(A) dependent
(B) depends
(C) depend
(D) dependable

13. At the staff meetings, management typically ------- to any questions regarding workplace policies.

(A) responds
(B) retains
(C) submits
(D) pronounces

14. The department head ------- Mr. Russell assistance with his product research project, which is due next week.

(A) produced
(B) donated
(C) offered
(D) suggested

15. The Vice President ------- the senior staff to always act in the best interest of the company.

(A) alleged
(B) vowed
(C) pursued
(D) urged

16. Please ------- Ms. Lee that her order will be sent to her office by the end of the week.

(A) announce
(B) mention
(C) report
(D) inform

17. Café Celeste ------- patrons a complimentary dessert now through the end of June.

(A) are offered
(B) will be offering
(C) offering
(D) to offer

18. The aim of Kanashu University is to help students ------- their academic and professional goals.

(A) achieving
(B) achieve
(C) achievement
(D) achieved

19. Use a soft brush to clean any dust from your monitor so that the protective film can ------- to the screen of your laptop.

(A) comply
(B) utilize
(C) polish
(D) adhere

20. The revised contract contains information Mr. Pierre -------.

(A) correct
(B) has been corrected
(C) to correct
(D) will correct

시제

동사 시제 일치 문제는 해석보다는 문장 안에서 시제를 알려주는 단서인 시간 어구들을 찾아 재빨리 정답을 찾는 것이 관건이다. 토익에서 빈출되는 시제 문제로는 현재완료와 시간·조건의 부사절 시제 문제가 있다.

Tip!
시제 유형은 매회 0~2문제가 출제되고 있고, 1문제 출제 빈도가 가장 높아!

 **핵심 문법**

1. 단순 시제

▶ 과거 시제: 과거 사실 또는 이미 끝난 동작이나 상태를 나타낸다.

▶ 현재 시제: 일반적인 사실이나 반복되는 동작을 나타낸다.

▶ 미래 시제: 미래 상황에 대한 추측, 계획, 의지를 나타낸다.

>> 적중 포인트 1 과거 시제

Two weeks ago, Mr. Alvarez **implemented** some policies to improve the company's image.
2주 전에, 알베레즈 씨는 회사 이미지를 개선하기 위해 몇 가지 정책들을 실행했다.

과거 시제와 쓰이는 시간 어구							
yesterday	어제	this morning	오늘 아침	recently	최근에	previously	이전에
「시간 + ago」	~전에	「last + 시간」	지난 ~에	「in + 과거」	~에		

>> 적중 포인트 2 현재 시제

The HR manager **holds** a staff meeting **every Monday morning**.
인사팀 매니저는 매주 월요일 아침마다 직원회의를 연다.

현재 시제와 쓰이는 시간 어구	
usually, often, always, now, currently *Cf* presently (주로 현재 진행형과 자주 쓰임)	대개, 종종, 늘, 지금, 현재
occasionally, regularly / periodically	이따금씩, 정기적으로 / 주기적으로
each[every] month / year	매달 / 매년

>> 적중 포인트 3 미래 시제

Mr. Komiya **will address** the topic of workplace productivity at **next month's workshop**.
코미야 씨는 다음 달 워크숍에서 작업장 생산성을 주제로 다룰 것이다.

미래 시제와 쓰이는 시간 어구							
tomorrow	내일	「next + 시간」	다음 ~에	soon / shortly	곧	「later + 시점」	~후에
「in + 기간」	~후에	「sometime + 미래」	~중 언젠가	over the next ~	다음 ~간	as of	~부로

1. Mr. Barton will talk about the investor's conference he ------- in Cape Town last week.

   (A) attends   (B) attended   (C) will attend   (D) attend

2. Next month, Wildlife Preserver, an environmental group, ------- a thorough investigation of the construction of the canal.

   (A) conducted   (B) conducting   (C) will conduct   (D) will be conducted

3. Facilities ------- an air-conditioned dining room as well as a computer lab with 24-hour access to PCs.

   (A) including   (B) include   (C) is included   (D) to include

2. 진행 시제

▶ 과거 진행 시제: 과거 특정 시점에서 진행되고 있던 일을 나타낸다.

▶ 현재 진행 시제: 현재 시점에서 진행되고 있는 일을 나타낸다.

▶ 미래 진행 시제: 미래 특정 시점에 진행되고 있을 일을 나타낸다.

>> 적중 포인트 1   과거 진행 시제

Mr. Taylor **was attending** a seminar in Tokyo last weekend.
테일러 씨는 지난 주말에 도쿄에서 열린 세미나에 참석하고 있었다.

>> 적중 포인트 2   현재 진행 시제

The company **is making** significant growth in its sales profits.
그 회사는 판매 수익에서 상당한 성장을 보이고 있다.

✔ 현재 진행 시제는 가까운 미래의 예정된 계획을 나타낼 수 있다.

Mr. Anderson **is coming** for the groundbreaking ceremony **next week.**
앤더슨 씨은 다음 주 기공식에 올 예정이다.

>> 적중 포인트 3   미래 진행 시제

Our new software system **will be providing** differentiated services to our customers.
우리의 새로운 소프트웨어 시스템이 고객들에게 차별화된 서비스를 제공하게 될 것이다.

1. Beginning next month, Chow Manufacturing Inc. ------- free snacks and beverages to all its workers.

   (A) will be providing   (B) has provided   (C) will have provided   (D) has been providing

2. At this time, the safety procedures for the assembly line ------- to fix the problems indicated at the annual factory inspection.

   (A) are revising   (B) are being revised   (C) be revised   (D) have revised

3. Due to the lack of time given to Mr. Sato when he ------- for his presentation, he was not able to include all the charts.

   (A) to prepare   (B) preparing   (C) prepare   (D) was preparing

3. 완료 시제

▶ 과거 완료 시제: 과거 특정 시점 이전에 발생한 일을 나타낸다.

▶ 현재 완료 시제: 과거에 시작된 일이 현재에 영향을 미칠 때를 나타낸다.

▶ 미래 완료 시제: 어떤 사건이나 동작이 미래의 특정한 시점에 완료될 때를 나타낸다.

>> 적중 포인트 1 과거 완료 시제

After Ms. Javier **had acquired** the necessary expertise, she started her own business.
하비에르 씨는 필요한 전문성을 익힌 후에, 자기 사업을 시작했다.

과거 완료와 어울리는 시간 표현	
「before / after + 주어 + 과거 시제」	(과거에) ~하기 전에 / ~한 후에
「by the time / when + 주어 + 과거 시제」	(과거에) ~했을 때

>> 적중 포인트 2 현재 완료 시제

A lot of things **have changed** over the past three years.
지난 3년 동안 많은 것들이 변해 왔다.

현재 완료와 어울리는 시간 표현	
「since + 과거」	(과거 시점) 이후로 (지금까지)
「over / in / for / during + the past[last] 기간」	지난 ~동안
recently	최근에
so far	지금까지

>> 적중 포인트 3 미래 완료 시제

Sophie **will have worked** for five years at this company by next December.
내년 12월이면 소피는 이 회사에서 5년 동안 근무한 셈이다.

미래 완료와 어울리는 시간 표현	
「by + 미래 시점」	~가 되면
「by the time + 주어 + 현재 시제」	~할 때까지면, ~할 때쯤이면

+ check .... 해설서 p.5

1. In order to attract more customers, many local businesses ------- offering new services in the past few months.

   (A) to begin   (B) will begin   (C) will have begun   (D) have begun

2. Andrew Flinter ------- one of the best teachers at Landon High School for many years.

   (A) to be considering   (B) having considered

   (C) had been considering   (D) has been considered

3. Groovy Motors' new car design was much more appealing to young drivers than the company -------.

   (A) anticipate   (B) are anticipating   (C) were anticipated   (D) had anticipated

4. 시제 일치 예외

▶ 시간·조건의 부사절은 주절의 시제가 미래라고 할지라도 종속절은 현재 시제를 사용한다.

▶ 주장, 명령, 요구, 추천, 제안 등을 나타내는 동사나 필요성, 당위성을 나타내는 형용사 뒤에 오는 that절은 문맥상 '~해야 한다'를 나타내므로 조동사 should를 쓰는데 should는 대개 생략된다.

>> 적중 포인트 1 시간·조건 부사절

Unless you **have** the confirmation number, you **will not** be able to change your booking.
만약 확인 번호가 없으면, 예약을 변경할 수 없을 것이다.

시간의 부사절 접속사			
when	~할 때	by the time	~할 때쯤에
after	~이후에	before	~전에
until	~할 때까지	while	~하는 동안에
as soon as, once	~하자마자		
조건의 부사절 접속사			
if	만약 ~한다면	unless	만약 ~하지 않는다면
as long as	~하는 한, ~이기만 하면	provided (that)	~한다면

>> 적중 포인트 2 「(should) + 동사원형」

It is imperative that the deadline **(should) be extended** until next week.
마감일은 반드시 다음 주까지로 연장되어야 한다.

[주장 / 명령 / 요구 / 추천 / 제안 동사 + that + 주어 + (should) + 동사원형]			
ask, request, demand	요청하다	recommend, suggest	추천하다, 제안하다
[It is + 필요성 / 당위성 형용사 + that + 주어 + (should) + 동사원형]			
imperative	의무인	necessary, essential, vital	필수적인
important, critical	중요한		

+ check .... 해설서 p.5

1. Until Mr. Bennett finishes his special project, Ms. Chang ------- most of his regular duties.

   (A) had been covering   (B) covered   (C) will cover   (D) will be covered

2. Many employees have demanded that the managers ------- with the executive board about providing more flexible working hours.

   (A) negotiate   (B) will negotiate   (C) was negotiating   (D) to negotiate

3. To ensure that the clients enjoy their visit to our office next Friday, it is crucial that some entertainment ------- for that afternoon.

   (A) were prepared   (B) are preparing   (C) will prepare   (D) be prepared

1. Several industry experts forecast that demand for organic food ------- by 50 percent over the coming 5 years.

(A) be increased
(B) will increase
(C) increasing
(D) has increased

2. Hafon Foods, a major food manufacturer, ------- 3,000 cans of meat to the city's homeless shelters each year.

(A) donates
(B) to donate
(C) donating
(D) are donated

3. Last week's meeting ------- opportunities for new employees to learn about the company culture.

(A) creating
(B) creates
(C) created
(D) will create

4. Pit Stops ------- customers a complimentary window cleaning on weekends.

(A) offer
(B) had offered
(C) was offered
(D) offers

5. The Marketing Department ------- a welcome party for new employees later today.

(A) is held
(B) is holding
(C) will be held
(D) had been holding

6. ------- the past decade, the number of speed-related car accidents has decreased by 10 percent.

(A) Over
(B) On
(C) At
(D) Of

7. DNB Incorporated ------- a thorough survey before it opened a new branch in Sydney.

(A) have conducted
(B) would conduct
(C) had conducted
(D) was conducting

8. It is necessary that each applicant ------- the documents no later than October 15.

(A) submit
(B) be submitted
(C) submits
(D) to submit

9. Oberlin Bakery ------- a delicious range of cakes and pastries since it was founded in 1998 by Mr. Oberlin.

(A) will have produced
(B) has produced
(C) was producing
(D) would produce

10. The next executive board meeting will be postponed ------- the CEO returns from her trip to Asia.

(A) since
(B) until
(C) in
(D) around

11. Keane Supermarket's steady sales have made the company's profits soar ------- it was established in 1987.

(A) if
(B) how
(C) than
(D) since

12. After all the submissions have been considered, Mr. Cruise ------- the winning photograph.

(A) will choose
(B) has chosen
(C) chose
(D) are choosing

13. K12 Camping ------- in operation in Charleston for 10 years by the end of this month.

(A) has been
(B) would be
(C) will be
(D) will have been

14. By the time Ms. Min joined our firm as a market analyst, she ------- in the financial sector for over 15 years.

(A) has worked
(B) works
(C) will have worked
(D) had worked

15. Mr. Lowe, the new head of the IT Department, ------- authorization to replace any software he thinks is outdated.

(A) to obtain
(B) obtain
(C) obtaining
(D) will obtain

16. Since Mr. Schmidt cannot participate in the meeting, we ------- that Ms. Lee take his place.

(A) recommended
(B) introduced
(C) reported
(D) announced

17. Every member that signed up for the home business course ------- a confirmation e-mail last week.

(A) was sending
(B) would send
(C) will be sent
(D) was sent

18. Security at WCX Technology has greatly improved since the revised safety procedures ------- implemented.

(A) were
(B) to be
(C) will be
(D) been

19. ------- we meet at our bank next week, all of your financing details will have been finalized.

(A) By the time
(B) In order for
(C) As much as
(D) Now that

20. The provincial government has obtained the ownership of Austin Theater and will ------- reopen it as a history museum.

(A) soon
(B) recently
(C) such
(D) very

능동태와 수동태

동사의 태를 묻는 문제는 주어와 동사의 관계가 능동인지 수동인지를 파악해야 한다. 3형식 동사의 태를 묻는 문제가 주로 출제되며, 3형식 동사의 태는 뒤에 목적어가 있는지의 여부로 빠르게 확인할 수 있다.

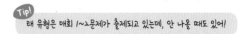

Tip!
태 유형은 매회 1~2문제가 출제되고 있는데, 안 나올 때도 있어!

핵심 문법

1. 능동태 vs. 수동태

▸ 보통 동사 뒤에 목적어가 있으면 능동태를, 목적어가 없으면 수동태를 선택한다.

▸ 수동태 뒤에는 명사가 나올 수 없지만, 4형식·5형식 동사의 경우에는 수동태 뒤에 명사가 나올 수 있다.

▸ 목적어가 없는 자동사는 수동태가 불가하다.

≫ 적중 포인트 1 3형식의 수동태

(능동태) **They renovated our office** last month.
그들이 지난달에 우리 사무실을 개조했다.

(수동태) **Our office was renovated** last month (**by them**).
우리 사무실은 (그들에 의해) 지난달에 개조되었다.

✔ 수동태를 빨리 구분하는 방법

능동태	「동사 + 명사(목적어)」
수동태	「be + p.p.」 | 「be + p.p. + 전치사구」 | 「be + p.p. + 부사」

≫ 적중 포인트 2 4형식·5형식의 수동태

목적어가 두 개인 4형식 동사나 목적격 보어로 명사가 나오는 5형식 동사는 수동태가 되었을 때 동사 뒤에 바로 명사가 나올 수 있으므로 문제 풀이 시 해석을 통해서 태를 결정해야 한다.

(능동태) **We sent you** a list of new products.
우리는 당신에게 새로운 제품들의 목록을 보냈다.

(수동태) **You were sent** a list of new products (**by us**).
당신에게 새로운 제품들의 목록이 (우리에 의해) 보내졌다.

4형식 동사					
give	주다	send	보내다	offer	제공하다
grant	수여하다	award	수여하다	assign	할당하다
5형식 동사					
consider	~을 …이라고 여기다			name	~을 …으로 이름 짓다
elect	~을 …으로 뽑다			appoint	~을 …으로 임명하다

>> 적중 포인트 3 목적어가 없는 자동사

수동태는 능동태의 목적어가 주어 자리에 오는 것이므로 반드시 목적어가 있는 타동사만이 수동태가 될 수 있다.

The initial plan was (objected, **rejected**) by the clients.
초기 계획이 고객들에 의해서 거절되었다.
⋯→ object는 전치사 to를 동반하는 자동사이므로 수동태가 불가하다.

(능동태) **The salesperson dealt with the customer complaint** in a timely manner.
판매원이 시기적절하게 고객 불만을 처리했다.

(수동태) **The customer complaint was dealt with** in a timely manner (**by the salesperson**).
고객 불만이 (판매원에 의해) 시기적절하게 처리되었다.

「be p.p. + 전치사」의 수동태로 표현되는 「자동사 + 전치사」			
account for	~을 설명하다 ⋯⋯→	be accounted for	설명되다
deal with	~을 다루다 ⋯⋯→	be dealt with	다뤄지다
refer to	~을 참고하다 ⋯⋯→	be referred to	참고되다

+ check ⋯⋯ 해설서 p.7

1. Any mail that is not addressed to a specific department can be ------- to our regional headquarters.

   (A) forwarding   (B) forward   (C) forwards   (D) forwarded

2. The new guidelines for submitting expense reports ------- in early spring.

   (A) will be implemented   (B) are implementing
   (C) implementing   (D) had been implementing

3. Products for customers in East Asia will be ------- out of the company's fulfillment center in Malaysia.

   (A) shipped   (B) returned   (C) included   (D) arrived

2. 감정 동사

▶ 감정 동사는 주어가 사람일 때는 수동태, 사물일 때는 능동태로 쓴다.

be interested in	~에 흥미를 느끼다	be satisfied with	~에 만족하다
be dissatisfied with	~에 불만족스러워하다	be disappointed with	~에 실망하다
be delighted[pleased] with/to부정사	~에 기뻐하다	be concerned about	~에 대해 걱정하다

>> 적중 포인트 「사람 주어 + 감정 동사」의 수동태

We **are pleased** to announce that we are opening another branch in New York.
저희가 뉴욕에 또 다른 지점을 열게 될 것을 알리게 되어 기쁩니다.

··· 해설서 p.7

+ check

1. Ms. Klein is ------- in finding out more about Reiko Tech's Internet services.

   (A) interest   (B) interests   (C) interested   (D) interestingly

2. The committee is ------- to announce the Employee of the Year at tonight's company dinner.

   (A) excite   (B) excites   (C) excitedly   (D) excited

3. In order to keep the customers of KC Cellular Phone -------, we do our best to give premium customer service.

   (A) satisfy   (B) satisfying   (C) satisfaction   (D) satisfied

3. 수동태 숙어 표현

▶ 수동태에서 by 이외의 전치사를 갖는 관용적인 표현들을 평소에 암기해 두자.

▶ 「be p.p. + to부정사」

▶ 「be p.p. + that절」

>> 적중 포인트 1 by 이외의 수동태 전치사

be equipped with	~으로 갖춰져 있다	be committed to	~에 전념하다
be outfitted with	~으로 갖춰져 있다	be dedicated to	~에 전념하다
be associated with	~과 연관되어 있다	be devoted to	~에 전념하다
be exposed to	~에 노출되다	be involved in	~에 개입되다
be related to	~과 관련되어 있다	be engaged in	~에 종사하다
be limited to	~으로 제한되어 있다	be based on	~에 기초하고 있다
be known for	~으로 알려져 있다		

>> 적중 포인트 2 「be p.p. + to부정사」

be asked[requested / required] to부정사	~을 하도록 요청받다[요구받다]
be advised to부정사	~을 하도록 권고되다
be enabled to부정사	~을 하는 것이 가능해지다
be encouraged to부정사	~을 하도록 권장되다
be allowed[permitted] to부정사	~을 하도록 허락되다[허가되다]
be intended to부정사	~을 하도록 의도되다

>> 적중 포인트 3 「be p.p. + that절」

inform / notify / remind / assure + 목적어 (사람) + that절 → 목적어 (사람) + be + informed / notified / reminded / assured + that절	알리다 / 통보하다 / 상기시켜 주다 / 확언하다

+ check .... 해설서 p.7

1. The imported materials used exclusively for our new products should be ------- with cheaper ones in order to reduce manufacturing costs.

   (A) coordinated   (B) replaced   (C) requested   (D) worked

2. As taking pictures in the museum is strictly prohibited, visitors to the exhibition ------- to leave their cameras or camcorders at home.

   (A) had advised   (B) will be advising   (C) were advising   (D) are advised

3. Please be ------- that we will complete our purchase of Sawyer Engineering tomorrow, and it will officially merge with us next month.

   (A) recommended   (B) allowed   (C) ensured   (D) informed

1. While Peach Street's parking lot -------, visitors are strongly encouraged to use public transportation.

(A) repairs
(B) is being repaired
(C) have repaired
(D) repair

2. The guided tour will be led ------- Ms. Davinch and will include visits to several award-winning wineries.

(A) up
(B) by
(C) on
(D) as

3. Until a security system ------- in the operations area of our new office, please keep confidential documents in the old location.

(A) were implementing
(B) would be implementing
(C) has implemented
(D) has been implemented

4. Once the new annual sales targets -------, managers should meet with their teams right away to discuss marketing strategies.

(A) have been announced
(B) announce
(C) will announce
(D) announced

5. Clients whose product is out of stock ------- a similarly-priced item or receive a voucher for store credit.

(A) choosing
(B) may choose
(C) to be chosen
(D) should be chosen

6. To maintain optimum suction power for your vacuum cleaner, the bin ------- prior to the vacuuming process.

(A) must be emptied
(B) have emptied
(C) would be emptying
(D) are emptying

7. Because sales of Olga Tech's home appliances were ------- last year, the company will lower the prices of some of its products.

(A) disappoint
(B) disappointed
(C) disappointing
(D) disappointment

8. All instructional materials prepared for trainees must be ------- carefully to ensure compliance with company policy.

(A) edit
(B) edited
(C) editing
(D) edits

9. Technicians are ------- to wear safety helmets at all times while working in the plant.

(A) inquired
(B) insisted
(C) appealed
(D) required

10. The replacement parts that Edwin installed in the grain elevator worked much better than we -------.

(A) expect
(B) are expecting
(C) was expected
(D) had expected

11. Elco Airline's seats are ------- with a high-tech entertainment system to make its flights as enjoyable as possible.

(A) equip
(B) equipment
(C) equipped
(D) equipping

12. As a former editor-in-chief of *Occasions*, Ms. Chan recently ------- Journalist of the Year by the National Association.

(A) named
(B) is named
(C) was named
(D) has named

13. It is essential that no one ------- to the building after 10 P.M. unless accompanied by a security officer.

(A) admit
(B) are admitted
(C) be admitted
(D) is admitting

14. The Investor Support Department resources ------- mainly for users of our online trading platform.

(A) intended
(B) have been intending
(C) intention
(D) are intended

15. The office space that Mr. Carlos is going to sign the lease for is ------- across from the Metiz Building.

(A) locate
(B) located
(C) locating
(D) location

16. Mr. Greg ------- to deliver a presentation at the monthly business workshop, but he declined the invitation.

(A) encouraged
(B) has encouraged
(C) was encouraged
(D) was encouraging

17. The Joseph Foundation ------- nearly 2,000 books to public libraries across the country over the past five years.

(A) will be donated
(B) is donated
(C) was donated
(D) has donated

18. Fontere Industries was ------- the contract because its bid price was the most competitive.

(A) awarding
(B) award
(C) awarded
(D) to award

19. The crew at Bulut Diagnostic is ------- to setting the highest standards of service in our industry.

(A) admired
(B) committed
(C) attempted
(D) supposed

20. Please be ------- that every inquiry from our customers will receive prompt attention.

(A) assuring
(B) assure
(C) to assure
(D) assured

REVIEW TEST 01

해설서 p.9 / ⏱ 제한 시간 6분

1. A total of $253,850 ------- anonymously to Edinburgh Children's Hospital in April.

(A) was contributed
(B) contribution
(C) contributed
(D) contribute

2. Road repairs on King Expressway ------- creation of a detour through the suburbs.

(A) require
(B) requires
(C) requiring
(D) requirement

3. In order to be considered for admission, prospective students must ------- at least 85 points on the university's entrance exam.

(A) scoring
(B) scored
(C) score
(D) to score

4. Guests who attended the launch of YZ Motors' new line of vehicles found the various designs very -------.

(A) attractive
(B) attraction
(C) attracted
(D) attracts

5. Tipton Freight's union leaders meet monthly with staff to make sure that labor laws ------- properly.

(A) would have followed
(B) are being followed
(C) to be followed
(D) had been followed

6. Until the labor dispute is resolved, Recoma Motors expects production numbers ------- significantly.

(A) have suffered
(B) suffer
(C) suffering
(D) to suffer

7. Every representative is required to ------- with the firm's regulations regarding outside employment.

(A) inform
(B) update
(C) observe
(D) comply

8. All electrical technicians should ------- their manager of any repair requests made by customers.

(A) recommend
(B) inform
(C) offer
(D) review

9. While the lobby is -------, employees must use the back entrance to enter and exit the building.

(A) renovate
(B) being renovated
(C) to renovate
(D) renovation

10. Analysts anticipated that Cantan Technology's stock price ------- to 70 to 80 dollars a share by now.

(A) rose
(B) has risen
(C) would rise
(D) rising

42 파고다 토익 고득점 완성 RC

11. The responses that follow ------- by a large group of employees interviewed during our research study.

(A) are giving
(B) have given
(C) were given
(D) has been given

12. Clayton Museum's exhibits appeal ------- to art lovers of all ages.

(A) wide
(B) wider
(C) widely
(D) widest

13. At Ghent Co., professional development courses for employees ------- to nurture leadership skills.

(A) will design
(B) designed
(C) designs
(D) have been designed

14. The purpose of today's meeting is to discuss ------- to improve customer satisfaction.

(A) initiatives
(B) initiating
(C) initiated
(D) initiate

15. Inovax Tech designs and offers solutions to help companies like yours ------- issues that may limit an organization's success.

(A) diagnose
(B) diagnosed
(C) can diagnose
(D) are diagnosing

16. Most of our products are designed for commercial buildings, but some are ------- for use at home.

(A) suit
(B) suitable
(C) suitability
(D) suitably

17. Mr. Kwon renewed the ------- to *Science Today* magazine one week before it expired.

(A) subscribing
(B) subscribed
(C) subscribe
(D) subscription

18. Ben Miller ------- our building plans by the time he visits Kandall Inc.'s corporate headquarters tomorrow.

(A) finalizes
(B) is finalizing
(C) finalized
(D) will have finalized

19. If sending confidential information to a client, keep such documents ------- by using reliable courier service.

(A) securely
(B) securing
(C) secure
(D) security

20. At APA International, the maximum ------- for shipping containers is 50 metric tons.

(A) weighing
(B) weight
(C) weigh
(D) weighted

명사

명사 문제는 난이도는 낮지만 매회 3문제 이상 출제될 정도로 출제 비중이 높다. 특히, 가산 명사와 불가산 명사를 구분하는 문제나 형태가 비슷한 명사의 뜻을 구분하는 문제가 자주 출제되고 있다.

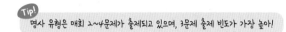

Tip!
명사 유형은 매회 2~4문제가 출제되고 있으며, 3문제 출제 빈도가 가장 높아!

 핵심 문법

1. 명사는 주어, 목적어, 보어 자리에 온다.

▶ 명사는 문장에서 주어, 목적어, 보어 역할을 한다.

>> 적중 포인트 명사: 주어, 목적어, 보어 자리

❶ 주어 자리

Confirmation of your hotel reservation will be emailed to you before your departure.
귀하의 호텔 예약 확인서가 귀하의 출발 전에 이메일로 보내질 것입니다.
···› 동사 will be emailed의 주어 자리에 Confirmation이 왔다.

❷ 목적어 자리: 동사의 목적어 자리

John Greener made a significant **contribution** to the contract negotiation with Macesoft.
존 그리너는 매스소프트와의 계약 협상에서 상당한 공헌을 했다.
···› 타동사 made의 목적어 자리에 contribution이 왔다.

❸ 목적어 자리: 전치사의 목적어 자리

In **response** to your job advertisement, I have sent my résumé for your consideration.
귀하의 구인 광고에 응해서, 고려하실 수 있도록 제 이력서를 보냈습니다.
···› 전치사 In 뒤의 목적어 자리에 response가 왔다.

❹ 주격 보어 자리

Ms. Marx will become the **head** of the company's Marketing Department.
마르크스 씨는 회사 마케팅 부서장이 될 것이다.
···› 2형식 동사 become 뒤의 주격 보어 자리에 명사 head가 쓰여 주어 Ms. Marx와 동격을 이룬다.

❺ 목적격 보어 자리

The supervisor considers Alfredo a dedicated **employee**.
그 상사는 알프레도를 열심히 하는 직원으로 여긴다.
···› 5형식 동사 considers 뒤의 목적격 보어 자리에 명사 employee가 쓰여 목적어 Alfredo와 동격을 이룬다.

1. A recent survey indicates that many customers use our gift cards to make ------- for food and beverage purchases in our bookstores' cafes.

(A) pays   (B) paying   (C) payable   (D) payments

2. ------- of the online ordering system is our top priority for making the company more responsive to customer needs.

(A) Complete   (B) Completion   (C) Completed   (D) Completely

3. Any changes to the construction plan must be made in ------- with both the client and our suppliers.

(A) coordinate   (B) coordinates   (C) coordinated   (D) coordination

2. 명사는 관사, 소유격, 형용사, 분사 뒤에 온다.

▶ 명사 앞에는 명사의 수나 대상을 한정하는 관사나 소유격 등이 온다.

▶ 명사를 꾸며주는 형용사나 분사도 명사 앞에 올 수 있다.

>> 적중 포인트 1 「관사/소유격 + 명사」

❶ 관사 (a/an, the) 뒤

The **process** of applying for a driver's license varies by state.
운전면허증을 신청하는 절차는 주마다 다르다.

❷ 소유격 뒤

To promote its **growth**, Lupina is investing heavily in product development.
성장을 촉진하기 위해서, 루피나는 제품 개발에 크게 투자하고 있다.

>> 적중 포인트 2 「형용사/분사 + 명사」

❶ 형용사 뒤

Due to his lack of relevant **qualifications**, Mr. Carlton was not offered the marketing manager position.
관련된 자질 부족으로, 칼튼 씨는 마케팅 매니저직을 제안받지 못했다.

❷ 분사 뒤

The employees at Mason have gone through many exciting **challenges** since it expanded into Asia.
메이슨 사가 아시아로 확장한 이래로 직원들은 많은 흥미로운 일들을 했다.

1. Giorgio Corporation's latest appliance is a ------- of a food processor and a high-speed blender.

(A) combine   (B) combination   (C) combines   (D) combined

2. Pilanti Production would like to reduce its ------- on contract workers in the next few years.

(A) rely   (B) relies   (C) reliance   (D) reliable

3. Clayton Sinclair, a board member of the Linton Press Association, has no ------- of running for president anytime soon.

(A) intends   (B) intending   (C) intended   (D) intention

3. 가산 명사 vs. 불가산 명사

▶ 기본적으로 명사 문제가 나오면 가산/불가산 여부를 확인하고, 가산 명사인 경우에는 반드시 단수/복수를 확인해야 한다. 단수일 때는 앞에 부정관사 a/an을, 복수일 때는 단어 뒤에 -s/es를 붙인다. 하지만 불가산 명사는 앞뒤에 아무것도 붙이지 않는다.

▶ 가산 명사와 함께 쓰이는 수량 형용사와 불가산 명사와 함께 쓰이는 수량 형용사가 있다.

≫ 적중 포인트 1 가산 명사와 불가산 명사의 구별

It is our policy to offer (discount, **discounts**) up to 10 percent to VIP members.
우수 회원들에게 최대 10%까지 할인을 제공하는 것이 우리의 정책이다.
⋯→ discount는 가산 명사이므로 앞에 a/an이나 뒤에 -s/es를 붙여야 한다.

The HR manager has (**access**, accesses) to confidential employee information.
인사팀 매니저는 기밀 직원 정보에 접근할 수 있다.
⋯→ access는 불가산 명사이므로 앞에 a/an이나 뒤에 -s/es를 붙이지 않는다.

가산 명사		불가산 명사	
a permit	허가(증)	permission	허가, 승인
an approach	접근법	access	접근
a detail	세부 사항	information	정보
a certificate	증명(서)	certification	증명서
a suggestion	제안	advice	조언
a survey	설문 조사	research	연구
a decision	결정	approval	승인
a refund	환불	equipment	장비
a request	요청	operation	운영

-ing로 끝나는 불가산 명사			
understanding	이해	accounting	회계
planning	계획	training	훈련
cleaning	청소	handling	처리
photocopying	복사	widening	확장
housing	주거, 숙소	advertising	광고, 광고업
seating	좌석	banking	은행 업무
processing	처리	dining	식사
writing	글쓰기	ticketing	티켓 발급

>> 적중 포인트 2 가산 명사와 불가산 명사 앞에 오는 수량 형용사

(**All**, ~~Every~~, ~~Another~~) managers are expected to familiarize themselves with the revised policy.
모든 관리자가 수정된 정책에 익숙해질 것으로 기대된다.

⋯→ managers는 복수 명사이므로 단수 명사와 함께 쓰이는 수량 형용사 Every와 Another의 수식을 받을 수 없다.

단수 가산 명사 수식		복수 가산 명사 수식		불가산 명사 수식		복수 가산 명사/불가산 명사 수식	
one	하나의	a few	몇 개의	a little	약간의	all	모든
each	각각의	few	몇 개 없는	little	거의 없는	any / some	어떤
every	모든	many	많은	less	더 적은	more	더 많은
another	다른	several	몇몇의	much	많은	most	대부분
		numerous	많은			other	다른
		various	다양한			a lot of	많은
		diverse	다양한			(= lots of)	
		multiple	다수의				

+ check .... 해설서 p.11

1. Starting this Saturday, Mika's Sporting Goods will be giving a 30 percent discount on all hiking gear -------.

    (A) purchase   (B) purchases   (C) purchaser   (D) purchasers

2. The Chopmaster 2000 food processor has become our top-selling item following its ------- to the Indian market last year.

    (A) introduce   (B) introduced   (C) introduction   (D) introductions

3. Almost without exception, ------- package that is misplaced due to sorting errors is found and delivered to the client within three days.

    (A) every   (B) all   (C) much   (D) few

4. 사람 명사 vs. 사물/추상 명사

▶ 형태가 비슷한 사람 명사[→ 가산 명사]와 사물/추상 명사[→ 주로 불가산 명사]를 구분하는 문제가 출제된다.

▶ 사람 명사는 가산 명사이므로 단수/복수를 구분해서 사용해야 한다. 즉, 단수는 앞에 a/an을, 복수는 뒤에 -s/es를 붙여야 한다.

▶ 사물을 나타내는 명사는 가산 명사도 있지만 불가산 명사도 있다.

>> 적중 포인트 사람 명사와 사물/추상 명사의 구별

Ms. Hilo called our technical team for (**assistance**, ~~assistant~~) with the wireless connection.
힐로 씨는 무선 연결의 도움을 받기 위해 기술팀에 연락을 취했다.

⋯→ assistant는 사람 명사로 앞에 관사 a/an이나 뒤에 -s/es를 붙여야 한다.

사람 명사		사물/추상 명사	
architect	건축가	architecture	건축
analyst	분석가	analysis	분석
applicant	지원자	application	지원
assistant	보조, 비서	assistance	도움
accountant	회계사	accounting	회계
competitor	경쟁자	competition	경쟁
correspondent	특파원, 기자	correspondence	서신 왕래, 서신
distributor	유통업자	distribution	유통
delegate	대표	delegation	대표단, 위임
enthusiast	애호가	enthusiasm	열정
authority	권한, 권위자	authorization	승인
professional	전문가	profession	직업
manufacturer	제조자, 제조사	manufacture	제조
producer	생산자, 제작자	product	제품

+ check ·········· 해설서 p.12

1. If there are ------- who can work the night shift at the restaurant, they will get higher preference.

    (A) applicants   (B) apply   (C) applications   (D) applicable

2. Merason Landscaping has recently included the ------- of garden and plant waste to their services.

    (A) recyclable   (B) recycling   (C) recycled   (D) recycler

3. Xiaoqing Mills is the ------- of the machinery that produces flour for our bakery.

    (A) operator   (B) operate   (C) operations   (D) operates

5. 복합 명사

▶ 「명사 + 명사」 형태로 쓰이는 관용적 표현을 익혀야 한다.

>> 적중 포인트 「명사 + 명사」

Perderson Inc. has provided a variety of office (~~supplier~~, **supplies**) to our company for 5 years.
퍼더슨 사는 5년 동안 우리 회사에 여러 가지 사무용품을 제공해왔다.

···→ a variety of 뒤에는 복수 명사가 와야 하는데 office가 단수이므로 복합 명사 office supplies가 적합하다.

customer satisfaction	고객 만족	account number	계좌번호
identification card	신분증	application form	신청서
assembly line	조립 라인	pay increase	급여 인상
job opening	공석	expiration date	만기일, 유효 기간
job performance	직무 수행	bank transaction	은행 거래
training session	교육 기간	delivery company	배송 회사
working environment	업무 환경	keynote address	기조연설
dedication ceremony	헌정식	office supplies	사무용품
worker productivity	직원 생산성	travel arrangement	여행 준비
job opportunity	고용 기회	sales representative	판매직원, 영업사원
return policy	반품 정책	benefits package	복지 혜택
confirmation number	확인 번호	savings bank	저축 은행
living expenses	생활비	evaluation form	평가서
travel itinerary	여행 일정	maintenance work	정비 작업
award ceremony	시상식	public relations	홍보
meal/food preference	식사/음식 선호	cooking competition	요리 경연대회
contingency plan	비상 대책	attendance record	출석 기록

+ check .... 해설서 p.12

1. The insurance plan is designed to cover the healthcare ------- of all current employees and their families.

    (A) needs   (B) needed   (C) to need   (D) is needed

2. Marisa Burton is not expected to join our team ------- seminar today.

    (A) to develop   (B) has developed   (C) developing   (D) development

3. Staff members should submit travel ------- requests by the last day of the month.

    (A) reimbursable   (B) reimbursing   (C) reimburse   (D) reimbursement

1. If the board of directors gives its approval, a ------- of our main manufacturing operation will be carried out in September.

   (A) restructure
   (B) restructured
   (C) restructuring
   (D) restructures

2. Since its ------- two years ago, the international sales department has proven valuable to our operations overseas.

   (A) find
   (B) founder
   (C) foundation
   (D) found

3. Every ------- who has submitted a résumé for the managerial position will receive a call for an interview.

   (A) application
   (B) applicant
   (C) applied
   (D) applicants

4. A request for a building ------- should be submitted at least four weeks before the work begins.

   (A) permit
   (B) permitted
   (C) permission
   (D) permits

5. Ms. Gutierrez's impressive presentation is the ------- of weeks of research and preparation.

   (A) resulted
   (B) result
   (C) results
   (D) resulting

6. For ------- purposes, the name and contact information of the client will be removed from the document.

   (A) confided
   (B) confiding
   (C) confidentially
   (D) confidentiality

7. St. Peter's Church was designed by a famous local ------- who received numerous prestigious awards.

   (A) architecture
   (B) architect
   (C) architectural
   (D) architects

8. For a detailed ------- of our writing seminar, please download a copy of the program from our website.

   (A) information
   (B) description
   (C) subscription
   (D) attention

9. Prior to the start of the conference, each ------- will be assigned a seat and given a detailed schedule of the day's events.

   (A) delegating
   (B) delegate
   (C) delegates
   (D) delegated

10. Tara never expressed any ------- to switch departments until this year.

    (A) inclined
    (B) incline
    (C) inclining
    (D) inclination

11. *Global Economic Times* is a new financial ------- for business professionals.

(A) publish
(B) publication
(C) publishers
(D) is publishing

12. Mr. Dawson has consulted a ------- about his plan to establish a new business in Tokyo.

(A) professional
(B) professionals
(C) professionalism
(D) professionally

13. While the roads are being repaired, motorists are advised to use ------- when driving on Highway 10.

(A) cautious
(B) cautiously
(C) cautioned
(D) caution

14. Pinewood Group will open new shopping centers in ------- that are more accessible to customers who use public transportation.

(A) locate
(B) located
(C) location
(D) locations

15. Despite intense -------, our brand's market share has continued to grow.

(A) competition
(B) compete
(C) competing
(D) competitor

16. Every event planner knows that organizing a successful event depends on close ------- between different suppliers.

(A) collaborator
(B) collaborate
(C) collaboration
(D) collaborated

17. The Shelrin Company is the main ------- for Anpo Manufacturing, which produces a variety of auto parts.

(A) to distribute
(B) distributing
(C) distributor
(D) distribution

18. ------- to borrow presentation equipment must be made via e-mail to the Technical Support Department one week in advance of your event.

(A) Request
(B) Requested
(C) Requesting
(D) Requests

19. Development plans for the industrial zone include ------- of the nearby freeway and expansion of adjacent parking space.

(A) widening
(B) wide
(C) widen
(D) width

20. Shen Hing Corporation advises visitors to reserve hotel ------- well in advance of arriving in Hong Kong.

(A) accommodates
(B) accommodated
(C) accommodating
(D) accommodations

형용사

UNIT 05

형용사 문제는 주로 명사를 수식하거나 보어 자리를 묻는 문제로 출제된다. 혼동하기 쉬운 형용사를 구분하는 문제나 형용사가 들어가는 관용표현을 묻는 문제도 빈번하게 등장하고 있다.

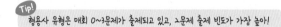

Tip!
형용사 유형은 매회 0~3문제가 출제되고 있고, 2문제 출제 빈도가 가장 높아!

핵심 문법

1. 형용사 자리

▶ 형용사는 명사 앞이나 구 형태로 뒤에서 명사를 꾸며주는 역할을 한다.
▶ 2형식 동사 뒤의 주격 보어나, 5형식 동사 뒤의 목적격 보어 자리에 온다.

>> 적중 포인트 1 명사 수식

❶ 명사 앞 수식

Mr. Lee has been nominated for the Employee of the Year award for his <u>exceptional</u> **performance** this year.

이 씨는 올해 뛰어난 업무 수행으로 올해의 직원상 후보로 추천되었다.

❷ 명사 뒤 수식

Mr. Kim is **the person** <u>responsible</u> for repairing all the damaged goods in the store.

김 씨는 매장의 모든 손상된 물품들의 수리를 담당하고 있는 사람이다.

>> 적중 포인트 2 보어 자리

❶ 주격 보어 자리

Although this year's sales **are** <u>high</u>, the management expects us to boost sales even more.

비록 올해의 매출액이 높긴 하지만, 경영진은 우리가 판매량을 훨씬 더 높이기를 바란다.

2형식 동사	
be	~이다
become	~이 되다
remain	계속 ~한 상태이다
stay　　　　+ 형용사	~한 상태로 남아있다
seem	~하게 보이다
appear	~하게 보이다
prove	~으로 판명되다

❷ 목적격 보어 자리

Most customers **consider** our company's new products <u>innovative</u>.
대부분의 고객이 우리 회사의 신제품을 혁신적이라고 여긴다.

5형식 동사		
make		∼을 …하게 만들다
find		∼가 …한 것을 알게 되다, ∼를 …하다고 여기다
leave	+ 목적어 + 형용사	∼을 …한 채로 두다
consider		∼을 …하다고 여기다
deem		∼을 …으로 여기다
keep		∼을 …하도록 유지하다

☑ 주의해야 할 형용사

「명사 + -ly」 → 형용사					
costly	비싼	friendly	친절한	daily	매일의
orderly	정돈된	weekly	매주의		
현재분사형 형용사 (V-ing)					
demanding	힘든	challenging	힘든	remaining	남아있는
outstanding	뛰어난	rewarding	보람찬	lasting	지속적인
existing	기존의	promising	유망한, 촉망되는		
과거분사형 형용사 (p.p.)					
damaged	손상된	enclosed	동봉된	experienced	숙련된
detailed	상세한	qualified	자격이 있는	skilled	숙련된
limited	한정된	written	서면의	accomplished	뛰어난

+ check .... 해설서 p.14

1. Employers have found students from local trade schools to be extremely ------- workers.

   (A) capable   (B) capability   (C) capacity   (D) capably

2. The offer of admission is ------- until all required documents have been received and checked.

   (A) conditionally   (B) conditions   (C) conditional   (D) condition

3. We do not believe that the software project will be ------- in the near future.

   (A) complete   (B) completely   (C) completion   (D) completing

2. 수량 형용사

▶ one / each / every / another + 단수 명사

▶ a few / few / many / several / both / various / multiple / numerous + 복수 명사

▶ a little / little / much + 불가산 명사

▶ a lot of / lots of / other / some / any / all / most / more + 복수 가산 명사 / 불가산 명사

>> 적중 포인트 1 「수량 형용사 + 단수 명사」

<u>Each</u> **conference participant** should submit a completed registration form.
각 회의 참가자들은 작성이 완료된 신청서를 제출해야 한다.

each 각각의 / every 모든	⋯ each / every employee 각각의 / 모든 직원
one 하나의 / another 또 다른 하나의	⋯ one / another item 하나의 / 또 하나의 상품

✅ 「every / another + 수사 + 복수 명사」: every two hours (2시간마다)

>> 적중 포인트 2 「수량 형용사 + 복수 명사」

<u>Few</u> **people** know how to use the new software.
새 소프트웨어의 사용 방법을 아는 사람들은 많지 않다.

many / a number of / numerous / multiple 많은 / 다수의	⋯ a number of / multiple places 많은 / 다수의 장소들
various / a variety of / an array of / a range of 다양한	⋯ a variety of reasons 다양한 이유들
few 수가 많지 않은(부정) / a few 약간의(긍정) / fewer 더 소수의	⋯ a few employees 몇 명의 직원들
each of ~의 각각 / one of ~중 하나	⋯ each / one of the applicants 지원자들 중 각각 / 한 명

>> 적중 포인트 3 「수량 형용사 + 불가산 명사」

He paid <u>little</u> **attention** to what I was saying.
그는 내가 말하고 있는 것에 거의 관심이 없었다.

much / a great deal of 많은	⋯ much information 많은 정보
little 거의 없는(부정) / a little 약간의(긍정) / less 더 적은	⋯ little time 시간이 거의 없는

>> 적중 포인트 4 「수량 형용사 + 복수 가산 명사 / 불가산 명사」

For <u>more</u> **information** on our service, visit our customer service website.
저희 서비스에 대한 자세한 내용을 원하시면, 고객 서비스 웹사이트를 방문하세요.

a lot of / lots of / plenty of 많은	⋯ a lot of books 많은 책 a lot of time 많은 시간
all 모든 / most 대부분의 / some 약간의 / any 어느 ~든지 / other 다른	⋯ most books 대부분의 책 most time 대부분의 시간

1. SG Car Company's ------- improvements to its hybrid cars will have a great effect on the automobile industry.

   (A) many   (B) each   (C) another   (D) much

2. Online quizzes are designed to grant players some hints after a reasonable number of -------.

   (A) attempting   (B) attempt   (C) attempts   (D) attempted

3. According to the majority of -------, solar panels allow homeowners to save between 2,000 and 4,000 dollars per year.

   (A) estimated   (B) estimating   (C) estimates   (D) estimate

3. 혼동하기 쉬운 형용사

▶ 형태는 비슷하지만 의미가 다른 형용사가 출제되므로 정확하게 구별할 수 있어야 한다.

>> 적중 포인트 형태가 비슷한 형용사

We always make sure that all our customers' information is strictly (confident, **confidential**).
우리는 항상 고객들의 정보가 엄격하게 비밀로 유지되도록 해야 한다.
⋯▶ be동사의 보어 자리로 형용사가 필요한데, 해석을 해보면 '기밀의, 비밀의'라는 의미가 들어가야 하므로 정답은 confidential이
된다.

impressive	인상적인	impressed	감명받은
considerable	상당한	considerate	사려 깊은
favorite	좋아하는	favorable	우호적인
reliant	의존적인	reliable	신뢰할 만한
weekly	매주의	weeklong	일주일간의
beneficial	유익한	beneficent	인정 많은
confident	자신감 있는	confidential	기밀의, 비밀의
arguable	논란의 여지가 있는	argumentative	논쟁적인
competitive	경쟁적인, 경쟁력 있는	competent	유능한
dependent	의존적인	dependable	믿을 만한
successful	성공적인	successive	연속의
appreciable	상당한, 주목할 만한	appreciative	감사하는
satisfactory	충족시키는	satisfied	만족스러운
responsible	책임이 있는	responsive	반응하는
respectable	존경할 만한	respectful	공손한, 예의 바른
respected	훌륭한, 높이 평가되는	respective	각각의, 각자의
extensive	광범위한, 폭넓은	extended	연장된
exhaustive	철저한	exhausted	지친

1. The historic Southport Theater in Curacao City is in need of ------- repairs.

   (A) extensive   (B) extend   (C) extension   (D) extending

2. We look forward to building a mutually ------- working relationship with you.

   (A) beneficial   (B) benefit   (C) benefited   (D) beneficent

3. Content on this website, including news, opinions, and editorial works belongs to their ------- authors.

   (A) respected   (B) respectable   (C) respective   (D) respectful

4. 형용사 관용표현

>> 적중 포인트 「be + 형용사 + 전치사」

Sports Gym will not be (**responsible**, responsive) for the loss of any items left in lockers overnight.
스포츠 짐은 간밤에 사물함에 남겨진 모든 물품의 손실에 관해서 책임을 지지 않을 것입니다.

···→ '~을 책임지고 있다'라는 뜻의 관용표현은 be responsible for이다.

「be + 형용사 + about」			
be enthusiastic about	~을 열심히 하다	be optimistic about	~에 대해 낙관하다
「be + 형용사 + for」			
be famous for	~으로 유명하다	be responsible for	~에 책임이 있다
be suitable for	~에 적합하다	be eligible for	~에 자격이 있다
be valid for	~에 유효하다	be honored for	~으로 상을 받다
「be + 형용사 + of」			
be afraid of	~을 두려워하다	be appreciative of	~에 감사하다
be aware of	~을 인식하다[알다]	be capable of	~할 수 있다
be representative of	~을 대표하다		
「be + 형용사 + with」			
be associated with	~과 관련되다	be compatible with	~과 호환되다
be compliant with	~을 준수하다	be pleased with	~에 기뻐하다
「be + 형용사 + to(전치사)」			
be accessible to	~에 접근 가능하다	be beneficial to	~에 이익이 되다
be accustomed to	~에 익숙하다	be exposed to	~에 노출되다
be attractive to	~에게 있어 매력적이다	be devoted to	~에 헌신하다
be available to	~에게 이용 가능하다	be entitled to	~할 자격이 있다
be subject to	~하기 쉽다, 영향을 받다	be equivalent to	~에 상응하다

「be + 형용사 + to부정사」			
be able to	~할 수 있다	be eligible to	~할 자격이 있다
be proud to	~하는 것을 자랑스러워하다	be qualified to	~할 자격이 있다
be entitled to	~할 자격이 있다	be ready to	~할 준비가 되다
be bound to	반드시 ~하게 될 것이다	be reluctant to	~하기를 꺼리다
be delighted to	~해서 기분이 좋다	be glad to	~해서 기쁘다
be supposed to	~하기로 되어 있다	be willing to	기꺼이 ~하다
be eager to	~하기를 열망하다	be likely to	~할 것 같다
be pleased to	~해서 기쁘다	be unable to	~할 수 없다

+ check .... 해설서 p.15

1. Please note that the comments and opinions featured on this website are not ------- of the News Media Society.

   (A) represents   (B) represented   (C) representative   (D) representatively

2. Employees are ------- about the launch of the new company website designed by Mobius Inc.

   (A) enthusiastic   (B) devoted   (C) respectable   (D) perceptive

3. The textile factory at Harlow Studios is subject to ------- quality inspections by our staff.

   (A) routinely   (B) routines   (C) routineness   (D) routine

Practice

1. The product specifications are ------- everything our engineers had requested.

   (A) consisted
   (B) consisting
   (C) consistency in
   (D) consistent with

2. This two-door convertible is the most popular ------- vehicle our dealership offers.

   (A) rent
   (B) renter
   (C) rented
   (D) rental

3. Many people are complaining that subway delays caused by mechanical faults are becoming more -------.

   (A) frequented
   (B) frequent
   (C) frequently
   (D) frequency

4. The CEO questioned whether the managers were doing ------- to maximize the productivity of their workers.

   (A) enough
   (B) many
   (C) other
   (D) such

5. For the first few months, Ernesto struggled to keep up with the ------- schedule of his new job.

   (A) demanding
   (B) demand that
   (C) demand to
   (D) demanded

6. The Nelta Manufacturing plant manager considered it ------- to suspend production while safety inspections were being conducted.

   (A) necessity
   (B) necessary
   (C) necessitate
   (D) necessarily

7. From January 3 to 6, Mr. Hunter will hold a number of workshops for ------- assistant managers.

   (A) either
   (B) all
   (C) each
   (D) few

8. All of the candidates for the promotion gave great responses, but Mr. Gutierrez's answers were particularly -------.

   (A) insightful
   (B) insight
   (C) insights
   (D) insightfully

9. Many countries are becoming increasingly ------- on petroleum imported from outside of the Middle East.

   (A) reliant
   (B) reliance
   (C) reliable
   (D) rely

10. A recent survey indicates that many consumers are ------- to buy the latest MX555 laptop because of its enhanced capabilities.

    (A) knowledgeable
    (B) decisive
    (C) anxious
    (D) exciting

11. According to the product satisfaction survey, Hardaway work boots are not as ------- as other similar brands.

(A) light
(B) lightly
(C) lightest
(D) lightness

12. The factory workers are now back on the job following ------- talks with union representatives.

(A) extends
(B) extend
(C) extensive
(D) extent

13. The factory's new assembly equipment has proven ------- in increasing production levels.

(A) effected
(B) effective
(C) effectively
(D) effectiveness

14. The marketing manager was ------- of the team members' efforts to make the new advertising campaign a success.

(A) willing
(B) appreciative
(C) fulfilled
(D) decisive

15. Regulations on handling dangerous chemicals in the laboratory should be set in a ------- manner to prevent injuries.

(A) time
(B) timely
(C) times
(D) timing

16. The rental agreement states that tenants are personally ------- for any destruction of property that occurs during the lease period.

(A) informed
(B) liable
(C) compatible
(D) prohibited

17. Prime Stationery is no longer ------- delivery orders for office supplies that are less than $100.

(A) accepting
(B) accepted
(C) acceptable
(D) accept

18. The owner's manual says that you should change the car's oil once ------- three months.

(A) total
(B) any
(C) only
(D) every

19. Passengers can receive vegetarian meals for ------- additional charge if they inform our airline at least 48 hours in advance.

(A) no
(B) not
(C) nothing
(D) nonetheless

20. In order to ensure compliance with all the new regulations, the company will implement a ------- internal audit program.

(A) comprehensive
(B) conceivable
(C) numerous
(D) potential

부사

UNIT 06

부사 문제는 부사 자리를 묻거나 부사 어휘, 부사의 문법적 특징을 묻는 문제들이 출제된다. 부사는 수식어이므로 생략되어도 문장에는 문법적 오류가 없다는 점에 유의한다. 부사 어휘는 함께 잘 쓰이는 어휘를 암기해 두면 정답을 더 신속하게 고를 수 있다.

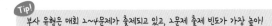

Tip!
부사 유형은 매회 2~4문제가 출제되고 있고, 2문제 출제 빈도가 가장 높아!

핵심 문법

1. 부사 역할

▶ 부사는 동사, 형용사, 부사 또는 문장 전체를 수식하며, 부사가 없어도 완전한 문장이 될 수 있다.

>> 적중 포인트 1 동사 수식

❶ 주어 + [부사] + 동사

The legislators **finally** decided to reform the law.
국회의원들이 마침내 법안을 개정하기로 결정했다.

❷ 자동사 + [부사]

The profits at Todax Corporation have increased **steadily.**
토닥스 사의 수익이 꾸준히 증가해왔다.

❸ have + [부사] + p.p.
   have + p.p. + [부사]

The company has **substantially** increased its profit margins.
그 회사는 이익이 상당히 증가했다.

❹ be + [부사] + 현재분사/과거분사
   be + 현재분사/과거분사 + [부사]

The new supermarket is **conveniently** located on William Street.
새 슈퍼마켓이 윌리엄 가에 편리하게 위치해 있다.

❺ 조동사 + [부사] + 본동사

This copy machine can **easily** be repaired.
이 복사기는 쉽게 수리될 수 있다.

❻ to부정사 수식

We are always trying to develop our products to **better** suit the needs of our customers.
우리는 고객들의 요구에 더 부합하기 위해 항상 제품 개발에 힘쓰고 있다.

❼ 동명사 수식

The project helps conserve the environment by **heavily** investing in clean energy.
그 프로젝트는 청정에너지에 대거 투자함으로써 환경 보호를 돕는다.

>> 적중 포인트 2 형용사 수식

It was an **absolutely** successful project.
그것은 틀림없이 성공적인 프로젝트였다.

>> 적중 포인트 3 부사 수식

Mr. Kent knows the city's streets **very** well.
켄트 씨는 이 도시의 거리를 매우 잘 안다.

>> 적중 포인트 4 문장 전체 수식

Alternatively, you can contact us by e-mail.
다른 방법으로는, 이메일로 저희에게 연락할 수 있습니다.

>> 적중 포인트 5 수사 수식

The plane will be landing in **approximately** 30 minutes.
비행기는 약 30분 후에 착륙할 것이다.

approximately, about, around, roughly	대략	nearly, almost	거의
more than, over	~보다 많은, ~이상	up to	최대 ~까지
at least	최소한, 적어도	only, just	단지, 겨우

+ check .... 해설서 p.17

1. No student attending McRae University may graduate without ------- fulfilling the requirements of their major.

   (A) satisfaction   (B) satisfied   (C) satisfactory   (D) satisfactorily

2. Upon receipt of the items, the payment will be deposited ------- to your company account.

   (A) direction   (B) directs   (C) directly   (D) directed

3. Leo's Dessert Shop has ------- been in business since January, but it is now the best-selling donut shop in the area.

   (A) only   (B) ever   (C) lately   (D) once

2. 주의해야 할 부사

>> 적중 포인트 1 still vs. yet 여전히, 아직도

Some managers are **still not** convinced that the system is beneficial to the company.
몇몇 관리자들은 그 시스템이 회사에 유익한지 아직 확신하지 못하고 있다.

···→ still은 부정문에서 not 앞에 온다.

Due to a lack of funds, the renovation of the bridge **has yet to** be discussed.
자금 부족 때문에, 다리 보수 공사는 아직 논의되지 않았다.

···→ yet은 부정문에서 주로 not 뒤 또는 문장 끝에 오지만, have[be] yet to do(아직 ~하지 못하다)의 관용표현으로도 쓰인다.

>> 적중 포인트 2 once 한번, (과거의) 한때

MCY Motors, one of the biggest vehicle manufacturers in Europe, **was once** a small car dealership.
유럽에서 가장 큰 자동차 제조업체 중 하나인 엠씨와이 자동차는 한때 작은 자동차 영업소였다.

···→ once는 과거 시제와 함께 쓰인다.

>> 적중 포인트 3 quite 꽤, 상당히

The food in the cafeteria is **quite good**.
여기 카페테리아 음식은 꽤 좋다.

···→ quite는 형용사와 함께 쓰인다.

>> 적중 포인트 4 증가/감소를 나타내는 말을 수식하는 부사

Since Hidy Norman was appointed CEO, the profit margin at Cordin Broadcasting has **increased significantly**.
하디 노먼이 전문경영인으로 임명된 이래로, 코딘 방송사의 수익이 급격하게 증가했다.

considerably, substantially, significantly, greatly	상당히
unexpectedly, surprisingly	뜻밖에, 의외로
sharply, dramatically, markedly	급격하게
remarkably, markedly	두드러지게
quickly, rapidly	빠르게
slowly, steadily, gradually	느리게, 꾸준히, 점차적으로

≫ 적중 포인트 5 형용사나 부사만 수식하는 부사

This quarter's sales figures were **relatively high**.
이번 분기의 판매 수치는 비교적 높았다.

so, very, quite	꽤
extremely, exceptionally	매우, 극도로
relatively	비교적

≫ 적중 포인트 6 otherwise 달리, 그렇지 않으면

❶ 「**unless + otherwise + 과거분사**」 **(달리)**
「**unless + 과거분사 + otherwise**」

Unless otherwise specified, attendance at the meeting will be limited to VIP members.
달리 명시 사항이 없으면, 회의 참석은 브이아이피 회원들로 제한될 것이다.

⋯→ Unless otherwise mentioned/stated/indicated/instructed/specified (달리 언급/지시 사항/명시 사항이 없으면)

❷ 「**S + V; otherwise, S + V**」 **(그렇지 않으면)**

You should record your working hours after shifts; **otherwise**, you will not be paid.
교대 근무 후에 근무 시간을 기록해야 한다. 그렇지 않으면, 보수를 받지 못할 것이다.

해설서 p.17

+ check

1. The customer who has shown interest in buying the home on Elm Road has ------- to sign the sales agreement.

   (A) so   (B) always   (C) yet   (D) almost

2. Over the past five years, household incomes have increased -------, accompanying a sharp decline in the unemployment rate.

   (A) markedly   (B) fashionably   (C) loudly   (D) importantly

3. Despite the lack of time, the design team managed to make the company's new logo ------- attractive.

   (A) much   (B) quite   (C) often   (D) well

3. 혼동하기 쉬운 부사

hard	adj 딱딱한, 어려운 adv 열심히	hardly	adv 거의 ~하지 않는
late	adj 늦은 adv 늦게	lately	adv 최근에
close	adj 가까운, 면밀한 adv 가깝게	closely	adv 면밀하게, 밀접하게
high	adj 높은 adv 높게	highly	adv 매우, 많이
near	adj 가까운 adv 가깝게	nearly	adv 거의
short	adj 짧은 adv 짧게	shortly	adv 곧, 이내

+ check ·· 해설서 p.17

1. Director Leila Ryu will answer questions from the audience ------- following the premiere of her new film.

   (A) short   (B) shorter   (C) shortly   (D) shortage

2. -------, Juliana has been staying at work until 8 or 9 P.M. almost every day.

   (A) Lately   (B) Lateness   (C) Later   (D) Late

3. Alice Ebihara, our head of accounting, plans to monitor this year's expenses much more -------.

   (A) close   (B) closer   (C) closely   (D) closed

4. 접속부사

▶ 접속부사는 두 문장을 연결해 주지만, 품사는 부사이지 접속사가 아니므로 두 문장을 이어줄 때 접속부사가 쓰일 수 있는 패턴을 익혀둔다.

「주어(S) + 동사(V). 접속부사, 주어(S) + 동사(V)」

「주어(S) + 동사(V); 접속부사, 주어(S) + 동사(V)」

「주어(S) + 동사(V) + 접속사 + 접속부사, 주어(S) + 동사(V)」

* 「접속사 + 접속부사」: and also 또한, and then 그리고 나서, and therefore 그러므로

결과	therefore, hence	그러므로
	then	그리고 나서
	consequently	결과적으로
	as a result	결과적으로
부가	in addition, besides, plus	게다가
	moreover, furthermore	더욱이
대조	however	그러나
	otherwise, or else	그렇지 않으면
	nonetheless, nevertheless	그럼에도 불구하고
	on the other hand	반면에
기타	for example	예를 들어
	instead	대신에
	as usual	여느 때처럼
	afterward(s)	그 후에

+ check .... 해설서 p.17

1. Some activities had to be held indoors due to the weather, but the company's annual employee workshop was ------- completed as scheduled.

   (A) accordingly   (B) nonetheless   (C) mutually   (D) furthermore

2. Lomita Logistics ships sensitive documents internationally and -------, requires a secure tracking system.

   (A) rather   (B) however   (C) since   (D) therefore

3. Mr. Grazie applied for the sales position; -------, his past jobs were all in accounting.

   (A) now that   (B) however   (C) in case   (D) otherwise

1. Consumers can support area farmers by purchasing fruits and vegetables that are grown -------.

(A) region
(B) regional
(C) regions
(D) regionally

2. Texahoma National Bank has discovered that some clients are responding ------- to its plans to close down neighborhood branches.

(A) negatively
(B) negative
(C) negativity
(D) negatives

3. Interviews with local business owners have shown that they are almost ------- in agreement with the new waterfront development plans.

(A) universe
(B) universality
(C) universal
(D) universally

4. Your meals at the buffet are ------- complimentary provided that you can confirm that you are a current guest of this hotel.

(A) completion
(B) completely
(C) complete
(D) completed

5. Khorshid Solar Power has ------- to announce whether it has accepted the terms of the merger.

(A) allowed
(B) soon
(C) yet
(D) likely

6. Staff must turn off all electronic machinery after finishing work every day, unless ------- advised.

(A) likewise
(B) otherwise
(C) daily
(D) repeatedly

7. As a result of Mr. Christopher's unexpected illness, he has cut back ------- on his current projects.

(A) significantly
(B) significant
(C) signifying
(D) significance

8. Heavy rain may cause flight schedules to change ------- this week.

(A) sincerely
(B) popularly
(C) virtually
(D) unexpectedly

9. Despite ------- examining your company's proposal, our board of directors has voted against proceeding with a joint venture at this time.

(A) thought
(B) thoughtful
(C) thoughtfully
(D) thoughtfulness

10. The firm's least profitable service was also, -------, the most highly advertised.

(A) surprise
(B) surprising
(C) surprisingly
(D) surprised

11. Garisop Inc. offers ------- priced products to customers by implementing a cost-effective manufacturing process.
(A) competitively
(B) competitive
(C) competed
(D) competition

12. The Morten Rattan Museum is housed in a beautiful mansion that was ------- the home of the famous writer, Max Thomas.
(A) such
(B) each
(C) more
(D) once

13. ------- situated near the international airport, Green Quay Resort is the perfect location for business conventions.
(A) Idealistic
(B) Ideal
(C) Ideals
(D) Ideally

14. The refrigerator was taken to the repair center almost a week ago, but it ------- has not been repaired.
(A) still
(B) yet
(C) already
(D) only

15. Thanks to the new quality assurance system, our customer complaints have decreased -------.
(A) potentially
(B) extremely
(C) respectively
(D) dramatically

16. ------- invited guests are allowed to attend the opening of Tarya Filonen's art show.
(A) Except
(B) Quite
(C) Only
(D) Before

17. The employee lunch meeting normally starts at noon and takes ------- 45 minutes.
(A) approximately
(B) appropriately
(C) actively
(D) alternatively

18. According to the contract, the insurance will go into effect ------- after the first payment is received.
(A) currently
(B) habitually
(C) immediately
(D) centrally

19. All furniture in this store can be ordered as a set or -------.
(A) individually
(B) individuality
(C) individualize
(D) individual

20. For security purposes, our managers ------- review customer account activity.
(A) formerly
(B) solely
(C) recently
(D) occasionally

대명사

대명사 문제는 인칭대명사, 재귀대명사, 지시대명사, 부정대명사가 골고루 나오는데, 그 중 인칭대명사는 매회 출제된다. 인칭대명사 문제의 난이도는 낮은 편이지만, 그 밖의 다른 대명사 문제 유형은 어렵게 출제되기도 하므로 반드시 대명사의 종류와 특징을 구분해서 익혀두자.

> **Tip!**
> 대명사 유형은 매회 1~3문제가 출제되고 있고, 그 문제 출제 빈도가 가장 높아!

핵심 문법

1. 인칭대명사

▶ 인칭대명사는 사람 명사를 대신하여 명사의 수, 인칭, 성별에 따라 알맞은 형태로 써야 한다. 주어로 쓰이면 주격, 명사 앞에는 소유격, 동사나 전치사 뒤에는 목적격으로 쓴다.

≫ 적중 포인트 1 주격은 주어 자리에 온다.

After **you** review all the details, you can contact us for more information.
모든 세부사항을 검토하신 후에, 더 많은 정보를 원하시면 저희에게 연락하실 수 있습니다.

≫ 적중 포인트 2 소유격은 명사 앞에 온다.

When employees are concerned about their performance, they can consult **their** supervisor.
직원들은 그들의 성과에 대해 염려되는 점이 있다면, 그들의 상관과 상의할 수 있다.

✓ **on one's own은 '스스로'라는 의미이다.**

Team members should be able to work efficiently **on their own**.
팀원들은 그들 스스로 효율적으로 일할 줄 알아야 한다.

≫ 적중 포인트 3 목적격은 타동사나 전치사 뒤에 온다.

If your order is defective, you can send **us** the product immediately. (타동사의 목적어)
주문한 물건에 결함이 있으면, 즉시 제품을 저희에게 보내주시면 됩니다.

Ms. Lee wants to propose a business plan to the investors, but the manager wants to talk with **her** first. (전치사의 목적어)
이 씨가 투자자들에게 사업 계획을 제안하고 싶어 하지만, 관리자는 그녀와 먼저 이야기해보기를 원한다.

≫ 적중 포인트 4 소유대명사는 「소유격 + 명사」로 주어, 목적어, 보어 자리에 온다.

John wanted to meet with a friend of **mine(= my friend)**.
존은 내 친구 중의 한 명을 만나고 싶어 했다.

1. Not only is Chad Pratt a university professor, but ------- is also the author of a best-selling book.

   (A) he   (B) his   (C) him   (D) himself

2. Weeton Catering Service assures us that ------- wheat products are allergy-free.

   (A) they   (B) its   (C) itself   (D) themselves

3. Those wishing to renew their subscription to *Gardener News Monthly* should send ------- the payment no later than June 30.

   (A) ourselves   (B) our   (C) us   (D) ours

2. 재귀대명사

▸ 목적어가 주어와 같을 때 '~ 자신'이라는 의미로 재귀대명사를 쓴다.

▸ 재귀대명사는 '직접, 스스로'라는 뜻으로 주어, 목적어, 보어 등을 강조하는 용법으로 쓰인다. 강조하는 말 바로 뒤에 오거나 문장의 끝에 올 수 있다.

>> 적중 포인트 1 재귀 용법

주어와 목적어가 의미하는 내용이 같을 때 타동사의 목적어 자리에 오며 생략할 수 없다.

Ms. Rushdie has shown **herself** to be competitive.
러쉬디 씨는 자기 자신이 경쟁력이 있다는 것을 보여왔다.

>> 적중 포인트 2 강조 용법

주어나 목적어를 강조할 때, 강조하는 명사 바로 뒤 또는 문장 끝에 위치하며 생략할 수 있다.

The president delivered the presentation to the new buyers **himself**.
사장이 직접 새 구매자들을 상대로 발표했다.

>> 적중 포인트 3 관용표현

by oneself(= on one's own)는 '혼자서, 혼자 힘으로'의 뜻이고, for oneself는 '스스로, 혼자 힘으로'를 뜻한다.

Ms. Kim has to train the new employee **by herself.**
김 씨는 혼자서 신입 직원을 교육해야 한다.

1. Many local distributors have already tried the program ------- and found it satisfactory.

   (A) themselves   (B) they   (C) their   (D) them

2. All newly hired staff must attend the orientation to familiarize ------- with the company's policies and regulations.

   (A) itself   (B) ourselves   (C) themselves   (D) yourself

3. Since the project manager's request for additional workers was not approved, she proceeded with two projects by -------.

   (A) her own   (B) herself   (C) her   (D) she

3. 지시대명사

▶ that/those는 앞에 언급된 명사를 반복할 때 쓰며, 단수 명사일 때는 that, 복수 명사일 때는 those를 쓴다.

▶ those는 뒤에 수식어를 취하여 '~한 사람들'이라는 의미로 쓰인다.

>> 적중 포인트 1 명사를 대신하는 「that/those + 전치사구」

The benefits of working at the Tokyo office are much better than **those** of working at any other branches in Japan.

도쿄 지사 근무의 혜택은 일본의 다른 어떤 지사에서 일하는 것보다 훨씬 좋다.

⋯➔ 비교급 문장으로 앞에 나오는 benefits라는 복수 명사를 받아 those로 쓴다. 이때 뒤에 전치사구의 수식을 받고 있어 인칭대명사 them은 쓸 수 없다.

>> 적중 포인트 2 「those(= people) + 수식어」

Those who work on weekends are entitled to extra vacation days.

주말에 근무하는 사람들은 추가 휴가를 받을 자격이 있다.

「those + who/-ing/p.p./전치사구」	~하는 사람들
「anyone/everyone + who/-ing/p.p./전치사구」	~하는 어느 누구나/모두

⋯➔ those는 복수로, anyone/everyone은 단수로 수 일치 시켜야 하는 차이가 있다.

 check ·· 해설서 p.20

1. Several construction projects are planned in the state, but Gardner is focused on ------ near the main highway.

   (A) them   (B) those   (C) which   (D) how

2. Only ------- who pass the final exam will be eligible to apply for a permanent position.

   (A) they   (B) if   (C) those   (D) anyone

3. ------- who thinks that they have a better strategy for increasing sales is welcome to talk to Mr. Ramirez.

   (A) Another   (B) Anyone   (C) Many   (D) All

4. 부정대명사

▶ one, some, any, many, much, all, each 등은 불특정한 사람이나 사물을 가리키는 부정대명사로 쓰인다.

>> 적중 포인트 1 전체 중 일부를 나타내는 표현

One of the customer service representatives is expected to give me a call.

고객 서비스 담당자 중 한 명이 나에게 전화할 것으로 예상된다.

one of the			~중 하나
each of the	+ 복수 명사	+ 단수 동사	~중 각각
either of the			~중 하나 (둘 중 하나)
much of the	+ 불가산 명사	+ 단수 동사	~중 많은 부분
little/a little/less of the			~중 거의 없음/약간/더 적음

several of the both of the many of the few / a few / fewer of the	+ 복수 명사	+ 복수 동사	~중 몇몇 ~중 둘 다 ~중 많은 사람들(것들) ~중 거의 없음 / 약간 / 더 적음
all of the most of the some of the any of the	+ 복수 명사 불가산 명사	+ 복수 동사 단수 동사	~의 전부 ~의 대부분 ~의 일부 ~의 아무도 / 어느 것도(아닌)

☑ _____ of the에 들어갈 수 없는 대명사

everyone / someone / anyone ✖ everybody / somebody / anybody ✖ everything / something / anything ✖ the one / this / that / these / those ✖	+ of the

PART 5 UNIT 07

>> **적중 포인트 2** one 정해져 있지 않은 단수, another 또 다른 하나, the other / the others 나머지(들)

I got **two job offers**: **one** is in New York, and **the other** is in L.A.
두 일자리를 제안받았는데, 하나는 뉴욕에서, 나머지 하나는 LA에서다.

one (단수) / the other (단수)	전체 범위가 **두 개**인 경우
one (단수) / another (단수) / the other (단수)	전체 범위가 **세 개**인 경우
one (단수) / the others (복수)	전체 범위가 **세 개 이상**인 경우

>> **적중 포인트 3** 불특정 다수 some / others

While **some** workers like flexible working hours, **others** prefer to work during regular working hours.
어떤 직원들은 탄력 근무제를 좋아하지만, 어떤 이들은 정규 근무 시간에 일하는 것을 선호한다.

>> **적중 포인트 4** each other / one another 서로 ···→ 주어 자리에 올 수 없고 동사와 전치사의 목적어 자리에만 올 수 있다.

Employees are expected to help **one another** in the workplace.
직장에서 직원들은 서로 도울 것으로 기대된다.

>> **적중 포인트 5** 형용사 no, 대명사 none, 부사 not

EZ Travel Store will replace any defective items at **no** cost.
이제트 여행 가게는 하자가 있는 상품은 무엇이든 무료로 교환해 드립니다.

None of the members is going to the festival.
회원 중 어느 누구도 축제에 가지 않을 것이다.

+ check ·· 해설서 p.20

1. The recruitment manager, Letita Fung, is seeking ------- qualified to head the Sales Department.

   (A) someone   (B) one another   (C) everyone   (D) whose

2. Ms. Yang will represent Ukran Technologies at the upcoming negotiation meeting as she knows the contract details better than -------.

   (A) most   (B) whichever   (C) much   (D) each

3. Though ------- disliked the decision, the new budget policy was implemented because expenses were too high in some departments of the company.

   (A) any   (B) many   (C) other   (D) himself

Practice

1. We need to inform HR that ------- interviews with the remaining candidates will be postponed.

(A) we
(B) our
(C) ours
(D) ourselves

2. This conference will give Mr. Brown a chance to voice his opinions on the changes ------- proposed about the management of the company.

(A) he
(B) that
(C) were
(D) until

3. Invitations to next month's fundraising event were mailed to over 100 people, but ------- have replied so far.

(A) little
(B) few
(C) whoever
(D) so

4. If you have difficulties setting up the new computer on -------, please call our Customer Support Center.

(A) yours
(B) yourself
(C) your own
(D) your

5. Nextcom's recently introduced DX-7000 is the first video conferencing product of ------- kind to address cost-conscious small businesses.

(A) our
(B) your
(C) their
(D) its

6. Ms. Welch has submitted her expense report, but Mr. Garrison has still not submitted -------.

(A) his
(B) him
(C) he
(D) himself

7. Thanks to her talent for multitasking, Ms. Choi has shown ------- to be an outstanding event coordinator.

(A) she
(B) her
(C) herself
(D) hers

8. According to Mr. Thomas, the district managers are likely to conduct interviews with the candidates -------.

(A) him
(B) himself
(C) theirs
(D) themselves

9. ------- who are interested in working at the new branch in Sydney are asked to notify the Personnel Department manager.

(A) Them
(B) Anyone
(C) That
(D) Those

10. Many of the guests ------- watched yesterday's performance have already posted their reviews online.

(A) which
(B) few
(C) those
(D) who

11. ------- of the complaints received by our office is investigated and taken care of thoroughly by our Customer Service Department.
(A) All
(B) Much
(C) Each
(D) Every

12. During the seminar, the participants were asked to organize ------- in groups based on previous work experiences.
(A) their
(B) theirs
(C) their own
(D) themselves

13. Although Ms. Bushra is a new employee, her decisions resemble ------- of a manager who has been in this business for many years.
(A) it
(B) those
(C) all
(D) them

14. These two are the most highly qualified, and it is very hard to choose one applicant over -------.
(A) one more
(B) the other
(C) all other
(D) some other

15. The fiberglass workers are experienced with ------- from making small car repairs to constructing entire boats.
(A) distinctions
(B) others
(C) approaching
(D) everything

16. The senior designer created two logos for the brand, but ------- was approved.
(A) either
(B) nobody
(C) neither
(D) all

17. Since many bids were made for the remodeling project, Mr. Flynn and Ms. Junko were delighted when ------- were selected.
(A) them
(B) their
(C) theirs
(D) they

18. Even though many consumers hope to purchase a house as quickly as possible, ------- just prefer the freedom of renting.
(A) some
(B) someone
(C) other
(D) another

19. Katy Leung, Director of Human Resources, chose to conduct the employee training -------.
(A) hers
(B) herself
(C) she
(D) her

20. Four firms were contacted about supporting the Kinder Holiday Outreach Program, and ------- donated large sums.
(A) any
(B) all
(C) anything
(D) everything

전치사

전치사 문제는 전치사 뒤의 빈칸에 들어갈 알맞은 품사를 고르는 문제와 전치사의 기본적인 의미와 용법을 묻는 문제가 빠지지 않고 출제되고 있다. 특정 동사나 명사, 형용사와 어울려 쓰이는 전치사의 관용적인 표현 문제도 매회 출제된다.

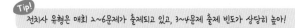

Tip!
전치사 유형은 매회 2~6문제가 출제되고 있고, 3~4문제 출제 빈도가 상당히 높아!

1. 전치사의 특징

▶ 전치사는 명사와 함께 쓰여, 형용사나 부사 역할을 한다.
▶ 전치사 뒤에는 명사 계열인 명사, 동명사, 명사절이 온다.

>> 적중 포인트 1 형용사나 부사 역할을 하는 전치사구

The deadline **for the monthly budget report** was postponed.
월간 예산 보고서의 마감일이 연기되었다.
···→ 앞 명사를 수식하는 형용사 역할을 한다.

The shipping company now has contracts **with 32 major clothing retailers**.
그 운송회사는 현재 32개 주요 의류 소매업체와 계약을 맺고 있다.
···→ 동사를 수식하는 부사 역할을 한다.

>> 적중 포인트 2 「전치사 + 명사/동명사/명사절」

In addition to the ability to speak English, applicants should have relevant experience.
영어를 말할 수 있는 능력 이외에도, 지원자들은 관련 경험이 있어야 한다.
···→ 「전치사 + 명사」

All technicians at Gelco Pharmaceuticals are expected to wash their hands **before** entering the laboratories.
젤코 제약의 모든 기술자는 실험실에 들어가기 전에 손을 씻어야 한다.
···→ 「전치사 + 동명사」

We have printed enough information packets to distribute **regardless of** how many guests attend.
우리는 얼마나 많은 손님이 참석하는 지와는 상관없이 나눠 줄 충분한 안내 책자를 인쇄했다.
···→ 「전치사 + 명사절」

+ check ··· 해설서 p.22

1. Amali Manufacturing won the Industry Innovation Award this month ------- its new line of electrical appliances.
   (A) but   (B) while   (C) also   (D) for

2. ------- his busy speaking agenda, the Vice President of Sales made time to speak with the new trainees.
   (A) Nevertheless   (B) Despite   (C) Unless   (D) Although

3. Pelican Pizza has decided that ------- local delivery service, it will start offering its product in the frozen food sections of supermarkets across the state.
   (A) regardless of   (B) in addition to   (C) based upon   (D) on account of

2. 시간 전치사: 시간, 시점, 기간 전치사

>> 적중 포인트 1 시간 전치사

「at + 정확한 시간/시점」	~에	at 2 P.M. at noon at the beginning	오후 2시에 정오에 ~초에
「on + 날짜/요일」	~에	on January 3 on Friday on Sunday afternoon on weekdays/weekends	1월 3일에 금요일에 일요일 오후에 주중에/주말에
「in + 월/계절/연도/시기」	~에	in April in summer in 2023 in the morning/evening	4월에 여름에 2023년에 아침에/저녁에

>> 적중 포인트 2 시점을 나타내는 전치사

「before(= prior to) + 시점」	~전에	before April prior to your arrival	4월 전에 도착 전에
「after(= following) + 시점/기간」	~후에	after a month following the meeting	한 달 후에 회의 후에
「since + 과거 시점」	~이래로	since last summer	지난 여름 이래로
「from + 시점」	~로부터	from today	오늘부터
「by + 시점」	~까지(완료)	by next Friday	다음 금요일까지
「until + 시점」	~까지(지속/계속)	until tomorrow	내일까지

>> 적중 포인트 3 기간을 나타내는 전치사

「for + 기간」	~동안에	for the last five years	지난 5년 동안에
「during + 특정 기간」	~동안에	during the business trip	출장 동안에
「within + 기간」	~이내에	within 30 days	30일 이내에
「over + 기간」	~동안에, ~이상	over the past three years	지난 3년 동안에
「in + 기간」	~후에	in two weeks	2주 후에
「throughout + 기간」	~내내	throughout the year	일 년 내내

1. Defective items bought at our retail locations must be returned ------- a week with proof of purchase.

   (A) with   (B) until   (C) from   (D) within

2. The chairman of the Herman Wright Foundation will make a speech ------- this evening's charity banquet.

   (A) except   (B) before   (C) as   (D) onto

3. There have not been any new developments on Carretown's historic seafront ------- more than a decade.

   (A) over   (B) until   (C) up   (D) in

3. 장소 전치사: 장소, 방향, 위치 전치사

>> 적중 포인트 1 장소를 나타내는 전치사

「at + 지점」	~에서/~에	at the library at JP Printing Services	도서관에서 제이피 프린트 회사에서
「on + 표면」	~위에/~에	on the table on the first floor	탁자 위에 1층에
「in + 공간」	~에서/~에	in Asia in the lobby	아시아에서 로비에서

>> 적중 포인트 2 방향, 위치를 나타내는 전치사

to	~로/~에게	to the headquarters	본부로
from	~로부터/~에서	from Cape Town	케이프 타운으로부터
beside / next to	~옆에	next to the building	건물 옆에
through	~을 통해	through the hall	복도를 통해
throughout	~곳곳에, ~전체에	throughout the city	도시 곳곳에
across	~을 건너, ~곳곳에	across the street	길을 건너
above / over	~위에	above the tree	나무 위에
under / below	~아래/~밑에	under the desk	책상 밑에
into	~속으로	into the water	물속으로
out of	~의 밖으로	out of the box	상자 밖으로
near	~가까이에	near the office	사무실 가까이에
past	~을 지나서	past the building	건물 지나서
between	(둘) ~사이에	between New York and Seattle	뉴욕과 시애틀 사이에
among	(셋 이상) ~사이에	among the employees	직원 사이에
along	~을 따라	along the street	거리를 따라
alongside	~의 옆을 따라	alongside the road	길옆을 따라
opposite	~맞은편에	opposite the library	도서관 맞은편에

해설서 p.22

+ check

1. The management of Kerrydown Accounting will meet ------- 402 Caledon Drive on Friday, July 21.

(A) between   (B) out   (C) at   (D) like

2. Workers ------- the automobile industry are entitled to paid vacation after 90 days of employment.

(A) onto   (B) about   (C) in   (D) over

3. As we sell our products at offline stores only, please visit any of our locations ------- the U.S. if you would like to purchase our recent tablet PC model.

(A) across   (B) onto   (C) between   (D) next

4. 비슷한 의미의 전치사

about, as to, as for, regarding, concerning, pertaining to, on, over	～에 관하여
due to, because of, owing to, thanks to, on account of	～때문에
in spite of, despite, notwithstanding	～에도 불구하고
besides, in addition to, plus, as well as, aside from, apart from, on top of	～뿐만 아니라
except (for), without	～을 제외하고
considering, given	～을 고려할 때

+ check

해설서 p.23

1. ------- road repairs on King Road and Savannah Street, traffic in the nearby areas will be subject to delays.

(A) Otherwise   (B) Because   (C) Due to   (D) Whereas

2. ------- a poor turnout at the grand opening event, our new location's sales for the year exceeded expectations.

(A) Despite   (B) While   (C) Even though   (D) Including

3. Additional information ------- the training seminar will be emailed to those who have expressed interest in participating.

(A) regarding   (B) across   (C) through   (D) notwithstanding

5. 헷갈리기 쉬운 전치사

by until	~까지(완료 시점) ~까지(계속 시점)	'완료'의 의미로 finish, submit, return, deliver, receive와 잘 쓰임 '지속/계속'의 의미로 stay, continue, last, postpone, keep과 잘 쓰임	
「for + 숫자 기간」 「during + 특정 기간」	~동안에 ~동안에	for five years during the summer vacation	5년 동안에 여름 방학 동안에
between among	(둘) ~사이에 (셋 이상) ~사이에	between July and September among customers	7월과 9월 사이에 고객들 사이에

+ check .... 해설서 p.23

1. Because of a software failure, design samples produced ------- the week of March 3 may be in the wrong format.

   (A) between　　　　　(B) under　　　　　(C) during　　　　　(D) above

2. Mr. Byron requests that all sales reports be submitted ------ the beginning of next week.

   (A) until　　　　　(B) if　　　　　(C) that　　　　　(D) by

3. ------- organizing a ceremony, look for a proper venue that accommodates all the guests and is easily accessible by public transportation.

   (A) How　　　　　(B) When　　　　　(C) During　　　　　(D) Since

6. 전치사 관용표현

>> 적중 포인트 1 「자동사 + 전치사」

account for	~을 설명하다[차지하다]	comply with	~을 준수하다
adhere to	~을 준수하다	deal with	~을 다루다
agree to[with/on/upon]	~에 동의하다	belong to	~에 속하다
consist of	~으로 구성되다	benefit from	~으로부터 혜택을 얻다
collaborate on/with	~에서/~와 협력하다	comment on	~에 대해 언급하다
compete with[against]	~와 경쟁하다	depend on[upon]	~에 의지하다
enroll in	~에 등록하다	rely on[upon]	~에 의지하다
register for	~에 등록하다	object to	~에 반대하다
refer to	~을 참조하다	succeed to/in	~을 계승하다/~에 성공하다
proceed with/to	~을 진행하다/~로 나아가다	participate in	~에 참가하다
respond to	~에 반응하다	contribute to	~에 공헌하다
apologize for	~에 대해 사과하다	refrain from	~을 삼가다
depart from	~로부터 떠나다	apply for/to	~에 지원하다/~에 적용되다

>> 적중 포인트 2 「명사 + 전치사」

access to	~에의 접근(권한)	interest in	~에 대한 관심
advance in	~에 대한 진보	benefit from	~에 대한 혜택
increase in	~에 대한 증가	demand for	~에 대한 수요
tax on	~에 대한 세금	dispute over	~에 대한 논쟁
commitment to	~에 대한 전념[헌신]	attention to	~에 대한 관심
effect[impact] on	~에 대한 영향	contribution to	~에 대한 공헌
investment in	~에의 투자	confidence in	~에 대한 자신

>> 적중 포인트 3 「be + 형용사 + 전치사」

be appreciative of	~에 감사하다	be capable of	~을 할 수 있다
be compatible with	~과 호환되다	be consistent with	~과 일치하다
be eligible for	~에 대한 자격이 있다	be aware of	~을 잘 알고 있다
be responsible for	~을 책임지다	be famous for	~으로 유명하다
be subject to	~쉽다	be entitled to	~에 자격을 부여받다
be absent from	~을 결석하다	be familiar with	~에 익숙하다
be suitable for	~에 적합하다	be relevant to	~에 관련이 있다

>> 적중 포인트 4 두 단어 이상의 전치사

as a result of	~의 결과로	in compliance with	~을 준수하여
in accordance with	~와 일치하여	in advance of	~보다 미리
in favor of	~에 찬성하여	in honor of	~을 기념하여
in observance of	~을 준수하여	in response to	~에 대한 응답으로
in the event of	~인 경우에	on behalf of	~을 대신하여

+ check 해설서 p.23

1. Consumers benefit ------- a greater choice of products at lower prices.

    (A) from   (B) at   (C) on   (D) for

2. Many survey respondents were familiar ------- the products made by Severn Labels, whose advertisements use cutting-edge photography.

    (A) of   (B) on   (C) with   (D) from

3. To make sure that they are not charged a fine, local stores are encouraged to renew their business licenses no later than a month ------- the expiration date.

    (A) depending upon   (B) as required by   (C) indicated as   (D) in advance of

해설서 p.23 / ⏰ 제한 시간 6분

1. Due to the reorganization, all hiring of new employees is on hold ------- further notice.

(A) of
(B) until
(C) with
(D) regarding

2. Dinner for tonight's alumni reunion is sponsored ------- Mike's Butchery.

(A) by
(B) for
(C) with
(D) since

3. Please call KNZ Inc.'s customer service center with any inquiries you may have ------- our shipping services.

(A) regard
(B) regards
(C) regarded
(D) regarding

4. ------- his overseas experience, Nakhwinder might be a good choice for the opening in the Dubai office.

(A) To consider
(B) Considered
(C) Considering
(D) Consider

5. Staff members interested in gaining qualifications ------- those required for their current jobs are welcome to enroll in any courses that interest them.

(A) prior to
(B) on top of
(C) likewise
(D) as opposed to

6. On Mondays ------- the holiday period, the store opens at 9:00 A.M. instead of 10:00 A.M.

(A) during
(B) since
(C) at
(D) if

7. Rumi Kwon is in charge of ordering all office supplies ------- those for the Design Team.

(A) aside
(B) even if
(C) except
(D) additionally

8. Customers have the right to inspect all items ------- delivery to ensure there are no defects in the merchandise.

(A) upon
(B) later
(C) about
(D) subsequently

9. The president believes that superior customer service gives Hanada Delivery a competitive advantage ------- other shipping companies.

(A) over
(B) including
(C) than
(D) especially

10. The staff meeting of the Marketing Department has been scheduled ------- 10 A.M. on Friday.

(A) between
(B) in
(C) our
(D) for

11. ------- just two years left before retirement, Giovanni suddenly decided to change careers.

(A) In
(B) With
(C) Even
(D) When

12. Crowe Trading announced earlier today that it is preparing to expand ------- China.

(A) at
(B) upon
(C) into
(D) of

13. Additional information ------- the training seminar will be emailed to those who have signed up to attend.

(A) pertaining to
(B) across
(C) in spite of
(D) through

14. Inquiries about our rental properties have increased threefold ------- the airing of a documentary about our city.

(A) regarding
(B) since
(C) before
(D) including

15. ------- rising food prices, consumers are spending less money on groceries these days.

(A) In that
(B) Even if
(C) Just as
(D) Owing to

16. A Daon Technology representative can be reached ------- calling our toll-free number.

(A) into
(B) to
(C) by
(D) as

17. Willem Conference Center is conveniently situated in downtown Starborough, ------- walking distance of several restaurants and hotels.

(A) within
(B) finally
(C) moreover
(D) until

18. News of the upcoming sales event is likely to spread rapidly ------- the staff of the Yokohama distribution center.

(A) in case
(B) into
(C) among
(D) here

19. Access to the performance by the London Philharmonic Orchestra is limited ------- 50 observers per show.

(A) by
(B) to
(C) for
(D) in

20. Mr. Hatch and his partners have agreed ------- a plan to expand the business overseas.

(A) upon
(B) from
(C) at
(D) by

REVIEW TEST 02

해설서 p.25 / 제한 시간 6분

1. The Marketing Director congratulated Anna King for ------- valuable contribution to the advertising campaign.

(A) her
(B) herself
(C) she
(D) hers

2. Part-time staff at Pencorp Inc. are always recruited ------- an employment agency.

(A) through
(B) around
(C) after
(D) as

3. To set up an online trading account, customers need to confirm personal ------- such as their date of birth and social security number.

(A) detail
(B) details
(C) detailing
(D) detailed

4. The new factory machinery should allow us to fill our orders more ------- than before.

(A) quickest
(B) quicker
(C) quick
(D) quickly

5. Modiva Outlet Mall offers ------- on a wide range of quality merchandise.

(A) discounted
(B) discount
(C) discountable
(D) discounts

6. Due to an unexpected contribution from a local company, the community center was built and opened ------- schedule.

(A) regardless of
(B) except for
(C) ahead of
(D) compared to

7. The Career Development Program is designed to be accessible to ------- employee in the company.

(A) all
(B) some
(C) every
(D) much

8. Before switching on the device, make sure to insert the battery in the slot with the ------- on top.

(A) writing
(B) written
(C) write
(D) writer

9. By replacing old appliances with energy-efficient ones, you can reduce your utility bills by ------- 20 percent.

(A) nears
(B) nearly
(C) neared
(D) nearing

10. Rikiya Tanaka offered to prepare the rest of the report ------- so that his coworkers could leave early.

(A) his
(B) him
(C) himself
(D) his own

11. Ms. Freedom deduced that a ------- RAM stick was the reason for the malfunction.

(A) tolerant
(B) agitated
(C) trivial
(D) faulty

12. ------- wishing to attend next week's sales workshop must register by this Friday.

(A) Them
(B) Whoever
(C) Anyone
(D) Who

13. Sapori di Foggia is planning to open a second location featuring a ------- different menu.

(A) completed
(B) completing
(C) completes
(D) completely

14. The board of directors has decided to distribute a ------- of this year's profits to employees as a special bonus.

(A) gratitude
(B) limit
(C) selection
(D) percentage

15. The joint venture was created ------- to allow both Esso Technology and the Lonellu Group to expand into international markets.

(A) specifying
(B) specifically
(C) specific
(D) specify

16. Local high schooler Danielle Kennedy will ------- the nation at the World Ski Championships this winter.

(A) acquire
(B) represent
(C) participate
(D) allow

17. We offer ------- a discount on all of our company products and services.

(A) retire
(B) retired
(C) retiree
(D) retirees

18. By implementing an online ordering system, Cruise Furniture will be able to deliver items ------- its warehouse to customers within two business days.

(A) from
(B) such
(C) when
(D) until

19. Ernie's Bakery's donuts are normally offered with a beverage, but if you prefer, they can always be bought -------.

(A) separating
(B) separated
(C) separately
(D) separation

20. The popularity of the latest issue of the magazine is ------- due to the artistic talents of Ms. Kim.

(A) likely
(B) liking
(C) liked
(D) like

명사절 접속사

명사절은 명사처럼 주어, 목적어, 보어 자리에 온다. that, what, whether가 이끄는 명사절을 묻는 문제가
자주 출제되며, 부사절 접속사와 혼동하지 않도록 해야 한다.

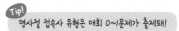
명사절 접속사 유형은 매회 0~1문제가 출제돼!

 **핵심 문법**

1. 명사절의 자리와 쓰임

▶ 명사절은 문장에서 명사 역할을 하며 주어, 목적어, 보어 자리에 온다.

≫ 적중 포인트 명사절의 자리

❶ **주어 자리**

Whether Ms. Kim has arrived from New York or Washington is unknown.
김 씨가 뉴욕에서 왔는지 워싱턴에서 왔는지가 알려지지 않았다.

❷ **동사의 목적어 자리**

I don't know **what happened at the company banquet**.
나는 회사 연회에서 무슨 일이 있었는지 모른다.

❸ **전치사의 목적어 자리**

The company is going to have a discussion as to **whether it will expand its business next year**.
회사는 내년에 사업을 확장할 것인지에 대해 논의를 할 것이다.

❹ **보어 자리**

The problem is **that Ms. Lucy will not be able to conduct interviews tomorrow**.
문제는 루시 씨가 내일 인터뷰를 할 수 없을 거라는 것이다.

+ check .... 해설서 p.27

1. Arca Corporation announced ------- they would not merge with Vista Corporation until they
   agree on the resignation of its CEO.

   (A) that   (B) because   (C) while   (D) what

2. Please inform Steve Ortiz that ------- will be working on the Schneider account.

   (A) he   (B) his   (C) him   (D) himself

3. ------- meets the technician must explain what problem has occurred.

   (A) In order to   (B) Whoever   (C) Despite   (D) Anyone

2. 명사절 접속사 that vs. what

▶ 명사절 접속사 that 뒤에는 완전한 문장이 오지만, what 뒤에는 불완전한 문장이 온다.

▶ the fact / idea / opinion / news / rumor 뒤에 오는 that절은 동격(~라는 사실 / 생각 / 견해 / 뉴스 / 소문)을 나타 낸다.

▶ 「be + 형용사 + that절」 형태의 관용표현을 익혀두자.

>> 적중 포인트 1 「that + 완전한 문장」 vs. 「what + 불완전한 문장」

The management announced (**that**, ~~what~~) performance evaluations will be conducted on a regular basis.

경영진은 업무 평가가 정기적으로 행해질 것이라고 발표했다.

···▷ 타동사 announce의 목적어 역할을 하는 명사절 접속사 자리이다. 빈칸 뒤에 완전한 문장이 나오므로 명사절 접속사 that이 와 야 한다.

Attendees need to consider (~~that~~, **what**) the keynote speaker suggested.

참가자들은 기조 연설자가 제안한 것을 고려해볼 필요가 있다.

···▷ 타동사 consider의 목적어 역할을 하는 명사절 접속사 자리이다. 빈칸 뒤에 suggest의 목적어가 없는 불완전한 문장이 나오므 로 명사절 접속사 what이 와야 한다.

>> 적중 포인트 2 동격의 that절

Everybody knows **the fact** that Mr. Kim will quit.

모든 사람은 김 씨가 그만둘 것이라는 사실을 안다.

···▷ the fact / idea / opinion / news / rumor that(~라는 사실 / 생각 / 견해 / 뉴스 / 소문)으로 종종 출제된다.

>> 적중 포인트 3 관용적인 표현

be aware that	~을 알다
be glad[happy / delighted / pleased] that	~해서 기쁘다
make sure(= be certain) that	~을 확실히 하다
be concerned[worried] that	~을 걱정하다
be afraid that	~을 두려워하다
be sorry that	~을 유감스러워하다
It is important that	~은 중요하다
It is necessary[essential] that	~은 필수이다
It is likely that	~일 것 같다
It is possible / impossible that	~은 가능 / 불가능하다

+ check .... 해설서 p.27

1. ------- a number of textile factories are advertising job openings may be an indication of renewed economic activity.

   (A) As long as   (B) Along with   (C) Pertaining to   (D) The fact that

2. ------- Mr. Wyatt proposed at the meeting definitely impressed the board of directors.

   (A) What   (B) That   (C) Unless   (D) So that

3. Users should be ------- that changes have been made recently to the format of our website.

   (A) in mind   (B) known   (C) advised   (D) awareness

3. 명사절 접속사 whether

▶ whether (or not)가 이끄는 명사절은 '~인지 아닌지'를 의미하며, 문장에서 주어, 목적어, 보어로 쓰인다.

>> 적중 포인트 명사 자리의 whether절

❶ 주어 자리

Whether the site for the new building is affordable remains to be seen.
새로운 건물을 위한 부지 가격이 적당한지는 두고 봐야 한다.

❷ 타동사의 목적어

Ms. Kim has not decided **whether she will hire the intern as a full-time employee**.
김 씨는 그 인턴을 정식 직원으로 채용할지를 아직 결정하지 않았다.

❸ 전치사의 목적어

The company will hire employees regardless of **whether applicants have a university degree**.
회사는 지원자들이 대학 학위가 있는가와 상관없이 직원을 고용할 것이다.

❹ 보어 자리

The problem is **whether customers are willing to buy the product at this high price**.
문제는 고객들이 제품을 이렇게 높은 가격에 기꺼이 구매할 것인가이다.

❺ 「whether + to부정사」

Committee members will decide **whether to nominate Mr. Kent for the board**.
위원회 회원들은 켄트 씨를 위원회에 후보로 임명할지 말지를 결정할 것이다.

☑ 부사절로 쓰인 whether

whether는 대표적인 명사절 접속사이지만, or 또는 or not과 함께 '~이든 (아니든)'을 뜻하는 부사절 접속사로도 쓰인다.

Whether a purchase is large or small, customers deserve the same high-quality service.
구매한 물건이 대량이든지 소량이든지, 고객들은 똑같은 고품질 서비스를 받을 자격이 된다.

+ check ·· 해설서 p.27

1. The marketing team will determine ------- launching a new version of the product now will be profitable or not.

   (A) while   (B) whether   (C) whichever   (D) whatever

2. The board is still debating ------- or not to promote Ms. Chen to sales manager despite her recent achievements.

   (A) whether   (B) neither   (C) either   (D) unless

3. We are going to have a discussion as to ------ we will expand our business next year.

   (A) because   (B) whether   (C) unless   (D) although

4. 복합관계대명사

▶ 복합관계대명사가 이끄는 명사절은 문장에서 주어와 목적어로 쓰이며, 「대명사 + 관계대명사」의 역할을 한다.

▶ 복합관계대명사는 명사절과 부사절을 이끌 수 있으나, 주로 명사절의 형태로 출제된다.

복합관계대명사	명사절		부사절	
whoever	= anyone who	~하는 사람은 누구나	= no matter who	누가 ~하든지
whomever	= anyone whom	~하는 사람은 누구나	= no matter whom	누구를 ~하든지
whatever	= anything that	~하는 것은 무엇이나	= no matter what	무엇을 ~하든지
whichever	= anything that	~하는 것은 어느 것이나	= no matter which	어느 것을 ~하든지

>> 적중 포인트 복합관계대명사 = 「대명사 + 관계사」

Whoever receives the best evaluation will get the manager position at the new branch.
최고의 평가를 받는 사람은 누구나 새로운 지점의 관리자 자리를 얻을 것이다.
⋯▶ 문장의 동사 will get의 앞은 주어 자리이므로 명사절 접속사 Whoever(= Anyone who)가 이끄는 명사절이 쓰였다.

 check ·· 해설서 p.27

1. ------- is last to leave should lock all the doors.

   (A) Who   (B) Which   (C) Whoever   (D) Whenever

2. As the contract is crucial for Polster Co. to expand in this area, they are willing to accept -------
   conditions we set for the deal.

   (A) wherever   (B) however   (C) whomever   (D) whatever

3. We assure you that ------- Benny's Pizzeria location you visit, you will be served top-quality
   pizza dishes.

   (A) some   (B) whichever   (C) these   (D) whose

1. Mr. Planck reviews the building designs created by our architects to determine ------- they comply with government regulations.

(A) while
(B) whether
(C) then
(D) because

2. ------- needs an income verification form for personal reasons should ask Ms. Roh in the Accounting Department.

(A) Each
(B) Another
(C) Whoever
(D) Someone

3. A recent survey indicates ------- most consumers prefer Everyday Bath shampoo over other hair-washing products.

(A) that
(B) but
(C) what
(D) like

4. ------- is particularly impressive about this album is that the singer incorporates many of her own personal experiences into her songs.

(A) Which
(B) That
(C) Why
(D) What

5. The secretary printed some invitations ------- he will send out tomorrow.

(A) which
(B) who
(C) whose
(D) what

6. It remains to be seen ------- Alex Grande will meet his sales target for the quarter.

(A) concerning
(B) whether
(C) with
(D) along

7. All team managers should encourage their staff to attend the training as it is important ------- employees know the safety precautions.

(A) to
(B) that
(C) should
(D) what

8. Senior management has reviewed Mr. Rivera's qualifications and will decide ------- to appoint him as a board member.

(A) whether
(B) after
(C) that
(D) about

9. The project proposal should be revised because the board believes ------- contains unrealistic expectations.

(A) they
(B) one
(C) that
(D) it

10. The recent statistics show ------- the number of auto accidents has been decreasing since the traffic signals were changed.

(A) because
(B) that
(C) while
(D) what

11. LMM has arranged a training program for ------- candidate is chosen as the new regional manager.

(A) its
(B) one
(C) whichever
(D) however

12. The fact ------- brand recognition can increase public demand is an important aspect of marketing.

(A) because
(B) that
(C) which
(D) unless

13. As soon as the management of Etello Trading has reviewed the bidding documents, they will determine ------- proposal will be chosen.

(A) whatever
(B) which
(C) why
(D) who

14. Customers who received defective products can return them to any of our locations regardless of ------- they have been opened or not.

(A) neither
(B) whether
(C) despite
(D) besides

15. Ms. Kagan at the headquarters asked us to find ways to increase revenue, ------- has decreased by 20 percent since last summer.

(A) which
(B) what
(C) who
(D) whom

16. ------- the year-end bonus is going to be half of last year's is disappointing news to the entire staff.

(A) What
(B) Although
(C) That
(D) Because

17. The Karrie Shoe Company, ------- is located in Waruville, is the second oldest shoe company in the country.

(A) that
(B) where
(C) who
(D) which

18. The employee handbook explains ------- new employees need to know regarding company benefits.

(A) which
(B) where
(C) how
(D) what

19. At the presentation, Mr. Meyer will explain ------- the company got started as a small local business 30 years ago.

(A) during
(B) about
(C) while
(D) how

20. The development plan should accurately state ------- is in charge of each task.

(A) when
(B) everything
(C) who
(D) some

UNIT 10 형용사절 접속사

형용사절은 관계대명사나 관계부사가 이끄는 절로, 바로 앞에 오는 명사(선행사)를 꾸며주는 형용사 역할을 한다. 관계대명사는 격(주격, 목적격, 소유격)을 결정하는 문제가 출제된다. 관계대명사와 관계부사의 차이를 구분하는 문제도 종종 등장하는데 관계대명사는 뒤에 불완전한 문장이 오고, 관계부사는 완전한 문장이 온다.

A-Z 핵심 문법

1. 형용사절 – 관계대명사

▶ 관계대명사의 역할: 「접속사 + 대명사」로 앞에 나오는 명사(선행사)를 수식한다.

▶ 관계대명사는 앞에 오는 선행사(사람/사물)에 따라 who, which, that을 구분해서 사용한다.

▶ 관계대명사는 절 안에서 주어, 목적어, 명사 수식어 역할을 하며, 각각 주격, 목적격, 소유격으로 쓴다.

▶ 관계대명사 종류

종류	선행사	주격	목적격	소유격
who	사람	who	whom	whose
which	사물	which	which	of which / whose
that	사람 / 사물	that	that	X

≫ 적중 포인트 1 관계대명사는 명사(선행사)를 수식한다.

The manager **who** is currently in charge of the project will resign next month.
현재 그 프로젝트를 책임지고 있는 관리자는 다음 달에 사임할 것이다.

≫ 적중 포인트 2 관계대명사는 주격, 목적격, 소유격이 있다.

❶ 주격 관계대명사

「선행사 + 주격 관계대명사 + 동사」

A special lunch menu, **which is** available for only $5, made our restaurant a famous attraction.
겨우 5달러만 내면 먹을 수 있는 특별 점심 메뉴는 우리 식당을 유명한 인기 장소로 만들었다.

「주격 관계대명사 + be동사」는 생략 가능하다.

The seminar, (**which was**) about the history of the company, was delivered by the founder.
회사 역사에 관한 그 세미나는 창업주에 의해 진행되었다.

❷ 소유격 관계대명사

「선행사 + 소유격 관계대명사 + 명사」

We need two additional mechanics **whose responsibilities** include inspecting our assembly line.
우리는 두 명의 추가 정비공들이 필요한데, 그들의 직무는 조립 라인 점검을 포함한다.

⋯→ 소유격 관계대명사 뒤에는 완전한 문장이 온다.

❸ 목적격 관계대명사

「선행사 + 목적격 관계대명사 + 주어 + 타동사」
「선행사 + 목적격 관계대명사 + 주어 + 동사 + 전치사」
「선행사 + 전치사 + 목적격 관계대명사 + 주어 + 동사」

Please check your new schedule, **which** you can **find** on the company's website.
회사 홈페이지에서 찾을 수 있는 여러분의 새로운 일정을 확인해주세요.
⋯▸ 앞에 있는 선행사 schedule을 받으며, find의 목적어가 없으므로 목적격 관계대명사 which가 필요하다.

The Melba Center, **which** DGC Industries has resided **in** since last year, needs to repair the elevators soon.
The Melba Center, **in which** DGC Industries has resided since last year, needs to repair the elevators soon.
작년부터 디지씨 산업이 입주해 있는 멜버 센터는 곧 엘리베이터들을 수리해야만 한다.
⋯▸ 전치사 in은 수식하는 동사 reside 뒤에 올 수도 있고, in의 목적어인 선행사 Melba Center 뒤에 올 수도 있다.

+ check .... 해설서 p.29

1. Most of the applicants ------- submitted their résumés for the accounting manager position were highly qualified.

   (A) which   (B) what   (C) who   (D) when

2. Dr. Coleman, a respected physicist ------- research has appeared in many scientific journals, has been offered a consulting contract with our engineering firm.

   (A) whose   (B) whereas   (C) because   (D) his

3. Our main goal is to create a world in ------- handicapped people have both the right and the opportunity to contribute their full value to society.

   (A) when   (B) which   (C) whose   (D) where

2. 관계대명사 that vs. what

▸ 관계대명사 that은 소유격이 없으며, 전치사의 목적어로 쓸 수 없다. 또한, 계속적 용법으로 콤마 뒤에 쓸 수 없다.

▸ 관계대명사 what(= the thing which/that)은 명사절 접속사로 선행사를 포함하고 있으므로 앞에 명사가 오면 쓸 수 없다.

≫ 적중 포인트 1 주의해야 할 관계대명사 that

Sirax Chemicals has been promoting its latest product, (~~that~~, **which**) was put on the market last month.
시랙스 화학은 지난달 시장에 출시된 최신 제품을 홍보하고 있다.
⋯▸ 콤마 다음에 that을 쓸 수 없으므로 which를 써야 한다.

≫ 적중 포인트 2 선행사가 필요없는 명사절 접속사 what

I bought the car (**that**, ~~what~~) my family wanted.
나는 우리 가족이 원했던 차를 샀다.
⋯▸ 앞에 선행사 the car가 있어서 what은 쓸 수 없고, 타동사 wanted의 목적어로 목적격 관계대명사 that이 필요하다.

I bought (~~that~~, **what**) my family wanted.
나는 우리 가족이 원했던 것을 샀다.
⋯▸ 앞에 선행사가 없고, 뒤에 불완전한 문장이 나오는 what이 필요하다.

1. Established about a hundred years ago, Fitzbon is a family-run business ------- specializes in homemade chocolate.

   (A) them   (B) that   (C) where   (D) what

2. Providing the best customer service is ------- makes Express Home Cable so popular with cable TV subscribers in Montreal.

   (A) which   (B) what   (C) whose   (D) who

3. ------- is impressive about our menu is the freshness of the ingredients directly delivered from our organic farms.

   (A) Which   (B) That   (C) Why   (D) What

3. 형용사절 – 관계부사

▶ 관계부사의 역할: 관계부사는 「접속사 + 부사」로 앞에 나오는 명사(선행사)를 수식한다.

▶ 관계부사 종류

종류	선행사	「전치사 + 관계대명사」 = 관계부사
when	시간	at / on / in which
where	장소	at / on / in which
why	이유	for which
how	방법	in which

* the way 선행사는 how와 함께 쓰이지 않는다.

>> 적중 포인트

Heavy traffic was the reason **why** Mr. Sanchez arrived late for the meeting.
차량 정체가 산체스 씨가 회의에 늦은 이유였다.

⋯→ 앞에 선행사가 the reason(이유)이고, 뒤에 완전한 문장이 나오므로 관계부사 why가 와야 한다.

1. We at Merdov Trading do our best to create an enjoyable working environment ------- which our employees work efficiently.

   (A) in   (B) from   (C) until   (D) down

2. During the tour, we will visit a candy factory ------- you can taste a variety of treats and purchase fascinating souvenirs.

   (A) not only   (B) together with   (C) instead of   (D) at which

3. Mazon Enterprises will hold a series of seminars ------- useful information will be provided for those wishing to start their own business.

   (A) beside   (B) until   (C) near   (D) where

4. 관계대명사 vs. 관계부사

▶ 관계대명사와 관계부사의 차이는 선행사의 차이도 있지만, 뒤에 오는 문장에 따라 구분한다. 관계대명사 뒤에는 불완전한 문장이 오고, 관계부사 뒤에는 완전한 문장이 온다.

>> 적중 포인트 「관계대명사 + 불완전한 문장」 vs. 「관계부사 + 완전한 문장」

The city **which** the Gamma Business Center will be relocated **to** is expected to be more convenient.
⋯ 관계대명사 which 뒤에는 불완전한 문장(전치사 to의 목적어 없음)이 나온다.

The city **to which** the Gamma Business Center will be relocated is expected to be more convenient.
⋯ 전치사 to는 관계대명사 which 앞으로 올 수 있다.

The city **where** the Gamma Business Center will be relocated is expected to be more convenient.
⋯ 관계부사 where 뒤에는 완전한 문장이 나온다.
⋯ 관계부사는 「전치사 + 관계대명사」로 바꿔 쓸 수 있다. (where=to which)

감마 사업 센터가 이전할 그 도시는 더 편리할 것으로 기대된다.

+ check ·· 해설서 p.30

1. We are planning to hold a real estate fair for anyone ------- is interested in purchasing a property in the suburban area.

   (A) where   (B) whoever   (C) when   (D) who

2. All of the newly registered customers are eligible for coupons with ------- they can purchase our products at a 20 percent discount.

   (A) what   (B) which   (C) where   (D) whose

3. To thank you for completing our survey, we have sent you a $10 gift certificate for Almont's Bistro, ------- you can enjoy various Italian dishes.

   (A) who   (B) where   (C) what   (D) which

1. We strongly recommend office workers ------- remain seated all day to get up and walk around at least once every hour.

(A) where
(B) whoever
(C) when
(D) who

2. Harington Paper, ------- managers have expressed concerns about meeting increasing demands, has revised the factory workers' schedules.

(A) whatever
(B) whose
(C) who
(D) which

3. Roberto Kitchenware, ------- specializes in traditional dish-making techniques, expanded its market to Asia last year.

(A) what
(B) which
(C) that
(D) where

4. R&C Manufacturing had a series of meetings with important clients yesterday, most of ------- are very satisfied with its products.

(A) who
(B) them
(C) that
(D) whom

5. Research and Development is doing ------- possible to finalize and prepare the prototype for demonstration at the trade show.

(A) that
(B) wherever
(C) everything
(D) most

6. Bourne Voyage caters to professionals ------- travel domestically and overseas.

(A) who
(B) what
(C) whose
(D) whatever

7. Mr. Schwartz is glad that he changed to his new position, ------- he is able to use his background in architecture.

(A) in which
(B) depending on
(C) along with
(D) compared to

8. Gyen Tech is offering a special free DVD to anyone who ------- the new XE 300 game before October 1.

(A) purchaser
(B) purchase
(C) purchasing
(D) purchases

9. Before you apply for a managerial position, it is important that you understand ------- the job entails.

(A) which
(B) what
(C) how
(D) when

10. The engineers discovered a defect in the factory machine's cooling system ------- must be fixed immediately.

(A) who
(B) that
(C) whose
(D) whoever

11. Separate files may be submitted via the online review site, in ------- case the files should be uploaded in the order of main text and tables.

(A) what
(B) which
(C) that
(D) whose

12. As promised, please find attached a copy of the presentation ------- the personnel director gave at the meeting.

(A) then
(B) what
(C) that
(D) when

13. Even though the IM100 is a fairly simple device to use, ------- not used to smartphones may need to refer to the user's manual.

(A) whose
(B) those
(C) these
(D) but

14. Those ------- experience problems with the new video equipment should speak with one of the service technicians.

(A) which
(B) who
(C) what
(D) where

15. Mr. Xia called the warehouse yesterday to check on the status of the replacement parts ------- ordered last week.

(A) he
(B) that
(C) were
(D) until

16. The vice president chose the place ------- the company will hold its press conference.

(A) where
(B) which
(C) until
(D) during

17. Only ------- who have received authorization from the orchestra manager are permitted to make recordings during the concert.

(A) one
(B) much
(C) other
(D) those

18. The recent issue of *Trade Forums Magazine* contains 20 articles, ------- of which are about the current state of the economy.

(A) several
(B) another
(C) nothing
(D) who

19. Slatington is the perfect location for restaurants and hotels, ------- will profit from the newly-completed highway near the town.

(A) how
(B) which
(C) when
(D) whose

20. Sylvan Beverages has recently renewed its contract with the supplier ------- orchards are in Connor Valley.

(A) whose
(B) where
(C) whatever
(D) which

부사절 접속사

부사절 접속사는 특히 선택지에서 전치사와 접속부사가 함께 나와서 문법적인 쓰임을 구별하는 문제가 출제되므로, 해석에 의존해서 풀기보다는 평소에 전치사, 접속사, 접속부사의 문법적 쓰임과 종류를 확실히 익혀 문제를 풀 수 있도록 해야 한다.

> Tip!
> 부사절 접속사 유형은 매회 출제되고 있고,
> 전치사 vs. 접속사를 구별하는 문제가 주로 나와!

핵심 문법

1. 부사절의 자리와 쓰임

▶ 부사절 접속사가 이끄는 부사절은 주절의 앞에 오거나 뒤에 온다.
▶ 부사절의 축약형인 분사구문 앞에는 부사절 접속사가 오기도 한다.

>> 적중 포인트 1 부사절은 주절의 앞이나 뒤에 온다.

Once the company arranges his residence, Mr. Nakamura will leave for the Tokyo branch.
= Mr. Nakamura will leave for the Tokyo branch **once** the company arranges his residence.
회사가 그의 거주지를 준비하게 되면, 나카무라 씨는 도쿄 지사로 떠날 것이다.

>> 적중 포인트 2 「부사절 접속사 + 분사」 구문

When you send your application form, you should enclose two letters of reference.
= **When sending** your application form, you should enclose two letters of reference.
귀하의 지원서를 보내실 때는, 두 장의 추천서를 동봉하셔야 합니다.

+ check ·· 해설서 p.32

1. ------- the deadline for course registration is next month, signing up early would increase your chances for enrollment.

   (A) While   (B) With   (C) Regarding   (D) Despite

2. Clients have to complete a consent form ------- personal data can be submitted to new accounting firms.

   (A) before   (B) rather   (C) plus   (D) except

3. ------- the venue arrangements for the 20th-anniversary ceremony have been made, the invitations should be sent out.

   (A) Due to   (B) As a result of   (C) In order to   (D) Now that

2. 시간·조건을 나타내는 부사절 접속사

>> 적중 포인트 1 시간

Mr. Park will give me rides to work this week **while** my car is being repaired.
내 차가 수리되는 동안 이번 주는 박 씨가 나를 회사까지 태워다 줄 것이다.

when, as	~할 때	as soon as, once	~하자마자
after	~후에	before	~전에
while	~하는 동안에, ~인 반면에	by the time	~할 때쯤에
until	~까지	since	~한 이래로

···→ after, before, until, since는 전치사로도 쓰인다.

>> 적중 포인트 2 조건

If you are not available on the designated date, please let us know as soon as possible.
만약 지정된 날짜에 귀하께서 시간이 없으시면, 되도록 빨리 저희에게 알려주세요.

if, provided (that)	만약 ~라면	unless	~하지 않으면
as long as	~하는 한	only if	~인 경우에만
as if, as though	마치 ~인 것처럼		

>> 적중 포인트 3 시간·조건의 부사절은 주절의 시제가 미래라고 할지라도 종속절에는 현재 시제를 사용한다.

Mr. Kim **will attend** tomorrow's meeting **if** no other sales manager **is** able to.
다른 영업 매니저가 참석할 수 없다면, 김 씨가 내일 회의에 참석할 것이다.

☑ By the time이 이끄는 절의 시제

[By the time + S + 과거, S + had p.p.] (과거에) ~했을 때, 이미 ~했었다
[By the time + S + 현재, S + 미래 완료] (미래에) ~할 때쯤이면, 이미 ~했을 것이다
···→ By the time절이 과거 시제이면 주절에는 과거 완료가 쓰이고, 현재 시제이면 미래 완료가 쓰인다.

By the time the merger **was announced**, Koxy Co. **had suffered** profit losses for a year.
합병이 공지되었을 때, 콕시 사는 일 년간 수익 손실을 겪었었다.

+ check ·· 해설서 p.32

1. ------- the huge success of Ms. Kwon's new novel, a play based on the book was performed.

   (A) Already   (B) Because   (C) When   (D) After

2. The Recruiting Department could not find the right candidate for the accounting manager position ------- Jason Croucher applied.

   (A) unless   (B) rather than   (C) until   (D) as though

3. ------- no one is here to receive the package, please leave it on the counter.

   (A) If   (B) That   (C) Only   (D) For

3. 이유·양보를 나타내는 부사절 접속사

>> 적중 포인트 1 이유

Because Ms. Pollock was ahead of schedule, she could take a few days off.
폴록 씨가 일정보다 앞서 있었기 때문에, 그녀는 며칠 휴가를 낼 수 있었다.

because, as, since, now that	~이기 때문에

>> 적중 포인트 2 양보

Even though Ms. Ying is enthusiastic about traveling, she seldom has time to travel.
잉 씨는 여행 다니는 것을 아주 좋아하지만, 그녀는 좀처럼 여행할 시간을 낼 수 없다.

although, though, even though, even if	비록 ~일지라도

+ check .... 해설서 p.32

1. ------- Hamilton Bookstore has done very well in O'Hara, it will open additional locations in Reeseville and Brownstone.

   (A) Unless   (B) Since   (C) Rather   (D) Therefore

2. Mr. Katner asked for a deadline extension for the quarterly sales report ------- he had been working on the ad campaign this week.

   (A) as   (B) if   (C) once   (D) whether

3. ------- it is easier to track a shipment online, some still prefer to call the company to check on their orders.

   (A) Although   (B) Therefore   (C) Whether   (D) Moreover

4. 목적·결과를 나타내는 부사절 접속사

>> 적중 포인트 1 목적

Mr. Alvarez postponed taking a vacation **so that** he could complete the project currently behind schedule.

알베레즈 씨는 현재 일정이 뒤처진 프로젝트를 끝내기 위해서 휴가 가는 것을 연기했다.

so that, in order that	~하기 위해서

>> 적중 포인트 2 결과

Mr. Chun's ideas were **so** creative **that** the advertising director immediately decided to employ him.

천 씨의 아이디어들이 아주 창의적이어서 광고 책임자는 그를 고용하기로 즉시 결정했다.

「so + 형용사/부사 + that」, 「such a + 형용사 + 명사 + that」	너무 ~해서 …하다

+ check .... 해설서 p.33

1. Employees wishing to attend the company picnic are required to register by next Tuesday ------- we can prepare a sufficient amount of refreshments.

   (A) unless   (B) so that   (C) in case   (D) either

2. All invoices should reach the Accounting Department by the 25th so that payments ------ in the first week of the following month.

   (A) will make   (B) be made   (C) make   (D) can be made

3. ------- the shipment arrives on time, it needs to be packed and ready to send out by noon today.

   (A) Even though   (B) Since   (C) In place of   (D) In order that

5. 기타 빈출 부사절 접속사

>> 적중 포인트

The new intern acted **as though** she was not nervous about her presentation.
새 인턴은 그녀의 발표에 대해 긴장하지 않은 것처럼 행동했다.

given that	~을 고려해 볼 때	in that	~이라는 점에서
considering (that)	~을 고려해 볼 때	assuming (that)	~을 가정해 볼 때
in the event (that)	~인 경우에	except that	~라는 점을 제외하고
in case (that)	~인 경우를 대비해서	as if, as though	마치 ~인 것처럼
whereas	반면에		

+ check .... 해설서 p.33

1. Mr. Kreitzler is a Pielert Marketing's specialist in business trends ------- Ms. Freeberg is an expert on social media.

   (A) whereas   (B) after all   (C) aside from   (D) despite

2. ------- there are no more changes in your order, building materials will be shipped to the indicated address on Wednesday morning.

   (A) Assuming   (B) Excluding   (C) Otherwise   (D) Furthermore

3. ------- the rent for this office will go up next year, we should start looking for a more affordable property.

   (A) Prior to   (B) Rather than   (C) Owing to   (D) Given that

6. 부사절 접속사 vs. 전치사

▶ 부사절은 「부사절 접속사 + 주어 + 동사」 형태이다.

▶ 전치사 뒤에는 명사나 동명사가 온다.

>> 적중 포인트 부사절 접속사 vs. 전치사

(~~Although~~, **Despite**) a thorough investigation, no evidence of misconduct has been found.
철저한 조사에도 불구하고, 어떠한 위법 행위의 증거도 발견되지 않았다.

⋯→ a thorough investigation이라는 명사 앞에 들어갈 수 있는 것은 전치사이므로, 정답은 Despite가 된다.

종류	부사절 접속사	전치사	의미
양보	although, (even) though	despite, in spite of, notwithstanding	비록 ~이지만
이유	because, as, since, now that	because of, due to, owing to, on account of	~때문에
시간	while after, before as soon as by the time, until	「during + 특정 기간」, 「for + 기간 명사」 following, prior to on[upon] -ing by (완료), until (계속/지속)	~하는 동안 ~후에/전에 ~하자마자 ~할 때까지
조건	unless in case (that), in the event (that)	without (~없이) in case of, in the event of	만약 ~가 아니라면 ~한 경우에, ~을 대비하여
목적	so that, in order that	「so as to[in order to] + 동사원형」	~할 수 있도록
제외	except that	except for	~을 제외하면
기타	given that - as if, as though	given regardless of like	~을 고려하면 ~와 상관없이 마치 ~인 것처럼
	-	about, on, over, as to, as for, regarding, concerning, pertaining to	~에 관하여
	-	apart from, aside from, in addition to, on top of	~뿐만 아니라

+ check .... 해설서 p.33

1. ------- efforts to save the historic Armstrong Theater, it was torn down last month for retail development.

   (A) Even   (B) Neither   (C) Although   (D) Despite

2. ------- the remodeling of our cafeteria, vouchers will be provided for a nearby restaurant.

   (A) Meanwhile   (B) During   (C) Though   (D) Unless

3. Mr. Fyodorov will present at the upcoming Nano Technology Symposium by himself ------- Ms. Walker is not able to attend.

   (A) due to   (B) because   (C) until   (D) likewise

7. 접속부사

▶ 접속부사는 문장을 연결하는 접속사 역할을 하지 못하지만, 문맥을 연결해 주는 역할을 하는 부사이다. Part 6에서 거의 매달 출제되므로 접속부사의 종류와 뜻을 잘 알아두도록 하자.

[주어(S) + 동사(V). 접속부사, 주어(S) + 동사(V)]

[주어(S) + 동사(V); 접속부사, 주어(S) + 동사(V)]

[주어(S) + 동사(V) + 접속사 + 접속부사, 주어(S) + 동사(V)]

* 「접속사 + 접속부사」: and also 또한, and then 그리고 나서, and therefore 그러므로

>> **적중 포인트** 접속부사는 접속사가 아니라 부사이다.

I appreciate your invitation to speak at the convention. **However**, I will not be able to attend due to my business trip to Singapore next week.
컨벤션에서 연설하도록 초대해 주셔서 감사합니다. 하지만 다음 주 싱가포르 출장 때문에 참석할 수 없습니다.

therefore, thus	그러므로	however	그러나
moreover, furthermore	더욱이	nevertheless, nonetheless	그럼에도 불구하고
then	그리고 나서	also	또한
rather	차라리	instead	대신에
besides, in addition	게다가	in other words	다르게 말하면
on the other hand	반면에	otherwise	그렇지 않으면
afterward(s)	이후에	likewise	그와 같이
on the contrary	대조적으로	in fact	사실상
if so	만약 그렇다면	namely	즉, 다시 말해

+ check .... 해설서 p.33

1. Employees should ensure they sign in before starting each shift; -------, working hours may not be accurately reflected in the following paychecks.

   (A) otherwise   (B) therefore   (C) moreover   (D) additionally

2. Zino Digital subscribers will be sent updates ------- changes to terms and conditions are made.

   (A) whenever   (B) although   (C) meanwhile   (D) accordingly

3. ------- the global recession, A-Techo Motors continues to sell many cars and increase its profits.

   (A) On the other hand   (B) As a matter of fact   (C) Notwithstanding   (D) Eventually

8. 복합관계부사

▶ 복합관계부사는 「관계부사 + ever」의 형태인 접속사로 '~든지'라는 양보의 의미로 해석되며, 완전한 문장이 뒤따라 나온다.

>> 적중 포인트 「관계부사 + ever」

As providing excellent service is our top priority, you are welcome to contact us **whenever** you need our assistance.

뛰어난 서비스를 제공하는 것이 저희의 최우선 과제이므로, 귀하께서 저희의 도움이 필요할 때 언제든지 저희에게 연락하실 수 있습니다.

복합관계부사		의미
whenever	no matter when	언제든지
wherever	no matter where	어디에서든지
「however + 형용사/부사」	「no matter how + 형용사/부사」	아무리 ~할지라도

* however는 접속사로 쓰일 때 단독으로 쓰일 수 없고 뒤에 형용사 또는 부사와 같이 쓰인다.

+ check .... 해설서 p.34

1. At Levy's Men's Attire, all of our retail staff are expected to assist customers ------- they inquire about any product in the store.

   (A) whenever   (B) even if   (C) no doubt   (D) as expected

2. To minimize disruptions to our scheduled shipments, El Mundo Industries utilizes its in-house delivery drivers ------- possible.

   (A) according   (B) constantly   (C) otherwise   (D) whenever

3. Since the software is new, it will experience technical errors no matter ------- hard the developers may have worked on the program.

   (A) if   (B) where   (C) how   (D) so

해설서 p.34 / ⏱ 제한 시간 6분

1. ------- Mr. Naveen could not board his train, he was still able to make it to the seminar.

(A) In cases
(B) Though
(C) Just like
(D) Despite

2. ------- Lenexa Diagnostic continues to grow at its current rate, it should be able to increase revenue by at least 20 percent next year.

(A) Assuming
(B) Excluding
(C) Otherwise
(D) Furthermore

3. ------- that Mr. McDermott is in charge of the department, work efficiency is expected to increase.

(A) From
(B) In
(C) Still
(D) Now

4. Zemicon Inc. has established a strong reputation as a provider of portable add-ons for laptop computers ------- last year.

(A) out of
(B) due to
(C) since
(D) through

5. ------- we can find a cheaper source of raw materials, we will need to start charging more for our mobile devices this year.

(A) Unless
(B) Since
(C) Assuming
(D) As soon as

6. All applicants must present two photos and a form of identification ------- applying for a passport.

(A) with
(B) since
(C) or
(D) when

7. Apong Group will implement a new dress code ------- the board of directors approves it next week.

(A) as well as
(B) since
(C) as soon as
(D) during

8. Ms. Hsieh ordered the office supplies by express mail ------- the team could receive them on the following day.

(A) in case
(B) in order to
(C) so that
(D) given that

9. The procedures for becoming one of Lizmore Club's regular members are ------- complicated that many prospective members complain about them.

(A) well
(B) very
(C) too
(D) so

10. Periodic maintenance checks, ------- carried out at an authorized service center, should maximize the safety and performance of your Kaminari ES360 electric scooter.

(A) if
(B) where
(C) though
(D) by

11. Residents are reminded that all plastic items ------- vinyl bags and wrappers should be discarded in the recycling bin marked "plastics."

(A) despite
(B) even
(C) except
(D) nevertheless

12. ------- our shareholder meeting is held, the board of directors will have selected a new Chief Financial Officer.

(A) In consideration of
(B) By the time
(C) Even if
(D) To ensure that

13. ------- Mr. Smith achieved very high performance ratings, he has a good chance of being promoted.

(A) So that
(B) Besides
(C) As
(D) Due to

14. ------- the results of the latest survey are released, the TV advertising campaign for the new footwear will be postponed.

(A) With
(B) Moreover
(C) Until
(D) Beyond

15. When ------- a purchase online, you should exercise caution because your personal information may not be fully secure.

(A) make
(B) making
(C) to make
(D) made

16. Internet access will be freely available ------- the seminar at several computer stations.

(A) while
(B) since
(C) during
(D) within

17. ------- uncomfortable they may be, drivers and passengers must wear seat belts while driving.

(A) No matter how
(B) Despite
(C) In order that
(D) Nevertheless

18. Those who wish to rent an apartment in a foreign country should examine the contract thoroughly ------- signing it.

(A) before
(B) earlier
(C) past
(D) ahead

19. ------- Mr. Norman has organized a team with representatives from relevant divisions, the deadline for the Alton project will be set.

(A) While
(B) Once
(C) Despite
(D) Whereas

20. According to a recent study, most employees check their work e-mail regularly ------- on vacation.

(A) so that
(B) during
(C) whether
(D) while

1. Mario Lucci's sales presentation was so convincing ------- all of the clients wanted to order the product.

(A) which
(B) about
(C) that
(D) during

2. As ------- in our rental contract, tenants must pay the first month's rent and a deposit in advance.

(A) state
(B) statement
(C) stated
(D) states

3. Customers may exchange defective items at our store ------- they show valid proof of purchase.

(A) provided that
(B) as though
(C) due to
(D) rather than

4. ------- Mr. Walken's concerns, Bosworth Technologies plans to launch its new product on June 1.

(A) As long as
(B) Nevertheless
(C) Regardless of
(D) Regrettably

5. Museum visitors are invited to drop by the gift shop, ------- small replicas of famous sculptures are sold.

(A) into
(B) thus
(C) what
(D) where

6. Mr. Raul will not be able to attend next week's conference in Barcelona, so Ms. Jung will go in ------- place.

(A) he
(B) him
(C) his
(D) himself

7. ------- our website is temporarily out of service, we cannot access your account at the moment.

(A) Regardless of
(B) Since
(C) In case of
(D) Besides

8. Some of the items ------- are on the company picnic shopping list have already been purchased.

(A) such
(B) around
(C) that
(D) what

9. Our products can be sent by express shipping ------- requested at the time of ordering.

(A) but
(B) if
(C) in order that
(D) in addition to

10. ------- the Accounting Director, Ms. Grant is in charge of ensuring the company's compliance with financial regulations.

(A) Since
(B) As
(C) Should
(D) From

11. ------- a power outage, it is the responsibility of the Facilities Management Team to ensure that the building remains secure.

(A) Contrary to
(B) In the event of
(C) Considering that
(D) For the sake of

12. All perishable items ------- the kitchen should be thrown away upon expiration.

(A) on
(B) in
(C) with
(D) via

13. Articles prepared ------- publication in this month's employee newsletter must be submitted by April 30 at the latest.

(A) to
(B) as
(C) by
(D) for

14. ------- all of the members of this city's professional baseball team were recruited from colleges in our state.

(A) Reasonably
(B) Fully
(C) Ever
(D) Almost

15. ------- sales representatives normally work at their respective branches, they are required to attend regular training sessions at the head office.

(A) Due to
(B) In view of
(C) Rather than
(D) While

16. The marketing team members found ------- struggling to promote the company's new line of home appliances.

(A) they
(B) theirs
(C) their own
(D) themselves

17. Air Pacifika announced a flight heading from London to New York had turned back shortly after takeoff ------- a technical problem.

(A) whereas
(B) due to
(C) otherwise
(D) instead of

18. Mr. Miller ------- backed up into a coworker's vehicle and caused some damage to the headlight.

(A) accident
(B) accidents
(C) accidental
(D) accidentally

19. Dr. Riana has committed herself ------- research in clinical psychology.

(A) to
(B) so
(C) that
(D) of

20. Once your meeting is finished, move ------- one table back to the neighboring room and leave the other three where they are.

(A) away
(B) just
(C) toward
(D) with

to부정사

UNIT 12

to부정사는 동사의 성질을 가지면서 명사, 형용사, 부사로 쓰인다. to부정사 용법 중에서 '~하기 위해서'라는 의미를 나타내는 부사적 용법이 가장 많이 출제되지만, 명사적 용법과 형용사적 용법을 묻는 문제도 종종 출제된다. 특히 to부정사가 쓰인 관용적인 표현이 출제 빈도가 가장 높으므로 평소에 익히도록 하자.

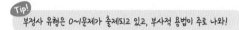
Tip!
부정사 유형은 0~1문제가 출제되고 있고, 부사적 용법이 주로 나와!

 핵심 문법

1. to부정사 자리

▶ 명사 자리: 주어, 목적어, 보어 자리에 쓰여 명사 역할을 한다.

▶ 형용사 자리: 명사를 뒤에서 수식하는 형용사 역할을 한다.

▶ 부사 자리: 문장을 수식하거나 목적(~하기 위해서)을 나타내는 부사어구로 쓰인다.

>> **적중 포인트 1** 명사적 용법: 주어, 목적어, 보어로 쓰이는 to부정사

❶ 주어

To boost sales is the Marketing Department's main goal.
판매량을 늘리는 것이 마케팅 부서의 주요 목적이다.

❷ 동사의 목적어: 「동사 + to부정사」

The new CEO wants **to reduce** the production costs this quarter.
새로 부임한 전문경영인은 이번 분기의 생산 비용을 줄이기를 원한다.

❸ 주격 보어: 「be동사 + to부정사」

The aim of the course is **to provide** attendees with new advertising strategies.
이 수업의 목적은 참가자들에게 새로운 광고 전략을 제공하는 것이다.

✔ goal / purpose / job / aim / objective / mission 등이 주어로 나오면 동사는 be to가 주로 나온다.

❹ 목적격 보어: 「동사 + 목적어 + to부정사」

Mr. Larkin asked Ms. Lawson **to deliver** a presentation at the conference.
라킨 씨는 로슨 씨에게 회의에서 발표해달라고 부탁했다.

>> 적중 포인트 2 형용사적 용법: 명사를 꾸며주는 to부정사

Mr. Lee is the person most likely **to get** the general manager position.
이 씨는 가장 총지배인 자리를 얻을 것 같은 사람이다.

>> 적중 포인트 3 부사적 용법: 문장 전체를 수식하거나 목적을 나타내는 to부정사

(In order) To qualify for the position, applicants must have strong communication skills.
그 직무에 자격을 갖추기 위해서, 지원자들은 뛰어난 의사소통 능력을 갖추어야 한다.

해설서 p.37

+ check

1. To ------- our donors, Elkhart Academy is hosting a dinner and awards ceremony this Saturday.

   (A) acknowledge   (B) acknowledging   (C) acknowledged   (D) acknowledgment

2. A data management company was hired ------- the customer files that cannot be discarded.

   (A) to store   (B) will store   (C) has been stored   (D) to have stored

3. The main purpose of this training session ------- new employees adapt to the company, eventually increasing staff productivity.

   (A) had helped   (B) is to help   (C) is helped   (D) help

2. to부정사를 취하는 동사, 명사, 형용사

>> 적중 포인트 1 목적어로 to부정사를 취하는 동사

want to do	~하는 것을 원하다	wish to do	~하는 것을 바라다
hope to do	~하는 것을 소망하다	need to do	~할 필요가 있다
plan to do	~하는 것을 계획하다	refuse to do	~하는 것을 거절하다
expect to do	~하는 것을 기대하다	choose to do	~하는 것을 선택하다
promise to do	~하는 것을 약속하다	manage to do	~하는 것을 해내다
fail to do	~하는 데 실패하다	aim to do	~을 목표로 하다
intend to do	~하는 것을 의도하다	decide to do	~을 결정하다
hesitate to do	~하는 것을 망설이다		

>> 적중 포인트 2 목적격 보어로 to부정사를 취하는 동사

ask + 목적어 + to do	~하라고 요청하다	require + 목적어 + to do	~하라고 요구하다
allow + 목적어 + to do	~하는 것을 허락하다	encourage + 목적어 + to do	~하라고 격려하다
intend + 목적어 + to do	~하도록 의도하다	remind + 목적어 + to do	~하라고 상기시키다
invite + 목적어 + to do	~하라고 요청하다	expect + 목적어 + to do	~할 것이라고 기대하다
advise + 목적어 + to do	~하라고 권고하다	force + 목적어 + to do	~하라고 강요하다
persuade + 목적어 + to do	~하라고 설득하다	enable + 목적어 + to do	~할 수 있게 하다
cause + 목적어 + to do	~하는 것을 야기하다	urge + 목적어 + to do	~하도록 권고하다

✓ 목적격 보어로 to부정사를 취하는 동사의 수동태

be asked to do	~하도록 요청받다	be required to do	~하도록 요구받다
be allowed to do	~하도록 허용되다	be encouraged to do	~하도록 권장되다
be intended to do	~하도록 의도되다	be reminded to do	~하도록 상기하게 되다
be invited to do	~하도록 요청받다	be expected to do	~하도록 예상되다
be advised to do	~하도록 권고받다	be forced to do	~하도록 강요받다
be persuaded to do	~하도록 설득되다	be enabled to do	~할 수 있게 되다

>> 적중 포인트 3 to부정사를 취하는 명사

decision to do	~할 결정	chance to do	~할 기회
plan to do	~할 계획	ability to do	~할 능력
opportunity to do	~할 기회	right to do	~할 권리
authority to do	~할 권한	attempt to do	~하기 위한 시도
effort to do	~하기 위한 노력	way to do	~하기 위한 방법
time to do	~할 시간	need to do	~할 필요

▶▶ 적중 포인트 4 to부정사를 취하는 형용사

be able to do	~할 수 있다	be likely / liable to do	~할 가능성이 있다
be about to do	막 ~하려고 하다	be ready to do	~할 준비가 되어 있다
be eager to do	~하는 것을 간절히 바라다	be willing to do	기꺼이 ~하다
be sure to do	반드시 ~하다	be hesitant to do	~하는 것을 망설이다
be reluctant to do	~하기를 꺼리다	be available to do	~할 시간이 있다
be eligible to do	~할 자격이 있다	feel free to do	마음껏 ~하다
be proud to do	~을 자랑스럽게 여기다		

☑ 전치사 to가 사용된 표현

be subject to -ing	~에 달려 있다	be committed to -ing	~에 헌신하다
be dedicated to -ing	~에 헌신하다	be devoted to -ing	~에 전념하다
be accustomed to -ing	~에 익숙하다	be opposed to -ing	~에 반대하다
contribute to -ing	~에 기여하다	look forward to -ing	~하기를 학수고대하다

☑ 「be p.p. + to부정사」 관용표현

be pleased to do	~하게 되어 기쁘다	be delighted to do	~하게 되어 기쁘다
be set to do	~하기로 예정되어 있다	be scheduled to do	~하기로 예정되어 있다
be prepared to do	~할 준비가 되다	be supposed to do	~하기로 되어 있다

+ check ·· 해설서 p.38

1. The firm promises ------- any funds spent on travel for business purposes.

   (A) reimburse   (B) reimbursement   (C) reimbursing   (D) to reimburse

2. The authentic food and atmosphere at Sawatdee Restaurant allow customers ------- that they are really having a meal in Thailand.

   (A) feel   (B) to feel   (C) felt   (D) feeling

3. Career development expert Dan Chung is expected ------- his popular seminar at Knowles university again this year.

   (A) to offer   (B) will be offering   (C) offer   (D) had been offered

Practice

1. Reine Systems recruited three experts ------- customers with computer-related issues.

(A) was assisted
(B) is assisting
(C) assistance
(D) to assist

2. The purpose of the board meeting ------- a successor to retiring president Rio Hong.

(A) had chosen
(B) is to choose
(C) is chosen
(D) choose

3. Inclement weather conditions caused flights ------- for more than three hours.

(A) delay
(B) to delay
(C) delaying
(D) to be delayed

4. Please make sure that the books ------- sent to the Book Fair in Seoul are ready by Wednesday.

(A) to be
(B) was
(C) are
(D) have been

5. ------- maintain its place as the leader in book publishing, Carson Printing has bought out two of its competitors.

(A) Nevertheless
(B) In order to
(C) As much as
(D) Therefore

6. Mr. Metzen urged his assistant ------- the summary report well in advance of the press release on Monday.

(A) type
(B) will type
(C) was typing
(D) to type

7. In order ------- Mr. Holt to contact you regarding your next appointment, he will need your phone number.

(A) to
(B) of
(C) for
(D) with

8. Dr. Walters was invited ------- at our 10th Global Partnership Ceremony in Las Vegas.

(A) spoke
(B) is speaking
(C) to speak
(D) speak

9. According to the new policy, website administrators are unable ------- photos of members without their consent.

(A) post
(B) posted
(C) to post
(D) posting

10. Explaining how to work towards a mutual goal is a great way ------- rapport with prospective clients.

(A) to build
(B) have built
(C) had built
(D) build

11. According to the employee survey, company workshops help employees ------- working relationships.

(A) would strengthen
(B) strengthen
(C) strengthened
(D) will strengthen

12. Our restaurant needs a device with the ------- to filter the air continuously in a large dining room.

(A) opportunity
(B) sense
(C) ability
(D) permission

13. The Sealife Heritage Society is dedicated to ------- the natural environment of Gorae Islands.

(A) preservation
(B) preserve
(C) preserved
(D) preserving

14. Considering the emergence of new online rivals, traditional financial services companies need to ------- to remain competitive.

(A) strive
(B) advise
(C) open
(D) expect

15. In an effort ------- duplication of work, office procedures will be reviewed thoroughly and simplified.

(A) to prevent
(B) prevented
(C) preventing
(D) preventive

16. Bellafor Fashion's board of directors pointed to the continued decline in revenues to explain their decision ------- retail sales in Western Europe.

(A) was suspending
(B) have suspended
(C) to suspend
(D) will suspend

17. The portable heater uses a rechargeable battery ------- the required electricity.

(A) to supply
(B) supplies
(C) supplied
(D) will supply

18. Even though the strict security policy can be troublesome at times, it is intended ------- both the firm and our clients.

(A) protecting
(B) protection
(C) to protect
(D) to be protected

19. Those who are preparing for interviews are ------- to do some research about the companies they want to join.

(A) criticized
(B) inquired
(C) accepted
(D) advised

20. Our president has considered ------- Ms. Myer as chief editor to succeed Mr. Jason, who is retiring next month.

(A) appoint
(B) to appoint
(C) appointed
(D) appointing

동명사

동명사는 동사의 성질을 가지고 명사 역할을 한다. 명사처럼 주어, 목적어, 보어 자리에 올 수 있으며, 동사처럼 목적어를 취하면서 부사의 수식을 받는다. 특히 명사와 동명사의 차이를 구별하는 문제가 거의 매회 출제가 되며, 동명사를 취하는 관용표현도 출제가 되니 평소에 잘 익혀두도록 하자.

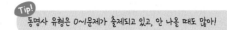

Tip!
동명사 유형은 0~1문제가 출제되고 있고, 안 나올 때도 많아!

핵심 문법

1. 동명사 자리: 주어, 목적어, 보어

▶ 동명사는 주어, 목적어, 보어 자리에 쓰여 명사 역할을 한다.

>> 적중 포인트 1 주어 자리

Assisting customers promptly is our top priority.
고객들을 신속하게 돕는 것이 저희가 최우선으로 하는 것입니다.

>> 적중 포인트 2 동사의 목적어 자리

We recommend **contacting** the sales representative if you have any problems with the product.
제품에 문제가 있으면 판매담당자에게 연락하시는 것을 권해 드립니다.

>> 적중 포인트 3 전치사의 목적어 자리

As a coordinator, you will be responsible for **arranging** shifts for employees.
코디네이터로서, 당신은 직원들의 근무 조를 조정하는 것을 책임질 것입니다.

>> 적중 포인트 4 보어 자리

Our responsibility as a tech support team is **helping** employees solve their IT issues.
기술지원팀으로서 우리의 책무는 직원들이 IT 문제들을 해결하도록 돕는 것입니다.

+ check ⋯⋯ 해설서 p.40

1. Despite our focus on ------- manufacturing costs, the rising price of raw materials and labor has made it difficult.

   (A) lowers   (B) lowered   (C) lowering   (D) lowest

2. Our new products were used by groups of testers and modified according to their responses ------- being placed on the market.

   (A) before   (B) initial   (C) ahead   (D) previous

3. ------- a parking permit for the library was a difficult task that took a lot of paperwork.

   (A) Obtain   (B) Obtained   (C) Obtains   (D) Obtaining

2. 명사 vs. 동명사

▶ 명사는 형용사의 수식을 받지만, 동명사는 부사의 수식을 받는다.

▶ 명사는 관사(a/an, the)와 함께 쓰일 수 있지만, 동명사는 관사와 함께 사용할 수 없다.

▶ 명사는 목적어를 취할 수 없지만, 동명사의 경우 타동사의 동명사는 목적어를 취할 수 있다.

>> 적중 포인트 1 「형용사 + 명사」, 「부사 + 동명사」

Jenhotu, Inc. will attract many customers by (effective, **effectively**) promoting its website.
젠호투 사는 웹사이트를 효율적으로 홍보하여 많은 고객을 유치할 것이다.

⋯→ 전치사 by 뒤에 나오는 promoting은 동명사로, 부사의 수식을 받으므로 답은 effectively이다.

>> 적중 포인트 2 「a/an, the + 명사」

The Leicester Library offers a (collecting, **collection**) of over 1,000 books of medical journals.
레스터 도서관은 1,000권 이상의 의학 학술지 소장품을 제공한다.

⋯→ 타동사 offer 뒤의 목적어 자리이며, 앞에 관사 a가 있으므로 동명사 collecting은 오답이다.

Mr. Kim suggested (support, **supporting**) environmental organizations in Asia.
김 씨는 아시아의 환경단체를 지원하는 것을 제안했다.

⋯→ 타동사 suggest 뒤의 목적어 자리이며, 명사인 support는 관사가 와야 하므로 오답이다.

>> 적중 포인트 3 「동명사 + 목적어」

If you want to return the defective items, please let us know within 10 days of (receipt, **receiving**) this notice.
만약 결함 있는 물건을 반송하고 싶다면, 이 공지를 받은 지 10일 안에 알려주세요.

⋯→ 전치사 of의 목적어 자리이며, 뒤에 this notice를 목적어로 받는 동명사가 필요하므로 답은 receiving이다.

+ check ⋯⋯⋯⋯⋯⋯⋯⋯⋯⋯⋯⋯⋯⋯⋯⋯⋯⋯⋯⋯⋯⋯⋯⋯⋯⋯⋯⋯⋯⋯⋯⋯⋯⋯⋯⋯⋯⋯ 해설서 p.40

1. In this taste test, consumers are asked to rank our new brand of coffee in order of ------- among several other brands.

   (A) prefer   (B) preferring   (C) preference   (D) preferential

2. By ------- pursuing innovation and growth, Lowena Hotel Group aims to become a leader in the hospitality industry.

   (A) to act   (B) more active   (C) acted   (D) actively

3. For inquiries pertaining to ------- events, please contact us at 212-555-5309.

   (A) reschedule   (B) rescheduling   (C) reschedule of   (D) reschedules

3. 목적어로 동명사를 취하는 동사

>> 적중 포인트 「동사+동명사」

consider -ing	~할 것을 고려하다	suggest -ing	~할 것을 제안하다
recommend -ing	~할 것을 추천하다	avoid -ing	~하는 것을 피하다
mind -ing	~하는 것을 꺼리다	include -ing	~하는 것을 포함하다
enjoy -ing	~하는 것을 즐기다	discontinue -ing	~하는 것을 중단하다
finish -ing	~하는 것을 끝내다	postpone -ing	~하는 것을 연기하다

✓ -ing로 끝나는 명사 (p.48 참조)

advertising	광고, 광고업	ticketing	발권
planning	계획, 입안	training	교육, 훈련
opening	공석	funding	자금, 자금 지원
housing	숙소, 주거	gathering	모임
seating	좌석, 자리	shipping	배송

+ check ·· 해설서 p.40

1. The research assistant's responsibilities include ------- for efficient ways to facilitate the experiment process.

   (A) search　　　　(B) searches　　　　(C) searching　　　　(D) searched

2. The Planning Department recommended ------- the new branch in a residential area away from downtown.

   (A) locate　　　　(B) locating　　　　(C) to locate　　　　(D) was locating

3. The president of Paxmata Apparel is considering ------- another factory in Vancouver next year.

   (A) built　　　　(B) to build　　　　(C) building　　　　(D) being built

4. 동명사 관용표현

look forward to -ing	~하는 것을 고대하다
be committed[dedicated / devoted] to -ing	~하는 데 헌신하다[전념하다]
have difficulty[a problem / trouble] -ing	~하는 데 어려움을 겪다
cannot help -ing	~하지 않을 수 없다
keep (on) -ing	계속해서 ~하다
be busy -ing	~하느라 바쁘다
spend 시간/돈 (in) -ing	~하는 데 시간/돈을 쓰다
object to -ing	~에 반대하다
contribute to -ing	~하는 것에 기여하다
be used to -ing	~하는 것에 익숙하다
on[upon] -ing	~하자마자
by -ing	~함으로써

+ check .... 해설서 p.40

1. Employees are encouraged to save paper ------- printing on both sides for internal documents.

   (A) therefore   (B) whether   (C) where   (D) by

2. With proven experience and professionalism, Supreme Travel Agency is ------- to providing the highest level of customer service.

   (A) designed   (B) committed   (C) scheduled   (D) expressed

3. Mr. Clements always has difficulty ------- contracts with his client in Chinese because of his lack of language skills.

   (A) negotiation   (B) negotiating   (C) negotiable   (D) negotiates

Practice

1. The CEO of Mentis Publishing plans on ------- the company's goals for this year at tomorrow's meeting.

(A) outline
(B) outlined
(C) outlining
(D) outlines

2. We at Wandosa Hotel strongly recommend ------- rooms more than six weeks in advance during summer.

(A) books
(B) to book
(C) booking
(D) be booked

3. We at Tarrab Textiles are serious about our commitment to ------- the environmental impact of our manufacturing.

(A) reduces
(B) reduced
(C) reducing
(D) reduction

4. Since ------- at the National Culture and Arts Center three years ago, classical pianist Eun-bin Cho has continued to develop her career.

(A) performers
(B) performing
(C) performance
(D) performable

5. Rolent Inc. was able to attract several potential buyers by ------- advertising its new products locally.

(A) effective
(B) effectively
(C) more effective
(D) most effective

6. In addition to ------- the existing clientele in Australia, Sleestak Consulting hopes to establish a new client base in Southeast Asia in the coming decade.

(A) retain
(B) retains
(C) retaining
(D) retention

7. KT Rail may change the departure times of all trains without ------- passengers in advance.

(A) notification
(B) notify
(C) notifying
(D) notified

8. Construction will not be able to break ground before obtaining full ------- from the city development board.

(A) to approve
(B) approval
(C) approves
(D) approve

9. All workers must know the safety rules for ------- heavy machinery.

(A) commanding
(B) handling
(C) encouraging
(D) staying

10. Lomkay Group is looking forward to ------- with Podhas Corporation to secure its current position in the food and beverage industry.

(A) negotiate
(B) negotiating
(C) have negotiated
(D) be negotiating

11. Marshall's daily routine includes ------- client account activity for unusual transactions.

(A) review
(B) reviews
(C) reviewing
(D) reviewed

12. The newly hired building designer is expected to ------- us meet the tight project deadline with her innovative ideas.

(A) help
(B) helping
(C) helps
(D) helped

13. The local travel brochure at Pakli Resort ------- walking through the forest during the daytime.

(A) offers
(B) avoids
(C) suggests
(D) refuses

14. Goodwill Mart expects all of its employees ------- to customer complaints in a courteous and professional manner.

(A) respond
(B) responding
(C) to respond
(D) respondent

15. According to a business report, a number of recently founded companies are ------- expanding investment in the media industry.

(A) considerable
(B) consideration
(C) considerate
(D) considering

16. By ------- these simple rules, you can help ensure our security even when outside the office.

(A) observation
(B) observing
(C) to observe
(D) observed

17. The marketing manager suggested ------- the logo to enhance the image of the company.

(A) change
(B) changing
(C) to change
(D) changes

18. Due to careful -------, the construction of the new stadium will cause very little inconvenience to the community.

(A) plan
(B) planner
(C) planning
(D) planned

19. Rox Station has created a charitable foundation ------- to mentoring talented local students.

(A) agreeable
(B) designed
(C) dedicated
(D) capable

20. Before ------- to buy an apartment in Charlton, Mr. Russell consulted his colleague about the area.

(A) decide
(B) decision
(C) decides
(D) deciding

UNIT 14 분사

분사는 동사의 성질을 가지면서 형용사처럼 명사를 수식하거나 보어 자리에 온다. 특히 명사를 뒤에서 수식하는 현재분사와 과거분사 구분 문제가 오답률이 높으므로 확실히 익혀두도록 하자.

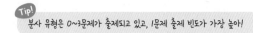

Tip!
분사 유형은 0~3문제가 출제되고 있고, 1문제 출제 빈도가 가장 높아!

핵심 문법

1. 분사의 자리와 쓰임

▶ 「동사원형 + -ing 형태」인 현재분사와, 「동사원형 + -(e)d」 형태인 과거분사는 형용사처럼 명사를 앞뒤에서 꾸며주는 수식어 역할을 한다.

▶ 수식을 받는 명사와 능동 관계이면 현재분사, 수동 관계이면 과거분사를 쓴다.

▶ 주어와 목적어를 설명하는 보어: 주어나 목적어와 능동 관계이면 현재분사, 수동 관계이면 과거분사를 쓴다.

>> 적중 포인트 1 명사 수식

❶ 명사 앞

With her fascinating **movie**, Bella Jung became a nationally renowned actress.
그녀의 매혹적인 영화로, 벨라 정은 전국적으로 유명한 여배우가 되었다.

❷ 명사 뒤

To attract investors, Fecor Tech will contact **businesses** interested in the project.
투자자들을 끌기 위해서, 페코르 전자는 그 프로젝트에 관심이 있는 사업체들에 연락할 것이다.

>> 적중 포인트 2 주격 보어, 목적격 보어

❶ 주격 보어

Survey results of our new products were **disappointing**.
신제품에 대한 조사 결과는 실망스러웠다.

❷ 목적격 보어

The new travel brochure will make tourists quite **excited** about visiting Bondi Beach.
새 여행책자는 관광객들이 본디 해변에 방문하는 것을 매우 들뜨게 할 것이다.

+ check ··· 해설서 p.42

1. Please closely consult the ------- documents before returning any item for a refund or a replacement.

   (A) enclose   (B) enclosing   (C) to enclose   (D) enclosed

2. Students should be prepared to show identification ------- their enrollment at the university.

   (A) confirm   (B) confirming   (C) confirms   (D) confirmation

3. Mr. Meyers, the founder of Smile Again Services, always emphasizes that the top priority of the company is to keep customers -------.

   (A) satisfied   (B) satisfyingly   (C) satisfaction   (D) satisfying

2. 분사 구문

▶ 「접속사 + 주어 + 동사, ~」 형태의 부사절을 분사를 이용해서 간결하게 나타낼 수 있다. 부사절의 주어가 주절의 주어와 같으면 생략하고, 부사절의 동사를 분사형으로 만든다.

▶ 의미를 분명하게 하기 위해 부사절 접속사를 생략하지 않고 「접속사 + 분사 구문」 형태로 쓰기도 한다.

▶ 분사 구문의 태는 주절의 주어와 능동 관계이면 현재분사를 쓰고, 수동 관계이면 과거분사를 쓴다.

>> 적중 포인트 1 「(접속사) + 분사 구문」

✓ 「접속사 + 주어 + 동사, 주어 + 동사」 = 「(접속사) + V-ing / p.p., 주어 + 동사」

After they signed the contract, the two rival companies held a press conference.
= **(After) signing** the contract, the two rival companies held a press conference.
계약서에 서명한 후, 두 경쟁사는 기자회견을 열었다.

⋯→ 부사절 접속사인 After를 생략한다.

⋯→ 주절의 주어 the two rival companies와 부사절의 주어 they가 같을 때는 부사절의 주어를 생략한다.

⋯→ 주절의 동사와의 관계에서 시제/태를 판단하여 시제가 signed와 held 둘 다 과거시제이고 능동이므로 signing이 된다. 때에 따라서는 부사절 접속사인 after를 생략하지 않고 After signing으로 쓰기도 한다.

>> 적중 포인트 2 현재분사(능동) vs. 과거분사(수동)

(Interviewing, ~~Interviewed~~) candidates, the manager tries to ask as many questions as possible.
지원자들을 면접 볼 때, 관리자는 가능한 많은 질문을 하려고 노력한다.

⋯→ 일반적으로 분사 구문은 부사절과 주절의 주어가 같을 때 만들기 때문에 분사 구문의 의미상 주어는 주절의 주어 the manager와 동일하다. the manager가 지원자들을 '면접하는' 것이므로 능동 관계를 나타내는 현재분사 Interviewing으로 쓴다.

(~~Preferring~~, **Preferred**) by young customers, our products have considerable market share.
젊은 소비자들에 의해 선호되기 때문에, 우리 제품들은 상당한 시장 점유율을 가지고 있다.

⋯→ 주절의 주어가 제품이고, 제품이 '선호되는' 것이므로 수동 관계를 나타내는 과거분사 Preferred로 쓴다.

Bahoz, Inc. announced it would merge with Maxhu Co. next month, (**confirming**, ~~confirmed~~) rumors that it plans to expand into Asia.
바호즈 사는 다음 달에 맥스후 사를 합병할 것이라고 발표하면서, 아시아 지역으로 확장할 것이라는 소문을 확인시켜 주었다.

⋯→ 완전한 문장 뒤에 콤마로 연결된 분사는 바로 앞에 오는 명사를 꾸며주는 수식어가 아니라 주어가 동시에 행하고 있는 또 다른 행위를 설명한다. 바호즈 사가 합병 발표를 하면서 동시에 아시아 진출에 대한 소문을 확인시켜 준 것이므로 콤마 뒤에는 현재분사가 온다.

분사 구문의 형태	
-ing	~한, ~하는
p.p.	~된
Having p.p.	~하고 난 후
「Having been p.p. ~, S+V」	~된 후
「S+V, -ing」	그래서 ~하게 되다, ~하면서 …하다

>> 적중 포인트 3 접속사가 포함된 분사 구문

「시간 접속사 when / while / after / before + 현재분사」	
when interviewing	인터뷰할 때
「조건 접속사 if / unless / once + 과거분사」	
unless otherwise mentioned[stated / indicated / instructed]	달리 언급되어 있지 않으면
unless mentioned[stated / indicated / instructed] otherwise	달리 지시받지 않으면
「as + 과거분사」	
as discussed / required / indicated / stated	논의된 / 요구된 / 표시된 / 명시된 대로

+ check

1. When ------- hot food from the microwave, make sure to use kitchen gloves to avoid burning your hands.

   (A) remove   (B) removes   (C) removed   (D) removing

2. An audit of the branch's finances revealed several inconsistencies, ------- further investigation.

   (A) requiring   (B) required   (C) require   (D) requirement

3. As -------, your salary will be $62,000 per year with incentives and company stock shares.

   (A) discussion   (B) discussing   (C) discussed   (D) discuss

3. 혼동하기 쉬운 현재분사와 과거분사

>> 적중 포인트 1 「현재분사 + 명사」

명사를 앞에서 수식하는 현재분사와 명사의 관계는 능동이다.

leading company	일류 회사	existing building	기존 건물
challenging task	힘든 일	opening remarks	개회사
promising member	전도유망한 구성원	lasting impression	오래 지속되는 인상
preceding years	지난 몇 년	emerging company	떠오르는 회사
rewarding effort	가치 있는 노력	remaining work	남아 있는 업무
increasing competition	증가하는 경쟁	mounting pressure	증가하는 압력
demanding job	힘든 업무	overwhelming demand	압도적인 수요
missing luggage	분실 수화물	remaining paperwork	남아 있는 서류 작업
the following year	다음 해	upcoming merger	곧 있을 합병

>> 적중 포인트 2 「과거분사 + 명사」

명사를 앞에서 수식하는 과거분사와 명사의 관계는 수동이다.

attached document	첨부 자료	detailed information	세부 정보
damaged item	손상된 제품	designated parking area	지정된 주차 공간
proposed plan	제안된 계획	written permission/consent	서면상 허가/동의
enclosed brochure	동봉된 안내책자	preferred means	선호되는 수단
reduced rates	할인된 가격	customized program	맞춤형 프로그램
unlimited access	무제한 이용	finished product	완제품
involved task	관련된 업무	revised edition	개정판
limited warranty	제한된 품질 보증기간	dedicated employee	헌신적인 직원
qualified candidate	자격 있는 지원자	experienced tour guide	경력 많은 관광 가이드
skilled engineer	숙련된 기술자	accomplished artist	기량이 뛰어난 예술가
renowned author	유명한 작가	distinguished sculptor	유명한 조각가

>> 적중 포인트 3 주의해야 할 감정 동사

사람의 감정을 나타내는 과거분사형 감정 형용사는 사람만 수식한다. 사물은 감정을 느낄 수 없으므로 현재분사형으로 나타낸다.

excite	흥미진진하게 만들다	please	기쁘게 하다
interest	흥미를 끌다	encourage	격려하다
frustrate	좌절시키다	disappoint	실망시키다
embarrass	당황하게 하다	distract	산만하게 하다
fascinate	매혹시키다	impress	깊은 인상을 주다
overwhelm	압도하다	satisfy	만족시키다

fascinated audience	매료된 청중	fascinating concert	멋진 공연
disappointed candidate	실망한 지원자	disappointing result	실망스러운 결과
excited audience	흥분한 청중	exciting game	흥미로운 경기
distracted people	산만한 사람들	distracting factor	산만한 요소

>> 적중 포인트 4 자동사의 현재분사형 형용사

자동사는 과거분사형으로 쓰지 못하고, 현재분사형으로 쓰인다.

remaining	남아 있는	rising	오르는
existing	존재하는, 기존의	lasting	지속되는
missing	사라진	emerging	떠오르는
participating	참석하는	culminating	최고조에 달한

+ check .... 해설서 p.43

1. Please submit the ------- expense report today for accounting manager Mark Blackmore's review.

   (A) update   (B) updated   (C) updating   (D) to update

2. Any structural changes, including renovations to ------- buildings, must be approved by the Construction Committee.

   (A) existence   (B) existed   (C) existing   (D) exist

3. The awards banquet is the ------- event of the Chamber of Commerce's annual expo.

   (A) culminate   (B) culminated   (C) culminating   (D) culminations

Practice

1. The enclosed brochure specifies the services ------- by Horax Shipping, and I have highlighted in green those which you inquired about.

(A) provide
(B) providing
(C) provided
(D) are provided

2. Ms. Ma must receive a ------- copy of her itinerary by this afternoon at the latest to make an appointment with an important client.

(A) revises
(B) revising
(C) revised
(D) revise

3. As per Fera Fitness's membership agreement, any belongings not ------- from lockers for more than 48 hours may be thrown away.

(A) remove
(B) removes
(C) removing
(D) removed

4. Employers must ------- committed to keeping the workplace safe to prevent injuries.

(A) remain
(B) exist
(C) plan
(D) make

5. Employees ------- in the office after 9 P.M. are required to inform the security guards at the front desk.

(A) work
(B) works
(C) working
(D) worked

6. A trip to Salcedo Ranch is seldom ------- since it has plenty of fun activities for the whole family.

(A) bored
(B) boredom
(C) boring
(D) bore

7. Following an impressive career as a market researcher at Defto Motors, Yunus now plans to seek an advanced degree in preparation for a ------- role in management.

(A) challenge
(B) challenging
(C) challenged
(D) challenges

8. Lester Robinson only appeared in the film for a few minutes, but his dramatic acting had an ------- impact on moviegoers.

(A) endure
(B) endures
(C) enduring
(D) endured

9. The express train ride from Seoul to Busan takes less than three hours with two ------- 5-minute stops.

(A) scheduling
(B) scheduled
(C) schedules
(D) schedule

10. When ------- an intersection, you should slow down and watch for traffic coming in every direction.

(A) approach
(B) approaches
(C) approached
(D) approaching

11. Anyone ------- to confer any comments during the shareholder meeting should first refer to Mr. Manning.

(A) wished
(B) wishing
(C) will wish
(D) had wished

12. Cheridom College will grant an ------- deadline for those students who were unable to access the school's website last week.

(A) extensive
(B) extends
(C) extension
(D) extended

13. You should submit all monthly reports by the 25th unless ------- otherwise.

(A) instructing
(B) instructor
(C) instructed
(D) instruct

14. ------- met the high expectations of clients and shareholders, Kevin was given a large salary raise after his annual review.

(A) To have
(B) Being
(C) Having
(D) To be

15. Visitors must park their cars in the ------- area of the Upper Campus parking lot.

(A) designated
(B) designation
(C) designating
(D) designates

16. Sanjeev completed the firm's three-year junior analyst program, ------- becoming eligible for hire as an investment banker.

(A) throughout
(B) instead
(C) thereby
(D) such as

17. Goodtrip Tours recently introduced new travel deals and is selling them at ------- rates in a promotional campaign.

(A) reduce
(B) reduced
(C) reducing
(D) reduction

18. Successful candidates will receive a ------- salary and one of the best benefits packages in the industry.

(A) satisfied
(B) competitive
(C) preventable
(D) experienced

19. ------- mentioned in the job description, all new employees are required to pass a licensing exam within three months of starting work here.

(A) Although
(B) When
(C) As
(D) On

20. Many people believe that the oil supply can rebound, ------- the trend of reinvigorated growth that was seen last year.

(A) continual
(B) continuing
(C) continues
(D) continued

UNIT 15 비교·가정법·도치

비교 구문은 원급, 비교급, 최상급 비교 구문의 유형을 파악하는 것이 중요하다. 가정법과 도치 구문은 출제 빈도가 매우 낮은 편이다. 매년 1회 정도 출제되거나 아예 출제되지 않을 때도 있지만, 고득점을 목표로 한다면 익혀두어야 한다.

Tip!
비교·도치 유형은 0~3문제가 출제되고 있고, 안 나올 때가 많아!

핵심 문법

1. 비교급

▶ 원급 비교(~만큼 …한/하게): 두 비교 대상이 정도 차이가 없이 동등함을 나타낸다.

▶ 비교급 비교(~보다 더/덜 …한/하게): 비교하는 대상이 정도 차이가 있어서 하나가 더 뛰어남을 나타낸다.

▶ 최상급 비교(~(중)에서 가장 …한/하게): 셋 이상의 비교 대상 중 하나가 가장 뛰어남을 나타낸다.

≫ 적중 포인트 1 원급 비교

✔ 「as + 형용사/부사의 원급 + as」 ~만큼 …한/하게

Icecool Soft Drinks is **as popular as** Tobias Bean Coffee.
아이스쿨 소프트 음료는 토바이어스 빈 커피만큼 유명하다.

≫ 적중 포인트 2 비교급 비교

✔ 「형용사/부사의 비교급 + than」 ~보다 더/덜 …한/하게

Ms. Sakamoto asked her boss if she could leave the office **earlier than** usual.
사카모토 씨는 평소보다 일찍 퇴근해도 되는지를 상사에게 물어봤다.

- 「형용사/부사 -er + than」: 형용사/부사가 2음절 이하의 단어
- 「more 형용사/부사 + than」: 형용사/부사가 3음절 이상의 단어
- 비교급 강조 부사는 much, even, still, far, a lot (훨씬) 등이 있다. (many X)
- the 비교급, the 비교급: ~하면 할수록 더욱 …하다
- 「the 비교급 + one of the two」: 둘 중에서 더 ~한 것

≫ 적중 포인트 3 최상급 비교

✔ 「the + 형용사/부사의 최상급 + in/of/among」 ~(중)에서 가장 …한/하게

Jane Cole's performance was **the most impressive** of all the performances.
제인 콜의 공연은 모든 공연 중에서 가장 인상 깊었다.

- 「the/소유격/'s 형용사/부사 + -est」: 형용사/부사가 2음절 이하의 단어
- 「the/소유격/'s most 형용사/부사」: 형용사/부사가 3음절 이상의 단어
- 최상급은 비교 범위를 나타내는 전치사 in/of/among(~(중)에서)과 함께 잘 쓰인다.

the same ~ as	~와 똑같은
no longer(= not ~ any longer)	더 이상 ~가 아닌
rather than	~보다는 오히려, ~대신에
other than	~이외에
more than/less than	~이상/~이하
at most/at best/at least	많아 봐야/기껏해야/적어도
no later than(= by)	~보다 늦지 않게, 늦어도 ~까지는

+ check .... 해설서 p.45

1. Owing to the highest sales increase in the company's history, the CEO announced that all employees will receive ------- larger bonuses than last year.

   (A) very   (B) too   (C) even   (D) so

2. Polanski Footwear produces the ------- handmade leather shoes of any manufacturer in Italy.

   (A) finely   (B) finest   (C) finer   (D) fine

3. ------- renting an apartment downtown, you should consider buying a house in a nearby suburb.

   (A) Considering how   (B) Rather than   (C) Assuming that   (D) Much less

2. 가정법

▶ 가정법은 어떤 상황에 반대되는 사실을 가정한 것이다. 대개 if절로 시작되며, 특별한 시제를 사용한다.

▶ 가정법 과거 완료(과거에 ~였더라면, …였을텐데): 과거의 반대 상황을 가정할 때 사용한다.

▶ 가정법 미래(혹시 ~라면, …일 것이다): 실현 가능성이 적은 일을 가정하거나, 매우 정중한 표현에 사용된다.

>> 적중 포인트 1 가정법 과거 완료: (과거에) ~였더라면, (과거에) …였을텐데 cf must have p.p. ~임에 틀림없다

If I **had arrived** earlier, I **could have helped** her with her presentation.
내가 일찍 도착했었더라면, 그녀가 발표할 때 도울 수 있었을 텐데.

「If 주어(S) + 과거완료(had + p.p.), 주어(S) + would/should/could/might + have p.p.」

>> 적중 포인트 2 가정법 미래: 혹시 ~라면, …일 것이다 / 혹시 ~라면, …해라

If you **should decide** to join our fitness club this month, you **can take advantage of** a special offer.
저희 헬스클럽에 이번 달에 가입을 결정하신다면, 특별 할인을 이용할 수 있습니다.

「If 주어(S) + should + 동사원형, 주어(S) + 조동사의 현재형(will/shall/can/may) + 동사원형」	혹시 ~라면, ~일 것이다
「If 주어(S) + should + 동사원형, 명령문(please + 동사원형)」	혹시 ~라면, ~해라

1. If you sign up for our membership online, you ------- a monthly newsletter containing information on upcoming events and sales.

(A) were sending   (B) would send   (C) will be sent   (D) were sent

2. If he ------- the building design earlier, Mr. Hoffman could have begun the project before the end of March.

(A) will revise   (B) revised   (C) revising   (D) had revised

3. If he had been notified that his office would be remodeled for two weeks, Mr. Alvarez ------- in a request for vacation during that time.

(A) will put   (B) put   (C) had been putting   (D) could have put

3. 도치

▶ 도치는 특정한 말을 강조하기 위해서 주어와 동사의 위치를 바꾼 것이다.

>> 적중 포인트 1 be동사의 보어가 문장의 맨 앞에 올 때

The meeting schedule is attached to this letter.
= **Attached to this letter** is the meeting schedule.
이 편지에 회의 일정표가 첨부되어 있습니다.

「Enclosed / Attached / Included + is / are + 주어(S)」	~가 동봉 / 첨부 / 포함되어 있다

>> 적중 포인트 2 부정어, only 또는 only가 들어간 부사구가 문장 맨 앞에 올 때

Only recently did the unemployment rate fall below five percent.
최근에서야 실업률이 5% 이하로 떨어졌다.

hardly		거의 ~하지 않는
seldom / rarely		좀처럼 ~않는
never	+ 동사(V) + 주어(S)	결코 ~않다
few / little		거의 ~않다
only recently		최근에서야
not only		~뿐만 아니라

>> 적중 포인트 3 So / as(~도 그렇다), Neither / Nor(~도 그렇지 않다)가 문장 / 절의 맨 앞에 올 때

Mr. Carlton transferred to the Tokyo office, **and so did** his assistant.
= Mr. Carlton transferred to the Tokyo office, **as did** his assistant.
칼튼 씨는 도쿄 사무실로 옮겼고, 그의 비서도 그러했다.

>> 적중 포인트 4 가정법에서 if가 생략될 때

❶ 가정법 과거 완료 도치

If the payment **had been made** on time, we could have avoided additional late fees.
= **Had** the payment **been made** on time, we could have avoided additional late fees.
만약 제시간에 돈이 지급되었다면, 추가 연체료는 피할 수 있었을 것이다.

❷ 가정법 미래 도치

If you **should have** any inquiries, our staff will be happy to assist you.
= **Should** you **have** any inquiries, our staff will be happy to assist you.
문의 사항이 있으시면, 저희 직원이 기꺼이 도와드릴 겁니다.

+ check .... 해설서 p.45

1. In no way did the news of the merger adversely ------- the stock price of Ramoro as its investors have confidence in the company's financial stability.

   (A) to affect   (B) affect   (C) affecting   (D) affected

2. Only recently have the factory managers ------- that more than 1,000 units of the new microphone were found to be defective.

   (A) to confirm   (B) confirming   (C) confirm   (D) confirmed

3. Designed by Michael Min, the Piwan Tower is an outstanding piece of work, ------- his other architectural projects.

   (A) while   (B) yet   (C) as are   (D) in fact

Practice

1. JHG Equipment's ------- photocopiers produce vivid color pictures and come with a three-year warranty.

(A) late
(B) lately
(C) latest
(D) later

2. Otsukuriyanka Restaurant uses only the ------- seafood available on the market for all of its dishes.

(A) most freshness
(B) freshest
(C) freshly
(D) more freshly

3. ------- along with the letter is an application form that needs to be filled out completely and returned within 7 days.

(A) Attach
(B) Attaching
(C) Attached
(D) To attach

4. If Mr. Gonzales had informed me that he was visiting New York for the conference, I ------- him up at the airport.

(A) have picked
(B) be picking
(C) will pick
(D) would have picked

5. Calston Exports concluded that replacing the broken equipment would be ------- cheaper than fixing it.

(A) much
(B) more
(C) as
(D) like

6. Only recently has Mr. Marshall ------- studying Chinese, even though he moves to Shanghai next month.

(A) starts
(B) started
(C) starting
(D) to start

7. The daily lives of smoking women are ------- affected than are those of male counterparts.

(A) more adversely
(B) more adverse
(C) most adverse
(D) adversely

8. Had hotel reservations ------- sooner, it might have been possible to accommodate all the participants at one hotel.

(A) making
(B) was made
(C) been made
(D) made

9. Among the convenience stores located in the area, F&C Store is the ------- to get to from our office.

(A) easily
(B) easiest
(C) more easily
(D) most easily

10. As the number of tourists visiting the Silver Museum increases, ------- does the need for tour guides.

(A) therefore
(B) so
(C) again
(D) however

11. Despite some additional options, the new SX500 model has almost the same features ------- the previous one.

(A) for
(B) as
(C) in
(D) than

12. Ms. Lynn was not satisfied with her paintings because she is her own ------- critic.

(A) harshly
(B) harsher
(C) most harshly
(D) harshest

13. Comparing the sales figures of the two items, Emmy Campfire's hiking outfits are as ------- as its hiking boots.

(A) popular
(B) most popular
(C) popularly
(D) more popular

14. Mr. Enrique ordered the ------- possible lights for the company's offices.

(A) brighter
(B) brightly
(C) brightest
(D) brighten

15. ------- all the candidates interviewed by HR, Rachel stood out as the most highly qualified.

(A) Upon
(B) Being
(C) Almost
(D) Of

16. It is necessary that every applicant submit their documents ------- May 15.

(A) more than
(B) rather than
(C) no later than
(D) no longer than

17. Piercent Paper's new CEO is considering much ------- actions to overcome their financial difficulties than his predecessor.

(A) boldness
(B) bolder
(C) boldest
(D) boldly

18. Major Korean companies' annual revenues have an even ------- influence on gross domestic product.

(A) strongly
(B) strength
(C) strongest
(D) stronger

19. ------- will Ms. Morris arrange interviews, but she will also be responsible for ordering office supplies.

(A) Not only
(B) So as to
(C) In spite of
(D) Just as

20. You may be asked to cover repair fees ------- damage to the vehicle be discovered after your lease has ended.

(A) instead
(B) should
(C) since
(D) let

1. All ------- products must be recorded in the database with a note explaining the customer's reasons.

(A) return
(B) returns
(C) returned
(D) was returned

2. Because we decided not to choose unnecessary options such as a sunroof, our new car was ------- cheaper than expected.

(A) much
(B) more
(C) as
(D) like

3. Luke Haimeia has been recognized as an ------- skilled programmer and designer by his company.

(A) excepting
(B) exceptional
(C) exception
(D) exceptionally

4. ------- cooperation between departments, we've set up a weekly review meeting.

(A) Facilitates
(B) Facilitation
(C) Is facilitating
(D) To facilitate

5. In ------- to popular demand, SanMarco Mart has agreed to extend its weekday hours and open on Sundays.

(A) counter
(B) response
(C) expression
(D) cooperation

6. As ------- in the contract, the items must be delivered on the 10th of every month.

(A) indicative
(B) indication
(C) indicating
(D) indicated

7. Our Investor Relations Department has posted a press release on our website stating that we ------- to launch our own line of smartphones this year.

(A) recommend
(B) foresee
(C) intend
(D) consider

8. Benjamin Martinez will most likely be offered the job as senior researcher on account of his ------- résumé.

(A) qualified
(B) skillful
(C) impressive
(D) informed

9. In addition to daffodils, Amy's Flowers Inc. also supplies a wide range of summer flowers to ------- across the country.

(A) distributing
(B) distributed
(C) distribution
(D) distributors

10. Call Frontiere Inc.'s customer service center ------- assistance with your product over the phone.

(A) will receive
(B) receives
(C) to receive
(D) receiving

11. KTCG Inc. is trying to encourage employees to park their vehicles in Area K because Area B is ------- under construction.

(A) current
(B) more current
(C) most current
(D) currently

12. Employees may request an unpaid leave of absence, which is subject to ------- by their supervisor.

(A) approving
(B) approved
(C) approval
(D) approvingly

13. XTM Sportswear's R&D team has been working on ------- new fabrics which can withstand extreme weather conditions.

(A) develop
(B) developed
(C) developing
(D) to develop

14. As positive as the current state of the e-commerce business is, the future looks even more -------.

(A) promises
(B) promised
(C) promising
(D) to promise

15. As ------- at the previous meeting, the company will not disclose the details of the contract.

(A) discuss
(B) discussed
(C) discussion
(D) discussing

16. A customer representative will confirm your discounts within three days ------- your information is received.

(A) upon
(B) still
(C) just
(D) once

17. Heimwerk Furnishings President Heinrich Nissen ------- supports nor opposes the proposal for the creation of an employee labor union.

(A) if
(B) because
(C) yet
(D) neither

18. In the ------- anticipated press conference, Mr. Cheung presented his company's latest line of solar paint.

(A) customarily
(B) effectually
(C) highly
(D) promptly

19. Due to seasonal demand, processing orders may take a day ------- than usual.

(A) longer
(B) longest
(C) length
(D) long

20. Gryphon Security will reply within one day to all customer complaints ------- through the company website.

(A) filed
(B) file
(C) files
(D) filing

VOCA

▲

RT 5

▼

단문 빈칸 채우기

동사 어휘 1

UNIT 01

1 **accelerate** 가속화하다 ● expedite
accelerate production 생산을 가속화하다

2 **accommodate** 수용하다, 숙박시키다
n accommodation 숙박시설
accommodate the audience/demand
청중들을/요구를 수용하다

3 **accompany** 동반하다, 따라가다
only if accompanied by the original receipt
영수증 원본을 지참할 경우에만

4 **account for** ~을 차지하다, ~의 원인이다, 설명하다
● explain
account for two thirds of production
생산량의 2/3를 차지하다
account for the price increase
가격 상승의 원인이다

5 **acquire** 취득하다, 인수하다
n acquisition 인수, 습득
acquire the company 회사를 인수하다
cf. merge는 '합병하다'의 뜻으로, merge with로 사용된다.

6 **address** 다루다, 처리하다 ● deal with ● treat
address the inquiries 요구를 다루다
address the issues[problems] 문제를 처리하다
address customer requests and complaints
고객의 요청과 불만을 처리하다
address concerns about ~에 대한 우려를 처리하다

7 **adhere to** ~을 고수하다, ~을 지키다, ~에 부착되다
● comply with ● observe ● conform to
adhere to policies/rules/standards
정책/규칙/기준을 지키다
adhere to the surface of the wood
나무 표면에 부착되다

8 **agree** 동의하다
agree on/upon + 의견 ~에 동의하다/뜻을 같이하다
agree to + 제안/의견 ~에 찬성하다
agree with + 사람 ~에 동의하다

9 **assemble** 조립하다, 모이다
n assembly 조립 (작업), 집회, 모임
assemble the components 부품을 조립하다

10 **assess** 평가하다 ● evaluate
assess the effectiveness of ~의 유효성을 평가하다

11 **assign (A to B)** (A를 B에게) 할당하다, 배정하다
assign work to each project member
업무를 각 프로젝트 구성원에게 할당하다

12 **assume** (직책·업무를) 떠맡다, 추측하다
assume the title/responsibility 직함/책임을 맡다
cf. undertake는 '(업무 등을 맡아) 착수하다'의 뜻으로 직함을 목적어
로 쓰지 않는다.

13 **attract** 끌다, 유치하다 ● draw
n attraction 끌림, 매력
adj attractive 매력적인
attract tourists 관광객을 유치하다
a tourist attraction 관광명소
attractive salary 괜찮은 급여

14 **attribute A to B** A를 B의 덕분이라고(탓이라고) 여기다
attribute high sales to efficient management
높은 판매를 효율적인 경영 덕분이라고 여기다
A is attributed to B A는 B 덕분이다

15 **authorize** ~을 인가하다
adj authorized 공인된 cf. ↔ unauthorized 허가받지 않은
n authorization 허가
n authority 권한, 권위자
an authorized service center 공인된 서비스 센터
unauthorized reproduction 불법 복제

16 **award A to B** B에게 A를 수여하다
award the contract to a new company
신생 기업에 계약을 맡기다
be awarded a contract 계약을 따내다

17 **benefit** 혜택을 보다, 이익을 얻다
benefit from ~으로부터 혜택을 보다

18 **collaborate** 협력하다
collaborate with + 사람 ~와 협력하다
collaborate on + 협력 내용 ~에 대해 협력하다

19 **commend** 칭찬하다, 추천하다 ● praise
adj commendable 칭찬받을 만한
commendable work 칭찬받을 만한 일
cf. comment 논평하다, 견해를 밝히다
commence 시작되다

20 **comply with** + 규정 ~을 준수하다[지키다]
● abide by ● adhere to ● follow ● obey
● observe ● conform to
n compliance 준수, 따름
comply with the rules 규칙을 준수하다

Practice

해설서 p.49 / ⏱ 제한 시간 5분

1. Overseas managers should ------- with all local laws regarding wages and working conditions.

(A) observe   (B) concern

(C) accommodate   (D) comply

2. Workers are required to ------- issues with manufacturing equipment in a prompt manner.

(A) inform   (B) stand

(C) arrive   (D) address

3. IU Solutions will open a new regional office in Birmingham to ------- the company's growth in Europe.

(A) insulate   (B) participate

(C) designate   (D) accommodate

4. When Smart Stories ------- Brilliant Books in September, some overlapping departments of the two publishers will be restructured.

(A) merges   (B) remains

(C) anticipates   (D) acquires

5. In a press conference, the CEO announced that Ms. Denis would ------- the new marketing manager position in April.

(A) engage   (B) assume

(C) evolve   (D) promote

6. Plumbers from City Shore Utilities will visit the Parat premises at 1:00 P.M. to ------- the water pipes.

(A) order   (B) assess

(C) record   (D) proceed

7. Individual access codes will be given to personnel who are ------- to work in the facility.

(A) accrued   (B) adapted

(C) authorized   (D) adjusted

8. Tando Co. has never ------- such a large bonus to a first-year employee before.

(A) accessed   (B) accepted

(C) assumed   (D) awarded

9. Sky Airways has ------- greatly from its merger with Cyan Continental.

(A) accounted   (B) benefited

(C) equipped   (D) reminded

10. World-renowned designer Sophie Penn ------- with True Art Co. employees to create an innovative advertisement for the company.

(A) recalled   (B) provided

(C) collaborated   (D) employed

VOCA UNIT 01

동사 어휘 2

1 conceive (생각·계획 등을) 마음속으로 하다, 상상하다

conceive the plot 줄거리를 구상하다

2 conduct 실행하다, 실시하다 ⊜ carry out

conduct the survey / investigation /
research / inspection / study / analysis
설문 조사 / 조사 / 연구 / 검사 / 연구 / 분석을 실시하다

3 consult 의견을 듣다, 참고[참조]하다 ⊜ refer to

consult the e-mail / manual
이메일 / 매뉴얼을 참고하다

4 cover (비용 등을) 보상하다, 포함하다, 다루다
n coverage 적용, 보도

cover the cost 비용을 충당하다
insurance coverage 보험 보상 범위
media coverage 언론 보도

5 encounter 맞닥뜨리다, 접하다

encounter problems 문제를 접하다

6 endorse 지지하다, 홍보하다
⊜ support ⊜ promote ⊜ recommend

endorse a product 제품을 홍보하다

7 enforce (법률을) 시행하다, 진행하다
n enforcement 시행, 실행

enforce the law 법률을 시행하다

8 entitle 자격[권리]을 주다

be entitled to + 명사 ~에 대한 자격이 주어지다
be entitled to부정사 ~할 자격이 주어지다

9 exceed 초과하다, 능가하다
⊜ go beyond ⊜ surpass ⊜ excel
n excess 과도, 과잉

exceed one's expectation ~의 기대를 뛰어넘다
in excess of ~을 초과하여

10 face (문제 등에) 직면하다 ⊜ confront

be faced with ~에 직면하다 ⊜ be confronted with
face / encounter the risk 위기에 직면하다

11 facilitate 촉진하다, 용이하게 하다

facilitate communication 의사소통을 쉽게 하다

12 feature 특징으로 하다, 특별히 포함하다 **n** 특징, 특집

feature a variety of workshops
다양한 워크숍들을 특징으로 하다

13 gauge 측정하다, 판단하다

gauge the pressure 압력을 측정하다
gauge customer preference 고객 선호를 측정하다

14 generate 창출하다, 만들어내다
⊜ produce ⊜ yield ⊜ create

generate revenue[income] 수입을 창출하다
generate electricity 전기를 만들어내다

15 hesitate 주저하다, 망설이다

Do not hesitate to ask for assistance.
주저하지 마시고 도움을 요청하세요.
be hesitant to ~하는 것을 주저하다

16 honor 존중하다, 표창하다, 이행하다 **n** 명예, 경의

honor the winner 우승자를 표창하다
in honor of success 성공을 기념하여
be honored for ~으로 상을 받다
be honored to ~해서 영광이다

17 implement 실행하다, (계획·정책·규정 따위를) 시행하다
⊜ carry out

implement a plan / policy / program / strategy
계획 / 정책 / 프로그램 / 전략을 시행하다

18 institute (제도·습관 등을) 도입하다, 시작하다

institute a new dress code / procedure
새로운 복장 규정 / 절차를 도입하다

19 last 지속되다
adj lasting 지속적인

last until ~까지 지속되다
lasting impression 오래 기억에 남는 인상

20 launch 착수하다, 시작하다, 출시하다
⊜ begin ⊜ start ⊜ initiate ⊜ commence

launch a campaign 캠페인에 착수하다
launch a new product 신제품을 출시하다

Practice

1. The research team led by Dr. Moreno will ------- a series of consumer surveys this month.

(A) conduct　　　　(B) detain
(C) foresee　　　　(D) associate

2. The Marketing Department plans to conduct a consumer survey in order to ------- the level of interest in our product.

(A) gauge　　　　(B) apply
(C) implement　　(D) gain

3. Kindly ------- the employee manual for details on our outside employment policy.

(A) refer　　　　(B) visit
(C) approach　　(D) consult

4. Tony Bibbo ------- the main character in his latest suspense thriller, *Behind the Scene*, from a person he met on a recent trip to Nepal.

(A) encountered　　(B) convinced
(C) inspired　　　　(D) conceived

5. The employee manual contains solutions to any problems you may ------- with a client.

(A) encounter　　(B) comprise
(C) reside　　　　(D) qualify

6. Actor Jimmy Cruz has agreed to ------- the new product line by Jenya Cosmetics and will appear in its TV advertisement.

(A) endorse　　　(B) persuade
(C) thrive　　　　(D) realize

7. Ms. Ming courteously ------- the position offered by Verrazano Imports Ltd.

(A) converted　　(B) declined
(C) lessened　　(D) restricted

8. This month's Creative Gardening Fair in London ------- plants and flowers from all over the world.

(A) features　　　(B) observes
(C) establishes　　(D) combines

9. Every device needs to be ------- after assembly is complete to confirm that it functions properly.

(A) assigned　　(B) delivered
(C) marketed　　(D) inspected

10. Last month, the immigration office ------- 7,000 entry permits to foreign visitors.

(A) constructed　(B) traveled
(C) issued　　　　(D) acted

VOCA UNIT 02

UNIT 03

동사 어휘 3

1 locate 찾다, 위치를 찾아내다, 위치하다 ⊜ find ⊜ spot

locate a nearby restaurant or movie theater
근처 음식점이나 영화관을 찾다

2 meet 만나다, 맞추다, 충족시키다 ⊜ satisfy ⊜ fulfill

meet a goal 목표를 이루다
meet a deadline 마감일을 맞추다
meet the needs 요구를 충족시키다
meet the requirements 요건을 충족시키다

3 modify 수정하다, 변경하다

modify the error 오류를 수정하다
cf. revise 잘못된 것을 올바르게 변경하다

4 obtain A from B B로부터 A를 얻다[획득하다]

obtain insurance from the agent
대리인으로부터 보험을 구매하다

5 prefer 선호하다
n preference 선호
adj preferred 우선의

prefer working with other people
다른 사람들과 함께 일하는 것을 선호하다
preference for ~에 대한 선호
preferred means 선호되는 수단
food/meal preference 음식/식사 선호도

6 proceed with[to] ~을 진행하다, ~로 나아가다

proceed with the meeting 회의를 진행하다

7 redeem 보완하다, 현금[상품]으로 바꾸다

The coupons could be redeemed for cash.
쿠폰을 현금으로 바꿀 수 있다.

8 reflect 반영하다, 심사숙고하다

reflect consumer preferences
소비자의 선호도를 반영하다

9 refrain from -ing ~을 삼가다

refrain from taking pictures 사진 촬영을 삼가다
cf. prohibit from -ing ~하는 것을 금지하다

10 resume 재개하다, 재개되다 **n** 이력서

resume negotiations 협상을 재개하다

11 solicit 요청하다, 구하다

solicit funds 기금을 구하다

12 strive to ~하려고 노력하다[애쓰다]

strive to win 이기려고 노력하다

13 substitute A for B B 대신 A를 쓰다[대신하다]

be used as a substitute for sugar
설탕 대용품으로 사용되다

14 suspend 중지하다, 잠시 보류하다

suspend production/service
생산/서비스를 중지하다

15 terminate 끝내다, 종결시키다

terminate a contract 계약을 종료시키다

16 unveil 공개하다, 베일을 벗기다 ⊜ launch ⊜ introduce

unveil the product 제품을 공개하다

17 urge 충고하다, 강력히 권고하다

urge people to follow the safety guidelines
사람들에게 안전 수칙을 지키라고 당부하다

18 utilize 활용하다, 이용하다

utilize concrete as a building material
콘크리트를 건축자재로 활용하다

19 verify (사실임을) 입증하다, 확인하다
n verification 증명, 입증, 확인

verify a certificate 수료증의 진위를 확인하다

20 waive (권리·요구를) 포기하다, 감면하다
n waiver 감면

waive the requirements 요구 사항을 철회하다
get a tuition waiver 학비를 감면받다

Practice

1. Municipal workers believe that the plans to implement the paperless office policy will ------- to reduced expenses.

(A) experience
(B) determine
(C) lead
(D) intend

2. Be sure to ------- all industry regulations when planning the construction project.

(A) establish
(B) observe
(C) cooperate
(D) adhere

3. Even though the new plan is very creative, it would cost a fortune for the company to ------- with it at the moment.

(A) examine
(B) treat
(C) urge
(D) proceed

4. Locating an ideal site for the warehouse is ------- more difficult than expected.

(A) saying
(B) proving
(C) reaching
(D) searching

5. Despite the opportunities to cut costs, Ronzone's Bakeries should ------- to maintain the highest standards of quality.

(A) strive
(B) take
(C) recommend
(D) believe

6. Mr. Jefferson's promotion to vice president will ------- Norvis, Inc.'s presence as one of the leaders in the biochemistry field.

(A) accomplish
(B) incline
(C) solidify
(D) merge

7. Manufacturing of Lumpini Chili Sauce had to be ------- due to a shortage of a key ingredient.

(A) directed
(B) expired
(C) suspended
(D) foretold

8. Chief Editor Tanya Madison ------- Rawson Press's public relations division to promote Luke Thayer's latest novel on all the national cable networks.

(A) alleged
(B) vowed
(C) pursued
(D) urged

9. The International Binders Confederation ------- the interests of book publishers worldwide.

(A) recreates
(B) represents
(C) functions
(D) contributes

10. Mr. Hwang, the new operations director, has just ------- several scheduling conflicts that had led to some late deliveries last quarter.

(A) resolved
(B) reminded
(C) finished
(D) offered

VOCA UNIT 03

REVIEW TEST 01

해설서 p.52 / ⏱ 제한 시간 10분

1. We encourage front-line workers to ------- us of all customer feedback, both positive and negative.

(A) respond   (B) request
(C) indicate   (D) inform

2. During this Friday's flash sale, ------- a pair of hiking boots from Sunrise Athletes and get an additional pair for half price.

(A) buy   (B) find
(C) spend   (D) place

3. In preparation for the summer sales event in July, Mendrak Department Store will need to ------- some seasonal workers.

(A) continue   (B) finish
(C) function   (D) hire

4. Hawthorne Industries ------- each of its employees to carry an identification badge at all times.

(A) enters   (B) requires
(C) specifies   (D) verifies

5. Renovations on Donegal town hall will commence as soon as the mayor has ------- the plan.

(A) approved   (B) presumed
(C) designated   (D) fabricated

6. Several lawyers specializing ------- corporate finance have been contacted by Kayoid Incorporated.

(A) with   (B) in
(C) from   (D) by

7. Dr. Ido employed an interior designer to ------- all aspects of the clinic's renovation work.

(A) strive   (B) oversee
(C) urge   (D) require

8. Comic artist Yukito Shirow's homepage ------- over 20,000 visitors every month.

(A) features   (B) proceeds
(C) attracts   (D) creates

9. Park rangers must be able to ------- how to survive in the wilderness.

(A) utilize   (B) arrive
(C) demonstrate   (D) concentrate

10. Using this application, you can ------- with coworkers wherever they may be.

(A) communicate   (B) notify
(C) express   (D) arrive

11. PGD Group has ------- as the leading institute in the field of foreign language education.

(A) emerged
(B) showed
(C) produced
(D) assigned

12. Our firm has always made it a policy to ------- to local charities focused on providing educational opportunities.

(A) help
(B) require
(C) agree
(D) donate

13. The CEO's announcement was ------- by a question-and-answer session with management for all current employees.

(A) caused
(B) followed
(C) decided
(D) conducted

14. At Arandale, we believe that all of our employees ------- a respectful working environment.

(A) conduct
(B) request
(C) deserve
(D) fulfill

15. The long-awaited Macro NB4 laptop computer will finally be ------- at the Shanghai Electronics Tradeshow.

(A) decreased
(B) solved
(C) contacted
(D) unveiled

16. Attendees arriving after 3 P.M. must check in at the automated kiosk to be ------- to the conference.

(A) dismissed
(B) admitted
(C) redeemed
(D) approached

17. Superior Instrumentation, Inc. is looking for a regional marketing director to ------- our latest products in Australia and New Zealand.

(A) enjoy
(B) investigate
(C) convince
(D) launch

18. The old Swansville plant will be converted ------- a warehouse after the new facility begins production.

(A) into
(B) for
(C) by
(D) over

19. Ms. Boumaza is ------- with launching several promotions that have greatly improved Raja Electronics' profits.

(A) evaluated
(B) credited
(C) announced
(D) believed

20. All decisions regarding personnel changes will be ------- until the merger completion scheduled for January 1.

(A) solved
(B) prepared
(C) deferred
(D) compiled

명사 어휘 1

1 access (장소로의) 접근, 접근 권한 ⓥ 접근하다, 이용하다

access to confidential information
기밀 정보 접근 권한

unlimited access 무제한 접근

cf. access (불가산) vs. approach (가산)

2 accordance 일치, 조화

in accordance with the rules 규칙에 따라

3 admission 입장, 들어갈 허가

get free admission to the seminar
세미나 무료 입장을 (허가) 받다

4 advance 진보, 발전 ⓥ 진전시키다 ᵃᵈʲ 사전의

ⁿ advancement 승진, 발전, 진보

advances in medical technology 의학 기술의 진보

advance booking 사전 예약

in advance 미리

5 appraisal 감정, 평가

performance appraisal 업무 평가

6 approval 승인

written approval 서면 허가

prior approval 사전 승인

7 array 집합체, 정렬

an array of 다양한

a wide array of services 다양한 서비스

make an array of products 다양한 제품을 생산하다

8 arrival 도착, 도착한 사람(물건)

on[upon] arrival 도착하자마자

9 assembly 조립 (작업), 집회, 모임

ⓥ assemble 조립하다

assembly line 조립 라인

assembly plant 조립 공장

10 authority 권한, 권위자, 당국

delegate authority 권한을 위임하다

a recognized authority 인정받는 권위자

cf. authorization 승인, 허락

written authorization 서면 허가

11 benefit 혜택, 이점 ⓥ 혜택을 보다, 이익을 얻다

a benefit from the change 변경으로 인한 혜택

as a benefit of membership 회원의 혜택으로

12 capability 능력, 성능

above one's capability ~의 능력 밖에 있는

13 capacity 수용력, 생산능력

seating capacity 좌석 수용 능력

beyond one's capacity ~의 능력 밖인

14 caution 주의, 경계

use[exercise] caution 조심하다

15 certificate 증명서

the enclosed certificate 동봉된 증명서

cf. certificate (가산) vs. certification (불가산)

16 change 잔돈, 거스름돈

exact change for purchasing beverages
음료를 사기 위한 정확한 액수의 동전

cf. change가 '동전, 잔돈, 거스름돈'이라는 뜻으로 쓰일 때는 불가산 명사이다.

17 collaboration 협력

in collaboration with universities
대학교들과 협력하여

18 competition 경쟁, 대회

ᵃᵈʲ competitive 경쟁력 있는

ⁿ competitiveness 경쟁력

a cut-throat competition 살벌한 경쟁

competitive salary 괜찮은(높은) 연봉

enhance one's competitiveness 경쟁력을 높이다

19 commitment 헌신, 전념

ⓥ commit 저지르다, 전념하다

commitment to top quality service
최상급 서비스를 위한 헌신

commitment to ~에 대한 헌신[전념]

be committed to -ing ~에 전념하다

20 conflict 충돌, 상충 ⓥ 겹치다

a scheduling conflict 일정상의 충돌

due to a conflict in his schedule
그의 일정이 겹치기 때문에

Practice

1. Be sure to take advantage of your special ------- to the *Iden Global Journal* website.

(A) access   (B) routine
(C) position   (D) advance

2. Staff members expressed ------- for their Vice President, Ms. Macomber, who planned and organized several successful major investment sales transactions for the company.

(A) admiration   (B) persistence
(C) authority   (D) reward

3. Mr. Aufrance firmly believes that friendly ------- between corporations spurs innovative ideas and processes.

(A) condemnation   (B) competition
(C) condescension   (D) congregation

4. The city of Morrison is inviting the public ------- on its plan to erect a new sculpture celebrating the city's birthday.

(A) arrangement   (B) interest
(C) comment   (D) order

5. At Keystone Limited, the branch with the highest profits will be awarded the largest marketing ------- for the upcoming year.

(A) survey   (B) budget
(C) collections   (D) capacity

6. Aeron Fabrics has experienced a rapid ------- in production over the last quarter.

(A) sector   (B) adequacy
(C) acceleration   (D) inclusion

7. Our company's new microwave received positive reviews for its user-friendly manual and its -------.

(A) appliance   (B) attraction
(C) affordability   (D) awareness

8. The two competing firms were praised for their ------- on environmental issues.

(A) payment   (B) condition
(C) manufacturing   (D) collaboration

9. Mr. Simpson expressed his full ------- to the business deal during the PR event last Monday.

(A) assessment   (B) reference
(C) selection   (D) commitment

10. With the new payment system, city buses will no longer require exact -------.

(A) coin   (B) number
(C) amount   (D) change

UNIT 05 명사 어휘 2

1 compliance 준수, 따름

compliance with the rules/standards
규칙/기준에의 준수

in compliance with ~을 준수하여

2 consent 동의, 합의 **v** 동의하다

give/obtain consent 동의를 해주다/얻다
written consent 서면 동의
prior consent 사전 동의

3 contingency 만일의 사태

contingency plans 비상 계획

4 correspondence 서신 교환, 통신

interoffice correspondence 사내 통신
cf. correspondent 특파원, 통신원

5 decline 감소, 하락 **v** 감소하다, ~을 거절하다

in decline 기울어, 쇠퇴하여
a sharp decline 폭락, 대폭 하락
decline in profits 수익 하락

6 delegate 대표(자) **v** (권한·업무 등을) 위임하다

a labor delegate 노동자 대표
cf. delegation 대표단, 위임

7 dimension 크기, 치수 ⊜ size

measure the exact dimensions of the rooms
방들의 정확한 치수를 재다

8 disruption 중단, 혼란

cause a disruption in development
개발 중단을 야기시키다

9 efficiency 효율, 능률, 유능함

improve/enhance energy efficiency
에너지 효율을 향상시키다

10 eloquence 말재주, 웅변술
adj eloquent 유창한
adv eloquently 유창하게, 설득력 있게

polished eloquence 세련된 능변
eloquent speech 유창한 연설

11 estimate 견적(서), 추정치 ⊜ quotation
v 견적을 잡다, 추정하다 ⊜ quote

a written estimate 서면 견적서

12 expenditure 지출, 비용, 경비 ⊜ expense

a reduction in public expenditures 공공지출 삭감

13 expertise 전문 지식

technical expertise 전문 기술 지식
core areas of expertise 핵심 전문 분야

14 feasibility 실행 가능성, 타당성

consider the feasibility of a plan
계획의 실현 가능성을 고려하다

15 figure 수치, (유명) 인물

sales figures 판매 실적, 매출액

16 fluctuation 변동, 불안정

price fluctuation 가격 변동

17 flexibility 융통성, 유연성

demonstrate one's flexibility 융통성을 발휘하다

18 function 연회, 기능 **v** 작용하다

attend an official function 공식 행사에 참가하다

19 grant 지원금, 보조금 **v** 승인하다, 수여하다

government grants 정부 보조금

20 incentive 장려금, 자극, 유인책

incentives to compete 경쟁을 위해 주어지는 장려금
offer customers extra incentives
고객들에게 추가 우대책을 제공하다

Practice

해설서 p.54 / ⏱ 제한 시간 5분

1. In ------- with new environmental regulations, we should set up the air ventilation system.

(A) compliance   (B) competence
(C) arrangement   (D) advancement

2. All factory workers should review the safety ------- plan so that they know what to do in an emergency.

(A) termination   (B) discharge
(C) contingency   (D) prevention

3. Ms. Talia Ghulal, a representative of Quartermain Solutions, emphasized her company's ------- for stricter quality standards.

(A) consciousness   (B) consent
(C) fairness   (D) support

4. ------- of duties can reduce a supervisor's workload and enable other staff members to try new assignments.

(A) Permission   (B) Reputation
(C) Qualification   (D) Delegation

5. ACT, Inc. would like to sincerely apologize for the ------- in its online network.

(A) disruption   (B) action
(C) precaution   (D) update

6. Before presenting an estimate for repainting, Mr. Delano needs to take some measurements to determine the ------- of each room.

(A) appearance   (B) objectives
(C) content   (D) dimensions

7. Senior researchers at TopPro Laboratory must avoid ------- of their recent findings.

(A) permission   (B) confession
(C) allowance   (D) disclosure

8. Mr. Han will receive ------- from some subcontractors and will select the one with the lowest costs.

(A) estimates   (B) sponsors
(C) deliveries   (D) relocations

9. Thanks to his ------- and neat appearance, Mr. Diego was chosen as the company's spokesperson.

(A) prevalence   (B) allowance
(C) eloquence   (D) abundance

10. Before making an investment, we need to determine the ------- of building houses in that section of the city.

(A) employment   (B) fascination
(C) reality   (D) feasibility

VOCA UNIT 05

UNIT 06 명사 어휘 3

1 initiative 솔선, 기획, 계획, 결단, 주도권

take initiative 솔선수범하다
online marketing initiatives 온라인 마케팅 계획

2 installment 할부 (금액), (전집·연재물의) 1회분

pay in installments 할부로 지불하다
the latest installment 가장 최근 연재물
cf. installation 설치

3 interruption 방해, 간섭, 중단

without interruption 방해 없이
a brief interruption in electrical supply
잠시 동안의 전기 공급 중단

4 lapse 실수, 과실

a minor lapse in product quality
제품 품질의 작은 하자

5 modification 수정, 변경

make necessary modifications
불가피한 수정을 하다

6 notice 공고, 통지 ⓥ 알아채다

at short notice 충분한 예고 없이, 촉박하게
until further notice 추후 통보가 있을 때까지

7 perspective 관점, 시각

from a historical perspective 역사적인 관점에서

8 phase 단계, 국면

at the final[last] phase of construction
공사 마지막 단계에

9 premises 부지, (토지를 포함한) 건물

on the premises 부지 내에서

10 priority 우선권, 우선순위

take priority over all other work
다른 모든 일보다 우선순위를 차지하다
top priority 최우선 순위

11 proof 증거, 증빙, 증명서

proof of purchase 구매 증빙
proof of employment 재직 증명서

12 property 부동산, 건물, 재산

intellectual property 지적 재산
exclusive property 독점 재산

13 proximity 가까움, 근접함

in close proximity to ~에 근접하여
in the proximity of ~의 부근에

14 reference 참고, 추천, 언급

a letter of reference 추천서
for quick reference 쉽게 참고할 수 있도록

15 reimbursement 배상, 환급
≡ compensation ≡ remuneration

receive reimbursement for the cost of training
강습비를 환급받다

16 reputation 평판, 명성

establish a reputation 명성을 확립하다
a reputation for ~에 대한 명성[평판]

17 revenue 수입, 소득

tax revenue 세수입
generate revenue 수입을 창출하다

18 sequence 순서, 연속

in sequence 차례차례로

19 surplus 나머지, 잔여 adj 나머지의, 잔여의

a surplus of certain products 남아 있는 특정 상품

20 transition 이동, 변화

a transition period 과도기
cf. transaction 거래, 매매

Practice

1. Employee identification cards will contain our company's vision and mission as part of our public relations -------.

(A) process   (B) evaluation
(B) asset   (D) initiative

2. Every package shipped from the warehouse must contain an invoice that lists the items it holds as well as the place of ------- of the contents.

(A) version   (B) origin
(C) foundation   (D) achievement

3. Star Shipping sent 100,000 tons of steel to Greendale Ltd. fulfilling its contractual ------- two months earlier than expected.

(A) surplus   (B) obligation
(C) forecast   (D) indication

4. Ms. Park is evaluating the ------- of the partnership agreement with Sauber GmbH.

(A) effort   (B) grip
(C) turn   (D) scope

5. Kensington Hotel is almost always at full capacity due to its ------- to many tourist attractions.

(A) proximity   (B) vacancy
(C) efficiency   (D) availability

6. There will be a brief ------- in the area's electricity service at 3 P.M. on Friday for regular maintenance.

(A) statement   (B) outline
(C) interruption   (D) production

7. ProBio has made a completely successful ------- to an automated reporting system.

(A) location   (B) cooperation
(C) transition   (D) suspension

8. I was convinced to try the new device after seeing all the ------- from users who said buying it was the best decision they had ever made.

(A) contradictions   (B) specifications
(C) comparisons   (D) testimonials

9. Hayward's Barbecue asks all customers to refrain from consuming outside food or beverages on the -------.

(A) safety   (B) sequence
(C) prospects   (D) premises

10. The health and happiness of our workers is our highest ------- here at Matazanos Manufacturing.

(A) idea   (B) quality
(C) occasion   (D) priority

VOCA UNIT 06

REVIEW TEST 02

1. The offices in the Rivero Tower are only open until 6 P.M., but personnel with valid ------- may enter after hours.

(A) consolidation   (B) capability
(C) authorization   (D) attendance

2. Leschmart Inc. needs a cashier to work in its San Jose ------- daily 5:00 A.M. to 11:00 A.M.

(A) branch   (B) cover
(C) shift   (D) duty

3. With a convenient public transit system and two recently constructed hotels, Major Cay is being advertised as a tourist -------.

(A) purpose   (B) destination
(C) intention   (D) commitment

4. The supermarket is temporarily accepting only ------- because of an undetermined issue with our credit card reader.

(A) earnings   (B) cash
(C) sums   (D) payment

5. Trioz Technology's new CEO, Jia Wong, called for an ------- of the company's marketing strategies.

(A) inaccuracy   (B) attendance
(C) enterprise   (D) overhaul

6. The manufacturing plant stopped ------- this morning so that the defective machinery could be fixed.

(A) fabrication   (B) construction
(C) production   (D) correction

7. Barin Ltd. utilizes the highest quality security ------- to ensure the protection of confidential client information.

(A) consent   (B) measures
(C) angles   (D) distance

8. Determined restoration ------- in the Bekaa Valley have helped increase tourists' interest in the area.

(A) efforts   (B) views
(C) responses   (D) shares

9. The ------- of the museum renovations was covered by donations from the community.

(A) fund   (B) cost
(C) benefit   (D) contribution

10. Users should review the contract ------- in the product guide before installing the program.

(A) terms   (B) duties
(C) repairs   (D) openings

11. Additional pay will be given to ------- trained to give on-site demonstrations to prospective clients.

(A) specialists   (B) samples
(C) installments   (D) accounts

12. A benefit of joining Draven Advertising is the agency's monetary ------- of excellent performance.

(A) recognition   (B) disregard
(C) neglect   (D) respect

13. The city council has decided on the suburb of Barthur as the ------- for the annual autumn festival.

(A) appointment   (B) moment
(C) location   (D) date

14. Fly High Tech's on-site IT supervisors are senior employees with a ------- of knowledge in a range of technologies.

(A) length   (B) staff
(C) wealth   (D) respect

15. Expansion strategy for the next two years will be the ------- of the meeting.

(A) focus   (B) scheme
(C) method   (D) talent

16. Margate Construction has finished the ------- of the Aylerville Train Station, which will reopen as a museum.

(A) fulfillment   (B) restoration
(C) achievement   (D) ceremony

17. The Samson Architects Awards Board introduced a new ------- for designs constructed with eco-friendly materials.

(A) superiority   (B) recruitment
(C) category   (D) engagement

18. Volodya Genrihovich was recognized for his exceptional ------- as leader of the Downtown Renovation team.

(A) title   (B) opportunity
(C) appearance   (D) work

19. We at National Dissiz Hospital make our best ------- to meet with patients at their booked times.

(A) output   (B) instance
(C) effort   (D) account

20. Due to the increase in the amount of rainfall in the past few months, the ------- of groundwater is now well above average.

(A) generalization   (B) accumulation
(C) collaboration   (D) designation

형용사 어휘 1

1 affordable 가격이 알맞은, (금전적·시간적으로) 감당할 만한
affordable rate 저렴한 요금
＝ low cost ＝ reasonable price

2 appropriate 적절한, ~에 어울리는
take the appropriate measure 적절한 조치를 취하다

3 authentic 진품인, 진정한
v authenticate 진짜임을 증명하다
authentic pottery 진품 도자기

4 available 이용 가능한, 구매 가능한
readily[freely] available 손쉽게 구할 수 있는

5 aware 알고 있는, 인지하는 ＝ conscious
be aware of[that] ~을 알다
be aware of the new law 새 법에 대해 알다

6 broad 폭넓은, 광대한
adv broadly 대략적으로
broad familiarity with our products
우리 제품들에 대한 폭넓은 이해
broad knowledge 폭넓은 지식
be broadly defined 대략적으로 설명되다

7 competent 유능한
a competent worker 능력 있는 직원

8 complicated 복잡한, 뒤섞인 ＝ complex
a complicated system 복잡한 시스템

9 compatible 호환성의, 양립할 수 있는
be compatible with ~과 호환되다
be compatible with all models 모든 모델과 호환되다

10 complimentary 칭찬의, 무료의
＝ free of charge ＝ at no cost
complimentary words 칭찬하는 말
cf. complementary 보충의, 상호 보완적인

11 comprehensive 종합적인, 포괄적인, 광범위한
a comprehensive study 종합적인 연구

12 confidential 기밀의, 비밀의
confidential documents 기밀문서
cf. confident 자신감 있는

13 consecutive 연속적인, 계속되는 ＝ successive
three consecutive days 3일 연속
cf. subsequent 이어지는

14 considerable 상당한
put in considerable effort 상당한 노력을 기울이다
cf. considerate 사려 깊은

15 convenient 편리한, 알맞은
n convenience 편의, 편리함
the most convenient time to call
전화하기 가장 편한 시간
at your earliest convenience 형편이 되는 대로 빨리

16 critical 비판적인, 중요한
n criticism 비평
n critic 비평가, 평론가
a critical report 비판적인 보고서
play a critical role 중요한 역할을 하다
sharp criticism 신랄한 비평

17 defective 결함 있는, 하자가 있는
a defective product 결함 있는 상품

18 deliberate 신중한, 심사숙고한, 고의적인
v 신중히 생각하다
deliberate for five days to make a decision
결정하는 데 5일을 심사숙고하다

19 dependent 의존하는, 달려있는 ＝ reliant
be dependent on[upon] ~에 의존하다
The success of our company is dependent on
product quality. 우리 회사의 성공은 제품의 품질에 달려 있다.
cf. dependable 신뢰할 만한 ＝ reliable

20 diverse 다양한
n diversity 다양성
v diversify 다양화하다
a diverse line of products 다양한 제품 라인
a diverse range of 다양한

Practice

해설서 p.58 / ⏱ 제한 시간 5분

1. It is ------- that the manager be made aware of any customer complaints when they occur.

(A) rapid   (B) hectic
(C) valid   (D) critical

2. Both sides were ------- to the terms of the merger and it was finalized last Wednesday.

(A) convinced   (B) focused
(C) appreciative   (D) agreeable

3. Ceylon Corporation's ------- customer service personnel provide callers with any kind of assistance they require.

(A) inevitable   (B) continuous
(C) dedicated   (D) established

4. You should be ------- that all stock market investing involves some risk of losing money.

(A) aware   (B) confirmed
(C) heard   (D) compensated

5. Every year, the Shimogamo Budokan organizes a demonstration by a variety of highly ------- martial artists.

(A) concerned   (B) probable
(C) comprehensible   (D) accomplished

6. Ms. Talofa is ------- that Mr. Ken will be promoted to vice president of the sales division this year.

(A) designated   (B) guaranteed
(C) important   (D) confident

7. Our region has enjoyed five ------- weeks of warm winter weather, but we're expecting a blizzard by tomorrow night.

(A) forecast   (B) interrupted
(C) delayed   (D) consecutive

8. The Courtyard Communications application is ------- with all major computing devices including smart phones.

(A) deriving   (B) compatible
(C) meeting   (D) compulsory

9. Workshops regarding ------- traffic laws are offered for free to all of our full-time drivers.

(A) extreme   (B) total
(C) creative   (D) complicated

10. In appreciation of loyal customers who have been with us for over a decade, Orange Travel is willing to provide ------- airline tickets to Hong Kong this month.

(A) receptive   (B) complimentary
(C) approximate   (D) experimental

VOCA UNIT 07

PART 5 VOCA ▪ UNIT 07. 형용사 어휘 1   **153**

형용사 어휘 2

1 durable 내구성이 있는, 오래가는 ⊜ sturdy

durable goods 내구성 있는 상품

2 eager 간절히 바라는, 열심인

be eager to부정사 ~을 열망하다[간절히 바라다]
be eager to expand its business
사업 확장을 열망하다

3 economical 검소한, 실속 있는, 경제적인

an economical car 경제적인 차
cf. economic 경제의

4 effective 효과적인, 유효한, 유능한
n effect 영향, 효과

an effective marketing campaign
효과적인 마케팅 캠페인
come[go] into effect 시행되다, 발효되다
effective + 날짜 날짜에 실행[시행]하여

5 eligible 자격이 있는, 적임의, 적격의

be eligible for[to부정사] ~의 자격이 있다
be eligible for paid holidays
유급 휴가를 받을 자격이 있다

6 extensive 광대한, 광범위한 ⊜ comprehensive

extensive repairs 광범위한 수리

7 favorable 호의적인, 유리한

a favorable comment 호평
in a favorable light 호의적인 관점에서
favorable conditions 유리한 조건

8 formidable 만만치 않은, 어마어마한

formidable obstacles 엄청난 장애들
a formidable challenge 엄청난 도전

9 fortunate 운이 좋은

be fortunate to have the position
직위를 갖게 되어 운이 좋다

10 fragile 깨지기 쉬운, 망가지기 쉬운 ⊜ breakable

fragile items 깨지기 쉬운 물건들

11 imperative 필수적인

It is absolutely imperative that you work
overtime. 시간 외 근무를 반드시 해야 한다.

12 impressive 인상적인, 장엄한

an impressive performance 인상적인 공연

13 inclement (날씨가) 궂은
⊜ poor ⊜ severe ⊜ bad

inclement weather conditions 악천후

14 lengthy 매우 긴, 장황한
n length 길이

a lengthy memo 긴 메모

15 notable 주목할 만한, 저명한 ⊜ renowned

be notable for ~으로 유명하다[저명하다]
notable economists 저명한 경제학자들

16 numerous 매우 많은, 수많은

in numerous cases 많은 경우에
cf. numerous[various / multiple] + 복수 명사

17 ongoing 계속하고 있는, 진행 중인

ongoing investigations 계속되는 수사
an ongoing debate 계속 진행 중인 토론

18 optimistic ~에 대해 낙관적인
⊜ confident ⊜ positive

be optimistic about/that ~에 대해/~을 낙관하다
be optimistic about a successful outcome
성공적인 결과에 대하여 낙관하다

19 outstanding 눈에 띄는, 뛰어난, 미지불된

outstanding services 훌륭한 서비스
an outstanding balance 미지불된 잔액[잔고]

20 overwhelming 압도적인, 굉장한

an overwhelming success 대단한 성공

Practice

1. Given the present real estate market, Cristobal Investments is ------- to acquire new property.

(A) delinquent   (B) worthy
(C) hesitant   (D) ineffective

2. With more than 40 electric vehicles, Stargaze Transportation presently runs the most ------- taxi fleet in South Hampton.

(A) internal   (B) attentive
(C) economical   (D) projected

3. Employees over 55 years old who have been with the company for 10 years or more are usually ------- for early retirement with full benefits.

(A) able   (B) optional
(C) suggestible   (D) eligible

4. From our recruiters' point of view, a stable history of prior employment in a related field is ------- to possessing a degree.

(A) equivalent   (B) acceptable
(C) recognized   (D) required

5. Although online orders may be ------- from certain state and local taxes, it is the purchaser's responsibility to confirm this.

(A) payable   (B) exempt
(C) derived   (D) supported

6. PennTech University is ------- to feature world-famous pianist Myra Jang in its annual festival this coming Friday.

(A) fortunate   (B) talented
(C) admired   (D) necessary

7. Transferring all paper records to an electronic database could pose a ------- challenge.

(A) formidable   (B) reversible
(C) cohesive   (D) imperative

8. Due to the ------- call volumes on Monday mornings, contacting our customer services may take longer than expected.

(A) multiple   (B) noisy
(C) heavy   (D) extended

9. The remodeling of the dining area, expected to be finished at the end of the year, will be delayed as a result of ------- issues with the local authorities.

(A) dissolved   (B) considerate
(C) restrained   (D) ongoing

10. I am ------- that the results of the product launch will be as favorable as the marketing surveys suggested.

(A) flattered   (B) excessive
(C) hopeful   (D) worrisome

VOCA UNIT 08

UNIT 09 형용사 어휘 3

1 pending 임박한, 미해결된
≒ imminent ≒ impending

The deadline for the report is pending.
보고서 마감일이 임박했다.

2 perishable 상하기 쉬운

perishable goods 잘 상하는 제품

3 promising 유망한, 장래가 밝은

a promising young writer 촉망받는 젊은 작가

4 prospective 장래의, 가망이 있는, 잠재적인

a prospective buyer 예상 구매자
prospective customers 잠재적인 고객들

5 reliable 신뢰할 만한, 믿을 만한

a reliable source 믿을 만한 정보원
reliable test results 신뢰할 만한 테스트 결과
Cf. reliant 의존하는

6 renowned 유명한

a renowned author 유명한 저자
a nationally renowned businessman
국내에서 유명한 사업가

7 respective 각각의

They are renowned in their respective fields.
그들은 각각의 업계에서 유명하다.
Cf. respectful 공손한, 정중한, respectable 존경할 만한

8 restricted 제한된

a restricted area 제한된 구역
be restricted to authorized personnel
허가를 받은 직원들로 제한되다

9 sturdy (물건이) 튼튼한, 견고한

a sturdy bed frame made of wood or metal
목재나 금속재로 만들어진 튼튼한 침대 프레임

10 subsequent (시간상으로) 뒤이어 일어난, 이어지는

subsequent to the meeting 회의 후에
subsequent events 뒤이어 일어난 사건들
subsequent years 그 후 몇 년

11 substantial 상당한

a substantial sum of money 상당한 액수의 돈
undergo substantial renovations
대대적인 수리를 거치다

12 sufficient (일·논리 등이) 충분한, 흡족한

a sufficient explanation 충분한 설명
sufficient time to discuss 상의할 충분한 시간

13 tentative 시험적인, 임시적인

tentative agreement 임시 계약서
tentative schedule 임시 스케줄

14 unanimous 만장일치의
adv unanimously 만장일치로

unanimous agreement 만장일치의 합의
Cf. anonymous 익명인, 익명으로 된

15 unprecedented 전례가 없는, 이례적인

an unprecedented event 전례가 없는 사건

16 upcoming 다가오는, 곧 있을

the upcoming election 다가오는 선거

17 valid 유효한, 합법적인

a valid driver's license 유효한 운전면허증

18 versatile 다재다능한, 다목적의

a versatile tool 다목적 도구

19 vulnerable 취약한, 피해를 입기 쉬운

be vulnerable to ~에 취약하다
be more vulnerable to damage 파손에 더 약하다

20 wasteful 낭비의

a wasteful use of rich resources
풍부한 자원의 낭비 사용

Practice

1. Wooden floors are attractive, but you must realize that they are highly ------- to water damage.

(A) frequent   (B) fond
(C) dangerous   (D) vulnerable

2. Industry analysts predict the ------- merger will be approved next Monday by JK Ltd.

(A) recent   (B) related
(C) pending   (D) attentive

3. We thank you in advance for your -------- response to our inquiry.

(A) prior   (B) prompt
(C) obvious   (D) quickly

4. Nordic Angler hires sales clerks that are ------- about fishing so that they can get customers excited about purchasing items.

(A) pleasant   (B) courteous
(C) enthusiastic   (D) logical

5. JTL Corporation's business objectives cannot be met without ------- personnel.

(A) content   (B) convinced
(C) reliable   (D) right

6. In July, Albert Museum will present 30 pieces by the ------- painter Damian Hill.

(A) estimated   (B) founded
(C) renowned   (D) allocated

7. Periodic updates made to personal files by Curtis Medical Group are completely ------ and ensure patients both safety and confidentiality.

(A) secure   (B) authentic
(C) particular   (D) dedicated

8. The story by a nomad traveler, David Muraz, will be featured in the ------- issue of *Travel Monthly*.

(A) nearest   (B) upcoming
(C) ahead   (D) forward

9. Tristone Library is not liable for any personal belongings left ------- on the premises.

(A) ineligible   (B) nonreturnable
(C) discontinued   (D) unattended

10. Due to an ------- increase in revenue last quarter, all sales representatives will be awarded special bonuses this month.

(A) unprecedented   (B) imminent
(C) unsalvageable   (D) extraneous

VOCA UNIT 09

REVIEW TEST 03

1. All work requests should be submitted in writing unless the issue requires ------- attention.

(A) shiny
(B) urgent
(C) calm
(D) smooth

2. New hires for the company cafeteria must pass the ------- health checkup before starting employment.

(A) substantial
(B) mandatory
(C) prescriptive
(D) ingenious

3. A ------- florist arranged some floral decorations for the mayor's inauguration ceremony.

(A) likely
(B) dominant
(C) local
(D) prospective

4. The new fruit baskets for employees will be ------- to be taken home at the end of the day.

(A) available
(B) content
(C) accurate
(D) reduced

5. Over her long tenure, Professor Reynolds has done ------- work in the field of accounting and discovered new techniques to analyze companies.

(A) extensive
(B) provisional
(C) contiguous
(D) simulated

6. During the renovations, workers will temporarily have ------- access to the restrooms.

(A) limited
(B) avoidable
(C) managing
(D) nearly

7. Your ------- admission ticket waives three hours of parking fees in case you leave late.

(A) validated
(B) distributed
(C) proved
(D) acquired

8. Vahva Financial, a Helsinki-based start-up company, surpassed all predictions when it experienced ------- growth last quarter.

(A) available
(B) grateful
(C) rapid
(D) sole

9. Promoting current staff is a ------- approach to finding qualified managers at Kilkenny Ltd.

(A) multiple
(B) practical
(C) skilled
(D) content

10. Bartleby Savings and Loan advises its customers to invest in a ------- range of companies.

(A) proportionate
(B) deep
(C) diverse
(D) graphic

11. Sales of the DW-234 printer have not been ------- to warrant its own section in the new product catalog.

(A) even
(B) more
(C) enough
(D) usual

12. Managing your firm's assets can be hard and even ------- without the help of a financial advisor.

(A) risky
(B) concentrated
(C) decreased
(D) worthy

13. The acquisition of Sam Hwan Co. is ------- by the year's end, as long as negotiations continue in a positive direction.

(A) honored
(B) blending
(C) feasible
(D) ultimate

14. Experts consider Hana Trading a ------- firm because it has maintained a steady record of profitability.

(A) routine
(B) stable
(C) distant
(D) whole

15. At Jesper & Hammond, financial statements are audited regularly to ensure ------- information.

(A) accurate
(B) ample
(C) effective
(D) constructive

16. ------- among the qualifications the firm is seeking is the ability to manage staff in several different countries.

(A) Primary
(B) Proficient
(C) Proper
(C) Probable

17. We respect our clients' confidentiality, so it is ------- that we protect their personal information.

(A) appreciative
(B) destructive
(C) remunerative
(D) imperative

18. To make the expense reimbursement procedure as ------- as possible, Mr. Keen will provide a detailed explanation of all approved spending.

(A) transparent
(B) concerned
(C) powerful
(D) extraordinary

19. The *Westwood Guide* presents the most ------- methods of training workers to be more productive.

(A) contained
(B) effective
(C) concerned
(D) reluctant

20. The report by Mr. Leigh emphasized a ------- approach for raising the organization's brand recognition in the next quarter.

(A) comprehensive
(B) pursuing
(C) respective
(D) comprising

부사 어휘 1

1 absolutely 완전히, 절대적으로

absolutely impossible 완전히 불가능한
be absolutely essential 절대적으로 필요하다

2 accidentally 우연히, 우발적으로

meet accidentally 우연히 만나다
be discovered accidentally 우연히 발견되다

3 accordingly 그에 따라서, 그러므로

Please mark the samples accordingly.
견본품을 그에 따라서 표시해 주세요.

4 accurately 정확히, 틀림없이

accurately reflect 정확하게 반영하다

5 adversely 역으로, 불리하게
adj adverse 부정적인, 불리한

adversely affect crops in the area
그 지역의 작물에 악영향을 입히다
adverse effect 악영향

6 agreeably 기분 좋게, 받아들일 만하게

He nodded agreeably. 그는 기분 좋게 고개를 끄덕였다.

7 approximately 약, 대략

approximately half of the assistant's work
조교 업무의 거의 절반

8 barely 겨우, 간신히; 거의 ~않다

Barely 50 of the manufactured products were
sold. 생산된 제품 중 겨우 50개가 팔렸다.

9 cleverly 솜씨 좋게, 교묘하게

a cleverly concealed pocket 교묘하게 감춰진 주머니

10 closely 밀접하게, 면밀히

be closely related to ~과 긴밀하게 연관되어 있다
Cf. close (시간적·공간적으로) 접하여, 밀접하여

11 consistently 일관성 있게, 지속적으로
= constantly = continuously
adj consistent 일관된

consistently strong economy 꾸준하게 건실한 경제
be consistent in ~에 있어 시종일관되다

12 cordially 진심으로, 정성껏

You are cordially invited to the party.
귀하를 파티에 진심 어린 마음으로 초대합니다.

13 currently 현재는, 지금은 = presently

be currently offering a discount
현재 할인을 하고 있다
Cf. currently는 현재, 현재 진행형과 잘 쓰인다.

14 deeply 매우, 깊이

deeply appreciate the fine work
훌륭한 업무에 매우 감사하다

15 definitely 분명히, 명확히
adj definite 확실한

I'll definitely be on time. 나는 시간에 확실히 맞춰 가겠다.
a definite answer 명확한 답변

16 dramatically 급격하게
adj dramatic 극적인

increase dramatically 급격히 증가하다
a dramatic increase 극적인 증가
Cf. 증가/감소에 잘 쓰이는 부사
dramatically / sharply / significantly / substantially / slightly

17 even 심지어, 훨씬(비교급 강조)

report even better results
훨씬 더 좋은 결과를 보고하다

18 evenly 고르게, 침착하게

evenly distributed 고르게 분배된
spread paint evenly on walls
벽에 페인트를 고르게 칠하다

19 exclusively 오로지, 독점적으로 = only = solely

focus exclusively on their own work
오로지 자신들의 일에만 집중하다

20 explicitly 명쾌하게, 분명하게

Company policy is explicitly outlined.
회사 정책은 분명하게 드러나 있다.

Practice

1. When all demographics data has been collected, the number of sales representatives for the district will be determined -------.

(A) accordingly   (B) typically
(C) immeasurably   (D) implicitly

2. Many Sentential Bank employees mentioned that they could ------- read last quarter's newsletter because the text was so blurry.

(A) barely   (B) nearly
(C) simply   (D) almost

3. Proper preparation and fresh ingredients are ------- important to Hestia Restaurant's cooking staff.

(A) enough   (B) gradually
(C) right   (D) equally

4. Mr. Kimura's order was not ------- delivered until August 9.

(A) enormously   (B) relatively
(C) periodically   (D) completely

5. Author Dalia Borne is ------- obligated to write a new novel every 10 months.

(A) contractually   (B) descriptively
(C) responsibly   (D) critically

6. The main office of G&B is ------- located in the center of New Hampton.

(A) conveniently   (B) gracefully
(C) evenly   (D) fluently

7. Owing to its ------- good reviews last month, Montana Roast has been selected as Best Diner by *Gourmet Weekly*.

(A) practically   (B) potentially
(C) consistently   (D) reluctantly

8. A recent study revealed that offering a free bicycle rental program ------- reduces air pollution in the city.

(A) intensely   (B) limitedly
(C) previously   (D) drastically

9. This year, the Green Auto Prizes will be awarded ------- to companies manufacturing electronic vehicles.

(A) exceptionally   (B) routinely
(C) traditionally   (D) exclusively

10. Marlon Electronics' warranty ------- states that all repairs must be performed by authorized technicians.

(A) hardly   (B) cautiously
(C) indefinitely   (D) explicitly

VOCA UNIT 10

부사 어휘 2

1 extremely 매우, 극도로

extremely urgent meeting 매우 긴급한 회의

2 fairly 꽤, 상당히

a fairly typical reaction
상당히 전형적인 반응

3 favorably 호의적으로, 순조롭게

respond favorably to the news
소식에 대해 호의적으로 반응하다

4 firmly 단단하게, 확고하게

press the device firmly 그 장치를 단단하게 누르다
firmly established 확고히 자리 잡은

5 formerly 전에, 옛날에

formerly known as AP Printing
전에는 에이피 프린팅으로 알려진

6 fully 완전히, 전적으로

be fully operational 완전히 가동 가능한 상태에 있다
fully understand the policy 정책을 완전히 이해하다

7 heavily 심하게, 몹시, 무겁게

rely heavily on their computers
컴퓨터에 지나치게 의존하다
heavily discounted 대폭 할인된

8 highly 매우, 높이

highly recommend 강력히 추천하다
highly respected 매우 존경받는
highly regarded 높이 평가받는

9 ideally 이상적으로, 원칙적으로

ideally matched 이상적으로 결합된

10 immediately 즉각, 즉시 ⊜ right away

begin working immediately 즉각 일을 시작하다
effective immediately 즉시 효력이 발생하는

11 inadvertently 부주의하게, 실수로 ⊜ mistakenly

inadvertently omit
실수로 빠뜨리다

12 largely 대체적으로, 크게

be largely responsible for the problem
그 문제에 크게 책임이 있다

13 markedly 눈에 띄게, 현저하게
⊜ noticeably ⊜ strikingly ⊜ remarkably

shrink markedly 눈에 띄게 줄어들다

14 moderately 중간 정도로, 적당히, 알맞게

a moderately successful career
적당히 성공적인 경력

15 mutually 상호 간에

a mutually beneficial relationship
상호 이익 관계

16 occasionally 때때로, 이따금씩

visit occasionally 때때로 방문하다

17 otherwise 달리, 그렇지 않다면

otherwise known as ~으로도 알려져 있는
unless otherwise indicated
달리 명시되어 있지 않는 한, 별다른 언급 사항이 없으면

18 persistently 지속적으로, 끈질기게

persistently high interest rates 지속적으로 높은 금리

19 presumably 아마도, 짐작건대

The order has presumably come from Josh.
그 명령은 아마도 조쉬에게서 나왔을 것이다.

20 primarily 주로, 우선적으로

work primarily on the reconstruction project
재건 프로젝트를 주 업무로 하다

Practice

1. Centerville, which was ------- a residential area, has started accommodating office complexes and commercial buildings.

(A) readily   (B) constructively
(C) immediately   (D) formerly

2. Dr. Cheng designed detailed charts to record the factory's energy needs -------.

(A) broadly   (B) relatively
(C) precisely   (D) dominantly

3. All urgent inquiries about our products should be ------- directed to the Customer Service Department.

(A) recently   (B) significantly
(C) nearly   (D) immediately

4. Designed last November, Fleet Footwear's new cross-training shoes will ------- begin production next week.

(A) extremely   (B) precisely
(C) finally   (D) recently

5. Residents in Burlington have become ------- worried about their safety since cracks in the road began appearing.

(A) barely   (B) virtually
(C) increasingly   (D) carefully

6. The relationship between Farraway Builders and Guru Furniture has been ------- beneficial.

(A) commonly   (B) dominantly
(C) exactly   (D) mutually

7. The Brighton City Zoo averages ------- 5,000 visitors per week.

(A) fairly   (B) nearly
(C) totally   (D) relatively

8. During the weekly meeting, Ms. Bentley ------- offers advice that helps the accounting team complete their tasks more efficiently.

(A) neatly   (B) frequently
(C) enormously   (D) feasibly

9. The brochure has an extensive listing of ------- priced hotels in the region that cater to events of all sizes.

(A) rapidly   (B) relatively
(C) moderately   (D) subsequently

10. As a senior manager of global marketing, Ms. Takashima frequently visits Korea, ------- Seoul.

(A) primarily   (B) relatively
(C) already   (D) temporarily

VOCA UNIT 11

부사 어휘 3

1 prominently 현저하게, 두드러지게
be prominently displayed / posted
눈에 띄게 전시되다 / 게시되다

2 promptly 신속하게, 즉시
respond promptly to all inquiries
모든 문의에 신속하게 응하다
The train will leave promptly at 4:00.
기차는 4시 정각에 출발할 것이다.

3 provisionally 임시로, 잠정적으로
a provisionally approved loan
임시로 승인된 대출

4 punctually 시간을 엄수하여, 정확하게
arrive punctually for the training session
교육에 제시간에 도착하다

5 rarely 드물게, 거의 ~않는
⊜ seldom ⊜ barely ⊜ scarcely ⊜ hardly
rarely receive the news 소식이 뜸하다

6 readily 손쉽게, 기꺼이 ⊜ easily
readily available 쉽게 이용할 수 있는

7 regrettably 유감스럽게도, 슬프게도
Regrettably, some jobs will be lost.
유감스럽게도, 몇몇 일자리가 없어질 것이다.

8 relatively 상대적으로, 비교적
a relatively small part of total revenue
총수익의 비교적 적은 부분

9 rigorously 엄격하게 ⊜ strictly
adj rigorous 엄격한
rigorously conducted research 엄격하게 진행된 연구
rigorous standards 엄격한 기준

10 seemingly 겉으로 보기에는
a seemingly irrelevant question
겉으로 보기에 관련 없는 질문

11 separately 별도로, 개별적으로, 따로따로
be ordered separately 따로따로 주문되다

12 severely 심하게, 엄격하게
severely damaged 심하게 손상된

13 skillfully 기술적으로, 능숙하게
skillfully handle customer complaints
고객 불만을 능숙하게 처리하다

14 solely 오로지, 단지, 단독으로 ⊜ only ⊜ exclusively
be solely responsible for 단독으로 ~의 책임을 맡다

15 somewhat 어느 정도, 약간
somewhat limited 다소 제한된

16 steadily 꾸준히
increase steadily 꾸준히 증가하다

17 strictly 엄격히
strictly limited 엄격히 제한된
adhere strictly to ~을 엄격하게 지키다

18 thoroughly 완전히, 철저하게 ⊜ completely
thoroughly research 철저하게 조사하다
Please read the user manual thoroughly.
이 사용자 매뉴얼을 철저하게 읽어보기를 바란다.

19 typically 보통, 전형적으로
typically right after lunch 보통 점심 직후에

20 widely 널리 ⊜ broadly
be widely advertised 널리 광고되다
widely admired 널리 존경받는

Practice

1. Jasper Roman's sample artwork will be ------- displayed in *Galleria Galore Magazine*.

(A) prominently   (B) critically

(C) intensely   (D) mutually

2. Heron Ltd. sells products for commercial use and ------- stocks items for personal use.

(A) mildly   (B) supremely

(C) rarely   (D) shortly

3. The price of Lennex Auto's Sedan 7 is ------- lower than those of vehicles manufactured by its competitors.

(A) rapidly   (B) efficiently

(C) relatively   (D) gradually

4. To check if your package has been shipped, ------- visit our Delivery Tracking page and enter your order number.

(A) rather   (B) quite

(C) simply   (D) mostly

5. Due to security concerns, access to the server room is ------- limited.

(A) strictly   (B) barely

(C) slightly   (D) casually

6. Tamara Jones reviewed the research report from MNT Laboratories ------- and pointed out that more investigation needs to be done in some areas.

(A) thoroughly   (B) considerably

(C) interestingly   (D) usefully

7. Sales manager Sophie Hilton mentioned that advertising ------- online is not a reliable approach to drawing prospective clients.

(A) almost   (B) closely

(C) solely   (D) otherwise

8. Unless customers choose the express service, the shipment of orders ------- takes three days to arrive at the indicated mailing address.

(A) substantially   (B) perpetually

(C) familiarly   (D) typically

9. Saltville City Council voted ------- to approve the proposal for road repairs on Lumin Drive.

(A) disparately   (B) numerously

(C) separately   (D) unanimously

10. Mr. Delanie ------- cannot attend this Friday's annual banquet due to a family emergency.

(A) regretfully   (B) mistakenly

(C) forgetfully   (D) eventually

VOCA UNIT 12

REVIEW TEST 04

해설서 p.65 / ⏱ 제한 시간 10분

1. Some staff members are needed to take photos at the anniversary celebration, ------- those who are experienced at event photography.

(A) specifically
(B) accordingly
(C) constantly
(D) gradually

2. In order to assess the autonomous car, the researchers ------- let it run until the gas tank was empty.

(A) intentionally
(B) greatly
(C) forcefully
(D) heavily

3. Koruma Design was hired to decorate the interior of the new branch office because Ms. Marina spoke so ------- of their past projects.

(A) high
(B) highest
(C) highly
(D) higher

4. In spite of several reminders, a few of the employees ------- have not submitted their tax returns.

(A) ever
(B) constantly
(C) still
(D) almost

5. The Poriha City office ------- receives job applications, so candidates are asked to be patient while reviews are underway.

(A) recently
(B) rapidly
(C) regularly
(D) equally

6. The weekly meetings are held in the large conference room on Mondays, unless ------- announced by the manager.

(A) otherwise
(B) about
(C) once
(D) all

7. Siva Rajh, the owner of the new Loire Cafe, ------- worked as a pastry chef in Paris.

(A) accordingly
(B) previously
(C) still
(D) constantly

8. Please call the restaurant ------ one day in advance to make a reservation.

(A) at least
(B) in order that
(C) including
(D) although

9. Acculang's new laptop achieves processing speeds of ------- double those of competing brands.

(A) apart
(B) almost
(C) continually
(D) further

10. Companies will be notified ------- concerning their bids for the Layman Complex construction project.

(A) much
(B) soon
(C) about
(D) fine

11. This month, the Marketing Department is ------- researching customer preferences to prepare for their next campaign.

(A) actively

(B) historically

(C) yearly

(D) excessively

12. Ms. Murphy is ------- the representative speaker for the union representing the factory workers.

(A) formerly

(B) consistently

(C) currently

(D) greatly

13. Phoneware Tech has announced the release of a ------- time-saving app for online banking.

(A) cautiously

(B) properly

(C) formerly

(D) potentially

14. Our research team feels ------- pleased to have made a contribution to the world of robotics.

(A) attentively

(B) extremely

(C) casually

(D) openly

15. BFS Corporation provides specially customized software to help you monitor your expenses more -------.

(A) accurately

(B) possibly

(C) immensely

(D) commonly

16. Revenue from the Builders Trade Show was anticipated to be lower than last year, but it was ------- much higher.

(A) actually

(B) strongly

(C) particularly

(D) broadly

17. Hansen Holdings was surprised to learn that customers reacted ------- to the company's plans to close down a branch location.

(A) unfavorably

(B) probably

(C) unlikely

(D) potentially

18. Professor Wong's research project has been canceled because it became ------- time-consuming.

(A) increasingly

(B) appropriately

(C) poorly

(D) differently

19. The IT support staff can access all employee computers ------- and fix any software issues from anywhere in the world.

(A) substantially

(B) cordially

(C) remotely

(D) sincerely

20. The editors ------- review each article before publication in our magazine.

(A) utterly

(B) just

(C) widely

(D) closely

RT6

장문 빈칸
채우기

PART 6

OVERVIEW

Part 6은 4문항의 문제가 있는 4개의 지문이 나와 총 16문항이 출제된다.
각각의 빈칸에 가장 적절한 단어나 구, 그리고 문장을 고르는 문제는
Part 5와 Part 7을 접목한 형태로 볼 수 있다.

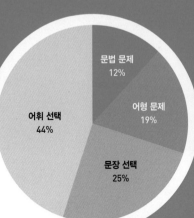

문법 문제
12%

어형 문제
19%

어휘 선택
44%

문장 선택
25%

문제 유형 분석

어형 문제 | 빈칸의 자리를 파악하여 선택지 중 알맞은 품사나 형태를 고르는 문제
어휘 선택 | 같은 품사의 네 개 어휘 중 정확한 용례를 파악하여 알맞은 단어를 고르는 문제
문법 문제 | 문장의 구조를 파악하여 구와 절을 구분하여 접속사나 전치사, 부사를 고르는 문제
문장 선택 | 앞뒤 문맥을 파악하여 네 개의 문장 중에 알맞은 문장을 고르는 문제

지문 유형

편지·이메일/기사/공지/지시문/광고/회람/설명서/발표문/정보문 등

최신 출제 경향

- 앞뒤 문맥을 통해 시제를 결정하는 문제의 출제 비중이 높다. 시제를 묻는 문제는 Part 5에서는
  시간 부사구로 결정하지만, Part 6에서는 맥락으로 파악해야 한다.
- 두 문장을 자연스럽게 이어주는 접속부사를 선택하는 문제가 많이 출제된다.
- 맥락상으로 파악해야 하는 대명사의 인칭 일치 문제, 수 일치 문제가 출제된다.
- 어휘는 그 문장만 보고는 문제를 풀 수 없고 앞뒤 문맥을 파악하여 고르는 문제가 출제된다.

핵심 학습 전략

- Part 5처럼 단순히 문장 구조나 문법을 묻는 문제도 출제되지만, 전체적인 내용이나 앞뒤 문장
  내용과 연결되는 어휘나 시제, 접속부사를 묻는 문제들이 주로 출제된다는 것에 유의한다.
- 문장 삽입 문제는 빈칸 앞뒤 문장의 대명사나 연결어 등을 확인하고 상관관계를 파악한다.
- 지문의 길이가 짧기 때문에 전체 내용을 파악하는 데 많은 시간이 걸리지 않으므로 정독해서
  읽으면 오히려 더 쉽게 해결할 수 있다.

문제 풀이 전략

Questions 143-146 refer to the following article.

Jakarta, INDONESIA (5 June) — An Indonesian steelmaker, Irwan Steel Company, announced that it had named Maghfirah Baldraf its new Chief Operating Officer of the Java Division effective 1 September. His 30 years of experience in the ------- made him the obvious choice for the position.
143.
Baldraf majored in metal engineering at the National University of Indonesia. After graduation, he then ------- his career in the quality control department at Putirai Metal. 15 years ago, he joined
144.
Irwan Steel Company. -------. Baldraf will go to Java to oversee the daily operations of Irwan Steel
145.
Company ------- its inauguration on September 1.
146.

1. 어휘 선택

Part 5 어휘 문제와는 달리 그 한 문장만 봐서는 여러 개가 답이 될 수 있을 것 같은 선택지들이 나온다. 따라서 Part 6의 어휘 문제는 앞뒤 문맥을 정확히 파악하여 답을 골라야 한다.

143.	(A) license	(B) industry	(C) outset	(D) program

이 문제에서는 '그 산업 분야에서의 30년 경력 때문에 그가 그 자리에 확실한 선택이었다'라는 의미를 파악해서 (B)를 골라야 한다.

2. 어형 문제

한 단어의 네 가지 형태가 나오는 문제를 어형 문제 또는 자리 찾기 문제라고 한다. Part 5와 마찬가지 방법으로 풀면 되지만, 동사 시제 문제는 문맥을 파악하는 까다로운 문제로 출제된다.

144.	(A) started	(B) had started	(C) was starting	(D) will start

이 문제는 동사의 시제를 고르는 문제로 문맥상 이 사람이 처음으로 직장 생활을 시작한 것을 이야기하고 있으므로 과거 시제인 (A)가 답이 되며, then도 힌트가 될 수 있다.

3. 문장 선택

Part 6에서 가장 어려운 문제로 전체적인 문맥을 파악하고, 접속부사나, 시제 등을 종합적으로 봐야 답을 고를 수 있다.

145.	(A) The company also has a division in Singapore.
	(B) He has been interested in engineering since he was young.
	(C) Most recently, he has served as Vice President of Development of Irwan Steel Company.
	(D) As soon as Baldraf is appointed, the company will go through a major restructuring.

이 문제에서는 대학교 졸업 후부터 이 사람의 경력을 시간 순서로 나열하고 있으므로 (C)가 답이 된다.

4. 문법 문제

문법 문제는 보통 문장의 구조를 파악하여 구와 절을 구분하는 문제이다.

146.	(A) by the time	(B) as soon as	(C) when	(D) after

이 문제에서는 빈칸 뒤에 명사구가 있으므로 명사를 목적어로 취하는 전치사가 답이 되어야 하는데 보기 중에 전치사로 쓰일 수 있는 것은 (D)뿐이다.

UNIT 01 시제

Part 6에서 많이 틀리는 문제 중 하나는 시제 문제이다. 느낌으로 답을 찾지 말고, 반드시 시제를 결정해 줄 수 있는 단서를 앞 문장 혹은 뒤 문장에서 빨리 찾아 답을 선택할 수 있도록 하자.

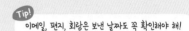

Tip!
이메일, 편지, 회람은 보낸 날짜도 꼭 확인해야 해!

📖 핵심 문제 유형

Question 1 refers to the following letter.

해설서 p.67

Hopper Auto Sales
November 1

Dear Valued Customer,
According to our records, the warranty on your car ------- this coming December.

(A) expired
(B) will expire
(C) expiring
(D) expiration

✓ PART 6에 자주 등장하는 시제

1. 시제를 빨리 확인하는 방법
▶ 상단에 있는 글을 쓴 날짜를 확인하면 시제를 빨리 찾을 수 있다.

2. 현재 시제를 사용하는 경우
▶ 회사의 현재 전문 분야, 가장 중요시하는 것
▶ 공연, 대중교통 등의 고정된 시간표나 일정
▶ 업무와 같은 주기적, 일상적, 반복적인 일
▶ 확정된 미래, 정해진 사실, 진리, 상식
▶ 규칙, 계약 등 문서화되는 내용

3. 현재 완료 시제를 사용하는 경우
▶ 과거부터 현재(또는 최근)까지 특정 기간 동안 발생하여 완료된 사실을 말할 때 쓴다.

4. 과거 시제를 사용하는 경우
▶ 빈칸을 포함한 문장에서 과거 시점 부사를 찾는다.
▶ 앞뒤 문장의 동사 시제를 통해서 일이나 사건의 전후 관계를 확인한다.

5. 미래 시제를 사용하는 경우 (미래 vs. 미래 완료)
▶ 미래 시제(will 동사원형)는 미래에 있을 사실을 나타낸다.
▶ 미래 완료 시제(will have p.p.)는 과거에 시작해서 미래 시점까지 계속되거나 완료되는 사실을 나타낸다.

▶ 빈칸에 들어갈 알맞은 보기를 고르세요.

1. [letter]

Dear Dr. Bradley,
As you know, Fontillo Services ------- in serving medical offices throughout the Hastings area with the most environmentally responsible cleaning methods.

(A) specializes
(B) will specialize
(C) specialized
(D) specializing

2. [advertisement]

The Best Agency Tour makes travelers' experiences pleasant and enjoyable. Each of our tour packages ------- admission fees, guides, transportation, and lunch.

(A) will be included
(B) used to include
(C) included
(D) includes

3. [memo]

From: Russell La Salle, Assembly Manager
To: Assembly Employees and Inspectors
Date: August 8
Subject: MK-X 20

I am writing to alert you that we ------- some e-mails from our customers regarding the top drawer in our new MK-X 20 refrigerators. Most of these e-mails indicate that customers are frustrated because the drawer does not close completely.

(A) have received
(B) will receive
(C) receiving
(D) receive

4. [notice]

Product Development Team,
The agenda for this week's meeting -------. Please find the final version attached to this e-mail.

(A) will be updated
(B) is updating
(C) has been updated
(D) will update

5. [press release]

For immediate release

2 February – KUB, Inc. announces the appointment of Margaret Lee as Chief Executive Officer. She is replacing Carl DuPont, who retired in January.

Ms. Lee ------- her career in the Human Resources Department of Dawson Hahn Asset Management. "Margaret Lee's experience and leadership will be invaluable as we enter our next phase of growth," said KUB spokesperson Stuart Wilsey.

(A) to begin
(B) begins
(C) began
(D) will begin

6. [notice]

Attention Employees: New Headquarters Completed

After several delays due to construction problems, Hasting Paper's new building was finally completed this week. All employees from our three separate offices ------- into the new building in small groups.

Employees' individual move dates can be found on our corporate website. The transition is scheduled to begin next week, and all employees should be settled into the new office by the end of July.

(A) will have moved
(B) did move
(C) have moved
(D) will be moving

7. [article]

City Marathon Planned

Berryville (April 1) — Mayor Regina Paget announced the creation of the Berryville Marathon yesterday. The race ------- every year in mid-August. The first one is scheduled for August 16 of this year.

(A) took place
(B) taking place
(C) has taken place
(D) will take place

8. [notice]

Channel 9 Celebrates 9 Years!

October 10 was Channel 9's 9-year anniversary. That's almost a decade's worth of entertaining programming. During that time, we ------- our viewers with live news, weather, and the very best dramas. That's why, this month, we are holding a contest, where 99 lucky winners will be invited to visit our studio on October 29 from 11 A.M. to 7 P.M. If you are selected, you can see what goes on behind our studio doors and meet several famous TV personalities. You will even get to watch how their shows are recorded. For complete details about the contest, visit our website. Do not miss out on this amazing opportunity!

(A) have provided
(B) will provide
(C) providing
(D) provides

9. [article]

The Autumn Cooking Carnival ------- to southern Milltown on September 16. For the past 10 years, this popular carnival has gone on tour around the state from September to November.

This year, the organizers wisely decided to arrange for more space. As expected, visitors showed up in record numbers to sample a variety of tasty dishes, enjoy rides and exhibits, and participate in food-themed contests.

(A) will come
(B) came
(C) comes
(D) was coming

10. [article]

BOULDER, Co. – June 1

A historic vase was discovered during an archaeological excavation in Southern Colorado. According to Selma Bavaria, the archaeologist who ------- the item, this is a remarkable discovery. "It is rare to see an item from this era that is still in one piece and great condition," she said. "We usually uncover only fragments."

(A) finds
(B) was finding
(C) has been finding
(D) found

Questions 1-4 refer to the following notice.

Sales Employees,

In the office, we try to maintain the maximum possible security for our electronic files. The same should be true when you travel to meet clients. It is ------- that you keep all work-related
1.
files on your computers protected. If you are transporting files on a memory stick, keep it in your possession at all times ------- the data on it. -------. Lastly, when you are having business
2. **3.**
discussions over the phone, avoid discussing detailed information about our company as much as possible. By ------- these simple rules, you can help ensure our security even when outside
4.
the office. Thank you.

Nikita Bayul
Director of Information Technology

---

1. (A) probable
(B) essential
(C) traditional
(D) conclusive

2. (A) is protecting
(B) protects
(C) to protect
(D) protected

3. (A) Be careful not to talk about business
on the phone, either.
(B) Do not remove any work-related files
from office computers.
(C) Employees are not allowed to copy any
files at the office.
(D) It would be best if you encrypt the files
as well.

4. (A) observing
(B) observed
(C) to observe
(D) observation

Dear Mr. Metzen,

Thank you for your recent ------- from Shields Brothers.
                     5.

All of our lighted signs are weatherproof and come with a five-year warranty. If you experience any problems with your sign due to faulty installation or parts, or weather damage during that time, we will repair it at no cost to you. -------. A representative will come to your business this
                  6.
Thursday ------- your installation options. We will charge your account for the remainder of your
        7.
bill ------- your sign has been securely mounted. Since you paid our standard 25% deposit, your
   8.
installation will be free.

Thank you again for coming to Shield Brothers for your advertising needs.

Sincerely,

Alan Shields

5. (A) donation
(B) visit
(C) purchase
(D) article

6. (A) You will be contacted by one of our employees next week.
(B) Please see the attached copy of our warranty for more details.
(C) When the repair work is done, you will be presented with a bill.
(D) We hope that the installation process will go smoothly for you.

7. (A) will discuss
(B) to discuss
(C) discussion
(D) discusses

8. (A) once
(B) afterward
(C) following
(D) upon

Questions 9-12 refer to the following e-mail.

To: Machiko Noguchi <nomachi@tokdesmail.com>
From: Olivia Mandig <oliviaman@eagdcmail.com>
Sent: Tuesday, February 2, 11:38 A.M.
Subject: Congratulations

Dear Ms. Noguchi,

Allow me to be the first to congratulate you on your official nomination for the annual Best Graphic Designer Award. As you may already know, this award ------- every year to an up-and-coming **9.** graphic designer. Your incredible computer design work ------- many companies with stunning **10.** graphics for their advertising campaigns. You were nominated by one or more of the companies that used your work over the course of the last year. -------. **11.**

The award will be presented at the opening night reception of the East Asian Graphic Design Conference on March 13 in Manila. As one of the four finalists, you will be offered airline tickets, a hotel reservation, and free passes to the convention for you and one guest. A dinner will ------- **12.** at the reception, so please let us know about any dietary restrictions you may have.

I look forward to hearing from you.

Sincerely,

Olivia Mandig
EAGDC Organizer

---

9. (A) are giving
(B) gives
(C) gave
(D) is given

10. (A) will be provided
(B) was provided
(C) has provided
(D) to be provided

11. (A) We hope you can be with us when the winner is announced.
(B) The excellent work you did will make you guaranteed to be the winner.
(C) Unfortunately, the awards ceremony has been postponed until fall.
(D) Thank you for participating, and we wish you better luck next time.

12. (A) serve
(B) be served
(C) be serving
(D) have served

From: Harrison Solomon, CEO
To: All Wimbledon Advertising employees
Subject: New VP of Sales
Date: May 3

-------. It is my great pleasure to inform you that the new Vice President of Sales ------- by the
 13.   **14.**
board of directors. The board would like to extend their thanks to everyone who was being

considered for the position for their patience and understanding. Effective May 19, Ms. Elizabeth

Cooke will be the new VP of the Sales Department. Ms. Cooke worked with us for over 10 years

in a variety of roles in other departments, but this experience is not the only reason she -------.
                                                                                       15.

Her leadership skills and numerous awards were also cited as important factors in the decision-

making process. We are sure that she ------- an excellent leader of our Sales Department. Please
                                   16.
congratulate her when you get the opportunity.

Harrison Solomon
WA CEO

13. (A) I regret to announce that Ms. Cooke
         has resigned.
     (B) We are still looking to fill an open
         position.
     (C) I have the news that you have all been
         waiting for.
     (D) Please consider applying for the Vice
         President's position.

14. (A) will appoint
     (B) is appointing
     (C) has been appointed
     (D) will be appointed

15. (A) is chosen
     (B) has chosen
     (C) will be chosen
     (D) was chosen

16. (A) is
     (B) will be
     (C) has been
     (D) was

대명사

Part 6에서 자주 출제되는 문제는 거의 정해져 있다. 그 유형 중 하나가 특정 지시대명사, 즉 앞에 나오는 명사를 받는 대명사 문제이다. 일단 무엇을 받는지를 빨리 찾아내는 것이 관건이다.

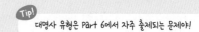

대명사 유형은 Part 6에서 자주 출제되는 문제야!

핵심 문제 유형

Question 1 refers to the following memo.

해설서 p.71

> To: All employees
> From: Bruce Kim
> Subject: New Security System
> Date: Friday, 1/13
>
> There will be technicians from Hidalgo Security Services in the office on Wednesday morning to set up our new entry system. It is important that all employees set aside time that afternoon to enter their personal identification codes and scan their fingerprints into the new system. ------- will be required when you arrive at work and when you depart.

(A) Many
(B) Another
(C) Some
(D) Both

✓ PART 6에 자주 등장하는 대명사

▶ 대명사 문제는 난도가 낮은 편이지만 종종 성급하게 문제를 풀어 틀리는 경우가 있으므로 주의하자.

앞에서 언급된 명사를 받는 대명사

▶ 앞에서 여러 사람을 등장시키면서 남자인지 여자인지를 묻는 경우

▶ 앞에 언급된 명사가 단수인지 복수인지를 묻는 경우

▶ 가산 명사를 받는 부정대명사: one, another, every, each, many, both, few, a few, several

▶ 불가산 명사를 받는 부정대명사: much, little, a little

▶ 가산/불가산 모두를 받는 부정대명사: some, any, most, all

▶ 빈칸에 들어갈 알맞은 보기를 고르세요.

1. [memo]

As you have probably heard, Wendy Zhang is retiring after a long career as marketing manager for Celine Dress Design. A party in honor of ------- many contributions to the company will be held on Friday, July 6, at 5 P.M.

(A) her
(B) your
(C) whose
(D) our

2. [letter]

We will be pleased to supply you with a new heater at no extra cost. However, per our company policy, you must send us the original receipt. Once we receive -------, we will contact you to set the time for our technician to visit.

(A) them
(B) it
(C) some
(D) one

3. [e-mail]

On behalf of Nathan Kellogg, I'm writing regarding ------- reservation at the Dragon Hill Inn. Mr. Kellogg's reservation was made last Wednesday through your website. However, the detailed confirmation information in the e-mail he received was inaccurate.

(A) my
(B) your
(C) his
(D) its

PART 6 UNIT 02

4. [advertisement]

At Crawford's Appliance Center, you can always find quality customer service and the best prices. For a limited time, installation and free delivery are being provided with your purchase of a major home appliance.

To qualify for this special offer, the appliance you purchase must be $300 or more. Only one free delivery is permitted per customer. Please contact ------- local store for further information about delivery options or visit our website, www.crawfordappliance.com.

(A) his
(B) her
(C) your
(D) their

5. [announcement]

The 10th annual Melbourne City Book Fair starts on Monday, March 3, and continues until Sunday, March 9. The event will kick off on Monday at 10 A.M. with a keynote discussion between best-selling novelists Jasmine Haroun and Victoria Tamimi on the topic of recent trends in the publishing industry. ------- of these speakers are Melbourne City natives.

(A) Few
(B) Both
(C) Another
(D) Any

6. [e-mail]

Although it is not common, an e-mail delivery failure could possibly be caused by our system rather than by an incorrect address. Therefore, if you are unable to send a message to ------- address, please contact Dauver Mail customer support.

(A) his
(B) their
(C) other
(D) any

7. [article]

Starting next month, Cowen Corporation will implement a new policy concerning working hours for all employees. However, ------- rules have not changed. As always, employees must be in the building 10 minutes prior to their starting times and at their workstations 5 minutes after this.

(A) every
(B) some
(C) each
(D) both

8. [e-mail]

I am updating our new employee directory to include the most recent contact information for our staff members. For this purpose, I need to confirm your home address and phone number. Please review the attached document and let me know if ------- has been changed.

(A) another
(B) either
(C) anyone
(D) whatever

9. [memo]

The Human Resources Department is in the process of updating the personnel system. To be sure that all the department managers are informed of the changes, ------- involved in tracking employee hours will need to attend one of our training sessions.

(A) that
(B) this
(C) those
(D) them

10. [letter]

Just mail the unwanted merchandise in its original box using the provided shipping label. Also, make sure to include all parts and accessories that came with the video equipment such as the carrying case, spare cords, and lens covers. If ------- are not returned, you may not receive a full refund. Otherwise, we will send you a full refund within two weeks of receiving the merchandise you purchased from us.

(A) these
(B) theirs
(C) either
(D) fewer

Questions 1-4 refer to the following article.

Shopping Center Begun

Construction began today on a new shopping center at the corner of Halifax Road and Surrey Avenue. -------. Once completed, the center will contain an assortment of different businesses
1.
including a hardware store, a dry cleaner, two clothing boutiques, a sporting goods shop, and
two restaurants. There will also be a parking garage. The project is expected to be completed
------- nine months. Many residents have said that the new shopping center will be a welcome
2.
------- to their neighborhood as there are currently few shops in the area. At the groundbreaking
3.
ceremony this morning, the mayor praised the developer for the boost to the local economy
created by projects ------- this.
4.

---

1. (A) The construction workers immediately went on strike.
   (B) Shoppers expressed satisfaction with the choices available to them.
   (C) The shopping center should be open within the next few days.
   (D) A textile factory once stood on the location of the site.

2. (A) toward
   (B) between
   (C) among
   (D) within

3. (A) product
   (B) addition
   (C) comment
   (D) viewpoint

4. (A) such as
   (B) similar
   (C) as well as
   (D) alongside

To: William Delchamps <willdelchamps@ontmail.com>
From: Michael Donegal <michaeldon@mthcsmail.com>
Sent: Tuesday, February 22
Subject: Your Reservations

Dear Mr. Delchamps,

We are pleased anytime you contact us regarding a business trip for you or your coworkers. However, we were, unfortunately, unable to process the ------- that you made on our website
5.
yesterday. Apparently, your company credit card has -------.
6.

If you would still like to have us hold these rooms for you, please call me at 555-9823. If you have not received your new credit card yet, direct money transfer is another ------- form of payment.
7.
-------. Thank you.
8.

Sincerely,

Michael Donegal
Customer Service Director
Montreal Tower Hotel

5. (A) plans
(B) parts
(C) reservations
(D) qualities

6. (A) expiration
(B) expires
(C) expiring
(D) expired

7. (A) acceptable
(B) capable
(C) proficient
(D) acquainted

8. (A) We no longer accept any payments by credit card.
(B) The bank confirmed the payment you wired arrived.
(C) Simply contact me, and I can instruct you how to do it.
(D) We appreciate your staying at our hotel.

Dear Mr. Valens,

I am sorry to hear that you are experiencing problems with your recently ------- Sonicus stereo
9.
receiver. For this product, you chose our extended warranty option, so your unit is still covered
by our guarantee. Unfortunately, the model you selected is no longer manufactured, and we
are unable to send you the same exact unit. However, we can offer you a ------- item from one
10.
of the newer Sonicus product lines. If this is acceptable, please see the form included in this
letter. Simply check the box ------- the stereo you would like to receive, and send it to us in the
11.
envelope provided. -------.
12.

Sincerely,

Britt Aguilar
Customer Service
SV Electronics

9. (A) purchases
(B) purchase
(C) purchased
(D) purchasing

10. (A) separate
(B) comparable
(C) balanced
(D) nutritional

11. (A) indicating
(B) will be indicating
(C) is to be indicating
(D) indicated

12. (A) You can learn about the Sonicus line
on our website.
(B) We hope that you got many hours of
enjoyment from your new stereo.
(C) You will be notified by us regarding
your interview next week.
(D) All shipping and handling fees will be
covered by us.

Attention all employees,

Technicians will be performing maintenance on the company e-mail system on Saturday morning at 2 A.M. Access to e-mail is going to be unavailable for approximately four hours ------- scheduled security improvements are made.
13.

------- the upgrade, employees will be prompted to choose a new password when logging in
14.
again for the first time. Passwords must contain seven to twelve characters and should not resemble any previous system passwords. -------.
15.

Please contact the Information Technology Department at extension 4867 with any questions or concerns about this matter. Thank you for your -------.
16.

13. (A) since
(B) while
(C) during
(D) along

14. (A) After
(B) Because
(C) Moreover
(D) Except

15. (A) Do not share your new password with anyone.
(B) We recommend using the same password as before.
(C) The system will be down for around twelve hours.
(D) Security is an issue that we need to think more about.

16. (A) recommendation
(B) clarification
(C) example
(D) patience

연결어

Part 6에서 자주 출제되는 문제 유형 중의 하나는 연결어이다. 앞뒤 문장을 읽고 글의 흐름과 어법상 알맞은 표현을 골라야 한다.

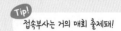
Tip!
접속부사는 거의 매회 출제돼!

 핵심 문제 유형

Question 1 refers to the following e-mail.

해설서 p.75

> Thank you for your interest in the position we have advertised. This e-mail serves as confirmation that we have received and reviewed your résumé and cover letter. Based on your education and employment history, it appears that you have sufficient qualifications for the job. -------, before we may begin discussing a contract, we need you to come to our office for an interview.

(A) Similarly
(B) Rather
(C) For example
(D) However

✔ PART 6에 자주 등장하는 연결어

Part 6에 나오는 연결어는 앞 문장과 뒤 문장의 해석도 중요하지만, 보기에 나온 품사를 먼저 구분하는 것도 중요하다.

1. 「전치사 + 명사/동명사」
   ㅡ 전치사 뒤에는 흔히 명사(구)가 온다. 명사와 동명사의 차이는 뒤에 나오는 목적어의 유무에 따라 달라진다. 「전치사 + 동명사 + 목적어」

2. 「접속사 + 주어 + 동사」
   (Despite, **Although**) he is just an assistant now, he is likely to be a successful businessman someday.
   그는 지금 비록 조수에 불과하지만, 언젠가는 성공한 사업가가 될 것 같다.
   ㅡ 접속사 뒤에는 「주어 + 동사」가 동반된다. 따라서 접속사인 Although가 답이 된다.

3. 「접속부사, 주어 + 동사」
   Customers have complained about long lines. **Therefore**, the bank will hire four new tellers.
   고객들은 긴 줄에 대해 항의했다. 그래서, 은행은 네 명의 신입 은행원들을 고용할 것이다.
   ㅡ 접속부사 뒤에는 콤마(,)와 「주어 + 동사」가 이어진다.

양보	however 그러나, otherwise 그렇지 않으면, nevertheless/nonetheless 그럼에도 불구하고
부가	in addition 게다가, besides 게다가, moreover 더욱이, furthermore 더욱이
결과	therefore/hence 그러므로, then 그러고 나서, consequently 결과적으로

▶ 빈칸에 들어갈 알맞은 보기를 고르세요.

1. [notice]

Dear Ms. Ellsworth,

This notice confirms that you have opted to cancel your telephone service, effective January 15. ------- the policies outlined in your contract, your final bill will include fees for the month before the date you moved out and will be sent to your new address.

(A) In the event of
(B) Under the circumstances
(C) In accordance with
(D) As a consequence

2. [article]

Sydney, Australia, 19 July — One of Australia's largest wood companies, Hinada Industries, has announced the appointment of Mr. Sherman Parkston, who was previously Hinada Industries' sales manager in the Hastings area, as global sales manager.

Mr. Parkston states that Hinada Industries will be able to establish new export markets. -------, he hopes that North America and Asia will emerge as markets for Hinada Industries' products.

(A) Nevertheless
(B) Rather
(C) As requested
(D) In particular

3. [e-mail]

Dear Mr. Rodriguez,

Your subscription to *Hamilton Magazine* will expire on August 31. Renew your subscription early for a reduced rate of $15.00 per month. -------, renewing now entitles you to reduced rates for other magazines produced by Golding Fox Publishing, including *Progressive Design* and *Fashionable Day*.

(A) However
(B) Consequently
(C) Instead
(D) Additionally

4. [notice]

Attention: All employees

Please be advised that all our offices will be closed on Friday, July 5, in observance of the holiday. -------, all requests for travel reimbursement must be submitted by Wednesday, July 3.

Any submissions received after that date will be processed during the week of July 8.

(A) Therefore
(B) Similarly
(C) For example
(D) Even if

5. [letter]

Dear Ms. Lynn,

The Customer Service department has received your request for the replacement of the water purifier you purchased last month. Please accept our apologies for any inconvenience.

We will be happy to provide you with a new one free of charge. -------, under the terms of the warranty, you must first send us the original receipt. Once we receive it, we will contact you to schedule immediate delivery of the replacement item.

(A) Namely
(B) Instead of
(C) Moreover
(D) However

6. [instruction]

Thank you for purchasing the GX-720 Toaster. For your safety, please read the instruction manual thoroughly before using the appliance. -------, follow these basic precautions:

* Do not attempt to reach inside the GX-720 with a fork or other metal utensil.
* Before cleaning the toaster oven, let it cool completely.

(A) On the other hand
(B) In addition
(C) As a result of
(D) In comparison

7. [notice]

Attention: All residents

As discussed at last month's tenant meeting, we have decided to add a second laundry facility for the benefit of our residents. Starting on April 5, some parts of the basement will be renovated. Please note that tenants will not be able to use the front entrance while work is in progress on this section of the building. -------, you will need to use the back entrance.

(A) Instead
(B) Otherwise
(C) For example
(D) However

8. [advertisement]

Crown's Shoe now offers customers the largest selection of brand-name shoes of any online retailer. We're also giving even more benefits to Crown's Shoe Club members! ------- paying no shipping fees, club members will receive 20 percent off their purchases when they order four or more pairs of shoes by December 3.

(A) In addition to
(B) Thus
(C) For example
(D) In comparison

9. [e-mail]

Please be advised that on June 20, XJ Store will implement a policy guaranteeing our customers a full refund for unused items purchased at our stores. Items may be returned within a month of purchase, ------- they show no signs of wear or damage.

(A) whereas
(B) moreover
(C) provided
(D) however

10. [flyer]

Are you interested in showing your talent to people in our area? -------, you are encouraged to apply for an opportunity to display your artwork at Humington Art Fair on March 3.
Applications are available online at www.humingtonartfair.org.

(A) Nevertheless
(B) If so
(C) After that
(D) Instead

Practice

Questions 1-4 refer to the following memo.

To: Marketing Team Members
From: Mina Kim, Director
Date: November 8
Re: Peter Chen's Retirement

There will be a retirement party for Peter Chen in conference room C on Friday, November 12 at 3:30 P.M. My assistant Gina will be collecting donations to be used to purchase a gift to ------- to Peter at the party. -------. There will be refreshments provided by the Valencia Deli.
1.   2.

Please contact Gina before 5 P.M. on November 10 to let her know ------- you will be attending or not. I hope ------- everyone will be able to attend this event to celebrate Peter's 15 years of
3.   4.
service to our company. Peter's last day of work with us will be Tuesday, November 30.

---

1. (A) place
   (B) inspect
   (C) present
   (D) state

2. (A) Thank you so much for attending the party.
   (B) We hope everyone will contribute to the fund.
   (C) Ask her to show you what the present looks like.
   (D) Peter really appreciated the sendoff we gave him.

3. (A) what
   (B) whether
   (C) whenever
   (D) whose

4. (A) these
   (B) that
   (C) through
   (D) then

Questions 5-8 refer to the following memo.

To: All employees
From: Allisa Carl, Payroll Coordinator
Date: March 1
Subject: Holiday Time Sheets

National Bank will not be open on March 15 in observance of the national holiday. Because of this, employees must submit their timesheets on Thursday, March 14, one day ------- than usual.
5.
This will apply to all branch employees as well as the off-site employees ------- submit their time
6.
sheets electronically. Contract employees should consult their supervisors to determine how this scheduled ------- will affect them.
7.

If you are unable to fill out the timesheet by 5 P.M. on March 14, please contact the payroll office to make alternative arrangements. -------. Thank you for your cooperation.
8.

PART 6 UNIT 03

5. (A) faster
(B) earlier
(C) previous
(D) advanced

6. (A) what
(B) where
(C) who
(D) whoever

7. (A) training
(B) payment
(C) increase
(D) closure

8. (A) Paychecks will be sent out on the 14th.
(B) It can be reached by dialing extension 704.
(C) All time sheets should be on my desk by the end of the day.
(D) We hope that everyone enjoyed the day off.

Questions 9-12 refer to the following report.

The dramatic ------- in the price of HAL Technology's stock has been attributed to their recently
9.
launched voice recognition software. The program's accuracy is unprecedented, and its logic
algorithms are the most advanced to date. -------. ------- 500,000 units have been sold since it
10. 11.
reached stores three weeks ago, and long lines have formed at many locations for the software.
Experts predict that HAL Technology will have a(n) ------- larger market share than Davida
12.
Electronics, the current market leader, by the year's end.

9. (A) decline
(B) hold
(C) interest
(D) rise

11. (A) Over
(B) Along
(C) Still
(D) Within

10. (A) Sales are currently not as high as
expected.
(B) The program resembles some
software released several months
ago.
(C) Critics are unanimous in their praise
of the product.
(D) Some users report mistakes in the
program's accuracy.

12. (A) more
(B) too
(C) even
(D) so

8 June
Karen Hirota
855 Daizo Road
Shibuya-ku, Tokyo,150-0043, Japan

Dear Ms. Hirota,

Thank you for submitting your application. We appreciate your considering a career with us.

Unfortunately, the posted executive assistant ------- has been filled.
                                              13.

-------, our Human Resources team was impressed with your educational background and work
14.

experience. Good applicants like yourself are hard to find. -------. You will be notified when -------
                                                            15.   **16.**

becomes available.

In the meantime, we wish you the best of luck in your future endeavors.

Best regards,

Bernie Hemmings
Human Resources Manager
Miyagi Investment Group

13. (A) open
(B) opening
(C) opened
(D) openness

14. (A) Likewise
(B) Nonetheless
(C) For example
(D) As a result

15. (A) Please confirm your choice on the
enclosed form.
(B) You have been selected to work at our
new branch.
(C) An interview will be scheduled for you
soon.
(D) We will keep your information on file for
future positions.

16. (A) which
(B) anybody
(C) one
(D) ours

UNIT 04 어휘 선택

PART 5 뿐만 아니라 PART 6에서도 어휘 선택은 어렵게 느껴지는 문제 중 하나이다. 무턱대고 해석에 의존해서 찾으려 하지 말고 빈출되는 어휘 유형이 어떤 것이 있는 지 파악하고 풀도록 한다.

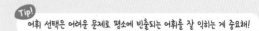

Tip! 어휘 선택은 어려운 문제로 평소에 빈출되는 어휘를 잘 익히는 게 중요해!

 핵심 문제 유형

Question 1 refers to the following article.

해설서 p.79

SAN FRANCISCO (2 May) — Luxuria, the global cosmetics company, has launched its annual Makeup Collection, showcasing its latest beauty product innovations. The ------- release is designed to offer customers new and exciting products, with many of the items developed based on feedback from surveys that aim to identify common beauty challenges and emerging trends.

(A) daily
(B) weekly
(C) monthly
(D) yearly

✔ PART 6에 자주 등장하는 어휘 선택

1. 동의어 & 패러프레이징 반복

영어는 똑같은 단어를 반복해서 사용하는 것을 싫어한다. 그러므로 동의어나 말을 바꿔쓰는 패러프레이징을 좋아한다.

본사	headquarters, head office, main office, -based
보수 공사	remodeling, renovation, redesign, upgrade, change

2. 궁합을 따지는 어휘(연어 collocation)

영어에서는 한 단어가 아닌 여러 단어의 궁합으로 같이 쓰이는 단어들이 있다.

conduct the survey 설문조사를 하다, meet the deadline 마감 날짜를 맞추다

3. 문법이 가미된 어휘

to부정사를 목적격 보어로 가지는 5형식 동사

ask, urge, encourage, cause, enable + 목적어 + to부정사

4. 최고급 어휘

비즈니스에 사용되는 익숙하지 않은 어휘들이 종종 출제되기도 한다. 이럴 경우 출제되었던 어휘가 또 시험에 등장하는 경우가 있으므로 빈출 어휘 또는 평소 문제나 지문에 나오는 어휘를 중심으로 익히도록 한다.

standing 고정(지속)적인, 상설의, standing order 자동이체

▶ 빈칸에 들어갈 알맞은 보기를 고르세요.

1. [e-mail]

To: jessica.smith@mail.net
From: FitnessNation@lilmail.com
Date: May 2
Subject: Re: Membership Changes

To our members:

We are excited to announce that our gym has experienced a significant ------- in membership this year, with the number of members doubling compared to last year. To improve the gym experience for everyone, we will upgrade our equipment and facilities, add more group fitness classes such as yoga and boxing, and hire more trainers to provide personalized attention and support. Your feedback is valuable to us, and we are committed to offering the best gym experience possible.

(A) interest
(B) request
(C) increase
(D) favor

2. [article]

SAN FRANCISCO (6 May) — Today, Tech Giant Xavier Corporation has completed the ------- of Yellowfield Corporation, a startup company that specializes in developing augmented reality (AR) software. Through this purchase, Xavier Corporation now has ownership of Yellowfield's cutting-edge AR technology, which is expected to accelerate Xavier's progress in the development of AR products. This deal demonstrates Xavier's commitment to innovation and its dedication to providing its customers with the most advanced technology.

(A) release
(B) cooperation
(C) network
(D) acquisition

PART 6 UNIT 04

3. [e-mail]

To: Mr. Rodriguez <jrodriguez@zoommail.com>
From: SkyRoutes Airlines <srresearch@srairlines.com>
Date: 7 June
Subject: Help us to improve!

Dear Mr. Rodriguez,

We hope this e-mail finds you well. Our records indicate that you have flown with SkyRoutes Airlines in the past, and we value your opinion. We request that you kindly take a few minutes to complete a brief online survey to share your thoughts about your overall experience with us. The survey is composed of four questions, and we would be grateful if you could answer them as candidly as possible. Your ------- is essential to aid us to enhance our services, and we appreciate your time and input.

(A) effort
(B) feedback
(C) creativity
(D) reservation

4. [Web page]

The latest addition to the website of Eastside Medical Center is a feature called "HealthConnect," which allows patients to view their medical information and connect with healthcare providers. Patients who wish to use this feature must first create an account by following a few simple steps. To begin, send an e-mail to register@eastsidehealth.com or text "Register" to 555-1212. Once you've received an activation code, you can visit the website and select the "HealthConnect" tab to complete the setup process using your computer, tablet, or smartphone.

Please note that the activation code is only valid for 72 hours, so you'll need to use it within that time frame. If you encounter any ------- during the registration process, you can contact technical support at support@eastsidehealth.com or by phone at 555-9876.

(A) ideas
(B) requests
(C) difficulties
(D) obligations

5. [advertisement]

If you're interested in trying out our new meal delivery service, JustFit, you can do so without any risk thanks to our 30-day trial period. During this time, you won't be charged anything and won't be locked into any sort of long-term contract. To enroll you in the trial, we'll need your contact information and payment details on file, but you won't be charged unless you continue using JustFit beyond the trial period. If you decide that the service isn't for you, ------- visit our website at www. justfit.com and go to the "membership" page. There, you can cancel your subscription by providing some basic information. It really is that easy!

(A) eventually
(B) frequently
(C) simply
(D) primarily

6. [e-mail]

To: John Davis <johndavis@email.com>
From: Mary Smith <marys@researchco.com>
Date: 2 June
Subject: Research Study

Dear Mr. Davis,

We are ------- conducting a research study to gather insights about user engagement patterns related to a new mobile application from a leading tech company. As a valued user of this app, your participation in a brief ten-question survey would be greatly appreciated. Your feedback would provide invaluable insights to the company on how to improve our user engagement strategies. Your responses will be treated with the utmost confidentiality and will only be used for research purposes. As a token of our appreciation, you will receive a £15 gift card that can be redeemed at any major retailer. To participate, please reply to this e-mail, and we will provide you with the survey link.

Thank you for your time and contribution to this study.

Sincerely,

Mary Smith
Survey Coordinator

(A) momentarily
(B) presently
(C) anonymously
(D) increasingly

7. [article]

(NEW YORK — 15 October) Green Growth Ventures, a sustainable agriculture company based in New York, announced that it has secured a $5 million investment to expand its indoor farming operations. The funding will be used to construct a new state-of-the-art facility and increase the production of fresh, locally-grown produce.

"I am ------- that this investment will allow us to continue our mission of providing sustainable, healthy food to our community," said Green Growth Ventures CEO Maria Rogers. "Our indoor farming technology allows us to grow produce year-round, using significantly less water and land than traditional farming methods. This not only benefits the environment but also ensures that our customers receive the freshest, most nutritious produce possible."

(A) expected
(B) confident
(C) obvious
(D) capable

8. [information]

ABC Company is ------- to announce the launch of its latest product line. This new collection showcases the latest technology and cutting-edge design to enhance customers' experiences. The launch event will take place on June 15, when customers and industry leaders will have the opportunity to preview the new products. Refreshments will be served from 10 A.M., and the product showcase will begin promptly at 11 A.M. Attendees are encouraged to stay and network until the event concludes at 1 P.M.

(A) familiar
(B) pleasant
(C) essential
(D) proud

9. [letter]

Landon's Lawn Services
23 Greenfield Way
Sunnyvale, California 94086.

Dear Valued Customer,

We want to take this opportunity to express our gratitude for your continued patronage of our lawn services. We take pride in maintaining your lawns and gardens with the utmost care and attention to detail. Unfortunately, we must inform you that we will be increasing our lawn care prices by 7 percent, ------- June 1st. The rising costs of equipment, fuel, and labor have made it necessary for us to adjust our prices. We believe that even with the price increase, our services remain a great value compared to the competition. Thank you for your understanding and support. We look forward to serving you for many years to come.

Sincerely,

Landon Johnson, Owner

(A) effective
(B) introductory
(C) upcoming
(D) apparent

10. [e-mail]

To: Anika Patel <apatel@abcinc.com>
From: John Smith <jsmith@defcorporation.com>
Date: May 15
Subject: Monthly Order Update

I hope this e-mail finds you well. I am reaching out to update our ------- order for the coming months. As you may recall, our previous orders included a significant number of BL 205 pens. However, we have noticed a decrease in demand for these pens among our team members. Therefore, we would like to reduce our order of BL 205 pens to just 10 per month starting next month. In place of these pens, we would like to increase our order of GN 301 markers to 16 per month.

I would like to note that we are not phasing out the BL 205 pens entirely at this point, but we will certainly keep you informed if there are any further changes to our order. Additionally, I request that you kindly send us a statement with an updated monthly bill reflecting these changes. Our Finance Department requires this information for their records.

Thank you for your attention to this matter, and please let me know if you have any questions or concerns.

(A) possible
(B) standing
(C) overdue
(D) reverse

Practice

해설서 p.83 / ⏱ 제한 시간 10분

Questions 1-4 refer to the following information.

Epicura Devices may occasionally lack inventory of items -------- are listed as available on our
website at the time of purchase. --------, due to the high volume of orders, this is an unavoidable
1.   **2.**
issue. If a payment has already gone through on an item that is sold out, it will be refunded
immediately. Alternatively, you can request to be put on a waitlist. This will ensure you receive
your item from our next --------. This will not incur any additional fees, but it may take several
3.
weeks to fulfill your order.

Epicura Devices is a growing company with three locations in Singapore. As a company that
cares about our customers, we are constantly looking for ways to improve our service. --------.
4.

1. (A) can
(B) upon
(C) then
(D) that

2. (A) To illustrate
(B) Regrettably
(C) Despite
(D) Therefore

3. (A) promotion
(B) batch
(C) estimate
(D) invitation

4. (A) If you have any comments, please get
in touch.
(B) Make sure to check back often.
(C) The final invoice will be sent shortly.
(D) We have signed a deal with a new
supplier.

Breathing New Life into Cubero City Zoo

Cubero City Zoo will reopen its doors to the public next month. This is the first time the public will see the newly designed museum since it was closed off for renovations last year.

One of the goals the renovations focused on was creating a family-friendly experience. Visitors to the museum will ------- enjoy more viewing platforms, restaurants, and informative signs about
       5.
all of the animals.

Visitors will also notice the zoo's increased sustainability efforts. -------, most of the lights and
       6.
signs in the zoo will be solar-powered. Additionally, the indoor exhibits will utilize more ------- air
       7.
conditioning systems that reduce the amount of power used.

Not all areas of the zoo will be open next month. The plan is to gradually reopen the zoo section by section over time. -------.
       8.

---

5. (A) nearly
(B) prior
(C) yet
(D) soon

6. (A) Consequently
(B) For instance
(C) Furthermore
(D) Despite

7. (A) efficiently
(B) efficiencies
(C) efficient
(D) efficiency

8. (A) A full schedule can be found on the zoo's website.
(B) Additional workers may be required for a new project.
(C) The air conditioning system will require further trials.
(D) A health inspection is due to take place.

Auto-adjusting Lightbulbs

Lighting technology has changed ------- in the past few years. One piece of emerging technology
     9.
is automatically adjusting lightbulbs, which are ------- alternatives to regular household
                                                10.
lightbulbs. These lightbulbs take into account the time of day as well as the Sun's natural shifts
in brightness to provide a stable level of brightness for your home.

Feedback from several local businesses who have been testing the lightbulbs out has been very
positive so far. -------. As an extra benefit, these lightbulbs end up consuming less energy than
                  11.
traditional lightbulbs, leading to cost savings. If they are installed correctly, the lightbulbs -------
                                                                                                  12.
significantly longer, presenting a more environmentally conscious option.

9. (A) expectedly
    (B) substantially
    (C) uniformly
    (D) certainly

10. (A) prolonged
     (B) minor
     (C) numerous
     (D) modern

11. (A) They have praised the comfort and
         ease of use.
     (B) They are available in a variety of
         different colors.
     (C) They accept all interested applicants.
     (D) They will go on sale starting next
         month.

12. (A) had lasted
     (B) would last
     (C) lasting
     (D) will last

Proposals for research project financing are now being ------- by Grayson City Council's
13.
Research Institute. Grants will be awarded to proposals that align with the Council's goal of
fostering more start-ups. We are seeking innovations that have commercially viable ------- in
14.
lucrative fields such as health, transportation, and computing. The ------- can be used in any
15.
appropriate way, such as for creating a prototype based on a design, recruiting skilled staff
members to bring an item to market, or applying for patents. If you think your project meets our
criteria, send a brief description to Grayson City Council Research Institute, 21 Kipling Point,
Grayson. -------.
16.

13. (A) accepted
(B) commenced
(C) invoiced
(D) questioned

14. (A) applications
(B) apply
(C) applicable
(D) applicably

15. (A) schedule
(B) product
(C) document
(D) funds

16. (A) This is the institute's sixth year in existence.
(B) Grayson is currently home to a number of startups.
(C) The deadline for all submissions is September 15.
(D) A well-designed website would be very helpful.

문장 선택

Part 6의 3문제는 알맞은 문법, 구조, 어휘 지식을 묻는다. 반면에, 1문제는 '빈칸에 알맞은 문장을 고르는 유형'으로 단순히 빈칸 주변보다는 앞뒤 문맥이나 전체 문맥을 파악해서 풀어야 하기 때문에 독해 실력을 더욱 요구한다.

> Tip!
> 문장 선택 유형은 Part 6에서뿐 아니라 RC 전체에서 가장 어려운 문제야!
> 앞뒤 문맥을 파악하는 게 관건이야!

핵심 문제 유형

Question 1 refers to the following brochure.

해설서 p.85

Please join us for our fifth annual Belmont Realty and Finance Seminar on Saturday, March 20, from 2:00 P.M. to 5:00 P.M. Our aim is to provide you with the information needed to prepare for home ownership.

Led by the top financial consultants in the country, this three-hour session will help you review the costs associated with buying a home and make knowledgeable decisions regarding your financial future. We'll teach you how to evaluate your income, make profitable investment decisions, and protect your capital. There will be a Q&A session at the end of the seminar. -------. Visit www.belmontrealtyfinance.com/marchseminar to register.

(A) We hope you enjoy your new home.
(B) You will find your membership very rewarding.
(C) Don't miss out on this opportunity.
(D) Improve your communication skills today.

✔ PART 6에서 가장 어려운 문장 선택

▶ 빈칸이 지문의 초반에 제시된 경우: 주로 지문의 주제나 목적을 나타내는 문장이 정답으로 출제된다.

▶ 빈칸이 지문의 중간이나 뒤에 제시된 경우: 빈칸 앞뒤 내용에 대한 부연 설명, 이유, 조건 등을 나타내는 문장이 정답으로 출제된다.

▶ 빈칸 앞뒤 문장에 대명사(this, these, it 등)나 연결어(however, therefore, in addition 등)가 나오는지 확인한다.

▶ 선택한 보기를 빈칸에 넣어서 문맥상 흐름에 맞는지 확인한다.

▶ 빈칸에 들어갈 알맞은 보기를 고르세요.

1. [memo]

To: All employees
From: Gabriel Funston
Date: February 5
Subject: website renovation

Greetings All,

Mirror Studio's IT team is currently renovating the company's website. They have recently completed the first stage. This stage focused on making the pages more user-friendly for our customers.

Before the new pages are made available to the public, we would like to have our employees test them out first to make sure that the work has been done satisfactorily. -------. A questionnaire will be emailed to you concerning the new website. Please take the time to answer all of the questions carefully. Your feedback is valuable to us.

Thank you,

Gabriel Funston
Systems Manager

(A) Also, make sure that you review the attached document.
(B) We respectfully request that everyone help out with this.
(C) Thus, you are required to provide an estimated completion date.
(D) Please describe the missing information in the space provided.

2. [memo]

To: All employees
From: Elton Roski
Re: Training
Date: 20 September

-------. To make sure all relevant library staff members are aware of the changes, those involved in tracking books and media materials will need to attend one of the training sessions that we will be holding. These have been scheduled for October 8, 9, and 10 from 1 P.M. – 2 P.M.

Please register by emailing tech@forestlakelibrary.org and make sure to indicate the date that is most convenient for you. If you are unavailable on these dates, contact me directly at eroski@forestlakelibrary.org, and I will provide individual training.

(A) As you all know, an open house will be held at the library next week.
(B) Forest Lake Library is committed to providing excellent service to the community.
(C) The library database system is being updated by the Technology Department.
(D) Starting next month, we will be extending our library hours.

3. [article]

Tucson Lake, November 10 — Rolo Toys has opened up its third location, this time at 500 Feather Road in the Kloud Shopping Center. Owner Arthur McGuire said that he could not pass up the chance to further expand his business. "-------."

Mr. McGuire also commented that although the Feather Road store is already operational, its official opening will be held on Sunday, November 15, at 11:00 A.M. with a special ribbon-cutting ceremony and a raffle drawing. This event is open to the public. Rolo sells the latest children's toys, games, and various party supplies, including balloons, banners, and birthday hats. Call 310-555-5462 or visit www.rolotoys.com for more information.

(A) The rent was so expensive that I had to find another location.
(B) Once I found out that retail space was available in the mall, I leased it immediately.
(C) Due to the decline in sales, I had no choice but to close down the store.
(D) I'm very excited about the construction of the new mall next year.

4. [e-mail]

To: Stefan Yoon <syoon@macvoylibrary.org>
From: Jessa Thompson <jthompson@hantechsystems.com>
Subject: Update
Date: January 4

Mr. Yoon,

I'm writing this e-mail to follow up on our discussion last week regarding the installation of the Wiz Turbo software on all of the computers at the Macvoy Library. As I mentioned, this system has been proven to reduce the amount of time it takes to track library materials by almost 35 percent.

Assuming that no unforeseen circumstances arise, the installation will take about an hour. -------. Please confirm at your earliest convenience if you wish to proceed with the project.

Thank you,

Jessa Thompson, Software Technician
Hantech Systems

(A) We would like to thank you again for the early confirmation.
(B) We are confident that you will be satisfied with the results.
(C) We could not have predicted the technical issue at that time.
(D) We will provide more information about the library if you wish.

5. [memo]

To: All staff members
From: Lorenzo Corales
Date: February 17
Subject: RVM-3

I would like to remind everyone that we will be transitioning to the RVM-3 e-mail program. As of 4:30 P.M. today, you will not be able to access Traxis, our current e-mail system. Therefore, it is crucial that you back up any important messages stored in Traxis before this time. Please keep in mind that once the Traxis system is removed, any messages that are unsaved will be deleted permanently.

To find out more about the new program, download the RVM-3 demo video, which describes all of its features: www.rvm.com/rvm3_video. -------. If you have further questions, contact supportcenter@encro.com.

(A) Customers will then be able to purchase the software.
(B) By doing so, you can enter the numbers of hours you worked.
(C) As such, you should transfer all of your important files.
(D) There is also a printable user manual available on the site.

6. [article]

Hongkong, June 1 — Ruben Sheerin, CEO of XED Motors, announced in a press conference this afternoon that the company is planning to release a new energy-efficient electric car at the end of the month.

According to Mr. Sheerin, this car features a dual electric motor, an advanced cruise control system, and a state-of-the-art GPS device.

Auto industry experts predict that this latest vehicle will bring even more attention to XED's recent line of compact cars. They attribute the company's consistently strong sales performance to its ability to constantly improve its automotive technology. -------.

(A) XED first revealed the car at an international motor show last year.
(B) XED has already exceeded its sales goals for this quarter.
(C) XED is planning to discontinue one of its vehicle lines.
(D) XED will provide financial compensation to its customers.

7. [e-mail]

To: Cindy Wilhem <cwilhem@zoommail.com>
From: Dylan Robins <drobins@johanauto.net>
Date: 7 November
Subject: Repair request

Dear Ms. Wilhem,

I am replying to your repair request (customer number 7695) which we received on 5 November via our online system. Based on the information that you provided, there is no need for you to bring in your car to be serviced. -------. You mentioned that the doors are set to lock automatically when the vehicle is in a stopped position. To deactivate this setting, first, locate the switch marked "auto lock" on the left side of the dashboard. Then simply flip the switch to the "off" position before pressing the "reset" button which is right next to the switch. If this fails to work, please contact me at 555-5735.

Sincerely,

Dylan Robins, Service Manager
Johan's Auto

(A) A technician will have the car repaired within 24 hours.
(B) We believe the issue can be resolved by you on your own.
(C) Our shop services all types of vehicles, including older models.
(D) Just include a brief description of the problem in your e-mail.

8. [article]

July 3 — Starting in September, the East Side School District will depend solely on Clifton Education Publishers for all English literature texts and teaching materials. In the past, Clifton was one of the two preferred suppliers for such content. However, as of September 1, the Board of Education will discontinue its contract with the other supplier. This decision was made based on a vote by teachers and other education officials, who praised the quality of Clifton's products. Even though the prices of Clifton's textbooks are relatively high, its supplementary materials such as teacher's guides and student workbooks are less expensive than those of other publishers. -------.

(A) This will enable the district to keep expenses within budget.
(B) This will be provided for free for a limited period.
(C) This will allow teachers to spend more time with their students.
(D) This will make it possible to create an effective curriculum.

9. [e-mail]

To: Evaline Patterson <epatterson@focaladvertising.com>
From: Chas Munoz <cmunoz@exposportsauthority.com>
Date: August 12
Subject: Marketing Campaign
Attachment: Images

Hello Evaline,

Expo Sports Authority will soon receive its fall inventory. Accordingly, I plan to start another advertising campaign in order to promote the season's new items. In particular, I would like to call attention to the Road Blazer hiking gear line, which is made of eco-friendly materials. Expo Sports Authority is one of the few local retailers to offer this product line, so we want it emphasized in all of our ads. -------. Please use these any way you wish in creating the ads.

Thank you,

Chas Munoz
Sales Director, Expo Sports Authority

(A) A budget estimate will be emailed to you by tomorrow.
(B) We would like to request some samples of your product.
(C) The ads are being displayed in stores across the city.
(D) Attached are some photos of the hiking gear.

10. [letter]

June 23

Gregory Valencia
1150 Spectacle Road
Montreal, QC H3A 1J7

Dear Mr. Valencia,

Please review the quote below for the delivery and installation of the Finesse Audio Home Theater System as per our discussion last Friday, June 20. The total amount comes to $489.99, which includes the purchase price, sales tax, and labor costs. Please understand that this is merely an estimate. -------.

Should you wish to proceed, please call me at 555-9483 to schedule a convenient time for you.

Thank you,

Tyrone Brown
Sales Manager, Finesse Audio Systems

(A) I would like to continue our discussion from last Friday.
(B) We will check our inventory to see if the item is in stock.
(C) Exact installation cost will vary slightly for each residence.
(D) Remember to submit your payment by the end of the week.

Questions 1-4 refer to the following e-mail.

To: Keiko Fukawa <keikofu@sapmail.com>
From: netoffice.com
Sent: Tuesday, October 21, 2:38 P.M.
Subject: Order

Thank you for placing an order with us. At 2:34 P.M. today, we received a purchase order from you for item #893-ch, a cherry-stained, roll-top computer desk. -------. As part of the special
1.
event we are currently having, you will also receive a matching desk chair at no extra charge.
Both items ------- hand-worked materials and come with our standard warranty. For the chair,
2.
some ------- will be required.
3.

If we have received this confirmation in error, please contact one of our ------- immediately at
4.
customerservice@netoffice.com. Otherwise, your order will be shipped within two business days.

1.
(A) It is currently unavailable.
(B) A warranty on it is not available.
(C) This item retails for a special price of $125.99.
(D) We hope that you would like to buy it.

2.
(A) feature
(B) contain
(C) measure
(D) seek

3.
(A) assemble
(B) assembles
(C) assembly
(D) assembled

4.
(A) producers
(B) demonstrators
(C) representatives
(D) applicants

To: Hye-rim Bae <hyerimbae@gsmmail.com>
From: Patricia Thorne <pattythorne@gsaccmail.com>
Sent: March 21, 11:31 A.M.
Subject: Changes

Greetings Ms. Bae,

In order to accommodate the new staff that will be hired for your department, your office will be expanded to take up the entire third floor. Unfortunately, this means that your teams will have to deal with some inconvenience over the next few months. Your office will be ------- relocated to
5.
the two conference rooms on the fifth floor. We cannot say as of yet how long this situation will last, but a contractor is coming next week to give us an estimate of how ------- the renovations
6.
will need to be.

The conference rooms will be somewhat cramped, so you will be permitted a more flexible work schedule. Employees will be permitted to work from home up to two days a week. However, the personnel ------- from home must have a mobile phone and high-speed Internet in their homes.
7.
-------. If you have any questions or requests concerning the renovations, please let me know.
8.

Sincerely,

Patricia Thorne

5. (A) generally
(B) temporarily
(C) permanently
(D) belatedly

6. (A) extend
(B) extensive
(C) extensively
(D) extent

7. (A) working
(B) workable
(C) workably
(D) worked

8. (A) Be sure to make your staff aware of these two requirements.
(B) You can contact Doug Peterson at extension 46 with your inquiries.
(C) These items can be obtained by contacting my office anytime.
(D) This matter should be considered settled and is not up for discussion.

Questions 9-12 refer to the following memo.

To: All Human Resources Staff
From: Jamila Ringit, HR Director
Date: Tuesday, May 4
Re: Meeting

As many of you already know, I attended a human resources management seminar in Chicago over the weekend. While I was there, I learned many techniques that I think would help us improve overall work conditions in the company. -------. Tomorrow morning, we will have a
9.
meeting at 10:00 to discuss those techniques. Then, I will ------- assign each of you a department
10.
to meet with on Thursday. At your meeting, you will discuss any and all problems or complaints they may have. I want you to encourage the employees in that department to come to you -------
11.
with any issues they aren't comfortable discussing in front of others. It is our responsibility to create an environment in which personnel collaborate ------- with each other. Next Monday, we
12.
will meet again to share what you have learned.

9. (A) What I learned at that staff meeting was incredible.
(B) I'd like to share the knowledge that I learned with you all.
(C) Please let me know if you'd like to attend the upcoming seminar.
(D) This should be an opportunity everyone can take advantage of.

10. (A) personal
(B) personally
(C) personalize
(D) personality

11. (A) rarely
(B) completely
(C) evidently
(D) individually

12. (A) ready
(B) readied
(C) readily
(D) readiness

NOTICE

-------. Due to the renovations to the lobby that will commence next week, the usual lateness
   13.
------- will be suspended. The building only has two stairwells and three elevators that reach
   14.
------- floor. Because ------- of the routes may not be accessible at certain times until the work
   15.   16.
is completed, concessions must be made. Therefore, employees may arrive as late as 10:00 as

long as they make up the time after 6:00. Thank you.

Katya Borozhny
Human Resources Director

---

13. (A) We are considering doing some work
    in the lobby in a month.
  (B) The renovations on the first floor have
    just been completed.
  (C) Thank you for your patience during
    the repair work on the building.
  (D) As announced last month, some
    construction work on the building will
    start soon.

14. (A) projection
   (B) policy
   (C) grant
   (D) ranking

15. (A) its
   (B) his
   (C) our
   (D) their

16. (A) it
   (B) all
   (C) every
   (D) none

REVIEW TEST

해설서 p.91 / ⏱ 제한 시간 10분

Questions 1-4 refer to the following letter.

Dear Ms. Chambers,

I am writing concerning your ------- of 20 of the 300 dinner plates that you received on May 7. At
      1.
Maestro Pottery, we pay careful attention to the quality of all our merchandise. Any defects in our

products are ------- unacceptable.
    2.

Your retail outlets are among our most loyal clients. -------, we will go ahead and refund the total
        3.
cost of the defective plates to your account.

-------. Do not hesitate to contact me regarding this or any other concerns or issues.
  4.

Sincerely,

Harold Shin
Director of Sales
Maestro Pottery

---

1. (A) coordination
    (B) creation
    (C) disposal
    (D) rejection

2. (A) considered
    (B) considers
    (C) considering
    (D) to consider

3. (A) Therefore
    (B) However
    (C) Regardless
    (D) Additionally

4. (A) Please confirm that you wish to
        proceed with this delivery.
    (B) Please send me a price estimate by
        next week.
    (C) Please return the items whenever it is
        most convenient for you.
    (D) Please visit our website to sign up.

Questions 5-8 refer to the following letter.

Justin Humphrey
2050 Rafael Drive
Atlanta, GA 30301
November 5

Dear Mr. Humphrey,

Thank you for your application for the marketing manager position with Laxco Global Co. ------- **5.** our assessment of your qualifications, we have decided that you are a suitable candidate for the position. -------. A member of our Human Resources staff will contact you on Wednesday, **6.** November 12, to arrange a meeting.

During the interview, you ------- to talk about your past work experience in detail. The day after **7.** the interview, a staff member will inform you whether you have been selected for the position or not. If you are not chosen, we will keep your details on file for nine months and will consider ------- for other positions as they become available. **8.**

We look forward to meeting you.

Sincerely,

Norah Cruz, Human Resources Manager
Laxco Global Co.

5. (A) Based on
    (B) Therefore
    (C) In order to
    (D) Consequently

6. (A) Please call our office today to schedule a time to come in.
    (B) We would like to offer you the position.
    (C) I have enclosed my résumé and thank you in advance for your consideration.
    (D) The next step in the recruitment process is an in-person interview.

7. (A) would have asked
    (B) will be asked
    (C) were asked
    (D) had asked

8. (A) you
    (B) him
    (C) myself
    (D) us

Questions 9-12 refer to the following memo.

To: Everclear Apartment Complex Tenants
From: FMP Maintenance Company
Date: April 2
Subject: Water Pipe Work

Please be informed that on May 19, from 10:00 A.M. to 2:00 P.M., FMP Maintenance Company will be ------- some water pipes at the Everclear Apartment Complex. While our crew members
9.
install the new pipes, the building's water service will be temporarily interrupted.

-------, all tenants of Everclear Apartment Complex are ------- not to turn on any water faucets
10.   11.
during this time. When water service resumes, please run the faucets for a few minutes. -------. If
12.
you have any questions or concerns, please contact the building manager.

We apologize in advance for the inconvenience.

9. (A) cleaning
    (B) opening
    (C) unloading
    (D) replacing

10. (A) Likewise
    (B) Accordingly
    (C) Even so
    (D) In contrast

11. (A) asking
    (B) having asked
    (C) asked
    (D) to ask

12. (A) Make sure to read the installation
        instructions first.
    (B) We will include the charge on your next
        utility bill.
    (C) Please remember to renew your lease
        before it expires.
    (D) This will ensure that the water is safe to
        use.

Aug. 10 — Carlsbad Town Council announced its decision to contract with Badmaev Construction for a new project. According to the terms, Badmaev ------- the 300-yard stretch of
13.
the beach north of Highway 78. The town's mayor, Miguel Cervantes, anticipates that the -------
14.
activities offered at the renovated facilities will make it popular with families. "Children need a place where they can learn to swim, surf, and enjoy the water safely," Mr. Cervantes said. "This is exactly what this community needs." -------. Badmaev spokesperson Joe Marsh notes that the
15.
area will have a medical clinic and professional lifeguards, but also points out that it's impossible to prevent every accident. "Naturally, we will give our best -------, but there is simply no way to
16.
eliminate all potential dangers from the beach."

13. (A) upgraded
(B) upgrades
(C) will upgrade
(D) to upgrade

14. (A) expensive
(B) mandatory
(C) recreational
(D) unforeseen

15. (A) On the other hand, the city has yet to make a decision on a construction company.
(B) Recently, many residents have made complaints about the waste at the beach.
(C) However, even with a more secure environment, activities near the ocean can never be completely risk-free.
(D) For the time being, the project cannot be approved because of budget limitations.

16. (A) value
(B) anticipation
(C) rate
(D) effort

PAF

RT 7

▼

독해

OVERVIEW

지문을 읽고 그에 해당하는 질문에 알맞은 답을 고르는 문제이다. 지문은 문자 메시지와 온라인 채팅과 같은 문자 대화문부터 신문 기사나 웹사이트 페이지까지 그 종류가 다양하며, 그 형태도 1개의 지문으로 된 단일 지문, 2개의 지문으로 된 이중 지문, 3개의 지문으로 이루어진 삼중 지문 문제로 구분할 수 있다. 단일 지문 29문항, 이중 지문 10문항, 삼중 지문 15문항씩 총 54문항이 출제된다.

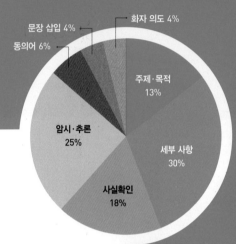

문제 유형 분석

단일 지문(10개) ┃ 이메일, 편지, 문자 메시지, 온라인 채팅, 광고, 기사, 양식, 회람, 공지, 웹페이지 등

이중 지문(2개) ┃ 이메일–이메일, 기사–이메일, 웹페이지–이메일, 웹페이지(광고)–웹페이지(사용 후기) 등

삼중 지문(3개) ┃ 다양한 세 지문들의 조합

최신 출제 경향

- 지문과 문제의 길이가 점점 길어지고 있다. 지문과 선택지를 일일이 대조할 필요가 있는 사실 확인 문제 유형의 비중을 늘려서 난이도를 조절하기도 한다.
- 암시·추론 문제의 비중이 증가하고 있다. 지문에 나와 있는 정보를 토대로 알 수 있는 사실 확인 및 암시·추론 문제가 많이 등장하고 있다.
- 동의어 문제가 매회 1~4문제의 출제 비율을 유지하고 있다.

핵심 학습 전략

- Part 7은 지문과 문항 수가 증가했고, 글의 흐름 파악이 중요해졌기 때문에 빠르고 정확한 독해력이 필요하다. 어휘력을 쌓고 문장의 구조를 파악하는 훈련을 통해 독해력을 뒷받침하는 기본기를 다져야 한다.
- 문자 메시지나 온라인 채팅은 난이도가 비교적 높지 않다. 그러나 구어체적 표현이 많이 나오고 문자 그대로의 사전적인 의미가 아닌 문맥상 그 안에 담겨 있는 숨은 뜻을 찾는 화자 의도 파악 문제가 꼭 출제되기 때문에 평소 구어체 표현을 숙지하고 대화의 흐름을 파악하는 연습을 한다.
- 질문의 키워드를 찾고 질문이 요구하는 핵심 정보를 본문에서 신속하게 찾아내는 연습이 필요하다.
- 본문에서 찾아낸 정답 정보는 선택지에서 다른 표현으로 제시되므로 같은 의미를 여러 가지 다른 표현들(paraphrased expressions)로 전달하는 패러프레이징 찾기 연습이 필요하다.

문제 풀이 전략

1. 지문 순서대로 풀지 말자.

Part 7은 처음부터 또는 마지막부터 순서대로 풀지 않아도 된다. 15개의 지문 중에서 당연히 가장 쉬운 것부터 먼저 풀고 어려운 문제는 시간이 남으면 푼다는 마음으로 풀어야 한다. 다음과 같은 순서로 문제를 풀어 보도록 한다.

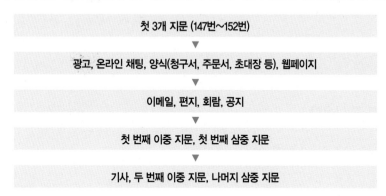

첫 3개 지문 (147번~152번)

▼

광고, 온라인 채팅, 양식(청구서, 주문서, 초대장 등), 웹페이지

▼

이메일, 편지, 회람, 공지

▼

첫 번째 이중 지문, 첫 번째 삼중 지문

▼

기사, 두 번째 이중 지문, 나머지 삼중 지문

2. 패러프레이징(Paraphrasing)된 정답을 찾는 것이 핵심이다.

같은 표현은 절대 반복되지 않는다. 정답은 지문에 나온 표현을 다른 말로 바꿔 나온다.

> - **지문에서 나오는 표현** National Museum is <u>located just minutes from Oxford Street Station</u> in Richmont's shopping district. 국립 박물관은 리치몬트의 쇼핑가에 있는 옥스퍼드 가 역에서 단 몇 분 거리에 있다.
>
> - **문제** What is suggested about the National Museum? 국립 박물관에 관하여 암시되는 것은?
>
> - **정답** It is <u>conveniently located</u>. 편리한 곳에 위치해 있다.

3. 지문 내용에 기반하여 정답을 찾는다.

정답은 반드시 지문 내용에 기반하여 사실인 것만 고른다. 절대 '그럴 것 같다, 그렇겠지'라고 상상하여 답을 고르면 안 된다. Part 7 문제 유형 중에는 추론해야 하는 문제들이 많이 나오기는 하지만 아무리 추론 문제이더라도 지문에 있는 근거 문장을 패러프레이징한 보기를 찾는 문제일 뿐이다. 추론 이상의 상상은 금물이다.

4. 문제를 먼저 읽고 키워드를 파악하자!

지문 유형 확인 ▶ 문제의 핵심어 확인 ▶ 지문 읽기 ▶ 문제 풀이

- 주제나 목적, 대상을 묻는 문제는 대개 지문의 첫머리에 단서가 제시되므로 도입부 내용을 잘 확인하여 이 내용을 포괄할 수 있는 선택지를 고른다.

- 세부 사항, 사실 확인 문제의 경우 핵심 단어 및 표현에 집중하여 질문에서 키워드를 파악하고 관련 내용이 언급된 부분을 지문에서 찾아 문제를 해결한다.

- 동의어 문제에서는 해당 단어의 대표적인 의미를 무작정 선택하는 것이 아니라 반드시 문맥상 어떤 의미로 쓰였는지 확인하여 정답을 찾는다.

UNIT 01 문자 대화문과 화자 의도

비즈니스 또는 일상생활에 관련된 정보를 주고받는 두 사람 사이의 문자 대화인 문자 메시지와 여러 사람 사이의 온라인 채팅이 각 한 지문씩 매회 2지문이 출제된다.

🔍 지문 유형 확인하기

1. 이런 지문 꼭 나온다

회사/비즈니스	· 회사 동료들 사이의 업무에 관한 내용 · 회의나 일정 변경에 관한 내용
고객 응대	· 고객과 고객을 응대하는 사람과의 문제 해결에 관한 내용
일상생활	· 행사 초대, 도움 요청 및 문의에 관한 내용

2. 이런 문제 꼭 나온다

▶ 대화를 하고 있는 사람들에 관한 세부 정보 문제

What is suggested about Ms. Stevens?/Where most likely is Suzanna?/At what kind of company do the writers most likely work?
스티븐스 씨에 대해 무엇이 암시되는가?/수잔나는 어디에 있겠는가?/필자는 어떤 종류의 회사에서 일하겠는가?
⋯▶ 인물들 간의 관계나 장소 등은 문자 대화의 시작 부분에 나오는 대화의 목적이나 주제를 통해 알 수 있다.

▶ 화자의 의도 파악 문제

At 9:40 A.M., what does Ms. Stevens mean when she writes, "Never mind"?
오전 9시 40분에, 스티븐스 씨가 "신경 쓰지 마세요"라고 쓴 것은 무슨 의미인가?
⋯▶ 문자 대화에서 특정 인물이 언급한 말의 의도를 묻는 문제는 지문에서 해당 표현을 찾아 앞뒤 문맥을 확인한다.

3. 독해 필살기

▶ 평소에 문자 메시지나 온라인 채팅 대화문에 익숙해져야 한다.

▶ 화자에 관한 세부 정보 문제, 예를 들어, 화자 간의 관계, 화자의 직업 혹은 직종에 관한 문제는 반드시 나온다.

▶ 화자의 의도 파악 문제는 바로 앞뒤 문장에 단서가 있으므로 잘 파악하도록 한다.

▶ 서로 한마디씩 문자나 채팅을 주고받는 형식이므로 특히 지문의 흐름을 따라가는 것이 중요하다. 간혹 화자 간의 관계를 혼동하여 오답을 선택하는 경우가 있으므로 주의한다.

Questions 1-2 refer to the following text message chain.

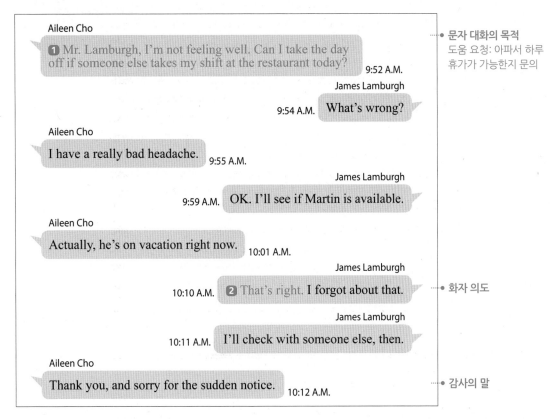

Aileen Cho

❶ Mr. Lamburgh, I'm not feeling well. Can I take the day off if someone else takes my shift at the restaurant today? 9:52 A.M.

James Lamburgh

9:54 A.M. What's wrong?

Aileen Cho

I have a really bad headache. 9:55 A.M.

James Lamburgh

9:59 A.M. OK. I'll see if Martin is available.

Aileen Cho

Actually, he's on vacation right now. 10:01 A.M.

James Lamburgh

10:10 A.M. ❷ That's right. I forgot about that.

James Lamburgh

10:11 A.M. I'll check with someone else, then.

Aileen Cho

Thank you, and sorry for the sudden notice. 10:12 A.M.

• 문자 대화의 목적
도움 요청: 아파서 하루
휴가가 가능한지 문의

• 화자 의도

• 감사의 말

1. What is suggested about Ms. Cho?

(A) She works under Mr. Lamburgh.
(B) She prefers night shifts.
(C) She is currently on vacation.
(D) She recently visited a hospital.

2. At 10:10 A.M., what does Mr. Lamburgh mean when he writes, "That's right"?

(A) He remembers that an employee is not available.
(B) He has spoken with his supervisor about an issue.
(C) He will confirm some information for Ms. Cho.
(D) He does not acknowledge that he made a mistake.

Questions 3-6 refer to the following online chat discussion.

Gwen Lynn [10:02 A.M.]:

Hello. ❸ Have you two looked over the cover designs for Kevin Brunswick's *Sleepless Bliss*?

Matt Halpert [10:03 A.M.]:

Out of the four, I think the first option is best because it's simple yet stylish. Options 2 and 3 are quite complicated while ❸ the last one is too similar to the cover of Mr. Brunswick's last novel.

Huey Park [10:03 A.M.]:

Yes. ❹ The first one does seem to stand out from the rest. In addition, the image on the front cover really suits the title.

Gwen Lynn [10:04 A.M.]:

❺ I'm glad we're all on the same page. I especially like how the artwork and the background colors really complement each other. Does anyone have any other comments or suggestions?

Huey Park [10:07 A.M.]:

I have one. Instead of having Mr. Brunswick's name appear right below the title, I think the text should be placed at the very bottom of the cover.

Matt Halpert [10:08 A.M.]:

Right. That way, the illustration can be seen more easily.

Gwen Lynn [10:09 A.M.]:

Mr. Brunswick was very specific about the placement of his name. However, I will bring it up with him during our meeting tomorrow. Anything else?

Matt Halpert [10:10 A.M.]:

Yes. Tom Patterson called while you were away from your desk earlier. ❻ He wanted to know if you made a decision about the candidates for the open position in our department.

Gwen Lynn [10:12 A.M.]:

Thank you for letting me know. I'll talk to Tom about it right now.

● **문자 대화의 목적**
용건 설명: 책 표지 디자인에 관한 의견 교환

● **화자 의도**

● **추가 정보**
신입 직원 선발을 결정했는지 문의

● **마무리 말**
담당자와 직접 처리하기로 함

3. What type of business does Ms. Lynn most likely work for?

(A) A publishing firm
(B) An interior design company
(C) An art gallery
(D) A clothing retailer

4. What is mentioned about the first design?

(A) It does not contain any text.
(B) It is complicated and attractive.
(C) It is more noticeable than the other designs.
(D) It needs more colors than it currently has.

5. At 10:04 A.M., what does Ms. Lynn mean when she writes, "I'm glad we're all on the same page"?

(A) She is pleased that a deadline has been met.
(B) She approves the proposal for a project.
(C) She is satisfied with recent sales figures.
(D) She agrees with the opinions of her coworkers.

6. What is suggested about Mr. Halpert's team?

(A) It is relocating to a new office.
(B) It is planning to hire a new employee.
(C) One of its members is retiring.
(D) All of its staff will receive training.

Questions 1-2 refer to the following text message chain.

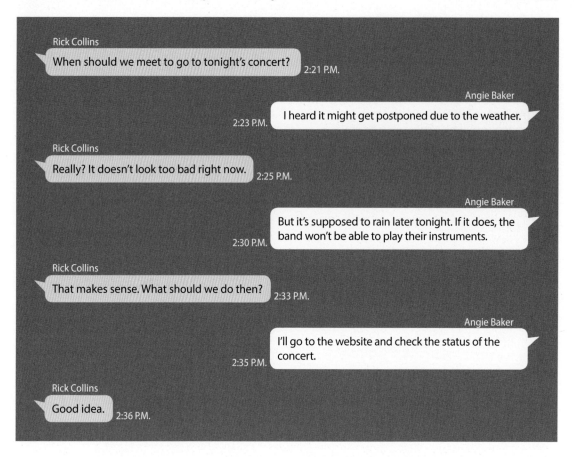

Rick Collins
When should we meet to go to tonight's concert?   2:21 P.M.

Angie Baker
2:23 P.M.   I heard it might get postponed due to the weather.

Rick Collins
Really? It doesn't look too bad right now.   2:25 P.M.

Angie Baker
2:30 P.M.   But it's supposed to rain later tonight. If it does, the band won't be able to play their instruments.

Rick Collins
That makes sense. What should we do then?   2:33 P.M.

Angie Baker
2:35 P.M.   I'll go to the website and check the status of the concert.

Rick Collins
Good idea.   2:36 P.M.

1. What is suggested about the concert?

(A) It will feature local artists.
(B) It will be held outdoors.
(C) It is free of charge.
(D) It is an annual event.

2. At 2:33 P.M., what does Mr. Collins mean when he writes, "That makes sense"?

(A) He sees why a show might be rescheduled.
(B) He knows why a website is not working.
(C) He understands why Ms. Baker will be late.
(D) He realizes why a concert is expensive.

Questions 3-5 refer to the following text message chain.

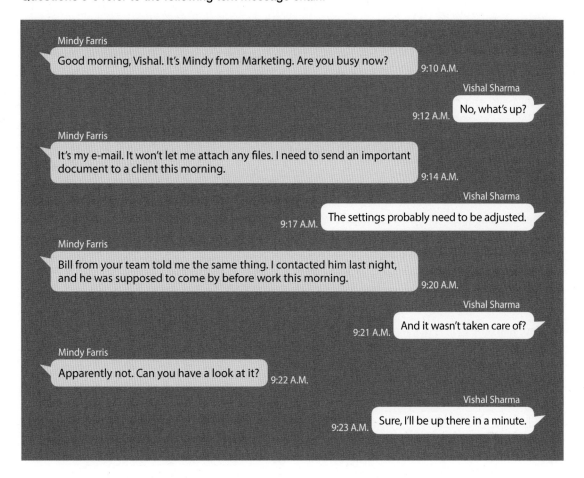

Mindy Farris
Good morning, Vishal. It's Mindy from Marketing. Are you busy now?
9:10 A.M.

Vishal Sharma
9:12 A.M.
No, what's up?

Mindy Farris
It's my e-mail. It won't let me attach any files. I need to send an important document to a client this morning.
9:14 A.M.

Vishal Sharma
9:17 A.M.
The settings probably need to be adjusted.

Mindy Farris
Bill from your team told me the same thing. I contacted him last night, and he was supposed to come by before work this morning.
9:20 A.M.

Vishal Sharma
9:21 A.M.
And it wasn't taken care of?

Mindy Farris
Apparently not. Can you have a look at it?
9:22 A.M.

Vishal Sharma
9:23 A.M.
Sure, I'll be up there in a minute.

3. What department does Mr. Sharma most likely work in?

(A) Accounting
(B) Marketing
(C) Human Resources
(D) Information Technology

4. What is suggested about Ms. Farris?

(A) She spoke to Mr. Sharma's team member yesterday.
(B) She has to leave for a business trip.
(C) She works in a different building from the one Mr. Sharma works in.
(D) She is unable to find an important document.

5. At 9:22 A.M., what does Ms. Farris mean when she writes, "Apparently not"?

(A) A client has not been contacted.
(B) A technical issue has not been resolved.
(C) A project has not been completed.
(D) A meeting room has not been reserved.

Questions 6-9 refer to the following online chat discussion.

Walters, David [9:20 A.M.]: Good morning. Samuel Tyson's last day at Vinex Marketing is next Thursday, so I would like to hear your suggestions on where to hold his farewell dinner. The accounting manager has told me that we're limited to $20 per person, so keep that in mind.

Chu, Martina [9:21 A.M.]: I went to Chaka's Indian Kitchen last week, and their food was amazing. I read that the head chef there, Shruti Shah, traveled throughout Mexico tasting and learning about local foods, and incorporating various ingredients into her curry dishes.

Walters, David [9:21 A.M.]: I'm not sure that's a good idea. Samuel can't handle spicy foods.

Chu, Martina [9:22 A.M.]: I forgot about that. Leslie, you sit right next to Samuel. Do you know where he likes to go for lunch?

Mingo, Leslie [9:24 A.M.]: He usually brings food from home. But I did notice that he frequently eats noodles. How about the new Chinese place across the street?

Chu, Martina [9:26 A.M.]: Do you mean Zao Chow Mein? I've heard good things about that place.

Walters, David [9:31 A.M.]: I'm reading testimonials on Zao's website, and a lot of them say how courteous and professional the servers are. In addition, their prices are quite affordable. If everyone is OK with this, I will go ahead and book a table at Zao for next Monday at 6:00 P.M.

Mingo, Leslie [9:32 A.M.]: Actually, I'll be out of the office that day for a business trip. But I'm free the next day.

Chu, Martina [9:32 A.M.]: Me, too.

Walters, David [9:33 A.M.]: OK, I'll make the reservation for that evening then. Please let me know if anything else comes up before then.

SEND

6. At 9:20 A.M., what does Mr. Walters mean when he writes, "keep that in mind"?

(A) He is reminding employees to attend a meeting.
(B) He would like ideas for meal options.
(C) He is reporting on the progress of a project.
(D) He wants staff members to be aware of the budget.

7. According to the discussion, what is true about Ms. Shah?

(A) She cannot eat spicy food.
(B) She was recently hired at Chaka's Indian Kitchen.
(C) She uses ingredients from a different country.
(D) She is a colleague of Ms. Chu.

8. What is suggested about Zao Chow Mein?

(A) It has increased its staff numbers.
(B) It posts reviews by customers online.
(C) Its ad campaigns were created by Vinex Marketing.
(D) Its menu items change regularly.

9. When will the dinner most likely be held?

(A) On Monday
(B) On Tuesday
(C) On Wednesday
(D) On Thursday

Questions 10-13 refer to the following online chat discussion.

David Kilday [3:24 P.M.] Teresa, have you already completed the VB34A model for the CEO? He wants you to customize it with an XPS-83.

Teresa Paul [3:26 P.M.] You mean that new microphone? It usually takes two days to order and install it.

David Kilday [3:27 P.M.] That will be too late. The CEO said he would like it before this Wednesday's product demonstration here at the factory.

Teresa Paul [3:28 P.M.] OK, I'll see if it can be done faster. I'll contact the production manager right now.

Teresa Paul [3:29 P.M.] Kevin, can your team obtain and install a new microphone (XPS-83) by tomorrow? It's going to be incorporated into the VB34A.

Kevin Sato [3:31 P.M.] I think so. Is it OK if it's done by tomorrow afternoon?

David Kilday [3:32 P.M.] Yes, that should be fine. I really appreciate it.

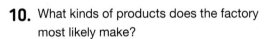

SEND

---

10. What kinds of products does the factory most likely make?

(A) Vehicles
(B) Ceramics
(C) Furniture
(D) Electronics

11. What does the CEO want to do?

(A) Move a presentation date
(B) Reduce an expense
(C) Call a vendor
(D) Modify a product

12. Why did Ms. Paul contact Mr. Sato?

(A) To announce a change to his vacation days
(B) To check the status of a shipment
(C) To see if a proposed deadline is acceptable
(D) To report on the results of a meeting

13. At 3:32 P.M., what does Mr. Kilday most likely mean when he writes, "that should be fine"?

(A) The CEO will be pleased if a task is done by tomorrow.
(B) He is happy with how a finished product looks.
(C) The production team will be okay with their new work shifts.
(D) He approves the purchase of some new equipment.

편지·이메일·문장 삽입

편지와 이메일은 비즈니스 또는 일상생활과 관련된 여러 정보를 주고받는 글로, 매회 3-5개 정도의 지문이 출제되며, 독해 전체 비중의 40%를 차지한다. 문장 삽입 문제는 지문 흐름상 주어진 문장의 적절한 위치를 고르는 문제이다. 지문당 1문제씩 총 2문제가 출제된다. 단순하게 세부정보를 찾기보다는 글의 흐름을 파악해서 적절한 위치를 골라야 하므로 전체적인 문맥 파악이 무엇보다 중요하다.

🔍 지문 유형 확인하기

1. 이런 지문 꼭 나온다

회의/행사 참석 요청	콘퍼런스 참석/행사 참여/연설을 요청하는 내용
할인 제공 안내	서비스의 이용이 뜸한 고객에게 보내는 할인 혜택 제공
항의·불평·불만	상품이나 서비스에 대한 항의·불평·불만 내용
배송 지연 사과	배송 지연에 따른 사과 내용
예약 일정	예약이나 일정을 취소 또는 확정하는 내용
구직자 합격, 불합격 통보	구직자의 합격 또는 불합격을 통보하는 내용
회원 가입 권유	회원 가입이나 회원 갱신을 권유하는 내용

2. 이런 문제 꼭 나온다

▶ 주제 파악 – What is the purpose of the e-mail? / Why was this letter written?
이메일의 목적을 무엇인가? / 편지는 왜 쓰여졌는가? ⋯ 특별한 몇몇 경우를 제외하고 주로 지문의 첫 도입부에 정답이 노출된다.

▶ 요청 사항 – What is Paul asked to do? 폴은 무엇을 하도록 요청받았는가?
⋯ 끝 문단에 명령문, if, should, must가 속한 문장에 정답이 노출된다.

▶ 첨부 사항 – What is enclosed with this letter? / What does Mr. Kim send with his e-mail?
이 편지에는 무엇이 동봉되어 있는가? / 김 씨는 이 이메일에 무엇을 함께 보내는가?
⋯ enclosed, attached, included, sent가 언급된 곳에서 정답이 노출된다.

▶ 문장 삽입 – In which of the positions marked [1], [2], [3], and [4] does the following sentence best belong? [1], [2], [3], [4]로 표시된 곳 중에서 다음 문장이 들어가기에 가장 적절한 곳은 어디인가?
⋯ 다른 문제들을 먼저 풀면서 전체적인 문맥을 파악한 후 마지막에 푼다.

3. 독해 필살기

▶ 발신자와 수신자 정보를 꼭 확인한다. 편지라면 주소를 확인하는 문제도 종종 출제된다.

▶ 본문을 읽기 전에 제목(Subject 혹은 Re로 적힌 부분)과 주제와 글을 쓴 목적이 언급된 앞부분을 꼼꼼히 읽는다.

▶ 첨부 사항이나 요청/당부/제안/부탁은 주로 글의 중반 이후에 나온다.

▶ 질문의 핵심적인 키워드를 기억하여 지문에서 상응하는 단어나 표현을 찾는다.

▶ 문장 삽입의 경우 주어진 질문을 먼저 읽고, 주어진 문장 안에서 핵심이 되는 키워드를 빨리 파악한다. 예컨대, 지시대명사(these, this, it 등)나 연결 어구(therefore, however, also 등)를 최대한 활용하여, 앞뒤 문장에 자연스럽게 이어질 수 있는지를 확인한다.

Questions 1-2 refer to the following e-mail.

From: <t.harrion@almometas.com>
To: <ptroung@transfreelance.com>
Subject: Your work
Date: September 20
Attachment: trans work

Dear Ms. Troung,

We received the translations of the technical instructions you did for us last week. – [1] –. Your work was excellent, and we hope to continue having you take care of our translation needs.

I am sending you this e-mail for a couple of reasons. – [2] –. ❷ First, I did not receive the original copies of the directions that I sent you. – [3] –. ❶ Also, I would like you to give me an estimate on the cost of translating the additional documents I have attached to this e-mail. – [4] –. Please send it to me as soon as possible.

Sincerely,

Timothy Harrison

• 발신인
• 수신인
• 제목
• 보내는 날짜
• 첨부

• 수신인

• 이메일의 목적
기술 번역을 계속해주길
요청

• 세부 정보:
원본 설명서 전달 요청,
번역 비용 견적서 요청

• 발신인

1. What did Mr. Harrison request from Ms. Troung?

(A) An e-mail address
(B) A marketing plan
(C) A price quote
(D) An updated résumé

2. In which of the positions marked [1], [2], [3], and [4] does the following sentence best belong?

"If you still have them, could you please return them to me?"

(A) [1]
(B) [2]
(C) [3]
(D) [4]

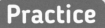
Questions 1-3 refer to the following letter.

Dustin Lingen
Top Show Enterprises
3484 Tolmie St.
Vancouver, BC V6B 6LB
February 29

Dear Mr. Lingen:

This letter is written in response to the request made on behalf of Elizabeth Atkins, the promotions manager of Top Show Enterprises. The request was for the use of official photos and logo for artist Frank Portugal who will be performing at the Sounds of the Valley Music Festival.

After much consideration, Mr. Portugal has decided to grant his permission. Go to xctalent.com/webbox, and enter the password SVMF229 to access the requested materials.

Please also be advised that any posters or flyers using Frank Portugal's photos or logo must be sent to our agency for review before it is made public. Enclosed you will find a document explaining the terms of use for the marketing material mentioned above.

Please contact me via e-mail at ziggya@xctalent.com for material approval or if you have any further questions.

Sincerely,

Ziggy Akinola

Ziggy Akinola, Talent Manager
XC Talent Agency

Enclosure

---

1. Why did Mr. Akinola write the letter?

(A) To obtain a password for a website
(B) To inquire about tickets to a music festival
(C) To request photos for advertisements
(D) To approve the use of graphics

2. Who most likely is Mr. Lingen?

(A) Ms. Atkins' assistant
(B) A music producer
(C) Mr. Portugal's band member
(D) A logo design artist

3. What must be sent to the XC Talent Agency?

(A) Audio samples
(B) A signed contract
(C) Promotional material
(D) Performance schedules

Questions 4-7 refer to the following e-mail.

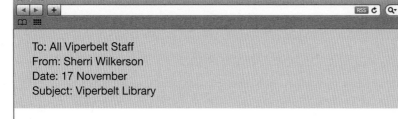

To: All Viperbelt Staff
From: Sherri Wilkerson
Date: 17 November
Subject: Viperbelt Library

Dear Colleagues,

As an employee of the Viperbelt Group, you have full access to the company library. In case you have not heard about the services being offered at the library, the library is more than just a place for our books and documents. — [1] —. Over the years, our employees have donated thousands of books from their own personal collections. On top of that, we have subscriptions to a wide range of magazines, and we even have licenses to some excellent self-learning programs. A popular one amongst employees is the music-learning program! Additionally, if you are looking for something the library currently does not have, you can put in a request. Simply state what you would like and when you would like it, and we can liaise with other libraries to locate you a copy. — [2] —.

Finally, something new we have been working on is a new app, which is now officially available. — [3] —. The app will allow you to download e-books and e-learning content onto your phone or tablet. This means you can access library materials anywhere, whether you're sitting on a bus or resting at home. Our recently expanded library team is always here to assist you with anything, so contact us by emailing library@viperbelt.co.uk. — [4] —.

Sherri Wilkerson
Director, Viperbelt Library

4. According to the e-mail, what is a service offered by the library?

(A) Membership at fellow libraries
(B) Conference rooms for meetings
(C) Access to self-learning programs
(D) Assistance for research-related tasks

5. Why does Ms. Wilkerson mention the library's app?

(A) To request donations for further development
(B) To announce the launching of a recent project
(C) To encourage employees to buy smartphones
(D) To justify the implementation of a membership fee

6. What does Ms. Wilkerson indicate about the library?

(A) It is closed every other weekend.
(B) It has recently hired more librarians.
(C) It will waive late fees for employees.
(D) It was recently renovated.

7. In which of the positions marked [1], [2], [3], and [4] does the following sentence best belong?

"It has been in development for two years."

(A) [1]
(B) [2]
(C) [3]
(D) [4]

Questions 8-11 refer to the following e-mail.

From	nmcclintock@mcinno.net
To	<All Staff>
Subject	Greetings
Date	September 12

McClintock InnoNet is excited to have such a dedicated group of staff members join our growing firm. Over the coming week, we hope you will carefully look over and become familiar with the requirements and amenities of our office building listed below.

Please note that all computers have security stickers on the CD tray. Any computer-related issues are handled by our Technical Department, so if you need to use the CD drive, please contact them directly. They can be reached at extension 334.

The security office requires all building employees to use their digital ID cards when inside the building. This card will let you through the lobby gates to the building's main elevators. Additional security locks are located throughout the building, so please carry your identification with you wherever you go.

The company's lounge room is located on the fourth floor and is open during business hours. There, you will find comfortable resting areas and a small café. All purchases made in the lounge should be made with your ID card, which is just like a credit card, except it only works in this building.

There is a recreation center on the ninth floor available for all employees at no charge, which is open from 5:30 A.M. to 11 P.M. Monday through Friday.

Lastly, the basement parking garage is accessible only from the public elevator in the lobby, just outside the security gates.

Sincerely,

Nathan McClintock
COO, McClintock InnoNet

---

8. What is the purpose of the e-mail?

(A) To describe a software installation procedure
(B) To give information to newly recruited employees
(C) To announce an increase in parking fees
(D) To request that managers send an office supply form

9. The word "growing" in paragraph 1, line 1, is closest in meaning to

(A) producing
(B) spreading
(C) expanding
(D) gaining

10. Where can staff purchase refreshments?

(A) In the basement
(B) In the lobby
(C) On the fourth floor
(D) On the ninth floor

11. According to the e-mail, what is provided for free?

(A) A meal
(B) Gym membership
(C) A parking permit
(D) Personal laptops

Questions 12-14 refer to the following letter.

July 21

Shannon Bryce
3475 E. Laurel Road
North Saint Marys
NSW 2760
Australia

Dear Ms. Bryce,

This letter is to inform you of your successful enrollment into the Sydney Institute of Aero Technology (SIAT). — [1] —. Your initial payment of $495 has been processed and covers your first three-month class period, course materials, and test session. When you log in to your online account, you will see your available courses. — [2] —. Theory, design, and application methods will be part of each course component.

Please note that your enrollment package does not include a meal plan. If you are interested in signing up for one, just let me know. — [3] —.

We have enclosed an agreement detailing class policies and a form for any other supplies you may need. We would appreciate it if you could sign and return the agreement at least a week before the first day of classes. — [4] —.

We welcome you to the first step of a fulfilling career.

Sincerely,

Anna Cornwall

Anna Cornwall
Manager, SIAT Student Services

ENCLOSURES

12. Why did Ms. Cornwall write the letter?

(A) To advertise a new course
(B) To ask for a transcript
(C) To confirm a payment
(D) To announce a fee increase

13. What is Ms. Bryce asked to submit in advance?

(A) A request form
(B) An invoice
(C) An internship application
(D) A contract

14. In which of the positions marked [1], [2], [3], and [4] does the following sentence best belong?

"For a complete pricing list, visit our cafeteria's website."

(A) [1]
(B) [2]
(C) [3]
(D) [4]

Questions 15-19 refer to the following Web page and e-mail.

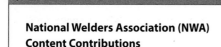

www.nationalweldersasso.org/content

National Welders Association (NWA)
Content Contributions

In the last few e-mail newsletters, we asked members to give feedback and suggestions for how to improve the *Monthly Welder*. We were quite impressed by your excellent ideas, and we will be adding one of them to our very next newsletter. Starting next month, the newsletter will have a new page called Real Welders. This section will feature videos, pictures, and other member-created material. The board members and senior decision-makers all agree that this will be an excellent way for members to feel more connected to the NWA and fellow members.

Many of you already have videos and pictures that you have taken at welding conferences, NWA division meetings, or other related events. We especially encourage those from our more remote divisions – like Division 429 in Alaska – to submit content, so we can learn more about what you do.

You can check out some sample videos by following this link. If you have something you would like to share, send it in an e-mail with a brief description to Jack Decker at jackd54@natwelder.com. Those received by October 15 may be included in the next newsletter.

To wrap up, this will only be the first of many improvements we plan to make to the *Monthly Welder*. Revisit this website in a few weeks' time when we unveil the new layout and several new language options in our November issue!

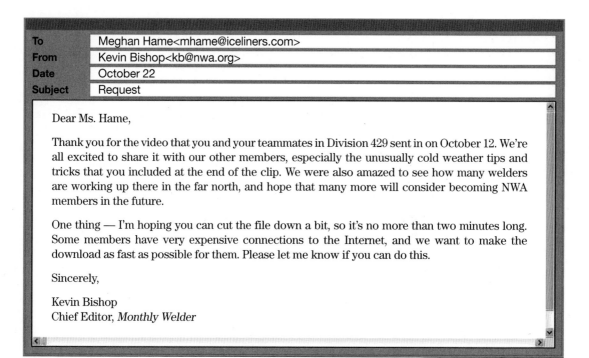

To	Meghan Hame<mhame@iceliners.com>
From	Kevin Bishop<kb@nwa.org>
Date	October 22
Subject	Request

Dear Ms. Hame,

Thank you for the video that you and your teammates in Division 429 sent in on October 12. We're all excited to share it with our other members, especially the unusually cold weather tips and tricks that you included at the end of the clip. We were also amazed to see how many welders are working up there in the far north, and hope that many more will consider becoming NWA members in the future.

One thing — I'm hoping you can cut the file down a bit, so it's no more than two minutes long. Some members have very expensive connections to the Internet, and we want to make the download as fast as possible for them. Please let me know if you can do this.

Sincerely,

Kevin Bishop
Chief Editor, *Monthly Welder*

15. For whom is the Web page information most likely intended?

(A) Magazine editors
(B) Students from welding schools
(C) NWA members
(D) Website designers

16. According to the Web page, what is true about the newsletter?

(A) Several of its sections will be changed.
(B) It will be published in different languages.
(C) It focuses on various regions of Alaska.
(D) A hard copy version is available.

17. On the Web page, the word "remote" in paragraph 2, line 2, is closest in meaning to

(A) far
(B) unrelated
(C) inaccessible
(D) slight

18. What is suggested about Ms. Hame's submission?

(A) It contains revised guidelines for NWA members.
(B) It will be included in the newsletter's next issue.
(C) It was received by Mr. Bishop on October 15.
(D) It is not compatible with a computer system.

19. What is Ms. Hame asked to do?

(A) Offer additional tips
(B) Edit her content
(C) Refer *Monthly Welder* to her friends
(D) Update her contact information

Grierton (Nov 18) – The Grierton Town Council has started discussing what to do about Autumn Lane, an old walking street that requires significant improvements. The biggest dilemma is that the repair work may endanger several historical landmarks.

"Bringing the street's buildings up to modern standards will cause some short-term economic stress," said urban planner Kylie Kim. "We've decided that tearing down several buildings would be cheaper than restoring them."

In addition to cost factors, there are concerns that some of the older buildings pose health risks. "New food and safety regulations for restaurants will go into effect at the end of the year," explains Brian Gould, a city inspector. "Many structures on Autumn Lane won't be able to comply fully with stricter standards. Thus, I think constructing new buildings in their places is the best option."

Locals who would like to learn more or express their thoughts are invited to attend a community forum at Grierton Town Hall next Saturday at 4 P.M.

November 19

Dear Editor:

This letter is in regard to the article published yesterday about the construction on Autumn Lane. The older buildings on this street are important Grierton sites and should not be torn down. Many local businesses also benefit from these historic locations as they draw quite a few tourists to the area. Therefore, the destruction of these landmarks would cause significant economic damage.

Sincerely,

Wes Smith
Vice Chairman, Grierton Preservation Alliance (GPA)

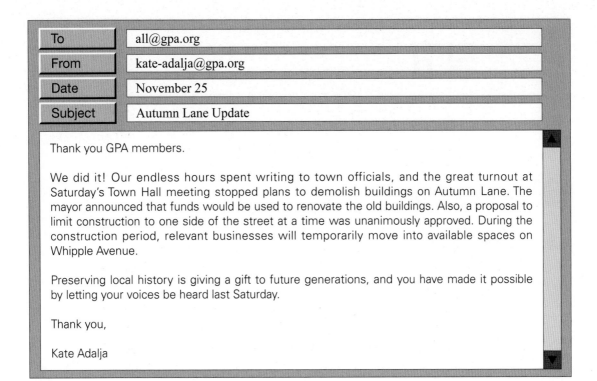

To	all@gpa.org
From	kate-adalja@gpa.org
Date	November 25
Subject	Autumn Lane Update

Thank you GPA members.

We did it! Our endless hours spent writing to town officials, and the great turnout at Saturday's Town Hall meeting stopped plans to demolish buildings on Autumn Lane. The mayor announced that funds would be used to renovate the old buildings. Also, a proposal to limit construction to one side of the street at a time was unanimously approved. During the construction period, relevant businesses will temporarily move into available spaces on Whipple Avenue.

Preserving local history is giving a gift to future generations, and you have made it possible by letting your voices be heard last Saturday.

Thank you,

Kate Adalja

20. According to the article, what is mentioned about Grierton?

(A) It will begin giving guided bus tours.
(B) It will revise some local laws.
(C) It is going to lower the rent on some buildings.
(D) It is fining companies for safety violations.

21. What is NOT suggested about Mr. Smith?

(A) He read a newspaper article on November 18.
(B) He does not agree with Ms. Kim.
(C) He thinks certain buildings boost the city's economy.
(D) He is a colleague of Mr. Gould.

22. In the e-mail, the word "endless" in paragraph 1, line 1, is closest in meaning to

(A) limited
(B) many
(C) final
(D) completed

23. Why does Ms. Adalja thank GPA members?

(A) They helped determine a town's decision.
(B) They were mentioned in a news report.
(C) They earned an award at a recent event.
(D) They raised money for upcoming projects.

24. What is stated about GPA members?

(A) Some of them went to Grierton Town Hall.
(B) They have a meeting every Saturday.
(C) Some of them own businesses on Autumn Lane.
(D) They assisted with some renovation work.

광고

광고는 이메일과 편지 유형 다음으로 가장 많이 출제되고 있으며, 구인 광고와 일반 상업 광고로 나뉜다.

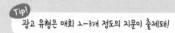

광고 유형은 매회 2-3개 정도의 지문이 출제돼!

🔍 지문 유형 확인하기

1. 이런 지문 꼭 나온다

구인 광고	· 경력직: 특정 업계의 근무 경력이 있는 경력직 구인 광고 · 신규 회원 모집: 헬스클럽이나 기타 여가 활동에서 신규 회원 모집
일반 광고 (제품, 서비스 업체 광고)	· 숙박 시설 광고: 호텔이나 리조트 이용에 관한 광고 · 제품 광고나 온라인 서비스 광고
할인 광고	· 회원 혜택, 점포 이전, 재고 정리 할인, 기념일 할인 광고

2. 이런 문제 꼭 나온다

☑ 구인 광고

▶ 주제 파악 – **What position is being advertised?** 어떤 자리가 광고되고 있는가?
⋯▸ 주로 지문의 앞부분에서 정답을 찾을 수 있다.

▶ 자격 조건 – **What is a requirement for the position?** 그 자리에 대한 한 가지 자격요건은 무엇인가?
⋯▸ 2~3번째 단락에서 정답을 찾을 수 있다.

▶ 지원 방법 – **How should the candidate apply for the job?** 지원자들은 그 자리에 어떻게 지원해야 하는가?
⋯▸ 제일 마지막 단락에서 정답을 찾을 수 있다.

☑ 일반 상업 광고

▶ 주제 파악 – **What is being advertised?** 무엇이 광고되고 있는가? ⋯▸ 주로 지문의 앞부분에서 정답을 찾을 수 있다.

▶ 대상 파악 – **For whom is this advertisement intended?** 이 광고는 누구를 대상으로 하고 있는가?
⋯▸ 주로 지문의 앞부분에서 정답을 찾을 수 있다.

▶ 제품 특징 – **What is NOT a feature of the product?** 제품의 특징이 아닌 것은 무엇인가?
⋯▸ detail, feature 등이 나오거나 비교 구문이 언급된 곳에서 주로 정답을 찾을 수 있다.

3. 독해 필살기

▶ 구인 광고는 제목에서 구인자의 직책이 언급되며, 지원자의 담당 업무와 지원 자격을 꼭 확인해야 한다.

▶ 일반 상업 광고는 광고 제품을 확인하고, 제품의 특징, 할인 혜택, 구매 방법 등을 확인해야 한다.

▶ 일반 상업 광고의 혜택, 장점, 특징은 주로 NOT/TRUE 문제가 많이 출제되기 때문에 해당 키워드를 찾아서 지문 내용을 파악해야 한다.

Questions 1-2 refer to the following advertisement.

Cowboy Jim's

Cowboy Jim's, the country's leading steak restaurant, is hiring servers for all of our locations. ❶ Join our team and work at a company that knows how to treat its employees. We offer numerous benefits and a pleasant working environment. With over 200 locations nationwide, we have plenty of positions available.

Requirements:
* Minimum two years of experience as a server
* Knowledge of the restaurant industry
* ❷ Good interpersonal skills and a positive attitude

If you are interested in joining our team, send your résumé to humanresources@cowboyjims.com or fax it to 303-555-6228.

• 회사 이름

• 회사 소개 및 구인 직책 소개
웨이터 모집

• 자격 요건
필요한 경력, 지식, 기술 및 태도

• 지원 방법 및 연락처
이메일 또는 팩스

1. What does the advertisement suggest about Cowboy Jim's?

(A) It has happy workers.
(B) It is looking for new chefs.
(C) It was established two years ago.
(D) It operates in other countries.

2. What is a stated requirement for the job?

(A) A good knowledge of the company's history
(B) Ability to work well with others
(C) A willingness to travel overseas
(D) Several years of management experience

PART 7 UNIT 03

Practice

Practice

Practice

해설서 p.105 / 제한 시간 20분

Questions 1-2 refer to the following advertisement.

Posted: SG Rocktrail 8 Mountain Bike
Asking: $1,300
Location: Metro Atlanta

Item Description:
- Purchased almost new from reseller a year ago. Bought for $1900.
- Came with a six-month manufacturer warranty.
- Buyer is responsible for replacing cracked handlebars.
- Has moderate wear and tear. (No pictures at this time.)

$1,300 or the best offer.

Will deliver within the metro area.

Contact: First come, first serve (404) 555-2794

1. What is NOT indicated about the bicycle?
(A) It has a broken part.
(B) Its price is flexible.
(C) It includes an extended warranty.
(D) It has belonged to several owners.

2. What is the seller willing to do?
(A) Provide photographs of the item
(B) Travel within the city
(C) Contact a manufacturer
(D) Reserve the item for a buyer

244   파고다 토익 고득점 완성 RC

Questions 3-4 refer to the following advertisement.

The GC Corp facility in Aspen is looking for an experienced in-house technical writer who will create manuals for the devices we develop for hospitals.

Applicants must have previously worked in some hospital or clinical setting.

Candidates should be able to communicate and coordinate with project managers and engineers smoothly.

Individuals who have an extensive portfolio of writing projects will get preferential consideration.

All applicants should have a bachelor's degree in English, journalism, or communications. In addition, they should have at least three years of technical writing experience.

3. What is stated about GC Corp?

(A) It recently expanded to Aspen.
(B) It produces specialized equipment.
(C) It is a well-regarded company.
(D) It is looking for a freelance worker.

4. What is NOT mentioned as a qualification for the writer position?

(A) Proficiency in two languages
(B) Experience in a medical environment
(C) The ability to collaborate with others
(D) Having a collection of work samples

Questions 5-7 refer to the following advertisement.

Watford Business Online   17 November

Attractive 200-square-meter storefront for rent on the ground floor in the 7-story Bakewell Building in Watford's business district. Available 20 November, €1750/month.

- Recently installed plumbing
- Car parking and loading area behind the building
- Public restroom in the lobby
- Back office with built-in wall safe
- Surveillance cameras are monitored 24/7
- Maintenance service expenses split between companies on floors 1 to 3
- Utilities not included
- Permission required before remodeling

Proof of property insurance is required at the time of contract signing.

Contact property manager John Admunson at 020 7946 0457.

5. What is mentioned about the Bakewell Building?

(A) It is located in a new commercial area.
(B) It has parking beneath the ground floor.
(C) Some of its tenants share maintenance fees.
(D) Some of its residents are moving out this month.

6. What is included in the monthly rent?

(A) Wireless internet
(B) Utility costs
(C) Housekeeping services
(D) Security systems

7. According to the advertisement, what are renters required to do?

(A) Agree to a long-term lease
(B) Meet with an insurance specialist
(C) Attend a safety course
(D) Provide some documents

Enjoy Art While Taking a Stroll!

The Cheyenne Arts Organization (CAO), established in 1981, is a commission that seeks to actively promote artists and galleries to interested collectors. Every weekend evening this month, guests are welcome to take a guided walk through the galleries and studios along Lupine Ave. All participating venues are part of the Cheyenne Arts Collective, which publishes the famous *Studio Guide* twice a year.

During the art walk, you can:

- Experience Cheyenne's art culture
- Buy recent pieces by renowned local artists at special, discounted prices
- Meet some of the artists and enjoy live music at a CAO-sponsored gathering at Café Boa starting at 7 P.M.

While the art walk is free, studios may request a small guest donation to go towards monthly expenses. The walk begins at 5 P.M. and lasts until 7 P.M. There is a limit of 15 participants per event. Note that while the pace of the walk is relaxed, there won't be many opportunities to sit down.

To find out more about the galleries, including what exclusive items are available for purchase, visit www.cheyennearts.org.

PART 7 UNIT 03

8. What is being advertised?

(A) A chance to buy artwork
(B) A famous painter
(C) A subscription to a magazine
(D) A university class

9. What will participants be expected to do?

(A) Arrive 15 minutes early
(B) Stand most of the time
(C) Complete a survey
(D) Submit a portfolio

10. What is mentioned about the CAO?

(A) It displays merchandise online.
(B) It trains museum guides.
(C) It organizes concerts every month.
(D) It has locations in different towns.

http://www.topadproductions.com

Top Ad Productions

Expand Your Customer Base by Creating a TV Advertisement for Your Business

At **Top Ad Productions**, we create cost-effective TV commercials that will help you reach new customers. We specialize in producing high-quality, customized ads in just a few weeks.

Our Services:

❦ **Customized identity** – Our graphic designers can create eye-catching logos for your business that will appear in the commercial.

🎞 **Professional actors** – We coordinate with various talent agencies to find skilled performers that represent your target audience and company image. Check our sample clips at www.topadproductions.com to see which actor would be the best for your ad.

🎬 **Original scripts** – Our talented writers can create an imaginative script that is customized to your business and the message you want to convey to customers.

♫ **Music production** – We work with professional producers to create background music to match the tone of your message.

Email info@topadproductions.com with your telephone number and a brief description of what you need. An agent will call you back the following day to learn more about the advertisement you would like to create and give you details about the production process.

To	info@topadproductions.com
From	dstapleton@stapletonlegal.com
Date	October 10
Subject	Inquiry

I saw your post in the *Stockton Herald*, and I would like to use your service to attract clientele to my law firm. I am looking to have an ad with a serious tone with professional music and logos. As for the concept, I would like your help in writing a script that would make potential clients feel like they can trust my firm. Please get in touch with me on my cell phone anytime between 8:00 A.M. and 6:00 P.M. I look forward to hearing from you.

Regards,

David Stapleton
Stapleton Legal
704-555-1265 (cell)
2484 Concord Street
Matthews, NC 28105

11. According to the advertisement, why are customers encouraged to visit the company website?

(A) To review customer feedback
(B) To make a reservation
(C) To get directions
(D) To watch some videos

12. What is suggested about Top Ad Productions?

(A) It offers legal advice.
(B) It is only open during the weekdays.
(C) It places advertisements in the newspaper.
(D) It recently won an award.

13. What is most likely true about Mr. Stapleton?

(A) He owns a business.
(B) He is an actor.
(C) He makes logos.
(D) He produces films.

14. What service does Mr. Stapleton NOT request from Top Ad Productions?

(A) Customized identity
(B) Professional actors
(C) Original scripts
(D) Music production

15. What will Mr. Stapleton most likely do on October 11?

(A) Film a commercial
(B) Design a graphic
(C) Talk to an agent
(D) Listen to some music

Questions 16-20 refer to the following advertisement, e-mail, and text message.

City Park Theater
1029 Elliott Ave, Calderdale
www.lloydfosterproductions.co.uk

Spend your summer nights in faraway places without ever leaving town! Come see productions of famous works, from the 18th century to the Modern Era, at the outdoor City Park Stage. Tickets are available at the City Park box office, or over the phone at 1-800-555-8649. Patrons with a membership to the theater may purchase additional tickets up to the day before a performance for 25 percent off.

- *Candid Dreamer*: Fall in love with this classic from June 1-24
- *Fisherman's Journey*: Enjoy the dramatic plot twists from June 27-July 25
- *Life of a Businessman*: Mark Brown's classic for one weekend only on July 26-27
- *Fields of Wheat*: Wrap up the season with showings from July 28-August 25

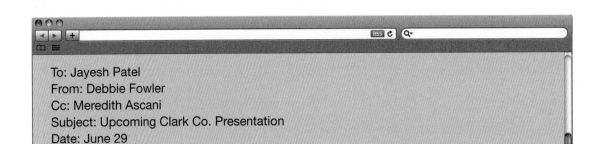

To: Jayesh Patel
From: Debbie Fowler
Cc: Meredith Ascani
Subject: Upcoming Clark Co. Presentation
Date: June 29

This e-mail is to confirm that your demonstrations of the new prototype have been finalized for July 25 and 26. The R&D conference room has been reserved for corporate security reasons. It is equipped with a laptop, printer, and video equipment. If you need anything else, inform me as soon as possible.

Marketing Vice President Meredith Ascani will attend both presentations to help conduct the Q&A session afterward. After your first day's session, she would like to take you out to eat with some of the other department heads and then to an outdoor theater show.

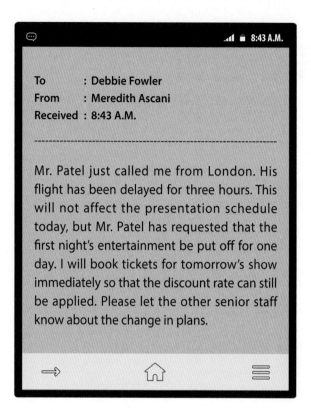

16. What is suggested about the City Park Theater?

(A) It has recently expanded its facilities.
(B) It features plays from various historical periods.
(C) It is recruiting new actors for the upcoming season.
(D) It is currently located in London.

17. What will Mr. Patel do during his trip?

(A) Explain how a product works
(B) Install some security software
(C) Discuss the history of Clark Co.
(D) Fix some video equipment

18. Which production was Mr. Patel originally scheduled to see?

(A) *Candid Dreamer*
(B) *Fisherman's Journey*
(C) *Life of a Businessman*
(D) *Fields of Wheat*

19. What will Ms. Fowler most likely do next?

(A) Change a dining reservation
(B) Contact some colleagues
(C) Review some presentations
(D) Book a new flight

20. Why most likely is Ms. Ascani planning to buy new tickets right away?

(A) She is unsure if Mr. Patel will enjoy the show.
(B) A performance has been suddenly canceled.
(C) She is a City Park Theater member.
(D) Mr. Patel will be arriving one day later.

UNIT 04 공지·회람

공지는 규정 변경이나 시행 방침 또는 행사에 관한 내용을 전달하기 위한 글이고, 회람은 회사 내에서 일정 변경이나 공지 사항을 알리는 글이다.

Tip!
공지·회람 유형은 매회 2개 정도의 지문이 출제되고 있어!

🔍 지문 유형 확인하기

1. 이런 지문 꼭 나온다

사내 공지	· 사용법: 기구/장비의 올바른 사용법 · 복장 규정, 주차장 공사, 회사 내 정책 변화 · 인사 발령 공지, 사내 세미나 교육 공지
관광 및 여행 시설 이용 안내 공지	· 호텔이나 숙박 시설 이용 안내 · 관광 및 여행에 관한 공지 · 안전 수칙이나 공공시설 이용 안내 공지
기타 공지	· 대회 및 콘테스트 공지 · 승객 대상 공지: 버스, 열차, 항공기 승객에 관한 공지 · 설문 조사 공지: 제품이나 서비스 구매 후 설문 조사 부탁 공지

2. 이런 문제 꼭 나온다

▶ 주제 파악 – What is the purpose of this notice? 이 공지의 목적은 무엇인가?
⋯→ 주로 지문의 앞부분에서 정답을 찾을 수 있다.

▶ 대상 파악 – Who is Maxwell Brenda?/For whom is this memo intended?
맥스웰 브렌다는 누구인가?/이 공지는 누구를 대상으로 하는가? ⋯→ 지문 앞부분에서 정답을 찾을 수 있다.

▶ 공지 출처 – Where would the notice most likely appear? 이 공지는 어디에 나와 있겠는가?
⋯→ 지문 앞부분에서 정답을 찾을 수 있다.

▶ 세부사항 – What will happen on April 5?/What will be announced next?
4월 5일에 무슨 일이 일어나겠는가?/다음에 무엇이 공지되겠는가?
⋯→ 날짜, 기간, 미래 시제가 언급된 문장 혹은 지문의 끝부분에서 정답을 찾을 수 있다.

▶ 사실 파악 – What is stated about the facility? 그 시설에 관하여 무엇이 언급되었는가?
⋯→ 질문의 키워드를 기억하여 정답을 찾을 수 있다.

3. 독해 필살기

▶ 공지와 회람의 기본 구성은 '글의 목적/주제 – 세부사항 – 요청/제안 사항'으로 이루어진다.

▶ 공지와 회람의 주제 찾기 문제는 반드시 출제되므로 제목이나 지문 앞부분을 절대로 놓치지 말자.

▶ 특히 고유명사와 특정 요일의 날짜는 잘 체크해 두고 답을 찾는다.

▶ 시간, 장소, 요청/제안 사항은 지문 중반 이후에서 답을 찾는다.

Questions 1-2 refer to the following memo.

Tivoli Community Center
To: George Connell
From: Don Martin
Date: August 30
Re: Budget Approval

I believe that our meeting on Thursday was quite productive. ❶ Of all the ideas we discussed for reducing the budget, I think our plan to close the facilities one day per week would be the most effective. I estimate that we will save over $1,000 per day, ❷ and I'm confident that President Jones will approve this idea at our next meeting on Monday. See you there!

Don Martin
General Manager

● 발신 기관
● 수신인
● 발신인
● 날짜
● 주제/제목

● 구체적인 내용

● 발신인
● 직책

1. What is mentioned in the memo?

(A) A budget must be increased.
(B) The community center wants to cut costs.
(C) Mr. Connell's presentation was successful.
(D) Mr. Martin will prepare a report.

2. What will happen on Monday?

(A) An executive will attend a meeting.
(B) Construction work will begin.
(C) A facility tour will be provided.
(D) A speech will be given.

해설서 p.109 / ⏱ 제한 시간 22분

Questions 1-2 refer to the following notice.

Dear Green Table Diners,

Management offers guests its apologies for not offering any hot dishes today. We are upgrading our ovens and stoves this weekend and will resume normal operations on Monday. The new setup will allow us to create an even greater variety of choices for your taste buds.

Please be assured that this will not reduce the number or quality of today's menu items. If we may do anything to make your experience better, please do not hesitate to let one of our employees know.

---

1. Where would the notice most likely appear?

   (A) In the back of a warehouse
   (B) In the back of a supermarket
   (C) At the front of a department store
   (D) At the front of a restaurant

2. What is being changed?

   (A) Some equipment
   (B) A guest list
   (C) A computer network
   (D) Some table arrangements

Questions 3-5 refer to the following memo.

NOTICE

Date: September 4

The Blast Pop vending machines in every break room in the office building will be removed this weekend. The company has decided not to renew the vendor's contract. Blast Pop's 5-year deal was signed when the company had only 10 employees. As the company has grown, management's vision and commitment to our employees' health have changed. So, two months ago, Hannah Collins was given the task of finding a more suitable vendor since she is responsible for all corporate financial transactions. After much research, Ms. Collins found the perfect supplier.

Today, we are pleased to announce an exclusive contract with Nutrilicious, who will install their new machines next Monday. The vending machines provide a variety of fresh fruits, low-fat dairy products, and healthy juices, which are all under $1. Also, Nutrilicious will give each employee a complimentary package of assorted nuts, as a sign of appreciation. If you have any questions about the change, please contact Ms. Collins.

3. In what department does Ms. Collins most likely work?

(A) Marketing
(B) Research
(C) Accounting
(D) Maintenance

4. For how many years did the company use Blast Pop vending machines?

(A) 1
(B) 4
(C) 5
(D) 10

5. What will NOT be included in the new vending machines?

(A) Fruits
(B) Juice
(C) Nuts
(D) Milk

Questions 6-8 refer to the following memo.

Jovian Furniture Carobville Store Preview Party
Jovian Furniture is inviting all employees to get a preview of its newest branch in the Carobville Mall. Although the originally scheduled celebration was postponed because of inclement weather, we are finally ready to welcome everyone. The event will now be on December 5 from 5 to 8 P.M., and it will have food catered by Ling's Diner.

How to get to the Carobville Mall from Headquarters
Go north on Wright Avenue and make your first right onto Main Street. At the intersection of Main and Fifth, turn right and keep going south until you reach Palm Drive. The shopping center is on the northeast corner. The store is on the third floor, next to the escalators.

Parking at Carobville Mall
All staff attending the event will not have to pay for parking that day as long as they show their Jovian employee badge. Just make sure to park in Lot A. For those taking public transportation, talk to Margaret in HR.

---

6. What was changed about the event?

(A) The guest number
(B) The date
(C) The location
(D) The food options

7. Where is the headquarters located?

(A) On Wright Avenue
(B) On Main Street
(C) On Fifth Street
(D) On Palm Drive

8. What is suggested about the Carobville Mall?

(A) It is near public transportation.
(B) It normally charges for parking.
(C) It is across the street from Ling's Diner.
(D) It closes at 8 P.M.

Spring Fun!

Celebrate spring in Mt. Vernon with these great events:

Mt. Vernon World Music Festival (April 20)
Go on a musical exploration with performers from Africa, Asia, South America, and Europe at the Mt. Vernon Cultural Center.

Mt. Vernon Theater Performances (April 21)
See plays such as *Easy Street*, *Maker's House*, and *Tea with Betty*. Performed by the Mt. Vernon Theater Group at the Mt. Vernon Cultural Center.

Mt. Vernon Book Fair (April 27)
Book readings and discussions showcasing the work of over 30 American writers. At various libraries and bookstores in the Mt. Vernon area.

Mt. Vernon Art Competition (April 28)
Local artists compete for the prestigious Baker Award. The competition will be judged by professors from Virginia University's Art Department at the Mt. Vernon Museum of Modern Art.

Mt. Vernon Community Center Grand Opening (May 4)
The much-anticipated community center opens at last. Come and enjoy a free lunch catered by Smith's Barbecue, and listen to the music of Stan Crocker and Little Cat at the Mt. Vernon Community Center.

For more details about the events, visit www.mtvernon.org/springevents.

9. What is suggested about all of the events?

(A) They are not open to the public.
(B) They might be delayed until the summer.
(C) They will take place in the Mt. Vernon area.
(D) They will not be rescheduled in case of rain.

10. What is NOT listed among the events?

(A) An art contest
(B) A free lunch
(C) A singing competition
(D) A theater show

11. Which event will take place at multiple venues?

(A) The Mt. Vernon World Music Festival
(B) The Mt. Vernon Theater Performances
(C) The Mt. Vernon Book Fair
(D) The Mt. Vernon Art Competition

12. What is indicated about Mr. Crocker?

(A) He will judge a competition.
(B) He is a local chef.
(C) He has organized the events.
(D) He will play at a new venue.

Questions 13-17 refer to the following memo and form.

From: Brian Barber, Human Resources Manager
To: All HR Staff
Date: January 2
Subject: Inventory Form
Attachment: officeinvent_list.doc

Please be advised that the yearly office inventory form must be submitted within the month. Every year, the Finance Department conducts an audit of the equipment used in the corporate office. The information gathered will help us determine our purchase budget for this year.

Attached you will find a form that is to be used to list any equipment, such as scanners and laptops, used by your department. Please indicate to the best of your knowledge how old the equipment is as well as its current condition. Photocopiers and printers that are over four years old will be replaced. Should this form be misplaced, please contact Mika Sato (msato@dmsat.com) to get another one.

As the lists must be finalized before the January 31 budget meeting, staff are asked to email the list by January 19 to Ryan Delap at ryandelap@dmsat.com. Please also be sure to coordinate with your other team members to ensure each item is only listed once on the form. Thank you in advance for your time and help with this matter.

Requestor's Name: _Daniela Morales_
Requestor's Department: _Sales_
Requestor's Manager: _Ronald Hamilton_
Building/Floor: _C/19th_
Submission date: _January 16_

Item	Model	Status			Years old
Scanner	CT3400	(Good)	OK	Bad	3
Photocopier	XZR650	Good	(OK)	Bad	5
Printer	HG8000	Good	(OK)	Bad	3
		Good	OK	Bad	
		Good	OK	Bad	

13. Why are the staff asked to fill out the form?

(A) To confirm which equipment should be repaired
(B) To arrange a date for an office inspection
(C) To report the condition of an office to supervisors
(D) To decide what equipment needs to be replaced

14. In the memo, the word "conducts" in paragraph 1, line 2, is closest in meaning to

(A) completes
(B) instructs
(C) guides
(D) drives

15. Who should employees contact to obtain additional forms?

(A) Mika Sato
(B) Ronald Hamilton
(C) Ryan Delap
(D) Brian Barber

16. When are staff asked to submit the form?

(A) By January 2
(B) By January 16
(C) By January 19
(D) By January 31

17. What can be inferred about Ms. Morales?

(A) She will receive a new photocopier.
(B) She purchased a new scanner last month.
(C) She was recently transferred to the sales team.
(D) She is Mr. Delap's manager.

PART 7 UNIT 04

Questions 18-22 refer to the following notice, instructions, and e-mail.

Help Wanted for Taste Testing

Unifique PR needs adults aged 19 to 55 for a special taste-testing event in the ballroom of Q Hotel in downtown Fort Wayne this Saturday. Participants will try a variety of proposed additions to Sunshine Burger's summer menu and provide feedback to a panel of moderators. Although taste testers will not be compensated, all food is free, and a number of prizes will be given away over the course of the evening. Please call Unifique PR at 1-800-555-2301 ext. 44 and take a brief survey, after which you will be given directions on how to finalize your registration if you are chosen.

Dear David,

Thank you for agreeing to facilitate the taste-testing event. Here are the details. To ensure their target market is well represented, the client requested that we locate 120 people who eat at fast-food restaurants at least three times a week. Each group will be provided with a distinct combination of menu items.

Dining Group	Time
1	5:30 P.M.
2	6:30 P.M.
3	7:30 P.M.
4	8:30 P.M

For each group of 30, you'll introduce the dishes as the meal is served. Then, after they've eaten, encourage them to share their opinions as much as possible with the panel. All meals will contain one item from each of the following four categories:

A: French fries, fried okra, fried sweet potatoes
B: Hawaiian burger, BBQ pork bun, fish sandwich
C: Apple slices, pineapple cookies, carrot sticks
D: Fig smoothie, iced tea, caramel latte

Make sure that the participant's name is recorded in the logbook during the feedback phase so that we know who we are discussing later on. Please let me know if you have any questions.

Patrick Scott

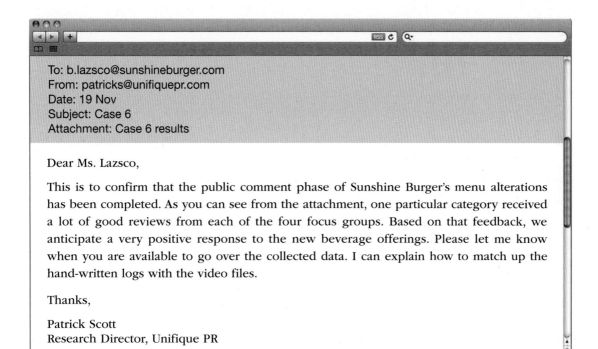

To: b.lazsco@sunshineburger.com
From: patricks@unifiquepr.com
Date: 19 Nov
Subject: Case 6
Attachment: Case 6 results

Dear Ms. Lazsco,

This is to confirm that the public comment phase of Sunshine Burger's menu alterations has been completed. As you can see from the attachment, one particular category received a lot of good reviews from each of the four focus groups. Based on that feedback, we anticipate a very positive response to the new beverage offerings. Please let me know when you are available to go over the collected data. I can explain how to match up the hand-written logs with the video files.

Thanks,

Patrick Scott
Research Director, Unifique PR

---

18. What is NOT suggested about the taste-testing participants?

(A) They regularly eat fast food.
(B) They will not be paid.
(C) They are hotel employees.
(D) They provided feedback over the phone.

19. In the instructions, the word "facilitate" in paragraph 1, line 1, is closest in meaning to

(A) forward
(B) speed up
(C) oversee
(D) walk through

20. What is mentioned about Case 6?

(A) The groups were not given information about their options.
(B) It was held at Sunshine Burger's head office.
(C) Every group had an equal number of members.
(D) It was only open to food and beverage industry professionals.

21. According to the e-mail, why was a logbook used?

(A) So participants could be identified.
(B) So the length of the study could be recorded.
(C) So participants could be contacted later.
(D) So the work hours of researchers could be tracked.

22. Based on the study's results, which category was the most popular?

(A) A
(B) B
(C) C
(D) D

기사

Part 7에서 기사는 지문의 길이도 길고 난이도가 있는 어휘들도 많이 나오기 때문에 가장 까다롭고 어렵게 느끼는 지문 유형이다. 하지만 문제 자체는 단순하고 평이하게 출제되는 경우가 많으므로 평소에 어휘력을 늘리고 다양한 신문 기사나 잡지를 미리 읽어 두는 것이 도움이 된다.

🔍 지문 유형 확인하기

1. 이런 지문 꼭 나온다

산업·기업·직업에 관한 사회성 기사	· 산업 전망: 소비 증가에 따른 업계 전망 기사 · 합병 인수에 관한 기사 · 외부 인물 영입: 신임 부사장 임명 기사 · 정책: 새로운 정책에 관한 기사
신제품 소개	· 신제품: 새로운 제품의 정보에 관한 기사 · 책 소개: 특정 작가의 출판물에 대한 소개
홍보성 기사	· 공사 정보: 새로운 다리·도로·지하철 노선 건설 · 홍보성 기사: 소설을 영화로 만든 기사
인터뷰 기사	· 성공 사례: 성공한 특정 인물이나 업체의 기사 · 특정 사업 성장 기사

2. 이런 문제 꼭 나온다

▶ 주제 파악 – **What does the article mainly discuss?** 기사는 주로 무엇을 논의하고 있는가?
⤵ 주로 지문의 앞부분 또는 뒷부분에서 정답을 찾을 수 있다.

▶ 세부사항 – **What is NOT stated about the Texas plant?** 텍사스주 공장에 관하여 언급되지 않은 것은 무엇인가?
⤵ 키워드를 이용하여 오답을 하나씩 소거한다.

▶ 추론/암시 – **What is suggested about Mr. Kim?** 김 씨에 대해 무엇이 암시되는가?
⤵ 추론/암시는 고유명사를 찾아 그 주변에서 정답을 찾는다.

▶ 미래 상황/전망/계획 – **What is likely to happen next?** 다음에 무슨 일이 일어나겠는가?
⤵ 지문 후반부의 미래 시제 동사를 단서로 정답을 찾는다.

3. 독해 필살기

▶ 평소에 기사에서 자주 등장하는 주제들을 익혀 지문이 낯설지 않도록 해야 한다.

▶ 기사의 주제는 도입부나 지문 끝부분에 나오므로 두 곳을 집중적으로 읽어야 한다.

▶ 고유명사(사람 이름, 회사 이름, 지명)가 많이 나와 혼동하는 경우가 많으므로 미리 체크하면서 읽어야 한다.

▶ 미래의 상황, 전망, 계획이나 제안 등은 지문 후반부에 정답이 제시되기 때문에 미래의 의미나 미래 시제의 동사를 잘 읽도록 한다.

해설서 p.114

Questions 1-2 refer to the following article.

Yamata Electronics Creates Fully Automated Plant

❶ Yamata Electronics recently announced that its Fukushima plant is now fully automated and operational. Using state-of-the-art robotic technology, the plant has eliminated the need for human input in the creation of its products. In fact, the only people who work in the plant are members of an automated production maintenance team. The team consists of engineers, software experts, and machine designers. These specialists maintain the robots and make any necessary changes to keep the production line running smoothly and efficiently.

Yamata claims that by automating the entire plant, it has cut its production costs in half. "This has had a huge impact on the value of the company. ❷ Our stock price has been steadily increasing since investors found out about our plans," said Ichiro Tanaka, the planning manager for Yamata Electronics.

Although Yamata Electronics has had to make a huge investment in creating all of the machinery necessary for full automation, it is clear that the company will benefit from this move in the long run.

• 기사 제목

• 기사의 주제
공장이 완전 자동화되어 가동 중임을 발표

• 특정 인물의 의견 인용
생산 원가 절감으로 주가가 오름

• 미래 상황 전망

1. What does the article mainly discuss?

(A) An electronics convention
(B) An environmental policy
(C) A drop in company sales
(D) A change at a factory

2. What is suggested about Yamata Electronics?

(A) It is attracting more investors.
(B) It was recently relocated.
(C) It introduced a new product.
(D) It has hired more workers.

Practice

Questions 1-3 refer to the following article.

> In a press conference yesterday, Taylor Stationery announced that it would be acquired by Edo Office World, a large office supply store chain. Taylor Stationery's founder, Sheryl Taylor, originally did not want to let the business go. However, after much consideration, she decided to accept Edo's purchase offer. In college, Ms. Taylor made decorative cards and envelopes for friends and family. After graduating, she launched the first Taylor Stationery store in her hometown of Palm Springs. A few years later, she expanded the business to Chula Vista, El Cajon, and La Jolla, and within 35 years, she managed to establish 60 locations across the country.

1. What is suggested about Ms. Taylor?

(A) She has allowed Edo Office World to buy her business.
(B) She has contracted Edo Office World to supply her stores.
(C) She was recently appointed as Edo Office World's CEO.
(D) She was selected to manage Edo Office World's newest branch.

2. According to the article, where is Ms. Taylor from?

(A) Chula Vista
(B) San Diego
(C) Palm Springs
(D) La Jolla

3. What is mentioned about Taylor Stationery?

(A) It has not been profitable lately.
(B) It has locations in other countries.
(C) It has just expanded to a new market.
(D) It has been operating for at least 35 years.

(2 January) Metro Wireless' spokesperson Deitrich Lang says that it will acquire four of its competitors over the next year, beginning next month with Electricall, a cell phone retailer in Madison. —[1]—. Metro Wireless, known for its favorable rates, will next take over Network Relay in nearby Gradyton in April. —[2]—. The details of the last one to be bought have not yet been revealed.

Metro Wireless branches have been opening up all over the state in the past several years. The stores have seen strong increases in their client numbers due to their wide selection of phones, friendly staff, and cheap data plans. According to Metro Wireless CEO Marianne Clow, this last reason really drives the company's growth in popularity. —[3]—. "Many mobile users these days want to download various content but can't afford other companies' expensive rates," says Clow. —[4]—. Last year, Metro Wireless hired Brent Smith as their marketing director, and a few months later, they announced the company's now-famous "Data for Everyone" initiative.

4. What is the article mainly about?

(A) Clients that are dissatisfied with their data plans
(B) A store relocating to a different town
(C) Cell phone retailers cutting their costs
(D) A company purchasing rival businesses

5. What does Ms. Clow say that customers like most about Metro Wireless?

(A) Its phone designs
(B) Its competitive pricing
(C) Its unique advertising
(D) Its convenient locations

6. In which of the positions marked [1], [2], [3], and [4] does the following sentence best belong?

"One more store, FoneCall Express in Darbyville, will be acquired in late August."

(A) [1]
(B) [2]
(C) [3]
(D) [4]

DUBLIN (10 May) After 27 years, Mary Craver will hand over the keys to her famous café, The Right Roast.

The location was originally a diner run by her husband, Daryl. However, once Ms. Craver took over, she stopped serving meals and focused instead on making top-quality beverages and desserts. —[1]—. The café gained a reputation for excellence by using only the highest-end suppliers for its coffee beans, cocoa, and milk, and Mary was nicknamed "The Coffee Queen." People from as far away as Tokyo and Johannesburg read about the shop's success, and visited to learn more about Mary's highly profitable business. —[2]—.

Ms. Craver's nephew, Louis Rast, will be taking over as the café's owner. —[3]—. Mr. Rast plans to carry on with business as usual but has been considering opening a new location. While asked about the possibility of a second location, Mr. Rast responded, "It might happen sometime next year, if all goes well." —[4]—.

Meanwhile, Ms. Craver is looking forward to retirement, though she will still stop by the café from time to time to make sure it is still business as usual. In the next several months, there will be a number of special events for patrons to bid Ms. Craver farewell and welcome Mr. Rast.

7. Why was the article written?

(A) To announce the closing of a local restaurant
(B) To promote a new line of beverages
(C) To explain the relocation of a company
(D) To report on a transition of business ownership

8. In what way did Ms. Craver change The Right Roast?

(A) She used better equipment.
(B) She added space for more customers.
(C) She changed the menu options.
(D) She redecorated the shop's interior.

9. What is mentioned about The Right Roast?

(A) It uses only one supplier.
(B) It is known internationally.
(C) It recently held a sale.
(D) It will change its name.

10. In which of the positions marked [1], [2], [3], and [4] does the following sentence best belong?

"For now, fans of The Right Roast around the country will just have to wait for more details."

(A) [1]
(B) [2]
(C) [3]
(D) [4]

Startup Energizes Portland

January 30 – Skylark, Inc. is opening its first retail store next week. Skylark's mission to provide low-cost solar panels involves opening three more retail stores in the next three years. —[1]—. Their store in Portland, Oregon is going to be Skylark's largest and is projected to make up nearly 40 percent of the company's sales this year.

Skylark's first store, located next to the main office, will offer a wide variety of home and commercial products. —[2]—. Already, more than 150 contractors have applied for the company's preferred-customer plan.

Skylark CEO Brian Kashani said that such a great start represents a milestone for the business and the industry as a whole.

"Starting this company, we knew that a lot of time, money, and hard work would be required. —[3]—. Thanks to the resources available to us here in Portland, we have been able to create many opportunities for not just residential buyers, but also the local construction industry," Mr. Kashani explained. "Our next store, in California, opens its doors at the end of the first quarter. The San Diego location is currently under construction, and we're already hearing from cities all over the country that are interested in hosting our stores."

Other retail stores will open in Montana and Colorado. These locations will all be smaller than the Portland branch, though they are expected to grow to serve their communities. —[4]—.

11. What is true about Skylark, Inc.?

(A) It has been recently acquired.
(B) It mainly does business with homeowners.
(C) It sells affordable energy products.
(D) It is relocating its main office.

12. What is mentioned about the store in Portland?

(A) It is the only location under construction.
(B) It earns less than other branches.
(C) It runs on solar power.
(D) It is the company's largest store.

13. Where will the next Skylark store be built?

(A) In Oregon
(B) In California
(C) In Montana
(D) In Colorado

14. In which of the positions marked [1], [2], [3], and [4] does the following sentence best belong?

"We are grateful for the help we received from building firms and the local government."

(A) [1]
(B) [2]
(C) [3]
(D) [4]

Dukeland Tech

5 December

Dear Investors:

Our company approaches the end of our second year as a public company, and we have made some great strides. We are now expanding our operations from solely online retail to now include a brick-and-mortar store in Melbourne.

This is a move that has been in the works for some time.
· In April, we secured retail space for our first flagship store at the Wirral Villas complex.
· In June, we contracted with Kuving Construction to start building our store.
· In October, we partnered with JP Homeware and DeProve Appliances to include their products in our stores.

The focus for next year will be on a successful grand opening of our store. We have plans to:
· Poll our customers beginning March on what they would like to see in our stores
· Invite focus groups into our store in May to gather feedback on the in-store experience
· Host a grand opening event for our store on July 17

We hope you are as excited as we are about our upcoming plans. I hope to share more with you soon.

Sincerely,
Elaine Townsend, CEO

MELBOURNE (12 August) — The Wirral Villas complex welcomed its doors to Dukeland Tech over the weekend. The electronics store joins Khyber Hall, one of the first stores to open since the complex's opening over two years ago. Within the week, an additional store, Snowelf Sports, will be making its debut.

The Wirral Villas management team also intends on opening up the west wing to additional stores. As the complex has seen a strong spike in business, the expectation is that the fight for retail space will be highly competitive. Tina Gordon, a spokesperson for Wirral Villas, commented that the team is very happy with the direction the company is moving in.

15. What is one purpose of the letter?

(A) To advertise a job opening
(B) To provide updates on a plan
(C) To gauge the interest in a product
(D) To seek a partnership on a project

16. According to the letter, when will consumers be surveyed?

(A) In March
(B) In June
(C) In July
(D) In October

17. What does the article indicate about Khyber Hall?

(A) It has multiple stores throughout the Melbourne area.
(B) It has been in the complex for at least two years.
(C) It recently underwent renovations at its store.
(D) It is the largest store in Wirral Villas complex.

18. What is suggested about the Dukeland Tech store?

(A) It is owned by JP Homeware.
(B) It is located in the west wing of the complex.
(C) It offers free deliveries of its products.
(D) It had to delay its grand opening.

19. In the article, the word "direction" in paragraph 2, line 8, is closest in meaning to

(A) path
(B) order
(C) range
(D) charge

Jasper Enterprises Rebranded

PORTLAND (22 OCT) Seattle's Fresh Dish Direct's acquisition of Jasper Enterprises, the company that runs half-dozen local health-conscious restaurants, has been completed. Fresh Dish Direct, with Jasper's properties, now manages 17 restaurants in Greater Portland.

Before Fresh Dish Direct's purchase of the chain, it was already well-known for its affordable menus, intended for price-conscious customers. Jasper's six locations, meanwhile, cater to those who want to spend a bit more for a special atmosphere and top-quality ingredients. The Raw Slice, a classic bistro established in 1935, and Heart Grain are some of the city's highest-rated vegetarian restaurants, now being managed by Fresh Dish Direct.

"Jasper's restaurants complement Fresh Dish Direct's portfolio," said Fresh Dish Direct's PR director Tony Alonzo. "Their popularity with customers and critics will make us a strong competitor in a new area of the business, while Jasper can now benefit from the financial resources of a large company."

Downtown Portland
Dining out? Whether you're on a budget or want to find out what the critics are raving about, Fresh Dish Direct has restaurants in Portland to suit everyone. The next time you're downtown, be sure to stop by one of the following eateries:

Cloud Nine
Café by day, fine dining by night, Cloud Nine specializes in using the freshest ingredients to make signature salads and pasta. The interior's elegance is unrivaled in the city.

Terry's Deli
Whether you're in the mood for a simple grilled cheese sandwich or a hearty beef soup, this neighborhood establishment is appealing due to its affordable prices.

Top Shelf
Specializing in Mediterranean cuisine, Top Shelf delivers flavorful, healthy, and fresh dishes seven days a week, year-round. The luxurious atmosphere and knowledgeable waitstaff make this a remarkable restaurant.

Coldwater Garden
Experience luxurious five-star dining on the waterfront. Enjoy an exceptional dinner with an extensive choice of beverages. Outdoor seating is now available on the recently completed deck overlooking the Willamette River. A formal dress code is required, and reservations are definitely recommended.

Take a look at our other renowned restaurants in the Greater Portland area on our website at www. freshdishdirect.com/locations.

Coldwater Garden

★★★★☆

This restaurant completely exceeded my expectations. The olive and cheese appetizer paired wonderfully with the drink selection recommended to me by my very patient waitress. The lobster was served exactly right and couldn't have been any fresher! However, the valet parking attendant was slow to retrieve my car, and I had to stand in the cold weather for almost half an hour. Other than that, I would highly recommend dining at this restaurant.

Samuel Ortez
Barcelona, Spain

20. What is suggested about Fresh Dish Direct?

(A) It has extensive experience in managing fine dining facilities.
(B) It plans to cater to a wider range of diners.
(C) It has a new head office in Portland.
(D) It offers discounts for regular customers.

21. What is stated about the four restaurants mentioned in the advertisement?

(A) They were all established in the 1930s.
(B) They have all received awards.
(C) They are all based in downtown Portland.
(D) They all require reservations.

22. Which restaurant is probably NOT a Jasper property?

(A) Cloud Nine
(B) Terry's Deli
(C) Top Shelf
(D) Coldwater Garden

23. What information is given in the restaurant in which Mr. Ortez dined?

(A) It is well-known for its sandwiches.
(B) It is open every day of the week.
(C) It has recently hired new staff.
(D) It has added another seating area.

24. What disappointed Mr. Ortez about his experience?

(A) An incorrect order
(B) An expensive bill
(C) A delay in a service
(D) The bad quality of food

양식

양식은 우리 주변에서 흔히 접할 수 있는 초대장, 영수증, 청구서, 일정표 등을 가리킨다. 다른 지문에 비해 비교적 텍스트의 분량이 적고 간단하기 때문에 지문의 유형만 잘 익히더라도 전체를 읽지 않고 문제를 풀 수 있어서 독해 시간을 단축시킬 수 있다.

🔍 지문 유형 확인하기

1. 이런 지문 꼭 나온다

청구서 (Invoice)	· 물품 거래 내역서
초대장 (Invitation)	· 행사에 초대하는 초대장
일정 (Schedule, Itinerary)	· 항공편이나 행사 일정, 여행 일정
설문 조사 (Survey form)	· 제품 또는 서비스 구매 후 고객 만족도, 직원들의 업무 만족도
계약 (Contract)	· 계약 조항
전화 메시지 (Telephone message)	· 전화 메시지 메모
보증서 (Warranty)	· 제품이나 서비스에 대한 보증서

2. 이런 문제 꼭 나온다

▶ 주제 파악 – What is the purpose of this form? / What is this coupon for?
　이 약식의 목적은 무엇인가? / 이 쿠폰은 무엇을 위한 것인가? ⋯→ 주로 지문의 앞부분에서 정답을 찾을 수 있다.

▶ 지문의 대상 – For whom is this information most likely intended?
　이 정보는 누구를 대상으로 하겠는가? ⋯→ 주로 지문의 앞부분에서 정답을 찾을 수 있다.

▶ 사실 파악 – What is NOT a service offered at the event?
　행사에서 제공되는 서비스가 아닌 것은 무엇인가? ⋯→ 키워드를 찾아 하나씩 제거하는 소거법을 이용한다.

3. 독해 필살기

▶ 양식이 작성된 이유, 목적, 용도 혹은 수신자, 발신자 질문은 지문 첫 부분에서 답을 찾을 수 있다.

▶ 금액, 수량, 날짜, 일정, 숫자에 관련된 질문은 먼저 읽고 파악해 둔다.

▶ 지문 후반부에 주의 사항이나 예외 사항이라고 해서 별표(*) 또는 Note가 적혀 있는 부분은 주의해서 읽도록 한다.

▶ 평소에 자주 나오는 양식 유형을 익혀두면 전체 글을 읽지 않고 빨리 답을 찾을 수 있다.

▶ 청구서는 주문받는 사람과 대금 지급자가 다를 수 있음에 유의한다.

▶ 전화 메시지 같은 경우 전화를 건 사람, 받는 사람, 제 3자 등이 등장하므로 각 인물이 누구인지를 파악해 둔다.

Questions 1-2 refer to the following invoice.

Westwood Photo and Video
Date: Oct. 22
Customer: Jeff Kitchener
Mailing address: Jeff Kitchener
　　　　　　　　2425 King St., Seattle, WA 89807

Billing address: Jeff Kitchener
　　　　　　　　7876 Cornwell Lane, Tacoma, WA 88745

Customer account number: 8823142
Shipping tracking number: DVL-33978
Method of payment: Credit Card (8872-0797- XXXX)

❷ Items purchased	Price
Pentax Optima Camera	$349.00
64GB memory card	$46.00
Tenba camera bag	$25.00

❶ Shipping: $0.00
Total: $420.00

❶ *Customers who have been doing business with us for 10 years or more are eligible for free shipping.

Thank you for doing business at Westwood Photo and Video. Your order should arrive in three business days. If you have any questions regarding your order, please call our customer service office toll free at 1-800-555-9654. Thank you.

→ 물품 판매자
→ 물품 주문 날짜
→ 물품 주문자
→ 배송지 주소

→ 청구지 주소 및 대금 지급자 정보

→ 주문자와 물품에 대한 세부 정보:
주문한 물품 수량, 단가, 총액 등

→ 기타 사항 혹은 연락처

1. What is suggested about Mr. Kitchener?

(A) He is a long-time customer.
(B) He chose the express shipping option.
(C) He is a professional photographer.
(D) He recently moved to Tacoma.

2. What item did the customer NOT order?

(A) A memory card
(B) A bag
(C) A camera
(D) A tripod

해설서 p.120 / ⏱ 제한 시간 20분

Questions 1-2 refer to the following receipt.

BRIGHT CENTER

13 W. Peachtree Street
Atlanta, GA 30309
(404) 258-3921

Thank you for shopping at Bright Center!

#72934	2 pkg. Glossy paper	$9.98
#32948	Drawing pad	$6.00
#92843	Foam brush	$1.99
#09232	Graphic pen	$4.95
	Subtotal	$22.92
	Tax (8%)	$1.83
	TOTAL	$24.75

Cash tendered: $24.75

Unused items may be exchanged or refunded within 15 days of purchase with the receipt.

Stop by the guest desk or ask a supervisor about the store's refund and exchange policy.

Fill out and hand in a comment card to a cashier, and get 20% off on your next purchase (up to $50)!

---

1. What type of business most likely is Bright Center?

(A) A computer repair shop
(B) A supermarket
(C) A printing center
(D) An art supply store

2. According to the receipt, how can customers receive a discount?

(A) By making a purchase of $50 or more
(B) By providing some feedback
(C) By talking to a store supervisor
(D) By calling the guest desk

Carbon Copiers

Order #: PA4501L

Contact Info: Madeline Dunn
Arrowcorp, Inc.
m.dunn@arrowcorp.ca
555-7874

Description of Request: Annual Marketing Report
500 spiral-bound copies, 329 pages (A4)
plain white paper

Project Designated to: Jack Schupe

Received on: 7 November

Completed by: 10 November

Special Requirements: Return via overnight delivery; postage has been pre-paid.

3. Where does Mr. Schupe most likely work?

(A) At Arrowcorp, Inc.
(B) At the post office
(C) At Carbon Copiers
(D) At a stationery store

4. What does the document suggest about Ms. Dunn?

(A) She requested special colored paper.
(B) Her order will be delivered on November 11.
(C) She will stop by Carbon Copiers on November 7.
(D) Her purchase is eligible for a discount.

Sleep Disorder Association of America
New Member Form

For over 30 years, the Sleep Disorder Association of America (SDAA) has funded research to find better treatments and worked to connect specialists with those who need help. From physicians to clinical researchers, our members specialize in various areas.

SDAA membership benefits:
- Free entrance to our annual seminars
- 30 percent off on any items purchased on our website
- Complimentary SDAA monthly newsletter
- Access to our research archive

Sign up today!
Full name: _____
Organization: _____
Address: _____
E-mail: _____
Phone: _____

Price of annual membership
- ☐ Healthcare professionals - $125
- ☐ Researchers - $80
- ☐ Individuals with sleep disorders - No charge

Payment Information
Credit card number: _____
Date of Expiration: _____

SDAA
Sleep Disorder Association of America

---

5. What is offered at a reduced price?

(A) Magazine subscriptions
(B) Access to research
(C) Products sold online
(D) Medical consultations

6. What is NOT implied about the SDAA?

(A) It manages several clinics.
(B) It hosts a yearly event.
(C) It was founded over 30 years ago.
(D) It produces a newsletter.

7. Who can receive SDAA benefits for free?

(A) Physicians
(B) Researchers
(C) University students
(D) Patients

Bries Hotels

Bries Hotels appreciates your business! To help us provide a better experience for our clientele, please let us know your opinion about your stay. At your convenience, please complete this survey and present it upon checkout to receive a valuable book of coupons from local businesses.

Date: August 4
Customer: Jamie Bohem
Contact Info: (307) 555-7942

Reservation Date(s) / Location
August 1-3 / New Orleans Bries Hotel
Notes: Originally reserved a standard room but was moved to a suite

On a scale of 1 to 4, with 4 being the best, how would you rate each area?

• **Guest Service**

Professionalism	1	2	(3)	4
Booking System	1	(2)	3	4

• **Room**

Neatness / Cleanliness	1	2	3	(4)
Comfort	1	2	3	(4)

Would you stay with us again?	(YES)	NO	UNSURE
Would you recommend your stay to others?	YES	NO	(UNSURE)

Feedback:
I use Bries Hotels when I travel on business and have always been satisfied. Recently, however, when I arrived at the New Orleans location, I found out my reservation was canceled. While it's true that my flight was delayed, and I checked in much later than scheduled, the front desk should have called or sent an e-mail before doing this. I had no choice but to let the clerk put me in a more expensive room.

8. How will Bries Hotels most likely use the data they collect from the form?

(A) Measure staff performances
(B) Improve customer satisfaction
(C) Design a better check-in system
(D) Reduce costs in certain areas

9. What does Ms. Bohem indicate about the hotel room?

(A) It was quite comfortable.
(B) It was very dirty.
(C) Its price was discounted.
(D) It was originally booked as a suite.

10. What does Ms. Bohem indicate about the service she experienced?

(A) The hotel charged her more than expected.
(B) The reservation system was easy to use.
(C) The front desk closed too early.
(D) The cancellation delayed her flight.

Questions 11-15 refer to the following e-mail and document.

From	Davu Verma <diyav@xmail.com>
To	Help desk <help@federalrent.com>
Subject	Contract Inquiry
Date	April 9

I am a long-term member of your monthly rental program. However, I will be returning to St. Louis soon, so I will no longer need your service. Since my contract (#FR216) renews automatically, I would like to return the car before the automatic renewal happens. That way, I will not be charged for the next month.

I will be leaving on April 30 but have not purchased an airline ticket yet. I would like to use the car until at least April 29. However, if the contract renewal happens before then, I will return the vehicle on the final day of this month's contract.

Please get back to me about exactly which day the next renewal will happen so that I can make the appropriate arrangements.

Regards,

Davu Verma

Federal Rent

Current Monthly Rental Contracts

Last Day of the Monthly Lease	Monthly Rate	Type of Car	Contract Number
3	$250	Vocant	FR752
30	$310	Marwari	FR413
29	$285	Saxon	FR398
28	$305	Freisian	FR216

* When terminating a contract, the renter must return the vehicle no later than 5 P.M. on the day listed on the contract. Failure to do so will result in an automatic renewal of the contract.

11. What is the purpose of the e-mail?

   (A) To ask for contract details
   (B) To inquire about a service cost
   (C) To promote a rental offer
   (D) To confirm ticket purchase

12. What is most likely true about Mr. Verma?

   (A) He works at Federal Rent.
   (B) He has family in St. Louis.
   (C) He will book a flight soon.
   (D) He only uses his car on weekdays.

13. How much is Mr. Verma's monthly rate?

   (A) $250
   (B) $285
   (C) $305
   (D) $310

14. On what date should Mr. Verma return his car?

   (A) April 3
   (B) April 28
   (C) April 29
   (D) April 30

15. What is true about a monthly contract?

   (A) It expires on the last day of the month.
   (B) It includes a free navigation system.
   (C) It is extended after 5 P.M. on the last contract date.
   (D) It is only offered in six-month intervals.

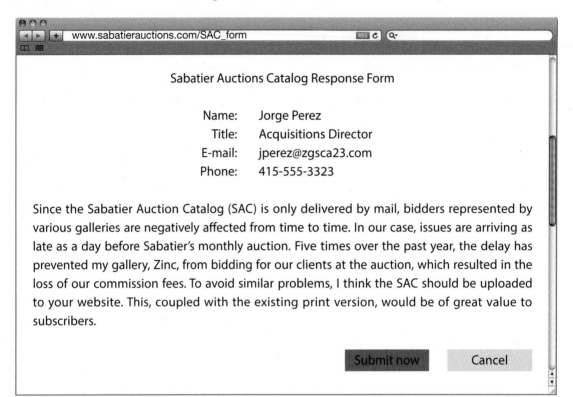

Sabatier Auctions Catalog Response Form

Name: Jorge Perez
Title: Acquisitions Director
E-mail: jperez@zgsca23.com
Phone: 415-555-3323

Since the Sabatier Auction Catalog (SAC) is only delivered by mail, bidders represented by various galleries are negatively affected from time to time. In our case, issues are arriving as late as a day before Sabatier's monthly auction. Five times over the past year, the delay has prevented my gallery, Zinc, from bidding for our clients at the auction, which resulted in the loss of our commission fees. To avoid similar problems, I think the SAC should be uploaded to your website. This, coupled with the existing print version, would be of great value to subscribers.

Submit now   Cancel

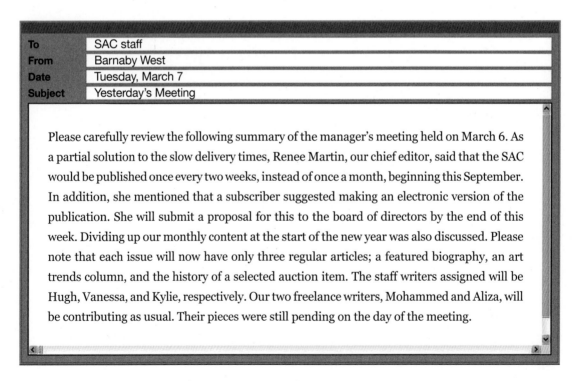

To	SAC staff
From	Barnaby West
Date	Tuesday, March 7
Subject	Yesterday's Meeting

Please carefully review the following summary of the manager's meeting held on March 6. As a partial solution to the slow delivery times, Renee Martin, our chief editor, said that the SAC would be published once every two weeks, instead of once a month, beginning this September. In addition, she mentioned that a subscriber suggested making an electronic version of the publication. She will submit a proposal for this to the board of directors by the end of this week. Dividing up our monthly content at the start of the new year was also discussed. Please note that each issue will now have only three regular articles; a featured biography, an art trends column, and the history of a selected auction item. The staff writers assigned will be Hugh, Vanessa, and Kylie, respectively. Our two freelance writers, Mohammed and Aliza, will be contributing as usual. Their pieces were still pending on the day of the meeting.

Sabatier Auctions Catalog November • Vol.27 • Number 11

CEO's Message:

This month, SAC is pleased to present online subscription services, to complement the print catalog (more information on page 30). Then, in December, Sabatier's new app, Auction Paddle, will be available to the public, free of charge. The application will let users see information about each lot, track bids in real time, and even place bids on items as though they are actually present at the auction house. Starting in February of next year, the SAC will be available on a biweekly basis, both in print and online versions.

Sincerely,

Adrien Mercier
Sabatier Auction House, CEO

16. What is true about Mr. Perez?

(A) He became a SAC subscriber 12 months ago.
(B) He will be interviewed by SAC.
(C) His suggestion will be put into action.
(D) His business sells art overseas.

17. Who will write about the background of an auction item?

(A) Renee
(B) Vanessa
(C) Hugh
(D) Kylie

18. What is implied about Aliza?

(A) She was present at the manager's meeting in March.
(B) Her office is located in another city.
(C) Her article was not submitted by the March 6 meeting.
(D) She has coauthored a book with Mohammed.

19. What is suggested about the SAC?

(A) It is 30 pages long.
(B) Its reader base is expanding.
(C) It postponed a plan to print two issues a month.
(D) It prints exclusively for Zinc's clientele.

20. What is mentioned about Auction Paddle?

(A) It will be launched in December.
(B) It has support for several languages.
(C) Only SAC readers can access it.
(D) It can be used to read SAC articles.

이중 지문

이중 지문은 서로 관련된 두 개의 지문을 읽고 총 5문제를 풀어야 한다. 이중 지문의 실제 난이도는 그렇게 높은 편은 아니지만 두 개의 지문을 읽어야 하고, 연계 문제가 출제되어 두 지문을 번갈아 봐야 하는 심리적 부담 때문에 체감 난이도가 높은 편이다. 무엇보다도 시간 관리가 중요하다.

Tip!
이중 지문 유형은 매회 ㄴ개의 지문이 출제돼!

🔍 지문 유형 확인하기

1. 이런 지문 꼭 나온다

편지 / 이메일 + 회신 편지 / 이메일	· 주문, 지원, 문의, 요청, 초대에 대한 상대방 회신 요구와 그 요구에 따른 수락 / 거절
광고 / 기사 / 평가 + 회신 편지 / 이메일	· 불특정 다수에게 보내는 광고나 공지 등장 · 그 광고나 공지에 대한 요청, 불만, 신청 회신 · 제품을 구매한 소비자가 불만을 제기하는 편지
편지 / 이메일 + 첨부 문서	· 주문, 지원, 문의, 요청에 관련된 편지 / 이메일 · 그 지문에 대한 세부적인 사항을 언급한 첨부 서류, 견적서, 일정
청구서 + 편지 / 이메일	· 받은 청구서에서 잘못된 금액 계산을 항의하는 편지 / 이메일
채용 광고 + 편지 / 이메일	· 채용 광고와 그와 관련된 지원 및 문의 편지 / 이메일

1. 편지와 이메일 관련

- 이메일 + 이메일   예약, 일정의 확인 등을 위한 이메일 교환
- 양식 + 이메일   행사나 일정표 등의 양식과 그에 대한 질문을 하는 이메일
- 편지 + 이메일   회사 내부 행사 또는 업무상 관련된 의견 교환 등을 담은 편지와 이메일
- 광고 + 이메일   상품, 프로그램 등에 대한 광고와 그에 관련된 질문을 하는 이메일
- 공지 + 이메일   행사 및 다양한 활동에 대한 공지와 그에 관련된 내용을 담은 이메일

2. 회람과 공지 관련

- 회람 + 이메일   승진, 모임 등 업무 관련 회람과 그에 관련된 질문/요청 등을 담은 이메일
- 회람 + 양식   업무 관련 회람과 신청서 등의 양식
- 공지 + 이메일   행사, 변경 사항 등에 대한 공지와 질문/요청 등을 담은 이메일
- 공지 + 양식   공사, 새로운 정책 등에 대한 공지와 신청서 양식

3. 광고 관련

- 광고 + 이메일   상품, 서비스 등에 대한 광고와 추가 정보나 질문을 담은 이메일
- 광고 + 편지   상품, 서비스에 대한 광고와 불만/만족 등의 내용을 담은 편지
- 광고 + 기사   상품, 서비스에 대한 광고와 회사의 광고된 내용에 대한 기사
- 광고 + 양식   상품, 프로그램 등에 대한 광고와 상품 평가와 같은 양식

4. 발표문과 기사 관련

- 발표문 + 이메일   변경 등에 대한 발표문과 질문/요청 등을 담은 이메일
- 기사 + 이메일   회사, 경제에 대한 기사와 그에 관련된 내용을 담은 이메일

5. 양식 및 기타 지문 관련

- 전화 메모 + 이메일   부재중 전화에 대한 메모와 관련 내용을 담은 이메일
- 청구서 + 이메일   물품 청구서와 그에 관련된 추가 정보나 요청 사항을 담은 이메일
- 설문서 + 이메일   각종 설문지와 그에 대한 감사의 내용을 담은 이메일
- 초대장 + 편지   다양한 행사에 대한 초대장과 그에 관련된 내용을 담은 편지
- 일정표 + 이메일   행사, 회의 등에 대한 일정표와 질문/요청 등을 담은 이메일

2. 이런 문제 꼭 나온다

단일 지문으로 풀 수 있는 질문 유형

According to the e-mail, when will the participants learn about the seminar?

이메일에 따르면, 참가자들은 언제 세미나에 관하여 알 수 있겠는가?

⋯▶ 이메일이라고 지문 유형이 주어졌으므로 해당하는 지문에 가서 정답을 찾을 수가 있다.

연계 지문으로 풀 수 있는 질문 유형

What item will Mr. Perez probably order? 페레즈 씨는 무슨 물품을 주문할 것인가?

⋯▶ 한 지문에서 주문할 수 있는 종류가 나오고, 또 다른 지문에서는 페레즈 씨의 정보가 나와서 두 지문을 연계해서 정답을 찾을 수가 있다.

3. 독해 필살기

▶ 우선 지문을 보면서 두 지문의 유형을 파악하고, 질문에 나와 있는 핵심 키워드를 확인한다.

▶ 질문을 읽을 때 5문제 중에서 단일 지문으로 풀 수 있는 문제와 연계 지문으로 풀 수 있는 문제를 구분한다.

    – 질문 중에서 3문제 정도는 단일 지문만으로 풀 수 있고, 1-2 문제 정도는 연계 지문 문제라고 보면 된다.

    – 질문의 보기에 숫자, 수치, 종류(사람 열거, 날짜 열거, 직업 열거)가 나오면 거의 연계 지문 문제라고 보면 된다.

▶ 지문의 전개 순서와 질문의 순서가 거의 동일하게 제시되는 경우가 많기 때문에, 질문의 순서에 따라 본문에서 답을 찾아 나간다. 하지만 질문의 순서와 내용의 순서가 다른 경우도 간혹 출제되기 때문에 주의가 필요하다.

해설서 p.125

Questions 1-5 refer to the following advertisement and e-mail.

Edgley Sporting Equipment (ESE)

ESE is one of the largest sporting equipment retailers in England, and ❶ we need to fill part-time openings at our Manchester location.

Clothing Department: Cashier experience necessary. Must be available Friday through Sunday. 10-20 hours per week.

Equipment Department: No ❷ prior sales experience is needed, but in-depth sports knowledge is necessary. ❹ Must be available Monday through Thursday. 25-40 hours per week.

Inventory Specialist: This is a special two-week position for the end of the year. Assist our warehouse manager in taking inventory of our stock. Must work nights on Saturdays and Sundays. 50 hours total.

Merchandising Assistant: Assist with the design and arrangement of in-store displays and merchandise. Must be available evenings on Saturdays and Sundays. 10-15 hours per week.

To apply for any of these positions, please contact Brandon Edgley at brandon@esemail.com.

- 회사 이름
- 글의 목적
  구인 광고
- 직책 설명, 자격 요건,
  근무 조건
- 연락 방법

To: Brandon Edgley <brandon@esemail.com>
From: Steven Mycroft <stevemy@balmail.edu>
Sent: Friday, November 23, 11:33 A.M.
Subject: Employment

Dear Mr. Edgley,

❺ I am a student at Balliol University, **and our winter holiday will be starting soon.** ❸ During that time, I would like to work and earn some money. ❹ As I have many club activities on the weekend, I would like to work on the weekdays.

❺ I'm on the university baseball team, and I have played many sports, such as tennis and badminton. **As a result, I know how to handle many different kinds of sports equipment.** ❺ I am also a frequent customer of your store, and I am always impressed with the quality of service and products.

I would like an opportunity to speak with you about filling one of your part-time positions. Thank you.

Sincerely,

Steven Mycroft

- 수신인
- 발신인
- 보낸 날짜
- 주제
- 이메일의 목적
  시간제 일자리 구직
- 이중 지문 연계 유형
  자격 요건 설명 또는
  발신자의 세부 정보
- 맺음말, 희망 사항

1. What is stated about the advertised positions?

   (A) They require no relevant work experience.
   (B) They all include weekend hours.
   (C) They are part-time positions.
   (D) They require working in several store locations.

2. In the advertisement, the word "prior" in paragraph 3, line 1 is closest in meaning to

   (A) current
   (B) earlier
   (C) direct
   (D) personal

3. What is the purpose of the e-mail?

   (A) To inquire about a job opening
   (B) To ask for Mr. Edgley's contact information
   (C) To recommend a colleague for a position
   (D) To request a reduction in working hours

4. What position is most suitable for Mr. Mycroft?

   (A) Clothing sales associate
   (B) Equipment sales associate
   (C) Inventory specialist
   (D) Merchandising assistant

5. What is NOT indicated about Mr. Mycroft?

   (A) He worked in the retail industry before.
   (B) He is a university student.
   (C) He enjoys playing many sports.
   (D) He often shops at Edgley's Sports Equipment.

해설서 p.126 / ⏱ 제한 시간 15분

Questions 1-5 refer to the following Web page and e-mail.

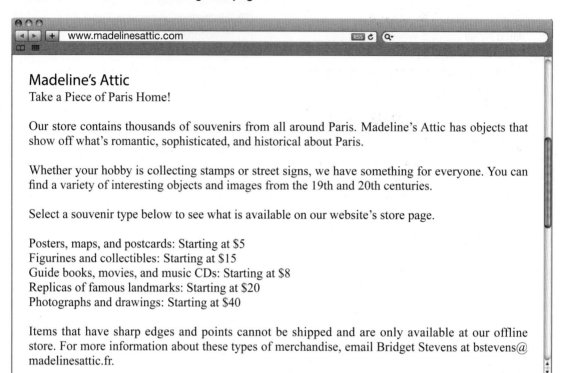

www.madelinesattic.com

Madeline's Attic
Take a Piece of Paris Home!

Our store contains thousands of souvenirs from all around Paris. Madeline's Attic has objects that show off what's romantic, sophisticated, and historical about Paris.

Whether your hobby is collecting stamps or street signs, we have something for everyone. You can find a variety of interesting objects and images from the 19th and 20th centuries.

Select a souvenir type below to see what is available on our website's store page.

Posters, maps, and postcards: Starting at $5
Figurines and collectibles: Starting at $15
Guide books, movies, and music CDs: Starting at $8
Replicas of famous landmarks: Starting at $20
Photographs and drawings: Starting at $40

Items that have sharp edges and points cannot be shipped and are only available at our offline store. For more information about these types of merchandise, email Bridget Stevens at bstevens@madelinesattic.fr.

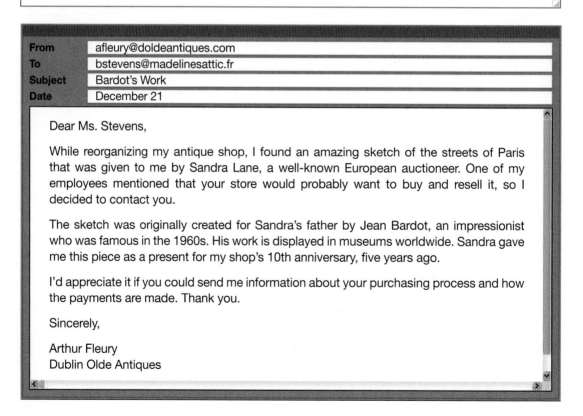

From	afleury@doldeantiques.com
To	bstevens@madelinesattic.fr
Subject	Bardot's Work
Date	December 21

Dear Ms. Stevens,

While reorganizing my antique shop, I found an amazing sketch of the streets of Paris that was given to me by Sandra Lane, a well-known European auctioneer. One of my employees mentioned that your store would probably want to buy and resell it, so I decided to contact you.

The sketch was originally created for Sandra's father by Jean Bardot, an impressionist who was famous in the 1960s. His work is displayed in museums worldwide. Sandra gave me this piece as a present for my shop's 10th anniversary, five years ago.

I'd appreciate it if you could send me information about your purchasing process and how the payments are made. Thank you.

Sincerely,

Arthur Fleury
Dublin Olde Antiques

1. What is NOT suggested about Madeline's Attic?

   (A) Its items come from different time periods.
   (B) It offers monthly discounts on artwork.
   (C) Its merchandise appeals to various interests.
   (D) It sells products related to French culture.

2. What is indicated about Madeline's Attic?

   (A) It has locations in several European countries.
   (B) All of its items are manufactured in Paris.
   (C) It was established in the 1960s.
   (D) Some of its products are not available online.

3. What is the lowest price Mr. Fleury's item would most likely sell for at Madeline's Attic?

   (A) $5
   (B) $15
   (C) $20
   (D) $40

4. What is suggested about Mr. Fleury?

   (A) He was a former employee at Madeline's Attic.
   (B) He will meet with Ms. Lane in Dublin.
   (C) He owns a product made by Mr. Bardot.
   (D) He regularly attends auctions in Europe.

5. What does Mr. Fleury ask about?

   (A) The procedure for selling merchandise to Madeline's Attic
   (B) The price of a photo he viewed at a shop
   (C) The background of an artist he will interview
   (D) The process for displaying work at a museum

Questions 6-10 refer to the following e-mail and report.

To	Quality Assurance Team
From	Pablo Evans
Date	13 September
Subject	Performance Testing

Greetings, All:

As you have probably heard, our company has come in for a lot of criticism in recent news reports. There are claims that our models are not meeting our stated performance standards. Most worrying of all are allegations that the gas mileage of our five "mini" models, which happen to be our top sellers, are not as efficient as advertised. We are concerned that this negative attention may damage our credibility, and of course, result in a drop in sales.

At Hidar Motors, we take pride in our vehicles and expect that each one will provide the same award-winning quality that our customers have come to appreciate over the last 40 years. As a result, we have hired the consulting firm, Glick Enterprises, to test these vehicles' gas mileages using industry-approved methods. Should it be revealed that one of our models is underperforming, we will take immediate action to correct the labeling and advertising.

This situation will allow us to reevaluate current procedures and ensure our vehicles are of the highest quality.

Pablo Evans

Chief Operations Officer

GAS MILEAGE PERFORMANCE RESULTS
Prepared for Hidar Motors
By Glick Enterprises

Car Model	Street-tested Gas Mileage*	Consumer-reported Gas Mileage*
Tarta Mini	38	35
Cosmos Mini	32	34
Extorma Mini	22	23
Bravoso Mini	28	26
Himalaya Mini	24	29

*in miles per gallon(mpg)

The performance tests on the models of greatest concern were conducted at the Glick Enterprises facilities as well as on public streets. Consumers were asked to report the gas mileage from their daily use as well. These numbers were then compared to the advertised gas mileage.

6. Why was the e-mail sent?

(A) To announce a new line of cars
(B) To propose a solution to a problem
(C) To discuss a potential partnership with Glick Enterprises
(D) To promote a company event

7. In the e-mail, the word "claims" in paragraph 1, line 2, is closest in meaning to

(A) demands
(B) ownerships
(C) interests
(D) accusations

8. What is NOT mentioned about Hidar Motors?

(A) It has been featured on the news.
(B) It has been in business for several decades.
(C) Its products have received recognition for their quality.
(D) Its sales numbers have been decreasing recently.

9. What is suggested about the vehicles that were used in the research?

(A) They were made by different manufacturers.
(B) They were launched this year.
(C) They are the company's most popular models.
(D) They have only been tested on highways.

10. According to the report, what vehicle performed the worst in fuel efficiency?

(A) Tarta Mini
(B) Extorma Mini
(C) Bravoso Mini
(D) Himalaya Mini

Questions 11-15 refer to the following letter and e-mail.

12 July

Mr. Jeffrey Harrington
SME Tax Consulting
80 W. Pilbert Lane
Vernon, BC

Dear Mr. Harrington,

I am considering opening my own tax preparation business in Kelowna.

I have been working for Kline-Vogel Tax Services in Vernon for the last 17 years. I believe the knowledge I gathered along the way and the ties I have with many people in the town will make this venture a success. Also, my wife runs a café in Kelowna, where over the course of many years, I have gotten to know the residents.

By opening as a member of your franchise, I believe that I can avoid many problems that small businesses face when they start up. Please let me know your availability for an in-person meeting and what kinds of documents you would like to see.

I look forward to hearing from you.

Sincerely,

Benjamin C. Schrader, CPA

To: <client-list for Kelowna SME Tax Consulting>
From: Ben Schrader
Date: 19 September
Subject: We're celebrating!

Valued clients,

When we opened the doors for business on September 19 of last year, my partners and I knew that we could make a difference by providing tax advice for the residents of Kelowna that would help them to save and prosper. As we mark the end of our first year, we hope to continue providing excellent services for our clients.

Within the first few months, we already had a solid client base because we displayed a firm resolve to make people's lives better. A middle-aged couple was worried about not having enough in savings to afford their child's college tuition. Our financial planning service helped them create a plan that also saved them extra money for retirement. Another client, Al's Computing, wrote a letter of thanks after paying the lowest amount in taxes ever in over a decade of operation.

Pleased customers are the reason why more and more people are choosing to hire us. We also owe a very large "thank you" to the SME Tax Consulting group for welcoming us into their network and assisting us every step of the way. I am honored to be a Kelowna business owner and a member of the SME family.

Benjamin C. Schrader, CPA

11. What is a purpose of the letter?

(A) To request additional funds
(B) To ask for an application form
(C) To promote a new product
(D) To describe job experience

12. In the letter, the word "ties" in paragraph 2, line 2, is closest in meaning to

(A) garments
(B) limits
(C) connections
(D) knots

13. Why did Mr. Schrader send the e-mail?

(A) To explain retirement savings plans
(B) To highlight a company's success
(C) To show support for a local program
(D) To extend an invitation to a celebration

14. What is mentioned about Kelowna SME Tax Consulting?

(A) It plans to purchase new computers.
(B) It has a new service for families.
(C) It will extend its office hours.
(D) It has been operating for a year.

15. What is suggested about Mr. Schrader?

(A) His proposal was accepted.
(B) He worked at his wife's café for a decade.
(C) He relocated to Vernon 17 years ago.
(D) His business is expanding overseas.

삼중 지문

가장 체감 난이도가 높은 문제 유형이다. 하지만 이중 지문처럼 도표, 서식, 목록과 같은 지문이 포함되어 있으므로, 각 지문의 관계만 잘 파악하면 어렵지 않게 답을 찾을 수가 있다. 이중 지문의 전략을 최대한 활용하도록 하자.

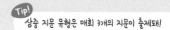

Tip!
삼중 지문 유형은 매회 3개의 지문이 출제돼!

🔍 지문 유형 확인하기

1. 이런 지문 꼭 나온다

광고 + 영수증/청구서 + 이메일	상품 광고 + 구매한 제품에 대한 영수증 + 제품에 관한 요청이나 수정 사항 이메일
광고 + 양식/주문서 + 이메일/편지	상품 광고 + 제품 주문서/양식 + 문의 사항이나 요청 사항 이메일/편지
광고 + 이메일/편지 + 이메일/편지	구인 광고 + 구직자의 자격 요건 문의/이메일/편지 + 인사 담당 답변의 이메일/편지
광고 + 이메일/편지 + 첨부 문서	구인 광고 + 구직자의 이메일/편지 + 이력서/지원서 첨부
공지 + 공지 사항 스케줄/표 + 이메일/편지	공지 + 공지 사항 스케줄/도표 + 공지에 관한 문의 이메일/편지
공지 + 기사 + 이메일	사내 공지 + 경제 불황 기사 + 경제 불황에 따른 회사 전략 요청 이메일
기사 + 이메일 + 이메일	인사이동에 관한 기사 + 승진 축하 이메일 + 답장 이메일
웹사이트 + 이메일 + 이메일	홍보 웹사이트 + 주문에 관한 이메일 + 문의 답변 이메일

2. 이런 문제 꼭 나온다

단일 지문으로 풀 수 있는 질문 유형

In the advertisement, what does Viola's Linens recommend customers to do?
광고에서, 비올라스 리넨스는 고객들이 무엇을 하도록 제안하는가?

⋯→ 광고라는 지문 유형이 주어졌으므로, 세 개 지문 중 해당하는 지문에 가서 정답을 찾을 수가 있다.

연계 지문으로 풀 수 있는 질문 유형

What tablecloth pattern did Katie Simms order? 케이티 심즈는 어떤 식탁보 무늬를 주문했는가?

⋯→ 한 지문에서 주문 목록이 나오고, 또 다른 지문에서는 케이티 심즈의 정보가 나와서 두 지문을 연계해서 정답을 찾을 수가 있다.

3. 독해 필살기

▶ 지문이 하나 추가되긴 했지만, 기존의 이중 지문을 푸는 전략으로 접근한다.

▶ 세 지문을 보면서 각각 지문의 유형을 파악하고, 질문에 나와 있는 핵심 키워드를 확인한다.

▶ 5문제 중에서 단일 지문으로 풀 수 있는 문제와 연계 지문으로 풀 수 있는 문제를 구분한다. 연계 문제는 첫 번째 와 두 번째 지문 연계 문제인지, 두 번째와 세 번째 지문 연계 문제인지를 파악한다.

▶ 평소에 여러 가지 서식(표, 스케줄, 청구서, 목록, 영수증 등)에 익숙해져야 한다.

Questions 1-5 refer to the following Web page and e-mails.

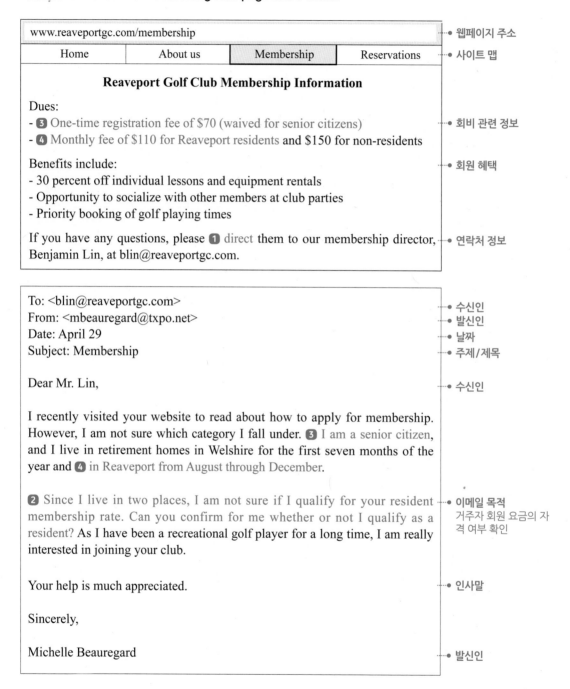

www.reaveportgc.com/membership ·····• 웹페이지 주소

| Home | About us | Membership | Reservations | ·····• 사이트 맵

Reaveport Golf Club Membership Information

Dues:
- ❺ One-time registration fee of $70 (waived for senior citizens) ·····• 회비 관련 정보
- ❹ Monthly fee of $110 for Reaveport residents and $150 for non-residents

Benefits include: ·····• 회원 혜택
- 30 percent off individual lessons and equipment rentals
- Opportunity to socialize with other members at club parties
- Priority booking of golf playing times

If you have any questions, please ❶ direct them to our membership director, ·····• 연락처 정보
Benjamin Lin, at blin@reaveportgc.com.

To: <blin@reaveportgc.com> ·····• 수신인
From: <mbeauregard@txpo.net> ·····• 발신인
Date: April 29 ·····• 날짜
Subject: Membership ·····• 주제/제목

Dear Mr. Lin, ·····• 수신인

I recently visited your website to read about how to apply for membership. However, I am not sure which category I fall under. ❸ I am a senior citizen, and I live in retirement homes in Welshire for the first seven months of the year and ❹ in Reaveport from August through December.

❷ Since I live in two places, I am not sure if I qualify for your resident ·····• 이메일 목적
membership rate. Can you confirm for me whether or not I qualify as a   거주자 회원 요금의 자
resident? As I have been a recreational golf player for a long time, I am really   격 여부 확인
interested in joining your club.

Your help is much appreciated. ·····• 인사말

Sincerely,

Michelle Beauregard ·····• 발신인

Dear Ms. Beauregard,

Thank you for your interest in our golf club. ❹ We consider anyone who lives in Reaveport for at least five months as a resident, so you certainly qualify for our resident membership fee. ❺ I recommend that you apply as soon as possible since our membership usually fills up by July. Please call me if you have further inquiries.

Sincerely,

Benjamin Lin
Membership Director, Reaveport Golf Club

• 수신인
• 발신인
• 날짜
• 주제/제목

• 수신인

• 문의에 대한 답변
5개월 이상 거주자는 주민으로 간주함. 가급적 등록을 서둘러 줄 것을 당부함

• 발신인

---

1. In the Web page, the word "direct" in paragraph 3, line 1, is closest in meaning to

(A) manage
(B) teach
(C) forward
(D) conduct

2. Why did Ms. Beauregard write the first e-mail?

(A) To cancel a service
(B) To renew her membership
(C) To request more information
(D) To provide a new address

3. What is suggested about Ms. Beauregard?

(A) She is a professional golf player.
(B) She does not have to pay a registration fee.
(C) She moved to Reaveport last year.
(D) She has met Mr. Lin before.

4. How much is Ms. Beauregard's monthly membership?

(A) $30
(B) $70
(C) $110
(D) $150

5. What is most likely true about the Reaveport Golf Club?

(A) It receives many membership applications.
(B) It is open only to Reaveport residents.
(C) It has been recently renovated.
(D) It has multiple locations.

PART 7 UNIT 08

Questions 1-5 refer to the following e-mails and record sheet.

From	m_leonard@tagetdata.com
To	billing@nationwidewater.com
Date	November 4
Subject	Invoice for Account #235923

Hello,

This is in regard to the invoice we recently received from your company. The total amount of our office's water usage for October came to $1050.20, which is far more than in the previous months.

We have paid in full, in keeping with our contract. However, to set up a plan to reduce water waste in the coming year, we request that you provide documentation about why the utility cost has increased. If it was made in error, please contact me directly.

Our maintenance supervisor has suggested, and I agree, that the issue might have been caused by a faulty underground pipe. Therefore, I would like you to send a representative out during our business hours to our office to check if there are any issues.

Sincerely,

Mina Leonard, Taget Data

Service Record Sheet
November 12

Representative	Service Location	Arrival	Work Description
David Novello	1920 Fairlane Avenue	1:15 P.M.	Pipe replaced
Nadia Anderson	9932 Byers Drive	1:20 P.M.	Pipe fixed
Andrea Kim	1244 Central Avenue	3:20 P.M.	Pipe replaced
Tonya Garcia	1029 Wesleyan Drive	3:45 P.M.	Pipe fixed

From	dana_meyer@nationwidewater.com
To	m_leonard@tagetdata.com
Date	November 13
Subject	Re: Invoice for Account #235923

Dear Ms. Leonard,

We at Nationwide Water appreciate you getting in touch with us. This e-mail is to provide you with an update on the issue at the Byers Drive location, which our representative determined was caused by a leaking underground pipe. That is why the meter incorrectly read your building's water usage. The pipe has been fixed, and you have our word this will not happen in the future.

Your next month's bill will be credited $220.00.

If you have any further need of assistance, please get in touch at any time.

Sincerely,

Dana Meyer
Billing Department, Nationwide Water

1. Why did Ms. Leonard send the e-mail?

(A) To review a contract
(B) To discuss a charge
(C) To ask about discount rates
(D) To sign up for a monthly subscription

2. What is implied about Ms. Leonard?

(A) She will not be using Nationwide Water's services anymore.
(B) She correctly guessed the cause of a problem.
(C) She recently relocated to another branch.
(D) She is contacting Ms. Meyer for the first time.

3. Who visited Taget Data's office on November 12?

(A) David Novello
(B) Nadia Anderson
(C) Andrea Kim
(D) Tonya Garcia

4. In the second e-mail, the word "read" in paragraph 1, line 4, is closest in meaning to

(A) perceived
(B) looked
(C) browsed
(D) measured

5. What does Ms. Meyer mention in her e-mail?

(A) An additional fee will be applied.
(B) A satisfaction survey will be sent.
(C) A new pipe will be installed soon.
(D) A portion of the bill will be deducted.

Questions 6-10 refer to the following advertisement, online form, and review.

LoadUp Transportation Rental Service (LTRS)

Whether you are moving across town or the country, call LTRS today. Every vehicle is equipped with moving crates and plenty of helpful items, such as scissors, tape, and bubble wrap. Refrigerated units are also available upon request. Our vehicles can be picked up at locations all over California, or delivered to your address by one of our professional drivers.

Our available vehicles:

Type	Loading Device	Length (meters)	Floor Space (square meters)	Interior Capacity (cubic meters)
Class A	Ramp	5.5m	$13.75m^2$	$55m^3$
Class B	Electric Lift	9.0m	$22.5m^2$	$90m^3$
Class C	Electric Lift	12.5m	$31.25m^2$	$125m^3$
Class D	Electric Lift	15.0m	$37.5m^2$	$150m^3$

Contact us to schedule an appointment with one of our logistics experts to determine which vehicle type is right for you. For pricing info, visit our website at www.loaduprental.com.

Address: www.loaduprental.com/requestform

Fill out the form to request information about a vehicle:

Name: Aaron Diaz	Business: Diaz Cleaners
E-mail: aaron@dzclean.com	Date: January 27

Your business was recommended by an associate, Alissa Velle, who recently used your service when she moved across town. My company is growing very rapidly and needs to relocate, too. So, I would like to rent a truck for the weekend. As I have some heavy cleaning equipment, I will need an electric lift on the back, plus a large enough trailer space to hold everything. Also, it would be helpful if the vehicle had padding inside to prevent damage to my machines.

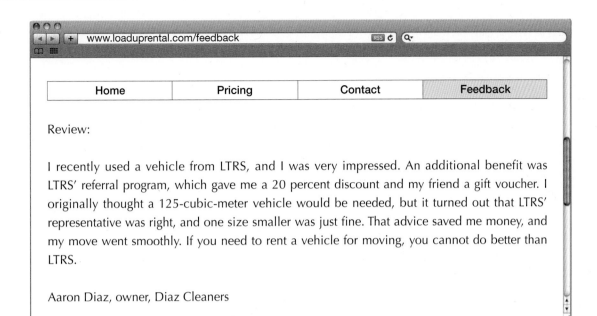

www.loaduprental.com/feedback

| Home | Pricing | Contact | **Feedback** |

Review:

I recently used a vehicle from LTRS, and I was very impressed. An additional benefit was LTRS' referral program, which gave me a 20 percent discount and my friend a gift voucher. I originally thought a 125-cubic-meter vehicle would be needed, but it turned out that LTRS' representative was right, and one size smaller was just fine. That advice saved me money, and my move went smoothly. If you need to rent a vehicle for moving, you cannot do better than LTRS.

Aaron Diaz, owner, Diaz Cleaners

6. What information about LTRS is NOT stated in the advertisement?

(A) The choice of loading method
(B) The mileage rates for its trucks
(C) The moving equipment provided
(D) The amount of internal space

7. What is most likely true about Ms. Velle?

(A) She works under Mr. Diaz.
(B) She was given a coupon.
(C) She plans to relocate to another country.
(D) She supplies equipment to cleaning companies.

8. What is implied about Diaz Cleaners?

(A) It has moved near Ms. Velle's business.
(B) It uses eco-friendly products.
(C) It is doing well.
(D) It has several locations.

9. Which vehicle did Mr. Diaz use?

(A) Class A
(B) Class B
(C) Class C
(D) Class D

10. In the review, the phrase "turned out" in paragraph 1, line 3, is closest in meaning to

(A) finished
(B) attended
(C) happened
(D) reversed

Questions 11-15 refer to the following letters and invoice.

Wingfield's Italian Antiques
75 W. Grand Street
St. Louis, MO 63112

Dear Ms. Wingfield,

Wingfield's Italian Antiques has been part of our town for as long as I can remember. I have often browsed through your shop and admired the quality of the merchandise on display. Recently, I decided to add several glass antiques you advertised on your website to my personal collection. Since I only purchase collectibles in near-perfect condition, I made sure to read each item's description carefully before ordering the antiques.

However, upon receiving my order, I found that the Aureliano Toso piece appears to have been broken in half and poorly glued back together.

I would appreciate it if you could reply as soon as possible to resolve this issue.

Sincerely,

Lanie Dalton
Lanie Dalton

Wingfield's Italian Antiques
75 W. Grand Street
St. Louis, MO 63112

Murano Venini Glass saucer	$212.00
Salviati d'Arte Amber faceted glass platter	$90.00
Cenedese Unicorn glass figurine	$55.00
Murano Sommerso Azure glass vase	$120.00
Aureliano Toso Marbled glass pitcher	$325.00
Total	$802.00

*Note: All sales at Wingfield Antiques are final.

Wingfield's Italian Antiques
75 W. Grand Street
St. Louis, MO 63112

Lanie Dalton
1022 Minnow Drive
St. Louis, MO 63105

Dear Ms. Dalton,

Please know that all our glassware is inspected carefully before being advertised for sale. I remember the piece you are describing, and I can assure you it was carefully looked over both upon arrival and again before it was shipped to your home. As a long-time antique dealer, I believe that this antique was put back together over 100 years ago by the original craftsman. So, the item is actually in its original condition.

I understand that you may be upset, so I would like to refund the charge for the Cenedese unicorn, which you may keep as my gift to you.

Please let me know if you have any other questions.

Best regards,

Esther Wingfield
Esther Wingfield

11. What is the purpose of Ms. Dalton's letter?

(A) To request a return mailing address
(B) To check on the availability of some merchandise
(C) To ask about a late delivery
(D) To express dissatisfaction with the condition of a product

12. What antique is Ms. Dalton worried about?

(A) The glass saucer
(B) The amber-faceted glass platter
(C) The azure glass vase
(D) The marbled glass pitcher

13. What is implied about Wingfield's Italian Antiques?

(A) It does not accept returns.
(B) It does not sell rare antiques online.
(C) It provides discounts to residents.
(D) It is run by a famous art collector.

14. What is mentioned in the second letter?

(A) Ms. Dalton's shipment has not yet arrived.
(B) Ms. Wingfield will submit some documentation.
(C) Ms. Dalton will add additional items to the order.
(D) Ms. Wingfield examined an item herself.

15. How much will Ms. Dalton be refunded?

(A) $55
(B) $90
(C) $120
(D) $212

REVIEW TEST

해설서 p.134 / ⏱ 제한 시간 54분

Questions 1-2 refer to the following product review.

The Scantech DB40-SL portable fan is fantastic. Its compact size allows it to fit into any pants or jacket pocket. I take the DB40-SL with me wherever I go, and it really comes in handy during those hot subway rides to and from the office. I do have one complaint: there is no way to know when the fan is about to run out of power. It would be great to have a new version with some sort of indicator light to warn us when the battery needs to be recharged. I would even consider buying an upgraded version.

-Robert Hanna

1. What is suggested about Mr. Hanna?

(A) He uses public transportation often.
(B) He has tried several portable fans.
(C) He recently started a new job.
(D) He lives far from his office.

2. According to Mr. Hanna, what improvements could be made to the Scantech DB40-SL?

(A) It could be smaller.
(B) An extra battery could be enclosed.
(C) A warning light could be added.
(D) It could be easier to grip.

Questions 3-4 refer to the following notice.

Dear *Roubaix Register* Subscribers:

Please note that due to an increase in printing costs, the *Roubaix Register* will be cutting down on the length of the daily print edition. Consequently, starting next month, the Opinion section will no longer be printed, and instead, it will appear on our website, www. roubaixregister.com.

A sample of the Opinion section will be posted online next week. Once this happens, we encourage all of you to check it out. If you think that there should be changes to the format or style, please email me at ttyrell@roubaixregister.com, and I'll look into it right away.

Thank you,

Todd Tyrell
Editor-in-Chief

3. What change is the *Roubaix Register* making?

(A) It will be replacing an editor.
(B) It will be adding a new section.
(C) It will move some content online.
(D) It will no longer be available daily.

4. According to the notice, why might subscribers contact Mr. Tyrell?

(A) To extend a service
(B) To request a refund
(C) To provide some suggestions
(D) To submit some articles

Questions 5-6 refer to the following text message chain.

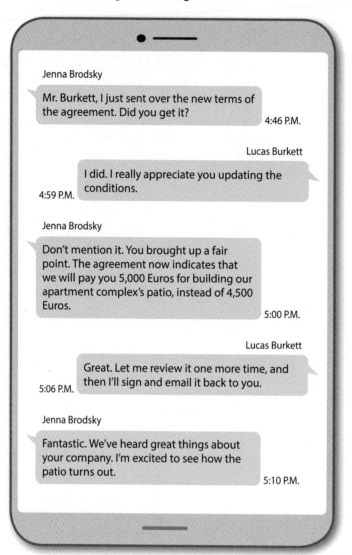

Jenna Brodsky

Mr. Burkett, I just sent over the new terms of the agreement. Did you get it?

4:46 P.M.

Lucas Burkett

4:59 P.M. I did. I really appreciate you updating the conditions.

Jenna Brodsky

Don't mention it. You brought up a fair point. The agreement now indicates that we will pay you 5,000 Euros for building our apartment complex's patio, instead of 4,500 Euros.

5:00 P.M.

Lucas Burkett

5:06 P.M. Great. Let me review it one more time, and then I'll sign and email it back to you.

Jenna Brodsky

Fantastic. We've heard great things about your company. I'm excited to see how the patio turns out.

5:10 P.M.

5. At 5:00 P.M., what does Jenna Brodsky mean when she says, "Don't mention it"?

(A) She already understands some instructions.
(B) She wants to address an issue.
(C) She was glad to complete a task.
(D) She does not want to discuss a subject.

6. Where most likely does Mr. Burkett work?

(A) An accounting company
(B) A construction firm
(C) A real estate agency
(D) A law office

Questions 7-8 refer to the following contract form.

Work Change Form

Landscape Contractor: Florence Rosales, Greenthumb Gardeners, 475 Archer Avenue, San Diego, CA

Property Manager: William Yamamoto, 7534 Weaver Road, San Diego, CA

First Day of Project: April 4

Last Day of Project: April 10

The contractor is hereby directed to review and make the following changes to the initial contract:

Details of the Change:

The client will now provide the seeds, soil, and flowers. As a result, the total cost of the project will be adjusted to include only the cost of labor.

Original Contract Amount: $1,223

Adjustment This Change Order: -$546

Revised Total with Change Order: $677

The New Payment Schedule:

25% ($169) of the new total amount will be collected at the signing of the contract, and $150 must be paid on the first day of the project. The remainder ($358) must be paid on the project's completion date.

Contractor: Florence Rosales

Property Manager: William Yamamoto

7. Why has the cost of the project been adjusted?

(A) The contractor underestimated the price of supplies.

(B) The contractor planted the wrong type of seeds.

(C) The client will supply all the materials.

(D) The client wants to negotiate labor costs.

8. How much money will Mr. Yamamoto most likely give Ms. Rosales on April 10?

(A) $169

(B) $358

(C) $546

(D) $677

Questions 9-11 refer to the following job advertisement.

Work at WT Health!

While most firms ask their sales forces to be pushy and sell products the customer doesn't really need, our team prides itself on being honest and straightforward with all of our clients. Instead of being aggressive, WT Health strives to educate community members on the benefits of our technology. Our commissions are not based on the number of customers you bring in, but on the number of participants attending your product demonstrations.

Earn money while taking our three-week training course. If you pass and become a Certified Sales Representative, you will become eligible for a permanent position on our team.

A college degree and a background in medical technology are a plus, but we'll consider the application of any passionate and articulate individual. Since our customers are located in a variety of regions, you may be asked to travel up to 100 kilometers from headquarters, but you will be reimbursed for any fees incurred in the process.

To apply for the position, log in to your Caliente Jobs account and submit a CV and cover letter. Don't forget to include your phone number. We prefer to correspond by text message. Send a message to 919-555-2333 if you have questions. Most successful applicants take the time to familiarize themselves with our products before coming in for an interview. Visit www.wthealth.com to do so.

9. According to the advertisement, what is the stated duty of the job?

(A) Presenting company products
(B) Attending medical conventions
(C) Developing new technology
(D) Meeting weekly sales commission goals

10. What is the requirement to obtain a permanent position?

(A) A sales associate certificate
(B) References from previous employers
(C) Experience with medical technology
(D) A college degree

11. According to the advertisement, why should an applicant go to WT Health's website?

(A) To submit a job application
(B) To register for a health conference
(C) To get directions to an office
(D) To read about some merchandise

Questions 12-14 refer to the following memo.

To: IRM Technology Division staff
From: Pat Zhao, CEO
Date: December 2
Subject: Important Notice

As most of you know by now, our Chief Technology Officer Tam Pradesh will be retiring at the end of this quarter. We will be having a company-wide dinner in his honor on December 21 at 6:30 P.M. at the Crystal Hotel. Everybody is welcome to attend.

At this time, I would also like to announce Mr. Pradesh's replacement. Jamie Hayes will be joining us on December 26. Ms. Hayes was the Vice President of Software Development at Sci-render Tech and the CTO at Securikey, where she won accolades for training and leading a team that developed an improved virus protection program. I look forward to her being a part of our organization.

Ms. Hayes' introduction will take place during the first quarter shareholders' meeting on December 30 at 10 A.M. and will be viewable on our website. At the meeting, she and CFO Charlotte Wisner will discuss their plans for IRM, Inc. for the coming year. Although this event is optional for employees, attendance is mandatory for department heads.

12. What is the memo announcing?

(A) A personnel change
(B) A press release for a new product
(C) A scheduling change for a meeting
(D) A staff promotion

13. According to the memo, what will happen on December 21?

(A) Mr. Pradesh will attend a dinner.
(B) Mr. Zhao will address investors.
(C) Ms. Hayes will conduct a training seminar.
(D) Ms. Wisner will hand out prizes.

14. Who is Ms. Hayes?

(A) A hotel manager
(B) A financial expert
(C) A job applicant
(D) A recently hired executive

Questions 15-18 refer to the following article.

Roast Meals a Hit in Seoul

SEOUL (November 12) — Maxine Lee has been living in South Korea for six years. Throughout that time, she had not seen a restaurant serving her favorite meal: a traditional Sunday roast. Sunday roasts, consisting of meat, potatoes, and carrots drizzled with gravy, had been a staple of Ms. Lee's childhood in New Zealand.

— [1] —. After speaking to other New Zealanders in South Korea, Ms. Lee made the decision to start her own restaurant, Hearty Delights, specializing in serving roast meals. The first restaurant was a tiny kitchen, barely able to seat 10 people. The initial response was slow as locals were unfamiliar with roast meals. However, word started spreading and soon, there were lines going outside the door.

"I've been surprised to see how many locals we started seeing," Ms. Lee said. "Admittedly, it has been difficult sourcing food from within the country. Lamb, for instance, is hard to come by. — [2] —. For that, I've had to resort to buying food from overseas. But I've tried my hardest to stay local in order to support the farmers here."

Ms. Lee started her restaurant through a grant provided by New Zealand International Trade (NZIT), who wanted to spread New Zealand culture. — [3] —. "I couldn't have done it without them. They were amazing to work with," she said.

Ms. Lee will be opening a larger, second location on November 26. Located in the heart of Seoul, in Gangnam district, the new premises will have the capacity to seat 100. — [4] —. Additionally, Hearty Delights will also begin offering an order-and-collect service through their website. Visit www.heartydelights.co.kr/order for more details.

---

15. What is indicated about Ms. Lee?

(A) She inherited a business.
(B) She originally trained as an accountant.
(C) She frequently moves due to work.
(D) She is not a Seoul native.

16. What does Ms. Lee say about the roasts?

(A) They include imported ingredients.
(B) They follow a traditional family recipe.
(C) They change depending on the season.
(D) They take a significant amount of time to prepare.

17. What is indicated about the NZIT?

(A) It helped advertise roast meals in Seoul.
(B) It shared industry contacts with Ms. Lee.
(C) It suggested locations for new restaurants.
(D) It provided capital for Ms. Lee's restaurant.

18. In which of the positions marked [1], [2], [3], and [4] does the following sentence best belong?

"Asia has been its latest focus."

(A) [1]
(B) [2]
(C) [3]
(D) [4]

Questions 19-21 refer to the following agenda.

Bob Roberts Presents:
Unlock Your Hidden Potential
May 27 (1–6 P.M.)
Seminar Tickets Starting at $99

1:00 P.M.: Where Do You Want to Go?
To advance your personal development, you need to know what to improve. This session will help students who just graduated to create achievable goals and increase their chances of getting a good job.

2:00 P.M.: Who Can You Count On?
Learn to build strong, supportive relationships, and how to discard ones that get in the way of your success.

3:00 P.M.: What Is Your Fuel?
Participants will also learn the importance of physical fitness and nutrition. Our master chef will share recipes and tips, and provide delicious free samples.

4:00 P.M.: Group Exercises
Attendees share stories of their personal journeys, and get honest feedback and affirmation regarding their action plans.

5:00 P.M.: Progress Checks
Keep track of improvements to your health and career. Learn to objectively evaluate how far you've come and what you need to focus on next.

---

19. Who is the seminar most likely intended for?

(A) Job recruiters
(B) Recent graduates
(C) Fitness instructors
(D) Medical students

20. Which section involves setting objectives?

(A) Where Do You Want to Go?
(B) Who Can You Count on?
(C) Group Exercises
(D) Progress Checks

21. What is NOT indicated about the seminar?

(A) It will provide résumé consultations.
(B) It is held for one day.
(C) It costs money to attend.
(D) It offers free food.

Questions 22-25 refer to the following online chat discussion.

Carl Lemieux [1:04 P.M.]
I'm going to be out with the Jennings group for a little longer. Is everything going to be in order for the CEO's visit on Monday?

April Poindexter [1:04 P.M.]
I think so. I'm having the entire floor cleaned over the weekend in preparation for the visit.

Anika Mattu [1:06 P.M.]
Since we upgraded our machines a few weeks ago, production of this year's truck model has been running smoothly without any major incidents. But we really should schedule another employee safety seminar soon.

Carl Lemieux [1:07 P.M.]
Didn't we have one earlier this year?

Anika Mattu [1:07 P.M.]
We've brought in a lot of new employees since then.

Carl Lemieux [1:09 P.M.]
Good point. When shall we arrange a session?

April Poindexter [1:10 P.M]
Also, Anika and I have been taking turns inspecting our assembly line at the end of every day.

Anika Mattu [1:10 P.M.]
Maybe next Tuesday. I can make the arrangements this afternoon.

Carl Lemieux [1:11 P.M.]
Thanks, guys. Actually, Anika, let's discuss that at a later time. We need to make sure everything is set for today's staff appreciation party. I'll head over in half an hour to assist you.

SEND

22. Where do the writers most likely work?

(A) At an auto repair shop
(B) At a car rental agency
(C) At a vehicle manufacturer
(D) At a transportation company

23. What recently happened?

(A) Some equipment was updated.
(B) A trade show was held.
(C) Some workers were retired.
(D) A penalty fee was issued.

24. At 1:09 P.M., what does Mr. Lemieux most likely mean when he writes, "Good point"?

(A) Some training needs to be provided.
(B) A deadline needs to be extended.
(C) Some recruiting guidelines should be revised.
(D) A product feature should be added.

25. What will Ms. Mattu most likely do next?

(A) Fix a machine
(B) Pick up a package
(C) Get ready for an event
(D) Meet with an executive

A New Era for the Palais Royale

Charleston (August 2)—The famous Palais Royale has long been a landmark on Colfax Avenue, but it is about to undergo a major transformation. The ballroom has recently changed ownership, with the New Brunswick-based Thomas Enterprises purchasing the 125-year-old facility last week from its long-time owner. The company's president, Ebonee Salem, says that they plan to shut down the ballroom this winter while crew members work to restore the facility's original woodwork and replace the current ceiling lights with an old-fashioned chandelier. —[1]—.

"But," Ms. Salem added, "we will keep the building's modern sound system, so the space can still be used for live concerts and other social functions."

In recent years, the Palais Royale has hosted a limited number of events. —[2]—. The former owner, Jessica Grassley, tried for years to make the ballroom a center of civic life as it was prior to the 1970s. "This was my passion project," said Grassley. "so it was tough for me. I didn't want to give the Palais Royale up, but in the end, I think Thomas Enterprises is going to give the old ballroom a new spark." —[3]—.

The new ownership group hopes the ballroom will attract more weddings, school dances, and big-ticket corporate events. The Palais Royale will also continue to host its annual charity event. This year's gathering will be held on April 11. The event, as always, will be open to the general public, but this year, all attendees will be required to wear formal attire. Also, it will no longer be known as the Palais Charity Drive. Instead, it will be called the PR Charity Gala. —[4]—.

26. What is implied about the Palais Royale?

(A) It was opened in the 1970s.
(B) It will raise its admission fees.
(C) It was previously a family-run facility.
(D) It will be renovated soon.

27. According to the article, what was hard for Ms. Grassley?

(A) Deciding to sell the ballroom
(B) Trying to retain good employees
(C) Choosing an appropriate design
(D) Finding interested buyers

28. What was renamed?

(A) A charity event
(B) A job title
(C) A local business
(D) A city street

29. In which of the positions marked [1], [2], [3], and [4] does the following sentence best belong?

"Traditional wallpaper will also be added."

(A) [1]
(B) [2]
(C) [3]
(D) [4]

Questions 30-34 refer to the following notice and e-mail.

Round the Bays Race

Round the Bays Race is back again this year, and the date has been confirmed to be March 14. As with every year, the route will involve beautiful scenes of the ocean as well as clifftop views. This year, we will introduce some variety by running through Matauri Bay, a new addition to our lineup. The main event will stretch 21 kilometers. However, we will also offer a 10-kilometer (10K) run and a 5-kilometer (5K) run for our more casual runners.

All participants will receive personalized water bottles as well as race bibs. Mailing out the items to you will take 7 business days, so the deadline to register and pay will be March 4. Late registrations will also be available, but you will have to pick up your items on the day of the event.

Register today by heading over to www.roundthebays.com/register. The main race is $50, the 10K is $30, and the 5K is $20. All proceeds will go towards cleaning up our beautiful beaches. Any questions should be emailed to Eric Chavez at e.chavez@roundthebays.com.

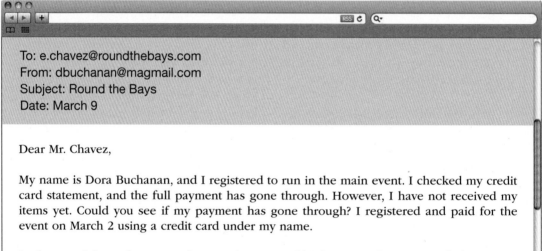

To: e.chavez@roundthebays.com
From: dbuchanan@magmail.com
Subject: Round the Bays
Date: March 9

Dear Mr. Chavez,

My name is Dora Buchanan, and I registered to run in the main event. I checked my credit card statement, and the full payment has gone through. However, I have not received my items yet. Could you see if my payment has gone through? I registered and paid for the event on March 2 using a credit card under my name.

In the case it is too late to send me my items, would it be easier for me to pick them up at the event instead?

Sincerely,

Dora Buchanan

30. What is suggested about the route of the Round the Bay Race?

(A) It changes every year.
(B) It is a new route this year.
(C) It has been shortened.
(D) It ends at a national park.

31. In the notice, the word "stretch" in paragraph 1, line 4, is closest in meaning to

(A) cover
(B) develop
(C) strain
(D) create

32. What is true about the various races being held on March 14?

(A) There are various age requirements for each race.
(B) There is a maximum number of participants per race.
(C) They give out prizes for the winners.
(D) They are intended to raise money for a cause.

33. What is indicated about Ms. Buchanan?

(A) She attends the race every year.
(B) She signed up late for the event.
(C) She helped plan out the route.
(D) She made a payment of $50.

34. What is one purpose of Ms. Buchanan's e-mail?

(A) To change a condition
(B) To verify a payment
(C) To make a suggestion
(D) To confirm the location

Questions 35-39 refer to the following expense report and e-mail.

Xin Collections Monthly Expense Report

Month	July
Submission date	9 August
Submitted by	Courtney Flowers
Head of office	Tami French
Office branch	California

Item No.	Date	Expense Amount	Description
1	3 July	$60.51	Client lunch meeting
2	7 July	$201.23	Return flights to Nevada for conference
3	12 July	$40.84	Package to Colorado
4	18 July	$130.11	Employee birthday dinner
5	25 July	$52.75	Office supplies
Total		$485.44	

Advance check from HQ	$500.00
Expenses paid by HQ	
Balance Due to HQ	$14.56

From:	Tami French <tfrench@xincollections.com>
To:	Courtney Flowers <cflowers@xincollections.com>
Date:	13 August
Subject:	Expense report adjustments

Dear Courtney,

I have looked over the monthly expense report you sent me. I would like to request the following adjustments. As a general rule, our Ohio headquarters likes to receive these reports at the beginning of every month. I understand you are still getting situated with your new responsibilities as a manager. However, an important part of being a good manager is being able to stay on top of the necessary paperwork.

Additionally, could you remove item 4 from your report? This expense is covered by headquarters. This has been the case for several years now. You should report this under "Expenses paid by HQ." Doing so will result in adjustments to the "Advance check from HQ" and "Balance Due to HQ" totals, so please calculate the new figures and write a check for the new amount.

Sincerely,

Tami French

35. According to the expense report, what did Ms. Flowers most likely do in July?

(A) Made an office repair
(B) Attended a business meeting
(C) Returned some books
(D) Conducted a survey

36. Where do Ms. Flowers and Ms. French work?

(A) In Colorado
(B) In Boston
(C) In California
(D) In Ohio

37. In the e-mail, the word "case" in paragraph 2, line 2, is closest in meaning to

(A) shell
(B) promise
(C) complaint
(D) policy

38. According to the e-mail, what is most likely true about Ms. Flowers?

(A) She did not receive adequate training.
(B) She exceeded her given budget in July.
(C) She was recently promoted to her position.
(D) She often submits paperwork late.

39. According to the e-mail, what item did Ms. Flowers list incorrectly on her report?

(A) Delivery service
(B) Celebration event
(C) Flight tickets
(D) Office supplies

Our Policy on Schedule Changes

Here at Andes Rail, we do everything we can to help you have the smoothest possible trip. For your convenience, schedules are made available on our website seven days ahead of time. However, unforeseen circumstances such as weather or unscheduled maintenance can lead to delays and cancellations.

Where to Find Information on Schedule Changes
All current train times are posted on the Andes Rail app and updated whenever a change occurs. If you buy your ticket directly from Andes Rail, we'll also send you an immediate notification via your selected mode of communication as soon as a change takes place. If you got your tickets through a third-party vendor, that company is obligated to contact you to provide updates within four hours of any change.

What to Do if Delays Create a Scheduling Conflict
The large majority of changes will affect your original arrival time by less than one hour. However, if excessive delays occur, or if scheduling makes it impossible to complete your trip as originally booked, we ask that you email our customer service team at customerservice@andesrail.com.

When You Are Eligible for Reimbursement
In a very small number of cases, we may not be able to accommodate you on another train. In these cases, you may qualify for full reimbursement, but be aware that to receive one, your rescheduling must meet the following conditions:
- Your original arrival or departure time was changed by at least three hours.
  OR
- The scheduling change results in a missed train.

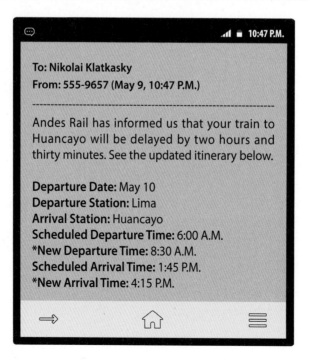

To: Nikolai Klatkasky
From: 555-9657 (May 9, 10:47 P.M.)

Andes Rail has informed us that your train to Huancayo will be delayed by two hours and thirty minutes. See the updated itinerary below.

Departure Date: May 10
Departure Station: Lima
Arrival Station: Huancayo
Scheduled Departure Time: 6:00 A.M.
***New Departure Time:** 8:30 A.M.
Scheduled Arrival Time: 1:45 P.M.
***New Arrival Time:** 4:15 P.M.

From:	Nikolai Klatkasky
To:	Vince Rhames
Date:	May 9
Subject:	Change of Plans
Attachment:	Quarterly Projections

Vince,

My morning train up to Huancayo is going to be delayed. Would you mind leading the Grissom Group meeting? I'll still be en route at that time. I've attached a slide show with our quarterly revenue projections. Their team is concerned about the performance of their investment, but I think they'll be pleased to see how successful our new laptops and smartphones have been in overseas markets.

Best,

Nikolai

40. What is true about Andes Rail?

(A) It has recently launched a new website.
(B) Its trains are frequently late.
(C) It posts schedules one week in advance.
(D) Its tracks are undergoing routine maintenance.

41. According to the notice, how can any Andes Rail passenger obtain up-to-date train information?

(A) By paying a small fee
(B) By visiting the Andes Rail ticketing office
(C) By speaking with an Andes Rail manager
(D) By checking an application

42. What is implied about Mr. Klatkasky?

(A) He will miss a connecting train.
(B) He will receive full reimbursement.
(C) He did not purchase his ticket from Andes Rail directly.
(D) He regularly uses Andes Rail when he goes on trips.

43. What is most likely true about the Grissom Group meeting?

(A) It will start before 4:15 P.M.
(B) It will be led by Mr. Klatkasky.
(C) It will take place in Lima.
(D) It will be postponed.

44. What kind of business does Mr. Klatkasky most likely work for?

(A) A travel agency
(B) An investment firm
(C) An electronics maker
(D) A rail company

Questions 45-49 refer to the following advertisement, e-mail, and Web page feedback.

Vincenzo's Dream Tours

Rome, Italy

Vincenzo's Dream Tours is excited to announce an end-of-summer 20 percent discount for all available tours. Act fast, as this offer is only valid for reservations made before 1 August. Come find out why we were named Top Tour Operator in Italy by *Roma Leisure Magazine*.

Below are some of our most popular tours:

- **Campania Region (two-day tour):** Walk through the ancient city of Pompeii to see what life was like in the Roman Empire. Then, make your way up to Mount Vesuvius to get an up-close look at the volcano that destroyed the city. Afterward, enjoy breathtaking views on a drive along the narrow cliff roads of the Amalfi Coast.

- **Gargano and the Tremiti Islands (three-day tour):** This tour is for nature lovers. The Gargano Peninsula features sandy beaches, romantic nature trails, and lush vegetation. On this tour, enjoy a night hike through the Foresta Umbra, boating and swimming around the Tremiti Islands, and a visit to the Unesco World Heritage Site, Monte Sant'Angelo.

- **Vatican City (one-day tour):** See some of the world's greatest artistic and architectural masterpieces at St. Peter's Square, the Sistine Chapel, and the Vatican Museums. Night tours are also available.

Private packages are also available upon request for organizations with large groups.

To	tlorenz@hotspot.com
From	info@vincenzosdream.com
Subject	Reservation Receipt
Date	25 July

Dear Ms. Lorenz,

Here is the receipt for your tour package. Please double-check to make sure all the information is correct.

Tour Package: Campania Region	
Start Date and Time: 7 August at 8 A.M.	
End Date and Time: 8 August at 8 P.M.	
Total Amount: €215	

If there is a mistake or you have any questions, our customer service representatives are ready to help you. Email us at cs@vincenzosdream.com or call us at +39 (06) 5555 8294.

We appreciate your business and look forward to seeing you soon!

Tour Feedback

As someone who loves history, I had wanted to go to Italy. This tour met all my expectations. Gian Ricci, our tour guide, was well-prepared and engaging. Because he grew up in the area, he took us to areas that are unknown to most visiting tourists. He was very knowledgeable and responded accurately to all of my questions about the area's architecture, traditions, and culture. I would recommend this tour to everyone.

Review by Tammy Lorenz

45. What is indicated about Vincenzo's Dream Tours?

(A) It has added more destinations.
(B) It only operates during the summer.
(C) It is a highly rated business.
(D) It will open locations in other European cities.

46. According to the advertisement, what can Vincenzo's Dream Tours offer customers?

(A) Exclusive tours for groups with many members
(B) Special discounts for first-time clients
(C) Complimentary gifts from a souvenir shop
(D) Transportation service from the local airport

47. What is implied about Ms. Lorenz's tour?

(A) It will last three days.
(B) It includes daily meals.
(C) It was booked at a lower rate.
(D) It was designed specifically for families.

48. In the Web page feedback, the word "met" in line 1, is closest in meaning to

(A) complied
(B) joined
(C) satisfied
(D) performed

49. What is suggested about Mr. Ricci?

(A) He works for a local magazine.
(B) He is a native of Campania.
(C) He is a university student.
(D) He speaks multiple languages.

Questions 50-54 refer to the following store offer and e-mails.

Wuerfel Supply Company

Bartertown's best wholesale source for all your disposable drinking cups, straw, and lid needs.

Order Today and Save

As part of our special promotion, new customers are eligible for the discounts listed below.

- $5 off purchases over $50
- $15 off purchases over $150
- $30 off purchases over $250
- $50 off purchases over $300

The shipping fee will also be waived for purchases of $250 or more.

To receive your discount, use the code found at the bottom of this page. Offer good until 31 July.

46EUEEEE

*This is a single-use code. Certain restrictions may apply.

To	customerservice@wuerfelsupplyco.nz
From	nbrie@dawsoncatering.com.nz
Date	19 July
Subject	Order Number 37991

To Whom It May Concern,

I ordered a box of 500ml coffee cups and straws a few days ago. I entered the promotional code (46EUEEEE), as your offer directed. And while my shipping charge was waived, I did not receive the $30 discount you advertised. Can I ask you to wire that amount to my company's account?

Aside from this issue, everyone at the office really appreciated the high quality of the cups and their heatproof lining in particular. In any case, after we receive the reimbursement, I plan to place another order. As a growing catering company, we are going to need these supplies restocked frequently. I saw on your website that you offer monthly deliveries. The first Tuesday or the first Thursday of the month is ideal for us. Do those days fit in your schedule?

Best,

Nora Brie
Dawson Catering Operations Team

To	nbrie@dawsoncatering.com.nz
From	mmaron@wuerfelsupplyco.nz
Date	19 July
Subject	Re: Order Number 37991

Dear Ms. Brie,

Thank you for taking the time to bring this matter to our attention. We apologize for not applying the promotional discount to your purchase. I have already gone ahead and reimbursed you. As compensation, I will also send you an extra set of coffee cups and straws at no charge. You should receive the package within the week.

I can also help you arrange regular shipment dates. Our drivers already deliver to your area the first Wednesday, Thursday, and Friday of every month, so we should be able to include you on our route. We can start as soon as next month if you like.

Let me apologize once again for the recent oversight, and we thank you for your continued business. We look forward to meeting all your future needs.

Best,

Marcus Maron, Customer Service Team

50. What is indicated about the offer?

(A) It expires before July 31.
(B) It is valid for one product.
(C) It excludes small businesses.
(D) It is for first-time customers.

51 Why was the first e-mail sent?

(A) To revise an order quantity
(B) To point out some defects
(C) To bring attention to a billing mistake
(D) To ask for directions to a building

52. How much did Ms. Brie spend at Wuerfel Supply Company?

(A) Over $50
(B) Over $150
(C) Over $250
(D) Over $500

53. In the second e-mail, what does Mr. Maron offer to Ms. Brie?

(A) Complimentary items
(B) Expedited delivery
(C) A discount coupon
(D) A membership card

54. When will Wuerfel Supply Company most likely deliver to Dawson Catering?

(A) The first Tuesday of the month
(B) The first Wednesday of the month
(C) The first Thursday of the month
(D) The first Friday of the month

MEMO

MEMO

MEMO

파고다 토익 RC 해설서

RC

해설서

4th Edition

파고다교육그룹 언어교육연구소, 라수진 I 저

고득점 완성

PAGODA Books

파고다 토익

토익 RC 해설서

4th Edition

파고다교육그룹 언어교육연구소, 라수진 l 저

고득점 완성

PAGODA Books

PART 5

UNIT 01. 문장의 구조와 수 일치

1. + check 　1. (D)　2. (C)　3. (D)　_{본서 p.22}

1. 낡은 사원의 복원은 문화유산 보존 위원회가 올해 완료할 첫 번째 프로젝트이다.

해설　관사 뒤의 빈칸이므로 명사인 (D) restoration이 정답이다.

어휘　temple 사원 ▎complete 완료하다

2. 스워브 마케팅 직원들은 본사에서 5년을 근무한 후에 해외지사로 전근갈 자격이 주어질 것이다.

해설　동사 앞에 들어가야 하는 인칭대명사는 주격이므로 (C) they가 정답이다.

어휘　be eligible to ~할 자격이 있다 ▎transfer to ~로 전근가다 ▎overseas 해외의 ▎branch 지사 ▎main office 본사

3. 고객님이 페어필드에 살고 계신다면 주문하신 피자를 40분 이내에 배달해 드리는 것이 피자 러버의 정책입니다.

해설　문장에 동사가 이미 나와 있으므로, (A), (B), (C)는 탈락이 되어 (D) to deliver가 정답이다. 이 문장은 「가주어 It + 동사 + ~ + 진주어 to부정사」구문이다.

어휘　policy 정책 ▎as long as ~하는 한 ▎live in ~에 살다

2. + check 　1. (B)　2. (B)　3. (A)　_{본서 p.23}

1. 캠벨 하우스는 우리 회사가 구독하는 주간 패션 잡지를 출판한다.

해설　빈칸은 동사 자리로 보기에서 동사는 (B)밖에 없으므로 (B) publishes가 정답이다.

어휘　subscribe to ~을 구독하다 ▎publisher 출판사 ▎publicity 홍보 ▎publication 출판(물)

2. 램버트 산업은 재고 추적 프로그램 설계를 간소화해 그것을 사용하기 위한 교육을 덜 받도록 했다.

해설　has 뒤에는 현재 완료 시제를 완성하는 p.p. 형태가 나와야 하므로 (B) simplified가 정답이다.

어휘　design 설계 ▎inventory tracking program 재고 추적 프로그램 ▎so that ~하도록 ▎simplify 간소화하다, 단순화하다 ▎simplification 단순화, 간소화

3. 미쉘란 식당에 가려면, 건물의 동쪽 끝에 있는 계단을 이용하시오.

해설　빈칸은 뒤에 목적어를 취하는 동사 자리로 주어가 생략된 명령문이므로 동사원형인 (A) use가 정답이다. 보통 if, when, in order to, to부정사는 명령문을 동반해서 자주 출제된다.

어휘　get to ~에 도착하다 ▎stair 계단

3. + check 　1. (C)　2. (D)　3. (A)　_{본서 p.25}

1. 사진 대회에 참가하는 데 관심 있는 직원들은 3월 23일까지 출품작을 제출해야 한다.

해설　문장에 이미 동사가 있고, 빈칸은 앞에 주어인 Those employees를 수식하는 형태가 와야 하므로 정답은 '관심 있는 직원들'이라는 의미를 만드는 (C) interested이다.

어휘　competition 대회 ▎entry 출입, 출품작

---

2. 실험실의 안전 수칙은 직원 안내서의 9-D 섹션에 서술되어 있다.

해설　빈칸은 동사 자리이며, 빈칸 뒤에 목적어가 없어 수동태가 적절한데, 문장의 주어가 procedures로 복수이므로 (D) are outlined가 정답이다.

어휘　safety procedure 안전 수칙 ▎laboratory 실험실 ▎handbook 안내서 ▎outline 서술하다

3. 귀하가 선택하신 원하는 카메라의 색상이 지금은 없지만, 똑같은 모델의 메탈블루 색상이 있습니다.

해설　이미 동사가 is로 나와 있으므로 (C), (D)는 탈락이 되며, '귀하가 선택하신'이라는 의미가 적합하므로 the camera (that) you selected를 만드는 (A) you가 정답이다.

어휘　select 선택하다 ▎currently 현재 ▎unavailable 이용할 수 없는 ▎desired 희망하는, 원하는

4. + check 　1. (D)　2. (B)　3. (D)　_{본서 p.27}

1. 자리가 한정되어 있으니, 최대한 빨리 내일 세미나에 참석할 수 있는지 매튜스 씨에게 알려주시기를 바랍니다.

해설　빈칸은 뒤에 the seminar를 목적어로 취하는 타동사 자리이며, 문맥상 '내일 세미나에 참석할 수 있는지 최대한 빨리 알려달라'는 의미가 자연스러우므로 (D) attend가 정답이다. (A)와 (C)는 뒤에 목적어를 취하기 위해 전치사가 필요한 자동사이므로 답이 될 수 없다.

어휘　due to ~으로 인해 ▎limited 제한된, 한정된 ▎spot 자리 ▎as soon as possible 가능한 한 빨리 ▎reply to ~에 답장을 보내다 ▎attend 참석하다

2. 메리스 사 직원들은 최근에 개정된 보안 정책에 익숙해지도록 회사 온라인 게시판을 방문해야 한다.

해설　become은 대표적인 2형식 동사로 뒤에 명사, 형용사가 주격 보어로 오며, 해석상 '익숙해지다'의 의미가 자연스러우므로 (B) familiar가 정답이다.

어휘　bulletin board 게시판 ▎revise 개정하다 ▎familiarize (oneself with) 익숙해지다 ▎familiarity 익숙함, 낯익음

3. 옌 씨가 회사 창립 기념 파티를 준비하고 있으니, 손님을 데려올지에 대해 그녀에게 알려 주십시오.

해설　사역동사 let은 「let + 목적어 + 동사원형」 '~가 …하게 하다' 패턴을 취하므로 목적격 대명사 (D) her가 정답이다.

어휘　organize 준비하다, 조직하다 ▎anniversary 기념일

Practice　_{본서 p.28}

1. (A)	**2.** (A)	**3.** (C)	**4.** (C)	**5.** (A)
6. (B)	**7.** (A)	**8.** (D)	**9.** (B)	**10.** (A)
11. (D)	**12.** (B)	**13.** (A)	**14.** (C)	**15.** (D)
16. (D)	**17.** (B)	**18.** (B)	**19.** (D)	**20.** (D)

1. 헐리스 카페의 새 아이스티를 마셔본 고객들은 그 음료가 충분히 달다고 말했다.

해설　be동사 뒤 보어 자리로, '음료가 달다'는 의미를 완성하는 형용사 보어 (A) sweet가 정답이다. 빈칸 앞에 정관사 the가 없으므로 최상급 형

용사인 (D) sweetest는 답이 될 수 없다. 참고로 enough는 명사 앞에 위치하면 형용사, 형용사 뒤에 위치하면 부사 역할을 한다.

어휘 **beverage** 음료 | **enough** 충분한; 충분히

2. 10주년 저녁을 위한 초대장이 곧 모든 직원에게 우편으로 보내질 것이다.

해설 빈칸은 주어 자리로 (A), (C)가 답으로 가능하다. 그러나 (C)의 경우 Inviting의 목적어가 없으며 문장의 의미 또한 어색하므로 답이 될 수 없다. 해석상 '초대장'이 보내져야 하므로 정답은 (A) Invitations가 된다.

어휘 **anniversary** 기념일 | **invitation** 초대장

3. 연구 개발팀에서 제안한 변화들은 작지만 회사에 상당한 영향을 미칠 것이다.

해설 문장의 주어는 The changes이고 suggested는 뒤에서 주어를 수식하는 과거분사이므로 빈칸은 동사 자리가 된다. 주어가 복수이므로 정답은 복수 동사인 (C) are가 된다.

어휘 **research and development** 연구 개발 | **significant effect on** ~에 대한 상당한 영향

4. 아파트 주민들은 업그레이드된 재활용 시스템이 쓰레기를 줄이는 데 효과적이라는 것을 알게 됐다.

해설 find는 대표적인 5형식 동사로 목적격 보어로 형용사를 취한다. 목적어로 the upgraded recycling system이 나왔으므로 정답은 형용사인 (C) effective가 된다.

어휘 **resident** 주민 | **recycling** 재활용 | **waste** 쓰레기

5. 인사부는 신입 직원들이 회사 정책에 친숙해지도록 돕는다.

해설 문장의 주어가 3인칭 단수 The Personnel Department이므로 빈칸에 (A) helps가 알맞다. become은 준사역 동사(help)의 목적격 보어로 나온 것이다.

어휘 **personnel department** 인사부 | **familiar with** ~에 친숙한 | **help + 목적어 + (to) do** 도와서 ~하게 하다, ~하는 것을 도와주다

6. 고객에게 중요한 문서를 우편으로 보낼 때, 그것을 보내기 전에 수령인에게 알리세요.

해설 「When / If절, 명령문 ~.」 구조이므로 빈칸에 동사원형이 와야 한다. 정답은 동사원형인 (B) notify가 된다.

어휘 **receiver** 수령인 | **notification** 알림, 통지 | **notify** 알리다

7. 티에프브이 전자는 회사의 성공에 기여한 20명의 훌륭한 직원들을 축하하는 연례 시상식을 개최했다.

해설 문장의 주어는 TFV Technology이고 동사는 held이다. 한 문장 안에 동사 두 개가 올 수 없으므로 (B), (D)는 답이 될 수 없으며, (A), (C)는 분사로 award ceremony라는 명사를 수식할 수 있다. '축하하는 시상식'이라는 의미가 되어야 하므로 정답은 현재분사인 (A) honoring이 알맞다.

어휘 **annual** 연례의 | **award ceremony** 시상식 | **outstanding** 뛰어난, 미지불된 | **contribute to** ~에 기여하다

8. 매년 최신의 콘셉트 자동차를 선보이는 모터쇼는 많은 방문객들을 끌어모은다.

해설 주어(The Motor Show) 다음에 콤마가 있으므로 관계대명사 that은 올 수 없고, 선행사를 포함하는 what은 앞에 선행사 Motor Show라는 명사가 나오므로 답이 될 수 없다. 그리고 where는 관계부사로 뒤에 완전한 문장이 나와야 하는데 뒤는 불완전한 문장이므로 정답은 (D) which가 된다.

어휘 **demonstrate** 입증하다, 보여주다 | **attract** 끌어들이다 | **visitor** 방문객, 손님

9. 연장된 이 지하철 노선으로 운행될 지역들은 몬트레스 미술관과 아루바 공원을 포함한다.

해설 문장의 주어는 Locations이고 동사는 include이다. 빈칸에는 주어 (Locations)를 수식할 수 있는 분사구나 to부정사구가 나오는 것이 알맞다. 의미상 수동의 의미인 '운행될'이 들어가야 하므로 정답은 (B) to be serviced가 된다. 분사구가 답이 되려면, serviced라는 과거분사가 나오면 된다.

어휘 **location** 지역, 위치 | **extended** 연장된

10. 코크 가전에서 무료 배송 자격을 얻으려면, 우편으로 보내진 바우처를 보여주셔야 합니다.

해설 본동사가 must present로 이미 존재하므로 동사 (C), (D)는 탈락이 되며, 빈칸 뒤에 목적어가 없다는 점에서 목적어를 취해야 하는 동명사 sending도 형태상 들어갈 수 없으므로 답에서 제외시킨다. 따라서 명사 voucher를 수식하는 수동태 관계절인 (A) that was sent가 정답이다.

어휘 **qualify** 자격을 얻다 | **shipping** 배송 | **appliance** 기기, 가전제품 | **present** 보여주다

11. 만약 절차에 대해서 추가 질문이 있다면 2월 4일에 보내진 김 씨의 이메일을 참조하세요.

해설 (A), (B), (C)는 뒤에 전치사와 함께 쓰이는 자동사이다. 뒤에 목적어 e-mail과 함께 쓰이는 타동사가 필요하므로 답은 '참조하다'의 뜻을 가진 (D) consult가 된다.

어휘 **procedure** 절차 | **inquire** 묻다, 문의하다 | **appeal** 호소하다, 흥미를 끌다 | **consult** 참조하다, 상담하다

12. 소포의 예상 도착 시간은 기사가 내일 배달해야 하는 횟수에 따라 달라집니다.

해설 빈칸은 동사 자리이다. 동사는 수, 시제, 태를 일치시켜 주는데, 동사 자리에 못 들어가는 (A), (D)는 탈락이며, 수 일치에서 주어가 단수이므로 동사의 복수형인 (C)도 탈락이다. 정답은 (B) depends가 된다.

어휘 **anticipated arrival time** 예상 도착 시간 | **package** 소포 | **depend on** ~에 따라 다르다, ~에 의존하다 | **dependent** 의존하는 | **dependable** 믿을 수 있는

13. 직원회의에서, 경영진은 보통 직장 정책에 관한 모든 질문에 답한다.

해설 빈칸은 주어 management의 동사 자리이다. 질문에 답한다는 의미가 되어야 문맥상 자연스러우며 빈칸 뒤에 to가 있으므로 전치사 to를 동반하는 자동사인 (A) responds가 정답이다.

어휘 management 경영진 | typically 보통 | regarding ~에 관하여 | workplace 직장 | policy 정책 | respond to ~에 답하다 | retain 유지하다 | submit 제출하다 | pronounce 발음하다, 표명하다

14. 부서 책임자는 다음 주가 마감인 제품 조사 프로젝트에 대해 러셀 씨에게 도움을 주었다.

해설 문장의 주어는 The department head이고 빈칸에는 동사가 와야 한다. 목적어가 두 개(Mr. Russell, assistance) 나오므로 4형식 동사를 찾는 문제이다. 그러므로 정답은 (C) offered이다.

어휘 department head 부서 책임자 | assistance 도움 | due ~하기로 되어 있는 | donate A to B A를 B에 기증하다 | offer A B(= offer B to A) A에게 B를 주다[제공하다] | suggest A to B A를 B에게 제안하다

15. 부사장은 상급 직원들에게 항상 회사의 이익을 위해서 행동해 달라고 요청했다.

해설 목적격 보어로 to부정사를 가지는 대표적인 5형식 동사를 찾는 문제이다. 요구, 설득, 허락 등의 의미를 가진 (D) urged가 답으로 알맞다.

어휘 interest 이익 | allege (근거 없이) 주장하다 | vow 맹세하다 | pursue 추구하다 | urge 권하다, 충고하다

16. 리 씨에게 그녀의 주문품이 이번 주 말까지 사무실로 배송될 것이라고 알려 주세요.

해설 빈칸 뒤에 목적어(사람)를 가지며 that을 가지는 동사를 찾는 문제이다. (A), (B), (C)는 바로 that을 취하므로 오답이다. 정답은 「inform + 목적어 + that」을 취하는 (D) inform이 된다.

어휘 announce 발표하다, 알리다 | mention 언급하다 | inform 알리다, 통지하다

17. 카페 첼레스떼는 단골 손님에게 지금부터 6월 말까지 무료 디저트를 제공할 것이다.

해설 빈칸은 문장에서 동사 역할을 하면서 뒤에 두 개의 목적어가 온 4형식 능동태 문장이므로 (B) will be offering이 정답이다.

어휘 patron 단골 손님 | complimentary 무료의

18. 가나슈 대학의 목적은 학생들이 그들의 학구적이고 전문적인 목표를 성취할 수 있게 도와주는 것이다.

해설 help라는 준사역 동사가 5형식으로 쓰였을 때는 목적격 보어로 to부정사 또는 동사원형이 와야 한다. 따라서 (B) achieve가 정답이다.

어휘 aim 목표, 목적 | achieve 달성하다, 성취하다

19. 당신의 노트북 컴퓨터 화면에 보호필름이 붙어 있도록 모니터에서 먼지를 제거하기 위해 부드러운 솔을 이용하시오.

해설 빈칸은 부사절 접속사 so that이 이끄는 종속절의 동사 자리이며, 빈칸 뒤에 전치사 to가 있으므로 to와 짝을 이뤄 adhere to '~에 들러붙다, ~을 고수하다'를 완성하는 (D) adhere가 정답이다.

어휘 clean 닦다, 청소하다 | dust 먼지 | so that ~하도록 |

---

protective 보호하는 | laptop 휴대용 컴퓨터 | comply 따르다 | utilize 활용하다 | polish 닦다 | adhere 들러붙다

20. 수정된 계약서는 피에르 씨가 수정할 정보를 포함하고 있다.

해설 빈칸 뒤에 목적어가 없어서 자칫 수동태 (B)를 선택할 수 있는데, 빈칸은 동사 자리로 동사 자리에 들어갈 수 없는 (C)가 탈락이 되며, 수 일치에 따라 (A)도 탈락된다. information 뒤에 목적격 관계대명사 that이 생략되어 「주어 + 동사」가 앞에 나오는 명사 information을 수식하는 문제로 정답은 (D) will correct가 된다. 해석을 해봐도 피에르 씨가 수정해야 할 정보이지, 수정되는 정보는 아니다.

어휘 revised 수정된 | contract 계약서 | correct 수정하다

UNIT 02. 시제

1. `+ check` 　　1. (B) 　　2. (C) 　　3. (B) 　　본서 p.31

1. 바튼 씨는 지난주 케이프타운에서 그가 참석했던 투자자 회의에 관하여 이야기를 할 것이다.

해설 빈칸은 동사 자리로, 시간을 나타내는 last week이 나오므로 과거 동사인 (B) attended가 정답이다.

어휘 investor 투자자 | conference 회의, 학회

2. 다음 달에, 환경 단체인 와일드라이프 프리저버는 운하 건설에 대한 철저한 조사를 실시할 것이다.

해설 빈칸은 동사 자리로, 일단 동사 자리에 들어갈 수 없는 (B)는 탈락이 된다. 미래를 나타내는 시간 어구 next month가 나오므로 정답은 (C), (D)가 가능하지만, 뒤에 목적어를 동반하여 수동태 (D)는 탈락이 되어 (C) will conduct가 정답이다.

어휘 thorough 철저한 | investigation 조사 | canal 운하

3. 시설들은 24시간 PC를 사용할 수 있는 컴퓨터실은 물론 냉난방 시설이 되어 있는 식당을 포함하고 있다.

해설 빈칸은 동사 자리로, 동사 자리에 들어갈 수 없는 (A), (D)는 탈락이 되며, 수 일치에 의해서 (C)가 탈락이 되어 (B) include가 정답이다.

어휘 facility 시설, 설비 | air-conditioned 에어컨이 설치된 | access to ~으로의 접근[접속]

2. `+ check` 　　1. (A) 　　2. (B) 　　3. (D) 　　본서 p.31

1. 다음 달부터, 차우 제조사는 그곳의 모든 근로자에게 무료 간식과 음료를 제공할 것이다.

해설 빈칸은 동사 자리로, 미래 시제를 나타내는 시간 어구인 Beginning next month가 나오므로, (A), (C)가 답이 될 수 있으며, 미래 완료 시제 (C)는 by next ~/by the end of ~/by the time ~을 동반해야 하므로 오답이다. 따라서 정답은 (A) will be providing이다.

어휘 beverage 음료

2. 지금, 연례 공장 조사에서 지적받은 문제점들을 해결하기 위해서 조립 라인을 위한 안전 수칙이 수정되고 있다.

해설 빈칸은 동사 자리로, 빈칸 앞에 복수 주어가 나오며 뒤에 전치사가

나오므로 수동태가 나와야 한다. 그러므로 (B) are being revised가 정답이다.

어휘 **at this time** 이때에, 현재 | **safety procedure** 안전 수칙 | **assembly** 조립 | **fix a problem** 문제를 해결하다 | **indicate** ~을 보여주다[지적하다] | **annual** 연례의 | **inspection** 점검 | **revise** ~을 수정하다

3. 사토 씨가 발표 준비를 하고 있었을 때, 그에게 주어진 시간이 부족해서 모든 차트를 포함할 수 없었다.

해설 빈칸은 동사 자리로, 동사 자리에 들어갈 수 없는 (A), (B)가 탈락이 되고, 수 일치로 (C)가 탈락되므로 (D) was preparing이 정답이다.

어휘 **due to** ~때문에 | **chart** 도표, 차트

3. (+ check)   1. (D)   2. (D)   3. (D)   본서 p.32

1. 더 많은 고객을 유치하기 위해, 많은 지역 사업들이 지난 몇 달간 새로운 서비스들을 제공하기 시작했다.

해설 빈칸은 동사 자리로 시간 어구 in the past few months는 현재 완료와 쓰이므로 (D) have begun이 정답이다.

어휘 **attract** 유치하다, 끌다 | **local business** 지역 기업

2. 앤드류 플린터는 수년간 랜던 고등학교에서 최고의 선생님들 중 한 명으로 여겨져 왔다.

해설 빈칸은 동사 자리로 뒤에 for many years는 현재 완료와 잘 어울리므로 (D) has been considered가 정답이다. 동사 consider는 5형식 동사로 수동태로 쓰였을 때 명사 보어를 바로 이끌 수 있다.

어휘 **for many years** 수년간 | **consider** 여기다

3. 그루비 자동차의 신차 디자인은 회사가 예상했었던 것보다 젊은 운전자에게 훨씬 더 어필했다.

해설 빈칸은 동사 자리이고, 운전자들을 끌어모은 것은 과거이지만 회사가 예상한 것은 그 이전이므로, 과거 완료 (D) had anticipated가 정답이다.

어휘 **appealing** 호소하는, 매력적인 | **anticipate** 예상하다

4. (+ check)   1. (C)   2. (A)   3. (D)   본서 p.33

1. 베넷 씨가 특별 프로젝트를 마칠 때까지, 창 씨가 그의 일상적인 업무 대부분을 담당할 것이다.

해설 빈칸은 창 씨가 주어로 하는 주절의 동사 자리로, 시간절 「Until S + V」의 시제가 현재(finishes)이므로 주절의 시제는 미래가 되어야 하며, 빈칸 뒤에 목적어가 있으므로 능동태 문장을 완성하는 (C) will cover가 정답이다.

어휘 **regular** 일반적인 | **duty** 업무 | **cover** (~의 일을) 대신하다

2. 더 유연한 근무 시간을 제공하는 것에 대해 많은 직원은 관리자들이 이사회와 협상할 것을 요구했다.

해설 요구의 의미를 가지는 동사 demand의 목적어로 쓰인 절에는 should가 생략된 동사원형을 써야 하므로 (A) negotiate가 정답이다.

어휘 **demand** 요구하다 | **executive board** 이사회 | **flexible** 유연한 | **negotiate** 협상하다

3. 다음 주 금요일에 고객들이 우리 사무소를 즐겁게 방문할 수 있도록, 그날 오후에 접대가 준비되어야 한다.

해설 「It is + 필요성을 나타내는 형용사(crucial) + 뒤에 오는 that절」은 should가 생략된 동사원형이 나오고 뒤에 전치사구가 나오는 수동태가 적합하므로 (D) be prepared가 정답이다.

어휘 **ensure** 확실하게 하다, 보장하다 | **crucial** 필수적인

Practice

본서 p.34

1. (B)	**2.** (A)	**3.** (C)	**4.** (D)	**5.** (B)
6. (A)	**7.** (C)	**8.** (A)	**9.** (B)	**10.** (B)
11. (D)	**12.** (B)	**13.** (D)	**14.** (D)	**15.** (D)
16. (A)	**17.** (D)	**18.** (A)	**19.** (A)	**20.** (A)

1. 몇몇 산업 전문가들은 유기농 식품에 대한 수요가 향후 5년 동안 50% 증가할 것으로 예측했다.

해설 빈칸은 동사 자리로 뒤에 over the coming 5 years라는 미래를 나타내는 시간 어구가 나오므로 정답은 (B) will increase가 되며, 앞에 '예측하다'라는 뜻의 동사 forecast가 나오면 뒤에는 미래 시제가 온다.

어휘 **expert** 전문가 | **forecast** 예측하다 | **demand** 수요 | **organic food** 유기농 식품

2. 가장 큰 식품 제조업체인 하폰 식품은 매년 시의 노숙자 쉼터에 3천 개의 고기 통조림을 기부한다.

해설 빈칸은 동사 자리로, 동사 자리에 들어갈 수 없는 (B), (C)는 탈락이 되고, 수 일치에서 Hafon Foods는 단수로 받기 때문에 (D)도 탈락이 된다. each year라는 시간 어구가 나와서 현재 시제를 나타내는 (A) donates가 답이 된다.

어휘 **manufacturer** 제조업체 | **homeless** 노숙자의 | **shelter** 피난처, 보호소 | **donate** 기부하다

3. 지난주 회의는 신입 직원들이 회사 문화를 알 기회를 제공했다.

해설 주어에 Last week이라는 과거를 나타내는 시간 어구가 나오므로 빈칸에는 과거 시제로 쓰인 (C) created가 들어가야 한다.

어휘 **opportunity** 기회

4. 피트 스톱스는 주말에 고객들에게 무료 창문 청소를 제공한다.

해설 보기에 주어진 동사 offer는 뒤에 2개의 목적어를 취하는 수여동사로 빈칸 뒤에 「사람 목적어(customers) + 사물 목적어(a complimentary window cleaning)」가 모두 있으므로 수동태인 (C)는 탈락이며, 주어가 고유명사로 단수이므로 복수 동사인 (A)도 답이 될 수 없다. Pit Stops가 주말에 무료 청소를 제공한다는 의미로, 보통의 주말(on weekends)을 나타낸다는 점에서, 현재 시제인 (D) offers가 정답이다. 과거 완료인 had p.p.는 보통 기준 시점이 되는 과거 시제가 있고, 이 과거의 이전 시점을 나타내므로 답과 거리가 멀다.

어휘 **complimentary** 무료의

5. 마케팅 부서는 오늘 늦게 신입 직원들을 위한 환영 파티를 열 예정이다.

해설 동사 문제가 나오면 수, 시제, 태를 일치시켜 준다. 주어는 단수이고 시

제는 later today를 통해서 미래임을 알 수 있다. 뒤에 목적어가 있으므로 수동태는 오답이며, 가까운 미래를 나타내는 현재 진행형인 (B) is holding이 정답이다.

어휘 welcome party 환영 파티 | hold 개최하다, 열다

6. 지난 10년간, 속도와 관련된 차량 사고가 10% 감소했다.

해설 has decreased라는 현재 완료와 잘 쓰이는 시간 어구는 「over/in/for/during the past/last + 기간」이므로 정답은 (A) Over가 된다.

어휘 decade 10년 | speed-related 속도와 관련된 | decrease 감소하다

7. 디엔비 사는 시드니에 새로운 지사를 열기 전에 철저한 설문 조사를 했다.

해설 접속사가 before '~하기 전에'이고 종속절의 시제가 과거(opened)이므로 빈칸에는 과거 이전의 시제를 나타내는 과거 완료 시제인 (C) had conducted가 와야 한다.

어휘 thorough 철저한 | open a new branch 새 지점을 열다 | conduct a survey 설문 조사를 하다

8. 각 지원자는 늦어도 10월 15일까지는 서류 제출을 해야만 한다.

해설 필요성을 나타내는 형용사 important/necessary/essential 다음의 that 뒤에는 should가 생략된 동사원형이 와야 하므로 정답은 (A) submit가 된다.

어휘 applicant 지원자 | no later than 늦어도 ~까지는 | submit 제출하다

9. 오벌린 제과점은 1998년 오벌린 씨에 의해 창립된 이래로 여러 가지 다양한 맛있는 케이크와 빵을 만들어왔다.

해설 접속사 since '~이래로'가 이끄는 절에 과거 시제(was founded)가 있으므로 주절의 시제에는 현재 완료가 들어가야 한다. 따라서 정답은 (B) has produced이다.

어휘 a range of 다양한 | pastry 빵 | found 설립하다

10. 다음 이사회 회의는 전문 경영인이 아시아 출장에서 돌아올 때까지 연기될 것이다.

해설 빈칸 앞뒤로 주어, 동사를 모두 갖춘 절이 연결되어 있으므로 부사절 접속사가 필요한 자리이며, 전문 경영인이 돌아올 때까지 연기될 거란 의미가 적절하므로 시간·조건의 부사절 접속사 (B) until이 정답이다.

어휘 executive board 이사회 | postpone 연기하다 | return from ~에서 돌아오다

11. 킨 슈퍼마켓의 꾸준한 판매가 설립 1987년 이래로 회사 수익을 급증하게 만들었다.

해설 주절의 시제가 have made로 현재 완료가 나오고, 종속절은 was established라는 과거 시제가 나오므로 정답은 접속사 (D) since가 된다. 접속사 since가 있는 문장은 일반적으로 주절에는 현재 완료가, 종속절에는 과거 시제가 쓰인다.

어휘 sale 판매 | soar 급증하다, 솟구치다

12. 모든 출품작이 다 검토되고 나서, 크루즈 씨가 수상 사진을 선택할 것이다.

해설 모든 출품작을 다 고려하면 그다음에 '~할 것이다'라는 미래의 의미가 들어가야 하므로 정답은 (A) will choose이다.

어휘 submission 출품작, 제출 | consider 검토하다, 숙고하다 | winning 승리의, 승리를 거둔

13. 케이12 캠핑은 이달 말이 되면 찰스턴에서 10년 동안 운영하게 되는 것이 된다.

해설 by the end of '~말까지'라는 미래 완료와 쓰이는 시간 어구가 나오므로 정답은 (D) will have been이다.

어휘 be in operation 작동 중이다, 운영 중이다

14. 민 씨가 시장 분석가로서 회사에 입사했을 즈음에, 그녀는 재무 분야에서 15년 넘게 일했었다.

해설 회사에 합류한 것은 과거이고 '그 시점에 15년 넘게 일했다'라는 의미가 되어야 하므로 과거 이전의 시제인 (D) had worked가 정답이 된다.

어휘 by the time ~할 즈음에 | analyst 분석가 | financial 재무의, 금융의

15. 정보통신 기술 부서의 새 책임자인 로위 씨가 구식이라고 생각되는 소프트웨어를 교체할 수 있는 허가를 받을 것이다.

해설 문장의 주어는 Mr. Lowe이므로 빈칸에는 3인칭 단수 동사가 와야 한다. 조동사의 경우 수 일치에 영향을 받지 않으므로 정답은 (D) will obtain이 된다.

어휘 head 장, 책임자 | authorization 허가 | replace 교체하다 | outdated 구식인 | obtain 얻다, 구하다

16. 슈미트 씨가 회의에 참석할 수 없기 때문에, 우리는 그의 자리를 이 씨가 맡기를 추천했다.

해설 that절의 주어가 Ms. Lee이므로 단수 동사가 나와야 하는데 동사원형인 take가 나와서 앞에 should가 생략되었음을 알 수 있다. 주장/요구/명령/추천/제안 동사의 that 뒤에 「(should) + 동사원형」이 나오므로 정답은 (A) recommended가 된다.

어휘 participate in ~에 참석하다 | take (임무·일을) 맡다

17. 홈 비즈니스 과정에 등록했던 모든 회원은 지난주에 확인 이메일을 받았다.

해설 과거 시제를 나타내는 부사(last week)가 있고, 등록한 사람들이 확인 이메일을 '보내다'가 아니라 '받다'의 의미가 되어야 하므로 과거 시제 수동태로 쓰여야 한다. 따라서 정답은 (D) was sent가 된다.

어휘 sign up for 등록하다 | confirmation 확인

18. 더블유씨엑스 전자의 보안이 변경된 안전 절차가 시행된 이후 크게 개선되었다.

해설 '~이후로'의 의미를 나타내는 접속사 since는 주절이 현재 완료, 종속절은 과거 시제가 들어가야 하므로 정답은 (A) were가 된다.

어휘 greatly 대단히, 크게 | improve 개선되다 | revised 변경된 | safety procedure 안전 절차 | implement 실행하다, 시행하다

19. 우리가 다음 주에 은행에서 만날 때, 모든 융자에 관한 세부 사항들이 마무리되어 있을 것이다.

해설 주절의 시제(will have been finalized)가 미래 완료이며, 종속절은 현재(meet)가 나오므로 시간의 부사절 접속사인 (A) By the time이 정답이 된다. 시간의 부사절은 현재 시제가 미래 시제를 대신한다.

어휘 financing 융자, 자금 조달 | detail 세부 사항 | finalize 마무리 짓다 | in order for ~하기 위해 | as much as ~만큼, ~정도까지 많이, ~이지만, 사실상

20. 지방 정부가 오스틴 극장의 소유권을 획득해 곧 역사박물관으로 다시 문을 열 것이다.

해설 빈칸은 조동사와 동사 사이에서 동사를 수식하는 부사 자리이다. 미래 시제가 쓰였으므로 (A) soon이 정답이다. 시간부사 soon(곧)은 미래 시제와, recently(최근에)는 현재 완료 또는 과거 시제와 어울려 쓰인다.

어휘 provincial 지방의 | government 정부 | obtain 얻다 | ownership 소유권 | theater 극장 | reopen 다시 문을 열다

UNIT 03. 능동태와 수동태

1. + check   1. (D)   2. (A)   3. (A)   본서 p.37

1. 특정 부서로 발송되지 않은 우편물은 지역 본부에 전달될 수 있다.

해설 「be + p.p. + 전치사」 구조이며, 해석상 우편물이 전달될 수 있다는 의미의 수동태가 필요하므로 (D) forwarded가 정답이다.

어휘 mail 우편(물) | address (~에 우편물을) 보내다 | specific 특정한 | regional 지역의 | headquarters 본사 | forward 전달하다

2. 경비 보고서 제출에 관한 새로운 지침들이 초봄에 시행될 것이다.

해설 빈칸은 동사 자리로 타동사 implement는 뒤에 목적어를 동반하지만 뒤에 in이라는 전치사가 나오므로 수동태가 적합하다. 따라서 (A) will be implemented가 정답이다.

어휘 guideline 지침, 가이드라인 | submit 제출하다 | expense report 경비 보고서 | implement 실행하다, 시행하다

3. 동아시아 고객들을 위한 제품들은 말레이시아에 있는 회사의 물류포장 센터에서 배송될 것이다.

해설 어휘 문제로 문맥상 '제품들은 회사의 물류포장 센터에서 배송될 것이다'라는 의미가 적합하므로 (A) shipped가 정답이다. (D)도 의미가 그럴듯해 보이지만 자동사로 수동태가 될 수 없다.

어휘 out of ~의 밖으로 | fulfillment center 물류포장 센터 | ship 배송하다 | return 반품하다

2. + check   1. (C)   2. (D)   3. (D)   본서 p.38

1. 클라인 씨는 레이코 전자의 인터넷 서비스에 관하여 더 많은 것을 아는 데 관심이 있다.

해설 '~에 관심이 있다'로 be interested in이 적합하므로 (C) interested가 정답이다.

어휘 find out 알아내다, 알게 되다

2. 위원회는 오늘 밤 회사 저녁 만찬에서 올해의 직원을 발표하게 되어 기쁘다.

해설 be동사의 보어 자리로 '~하게 되어 기쁘다'로 be excited to가 필요하므로 (D) excited가 정답이다.

어휘 committee 위원회 | announce 발표하다, 안내하다 | employee 직원, 고용인

3. 케이씨 휴대폰의 고객들을 만족시키기 위해서, 저희는 최고의 고객 서비스를 제공하기 위해 최선을 다합니다.

해설 5형식 동사 keep은 목적격 보어로 형용사를 가질 수 있는데, 그 주체는 목적어 즉 customers로 감정 동사의 주체가 사람이므로 (D) satisfied가 정답이다.

어휘 do one's best 최선을 다하다 | premium 아주 높은, 고급의 | satisfy 만족시키다 | satisfaction 만족

3. + check   1. (B)   2. (D)   3. (D)   본서 p.39

1. 우리 신제품을 위해서만 독점적으로 사용되는 수입 재료들은 제조 비용을 절감하기 위해서 더 싼 것으로 교체되어야만 한다.

해설 더 싼 것으로 '교체되어'야 한다는 해석이 가장 자연스러우므로 (B) replaced가 정답이다. be replaced with '~으로 교체되다'로 암기하면 바로 답을 찾을 수 있다.

어휘 imported 수입된 | exclusively 독점적으로 | reduce 줄이다 | manufacturing cost 제조 비용 | coordinate 조직화하다 | replace 대체하다

2. 박물관에서 사진을 찍는 것이 엄격히 금지되므로, 전시장 방문객들은 카메라나 캠코더를 가져오지 않도록 권고받는다.

해설 빈칸은 동사 자리로 주어가 복수이며 뒤에 목적어가 없어 수동태가 적합하며, 해석을 해봐도 충고를 받는 것이므로 수동태 (D) are advised가 정답이다.

어휘 strictly 엄격히 | prohibit 금지하다 | exhibition 전시회

3. 내일 소여 엔지니어링 인수를 완료하고, 다음 달에 정식으로 합병할 예정임을 알려 드립니다.

해설 수동태 동사를 완성하면서 that절을 이끌 수 있는 동사를 골라야 하는 문제다. 보기 중 동사 inform은 뒤에 「사람 목적어 + that절」을 이끌고, 수동태로 쓰일 때 'be informed that절'의 문장 구조를 취하므로 (D) informed가 정답이다.

어휘 complete 완성하다 | purchase 구매, 인수 | officially 공식적으로 | merge with ~와 합병하다 | recommend 추천하다 | allow 허락하다 | ensure 확실하게 하다 | inform 알리다

Practice

본서 p.40

1. (B)	**2.** (B)	**3.** (D)	**4.** (A)	**5.** (B)
6. (A)	**7.** (C)	**8.** (B)	**9.** (D)	**10.** (D)
11. (C)	**12.** (C)	**13.** (C)	**14.** (D)	**15.** (B)
16. (C)	**17.** (D)	**18.** (C)	**19.** (B)	**20.** (D)

1. 피치 가의 주차장이 보수되고 있는 동안에, 방문객들은 대중교통을 이용하도록 강력히 권고받는다.

해설 종속절의 주어(Peach Street's parking lot)가 단수이고 뒤에 목적어가 없으므로 수동태가 필요하다. 따라서 정답은 (B) is being repaired가 된다.

어휘 parking lot 주차장 | strongly 강력하게 | encourage 권하다, 장려하다, 격려하다 | public transportation 대중교통 | repair 보수하다

2. 그 가이드 관광은 다빈치 씨에 의해 인솔될 것이며 여러 상을 수상한 포도주 양조장 방문을 포함할 것이다.

해설 전치사 문제로 '다빈치 씨에 의해 인솔되다'라는 의미가 되어야 한다. 빈칸에 수동태의 행위자 앞에 쓰이는 전치사 by가 나와야 하므로 (B) by가 정답이다.

어휘 guided tour 안내인이 동반하는 여행 | winery 포도주 양조장

3. 새 사무실의 운영 구역에서 보안 시스템이 실행될 때까지, 기밀문서를 이전 위치에 보관하십시오.

해설 '실행하다'를 뜻하는 동사 implement의 목적어가 주어(a security system)로 나와 있으므로 빈칸에는 수동태가 적합하다. 그러므로 정답은 (D) has been implemented가 된다. 시간 접속사 until이고 는 시간 부사절에는 미래를 대신하는 현재나 미래 완료를 대신하는 현재 완료가 온다.

어휘 security system 보안 시스템 | operations area 운영 구역 | confidential document 기밀문서 | implement 실행하다, 시행하다

4. 새로운 연간 판매 목표가 발표되는 대로, 매니저들은 마케팅 전략을 논의하기 위해 즉시 팀과 만나야 한다.

해설 빈칸에는 종속절의 주어(the new annual sales targets)의 수, 시제, 태를 일치시킨 동사가 들어가야 한다. 뒤에 목적어가 없으므로 수동태인 (A) have been announced가 정답이다.

어휘 annual 연례의 | sales target 판매 목표 | strategy 전략 | announce 발표하다

5. 제품이 품절된 고객들은 비슷한 가격의 제품을 선택하거나 매장에서 교환할 수 있는 쿠폰을 받을 수 있다.

해설 빈칸은 동사 자리로, 동사 자리에 들어갈 수 없는 (A), (C)는 탈락이 되며, 해석에만 의존해서 (D)를 고르지 않도록 조심한다. 뒤에 목적어가 나오는 능동태가 들어가야 하므로 (B) may choose가 정답이다.

어휘 out of stock 품절된 | similarly-priced 비슷한 가격의 | receive 받다 | voucher 상품권, 쿠폰 | store credit 스토어 크레딧, 교환권

6. 청소기의 흡입력을 최적으로 유지하기 위해, 청소 작업 전 통이 비워져만 합니다.

해설 빈칸은 문장의 동사 자리이며, 빈칸 뒤에 목적어가 없고, 의미상 '통이 비워져야 한다'는 수동 관계가 성립하므로 (A) must be emptied가 정답이다.

어휘 maintain 유지하다 | optimum 최고의, 최적의 | suction 흡입 | vacuum cleaner 청소기 | bin 쓰레기통, 통 | vacuum 진공청소기로 청소하다 | empty 비어 있는; 비우다

7. 작년에 올가 전자의 가정용 기기 판매량이 실망스러워서, 회사는 일부 제품의 가격을 내릴 것이다.

해설 disappoint는 감정 동사로 앞에 주어가 사람이 아닌 sales로 '(사람들을) 실망시키는'의 의미이므로 정답은 능동형의 (C) disappointing이 된다.

어휘 sales 판매 | home appliances 가정용 기기 | lower 낮추다, 내리다

8. 교육생을 위해 준비된 모든 교육 자료는 회사 방침에 부합하도록 주의 깊게 편집되어야 한다.

해설 빈칸 뒤에 목적어 없이 부사 carefully가 나오므로 수동태 형식이 되어야 한다. 따라서 (B) edited가 정답이다.

어휘 instructional material 교육 자료 | trainee 교육생, 훈련생 | ensure 보장하다 | compliance with ~의 준수 | company policy 회사 방침

9. 기술자들은 공장에서 작업하는 동안 항상 안전모를 착용해야 한다.

해설 require는 대표적인 5형식 동사로 목적격 보어로 to부정사를 가지며, 수동태는 「be required + to부정사」가 되어 (D) required가 정답이다.

어휘 technician 기술자 | safety helmet 안전모 | at all times 항상, 늘 | plant 공장 | inquire 묻다, 문의하다 | insist 주장하다 | appeal 호소하다, 관심을 끌다

10. 에드윈이 대형 곡물 창고에 설치한 교체 부품은 우리가 예상했던 것보다 훨씬 더 잘 작동했다.

해설 작동한 시점은 과거(worked)이고 예상한 것은 과거 이전이므로 정답은 (D) had expected가 된다.

어휘 replacement parts 교체 부품 | install 설치하다 | grain elevator 대형 곡물 창고 | expect 예상하다

11. 엘코 항공의 좌석은 되도록 즐거운 비행이 될 수 있도록 최첨단 엔터테인먼트 시스템을 갖추고 있다.

해설 equip은 '(장비를) 갖추다'라는 의미의 타동사이다. 목적어(Elco Airline's seats)가 주어 자리에 있으므로 수동태 문장이 되는 (C) equipped가 정답이다.

어휘 high-tech 최첨단의, 첨단 기술의 | enjoyable 즐거운 | be equipped with ~을 갖추고 있다

12. 〈오케이즌스〉의 이전 편집장으로서, 찬 씨는 최근에 내셔널 협회에서 올해의 기자로 명명되었다.

해설 name은 5형식 동사로 수동태가 되어도 뒤에 명사를 동반할 수 있으며, recently는 과거 혹은 현재 완료와 잘 쓰인다. 그러므로 정답은 과거 수동태인 (C) was named가 된다.

어휘 former 이전의, 예전의 | editor-in-chief 편집장 | recently 최근에 | journalist 기자 | association 협회 | name 명명하다

13. 경비원을 동반하지 않는다면 어느 누구도 저녁 10시 이후에 건물에 들어갈 수 없습니다.

해설 essential이라는 필요성을 나타내는 형용사 다음의 that절에는 should가 생략된 동사원형이 와야 한다. 또한, 뒤에 목적어가 아닌 전치사 to가 와서 수동태의 동사원형이 필요하므로 정답은 (C) be admitted가 된다.

어휘 essential 필수적인 | unless accompanied by ~와 동반하지 않는다면 | security officer 경비원, 안전 보안 요원 | admit 들어가게 하다, 인정하다

14. 투자자 지원 부서 리소스는 주로 온라인 거래 플랫폼의 사용자를 대상으로 합니다.

해설 목적어 없이 mainly라는 부사가 나오므로 빈칸에는 수동태의 동사형이 적합하다. 그러므로 정답은 (D) are intended이다.

어휘 investor 투자가 | support 지원 | department 부서 | resources 자원 | mainly 주로 | trading platform 거래 플랫폼 | intend 의도하다

15. 카를로스 씨가 임대할 사무실 공간은 메티즈 빌딩 바로 맞은편에 위치한다.

해설 locate는 '위치에 두다'라는 의미로 쓰이는 타동사이다. 건물이 주어(The office space)로 쓰였으므로 '위치되다'라는 수동태로 쓰여야 한다. 그러므로 (B) located가 정답으로 알맞다.

어휘 lease 임대 | across from 바로 맞은편에 | locate 위치에 두다 | location 위치

16. 그렉 씨는 매달 있는 사업 워크숍에서 발표하는 것을 요청받았지만, 초대를 거절했다.

해설 encourage는 5형식 동사로 목적격 보어로 to부정사를 가질 수 있다. 주어인 Mr. Greg가 encourage의 목적어에 해당하므로 빈칸에는 수동태로 쓰인 동사가 와야 한다. 그러므로 정답은 (C) was encouraged가 된다.

어휘 deliver a presentation 발표하다 | decline 거절하다 | encourage 독려하다, 권장하다

17. 조셉 재단에서 지난 5년간 전국 공공 도서관에 거의 2천 권의 책을 기부했다.

해설 문장의 주어는 The Joseph Foundation이고, 빈칸은 동사 자리인데 뒤를 보니 2,000 books라는 목적어가 나오므로 수동태인 (A), (B), (C)는 탈락이 된다. 그러므로 정답은 능동태인 (D) has donated가 된다.

어휘 public 공공의 | library 도서관 | across the country 전국에 | donate 기부하다

18. 폰테레 산업의 입찰 가격이 가장 경쟁력 있었기 때문에 계약을 따냈다.

해설 award는 4형식 동사로 간접목적어(Fontere Industries)가 주어 자리에 있는 문장이다. be awarded the contract는 '계약을 따내다'라는 의미로 쓰이므로 정답은 (C) awarded가 된다.

어휘 bid 가격 제시 | competitive 경쟁력 있는 | be awarded a contract 계약을 따내다

19. 블루트 다이에그노스틱의 직원들은 우리 업계에서 최고 수준의 서비스를 제공하기 위해 최선을 다하고 있습니다.

해설 빈칸 다음에 있는 to는 전치사이다. 따라서 '~하는 데 전념하다[헌신하다]'라는 의미로 쓰인 'be committed to -ing'가 알맞으므로 정답은 (B) committed가 된다.

어휘 crew 직원(전체), 팀, 조 | set 만들다, 세우다 | standard 기준, 표준 | industry 산업, 업계 | admire ~을 높이 평가하다 | committed 헌신적인, 열정적인 | attempt 시도하다 | suppose 가정하다

20. 모든 고객의 문의사항에 즉각적인 주의를 기울일 것을 보장합니다.

해설 assure '보증하다, 확신하다'는 「assure + 목적어(사람) + that절」을 가진다. 목적어(사람)가 생략되어 있고 that절이 바로 나온다는 것은 수동태라는 것이므로 정답은 (D) assured가 된다.

어휘 inquiry 질문, 문의 | prompt attention 즉각적인 주의 | be assured that ~을 확신하다[보증하다]

REVIEW TEST 01
본서 p.42

1. (A)	2. (A)	3. (C)	4. (A)	5. (B)
6. (D)	7. (D)	8. (B)	9. (B)	10. (C)
11. (C)	12. (C)	13. (D)	14. (A)	15. (A)
16. (B)	17. (D)	18. (D)	19. (C)	20. (B)

1. 4월에 에든버러 아동 병원에 익명으로 총 253,850달러가 기부되었다.

해설 빈칸은 문장의 동사 자리이며 빈칸 뒤에 목적어가 없고, 의미상 '총 253,850달러가 기부되었다'라는 수동 관계가 성립하므로 (A) was contributed가 정답이다.

어휘 anonymously 익명으로 | contribute 기여하다, 공헌하다, 기부하다

2. 킹 고속도로의 도로 수리 작업은 교외를 통과하는 우회로 신설을 필요로 한다.

해설 문장의 주어는 Road repairs이며 빈칸은 동사 자리이다. 주어가 복수이므로 정답은 (A) require이다.

어휘 road repair 도로 공사 | expressway 고속도로 | creation 신설, 창조 | detour 우회로 | suburb 교외 | require 필요로 하다

3. 입학이 고려되기 위해, 장래의 학생들은 대학 입학시험에서 적어도 85점을 받아야 한다.

해설 빈칸은 조동사 뒤 동사원형 자리이므로 (C) score가 정답이다.

어휘 consider 고려하다 | admission 입학 | prospective 장래의, 유망한 | entrance exam 입학시험 | score 점수를 받다

4. 와이지 자동차의 새 차량 제품 출시에 참석한 손님들은 여러 디자인이 몹시 매력적이라고 여겼다.

해설 빈칸은 부사 very의 수식을 받는 형용사 자리이고, 또 5형식 동사인 found의 목적격 보어에는 형용사가 나오므로 (A) attractive가 정답이다.

어휘 launch 출시 | vehicle 차량 | various 다양한 | attractive 매력적인 | attraction 끌림, 명소 | attract 마음을 끌다

5. 팁톤 화물의 노조 간부들은 노동법이 적절히 지켜지고 있는지 확인하기 위해 매달 직원들과 만남을 가진다.

해설 빈칸은 명사절 that절의 동사 자리이다. 뒤에 목적어가 없으므로 수동태가 와야 하고 수동태 (B)와 (D) 중에서 주절의 시제가 현재이고, 문맥상 '노동법이 제대로 지켜지고 있는지 확인하기 위해 매달 만난다'는 의미가 되어야 자연스러우므로 현재 진행 수동태의 (B) are being followed가 정답이다.

어휘 freight 화물 | union leaders 노조 간부진 | make sure 확인하다 | labor law 노동법 | properly 제대로, 적절히 | follow 지키다

6. 레코마 자동차는 노사분규가 해소될 때까지, 생산 대수가 크게 타격을 입을 것으로 보고 있다.

해설 expect는 5형식 동사로써 목적격 보어로 to부정사를 취하므로 정답은 (D) to suffer이다.

어휘 labor dispute 노사분규, 노동 쟁의 | resolve 해결하다 | production 생산 | significantly 상당히, 크게 | suffer 손해를 입다

7. 모든 담당자는 외부 고용에 관한 회사의 규정을 준수해야 한다.

해설 동사 어휘 문제로, 뒤에 전치사 with를 동반하는 자동사 문제이다. 해석하면 '모든 담당자는 회사의 규정을 준수해야 한다'이므로 '준수하다'라는 의미의 자동사 (D) comply가 정답이다.

어휘 representative 담당자 | require 필요하다 | firm 회사 | regulation 규정 | regarding ~에 관하여 | employment 고용 | inform 알리다 | update 개정하다 | observe ~을 지키다 | comply 준수하다

8. 모든 전기 기사들은 고객들의 수리 요청을 관리자에게 알려야 한다.

해설 동사 어휘 문제이다. 목적어인 their manager 뒤에 of를 취하는 동사를 찾으면 된다. 이러한 동사로는 inform, notify, advise 등이 있다. 정답은 (B) inform이다.

어휘 electrical 전기의 | technician 기술자, 기사 | repair 수리 | request 요청; 요청하다 | recommend 추천하다 | inform A of B A에게 B에 대해 알리다 | review 검토하다

9. 로비가 단장되는 동안, 직원들은 건물을 드나들 때 후문을 사용해야 한다.

해설 빈칸은 is와 함께 동사구를 이루며, 뒤에 목적어가 없으므로 수동태가 나와야 한다. 따라서 정답은 (B) being renovated가 된다.

어휘 back entrance 후문 | exit 나가다 | renovate 보수하다, 개조하다 | renovation 보수, 수리

10. 분석가들은 칸탄 전자의 주가가 이제 주당 70에서 80달러까지 오를 것이라고 예상했다.

해설 이 문장은 「hope[expect/predict/anticipate]+that+주어+미래 시제(will+동사원형)」의 형태인데, 동사가 과거형인 anticipated이므로 시제를 일치시켜서 (C) would rise가 답이 된다.

어휘 analyst 분석가 | anticipate 예상하다 | stock price 주가 | share 주, 주식 | by now 이제, 지금쯤

11. 이어진 응답은 연구 기간 동안 인터뷰한 많은 직원들에 의해 제공되었다.

해설 빈칸은 문장의 본동사 자리로, 뒤에 목적어 없이 by a large group of employees라는 전치사구가 왔으며 주어가 복수형(responses)이므로 빈칸은 수동태 복수 동사가 필요하다. 따라서 정답은 (C) were given이다.

어휘 response 응답 | employee 직원 | research study 연구

12. 클레이턴 박물관의 전시품들은 모든 연령대의 미술 애호가들에게 널리 어필한다.

해설 '~에게 어필하다'라는 의미의 구동사 appeal to 사이에 들어갈 수 있는 품사는 부사이므로 (C) widely가 정답이다.

어휘 exhibit 전시품 | appeal 관심을 끌다 | art lover 미술 애호가 | all ages 전 연령대 | wide 폭넓은

13. 겐트 사에서는 리더십 능력을 키우기 위해 직원들을 위한 전문 개발 코스가 디자인되었다.

해설 빈칸은 문장의 동사 자리이며 전문 개발 코스가 디자인되었다는 수동 관계가 성립하므로 (D) have been designed가 정답이다.

어휘 professional 전문적인; 전문가 | nurture 육성하다, 키우다

14. 오늘 회의의 목적은 고객 만족을 개선하는 계획들을 논의하는 것이다.

해설 빈칸은 타동사 discuss의 목적어 자리로써 명사가 들어가야 하므로 정답은 (A) initiatives가 된다.

어휘 purpose 목적 | customer satisfaction 고객 만족 | initiative 계획, 기획, 진취성 | initiate 개시되게 하다

15. 이노백스 전자는 귀사와 같은 회사들이 조직의 성공을 제한할지도 모르는 문제들을 진단하는 데 도움을 주고자 해결책을 고안하고 제공합니다.

해설 빈칸 앞에 준사역 동사인 help가 있으므로, 빈칸에는 to부정사 혹은 동사원형이 나와야 한다. 따라서 정답은 (A) diagnose가 된다.

어휘 solution 해결책 | issue 문제, 이슈 | limit 제한하다 | diagnose 진단하다

16. 우리 제품 중 대부분은 상업용 건물을 위해서 고안되었지만, 일부는 가정용으로 적합하다.

해설 be동사의 보어 자리에 올 수 있는 형용사를 고르는 문제이다. 정답은 (B) suitable이다.

어휘 design 고안하다 ǀ commercial 상업용의 ǀ suit 적합하다 ǀ suitable 적합한 ǀ suitability 적당, 적합

17. 권 씨는 만료되기 일주일 전에 〈과학 오늘〉 잡지 구독을 갱신했다.

해설 빈칸은 동사 renewed의 목적어 자리이다. 목적어 자리에 명사를 고르는 문제로 정답은 (D) subscription이 된다. 동명사 (A)는 앞에 관사를 보고 지운다.

어휘 renew 갱신하다 ǀ expire 만료되다 ǀ subscribe 구독하다

18. 벤 밀러가 내일 칸달 사의 본사에 방문할 때쯤이면 그가 우리의 건축 계획을 확정했을 것입니다.

해설 시간을 나타내는 부사절 by the time이 나오고 뒤에 현재 시제 visits이 나오므로, 주절에는 미래 시제인 (D) will have finalized가 필요하다. 때와 조건의 부사절에서 주절의 시제가 미래일 때 종속절은 현재를 쓴다.

어휘 by the time 그때까지, ~할 때까지 ǀ headquarter 본사 ǀ finalize 확정하다

19. 고객에게 기밀 정보를 보낼 경우, 믿을 수 있는 택배 서비스를 이용하여 서류를 안전하게 해 주세요.

해설 빈칸은 동사 keep의 목적격 보어 자리이다. 문맥상 '서류들을 안전하게 해준다'는 의미가 되어야 자연스러우므로 형용사 (C) secure가 정답이다.

어휘 confidential 기밀의 ǀ reliable 믿을 수 있는 ǀ courier 택배 회사

20. 에이피에이 인터내셔널에서, 선적 컨테이너의 최대 무게는 50 미터톤이다.

해설 빈칸은 관사와 형용사의 수식을 받는 문장의 주어 자리이므로 명사 (B) weight가 정답이다.

어휘 maximum 최고의, 최대의 ǀ shipping container 선적 컨테이너 ǀ metric ton 미터톤 ǀ weight 무게 ǀ weigh 무게를 달다 ǀ weighted 치우친, 편중된

UNIT 04. 명사

1. + check　　1. (D)　　2. (B)　　3. (D)　　본서 p.45

1. 최근 조사에 따르면 많은 고객들이 우리 서점의 카페에서 식음료 구매에 대한 지불을 위해 우리의 기프트 카드를 사용하고 있는 것으로 나타났다.

해설 타동사 make의 목적어 자리로 들어갈 수 있는 품사는 명사이므로 (D) payments가 정답이다.

어휘 survey 조사 ǀ indicate 나타내다, 보여주다 ǀ food and beverage 식음료 ǀ purchase 구매(품); 구매하다 ǀ pay 지불하다 ǀ payment 지불

2. 온라인 주문 시스템의 완성은 회사가 고객 요구에 보다 신속하게 대응하는 것이 가장 중요한 우선순위의 일이다.

해설 빈칸은 주어 자리로 명사가 적합하므로 (B) Completion이 정답이다.

어휘 top priority 최우선 순위 ǀ responsive 반응하는, 대응하는 ǀ customer needs 고객 요구 ǀ completion 완성, 완료

3. 건설 계획에 대한 어떠한 변경도 고객과 우리의 공급자들 모두와 협조해서 이루어져야 한다.

해설 전치사 in 뒤에 명사가 필요하므로 (D) coordination이 정답이다. 그리고 in coordination with '~와 협조하여'라고 덩어리째 암기해 두자.

어휘 construction 건설 ǀ client 고객 ǀ supplier 공급자 ǀ coordination 협조

2. + check　　1. (B)　　2. (C)　　3. (D)　　본서 p.45

1. 조르지오 사의 최신 가전제품은 만능 조리 기구와 고속 분쇄기가 결합된 것이다.

해설 관사 a 뒤에는 명사가 나오는 것이 적합하므로 (B) combination이 정답이다.

어휘 corporation 회사, 기업 ǀ latest 최신의 ǀ appliance 가전제품 ǀ food processor 만능 조리 기구(식재료를 자르고 섞을 때 쓰는 기구) ǀ blender 분쇄기, 믹서기 ǀ combine 결합하다 ǀ combination 조합

2. 필란티 제작사는 향후 몇 년 안에 계약직 직원들에 대한 의존도를 낮추기를 원한다.

해설 소유격 its 뒤에는 명사가 나오는 것이 적합하므로 (C) reliance가 정답이다.

어휘 would like to ~하고 싶다 ǀ contract worker 계약직 직원 ǀ rely 의존하다 ǀ reliance 의존, 의지 ǀ reliable 믿을 수 있는, 믿을 만한

3. 린튼 출판인 협회의 이사인 클레이턴 싱클레어는 가까운 시일 안에 회장직에 출마할 의도가 없다.

해설 no라는 형용사 뒤에는 명사가 나오는 것이 적합하므로 (D) intention이 정답이다.

어휘 board member 이사 ǀ association 협회 ǀ run for ~에 출마하다 ǀ anytime soon 곧 ǀ intention 의도

3. + check　　1. (B)　　2. (C)　　3. (A)　　본서 p.47

1. 이번 주 토요일부터, 미카 스포츠용품점은 모든 등산용 장비 구매 물건들에 대해 30% 할인을 제공할 예정이다.

해설 해석해 보면 '등산용 장비 구매 물건'이라는 의미가 적합하므로 명사인 (A), (B)가 답이 될 수 있는데, purchase는 명사로 쓰일 때 '구매 행위'를 뜻하는 불가산 명사와 '구매한 물건'을 뜻하는 가산 명사로 쓰인다. 의미상 구매 행위에 대한 할인이 아닌, 구매 물건에 대한 할인이 적절하다. 또한, 앞에 쓰인 한정사 all은 가산 복수 명사 또는 불가산 명사를 취하므로 빈칸은 '구매 물건'을 뜻하는 가산 명사의 복수형이 와야 하므로 (B) purchases가 정답이다.

어휘 **sporting goods** 스포츠용품 | **hiking gear** 등산용 장비 | **purchase** 구입, 구입한 것

2. 쵸프마스터 2000 푸드 프로세서는 작년에 인도 시장에 출시된 이후 우리의 가장 많이 팔리는 품목이 되었다.

해설 빈칸은 소유격 its 뒤의 명사 자리로 (C), (D)가 들어갈 수 있는데, introduction은 '(사람의) 소개'를 의미할 때는 가산 명사로 쓰이지만, '(물건의) 도입'을 의미할 때는 불가산 명사로 쓰인다. 인도 시장에 푸드 프로세서를 새로 도입했다는 의미이므로 불가산 명사인 (C) introduction이 정답이다.

어휘 **food processor** 푸드 프로세서(식재료를 자르고 섞을 때 사용하는 기구) | **top-selling** 가장 많이 팔리는 | **following** ~후에 | **introduction** 도입, 소개

3. 거의 예외 없이, 분류상의 실수로 인해 잘못 놓여진 모든 소포는 3일 이내에 발견되어 고객에게 배달됩니다.

해설 빈칸은 package라는 단수 명사 앞에 들어가야 하는 것으로 단수 명사를 수식하는 (A) every가 정답이다. all은 복수 가산 명사 또는 불가산 명사를 취한다.

어휘 **without exception** 예외 없이 | **misplace** 제자리에 두지 않다 | **sorting error** 분류상의 실수 | **find** 발견하다 | **deliver** 배달하다

4. ➕ check   1. (A)   2. (B)   3. (A)   본서 p.48

1. 만일 식당에서 저녁 교대 근무를 할 수 있는 지원자가 있다면, 더 우대를 받을 것이다.

해설 there are가 나오므로 빈칸에는 복수 명사가 들어가야 하고 뒤에 사람 선행사를 받는 주격 관계대명사 who가 있으므로 (A) applicants가 정답이다.

어휘 **shift** 근무조 | **preference** 선호, 우대 | **applicant** 지원자 | **application** 지원, 적용, 신청서 | **applicable** 적용할 수 있는

2. 메라손 조경은 최근에 정원과 식물 쓰레기의 재활용을 그들의 서비스에 포함시켰다.

해설 빈칸은 명사 자리로 (B), (D)가 답이 될 수 있는데, 해석하면 '재활용'이라는 의미가 들어가야 하므로 (B) recycling이 정답이다.

어휘 **landscaping** 조경 | **plant** 식물, 공장 | **waste** 쓰레기, 폐기물 | **recycler** 재생 처리기

3. 샤오칭 제분소는 우리 제과점의 밀가루를 제조하는 기계 공장이다.

해설 빈칸은 명사 자리로 (A), (C)가 답이 될 수 있는데, be동사의 주격 보어로 명사 자리에는 주어와 동격의 의미가 들어가야 하므로 Xiaoqing Mills와 동격의 의미인 (A) operator가 정답이다.

어휘 **mill** 제분소 | **machinery** 기계류, 장치 | **produce** 제조하다, 생산하다 | **flour** 밀가루 | **bakery** 제과점, 베이커리

5. ➕ check   1. (A)   2. (D)   3. (D)   본서 p.49

1. 그 의료 보험은 모든 현직 직원과 그 가족의 건강 관리 요구를 보장하기 위해 고안되었다.

해설 빈칸은 타동사 cover의 목적어 자리로 '요구를 보장하다'라는 의미가 적합하므로 (A) needs가 정답이다. 그리고 앞에 healthcare와 복합 명사를 이루는 needs를 선택해서 답을 골라도 된다.

어휘 **insurance plan** 의료 보험 | **design** 고안하다, 설계하다 |

cover (보험으로) 보장하다, 다루다, 포함시키다 | **healthcare** 건강 관리 | **current** 현재의

2. 마리사 버튼은 오늘 우리 팀 개발 세미나에 참석하지 않을 것으로 예상된다.

해설 '팀 개발 세미나'라는 의미의 복합 명사가 적합하므로 (D) development가 정답이다.

어휘 **expect** 예상하다, 기대하다 | **join** 합류하다, 함께 하다

3. 직원들은 이달 말일까지 여행 환급 요청서를 제출해야 한다.

해설 빈칸 앞에 travel이라는 명사가 나오고, 뒤에 requests라는 명사가 나와서 '여행 환급 요청서'라는 복합 명사를 완성하는 (D) reimbursement가 정답이다.

어휘 **submit** 제출하다 | **reimburse** 상환하다

Practice
본서 p.50

1. (C)	**2.** (C)	**3.** (B)	**4.** (A)	**5.** (B)
6. (D)	**7.** (B)	**8.** (B)	**9.** (B)	**10.** (D)
11. (B)	**12.** (A)	**13.** (D)	**14.** (D)	**15.** (A)
16. (C)	**17.** (C)	**18.** (D)	**19.** (A)	**20.** (D)

1. 이사회가 승인하면, 주력 제조 사업장의 구조 조정이 9월에 단행될 것이다.

해설 「a + 명사 + of」가 들어가야 하므로 정답은 명사 (C) restructuring이 된다.

어휘 **board of directors** 이사회 | **approval** 승인 | **main** 주된, 주요한 | **manufacturing operation** 제조 사업장 | **carry out** 수행하다 | **restructure** 구조 조정하다 | **restructuring** 구조 조정

2. 2년 전에 해외 영업부가 설립된 이래로, 우리 해외 사업이 가치 있음을 증명했다.

해설 소유격 뒤이므로 명사가 와야 한다. (B), (C)가 답으로 가능한데, '창립 이래로'의 의미가 적합하므로 정답은 (C) foundation이 된다.

어휘 **international** 국제적인 | **prove** 증명하다 | **valuable** 귀중한, 가치 있는 | **overseas** 해외의, 해외에 | **founder** 창립자, 설립자 | **foundation** 창립, 설립

3. 관리직에 이력서를 제출한 모든 지원자는 면접을 위해 전화를 받게 될 것입니다.

해설 every 뒤에는 단수 명사가 와야 한다. who 주격 관계대명사 뒤에 has submitted라는 단수 동사가 있어 사람 단수 형태가 나와야 하므로 정답은 (B) applicant가 된다.

어휘 **submit** 제출하다 | **managerial position** 관리직 | **application** 지원, 적용, 신청서 | **applicant** 지원자

4. 건물 허가에 대한 신청은 일이 시작되기 최소 4주 전에는 제출되어야 한다.

해설 '허가'라고 할 때 permit, permission 둘 다 사용할 수 있지만, 앞에

관사 a가 있으므로 가산 명사가 들어가야 한다. permission은 불가산 명사이므로 정답은 가산 명사인 (A) permit가 된다.

어휘 request 요청, 신청 | at least 최소한 | permit 허가(증) | permission 허가, 허락

5. 쿠티에레즈 씨의 인상적인 발표는 몇 주간 연구와 준비를 한 결과이다.

해설 빈칸은 정관사 뒤에 명사 자리이며, 의미상 결과의 대상이 발표 하나이므로 단수 명사인 (B) result가 정답이다.

어휘 impressive 인상적인 | preparation 준비

6. 기밀 유지를 위해, 고객의 이름과 연락처 정보가 문서에서 삭제될 것입니다.

해설 복합 명사 문제로 '기밀 유지를 위해'는 for confidentiality purposes로 표현하므로 정답은 (D) confidentiality이다.

어휘 contact information 연락처 정보 | remove 제거하다, 삭제하다 | document 서류, 문서 | confide 터놓다 | confidentiality 기밀 유지, 비밀

7. 성 베드로 성당은 수많은 명망 높은 상을 받은 한 유명 지역 건축가에 의해서 설계되었다.

해설 빈칸에는 주격 관계대명사(who)의 선행사로 사람이 와야 한다. 의미상 '건축가'가 들어가야 하고, 앞에 관사 a가 있으므로 단수 형태인 (B) architect가 답으로 알맞다.

어휘 design 설계하다 | numerous 수많은 | prestigious 명망 있는 | architecture 건축학 | architect 건축가

8. 작문 세미나에 관한 세부적인 설명을 위해서, 웹사이트에서 프로그램 사본 한 부를 다운 받으세요.

해설 해석을 하면 '세부적인 정보/설명'이라는 의미가 들어가야 하므로 (A)와 (B)가 답이 될 수 있다. 그러나 information은 불가산 명사로 앞에 관사 a가 올 수 없으므로 정답은 (B) description이 된다.

어휘 detailed 상세한 | copy 사본, 복사본 | description 설명

9. 학회 시작 전에 각 대표에게 좌석이 할당되고 당일 이벤트에 대한 세부 일정이 제공됩니다.

해설 수 일치를 묻는 문제이다. 빈칸 앞에 단수 명사를 받는 한정사 each가 있으므로 정답은 '대표자'라는 의미의 (B) delegate가 된다.

어휘 prior to ~에 앞서 | conference 학회 | assign 할당하다 | delegate 대표; 위임하다, 뽑다

10. 타라는 올해가 되어서야 부서를 바꾸겠다는 의사를 표명했다.

해설 express라는 타동사의 목적어 자리로 명사가 필요하므로 정답은 (D) inclination이 된다. (C) inclining도 inclination과 유사한 의미의 명사이긴 하지만, 동사 express와 함께 쓰이지 않는다.

어휘 express inclination to do ~할 의사를 표하다 | switch 바꾸다, 전환하다 | department 부서

11. 〈세계 경제 타임지〉는 경영 전문가들을 위한 새로운 금융 출간물이다.

해설 빈칸은 형용사(financial)의 수식을 받는 명사 자리인데, Global

Economic Times와 동격 관계를 이루어야 하므로 '출간물'을 뜻하는 (B) publication이 정답이다.

어휘 financial 재정의 | professional 전문가 | publication 출판, 발행, 출판물

12. 도슨 씨는 도쿄에서 새 회사를 설립하는 그의 계획에 대해 전문가와 논의해 왔다.

해설 빈칸에 알맞은 명사를 찾는 문제이다. 관사 a 다음에 왔으므로 단수 형태이면서 의미상 '전문가'라는 단어가 나와야 하므로 답은 (A) professional이 알맞다.

어휘 consult 논의하다 | establish 설립하다 | professional 전문가 | professionalism 프로정신, 전문성

13. 도로가 보수되는 동안에, 운전자들은 10번 고속도로를 운전할 때 조심하라는 권고를 받는다.

해설 빈칸은 타동사 use의 목적어 자리로 명사가 들어가야 하므로 정답은 (D) caution이 된다. 동사 뒤라고 해서 성급하게 부사인 (B)를 선택하지 않도록 조심한다. use caution은 '조심하다'라는 뜻이다.

어휘 repair 보수하다 | motorist 운전자 | use(= exercise) caution 조심하다 | cautiously 조심히

14. 파인우드 그룹은 대중교통을 이용하는 고객들이 좀 더 접근할 수 있는 지역에 새 쇼핑센터를 열 것이다.

해설 주격 관계대명사(that) 뒤에 나온 be동사의 형태(are)로 미루어 보아 선행사는 복수 명사가 알맞다. 따라서 정답은 (D) locations이다.

어휘 accessible 접근할 수 있는 | public transportation 대중교통

15. 치열한 경쟁에도 불구하고, 우리 브랜드의 시장 점유율은 계속 성장하고 있다.

해설 형용사 intense 다음에 들어갈 명사로 (A)와 (D)가 가능한데, (D)는 사람 명사이므로 앞에 관사가 들어가야 한다. 따라서 정답은 '경쟁'을 뜻하는 (A) competition이 된다.

어휘 despite ~에도 불구하고 | intense 치열한 | market share 시장 점유율 | continue 계속되다

16. 모든 행사 기획자는 성공적인 행사를 준비하는 것은 서로 다른 공급업체 간의 긴밀한 협업에 달려 있다는 것을 알고 있다.

해설 형용사 close 다음에 들어갈 명사로 (A)와 (C)가 가능한데, (A)는 사람 명사이므로 앞에 관사가 들어가야 한다. 따라서 정답은 '협업'을 뜻하는 (C) collaboration이 된다.

어휘 organize 준비하다 | depend on ~에 달려 있다 | close 긴밀한 | supplier 공급업체

17. 셀린 사는 양포 제조의 주요 유통업체로 여러 가지 자동차 부품을 생산한다.

해설 빈칸이 형용사 main 다음에 있으므로 명사가 와야 한다. 의미상 빈칸에는 문장 주어인 The Shelrin Company와 동격의 형태가 와야 하므로 '유통업체'를 의미하는 (C) distributor가 답으로 알맞다.

어휘 a variety of 다양한 | auto parts 자동차 부품 | distributor 유통

업체, 배급업체 | **distribution** 유통, 배분

18. 발표 장비를 빌리는 요청서는 행사가 있기 일주일 전에 기술지원부로 이메일을 통해서 보내져야 한다.

해설 빈칸은 주어 자리로 명사 형태가 들어가야 한다. '요청서가 이메일을 통해서 보내져야 한다'는 의미로, 빈칸 앞에 관사가 없으므로 복수형인 (D) Requests가 정답이 된다.

어휘 **borrow** 빌리다 | **equipment** 장비 | **via** ~을 통해서 | **in advance** 미리 | **request** 요청, 요청서

19. 공업지대의 개발 계획에는 인근 고속도로의 확장과 인접한 주차 공간의 확대가 포함된다.

해설 동사 include의 목적어 자리에 「명사 + of + 명사」의 형태로 명사가 들어가야 한다고 성급하게 (D)를 선택하지 않도록 조심한다. -ing로 끝나는 (A)도 명사로, width는 '폭, 너비'라는 뜻이고, widening은 '확장'이라는 뜻이다. 해석을 해보면 '확장'이라는 의미가 들어가야 자연스러우므로 정답은 (A) widening이 된다.

어휘 **development plan** 개발 계획 | **industrial zone** 공업 지대 | **nearby** 인근의, 가까운 곳의 | **freeway** 고속도로 | **expansion** 확장 | **adjacent** 인접한, 가까이에 있는 | **parking space** 주차 공간 | **widening** 확장 | **widen** 넓어지다, 넓히다 | **width** 폭, 너비

20. 셴 힝 사는 방문객들에게 홍콩에 도착하기 훨씬 전에 호텔 숙박을 예약하라고 조언한다.

해설 '호텔 숙박'이라는 복합 명사가 나와야 하므로 빈칸에는 (D) accommodations가 들어가야 한다.

어휘 **advise** 조언하다, 권고하다 | **visitor** 방문객 | **reserve** 예약하다 | **hotel accommodations** 호텔 숙박 | **well in advance of** ~ 훨씬 전에

UNIT 05. 형용사

1. + check   1. (A)   2. (C)   3. (A)   본서 p.53

1. 고용주들은 지역 직업 학교의 학생들이 매우 유능한 근로자들임을 알게 되었다.

해설 빈칸은 명사 workers를 수식하는 형용사가 적합하므로 (A) capable이 정답이다.

어휘 **employer** 고용주 | **find** 알게 되다, 발견하다 | **trade school** 직업 학교 | **extremely** 매우, 극도로 | **capable** 유능한

2. 가입 제의는 모든 필요 서류들이 제출되어 확인될 때까지 조건부이다.

해설 빈칸은 be동사의 보어 자리로 '가입 제의는 조건부이다'라는 의미로 형용사가 들어가야 하므로 (C) conditional이 정답이다.

어휘 **admission** 가입, 입장 | **conditional** 조건부의 | **condition** 조건

3. 우리는 그 소프트웨어 프로젝트가 가까운 시일 내에 완성될 것으로 생각하지 않는다.

해설 빈칸은 be동사의 보어 자리로 의미상 '완성한'이라는 형용사가 들어가야 하므로 (A) complete가 답이 된다. complete는 동사뿐만 아니라 형용사로도 사용된다.

어휘 **in the near future** 가까운 장래에 | **complete** 완성한, 완전한

2. + check   1. (A)   2. (C)   3. (C)   본서 p.55

1. 에스지 자동차 회사의 하이브리드 차량에 대한 많은 개선이 자동차 산업에 커다란 영향을 미칠 것이다.

해설 빈칸에는 복수 명사 improvements를 수식하는 형용사가 필요하므로 (A) many가 정답이다.

어휘 **improvement** 향상, 개선 | **have a(n) effect on** ~에 영향을 미치다 | **automobile industry** 자동차 산업

2. 온라인 퀴즈는 상당수의 시도 후에 참가자에게 힌트를 주도록 설계되어 있다.

해설 빈칸은 수량 형용사 a number of '많은'의 수식을 받는 명사 자리이며, a number of는 복수 명사를 취하므로 (C) attempts가 정답이다.

어휘 **design** 설계하다 | **grant** 주다 | **hint** 암시, 힌트 | **a number of** 많은 | **reasonable** 합당한, 적당한 | **attempt** 시도

3. 다수의 추정치에 따르면, 태양 전지판은 집주인들이 연간 2,000에서 4,000달러 사이의 돈을 절약할 수 있게 해준다고 말한다.

해설 the majority of 뒤에는 복수 명사가 나와야 하므로 (C) estimates가 정답이다.

어휘 **the majority of** 다수의 | **solar panel** 태양 전지판 | **allow** 허용하다 | **homeowner** 집주인 | **save** 절약하다 | **estimate** 추정, 추산; 추정하다

3. + check   1. (A)   2. (A)   3. (C)   본서 p.56

1. 퀴라소 시에 있는 역사적인 사우스포트 극장은 대대적인 보수가 필요한 상태이다.

해설 빈칸은 repairs라는 명사를 수식하는 형용사 또는 분사 자리로 (A), (D)가 될 수 있는데 '대대적인 보수'라는 의미가 적합하므로 (A) extensive가 정답이다. 보통 형용사와 분사가 나오면 형용사를 정답으로 우선시한다.

어휘 **historic** 역사적인, 역사적으로 유명한 | **in need of** ~을 필요로 하는 | **repair** 보수, 수리 | **extensive** 광범위한 | **extension** 확장

2. 우리는 귀사와 상호 유익한 업무 관계를 구축하기를 기대합니다.

해설 빈칸은 뒤의 working relationship이라는 명사를 수식하는 형용사 자리로, 해석상 '상호 유익한 업무 관계'라는 의미가 적합하므로 (A) beneficial이 정답이다.

어휘 **look forward to -ing** ~하기를 고대하다 | **build** 구축하다, 짓다 | **mutually** 서로, 상호 간에 | **beneficial** 유익한 | **benefited** 혜택을 받은 | **beneficent** 인정 많은

3. 뉴스, 견해 및 사설을 포함한 본 웹사이트의 내용은 각 작성자의 것입니다.

해설 authors라는 명사를 수식하는 형용사 자리로 해석을 해보면 '각 저자'란 의미가 적합하므로 (C) respective가 정답이다.

어휘 **including** ~을 포함하여 | **editorial** 사설 | **belong to** ~의 것이다 | **author** 저자 | **respected** 훌륭한, 높이 평가되는 |

respectable 존경할 만한 | respective 각자의, 각각의 | respectful 존경심을 보이는, 공손한

4. + check   1. (C)   2. (A)   3. (D)   본서 p.57

1. 이 웹사이트에 올라와 있는 논평들과 의견들은 뉴스 미디어 소사이어티를 대표하지 않는다는 것을 알아 두십시오.

해설 be동사 뒤에 보어로 주로 형용사가 들어갈 수 있으며, '대표하다'라는 의미의 be representative of가 적합하므로 (C) representative가 정답이다.

어휘 comment 논평 | represent 대변하다 | representative 대표; 대표하는

2. 직원들은 뫼비우스 사에서 설계한 신규 회사 웹사이트의 출시에 열광적이다.

해설 be동사 뒤에 보어로 주로 형용사가 들어갈 수 있으며, '열광적이다'라는 의미의 be enthusiastic about이 적합하므로 (A) enthusiastic이 정답이다.

어휘 launch 출시, 개시 | design 설계하다 | enthusiastic 열광적인 | devoted 헌신적인 | respectable 존경할 만한 | perceptive 통찰력 있는

3. 할로우 스튜디오의 직물 공장은 우리 직원의 정기 품질 검사 대상이다.

해설 quality inspections라는 복합 명사를 수식하는 형용사 자리로 해석을 해보면 '정기 품질 검사'라는 의미가 적합하므로 (D) routine이 정답이다.

어휘 textile factory 직물 공장 | be subject to ~의 대상이다 | quality inspection 품질 검사 | staff 직원 | routine 상례적인, 정례적인

Practice   본서 p.58

1. (D)	2. (D)	3. (B)	4. (A)	5. (A)
6. (B)	7. (B)	8. (A)	9. (A)	10. (C)
11. (A)	12. (C)	13. (B)	14. (B)	15. (B)
16. (B)	17. (A)	18. (B)	19. (A)	20. (A)

1. 제품 사양은 우리 엔지니어들이 요청했던 모든 내용과 일치합니다.

해설 be동사의 보어 자리로 형용사가 들어가야 하며 '~과 일치하다'라는 의미의 be consistent with가 적합하므로 정답은 (D) consistent with이다. consist는 자동사이므로 수동태가 되거나 목적어로 명사를 바로 취할 수 없다.

어휘 product specifications 제품 사양 | request 요청하다 | consist 이루어져 있다 | consistency in ~의 일관성 | consistent with ~과 일치하는

2. 이 2도어 컨버터블은 우리 대리점에서 제공하는 가장 인기 있는 렌터카이다.

해설 복합 명사 문제로 '렌터카(rental vehicle)'가 적합하므로 정답은 (D) rental이 된다.

어휘 convertible 컨버터블(차량 지붕을 접었다 펴거나 떼었다 붙였다 할 수

있는 차량) | rental vehicle 임대 차량, 렌터카 | dealership 대리점 | rent 세내다 | renter 임차인, 세입자 | rental 임대료, 임대 물건, 임대; 임대의

3. 많은 사람이 기계적인 결함으로 야기된 지하철 지연이 자주 있는 것에 대해 불만을 토로하고 있다.

해설 동사 become은 2형식 동사로 빈칸에는 '자주'를 의미하는 형용사가 오는 것이 알맞다. 정답은 (B) frequent가 된다.

어휘 delay 지연 | mechanical fault 기계적 결함 | frequent 자주 일어나는 | frequently 자주, 여러 번 | frequency 빈번, 빈도, 주파수

4. 전문경영인은 과연 관리자들이 직원들의 생산성을 극대화하기 위해 최선을 다했는지 의문을 품었다.

해설 빈칸은 앞의 동사 were doing을 수식하는 부사 자리이므로 부사 역할을 할 수 없는 (B), (C), (D)는 모두 답이 될 수 없다. 따라서 '생산성을 극대화하기 위해 관리자들이 충분히 일했는지'라는 의미를 완성하는 (A) enough가 정답이다.

어휘 question 의문을 갖다 | maximize 극대화하다 | productivity 생산성

5. 처음 몇 달 동안, 에르네스토는 그의 새로운 직업의 힘든 일정을 따라가기 위해 고군분투했다.

해설 schedule이라는 명사를 수식하는 형용사 문제로, 의미상 '힘든, 어려운'이라는 뜻이 나와야 하므로 정답은 (A) demanding이 된다.

어휘 struggle 힘겹게 하다, 고군분투하다 | keep up with ~을 계속 따라가다 | demanding 부담이 큰, 힘든 | demand 요구 (사항); 요구하다, 필요로 하다

6. 넬타 제조 공장 운영자는 안전 검사가 시행되는 동안에 생산을 중단할 필요가 있다고 생각했다.

해설 consider '고려하다'는 5형식 동사로 목적격 보어로 형용사 또는 분사를 취할 수 있다. 따라서 (B) necessary가 답으로 알맞다. 문장의 구조는 「consider + 가목적어(it) + 형용사 + 진목적어(to부정사)」로 이루어져 있다.

어휘 suspend production 생산을 중단하다 | safety inspection 안전 검사 | conduct 시행하다 | necessity 필요성 | necessitate 필요로 하다

7. 1월 3일부터 6일까지 헌터 씨는 모든 부관리자들을 위해 다양한 워크숍을 개최할 것이다.

해설 assistant managers라는 복수 명사를 수식하는 수량 형용사를 찾는 문제이다. 이 문장에서는 '모든 부관리자들'이라는 의미가 들어가야 하므로 정답은 (B) all이 알맞다. (A) either가 답이 되려면 두 가지를 언급해야 하는데 그렇지 않았다. (C)는 단수 명사가 나와야 하므로 답이 될 수 없다. (D)는 '거의 없는'의 의미로 문맥상 알맞지 않다.

어휘 hold 개최하다 | a number of 많은 | assistant 조수, 부 | either (둘 중) 어느 하나의 | few 거의 없는

8. 승진 대상자들은 모두 좋은 반응을 보였지만, 쿠티에레즈 씨의 답변은 특히 통찰력이 있었다.

해설 빈칸은 be동사의 보어로 부사 particularly의 수식을 받는 형용사가 와야 한다. 따라서 (A) insightful이 정답이 된다.

어휘 candidate 후보자, 지원자 | promotion 승진 | particularly 특히 | insightful 통찰력 있는 | insight 통찰력

9. 많은 나라가 중동 지역 밖에서 수입해 오는 석유에 점점 의존하고 있다.

해설 빈칸에는 부사 increasingly의 수식을 받고, 2형식 동사 become의 보어 역할을 하는 형용사가 들어가야 한다. be reliant on은 '~에 의존하다'라는 의미이므로 정답은 (A) reliant가 된다.

어휘 increasingly 점점 | petroleum 석유 | import 수입하다 | be reliant on ~에 의존하다 | reliable 믿을 수 있는 | rely 의지하다

10. 최근 설문 조사에서 보여주는 바는 많은 소비자들이 향상된 성능 때문에 최신 엠엑스555 노트북을 구입하기를 열망하고 있는 것으로 나타난다는 것이다.

해설 because of 이하의 내용으로 보아 빈칸에는 'MX555 노트북 구매를 바란다'는 내용에 부합하는 형용사가 와야 한다. be anxious to는 '~하는 것을 열망하다[간절히 바라다]'의 의미로 정답은 (C) anxious가 된다.

어휘 recent 최근의 | indicate 나타내다 | latest 최신의 | enhanced 향상된 | capability 능력 | knowledgeable 아는 것이 많은, 박식한 | decisive 결정적인 | anxious 열망하는, 간절히 바라는

11. 제품 만족도 조사에 따르면, 하드웨이 작업 장화는 다른 유사 브랜드만큼 가볍지 않다.

해설 as와 as 사이에는 형용사 또는 부사가 들어갈 수 있는데, 앞에 be동사(are)가 있으므로 빈칸에는 보어로 '가벼운'이라는 의미의 형용사가 필요하다. 따라서 정답은 (A) light이다.

어휘 product satisfaction 제품 만족 | as ~ as … …만큼 ~한 | similar 유사한

12. 노조 대표들과의 광범위한 회담 이후 공장 근로자들은 이제 다시 업무에 복귀했다.

해설 talks '회담'이라는 명사 앞에 들어갈 알맞은 형용사는 (C) extensive이다.

어휘 be back on the job 업무에 복귀하다 | following ~이후에 | union representative 노조 대표 | extend 확장하다 | extensive 광범위한 | extent 넓이, 정도, 확대될 것

13. 공장의 새 조립 기기는 생산 수준을 향상하는 데 효율적임을 보여주었다.

해설 prove는 2형식 동사로 보어로 형용사를 취하므로 정답은 (B) effective가 된다.

어휘 assembly 조립

14. 마케팅 매니저는 새 광고 캠페인을 성공시키기 위한 팀원들의 노력에 감사해했다.

해설 be동사의 보어 자리에 알맞은 형용사 어휘를 물어보는 문제이다. be appreciative of는 '~에 감사하다'라는 의미로 정답은 (B) appreciative가 된다.

어휘 advertising 광고 | be willing to 기꺼이 ~하다 | be appreciative of ~에 감사하다 | fulfilled 성취감을 느끼는 | decisive 결정적인, 결단력 있는

15. 실험실에서 위험한 화학 물질을 다루는 것에 관한 규정은 부상을 막기 위해서 시기적절하게 정해져야 한다.

해설 명사인 manner 앞에 들어가는 형용사 문제이다. 「명사 + -ly」는 형용사이므로 정답은 (B) timely가 된다.

어휘 regulation 규정 | handle 다루다 | chemical 화학 물질 | laboratory 실험실 | prevent 막다 | injury 부상 | in a timely manner 시기적절하게 | timing 시기, 타이밍

16. 임대 계약서에는 세입자가 임대 기간 동안 발생하는 모든 재산 파손에 대해 개인적으로 책임진다는 것을 명시하고 있다.

해설 '~에 (금전적인) 책임을 지다'라는 의미가 알맞으므로 be liable for의 (B) liable이 정답이 된다.

어휘 rental agreement 임대 계약서 | state 명시하다 | tenant 세입자 | personally 개인적으로 | destruction 파손 | property 건물, 부동산 | occur 발생하다 | lease period 임대 기간 | inform 알리다 | liable 법적 책임이 있는 | compatible 양립될 수 있는, 화합할 수 있는 | prohibit 금하다, 하지 못하게 하다

17. 프라임 문구는 더 이상 100달러 이하의 사무용품 주문 배달을 받지 않는다.

해설 빈칸 앞의 no longer는 '더 이상 ~하지 않는'이라는 뜻의 부사적 관용표현이므로 생략하고 보면, 빈칸은 명사 delivery orders를 목적어로 취할 수 있는 동사 자리이므로 앞의 is와 현재진행형 능동태를 완성하는 (A) accepting이 정답이다.

어휘 stationery 문구 | no longer 더 이상 ~하지 않는 | office supply 사무용품 | acceptable 받아들일 수 있는

18. 사용 설명서에는 석 달에 한 번 자동차 오일을 교환해야 한다고 적혀 있습니다.

해설 '3개월마다'는 every three months로 표현한다. 따라서 정답은 (D) every이다.

어휘 manual 사용 설명서

19. 승객들은 최소 48시간 전에 우리 항공사에 알려주면 추가 요금 없이 채식주의 식사를 받을 수 있다.

해설 빈칸에는 additional charge를 수식할 수 있는 형용사가 와야 하므로 no가 알맞다. not, nonetheless는 부사, nothing은 대명사로 빈칸에 올 수 없다. 그러므로 정답은 (A) no가 된다.

어휘 passenger 승객 | receive 받다 | additional charge 추가 요금 | inform 알리다 | at least 적어도, 최소한

20. 새로운 모든 규정을 준수하기 위해, 회사는 종합적인 내부 감사 프로그램을 시행할 것이다.

해설 빈칸을 포함한 목적어(a ~ program)는 단수이므로, 복수 명사와 쓰이는 numerous는 답이 될 수 없다. 의미상 '종합적인 내부 감사 프로그램'이 되어야 하므로 (A) comprehensive가 정답이다.

어휘 ensure 보장하다 | compliance with ~의 준수 | regulations 규정 | implement 시행하다, 이행하다 | internal audit 내부 감사 | comprehensive 종합적인 | conceivable 상상할 수 있는, 가능한 | numerous 다양한 | potential 가능성이 있는

UNIT 06. 부사

1. + check   1. (D)   2. (C)   3. (A)   본서 p.61

1. 멕레이 대학교에 다니는 어떠한 학생도 그들의 전공 필수조건을 만족스럽게 이행하지 않으면 졸업하지 못할 수도 있다.

해설 빈칸 앞에 전치사 without과 동명사 fulfilling 사이에 들어가서 동명사를 수식하는 품사는 부사이므로 (D) satisfactorily가 정답이다.

어휘 fulfill (의무·약속 등을) 이행하다, 수행하다 | requirement 필수조건 | major 전공

2. 상품 수령 즉시, 대금은 당신의 회사 계정으로 바로 입금될 것이다.

해설 빈칸은 수동태 동사와 전치사구 사이의 수식어 자리이므로 부사 (C) directly가 정답이다.

어휘 receipt 수령 | payment 지불금 | deposit 예금되다 | direction 제시, 방향 | direct ~로 향하다 | directly 바로, 즉시

3. 레오 디저트 가게는 겨우 1월부터 영업을 시작했지만, 현재 이 지역에서 가장 많이 팔리는 도넛 가게입니다.

해설 해석을 해보면 '겨우 1월부터 영업을 시작했다'라는 의미가 적합하므로 (A) only가 정답이다.

어휘 be in business 영업 중이다 | best-selling 베스트 셀러의 | lately 최근에 | once 한 번

2. + check   1. (C)   2. (A)   3. (B)   본서 p.63

1. 엘름 가에 있는 주택 구매에 관심을 보였던 고객이 아직 매매 계약서에 사인을 하지 않았다.

해설 의미상 have yet to '아직 ~하지 못하다'가 적합하므로 (C) yet이 정답이다.

어휘 interest 관심, 흥미 | agreement 계약(서) | have yet to do 아직 ~하지 못하다

2. 지난 5년간 가계 소득은 현저하게 상승했고, 이는 실업률의 급격한 감소를 가져왔다.

해설 빈칸 앞에 increase '증가하다'라는 동사가 나오며, '증가하다, 감소하다'라는 동사를 수식하는 부사는 markedly가 적절하므로 (A) markedly가 정답이다.

어휘 household income 가계 소득 | accompany 동반하다 | sharp 급격한 | decline 하락 | unemployment rate 실업률 | markedly 급격하게 | fashionably 멋지게 | loudly 큰소리로 | importantly 중요하게

3. 시간 부족에도 불구하고, 디자인 팀은 용케도 회사의 새 로고를 아주 멋지게 만들었다.

해설 빈칸 뒤의 형용사 attractive를 수식하는 부사로, '상당히, 꽤 매력적

인'이라는 의미가 적합하므로 (B) quite가 정답이다.

어휘 manage to do 간신히 ~하다

3. + check   1. (C)   2. (A)   3. (C)   본서 p.64

1. 레일라 류 감독은 신작 영화 시사회에 이어 직후 관객의 질문에 답할 것이다.

해설 빈칸이 없어도 완전한 문장이므로 부사가 적합하므로 (C) shortly가 정답이다.

어휘 director 감독 | audience 관객, 청중 | following ~후에 | premiere 시사회 | film 영화

2. 최근에, 줄리아나는 거의 매일 오후 8시나 9시까지 직장에 남아 있다.

해설 「~, S + V」에서 빈칸은 문장 전체를 수식하는 부사 자리로 보기에서 (A), (D)가 부사인데, 해석을 해보면 '최근에'라는 의미가 적합하므로 (A) Lately가 정답이다.

어휘 stay at work 직장에 머무르다

3. 우리 회계 책임자인 엘리스 에비하라는 올해 경비를 훨씬 더 면밀하게 감시할 계획이다.

해설 빈칸 앞에 비교급을 완성하는 부사 more가 있다는 점에서 more가 필요 없는 비교급 형태인 closer는 답에서 먼저 제외시킨다. 의미상 빈칸은 동사 monitor를 수식하는 부사 자리인데, close는 '(거리상) 가깝게', closely는 '자세히, 면밀하게'라는 뜻으로 면밀하게 감시할 것이라는 의미가 적절하므로 (C) closely가 정답이다.

어휘 head of accounting 회계 책임자 | plan to ~할 계획이다 | monitor 감시하다 | expense 경비 | closely 빈틈없이, 면밀히

4. + check   1. (B)   2. (D)   3. (B)   본서 p.65

1. 날씨 때문에 일부 활동은 실내에서 진행해야 했지만, 그럼에도 회사의 연례 직원 워크숍은 예정대로 완료되었다.

해설 「be + p.p.」 사이에 들어가는 부사 자리로 해석을 해보면 '그럼에도'의 의미가 적합하므로 (B) nonetheless가 정답이다.

어휘 hold 열리다, 개최하다 | indoors 실내에서 | annual 연례의 | complete 완료하다 | as scheduled 예정대로

2. 로미타 물류는 기밀 서류를 국제 배송하며, 따라서, 보안 추적 시스템을 필요로 한다.

해설 이미 두 절 사이에 접속사 and가 나와 있으므로 빈칸은 부사 자리가 된다. 앞뒤 절의 의미를 인과관계로 연결시켜주는 접속부사가 들어가야 하므로 (D) therefore가 정답이다.

어휘 logistics 물류 관리 | ship 배송하다 | sensitive 민감한, 기밀을 요하는 | internationally 국제적으로 | secure 안전한 | tracking 추적

3. 그레이지 씨는 영업직에 지원했지만, 그가 전에 한 일들은 모두 회계 분야였다.

해설 빈칸이 없어도 완전한 문장이므로 부사가 들어가야 하며, (A), (C)는 접속사라서 탈락이 되고, 해석을 해보면 '역접'의 의미가 들어가야 하므로 (B) however가 정답이다.

어휘 apply for ~에 지원하다[신청하다] | accounting 회계 (업무) | now that ~라는 점에서 | in case ~인 경우에 | otherwise 그렇지 않으면

1. (D)	2. (A)	3. (D)	4. (B)	5. (C)
6. (B)	7. (A)	8. (D)	9. (C)	10. (C)
11. (A)	12. (D)	13. (D)	14. (A)	15. (D)
16. (C)	17. (A)	18. (C)	19. (A)	20. (D)

1. 소비자들은 지역에서 재배되는 과일과 채소를 구매하여 지역 농가를 지원할 수 있다.

해설 are grown은 수동태 문장이다. 빈칸은 동사 grown을 수식하는 부사가 오는 것이 적절하므로 (D) regionally가 정답이다.

어휘 support 지원하다 | purchase 구매하다 | region 지역 | regional 지역의 | regionally 지역에서

2. 택사호마 국립 은행은 일부 고객들이 인근 지점들을 폐쇄하려는 계획에 부정적인 반응을 보이고 있다는 것을 발견했다.

해설 respond to는 「자동사 + 전치사」 구조로 '~에 반응하다'란 의미이다. 자동사와 전치사 사이에 들어갈 수 있는 품사는 부사이므로 정답은 (A) negatively가 된다.

어휘 discover 발견하다 | client 고객 | respond to ~에 반응하다[대응하다] | close down 폐쇄하다 | neighborhood 인근, 이웃 | branch 지점, 지사

3. 지역 사업주들과의 인터뷰는 그들이 새로운 해안가 개발 계획에 거의 보편적으로 동의한다는 것을 보여주었다.

해설 be in agreement with는 '~에 동의하다, ~와 일치하다'라는 의미이다. 따라서 빈칸에는 부사가 들어가야 하므로 (D) universally가 정답이다.

어휘 local 지역의 | business owner 사업주 | in agreement with ~에 동의하여, ~와 일치하여 | waterfront 해안가 | development 개발 | universe 우주 | universality 보편성, 일반성 | universal 일반적인, 보편적인

4. 귀하가 이 호텔의 현재 투숙객임을 확인할 수 있는 경우 뷔페에서의 식사는 완전히 무료입니다.

해설 빈칸은 be동사와 형용사 complimentary 사이의 부사 자리이므로 (B) completely가 정답이다. 참고로 provided가 '~을 조건으로 하여'라는 뜻의 부사절 접속사로 쓰였다는 점에 주의한다.

어휘 meal 식사 | buffet 뷔페 | complimentary 무료의 | provided ~을 조건으로 하여 | confirm 확인해주다 | current 현재의 | complete 완전한; 완성하다

5. 코르시드 태양광 발전은 합병 조건을 수락했는지의 여부를 아직 발표하지 않았다.

해설 '아직 ~하지 못하다'라고 할 때, have[be] yet to를 쓴다. 그러므로 정답은 (C) yet이 된다.

어휘 solar power 태양광 발전 | announce 발표하다 | whether ~인지 아닌지 | accept 수락하다 | term 조건 | merger 합병

6. 직원들은 별도의 권고 사항이 없는 한 매일 일을 마친 후 모든 전자기기를 꺼야 한다.

해설 '별도의 권고 사항이 없으면'은 unless otherwise advised로 표현한다. 따라서 (B) otherwise가 정답이다. unless otherwise mentioned/stated/indicated/instructed는 '별도의 언급/지시 사항이 없으면'의 의미로 자주 사용된다.

어휘 turn off 끄다 | electronic machinery 전자기기

7. 크리스토퍼 씨가 예상치 못한 병을 앓고 난 결과, 그는 현재의 프로젝트를 상당히 줄였다.

해설 cut back on이 하나의 구동사로 '~을 줄이다'라는 의미이다. '상당히 줄이다'라는 의미가 알맞으므로 부사 (A) significantly가 정답이다.

어휘 as a result of ~의 결과로 | unexpected 예상하지 못하다 | illness 병 | cutback 줄이다, 축소하다 | current 현재의 | significant 상당한 | signify ~을 나타내다, 중요하다, 영향을 끼치다 | significance 중요성, 의의, 의미

8. 폭우로 인해 이번 주 비행 일정이 갑자기 변경될 수 있다.

해설 빈칸은 동사 change를 수식하는 부사 자리이다. '폭우로 비행 일정이 갑자기 변경될 수 있다'는 의미가 되어야 문맥상 자연스러우므로 (D) unexpectedly가 정답이다.

어휘 heavy rain 폭우 | cause 야기하다 | flight 비행, 항공편 | schedule 일정 | sincerely 진심으로 | popularly 일반적으로 | virtually 가상으로 | unexpectedly 갑자기

9. 귀사의 제안을 심사숙고하여 검토했음에도 불구하고, 저희 이사회는 현재 합작법인을 진행하는 데 반대표를 던졌습니다.

해설 동명사 examining을 수식하는 부사가 들어가야 하므로 (C) thoughtfully가 정답이다.

어휘 despite ~에도 불구하고 | examine 검토하다 | proposal 제안(서) | board of directors 이사회 | vote against ~에 반대표를 던지다 | proceed 진행하다, 계속해서 ~을 하다 | joint venture 합작투자회사 | thought 생각, 사고 | thoughtful 사려 깊은 | thoughtfulness 사려 깊음

10. 회사의 수익이 가장 적은 부문은 또한, 놀랍게도, 가장 많이 광고한 것이었다.

해설 두 콤마(,) 사이에 있는 빈칸은 삽입된 것을 의미한다. 이곳에 들어갈 수 있는 품사는 부사이므로 정답은 (C) surprisingly가 된다. 동사 was를 보고 빈칸에 형용사(surprising, surprised)가 들어가야 한다고 생각하지 않도록 한다.

어휘 least 가장 덜, 최소로 | profitable 수익성이 있는

11. 가리솝 사는 비용 효율적인 제조 과정을 실행함으로써 고객들에게 매우 합리적인 가격의 제품을 제공한다.

해설 priced라는 형용사를 수식하는 부사가 필요하므로 정답은 (A) competitively이다.

어휘 implement 실행하다 | cost-effective 비용 효율적인 | manufacturing 제조 | competitively priced(= reasonably priced) 가격 경쟁력 있는, 합리적인[저렴한] 가격의 | competitive 경쟁력이 있는 | compete 경쟁하다 | competition 경쟁

12. 모튼 라탄 박물관은 한때 유명한 작가 맥스 토마스의 거주지였던 아름다운 저택에 위치하고 있다.

해설 빈칸은 문장에 영향을 못 미치는 부사가 들어가는 것이 알맞다. '한때'라는 의미의 부사 (D) once가 정답이다.

어휘 be housed in ~에 수용되다[보관되다] | mansion 대저택 | once 한때

13. 국제공항 근처에 이상적으로 위치한 그린 퀘이 리조트는 비즈니스 컨벤션에 완벽한 장소이다.

해설 빈칸 뒤 situated ~ airport는 주절의 주어 Green Quay Resort를 수식하는 분사구문으로써 situated가 과거분사이므로 빈칸은 분사 형용사를 수식하는 부사 자리이다. 따라서 (D) Ideally가 정답이다.

어휘 situate 위치하다

14. 냉장고가 거의 일주일 전에 수리센터에 보내졌지만, 아직도 수리가 안되었다.

해설 '아직 수리되지 않았다'는 의미가 되어야 한다. not을 중심으로 yet은 not 뒤에, still은 not 앞에 와야 하므로 정답은 (A) still이 된다.

어휘 refrigerator 냉장고 | repair center 수리센터 | repair 수리하다

15. 새로운 품질 보증 시스템 덕분에, 고객 불만이 급격히 감소했다.

해설 해석을 해보면 '매우 감소했다'라고 해서 extremely도 답이 될 것 같지만, extremely는 형용사 또는 부사를 수식하는 부사이다. 증가나 감소를 나타내는 동사와 궁합이 맞는 부사는 dramatically, sharply, significantly와 같은 부사이다. 그러므로 정답은 (D) dramatically이다.

어휘 thanks to ~ 덕분에 | quality assurance system 품질 보증 시스템 | customer complaint 고객 불만 | decrease 감소하다 | potentially 잠재적으로 | extremely 매우, 몹시 | respectively 각각, 제각기 | dramatically 급격히

16. 타리아 필로넨의 미술 전시회 개막식에는 초대받은 손님만 참석할 수 있다.

해설 전치사는 「주어 + 동사」의 구조를 이끌 수 없고, 빈칸에 접속사가 들어가면 부사절만 있는 문장이 되므로 전치사 (A)와 접속사 (D)는 먼저 답에서 제외시킨다. 의미상 '초대받은 손님만 참석하도록 허용된다'가 자연스러우므로 (C) Only가 정답이다.

어휘 allow 허용하다 | except 제외하고 | quite 꽤, 아주 | only 오직 ~만 | before ~이전에

17. 직원 점심 회의는 보통 정오에 시작하고 약 45분 정도 걸립니다.

해설 숫자나 수치 앞에는 '거의, 대략'의 의미인 (A) approximately가 들어갈 수 있다.

어휘 normally 보통 | take (시간이) 걸리다 | approximately 대략, 거의 | appropriately 알맞게, 적당하게 | actively 적극적으로 | alternatively 양자택일로, 대신으로

18. 계약서에 따르면, 그 보험은 첫 보험료가 지불되고 나서 바로 적용될 것이다.

해설 '바로, 직후'라는 의미로 「directly / immediately / shortly + after」가 쓰인다. 그러므로 정답은 (C) immediately가 된다.

어휘 insurance 보험 | go into effect 효력이 발생하다 | currently 현재에 | habitually 습관적으로 | immediately 즉시, 바로 | centrally 중심에, 중앙에

19. 이 상점의 모든 가구는 세트로 혹은 개별적으로 주문할 수 있다.

해설 as a set '한 세트로'는 부사 역할을 하므로 등위접속사 or 뒤에도 부사인 (A) individually가 들어가는 것이 맞다.

어휘 order 주문하다 | as a set 한 세트로 | individually 개별적으로, 각각 따로 | individuality 개성, 특성 | individualize 개인의 요구에 맞추다 | individual 개개의; 개인

20. 보안을 위해, 우리 매니저는 가끔 고객 계정 활동을 검토한다.

해설 문장의 동사가 review로 현재 시제를 가리킨다. (A)는 과거 시제와 쓰이며, (C)는 과거 혹은 현재 완료 시제와 잘 쓰인다. 따라서 현재 시제와 어울리는 (D) occasionally가 정답이다.

어휘 security 보안 | review 검토하다 | customer account 고객 계정 | formerly 이전에 | solely 홀로 | recently 최근에 | occasionally 종종, 이따금씩

UNIT 07. 대명사

1. +check   1. (A)   2. (B)   3. (C)   본서 p.69

1. 채드 프랫은 대학교수일 뿐만 아니라, 그는 베스트셀러의 저자이기도 하다.

해설 동사 앞에 들어가는 주어 자리로 주격이 들어가야 하므로 (A) he가 정답이다.

어휘 author 저자 | best-selling 베스트셀러의

2. 위튼 출장연회 서비스는 우리에게 그 회사의 밀 제품들은 알레르기를 일으키지 않는다는 것을 장담한다.

해설 명사(구)인 wheat products 앞에 들어가는 소유격이 적합하므로 (B) its가 정답이다.

어휘 assure 장담하다, 확언하다 | wheat 밀 | allergy-free 알레르기가 없는

3. 〈가드너 뉴스 월간지〉 구독 갱신을 희망하시는 분들은 저희에게 늦어도 6월 30일까지 납부하셔야 합니다.

해설 send는 4형식 동사로 목적어가 두 개 나오는데 빈칸은 간접목적어 자리로 목적격이 나와야 하므로 (C) us가 정답이다.

어휘 renew ~을 갱신하다 | subscription 구독 | payment 지불, 납입 | no later than 늦어도 ~까지

2. + check　1. (A)　2. (C)　3. (B)　　본서 p.69

1. 많은 지역의 유통업자들은 이미 그 프로그램을 직접 시도해 보았고 그것을 만족스러워했다.

해설　주어인 local distributors를 강조하는 재귀대명사의 강조 용법으로 (A) themselves가 정답이다.

어휘　distributor 유통업자 | satisfactory 만족스러운

2. 새로 채용된 전 직원들은 회사의 정책과 규정들에 익숙해질 수 있도록 오리엔테이션에 참석해야만 한다.

해설　하나의 숙어적인 표현으로 familiarize oneself with로 익히면 바로 풀 수 있는 문제이다. 타동사 familiarize의 목적어 자리 앞에 staff를 받는 재귀대명사의 재귀 용법이 필요하므로 (C) themselves가 정답이다.

어휘　regulation 규정 | familiarize oneself with ~에 익숙해지다

3. 프로젝트 매니저의 추가 직원 요청이 승인되지 않아서, 그녀는 두 개의 프로젝트를 혼자서 진행시켰다.

해설　해석상 '혼자서'의 의미가 적합하므로 by oneself가 들어가는 (B) herself가 정답이다.

어휘　approve 승인하다 | proceed with ~을 진행하다

3. + check　1. (B)　2. (C)　3. (B)　　본서 p.70

1. 이 주에서는 여러 건설 프로젝트들이 계획되어 있지만, 가드너는 주요 고속도로 근처의 프로젝트들에 초점을 맞추고 있다.

해설　빈칸은 앞의 projects를 받는 대명사가 적합하므로 (B) those가 정답이다.

어휘　construction 건설 | A be focused on B A가 B에 집중하다 | highway 고속도로

2. 마지막 시험을 통과한 사람들만이 정규직에 지원할 자격이 될 것이다.

해설　'~하는 어느 누구나/사람들'를 나타내는 anyone/those who가 적합한데, 뒤에 복수 동사 pass가 나오므로 복수를 받는 (C) those가 정답이다.

어휘　eligible ~할 자격이 있는 | apply for 지원하다 | permanent position 정규직

3. 매출액을 늘리기 위한 더 나은 전략을 가지고 있다고 생각하는 사람은 누구든지 라미레즈 씨와 이야기해도 좋습니다.

해설　'~하는 어느 누구나'의 뜻을 가진 anyone who가 적합하며, 뒤에 단수 동사 thinks가 나오므로 (B) Anyone이 정답이다.

어휘　strategy 전략 | sales 매출액, 판매량

4. + check　1. (A)　2. (A)　3. (B)　　본서 p.71

1. 채용 담당 매니저 레티타 풍은 영업 부서를 이끌 자격을 갖춘 누군가를 찾고 있다.

해설　빈칸은 qualified의 수식을 받으며, 타동사 seek의 목적어 자리이다. 해석상 '누군가'의 의미가 적합하므로 (A) someone이 정답이다.

어휘　recruitment 채용 | qualified 자격을 갖춘 | head 이끌다 | someone 어떤 사람 | one another 서로

2. 그녀가 대부분의 사람들보다 계약의 세부 사항을 잘 알기 때문에 양 씨는 다가오는 협상 회의에서 우크란 전자를 대표할 것이다.

해설　해석을 해보면 '대부분의 사람들보다 잘 알다'라는 의미가 적합하므로 (A) most가 정답이다.

어휘　represent 대표하다 | upcoming 다가오는 | negotiation 협상 | contract 계약 | detail 세부 사항

3. 비록 많은 사람이 그 결정을 마음에 들어 하지 않았지만, 사내 일부 부서의 경비가 너무 높아서 새로운 예산 정책이 시행되었다.

해설　타동사 dislike 앞에 들어가는 주어 자리로 해석을 해보면 많은 사람들이 들어가야 하므로 (B) many가 정답이다.

어휘　dislike 싫어하다 | budget policy 예산 정책 | implement 실행하다, 시행하다 | expense 경비, 비용

Practice　　본서 p.72

1. (B)	**2.** (A)	**3.** (B)	**4.** (C)	**5.** (D)
6. (A)	**7.** (C)	**8.** (D)	**9.** (D)	**10.** (D)
11. (C)	**12.** (D)	**13.** (B)	**14.** (B)	**15.** (D)
16. (C)	**17.** (C)	**18.** (A)	**19.** (B)	**20.** (B)

1. 우리는 나머지 후보자들에 대한 면접이 연기될 것이라고 인사부에 알려야 합니다.

해설　빈칸 뒤에 오는 interviews는 동사가 아닌 명사로 쓰였으므로, 명사 앞에 소유격이 오는 것이 적합하다. 따라서 (B) our가 정답이다.

어휘　inform 알리다 | remaining 남아 있는 | candidate 후보자, 지원자 | postpone 연기하다

2. 이 회의는 브라운 씨에게 회사 경영에 관해 그가 제안한 변화에 대한 견해를 표명할 기회를 줄 것이다.

해설　빈칸 이하는 앞에 나온 his opinions on the changes를 수식하는 것으로 중간에 목적격 관계대명사 that이 생략된 「명사+(that)+주어+동사」 형태가 적합하고, 해석상 '그가 제안했던'이라는 의미가 들어가야 하므로 정답은 (A) he가 된다. (B)가 답이 되려면 '제안되다'라는 수동의 의미가 들어가야 한다.

어휘　give ~ a chance ~에게 기회를 주다 | voice (말로) 나타내다, 표하다 | propose 제안하다 | management 경영

3. 다음 달 모금 행사를 위한 초대장이 백 명 이상에게 발송되었지만, 지금까지 거의 응답하지 않았다.

해설　접속사 but 뒤는 앞 문장과 반대되는 의미가 나오는 것이 적합하다. 해석을 해보면 '초대장을 보냈지만, 사람들이 거의 안 했다'라는 부정의 의미가 적합하므로 (A), (B)가 적합한데 앞에 사람들(people)이라는 가산 명사를 받으므로 (B) few가 정답이다.

어휘　invitation 초대장 | fundraising event 모금 행사 | reply 응답하다 | so far 지금까지

4. 만약 혼자서 새 컴퓨터를 설치하는 데 어려움을 겪는다면, 고객 지원 센터로 전화하세요.

해설　'혼자서, 스스로'는 on one's own으로 표현한다. 따라서 (C) your own이 정답이 된다.

어휘 have difficulty -ing ~하는 데 어려움을 겪다 | set up 설치하다 | on one's own 혼자서, 스스로

5. 넥스트컴이 최근 소개한 디엑스-7000은 화상 회의 제품으로는 최초로 가격에 민감한 중소기업들에 초점을 맞춘 제품이다.

해설 빈칸 앞뒤의 of와 kind를 힌트로 of its kind '같은 부류의 것 중'이라는 표현을 유추할 수 있어야 한다. 의미상으로도 빈칸에 들어갈 대명사는 앞에서 단수로 쓰인 명사 video conferencing product를 받기 때문에 정답은 (D) its가 된다.

어휘 video conference 화상 회의 | address 초점을 맞추다, (문제를) 다루다, 처리하다, 착수하다 | cost-conscious 가격에 민감한 | small business 중소기업 | of its kind 같은 부류의 것 중

6. 웰치 씨는 경비 보고서를 제출했지만, 게리슨 씨는 아직 그의 것을 제출하지 않았다.

해설 역접을 나타내는 등위접속사 but이 있으므로 앞 문장과 상반되는 내용이 나올 것이다. 빈칸은 submit이라는 타동사의 목적어 자리로, his(= Mr. Garrison's) expense report가 들어가야 한다. 이것을 소유대명사로 바꾸면 his가 된다. 따라서 (A) his가 정답이다.

어휘 expense 비용, 지출

7. 최 씨의 멀티태스킹 능력 덕택에, 그녀는 훌륭한 이벤트 진행 책임자로 자기 자신을 보여왔다.

해설 빈칸은 show라는 타동사의 목적어 자리로 주로 목적격 혹은 재귀대명사가 정답으로 출제된다. 여기서는 '최 씨가 자기 자신이 뛰어난 이벤트 기획자라는 것을 보여줬다'라는 의미가 되어야 하므로 Ms. Choi를 받는 재귀대명사의 재귀 용법인 (C) herself가 정답이다.

어휘 talent 재능, 소질 | multitasking 멀티태스킹, 동시에 몇 가지 일을 하는 것 | outstanding 뛰어난 | coordinator 조정자, 책임자, 진행자

8. 토마스 씨에 따르면, 지역 관리자들이 직접 후보자들을 면접볼 것 같다고 한다.

해설 완전한 문장 뒤에 재귀대명사의 강조 용법이 오는 구조로 district managers를 받는 (D) themselves가 정답이 된다.

어휘 district manager 지역 관리자 | be likely to ~할 것 같다 | conduct 수행하다 | candidate 후보자

9. 시드니의 새 지사에서 일하는 데 관심 있는 사람들은 인사부장에게 통보해야 한다.

해설 who의 수식을 받는 지시대명사 Anyone과 Those가 답으로 들어갈 수가 있는데, who 뒤에 복수 동사(are)가 나왔으므로 복수 취급하는 (D) Those가 정답이 된다.

어휘 branch 지점, 지사 | notify 통보하다, 알리다 | personnel 인사의; 인사과

10. 어제 공연을 본 많은 손님이 이미 온라인으로 후기를 올렸다.

해설 한 문장에 동사가 2개(watched, have posted)이고, 동사 watched 앞에 빈칸이 있으므로 빈칸은 앞의 명사(guests)를 선행사로 하는 주격 관계대명사 자리이며, 선행사가 사람이므로 (D) who가 정답이다.

어휘 performance 공연 | post 게시하다, 올리다 | review 평가, 리뷰, 비평

11. 우리 사무실에서 접수된 각각의 불만 사항은 조사되어 고객 서비스부에 의해 철저하게 처리된다.

해설 빈칸 자리는 부정대명사 자리로 그 자리에 들어갈 수 없는 (D)는 탈락되며, 불가산 명사를 취하는 (B)도 탈락된다. (A)의 경우는 주어가 뒤에 complaints가 되어 복수 형태의 동사가 나와야 하므로 탈락된다. 정답은 「each of the 복수 명사 + 단수 동사」 형태인 (C) Each이다.

어휘 investigate 조사하다 | take care of ~을 처리하다 | thoroughly 철저하게

12. 세미나에서, 참가자들은 이전 경력을 기반으로 자신들을 그룹으로 조직하라고 요청 받았다.

해설 빈칸은 동사 organize의 목적어 자리로 여기서는 '참가자들은 이전 경력을 기반으로 자신들을 그룹으로 조직하라고 요청 받았다'라는 의미가 되어야 하므로 participants를 받는 재귀대명사인 (D) themselves가 정답이다.

어휘 participant 참가자 | organize 조직하다 | based on ~에 근거하여 | previous 이전의 | work experience 경력

13. 비록 부쉬라 씨는 신입사원이지만, 그녀의 결정은 수년 간 이 사업을 해온 매니저의 것과 유사하다.

해설 '부쉬라 씨의 결정(decisions)이 수년 간 이 사업을 해온 매니저의 결정(decisions)과 유사하다'는 의미이므로 decisions라는 복수 명사를 대신 받는 대명사가 필요하다. 따라서 정답은 (B) those이다.

어휘 decision 결정 | resemble 닮다, 유사하다

14. 이들 두 명이 가장 자질이 뛰어나서, 한 지원자를 다른 지원자 대신 선택하기가 매우 어렵다.

해설 두 명의 지원자를 비교하는 것이므로 'one, the other'로 표현할 수 있다. 따라서 정답은 (B) the other가 된다.

어휘 highly qualified 높은 자격을 갖춘 | applicant 지원자 | over ~이상, ~을 넘어

15. 섬유 유리 노동자들은 사소한 자동차 수리부터 배 전체를 짓는 것까지 모든 것에 경험이 있다.

해설 빈칸은 전치사의 목적어로써 명사나 대명사가 필요하며 빈칸 뒤에 from A to B 'A에서부터 B에 이르기까지' 구문이 연결되어 있는 점을 고려해야 하므로 문맥상 정답은 (D) everything이 된다.

어휘 fiberglass 섬유 유리 | repair 수리 | construct 건설하다, 구성하다 | entire 전체의 | distinction 차이 | approach 다가가다; 다가감

16. 수석 디자이너는 브랜드를 위해 두 가지 로고를 만들어 냈지만, 어느 것도 승인되지 않았다.

해설 역접을 나타내는 등위접속사 but이 나왔으므로 '로고 둘 다 승인되지 않았다'라는 의미가 들어가야 한다. 빈칸에는 두 개를 언급하면서 부정어를 나타내는 (C) neither가 답으로 알맞다.

어휘 senior designer 수석 디자이너 l approve 승인하다 l either (둘 중의) 어느 것 하나 l nobody 어느 누구도 ~아닌 l neither (둘 중의) 어느 쪽도 ~아닌

17. 리모델링 프로젝트를 위한 많은 입찰 가격들이 있었기 때문에, 플린 씨와 준코 씨는 자신들의 것이 선택되었을 때 무척 기뻐했다.

해설 빈칸은 부사절의 주어 자리이므로 빈칸에 들어갈 수 없는 목적격 대명사 (A)와 소유격 대명사 (B)를 먼저 제외시킨다. 문맥상 플린 씨와 준코 씨의 입찰 가격이 선정되었다는 의미이므로 「소유격 + 명사」인 소유대명사 (C) theirs가 정답이다.

어휘 bid 입찰 가격 l delighted 아주 기뻐하는 l select 선택하다

18. 많은 소비자들이 가능한 한 빨리 집을 구입하기를 원하지만, 일부는 단지 임대하는 자유를 선호한다.

해설 '일부'의 의미가 되어야 하므로, 일부를 가리키는 명사 (A) some이 정답이다. (B), (D)는 단수로 취급하는데 뒤에 prefer라는 복수 동사가 나왔으며, (C) other는 혼자 쓰이지 않기 때문에 답이 될 수 없다.

어휘 consumer 소비자 l purchase 구입하다 l as quickly as possible 가급적 빨리 l prefer 선호하다 l freedom 자유 l renting 임대차 행위

19. 인사책임자인 케이티 렁은 직원 교육을 그녀가 직접 하기로 결정했다.

해설 주절은 빈칸이 없어도 완벽한 문장이므로 부사 등의 수식어가 들어갈 자리인데, 대명사 중 수식어 자리에 들어갈 수 있는 것은 강조 용법으로 쓰이는 재귀대명사이므로 (B) herself가 정답이다.

어휘 director 책임자, 감독관 l Human Resources 인사부 l choose to ~하기로 결정하다 l conduct 수행하다

20. 킨더 명절 봉사활동 프로그램의 지원을 위해 네 개의 회사에 연락이 갔고, 모두가 많은 액수를 기부했다.

해설 빈칸은 앞의 명사 Four firms를 가리키는 대명사 자리이며, 이 네 회사 모두가 많은 액수를 기부했다는 의미이므로 all firms=all인 (B) all이 정답이다.

어휘 firm 회사 l contact 연락하다 l outreach 봉사활동 l donate 기부하다 l sum 액수, 합

UNIT 08. 전치사

1. + check   1. (D)   2. (B)   3. (B)   본서 p.74

1. 아말리 제조는 새로운 전기 제품으로 이달에 산업 혁신상을 받았다.

해설 빈칸 뒤 명사 앞에는 전치사가 필요한데, (A), (B)는 접속사이므로 탈락이 되고, (C)는 부사이므로 탈락한다. 따라서 정답은 (D) for가 된다.

어휘 manufacturing 제조 l electrical appliance 전기 제품

2. 바쁜 연설 일정에도 불구하고, 영업 부사장은 신입 교육생들과 시간을 내어 이야기를 나누었다.

해설 빈칸 뒤에 명사구가 나오므로 전치사가 필요하다. (C)와 (D)는 접속사로 탈락되고, (A)는 부사이므로 탈락된다. (B) Despite가 정답이다.

어휘 agenda 안건 l trainee 교육생

3. 펠리컨 피자는 지역 배달 서비스 외에도, 주 전역의 슈퍼마켓의 냉동 식품 코너에서 제품을 제공하기 시작하기로 결정했다.

해설 빈칸 뒤의 명사구를 목적어로 취할 전치사 자리이며, '지역 배달 서비스 외에, 슈퍼마켓의 냉동 식품 코너에도 제품을 제공할 것'이라는 해석이 자연스러우므로 (B) in addition to가 정답이다.

어휘 delivery 배달 l frozen food 냉동식품 l regardless of ~에도 불구하고 l in addition to ~에 더해 l base upon ~에 기초를 두다 l on account of ~때문에

2. + check   1. (D)   2. (B)   3. (D)   본서 p.76

1. 저희 소매점에서 구입한 불량품은 구입 증명서와 함께 일주일 이내에 반송되어야 합니다.

해설 뒤에 명사가 나오므로 전치사가 필요하며, '일주일 이내에 반품되어야 한다'는 의미이므로 뒤에 기간을 받는 전치사 (D) within이 정답이다.

어휘 defective 결함이 있는 l retail location 소매점 l return 반품하다 l proof of purchase 구매 증명서 l until ~까지 l within ~이내에

2. 허먼 라이트 재단의 이사장은 오늘 저녁 자선 연회가 있기 전에 연설을 할 것이다.

해설 명사 앞에 들어가는 전치사 자리로 해석을 해보면 '~하기 전에'라는 의미가 적합하므로 (B) before가 정답이다.

어휘 chairman 의장, 회장 l foundation 재단 l make a speech 연설을 하다 l charity banquet 자선 연회

3. 캐럿타운의 역사적 해안 지구에서는 10여 년 동안 어떠한 새로운 개발도 없었다.

해설 뒤에 more than이 나오는 중복적인 의미로 (A) over를 고르지 않도록 조심한다. a decade와 함께 쓰이는 시간 전치사 (D) in이 정답이다.

어휘 development 발전 l historic 역사적인 l seafront 해안 지구 l decade 10년

3. + check   1. (C)   2. (C)   3. (A)   본서 p.77

1. 케리다운 회계법인의 경영진은 7월 21일 금요일, 칼레돈 가 402번지에서 만날 것이다.

해설 빈칸 뒤에 특정 장소 · 지점이 나오므로 특정 장소를 나타내는 전치사 (C) at이 정답이다.

어휘 management 경영진 l like ~처럼, ~같이

2. 자동차 업계의 근로자들은 고용 후 90일이 지나면 유급 휴가를 받을 자격이 생긴다.

해설 해석을 해보면 '업계 내에서'라는 의미가 적합하므로 (C) in이 정답이다.

어휘 be entitled to ~할 자격이 있다 l paid vacation 유급 휴가 l employment 고용

3. 저희는 제품을 오직 오프라인 매장에서만 판매하므로, 저희 회사의 최근 태블릿 피씨 모델을 구매하고자 하시면 미국 곳곳에 있는 저희 매장 중 어느 곳이라도 방문해 주십시오.

해설 '제품을 구매하기 위해 미국에 있는 아무 매장이나 이용하라'는 해석이 자연스러우므로 '곳곳에'라는 의미의 (A) across가 정답이다.

어휘 purchase ~을 구입하다 | across ~곳곳에

---

4. +check 1. (C) 2. (A) 3. (A) 본서 p.77

1. 킹 가와 사바나 가 사이의 도로 공사 때문에, 근처 구역의 교통이 지연될 것이다.

해설 빈칸은 뒤에 명사를 동반하는 전치사 자리로, (A)는 접속부사, (B), (D)는 접속사로 탈락이 되어 (C) Due to가 정답이다.

어휘 traffic 교통 | nearby 근처의 | be subject to ~하기 쉽다. ~의 대상이 되다 | otherwise 그렇지 않으면 | whereas 반면에

2. 개막식에서의 저조한 참석률에도 불구하고, 우리의 새 입지의 올해 판매량은 예상을 웃돌았다.

해설 뒤에 명사를 동반하는 전치사 문제로, (B), (C)는 접속사로 탈락이 되며, '저조한 참석에도 불구하고, 판매량이 예상을 웃돌았다'는 의미이므로 (A) Despite가 정답이다.

어휘 poor 저조한 | turnout 참석률, 참석자 수 | grand opening 개막식 | sales 판매량, 매출액 | exceed 초과하다 | expectation 예상

3. 연수 세미나에 관련된 추가 정보는 참가에 관심을 표한 사람들에게 이메일로 발송될 것이다.

해설 명사 앞에 오는 전치사 문제로 해석을 해보면 '~에 관하여'라는 의미가 적합하므로 (A) regarding이 정답이다.

어휘 additional 추가의 | training seminar 연수 세미나 | participate 참여하다 | regarding ~에 관하여 | across 가로질러 | notwithstanding ~에도 불구하고

---

5. +check 1. (C) 2. (D) 3. (B) 본서 p.78

1. 소프트웨어 고장 때문에, 3월 3일이 있는 주에 생산된 디자인 견본은 형식이 틀릴 수도 있다.

해설 빈칸 뒤에 '3월 3일이 포함된 주(the week of March 3)'라는 의미의 기간 명사구가 연결되어 있어 특정 기간과 어울리는 전치사가 필요하므로 (C) during이 정답이다.

어휘 failure 실패, 고장 | format 구성 방식, 형식

2. 바이런 씨는 모든 영업 보고서가 다음 주 초까지 제출되기를 요구한다.

해설 뒤에 명사구가 나오는 전치사 문제로 해석을 해보면 '다음 주 초까지'라는 의미가 들어가야 하므로 '~까지'의 전치사 by와 until이 들어갈 수 있는데, 앞에 submit이라는 동사는 '완료'의 의미인 by와 주로 사용되므로 (D) by가 정답이다. until은 '지속/계속'의 의미로 사용된다.

어휘 sales report 영업 보고서 | submit 제출하다

3. 기념식을 준비할 때, 모든 손님을 수용하고 대중교통으로 쉽게 올 수 있는 적절한 장소를 찾으십시오.

해설 빈칸 뒤에 분사구문이 쓰였으므로 부사절 접속사이면서 해석상 '~할 때'라는 의미가 들어가야 하므로 (B) When이 정답이다. (C) During은 기간을 지칭하는 명사와만 함께 쓰인다.

어휘 organize ~을 조직하다[준비하다] | proper 적절한 | venue 장소 | accommodate ~을 수용하다 | accessible 접근 가능한 | since ~때문에

---

6. +check 1. (A) 2. (C) 3. (D) 본서 p.79

1. 소비자들은 저렴한 가격의 제품에 대한 선택의 폭이 넓어지는 혜택을 볼 수 있다.

해설 '~으로부터 혜택을 얻다'라는 뜻의 benefit from이 적합하므로 (A) from이 정답이다.

어휘 benefit from ~으로부터 혜택을 얻다 | choice 선택

2. 많은 설문조사 응답자들은 서번 레이블스가 만든 제품들과 친숙했는데, 그곳의 광고들은 첨단 촬영술을 사용한다.

해설 '~에 익숙하다'는 뜻의 be familiar with가 적합하므로 (C) with가 정답이다.

어휘 survey 설문조사 | respondent 응답자 | familiar 친근한, 익숙한 | advertisement 광고 | cutting-edge 최첨단의 | photography 촬영술, 촬영기법

3. 과태료가 부과되지 않도록 하기 위해, 지역 상점들은 만기일 한 달 전까지 영업 허가를 갱신할 것을 권장한다.

해설 해석을 해보면 '만기일 이전에'라는 의미가 적합하므로 (D) in advance of가 정답이다.

어휘 charge 부과하다 | fine 벌금 | encourage 권장하다 | renew 갱신하다 | business license 영업 허가 | no later than 늦어도 ~까지 | expiration date 만료일, 만기일 | depending upon ~에 의존하여 | as required by ~가 요구하는 대로 | indicated as ~으로 표시되어 | in advance of ~이전에, ~보다 앞서

Practice

본서 p.80

1. (B)	**2.** (A)	**3.** (D)	**4.** (C)	**5.** (B)
6. (A)	**7.** (C)	**8.** (A)	**9.** (A)	**10.** (D)
11. (B)	**12.** (C)	**13.** (A)	**14.** (B)	**15.** (D)
16. (C)	**17.** (A)	**18.** (C)	**19.** (B)	**20.** (A)

---

1. 조직 개편으로 인해, 신입사원 채용은 추후 공지가 있을 때까지 모두 보류된다.

해설 until further notice는 '추후 공지가 있을 때까지'라는 의미의 관용표현으로 덩어리째 암기해 두는 것이 좋다. 따라서 정답은 (B) until이다.

어휘 due to ~때문에 | reorganization (조직 등의) 개편 | hiring 고용 | on hold 보류된, 연기된 | notice 공지

2. 오늘 밤 동창회 저녁 식사는 마이크 도축업에서 후원한다.

해설 빈칸은 Mike's Butchery를 목적어로 하는 전치사 자리이며 빈칸 앞 동사구가 「be + p.p.」 형태이므로 수동태 문장을 완성하는 (A) by가 정답이다.

어휘 alumni reunion 동창회 | sponsor 후원하다

---

3. 귀하가 배송 서비스에 관해 어떠한 문의라도 있으시다면 케이엔제트사 고객 서비스 센터로 연락 주시기 바랍니다.

해설 you may have가 삽입되어 앞에 inquiries를 수식한다. '배송 서비스에 관한 문의'란 의미가 되어야 하므로 정답은 (D) regarding이 된다.

어휘 **inquiry** 문의 | **shipping service** 배송 서비스 | **regarding** ~에 관하여

4. 해외에서의 경험을 고려할 때, 나크와인더는 두바이 사무실 개설을 위한 좋은 선택일 수 있다.

해설 overseas experience라는 명사 앞에 들어가는 전치사 문제이다. '해외에서의 경험을 고려할 때'의 의미가 적합하므로 정답은 (C) Considering이다.

어휘 **overseas** 해외의 | **opening** 개설 | **consider** 고려하다

5. 현재 업무에 필요한 자격 외에도 자격 취득에 관심이 있는 직원들은 관심 있는 모든 과정에 등록하는 것을 환영합니다.

해설 빈칸 뒤에 명사구(those required for their current jobs)가 오므로 전치사가 들어가야 한다. '현재 업무에 필요한 자격 외에도'라는 의미가 되어야 하므로 정답은 (B) on top of가 된다.

어휘 **gain** 얻다 | **qualification** 자격, 자격증 | **enroll in** ~에 등록하다 | **prior to** ~이전에 | **on top of** ~외에 | **likewise** 똑같이, 비슷하게 | **as opposed to** ~와는 대조적으로, ~이 아니라

6. 연휴기간 동안 월요일에는, 상점이 오전 10시가 아니라 오전 9시에 문을 연다.

해설 빈칸은 the holiday period를 목적어로 하는 전치사 자리이며 '연휴기간 동안'이라는 의미가 되어야 하므로 (A) during이 정답이다. 시간 전치사 during 뒤에는 기간을 나타내는 표현이, since와 at 뒤에는 시점을 나타내는 표현이 온다.

어휘 **holiday period** 연휴 기간 | **open** (상점 등이) 문을 열다 | **instead of** ~대신에

7. 루미 권은 디자인팀 것을 제외하고 모든 사무용품 주문을 담당하고 있다.

해설 뒤에 명사구(those ~ team)가 나와 있으므로 빈칸에는 전치사가 필요하다. '루미 권은 모두 담당하고 있다. 디자인팀 것만 빼놓고'의 의미가 알맞으므로 정답은 (C) except이다. (A) aside '따로, 별도로', (D) additionally '게다가'는 부사로 쓰이는 단어이다.

어휘 **be in charge of** ~을 담당하다[책임지다] | **office supplies** 사무용품 | **aside** 따로, 별도로 | **even if** ~라고 할지라도 | **except** ~을 제외하고 | **additionally** 게다가

8. 고객들은 상품에 결함이 없음을 보장하기 위해 배송되자마자 모든 물품을 검사할 권리가 있다.

해설 「upon[on] + 명사(구)」는 '~하자마자'의 의미로 쓰이며, 문맥상 '배송이 되자마자 점검하다'라는 의미가 적절하므로 정답은 (A) upon이다.

어휘 **right** 권리 | **inspect** 점검하다, 조사하다 | **upon delivery** 배송이 되자마자 | **ensure** 반드시 ~하다, 보장하다 | **defect** 결함 | **merchandise** 상품 | **subsequently** 그 뒤에, 나중에

9. 사장은 최고의 고객 서비스가 다른 배송 업체들보다 하나다 운송에 경쟁적 우위를 준다고 생각한다.

해설 '~보다 경쟁적 우위'라는 표현을 쓸 때 competitive advantage over라고 쓴다. '~보다'라고 해서 than을 쓰지 않도록 조심한다. 정답은 (A) over이다.

어휘 **superior customer service** 최고의 고객 서비스 | **competitive advantage over** ~보다 경쟁적 우위 | **shipping** 운송 | **including** ~을 포함하여

10. 마케팅 부서 직원회의가 금요일 오전 10시로 예정되었다.

해설 be scheduled for는 '~으로 예정되다'라는 의미이므로 정답은 (D) for가 된다.

어휘 **be scheduled for + 명사** ~으로 예정되다

11. 은퇴를 불과 2년 앞두고, 지오반니는 갑자기 직업을 바꾸기로 결심했다.

해설 '은퇴를 불과 2년 앞두고'라는 의미가 자연스러우므로 '~한 상황에서, ~인 채로'의 의미를 갖는 (B) With가 정답이다.

어휘 **retirement** 은퇴 | **career** 직업, 사회생활

12. 크로우 상사는 중국으로 확장을 준비 중이라고 오늘 일찍 발표했다.

해설 '~로 확장하다'는 expand into로 표현하므로 정답은 (C) into가 된다.

어휘 **announce** 발표하다 | **earlier** (예상보다) 일찍 | **expand into** ~로 확장하다

13. 교육 연수에 관한 추가적인 정보는 참석을 신청한 분들에게 이메일로 보내질 것입니다.

해설 '세미나에 관한 추가적인 정보'라는 의미가 되어야 한다. 따라서 '~에 관한'을 의미하는 전치사 (A) pertaining to가 답으로 알맞다.

어휘 **additional information** 추가적인 정보 | **pertaining to** ~에 관한 | **in spite of** ~에도 불구하고

14. 우리 도시에 관한 다큐멘터리가 방영되고 나서 임대 부동산에 대한 문의가 세 배나 증가했다.

해설 have increased라는 현재 완료가 주절의 동사로 나오며 뒤에는 '다큐멘터리의 방영'이라는 시점이 나오므로, '(과거) 시점 이후로'라는 의리의 (B) since가 정답이다.

어휘 **inquiry** 문의 | **rental** 임대 | **property** 부동산 | **threefold** 세 배의 | **airing** 방송 | **documentary** 다큐멘터리, 기록물 | **regarding** ~에 관하여 | **including** ~을 포함하여

15. 증가하는 음식 가격 때문에, 소비자들은 요즘 식료품에 대한 소비를 줄이고 있다.

해설 해석을 해보면 '증가하는 음식 가격 때문에'라는 '이유'의 의미가 들어가야 하므로 정답은 (D) Owing to가 된다.

어휘 **rising price** 증가하는 가격 | **grocery** 식료품 | **in that** ~라는 점에서 | **even if** ~에도 불구하고 | **just as** 꼭 ~처럼 | **owing to** ~때문에

16. 다온 전자의 직원은 수신자 부담 전화로 연락함으로써 연결될 수 있다.

해설 '~함으로써'의 의미가 적합하므로 'by -ing' 형태가 되어야 한다. 따라서 (C) by가 정답이 된다.

어휘 representative 직원 | reach 연결하다, 닿다 | toll-free number 수신자 부담 전화

17. 윌럼 콘퍼런스 센터는 스타버러 도심에 식당과 호텔에서 걸어갈 수 있는 거리 이내에 편리하게 위치하고 있다.

해설 '걸어갈 수 있는 거리 이내에'는 within walking distance로 표현하므로 빈칸에 (A) within이 들어가야 한다.

어휘 conveniently 편리하게 | situate 위치시키다 | downtown 시내 | within walking distance 걸을 수 있는 거리 이내에 | moreover 게다가, 더욱이

18. 다가오는 할인 행사 소식은 요코하마 물류센터의 직원들 사이에서 급속히 퍼질 것으로 보인다.

해설 빈칸 뒤의 명사구를 이끄는 전치사가 필요하며, '할인 행사 소식이 직원들 사이에서 빠르게 퍼질 것이다'라는 의미가 자연스러우므로 '~사이에서, ~중에서'라는 의미의 (C) among이 정답이다.

어휘 upcoming 다가오는 | spread 퍼지다 | rapidly 급속히 | distribution center 물류 센터 | in case ~인 경우에 대비해서 | among ~중에서, ~사이에

19. 런던 교향악단 공연에의 입장은 공연당 방청객 50명으로 한정된다.

해설 빈칸은 50 observers를 목적어로 하는 전치사 자리이며 be limited to '~으로 한정되다'를 완성하는 (B) to가 정답이다.

어휘 access 접근, 출입, 이용 | performance 공연 | philharmonic orchestra 교향악단 | limit 제한하다, 한정하다 | observer 관찰자, 방청인 | per ~당

20. 해치 씨와 그의 동업자들은 사업을 해외로 확장할 계획에 대해 동의했다.

해설 '~에 동의하다'라는 뜻의 agree upon이 들어가야 하므로 정답은 (A) upon이 된다.

어휘 expand 확장하다 | overseas 해외로 | agree upon ~에 동의하다

REVIEW TEST 02

본서 p.82

1. (A)	2. (A)	3. (B)	4. (D)	5. (D)
6. (C)	7. (C)	8. (A)	9. (B)	10. (C)
11. (D)	12. (C)	13. (D)	14. (A)	15. (B)
16. (B)	17. (D)	18. (A)	19. (C)	20. (A)

1. 마케팅 책임자는 광고 캠페인에 대한 애나 킹의 가치 있는 기여에 대해 그녀를 축하했다.

해설 빈칸은 명사 앞에 들어가는 소유격 자리이므로 (A) her가 정답이다.

어휘 valuable 가치 있는, 소중한 | contribution 기여, 헌신

2. 펜코프 사의 시간제 직원들은 항상 직업소개소를 통해 채용된다.

해설 빈칸은 전치사 자리로 해석을 해보면 '직원들이 채용 대행사를 통해 채용된다'라는 의미가 가장 적합하므로 '~을 통해'라는 의미의 (A) through가 정답이다.

어휘 recruit 채용하다 | employment agency 직업소개소

3. 온라인 거래 계좌를 개설하기 위해서, 고객들은 그들의 생년월일과 주민등록번호와 같은 개인 정보를 확인할 필요가 있다.

해설 빈칸은 형용사 personal의 수식을 받는 명사 자리이다. detail은 세부사항을 뜻하는 가산 명사인데 빈칸 앞에 관사 등의 한정사가 보이지 않으므로 복수형인 (B) details가 정답이다.

어휘 set up 개설하다 | trading account 거래 계좌, 매매 계정 | confirm 확인해주다 | such as ~와 같은 | social security number 주민등록번호, 사회보장번호 | personal details 신상 명세

4. 새로운 공장 기계는 우리가 이전보다 훨씬 더 빨리 주문을 받을 수 있게 해줄 것이다.

해설 빈칸은 동사 fill을 수식하는 부사 자리이므로 (D) quickly가 정답이다. 참고로 (C) quick이 사전에는 형용사와 부사가 모두 가능한 것으로 정의되어 있으나 현대 영어에서 quick은 형용사, quickly는 부사로 통용되고 있으니 기억해 두자.

어휘 machinery 기계(류) | allow 허용하다 | fill 채우다 | order 주문(품); 주문하다

5. 모디바 아울렛은 아주 다양한 고품질의 상품에 대해 할인을 한다.

해설 빈칸 앞에 있는 offers는 타동사로 뒤에 목적어가 있어야 하므로 정답의 후보는 (B)와 (D)가 된다. discount는 가산 명사인데 빈칸 앞에 a/an과 같은 관사가 없으므로 복수형인 (D) discounts가 정답이다.

어휘 a wide range of 아주 다양한 | quality 고급의 | merchandise 상품 | discount 할인 | discountable 할인할 수 있는

6. 지역 기업의 예상치 못한 성금으로, 주민센터가 예정보다 일찍 지어져서 문을 열었다.

해설 빈칸은 전치사 자리로 schedule과 함께 어울려 쓰인다. 따라서 '예정보다 빨리'라는 뜻의 ahead of schedule을 만드는 (C) ahead of가 정답이다. on schedule '예정대로', behind the schedule '예정보다 늦게'의 표현도 알아두자.

어휘 due to ~ 때문에 | unexpected 예상치 못한 | contribution 기부금, 성금 | regardless of ~에 상관없이 | except for ~을 제외하고 | ahead of ~보다 앞선 | compared to ~와 비교하여

7. 경력 개발 프로그램은 회사의 모든 직원이 접근할 수 있도록 설계되었다.

해설 빈칸은 employee 명사를 수식하는 형용사 자리이다. all과 some은 뒤에 가산 복수 명사가 와야 하므로 오답이며, much는 뒤에 불가산 명사를 동반한다. 따라서 (C) every가 정답이다.

어휘 career development program 경력 개발 프로그램 | design 고안하다, 설계하다 | accessible to ~에 접근할 수 있는

8. 장치의 스위치를 켜기 전에, 위에 글자가 있는 구멍에 배터리를 삽입하세요.

해설 앞에 한정사 the가 있으므로 빈칸은 명사 자리이다. 보기 중에서 명사는 (A)와 (D)인데, 해석을 해보면 '글자가 위에 있는'이라는 내용이 적절하므로 정답은 (A) writing이 된다.

어휘 switch on 스위치를 켜다 | device 장치 | make sure 확실하게 하다, 반드시 하다 | insert 삽입하다 | slot 가느다란 구멍 | writing 글, 글자

9. 옛날 가전제품을 에너지 효율이 높은 것으로 교체함으로써, 공과금을 약 20%까지 절약할 수 있다.

해설 숫자나 수치 앞에는 '대략, 거의'라는 표현의 부사가 적합하므로 정답은 (B) nearly이다.

어휘 replace A with B A를 B로 교체하다 | energy-efficient 에너지 효율이 높은 | utility bill (전기·가스·수도 등의) 공과 | nearly 거의

10. 리키야 타나카는 동료들이 일찍 퇴근할 수 있도록 나머지 보고서를 직접 준비하겠다고 제안했다.

해설 주절은 빈칸이 없어도 완벽한 문장이므로 대명사 중 수식어 자리에 들어갈 수 있는 것은 강조 용법으로 쓰이는 재귀대명사이므로 (C) himself가 정답이다.

어휘 offer 제안하다 | rest 나머지 | so that ~하도록 | coworker 동료 | oneself 직접

11. 프리덤 씨는 결함이 있는 램프 장치가 오작동의 이유라고 추론했다.

해설 빈칸은 관사와 명사구 사이의 형용사 자리이다. 문맥상 '결함이 있는 램이 문제의 근원이라고 추론했다'라는 의미가 자연스러우므로 (D) faulty가 정답이다.

어휘 deduce 추론하다 | RAM 램, 컴퓨터 기억 장치 | stick 막대기 모양의 것 | reason 이유 | malfunction 오작동 | tolerant 내성이 있는 | agitated 흔들리고 있는 | trivial 사소한 | faulty 결함이 있는

12. 다음 주 영업 워크숍에 참석하기를 희망하는 사람은 누구든지 이번 금요일까지 등록해야 한다.

해설 빈칸은 뒤에 wishing이라는 현재분사의 수식을 받고, 의미상 '원하는 어느 누구나'가 적합하므로 정답은 해당 의미를 가진 (C) Anyone이 된다. anyone who라는 의미를 가진 Whoever가 답이 되려면 whoever is wishing ~이라고 나와야 한다. anyone은 보통 뒤에 who/-ing/p.p./with 등이 따른다.

어휘 attend 참석하다 | register 등록하다

13. 사포리 디 포기아는 완전히 다른 메뉴를 특징으로 하는 두 번째 점포를 열 계획이다.

해설 빈칸 앞에 관사 a가 있고 뒤에는 「형용사(different) + 명사(menu)」가 있으므로, 그 사이에 들어갈 수 있는 품사로는 부사가 적합하다. 따라서 (D) completely가 정답이다.

어휘 feature ~을 특징으로 하다 | complete 가능한 최대의, 완전한; ~을 완전하게 만들다

14. 이사회는 올해 수익의 일부를 직원들에게 특별 상여금으로 나누어 주기로 결정했다.

해설 빈칸은 명사 자리로 해석상 '올해 수익의 일부를 나누어 주다'가 자연스러우므로 (D) percentage가 정답이다. a percentage of는 '~의 1%'가 아니라 '~의 일부'라는 뜻이다.

어휘 the board of directors 이사회 | distribute 분배하다, 나눠주다 | profit 수익 | gratitude 고마움 | limit 한계 | selection 선택 | percentage 수익의 일부, 퍼센트

15. 그 합작 투자는 특히 에쏘 전자와 로넬루 그룹, 두 회사가 해외 시장으로 확장할 수 있도록 하기 위해 만들어졌다.

해설 「be + p.p.」는 수동태인 완전한 문장으로 뒤에는 보통 전치사나 부사가 온다. 따라서 부사 (B) specifically가 정답이다.

어휘 joint venture 합작 투자 | expand into ~로 확장하다 | specifically 특별히, 분명하게 | specific 구체적인, 분명한 | specify 명시하다

16. 현지 고등학생 다니엘 케네디는 올겨울 세계 스키 챔피언십에서 국가를 대표할 것이다.

해설 빈칸은 조동사 뒤의 동사 자리이므로 '세계 스키 챔피언십에서 국가를 대표할 것'이라는 의미가 되어야 자연스러우므로 (B) represent가 정답이다.

어휘 local 현지의, 지역의 | high schooler 고등학생 | nation 국가 | acquire 획득하다 | represent 대표하다 | participate 참여하다 | allow 허락하다

17. 저희는 은퇴자에게 회사의 전 제품과 서비스에 대해 할인을 제공합니다.

해설 빈칸은 동사 offer의 목적어인 명사 자리이다. 빈칸 앞에 관사가 없으므로 복수 명사 (D) retirees가 정답이다.

어휘 offer 제공하다 | discount 할인 | retire 은퇴하다 | retiree 은퇴자

18. 온라인 주문 시스템을 시행함으로써, 크루즈 가구는 영업일 이틀 이내에 창고에서 고객들에게 물품을 배송할 수 있을 것이다.

해설 ~ its warehouse to customers는 'from ~ to'의 구조이므로 (A) from이 정답이다.

어휘 implement 실행하다, 시행하다 | warehouse 창고 | business day 영업일

19. 어니스 베이커리의 도넛은 보통 음료와 함께 제공되지만, 원하시면, 언제든지 따로 구매하실 수 있습니다.

해설 수동태(be p.p.)의 완전한 문장 뒤에는 동사를 수식하는 부사가 온다. 따라서 정답은 (C) separately이다.

어휘 normally 보통은 | prefer 원하다, 선호하다 | separate 분리된; 분리되다 | separately 따로따로, 각기 | separation 분리, 헤어짐

20. 그 잡지의 최신 호 인기는 아마도 김 씨의 예술적 재능 때문일 듯하다.

해설 빈칸은 형용사 due 앞의 부사 자리이다. likely는 형용사일 때는 '~인 것 같은', 부사일 때는 '아마도'라는 의미이다. 따라서 (A) likely가 정답이다.

어휘 popularity 인기 | latest 최신의 | issue 판, 호 | be due to ~때문이다 | artistic 예술적인 | talent 재능 | likely ~할 것 같은

UNIT 09. 명사절 접속사

1. **+ check** 1. (A) 2. (A) 3. (B) 본서 p.84

1. 아르카 사는 전문경영인이 사임하는 데 합의하기 전까지는 비스타 사와 합병하지 않을 것이라고 발표했다.

해설 빈칸은 announce라는 타동사의 목적어 자리로 뒤에 주어, 동사를 이끄는 완전한 문장을 동반하는 명사절 접속사가 필요하다. (B), (C)는 부사절 접속사로 탈락이 된다. 불완전한 문장에 쓰이는 (D) 역시 탈락이 되어 정답은 (A) that이 된다.

어휘 announce 발표하다 | merge with ~와 합병하다 | resignation 사임, 사직

2. 스티브 오티즈에게 그가 슈나이더 계정 작업에 착수하게 될 거라고 알려주세요.

해설 빈칸은 문장의 목적어 자리에 온 that 명사절 내 주어 자리이므로 주격 대명사 (A) he가 정답이다.

어휘 inform 알리다 | account 고객, 계좌

3. 그 기술자를 만나는 사람은 누구든지 어떤 문제가 발생했는지 설명해야 한다.

해설 동사가 meets, must explain 두 개가 나와서 접속사가 필요하므로, (B) Whoever가 정답이다.

어휘 technician 기술자 | occur 발생하다 | in order to ~하기 위해서 | despite ~에도 불구하고

2. **+ check** 1. (D) 2. (A) 3. (C) 본서 p.85

1. 다수의 섬유공장이 구인 광고를 하고 있다는 사실은 경제활동이 다시 활발해졌음을 보여주는 지표일 수 있다.

해설 동사가 두 개(are, may be) 나오므로 접속사가 필요하다. Along with, Pertaining to는 전치사구로 탈락이 된다. 해석상 '~라는 사실'이라는 의미의 명사절 접속사가 필요하므로 (D) The fact that이 정답이다.

어휘 a number of 다수의, 많은 | textile 섬유, 직물 | advertise 광고하다 | job opening 빈자리, 공석 | indication 지표, 조짐 | renewed 재개된 | economic 경제적인 | as long as ~하는 한 | along with ~와 함께, ~에 덧붙여 | pertaining to ~와 관련된 | the fact that ~라는 사실

2. 와이엇 씨가 회의에서 제안한 것은 분명히 이사진들에게 깊은 인상을 주었다.

해설 문장의 동사는 impressed이며 그 앞 전체가 주어 자리이다. 빈칸은 그 주어안에 주어와 동사가 있는 명사절 접속사 자리이다. 뒤에 타동사 proposed의 목적어가 없는 불완전한 문장을 받는 명사절 접속사가 필요하므로 (A) What이 정답이다.

어휘 propose 제안하다 | definitely 분명히 | impress 인상을 주다 |

board of directors 이사회 | unless ~하지 않는 한 | so that ~하기 위하여

3. 최근에 웹사이트의 형식이 변경되었음을 사용자에게 알려야 한다.

해설 빈칸이 be동사 뒤에 위치하여 that 명사절을 받아 be advised that '~을 명심하다'라는 의미를 만드는 (C) advised가 정답이다.

어휘 format 구성 방식, 포맷 | advise 알리다 | awareness 인식, 자각, 알고 있음

3. **+ check** 1. (B) 2. (A) 3. (B) 본서 p.86

1. 마케팅팀은 새로운 버전의 제품을 지금 출시하는 것이 수익성이 있을지 여부를 결정할 것이다.

해설 동사 determine의 목적어로서 절이 연결되어 있으므로 명사절 접속사가 필요하며, 문장 끝이 'A or B'의 구조이므로 '~인지 아닌지'를 의미하는 (B) whether가 정답이다.

어휘 determine 결정하다 | launch 출시하다 | profitable 수익성이 있는

2. 이사회는 첸 씨의 최근의 성과에도 불구하고 그녀를 영업부장으로 승진시킬지의 여부를 여전히 논의 중이다.

해설 타동사 debate의 목적어로 or not이 주로 함께 사용되는 명사절 접속사 (A) whether가 정답이다.

어휘 promote 승진시키다 | despite ~에도 불구하고 | achievement 성과

3. 우리는 내년에 우리의 사업을 확장할 것인지에 대해서 논의할 것이다.

해설 as to라는 전치사 뒤의 목적어 자리로 완전한 문장을 이끄는 (B) whether가 정답이다. 나머지 보기는 다 부사절 접속사이다.

어휘 as to ~에 대해서 | expand 확장하다

4. **+ check** 1. (C) 2. (D) 3. (B) 본서 p.87

1. 가장 늦게 떠나는 사람은 모든 문을 잠가야 한다.

해설 문장의 본동사는 should lock으로 빈칸은 불완전한 문장(is last to leave)을 이끌면서 주어 역할을 동시에 해야 하므로 anyone who의 의미를 갖는 복합관계대명사 (C) Whoever가 정답이다.

어휘 last 마지막으로 | leave 떠나다 | lock 잠그다

2. 폴스터 사가 이 지역에서 확장하기 위해서는 그 계약이 매우 중요하기 때문에, 그들은 거래를 위해 우리가 정한 조건들을 기꺼이 수락하고자 한다.

해설 accept의 목적어 역할을 할 명사절을 이끌 접속사가 필요하다. 명사절 내에 목적어가 없는 불완전한 구조이며 '우리가 요구하는 것은 무엇이든지 수락한다'라는 해석이 자연스러우므로 (D) whatever가 정답이다.

어휘 contract 계약 | crucial 아주 중요한 | expand 확장하다 | be willing to 기꺼이 ~하다 | condition 조건 | deal 거래

3. 고객님이 어느 베니스 피자리아 지점을 방문하시더라도, 최고의 피자 요리를 제공받게 될 것을 장담합니다.

해설 빈칸에는 명사 location을 수식하는 말이 필요하다. 문맥상 '어느 지점을 방문하더라도'라는 뜻이 되어야 한다. whichever는 '어느 ~이든지 간에'라는 의미의 복합관계형용사로 '양보'의 의미를 가지며, 빈칸 뒤의 명사 location을 문맥상 적절히 수식하므로 (B) whichever가 정답이다.

Practice

본서 p.88

1. (B)	2. (C)	3. (A)	4. (D)	5. (A)
6. (B)	7. (B)	8. (A)	9. (D)	10. (B)
11. (C)	12. (B)	13. (A)	14. (B)	15. (A)
16. (C)	17. (D)	18. (D)	19. (D)	20. (C)

1. 플랑크 씨는 정부 규정을 준수하고 있는지의 여부를 알아보기 위해 우리 건축가들이 만든 건물 디자인을 검토한다.

해설 빈칸은 to부정사구에서 동사 determine의 목적어인 명사 자리인데, 빈칸 뒤에 절이 연결되어 있으므로 빈칸은 명사절을 이끄는 접속사가 필요하다. 따라서 (B) whether가 정답이다.

어휘 review 검토하다 | architect 건축가 | determine 알아내다, 결정하다 | comply with ~을 준수하다 | regulation 규정

2. 개인적인 사유로 수익 증명서가 필요한 사람은 누구든지 회계부의 로씨에게 요청해야 한다.

해설 문장에서 needs 그리고 should ask라는 동사가 두 개 나오므로, 접속사가 필요한데, 보기에서 접속사는 Whoever밖에 없으므로 정답은 (C) Whoever이다.

어휘 income verification form 수익 증명서 | for personal reasons 개인적인 사유로 | accounting department 회계부

3. 최근 설문 조사는 대부분의 소비자가 다른 헤어 세정 제품들보다 에브리데이 베스 샴푸를 선호한다는 것을 보여준다.

해설 most consumers ~ products는 문장의 동사 indicates의 목적어에 해당하는 절이다. 따라서 목적어 역할을 하는 명사절을 이끄는 접속사 (A) that이 정답이다.

어휘 survey 설문 조사 | indicate 나타내다, 보여주다 | prefer A over B B보다 A를 선호하다

4. 이 앨범에 대해 특히 인상적인 것은 가수가 그녀 자신의 여러 개인적인 경험을 노래에 넣었다는 것이다.

해설 문장에서 동사가 두 개이며 두 번째 is가 문장의 본동사로 그 앞에는 주어 역할을 하는 명사절 접속사가 와야 한다. 따라서 빈칸에서 The thing which[that] 또는 What이 와야 하므로 (D) What이 정답이된다.

어휘 impressive 인상적인 | incorporate 포함하다 | personal experience 개인적인 경험

5. 비서는 그가 내일 발송할 초대장을 출력했다.

해설 빈칸 이하는 some invitations를 수식한다. 선행사(some invitations)가 will send의 목적어이며 사물이므로 관계대명사는 which나 that이 올 수 있다. 그러므로 정답은 (A) which가 된다.

어휘 secretary 비서 | invitation 초대장 | send out ~을 보내다

6. 알렉스 그란데가 이번 분기 매출 목표를 달성할지는 미지수다.

해설 문장의 주어가 가주어 It이고 진주어는 명사절 Alex Grande will meet ~ quarter이다. 이 명사절을 이끌 접속사를 찾는 문제로 정답은 '~인지 아닌지'를 의미하는 (B) whether가 된다.

어휘 meet 맞추다, 충족시키다 | sales target 판매 목표액 | quarter 사분기 | concerning ~에 관하여 | whether ~인지 아닌지 | along ~을 따라 | it remains to be seen whether ~인지 아닌지 두고 봐야 한다

7. 직원들이 안전 예방 조치들을 아는 것이 중요하기 때문에 모든 팀의 관리자들은 자신들의 직원들이 훈련에 참가하도록 장려해야 한다.

해설 주어, 동사 앞 빈칸에는 접속사가 들어가야 하며 뒤가 완전한 문장이며 가주어 it을 앞에 세우고 진주어 that이 들어가는 자리가 되므로 정답은 (B) that이 된다. it is important that '~하는 것이 중요하다'로 익혀두면 답을 빨리 찾을 수 있다.

어휘 encourage 독려하다, 장려하다 | safety precaution 안전 예방 조치

8. 고위 경영진은 리베라 씨의 자격을 검토해 왔고 그를 이사회 임원으로 임명할지를 결정할 것이다.

해설 will decide의 목적어에 해당하는 명사절을 이끌 접속사가 필요하다. 의미상 '~해야 할지 말아야 할지'에 해당하는 접속사가 와야 하므로 (A) whether가 정답이 된다. 「whether + to부정사」는 '~해야 할지 말아야 할지'를 의미한다.

어휘 senior management 고위 경영진 | review 검토하다 | qualification 자격 | appoint 임명하다 | board member 이사회 임원

9. 이사회는 프로젝트 제안서에 비현실적인 예상치가 포함되어 있다고 생각하기 때문에 그것은 수정되어야 한다.

해설 동사 believes 뒤에 명사절 접속사 that이 생략되어, contains 동사의 주어가 되며 앞에 project proposal을 받는 대명사가 빈칸에 적합하므로 (D) it이 정답이다.

어휘 proposal 제안(서) | revise 수정하다, 개정하다 | board 이사회 | contain 포함하다 | unrealistic 비현실적인 | expectation 예상, 기대

10. 최근 통계자료는 교통 신호들이 바뀐 이후에 자동차 사고들의 숫자가 줄고 있다는 것을 보여준다.

해설 빈칸에 목적어를 이끄는 명사절(the number ~ decreasing)을 이끄는 접속사가 들어가야 하므로 (B) that이 정답이다.

어휘 statistics 통계, 통계자료 | traffic signal 교통 신호

11. 엘엠엠은 새로운 지역 관리자로 선택된 어느 후보자를 위한 교육 프로그램을 마련했다.

해설 has arranged와 is chosen 두 개의 동사가 나오므로, 부사절을 이끄는 접속사 (C)와 (D)가 답으로 가능하다. (D) however는 뒤에 형용사나 부사가 와야 하는데 명사 candidate가 나왔으며, 해석상 '어느 후보자든지'라는 의미가 적합하므로 (C) whichever가 정답이다.

어휘 **arrange** 마련하다, 준비하다 | **candidate** 후보자, 지원자 | **choose** 선택하다, 선정하다 | **regional manager** 지역 관리자

12. 브랜드 인지도가 대중 수요를 증가시킬 수 있다는 사실은 마케팅의 중요한 측면이다.

해설 문제에서 can increase와 is라는 동사가 두 개 나오는데, the fact that ~이라고 해서 '~라는 사실'이라는 동격의 명사절이 필요하므로 정답은 (B) that이 된다.

어휘 **brand recognition** 브랜드 인지도 | **public demand** 대중 수요 | **aspect** 측면 | **the fact that** ~라는 사실

13. 에텔로 상사의 경영진이 입찰 서류를 검토하자마자, 그들은 어느 제안을 선택할지에 대해서 결정할 것이다.

해설 determine 이하는 목적어 역할을 하는 명사절이다. 빈칸에는 명사 proposal을 수식하는 형용사 역할의 의문형용사가 필요하다. 간접의문문의 형태로 정답은 (B) which가 된다. 「determine[decide/choose] + which + 명사 + 동사 ~」는 '어느 명사를 ~할지를 결정하다[선택하다]'라는 의미로 잘 쓰인다.

어휘 **management** 경영진 | **bidding** 입찰 | **proposal** 제안

14. 결함이 있는 물건들을 받은 고객들은 제품이 개봉되었는지의 여부와 상관없이 어느 지점으로든 그것들을 반품하실 수 있습니다.

해설 전치사구 regardless of '~에 상관없이' 다음에 목적어 역할을 하는 명사절이 나온다. 문장 마지막에 있는 or not과 호응하여 쓰이는 접속사로 (B) whether가 들어가야 한다.

어휘 **defective** 결함 있는 | **regardless of** ~에 상관없이 | **despite** ~에도 불구하고

15. 본사에 있는 케이건 씨가 수익을 늘릴 방법을 강구하도록 우리에게 요청했는데, 그 수익은 작년 여름부터 20% 감소했다.

해설 콤마(,) 다음에 나온 빈칸에는 선행사 revenue를 주어로 받는 계속적 용법의 관계대명사가 필요하므로 정답은 (A) which가 된다.

어휘 **headquarters** 본사 | **revenue** 수익

16. 연말 보너스가 지난해의 반밖에 되지 않으리라는 것은 전체 직원들에게 실망스러운 소식이다.

해설 문장의 본동사는 두 번째의 is이다. 빈칸에서 last year's까지가 문장의 주어 역할을 하므로 빈칸에는 명사절을 이끄는 접속사가 와야 한다. 빈칸 뒤가 완전한 문장이므로 정답은 (C) That이 된다. (B)와 (D)는 부사절을 이끄는 접속사이다.

어휘 **half** 반 | **entire** 전체의 | **although** 비록 ~이지만

17. 와루벨에 위치한 캐리 제화는 국내에서 두 번째로 오래된 신발회사이다.

해설 선행사 Company를 수식하는 관계대명사 문제로, 앞에 콤마가 있어서 (A)는 탈락이 되며, 사람 선행사가 아니므로 (C)도 탈락된다. 빈칸 뒤는 불완전한 문장이므로 완전한 문장에 쓰이는 (B) 역시 탈락된다. 정답은 (D) which가 된다.

어휘 **be located in** ~에 위치하다

18. 직원 안내서는 새로운 직원들이 회사의 복리후생에 관해 알 필요가 있는 것들을 설명해 준다.

해설 타동사 explains의 목적어 자리에 주어 new employees와 동사 need to know가 나오므로 빈칸에는 명사절 접속사가 필요하며, 타동사 know의 목적어가 없는 불완전한 문장이므로 정답은 명사절 접속사 (D) what이다.

어휘 **handbook** 안내서 | **regarding** ~에 대해서 | **company benefit** 회사 복리후생

19. 발표에서, 마이어 씨는 그 회사가 30년 전에 어떻게 소규모 지역 업체로 시작했는지를 설명할 것이다.

해설 빈칸은 타동사 explain의 목적어 자리로 뒤에 주어와 동사를 이끄는 명사절 접속사 자리가 된다. 전치사인 (A)와 (B)는 탈락이 되며, 부사절 접속사인 (C)도 탈락이 되어 정답은 (D) how가 된다.

어휘 **local** 지역의 | **while** ~하는 동안에, ~하는 반면에

20. 개발 계획은 각 업무를 누가 담당하는지를 정확하게 명시해야 한다.

해설 빈칸은 동사 state의 목적어인 명사절을 이끄는 접속사 자리이다. 빈칸 뒤에 바로 동사 is가 연결되어 있는 점에서 명사절 접속사와 주어 역할이 동시에 가능한 의문 대명사 (C) who가 정답이다.

어휘 **development** 개발, 발전 | **accurately** 정확하게 | **state** 명시하다, 진술하다 | **in charge of** ~을 담당하여 | **task** 일, 과제

UNIT 10. 형용사절 접속사

1. **+ check** 1. (C) 2. (A) 3. (B) 본서 p.91

1. 회계 관리직에 이력서를 제출한 지원자들 대부분이 매우 좋은 자격을 갖추었다.

해설 빈칸 앞 applicants를 수식하는 관계대명사 자리로, 사람 선행사를 받으며 동사 앞에 나오는 주격 관계대명사 (C) who가 정답이다.

어휘 **applicant** 지원자 | **submit** 제출하다 | **résumé** 이력서 | **accounting** 회계 | **highly** 매우 | **qualified** 자격을 갖춘

2. 많은 과학 잡지에 연구가 실렸던 존경받는 물리학자 콜먼 박사는 우리 엔지니어링 회사와의 컨설팅 계약을 제안받았다.

해설 앞에 사람 선행사 physicist를 받으면서 빈칸 뒤에 명사 research를 취하는 소유격 관계대명사가 필요하므로 (A) whose가 정답이다.

어휘 **respected** 소문난, 존경받는 | **physicist** 물리학자 | **appear** 나오다, 출연하다 | **scientific journal** 과학기술 잡지 | **consulting** 자문의; 자문 | **contract** 계약(서) | **engineering** 공학 기술 | **firm** 회사, 기업 | **whereas** ~에 반해서

3. 우리의 주요 목표는 장애인들이 그들의 모든 가치를 사회에 기여할 수 있는 권리와 기회를 모두 갖는 사회를 만드는 것이다.

해설 선행사인 world를 수식하면서 전치사 in 뒤에 목적격 관계대명사가 나와야 하므로 (B) which가 정답이다.

어휘 **handicapped people** 장애인들 | **contribute** 공헌하다, 기여하다

2. + check　　1. (B)　2. (B)　3. (D)　본서 p.92

1. 약 100년 전에 설립된 피츠본은 수제 초콜릿을 전문으로 취급하는 가족 경영 사업체다.

해설 빈칸 앞뒤에 절이 쓰였고, 뒤의 절에 동사가 바로 쓰인 불완전한 구조이므로 주격 관계대명사인 (B) that이 정답이다.

어휘 establish 설립하다 | family-run 가족 경영의 | specialize in ~을 전문으로 하다 | homemade 수제의

2. 최상의 고객 서비스를 제공하는 것이 고속 홈 케이블을 몬트리올의 케이블 TV 가입자들에게 아주 인기 있게 만드는 것이다.

해설 불완전한 문장에서 보어 역할을 하는 명사절을 이끌 접속사가 필요하며 '~하는 것'이라는 해석이 자연스러우므로 (B) what이 정답이다.

어휘 subscriber 구독자, 가입자

3. 우리 메뉴의 인상적인 점은 우리 유기농 농장에서 직접 배송되는 재료들의 신선도이다.

해설 명사절 접속사 자리로, 주어가 없는 불완전한 구조의 절을 이끌어 문장 전체의 주어 역할을 하는 명사절을 이끌 접속사가 필요하다. '~한 것'이라고 해석되므로 (D) What이 정답이다. (A) Which는 '어느 것'이라는 선택의 의미로 해석된다.

어휘 impressive 인상적인 | freshness 신선도 | ingredient 재료 | directly 바로 | organic 유기농의

3. + check　　1. (A)　2. (D)　3. (D)　본서 p.92

1. 저희 메르도브 상사에서는 직원들이 효율적으로 근무하는 즐거운 근무 환경을 만들기 위해서 최선을 다합니다.

해설 빈칸은 관계대명사 which 앞에 들어가는 전치사를 묻는 문제로 앞에 선행사 working environment와 잘 어울리는 (A) in이 정답이다.

어휘 do one's best 최선을 다하다 | working environment 작업 환경 | efficiently 효율적으로

2. 여행하는 동안, 우리는 다양한 것들을 맛보고 멋진 기념품을 구매할 수 있는 캔디 공장을 방문할 것이다.

해설 두 개의 절을 연결할 수 있어야 하고 앞에 선행사 factory를 받으며 뒤에 완전한 문장이 나오므로 관계부사 (D) at which가 정답이다.

어휘 treat 특별한 것, 선물, 대접 | fascinating 멋진 | souvenir 기념품

3. 마존 사는 개인 사업을 시작하고 싶어 하는 사람들을 위해서 유용한 정보가 제공되는 몇 개의 세미나를 개최할 것이다.

해설 명사 seminars를 수식하는 완전한 구조의 절을 이어주는 접속사를 쓸 자리이므로 관계부사인 (D) where가 정답이다.

어휘 enterprise 기업 | a series of 일련의 | beside 더하여, 게다가

4. + check　　1. (D)　2. (B)　3. (B)　본서 p.93

1. 우리는 교외 지역 부동산을 구매하는 데 관심이 있는 사람들을 위해 부동산 박람회를 개최할 계획이다.

해설 부정대명사 anyone 뒤에서 수식하는 주어가 없는 불완전한 구조의 절을 이끌 성분이 필요하므로 주격 관계대명사인 (D) who가 정답이다. (B) whoever도 주어가 없는 불완전한 구조의 절을 이끌지만 명사를 수식하는 절을 이끌 수 없다.

어휘 real estate 부동산 | fair 박람회 | property 부동산 | suburban 교외의

2. 새로 등록한 모든 고객은 최대 20%의 할인가로 저희 제품을 구입할 수 있는 할인 쿠폰을 받으실 자격이 있습니다.

해설 빈칸은 전치사 with 뒤의 목적격 관계대명사 자리로 앞에 선행사가 나오면 사용할 수 없는 (A)는 탈락시킨다. 전치사 뒤에 관계부사가 올 수 없으며 목적격이 필요하므로 (C)도 탈락시킨다. 소유격 관계대명사인 (D) 역시 탈락되므로 (B) which가 정답이다.

어휘 newly 새롭게 | register 등록하다 | be eligible for ~할 자격이 있다

3. 저희 설문을 작성하신 데 대해 감사드리고자, 다양한 이탈리아 요리를 즐기실 수 있는 알몬트 식당의 10달러 상품권을 보내드렸습니다.

해설 앞에 장소를 나타내는 선행사를 뒤에서 수식하며 완전한 문장을 이끄는 관계부사인 (B) where가 정답이다.

어휘 complete 작성하다 | gift certificate 상품권

Practice　본서 p.94

1. (D)	2. (B)	3. (B)	4. (D)	5. (C)
6. (A)	7. (A)	8. (D)	9. (B)	10. (B)
11. (B)	12. (C)	13. (B)	14. (B)	15. (A)
16. (A)	17. (D)	18. (A)	19. (B)	20. (A)

1. 하루 종일 앉아 있는 직장인들은 적어도 한 시간에 한 번은 일어나서 돌아다닐 것을 강력히 권한다.

해설 선행사 workers가 동사 remain의 주어가 되므로 빈칸에는 주격 관계대명사가 필요하다. 선행사가 사람이므로 (D) who가 정답이 된다.

어휘 strongly 강하게 | recommend 추천하다, 권하다 | remain seated 앉은 채로 있다 | at least 적어도, 최소한

2. 해링턴 페이퍼의 관리자들이 증가하고 있는 수요를 충족시키는 것에 대해 우려를 표명해서 공장 직원들의 일정들을 수정했다.

해설 Harington Paper를 선행사로 받고 뒤에 managers라는 명사를 가지는 소유격 관계대명사가 필요하므로 정답은 (B) whose가 된다.

어휘 express concern about ~에 대해 우려를 표명하다 | meet demand 수요를 충족시키다 | revise 수정하다, 고치다 | whatever 어떤 ~일지라도

3. 로베르토 키친웨어 사는 전통 접시 제조 기술을 전문으로 하는 회사로 작년에 시장을 아시아로 확장했다.

해설 두 콤마(,) 사이에 있는 절은 선행사 Roberto Kitchenware를 설명한다. 또한, 동사 specializes의 주어가 되며 접속사 역할을 할 수 있는 관계대명사가 필요하므로 정답은 (B) which가 되어야 한다.

어휘 specialize in ~을 전문으로 하다 | expand 확장하다

4. 알앤씨 제조사는 어제 중요한 고객들과 일련의 회의를 가졌으며, 그 고객들 대부분이 회사의 제품에 대해 만족해한다.

해설 빈칸은 of 전치사의 목적어 자리이며, 앞에 R&C Manufacturing had 그리고 뒤에 most of ~ are satisfied라는 두 절을 이끄는 접속사 역할을 해야 한다. 빈칸은 앞의 clients를 받는 대명사 자리이다. 따라서 접속사 역할과 대명사 역할을 하는 관계대명사가 필요하다. 전치사 뒤에 오므로 목적격 관계대명사 (D) whom이 정답이 된다.

어휘 a series of 일련의 I be satisfied with ~에 만족하다

5. 연구 개발에서는 무역 박람회 시연을 위한 시제품을 최종화하고 준비하는 데 가능한 모든 것을 하고 있다.

해설 빈칸은 형용사 possible의 후치 수식을 받는 목적어 자리로 '시제품을 최종화하고 준비하는 데 가능한 모든 것을 하고 있다'는 의미이므로 대명사 (C) everything이 정답이다.

어휘 development 개발 I finalize 마무리 짓다 I prototype 시제품, 원형 I demonstration 시연 I trade show 무역 박람회 I wherever 어디에나

6. 본 여행사는 국내와 국외로 여행하는 전문직 종사자들을 충족시킨다.

해설 caters와 travel 두 개의 동사가 나오고, 동사 travel 앞에 빈칸이 있으므로 빈칸은 앞의 명사 professionals를 선행사로 하는 주격 관계대명사 자리이다. 따라서 (A) who가 정답이다.

어휘 voyage 여행 I cater to ~을 충족시키다 I professional 전문직 종사자 I domestically 국내에서 I overseas 해외로, 국외로 I whatever 무엇이든지

7. 슈바르츠 씨는 자신의 건축 배경을 활용할 수 있는 새로운 직책으로 바꾼 것에 대해 기뻐하고 있다.

해설 빈칸 뒤는 완전한 문장으로 접속사를 찾아야 한다. 장소의 선행사 position과 연결되어야 하므로 「전치사 + 관계대명사」인 (A) in which가 정답이다.

어휘 glad 기쁜, 반가운 I position 직책 I background (개인의) 배경 I architecture 건축학[술] I depending on ~에 따라 I along with ~에 덧붙여, ~와 함께 I compared to ~와 비교하여

8. 견 전자는 새 엑스이 300 게임을 10월 1일 전에 구매하는 모든 사람에게 특별 무료 디비디를 제공할 것이다.

해설 주격 관계대명사 who 뒤에는 동사가 들어가야 하며 앞에 선행사 anyone은 단수로 받아야 하므로 단수 동사인 (D) purchases가 답이 된다.

어휘 offer 제공하다 I purchase 구매하다

9. 관리직에 지원하기 전에, 그 직업이 수반하는 것을 이해하는 것이 중요하다.

해설 동사 understand의 목적어이며 명사절을 이끄는 접속사 역할을 하는 것을 찾는 문제이다. 「선행사 + 접속사」 역할을 하는 관계대명사인 (B) what이 정답이 된다.

어휘 apply for ~에 지원하다 I managerial position 관리직 I entail 수반하다

10. 엔지니어들은 공장 기계의 냉각 시스템에서 즉시 수리되어야 하는 결함을 발견했다.

해설 discovered와 must be fixed 두 개의 동사가 나오고, 동사 must be fixed 앞에 빈칸이 있으므로 빈칸은 앞의 명사 defect를 선행사로 하는 주격 관계대명사 자리이다. 선행사가 사물이므로 (B) that이 정답이다.

어휘 defect 결함 I cooling system 냉각 시스템 I fix 수리하다 I immediately 즉시 I whoever 누구라도

11. 별도의 파일들은 온라인 검토 사이트를 통해 제출될 수 있으며, 이 경우 파일들은 본문과 표 순으로 업로드되어야 합니다.

해설 빈칸에는 콤마 뒤의 문장을 주절과 이어주면서 명사 case를 수식하는 관계형용사가 필요하다. 관계형용사로서 앞의 내용을 지칭하는 역할을 하는 (B) which가 정답으로 적절하다. in which case '이러한 경우에'를 묶어서 통째로 기억해 두자.

어휘 separate 별개의, 분리된 I submit 제출하다 I via ~을 통해서[거쳐서] I in the order of ~의 순서로 I main text 본문 I table 표 I in which case 이러한 경우에

12. 약속한 바와 같이, 회의에서 인사부장이 했던 발표문의 복사본이 첨부되었으니 참조하시기 바랍니다.

해설 a copy of the presentation은 gave의 목적어이며 빈칸 이하의 수식을 받는 선행사이다. 따라서 빈칸에는 목적격 관계대명사가 필요하므로 정답은 (C) that이 된다.

어휘 as promised 약속한 대로 I attached 첨부된 I personnel director 인사부장

13. 아이엠100은 사용하기 매우 간단한 장치이지만, 스마트폰에 익숙하지 않은 사람들은 사용 설명서를 참조해야 할 수도 있다.

해설 빈칸은 주절의 주어로 명사나 대명사가 올 수 있다. 문맥상 '스마트폰에 익숙하지 않은 사람들'이라는 의미가 알맞으므로 정답은 (B) those이다. 여기에서 those는 '~한 사람들'이라는 뜻으로 뒤에 「관계대명사 + be동사」인 who are가 생략되어 반드시 수식어가 따라온다.

어휘 even though 비록 ~이지만 I fairly 상당히, 꽤 I device 장치, 기기 I be used to ~에 익숙하다 I refer to ~을 참조하다 I user's manual 사용 설명서

14. 새 비디오 장비에 어려움을 겪는 사람들은 서비스 기술자 중 한 사람과 이야기해야 한다.

해설 Those는 people을 받는 대명사이고 빈칸 뒤에 동사 experience가 나오므로 주격 관계대명사 (B) who가 들어가야 한다. Those who는 '~하는 사람들'이라는 표현으로 잘 쓰인다.

어휘 equipment 장비 I technician 기술자 I those who ~하는 사람들

15. 시아 씨는 지난주에 주문한 교체 부품의 상태를 점검하기 위해 어제 창고에 전화했다.

해설 이미 called라는 동사가 나와 있으므로 (C)는 탈락이 되고, (B)는 들어갈 수 있지만 부품은 주문되어지기 때문에 수동의 형태인 be ordered의 형태로 들어가야 한다. 따라서 이 문장은 목적격 관계대명사(that/which)가 생략되어 「(that) + 주어 + 동사」 구조가 나오는 것이므로 (A) he가 정답이다.

어휘 warehouse 창고 | status 상태, 상황, 지위 | replacement 교체, 대체 | part 부품

16. 부사장은 회사가 기자회견을 할 장소를 선택했다.

해설 선행사 the place가 장소를 가리키며 수식하는 빈칸 이하가 완전한 문장으로 구성되어 있으므로 관계부사 (A) where가 정답이다.

어휘 vice president 부사장 | hold a press conference 기자회견을 열다

17. 오케스트라 매니저의 승인을 받은 사람들만 콘서트 동안 녹음이 허락된다.

해설 who ~ manager가 빈칸을 수식하는 형용사절로 동사 are가 복수형이므로 복수 취급하는 명사를 골라야 한다. those who가 '~하는 사람들'의 의미로 복수를 취하므로 정답은 (D) those가 된다.

어휘 authorization 승인, 인가 | permit 허락하다 | recording 녹음

18. 〈트레이드 포럼즈 매거진〉의 최신 호는 20개의 기사를 다루고 있는데, 그중 몇 개는 현재의 경제 상황에 관한 것이다.

해설 which가 수식하는 것은 20 articles이고, '20개의 기사 중에서 몇 개가 현재의 경제 상황에 관한 것이다'라는 의미가 적합하므로 정답은 (A) several이 된다.

어휘 issue (잡지의) ~호 | contain 담다, 다루다 | current 현재의 | state 상태, 상황

19. 슬레이팅턴은 식당과 호텔을 위한 완벽한 장소로써 마을 근처에 새로 완공된 고속도로에서 이익을 얻을 것이다.

해설 빈칸 앞의 사물 선행사인 restaurants and hotels를 수식하고 뒤에 동사가 바로 나오는 주격 관계대명사가 필요하므로 정답은 (B) which가 된다.

어휘 location 장소, 위치 | profit from ~에서 이익을 얻다 | newly-completed 새로 완공된 | highway 고속도로 | near ~근처에

20. 실번 음료는 최근 카너 밸리에 과수원이 있는 납품업체와 계약을 갱신했다.

해설 앞의 사람 선행사 supplier를 수식하면서 뒤에 orchards라는 명사가 뒤따라 나오므로 소유격 관계대명사 (A) whose가 정답이다. 복합관계대명사 (C) whatever는 선행사가 없을 때 사용할 수 있으며, 주격/목적격 관계대명사 (D) which는 뒤에 주어나 목적어가 없는 불완전한 문장이 와야 한다. 빈칸 뒤에 장소 부사구 in Connor Valley가 있으므로 장소의 관계부사 (B) where도 답이 될 수 없다.

어휘 beverage 음료 | renew 갱신하다 | supplier 공급업체, 납품업체 | orchard 과수원 | whatever 무엇이든지

UNIT 11. 부사절 접속사

1. +check 1. (A) 2. (A) 3. (D) 본서 p.96

1. 강좌 등록 마감일이 다음 달이긴 하지만, 일찍 등록하는 것이 당신의 등록 가능성을 높여줄 것이다.

해설 빈칸은 뒤에 주어, 동사를 취하는 접속사 자리인데 나머지 보기는 전치사이므로 (A) While이 정답이다.

어휘 deadline 마감기한 | registration 등록 | sign up 등록하다 | enrollment 등록

2. 고객들은 새 회계 법인에 개인 정보가 제출되기 전에 동의서를 작성해야 한다.

해설 빈칸 앞뒤로 절이 연결되어 있는 접속사 자리로 해석을 해보면 '~전에'라는 시간 접속사가 필요하므로 (A) before가 정답이다.

어휘 consent form 동의서 | personal data 개인 정보 | accounting firm 회계법인, 사무소 | rather ~라는 점만 제외하면 | except ~을 제외하고

3. 20주년 기념식을 위한 장소가 준비되었기 때문에, 초대장이 발송되어야 한다.

해설 빈칸은 뒤에 주어, 동사가 나오는 접속사 자리로, 해석상 '~이기 때문에'라는 의미가 적합하므로 (D) Now that이 정답이다.

어휘 venue 장소 | arrangement 준비 | anniversary ceremony 기념식 | invitation 초대 | as a result of ~의 결과로 | now that ~이므로, ~이기 때문에

2. +check 1. (D) 2. (C) 3. (A) 본서 p.97

1. 권 씨의 새 소설이 큰 성공을 거둔 후에, 그 책에 기반을 둔 연극이 공연되었다.

해설 빈칸에는 뒤의 명사구를 동반하는 전치사가 필요하고, 해석상 '~한 이후'라는 의미이므로 (D) After가 정답이다.

어휘 huge 큰, 엄청난 | based on ~에 기초한[기반을 둔] | perform 공연하다

2. 채용 부서는 제이슨 크라우처가 지원할 때까지 회계부장직의 적임자를 찾지 못했다.

해설 빈칸은 뒤에 주어, 동사를 이끄는 접속사 자리로 해석상 '~할 때까지'가 들어가야 하므로 (C) until이 정답이다.

어휘 recruiting 채용 | candidate 후보자 | accounting manager 회계부장 | apply 지원하다

3. 이곳에 소포를 받을 사람이 아무도 없다면, 카운터 위에 두세요.

해설 빈칸은 주어, 동사를 이끄는 접속사 자리로 해석을 해보면 '~한다면'이라는 조건의 접속사가 들어가야 하므로 (A) If가 정답이다.

어휘 package 소포 | counter 계산대, 카운터

3. +check 1. (B) 2. (A) 3. (A) 본서 p.98

1. 오하라에 있는 해밀턴 서점이 아주 잘 되어서, 리스빌과 브라운스톤에 지점들을 추가로 열 것이다.

해설 빈칸은 뒤에 주어, 동사를 동반하는 접속사 자리로 해석을 해보면 '~하기 때문에'라는 의미가 적합하므로 (B) Since가 답이다.

어휘 additional 추가의 | location 장소, 위치

2. 캐트너 씨는 이번 주에 광고 캠페인 작업을 했기 때문에, 분기 영업 보고서의 기한 연장을 요청했다.

해설 직원이 '다른 일을 했기 때문에 보고서의 기한을 연장해 달라고 요청했다'고 해석하는 것이 자연스러우므로 이유를 나타내는 (A) as가 정답이다.

어휘 ask for ~을 요청하다 | deadline 마감일 | extension 기한 연장 | quarterly 분기의

3. 온라인으로 배송 상황을 파악하는 것이 더 쉽지만, 일부는 여전히 주문 확인을 위해 회사에 전화하는 것을 선호한다.

해설 빈칸 뒤에 두 개의 절이 쓰였고, 빈칸은 부사절 접속사를 쓸 자리이므로 '비록 ~하지만'의 뜻을 가진 (A) Although가 정답이다.

어휘 track a shipment 배송 상황을 파악하다 | moreover 더욱이

---

4. + check   1. (B)   2. (D)   3. (D)   본서 p.99

1. 회사 야유회에 참석하고자 하는 직원들은 저희가 충분한 양의 간식을 준비할 수 있도록 다음 주 화요일까지 신청하셔야 합니다.

해설 빈칸 앞뒤에 절이 쓰였고, 준비를 제대로 '하기 위해' 화요일까지 등록을 하라고 요구하는 것이므로 목적의 의미를 가지는 부사절 접속사 (B) so that이 정답이다.

어휘 register 신청하다 | sufficient 충분한 | refreshment 간식

2. 다음 달 첫째 주에 지불될 수 있도록 모든 송장이 25일까지 회계부에 도착해야 한다.

해설 so that은 '~하기 위해서'라는 목적을 나타내는 접속사로 뒤에 can/could와 동반해서 주로 사용된다. '~할 수 있도록 하기 위해서'라는 의미를 만드는 (D) can be made가 정답이다.

어휘 invoice 송장 | reach 도착하다 | payment 지불

3. 화물이 제시간에 도착하기 위해서는, 오늘 정오까지 포장이 되어서 발송될 준비가 되어 있어야 한다.

해설 빈칸 뒤에 두 개의 절이 쓰였으므로 부사절 접속사가 와야 한다. 오늘 정오까지 포장되어서 발송 준비를 하는 것은 '화물이 제시간에 도착하기 위한' 것이니 (D) In order that이 정답이다.

어휘 shipment 배송(물) | arrive 도착하다 | on time 시간을 어기지 않고, 정각에 | pack 포장하다 | send out 발송하다 | noon 정오 | in place of ~을 대신해서 | in order that ~하기 위해서

---

5. + check   1. (A)   2. (A)   3. (D)   본서 p.100

1. 크라이슬러 씨는 피에르트 마케팅의 사업 동향 전문가인 반면에 프리버그 씨는 소셜 미디어 전문가이다.

해설 빈칸 앞뒤에 절이 쓰였으므로 접속사가 들어가야 한다. 문맥상 대조의 의미를 만드는 (A) whereas가 정답이다.

어휘 specialist 전문가, 전문의 | trend 경향, 추세 | expert 전문가 | whereas ~인 반면에 | aside from ~은 제외하고 | despite ~인 반면에

2. 귀하의 주문에 더 이상의 변동이 없는 것으로 가정하고, 건축 자재가 수요일 아침에 적혀 있는 주소로 배송될 것입니다.

해설 빈칸 뒤에 두 개의 절이 쓰였으므로 부사절 접속사가 필요한데 해석을 해보면 '~을 가정하면'의 의미가 적합하므로 (A) Assuming이 정답이다.

어휘 ship ~을 선적하다[배송하다] | indicate 표시하다, 나타나다 |

---

assuming (that) ~라고 추정하고 | excluding ~을 제외하고

3. 이 사무실 임대료가 내년에 오를 것을 고려해, 우리는 가격이 더 적당한 곳을 찾기 시작해야 한다.

해설 두 개의 절을 연결할 접속사를 쓸 자리이며, '임대료가 오를 것을 고려해 볼 때'라는 의미가 적합하므로 (D) Given that이 정답이다.

어휘 rent 집세, 임차료 | affordable (가격이) 알맞은, 적당한 | property 재산 | prior to ~이전에 | rather than ~라기 보다는 | owing to ~때문에 | given that ~을 고려하면

---

6. + check   1. (D)   2. (B)   3. (B)   본서 p.101

1. 역사적인 암스트롱 극장을 구하기 위한 노력에도 불구하고, 소매업 개발을 위해 그곳은 지난달 허물어졌다.

해설 빈칸 뒤에 efforts라는 명사가 왔으므로 명사를 취하는 전치사가 와야 한다. (D) Despite가 정답이다.

어휘 effort 노력, 수고 | tear down (건물 등을) 허물다 | retail 소매

2. 저희 카페테리아 리모델링 기간 동안, 근처 식당에서 이용할 수 있는 쿠폰이 제공될 것입니다.

해설 빈칸 뒤에 명사(remodeling)를 취하는 전치사 문제이다. (A)는 접속부사, (C), (D)는 접속사로, 전치사 (B) During이 정답이다.

어휘 remodeling 주택 개보수, 리모델링 | cafeteria 구내식당, 카페테리아 | voucher 상품권, 쿠폰 | nearby 인근의, 가까운 곳의

3. 워커 씨가 참석할 수 없어서, 표도로프 씨가 다가오는 나노 기술 심포지엄에 혼자 참석할 것이다.

해설 빈칸은 뒤에 주어, 동사를 취하는 접속사가 와야 한다. 해석상 '~때문에'라는 접속사가 적합하므로 (B) because가 정답이다.

어휘 present 참석하다 | upcoming 다가오는 | Symposium 심포지움 | by oneself 혼자서 | likewise 똑같이, 비슷하게

---

7. + check   1. (A)   2. (A)   3. (C)   본서 p.102

1. 직원들은 반드시 교대하기 전에 출근 기록을 해야 한다. 그렇지 않으면, 다음 급여에 근무 시간이 정확히 반영되지 않을 수도 있다.

해설 빈칸 앞뒤로 절이 연결되어 있으며, 빈칸 앞에는 세미콜론(;), 뒤에는 콤마(,)가 있으므로 의미상 알맞은 접속부사를 고른다. 근무 기록을 하지 않으면 급여에 제대로 반영되지 않을 수도 있다는 문맥이므로 '그렇지 않으면'의 의미인 (A) otherwise가 정답이다.

어휘 ensure 반드시 ~하다 | sign in 서명하다, ~의 이름을 기록하다 | shift 교대조, 교대근무 | accurately 정확히 | reflect 반영하다 | following 다음의 | paycheck 급료, 급여 | otherwise 그렇지 않으면 | moreover 더욱이 | additionally 게다가

2. 지노 디지털 가입자는 약관이 변경될 때마다 업데이트를 받을 것이다.

해설 빈칸은 두 개의 절을 연결하며, '약관이 변경될 때마다 업데이트를 받는다'는 문맥이 적절하므로 (A) whenever가 정답이다.

어휘 subscriber 구독자 | terms and conditions (계약) 조건 | meanwhile 한편, 그동안에 | accordingly 그에 맞춰

3. 세계적인 불황에도 불구하고, 에이테코 자동차는 계속해서 많은 차를 팔면서 수익을 늘리고 있다.

해설 the global recession이라는 명사 앞에 들어가는 전치사 자리로, 보기 중에 전치사는 Notwithstanding밖에 없으므로 정답은 (C) Notwithstanding이 된다.

어휘 global 세계적인 | recession 불황 | continue 계속하다 | increase 늘리다 | profit 이익 | on the other hand 다른 한편으로는, 반면에 | as a matter of fact 사실은 | notwithstanding ~에도 불구하고 | eventually 결국, 끝내

8. + check   1. (A)   2. (D)   3. (C)   본서 p.103

1. 리바이 남성복 코너에서, 모든 소매점 직원들이 고객이 매장 내에서 어떤 제품에 대해 문의할 때마다 도움을 줄 것으로 예상한다.

해설 빈칸 뒤에 완전한 문장이 나오므로 접속사가 와야 한다. 해석상 '~할 때마다'의 의미인 (A) whenever가 정답이다.

어휘 retail 소매 | expect 예상하다 | assist 도움을 주다, 지원하다 | inquire about ~에 관하여 문의하다 | even if 비록 ~일지라도 | no doubt 아마, 틀림없이 | as expected 예상대로

2. 예정된 선적에 대한 차질을 최소화하기 위해, 엘 문도 산업은 가능할 때마다 사내 배송 운전사를 활용한다.

해설 빈칸 뒤에 it is가 생략되었고 해석상 '~할 때마다'가 들어가는 (D) whenever가 정답이다.

어휘 minimize 최소화하다 | disruption 차질, 지장 | shipment 선적 | utilize 활용하다 | in-house 내부의 | delivery 배송

3. 그 소프트웨어는 새로 나온 것이어서, 개발자들이 아무리 열심히 프로그램 작업을 했을지라도 기술적인 오류를 겪게 될 것이다.

해설 빈칸 앞에 no matter와 뒤에 부사 hard로 보아 (C) how가 정답으로, no matter how는 '아무리 ~할지라도'의 의미이다.

어휘 experience 겪다, 경험하다 | hard 열심히 | developer 개발자 | no matter how ~할지라도

Practice   본서 p.104

1. (B)	2. (A)	3. (D)	4. (C)	5. (A)
6. (D)	7. (C)	8. (C)	9. (D)	10. (A)
11. (C)	12. (B)	13. (C)	14. (C)	15. (B)
16. (C)	17. (A)	18. (A)	19. (B)	20. (D)

1. 나빈 씨는 기차를 타지 못했지만, 세미나에 참석할 수 있었다.

해설 빈칸은 두 개의 절을 연결하는 부사절 접속사 자리인데, 보기 중 접속사는 '~이긴 하지만'이라는 뜻의 (B) Though뿐이다.

어휘 board 타다 | make it (간신히) 시간에 맞춰 가다, 성공하다 | just like 마치 ~처럼

2. 레넥사 다이애그노스틱이 현재와 같은 성장세를 이어가고 있다고 가정하면, 내년에는 최소 20% 이상의 매출을 올릴 수 있을 것으로 보인다.

해설 부사절에 들어가는 알맞은 접속사를 찾아야 하므로 정답은 (A) Assuming이다. (B)는 전치사이고 (C)와 (D)는 접속부사이다.

어휘 continue 계속하다 | current 현재의 | at one's rate ~의 비율로 | revenue 수입 | at least 적어도, 최소한 | assuming ~을 가정하면 | excluding ~을 제외하고 | otherwise 그렇지 않으면 | furthermore 더욱이

3. 맥더못 씨가 부서를 책임지고 있기 때문에, 업무 효율성이 증대될 것으로 기대된다.

해설 '~이기 때문에'에 해당하는 접속사를 찾는다. Now that은 '~이기 때문에'를 의미하므로 정답은 (D) Now가 된다.

어휘 be in charge of ~을 담당하다[책임지다] | work efficiency 업무 효율성 | now that ~이기 때문에

4. 제미콘 사는 지난해 이후 휴대용 노트북 컴퓨터 주변 기기의 공급업체로서 높은 명성을 쌓아왔다.

해설 앞에 현재완료 시제인 has established가 나오고 뒤에 과거 시제를 나타내는 시간어구인 last year가 나와 해석상 '~이래로'의 의미가 들어가야 하므로 정답은 (C) since가 된다.

어휘 establish 확립하다 | reputation 명성 | provider 공급업체 | portable 휴대할 수 있는 | add-on 주변 기기 | due to ~때문에 | since ~이후로

5. 우리가 더 싼 원자재 공급원을 찾을 수 없다면, 우리는 올해 우리의 모바일 기기에 더 많은 요금을 부과하기 시작할 필요가 있을 것이다.

해설 '더 싼 원자재 공급원을 찾을 수 없다면 요금을 더 부과해야 한다'는 의미가 되어야 하므로 알맞은 접속사를 찾는다. 정답은 '~하지 않는다면'의 의미인 (A) Unless가 된다.

어휘 cheap (값이) 싼 | source 원천, 출처, 공급원 | raw material 원자재 | charge 부과하다 | device 기기, 장치 | assuming 가령 ~라면

6. 모든 지원자는 여권을 신청할 때 사진 2장과 신분증을 제시해야 한다.

해설 '여권을 신청할 때'라는 의미가 적합하므로 분사구문 형태의 when -ing가 들어가는 (D) when이 적합하다.

어휘 present 제시하다, 보여주다 | a form of identification 신분증 | apply for ~을 신청하다 | passport 여권

7. 아퐁 그룹은 이사진이 다음 주에 새로운 복장 규정을 승인하자마자 그것을 실행할 것이다.

해설 빈칸 뒤에 주어, 동사를 이끄는 접속사로 주절의 시제가 미래일 때, 종속절을 이끄는 시간의 접속사가 필요하므로 정답은 (C) as soon as다.

어휘 implement 실행하다, 시행하다 | dress code 복장 규정 | board of directors 이사회 | approve 승인하다 | as well as 게다가 | since ~이후로 | as soon as ~하자마자 | during ~하는 동안

8. 셰이 씨는 그 팀이 다음 날 그것을 받을 수 있도록 사무용품을 속달로 주문했다.

해설 절의 형식으로 '~하기 위해서'는 so that ~ can[could]으로 표현한다. 그러므로 (C) so that이 정답이다. in order to도 '~하기 위해서'를 의미하지만 구의 형태로 쓰이므로 답이 될 수 없다.

어휘 office supplies 사무용품 | express mail 속달 | following day 이튿날, 그 다음 날 | in case ~인 경우에 대비해서 | in order to ~하기 위하여 | so that ~ can[could] ~하기 위해서 | given that ~을 고려하면

9. 리즈모어 클럽 정회원이 되는 절차들은 매우 복잡해서 회원이 되고 싶은 많은 사람들이 그것들에 대해서 불평한다.

해설 '너무 ~해서 …하다'는 「so ~ that + 절」이므로 (D) so가 정답이다.

어휘 procedure 절차 | regular member 정회원 | complicated 복잡한 | prospective 장래의, 유망한 | so + 형용사[부사] + that + 주어 + 동사 너무 ~해서 …하다

10. 공인 서비스 센터에서 정기 정비 점검을 수행할 경우, 카미나리 이에스360 전기 스쿠터의 안전성과 성능을 극대화할 수 있습니다.

해설 해석을 해보면 '~에서 수행된다면'이라는 조건의 의미가 적합하므로 정답은 (A) if가 된다. 접속사 if 뒤에 과거분사(carried out)가 들어가는 분사구문이다.

어휘 periodic maintenance check 정기 점검 | carry out 수행하다 | authorized service center 공인 서비스 센터 | maximize 극대화하다 | performance 성능 | electric 전기의 | scooter 소형 오토바이

11. 주민들은 비닐백과 포장지를 제외한 모든 플라스틱 물품은 '플라스틱'이라고 표시된 재활용품 용기에 버려야 한다는 점을 상기해야 한다.

해설 빈칸부터 wrappers까지가 문장에 삽입되는 부사구로 빈칸에 들어갈 알맞은 전치사를 찾아야 한다. 해석을 해보면 '~을 제외하고'라는 의미가 들어가야 하므로 정답은 (C) except가 된다.

어휘 resident 주민, 거주자 | remind 상기시키다 | plastic 플라스틱으로 된; 플라스틱 | vinyl bag 비닐봉지 | wrapper 포장지 | discard 버리다, 폐기하다 | recycling bin 재활용품 용기 | mark 표시하다

12. 주주총회가 열릴 시기에, 이사회는 새로운 최고 재무 책임자를 선출할 것이다.

해설 부사절을 이끄는 알맞은 접속사를 찾아야 한다. '주주총회가 열릴 즈음에'라는 시간의 접속사가 들어가야 하므로 정답은 (B) By the time이 된다.

어휘 shareholder meeting 주주총회 | hold 열리다, 개최하다 | board of directors 이사회 | select 선출하다 | Chief Financial Officer(= CFO) 최고 재무 책임자 | in consideration of ~을 고려해 볼 때 | by the time ~할 때쯤 | even if 비록 ~일지라도 | to ensure ~하기 위해

13. 스미스 씨가 매우 높은 인사고과 등급을 달성했기 때문에, 그는 승진할 좋은 기회를 가지게 되었다.

해설 승진할 기회가 생긴 이유가 나와야 하므로 빈칸에는 이유의 접속사가 들어가야 한다. 정답은 '이유'의 의미로 쓰인 접속사 (C) As가 된다. as는 때를 나타내는 '~할 때, ~하자마자'의 뜻으로도 쓰인다.

어휘 achieve 성취하다, 달성하다 | performance rating 인사고과 등급 | have a good chance of -ing ~할 좋은 기회가 생기다 | promote 승진시키다 | so that ~하기 위하여

14. 최근의 조사 결과가 공개될 때까지, 새로운 신발의 텔레비전 광고 캠페인은 연기될 것이다.

해설 부사절을 이끄는 접속사를 찾는 문제이다. 보기에서 접속사는 Until 밖

에 없으므로 정답은 (C) Until이 된다.

어휘 release 공개하다 | footwear 신발(류) | postpone 연기하다

15. 온라인 구매를 할 때는, 개인 정보가 완전히 안전하지 않을 수 있으니 주의해야 한다.

해설 빈칸 뒤에 주어가 생략되어 있으므로 「접속사(when) + 분사구문」으로 봐야 한다. When you make a purchase online이 주절의 주어 (you)와 동사의 현재 시제(should exercise)가 일치하므로 주어를 생략하고 동사를 현재분사로 바꾸면 된다. 따라서 (B) making이 정답이다.

어휘 exercise caution 주의를 기울이다 | personal information 개인 정보 | secure 안전한 | make a purchase 구매하다

16. 세미나가 진행되는 동안 몇몇 컴퓨터에서 인터넷을 자유롭게 접속할 수 있습니다.

해설 seminar라는 명사 앞에 들어가는 전치사 문제로, 해석을 해보면 '세미나하는 동안에'가 들어가야 하므로 정답은 (C) during이 된다.

어휘 internet access 인터넷 접속 | freely 자유롭게 | computer station 컴퓨터

17. 아무리 불편하더라도, 운전자와 승객들은 운전 중에 안전벨트를 착용해야 한다.

해설 '아무리 ~하더라도'의 의미가 되는 접속사를 찾아야 하므로 정답은 (A) No matter how가 된다.

어휘 uncomfortable 불편한 | wear a seat belt 안전벨트를 매다 | while -ing ~하는 동안에 | no matter how 아무리 ~하더라도 | in order that ~하기 위하여 | nevertheless 그럼에도 불구하고

18. 외국에서 아파트를 임대하길 희망하는 사람들은 계약서에 서명하기 전에 그것을 철저히 검토해야 한다.

해설 빈칸 뒤에 주어가 생략된 「접속사(before) + -ing」 형태의 분사구문이다. before they(= those who) sign이 분사구문으로 before signing이 되어 해석하면 '계약서에 서명하기 전에 철저히 검토해야 한다'는 의미가 되어야 하므로 알맞은 접속사는 (A) before다.

어휘 those who ~하는 사람들 | rent 빌리다 | examine 검토하다, 점검하다 | thoroughly 철저히, 완전히

19. 일단 노먼 씨가 관계 부서들에서 온 직원들과 팀을 조직하면, 알톤 프로젝트의 마감 시한이 정해질 것이다.

해설 빈칸 뒤에 주어(Mr. Norman), 동사(has organized)가 들어가는 접속사 문제로, 해석을 해보면 '일단 ~하면'이라는 조건의 의미가 들어가야 하므로 정답은 (B) Once가 된다.

어휘 representative 직원 | relevant division 관련된 부서 | deadline 마감 기한 | set 지정하다 | whereas 반면

20. 최근 연구에 따르면, 대부분의 직원들은 휴가 기간 동안 그들의 업무상 이메일을 정기적으로 확인한다.

해설 '휴가 중인 동안에'는 while on vacation이 들어가야 하므로 정답은 (D) while이 된다. '~동안에'라고 해서 during도 들어갈 수 있지만,

관용적으로 while (you are) on vacation[duty]이라고 사용한다.

어휘 **regularly** 정기적으로 | **so that** ~하기 위하여 | **while on vacation** 휴가 동안에

REVIEW TEST 03
본서 p.106

1. (C)	**2.** (C)	**3.** (A)	**4.** (C)	**5.** (D)
6. (C)	**7.** (B)	**8.** (C)	**9.** (B)	**10.** (B)
11. (B)	**12.** (B)	**13.** (D)	**14.** (D)	**15.** (D)
16. (D)	**17.** (B)	**18.** (D)	**19.** (A)	**20.** (B)

1. 마리오 루치의 영업 발표는 정말 설득력이 있어서 모든 고객이 제품을 주문하기를 원했다.

해설 '너무 A해서 B하다'라는 의미를 가진 so A that B 구문이므로 (C) that이 정답이다.

어휘 **presentation** 발표, 프레젠테이션 | **convincing** 설득력 있는 | **client** 고객

2. 우리 임대 계약서에 명시된 것처럼, 세입자들은 첫 달 임대료와 보증금을 미리 지불해야 한다.

해설 「부사절 접속사 + 분사」인 분사 구문 문제로, '명시된 대로'라는 의미인 As stated가 적합하므로 정답은 (C) stated가 된다. As와 stated 사이에 it is가 생략되었다고 보면 된다.

어휘 **rental contract** 임대 계약서 | **tenant** 세입자 | **rent** 임대료 | **deposit** 보증금 | **in advance** 미리 | **state** 진술하다, 명시하다 | **statement** 진술

3. 고객들은 유효한 영수증을 제시할 경우, 우리 상점에서 하자가 있는 제품을 교환할 수 있습니다.

해설 빈칸 뒤에 주어, 동사가 나오므로 접속사가 필요하며, 해석상 '구매 증거를 제시할 수 있다면'이라는 조건의 의미가 들어가야 하므로 (A) provided that이 정답이다.

어휘 **exchange** 교환하다 | **defective** 결함 있는, 하자가 있는 | **valid** 유효한 | **proof of purchase** 구매 증명, 영수증 | **provided that(= if)** ~한다면 | **as though** 마치 ~인 것처럼

4. 워켄 씨의 우려와 상관없이, 보스윅스 전자는 6월 1일에 신제품을 출시할 계획이다.

해설 빈칸은 전치사 자리이다. 보기 중 전치사는 (C)이며, 나머지는 부사이다. 해석상 '~의 우려와 상관없이'라는 내용이 들어가야 하므로 정답은 (C) Regardless of다.

어휘 **concern** 우려, 걱정 | **plan to** ~할 계획이다 | **launch** 출시하다 | **as long as** ~하는 한 | **nevertheless** 그럼에도 불구하고 | **regardless of** ~와는 상관없이 | **regrettably** 유감스럽게도

5. 박물관 방문객들은 선물 가게에 들를 수 있는데, 그곳에서는 유명 조각품의 소형 복제품이 판매된다.

해설 빈칸 앞뒤에 절이 있으므로 빈칸에는 접속사 역할을 하는 품사가 필요하다. 빈칸 앞의 gift shop이 선행사이므로 빈칸에는 gift shop을 수식하는 관계사가 나와야 한다. 따라서 관계부사인 (D) where가 정답이다.

어휘 **drop by** 들르다 | **replica** 복제품, 모형 | **sculpture** 조각품

6. 라울 씨가 다음 주에 바르셀로나에서 있는 회의에 참석하지 못하기 때문에 정 씨가 그를 대신해서 갈 것이다.

해설 빈칸은 명사인 place 앞에 있으므로 소유격인 (C) his가 들어가야 한다.

어휘 **attend** 참석하다 | **conference** 회의, 콘퍼런스 | **in one's place** ~대신

7. 우리 웹사이트를 일시적으로 이용할 수 없기 때문에, 우리는 지금 당신의 계좌에 접속할 수 없습니다.

해설 빈칸 뒤에 주어, 동사가 나오므로 접속사가 필요하다. 보기 중 접속사는 Since밖에 없으므로 정답은 (B) Since다.

어휘 **temporarily** 일시적으로, 임시로 | **out of service** 운영이 중단된 | **access** 접속하다 | **account** 계좌, 계정 | **at the moment** 지금 | **regardless of** ~에 상관없이 | **since** ~이므로, ~이기 때문에 | **in case of** ~의 경우에 | **besides** 게다가, 뿐만 아니라

8. 회사 야유회를 위한 쇼핑 목록에 있는 몇몇 항목은 이미 구매되었다.

해설 문장에 are와 have been purchased라는 두 개의 동사가 나오므로, 빈칸은 주어인 Some of the items를 수식하는 절이다. 주어가 선행사인 items이므로 주격 관계대명사인 (C) that이 정답이다.

어휘 **item** 물품, 품목 | **company picnic** 회사 야유회 | **purchase** 구입하다

9. 우리 제품은 주문 당시에 요청된다면, 빠른 배송으로 발송될 수 있다.

해설 해석을 해보면 '요청된다면'이라는 조건의 의미가 적합하며, 「접속사 + 과거분사」가 나오는 분사구문으로 쓰였다. 따라서 정답은 (B) if가 된다.

어휘 **express shipping** 빠른 배송 | **at the time of** ~하는 시간에 | **in addition to** ~에 더하여

10. 회계 이사로서, 그랜트 씨는 회사가 재무 규정을 준수하게 하는 책임을 지고 있다.

해설 빈칸은 the Accounting Director를 이끄는 전치사 자리로 '회계 이사로서'라는 자격의 전치사 (B) As가 정답이다.

어휘 **accounting** 회계 | **be in charge of** ~의 책임이 있다 | **ensure** 확실히 하다 | **compliance** 준수 | **financial** 재무의 | **regulation** 규정

11. 정전이 발생할 경우에 건물의 보안을 유지하는 것은 시설 관리팀의 책임이다.

해설 명사 앞에 들어가는 전치사 문제이다. (C)는 접속사이므로 탈락이며, 의미상 '정전이 일어날 경우 보안 유지는 시설 관리팀의 책임이다'가 적절하므로 정답은 (B) In the event of가 된다.

어휘 **power outage** 정전 | **responsibility** 책임, 책무 | **Facilities**

Management Team 시설관리팀 | ensure 보장하다, 반드시 ~하게 하다 | secure 안전한 | contrary to ~에 반해서 | in the event of ~의 경우에 | considering that ~을 고려하면 | for the sake of ~을 위해서

12. 부엌에 있는 썩기 쉬운 물품은 유통기한이 지나면 모두 버려야 한다.

해설 '부엌 안에 있는 물건들'이라는 의미가 되어야 하므로 정답은 (B) in이 된다.

어휘 perishable 잘 상하는 | throw away ~을 버리다 | upon expiration 만료 시

13. 이번 달 사원 소식지에 게재될 기사를 늦어도 4월 30일까지는 제출해야 한다.

해설 전치사 문제이다. '이번 달 사원 소식지에 게재될 기사'라는 의미가 되어야 하므로 정답은 '~을 위한'이라는 의미의 전치사 (D) for이다.

어휘 article 기사 | publication 출판, 발행 | newsletter 소식지, 사보 | submit 제출하다 | at the latest 늦어도

14. 이 도시의 프로 야구팀의 거의 모든 구성원들은 우리 주의 대학에서 모집되었다.

해설 빈칸은 all 앞에 들어가는 부사 문제로 해석상 '거의'라는 의미가 나와야 하므로 정답은 (D) Almost다. almost all of로 같이 암기해두면 좋다.

어휘 professional 프로(선수) | recruit 채용하다 | state 주 | reasonably 상당히, 꽤 | fully 완전히, 충분히 | ever 언제나, 항상 | almost 거의

15. 영업 사원들은 평소에는 각자의 지점에서 일하는 반면, 본사에서의 정규 트레이닝에 참석해야만 한다.

해설 빈칸은 두 개의 절을 연결해 줄 수 있는 부사절 접속사 자리인데, 보기 중 접속사는 '~인 반면에'라는 뜻의 While뿐이므로 정답은 (D) While이다.

어휘 sales representative 영업 사원 | normally 보통 | respective 각자의, 각각의 | branch 지점 | regular 정기적인 | in view of ~을 고려해서 | rather than ~보다는

16. 마케팅팀의 직원들은 자신들이 회사의 새 가전제품을 홍보하느라 분투하고 있다는 걸 알게 되었다.

해설 빈칸에는 타동사 find의 목적어가 들어가야 하고, 앞에 나오는 marketing team members를 받는 재귀대명사의 재귀 용법이 들어가야 하므로 정답은 (D) themselves다.

어휘 struggle 애쓰다, 발버둥치다 | promote 홍보하다 | home appliance 가전제품

17. 퍼시피카 항공은 런던에서 뉴욕으로 가던 항공편이 기술적인 문제로 인해 이륙 직후에 회항했다고 발표했다.

해설 빈칸은 명사구 a technical problem을 목적어로 하는 전치사 자리이다. 문맥상 '항공편이 기술적인 문제로 인해 이륙 직후에 회항했다'는 의미가 되어야 하므로 빈칸에는 '~으로 인해'라는 의미의 원인을 나타내는 전치사인 (B) due to가 와야 한다.

어휘 flight 항공편, 항공기 | head 향하다 | shortly after ~직후에 | takeoff 이륙 | technical problem 기술적 문제 | whereas ~임에 비하여 | otherwise 그렇지 않으면 | instead of ~대신에

18. 밀러 씨는 실수로 후진하다 직장 동료의 차량을 들이받는 바람에 전조등에 약간의 피해를 입혔다.

해설 빈칸 뒤에 동사구가 나오므로 형용사인 accidental은 오답이다. 명사인 accident와 accidents는 주어인 Mr. Miller와 복합 명사를 이루지 못하므로 역시 오답이다. 따라서 동사를 수식하는 부사인 (D) accidentally가 정답이다.

어휘 back up (차를) 후진시키다 | coworker 직장 동료 | vehicle 차량, 탈것 | cause damage to ~에 손상을 입히다[파손시키다] | headlight 전조등, 헤드라이트 | accident 사고 | accidental 우연한 | accidentally 우연히, 뜻하지 않게

19. 리아나 씨는 임상 심리학 연구에 헌신해 왔다.

해설 빈칸은 commit oneself to 구문의 전치사 to 자리이다. 따라서 (A) to가 정답이다.

어휘 research in ~에의 연구 | clinical psychology 임상 심리학 | commit oneself to ~에 헌신하다[충실하다]

20. 회의가 끝나면, 한 테이블만 옆 방으로 옮기고 나머지 세 테이블은 제자리에 두십시오.

해설 빈칸은 형용사 one을 수식하는 부사 자리로, '테이블을 단 한 개만 옮기고 나머지는 제자리에 두라'는 내용이 자연스러우므로 숫자 강조부사 (B) just가 정답이다.

어휘 neighboring 근처의, 인접한 | leave 남기다

UNIT 12. to부정사

1. +check   1. (A)   2. (A)   3. (B)   본서 p.109

1. 기부자들에게 감사를 표하기 위해, 엘크하트 아카데미는 이번 주 토요일에 만찬과 시상식을 개최할 예정이다.

해설 to부정사로 뒤에 동사원형이 들어가야 하므로 (A) acknowledge가 정답이다.

어휘 donor 기부자 | host 주최하다, 열다 | awards ceremony 시상식 | acknowledge 감사를 표하다, ~을 받았음을 알리다 | acknowledgment 감사, 인정

2. 버릴 수 없는 고객 파일을 저장하기 위해 데이터 관리 회사가 고용되었다.

해설 이미 문장에 동사가 나와 있으므로 (B), (C)는 탈락이 되고, '~하기 위해서'의 의미가 들어가는 (A) to store가 정답이다. (D) to have stored는 완료 부정사로 본동사와 시제 차이가 날 때 쓴다.

어휘 management 관리 | hire 고용하다 | discard 버리다, 폐기하다 | store 저장하다

3. 이 교육의 주된 목적은 신입 직원들을 회사에 적응시키게 도움을 주어서, 결국에는 직원 생산성을 높이는 것이다.

해설 빈칸은 동사 자리로 수 일치에서 (D)는 탈락이 되고, goal/purpose/job/aim/objective가 주어로 나올 때 동사는 be to가 보통 따라 나오므로 (B) is to help가 정답이다.

어휘 adapt to ~에 적응하다 | eventually 결국에 | staff productivity 직원 생산성

2. ╋check   1. (D)   2. (B)   3. (A)   본서 p.111

1. 그 회사는 사업 목적의 여행에 쓰인 모든 자금을 변제하겠다고 약속한다.

해설 '~할 것을 약속하다'라는 의미가 적합하므로 「promise + to부정사」인 (D) to reimburse가 정답이다.

어휘 firm 회사 | promise 약속하다 | fund 자금 | reimburse 변제하다 | reimbursement 변제, 상환

2. 사왓디 레스토랑의 정통 음식과 분위기는 손님들이 정말 태국에서 식사를 하고 있다고 느낄 수 있게 해준다.

해설 allow는 대표적인 5형식 동사로 목적격 보어로 to부정사를 취하므로 (B) to feel이 정답이다.

어휘 authentic 진짜인, 정통의 | atmosphere 분위기, 환경 | allow 허용하다 | meal 식사 | Thailand 태국

3. 경력 개발 전문가인 댄 정은 올해에도 놀스 대학교에서 인기 있는 세미나를 제공할 것으로 예상된다.

해설 be expected 뒤에는 to부정사가 들어가야 하므로 (A) to offer가 정답이다.

어휘 career development 경력 개발 | expert 전문가 | expect 예상하다

Practice   본서 p.112

1. (D)	2. (B)	3. (D)	4. (A)	5. (B)
6. (D)	7. (C)	8. (C)	9. (C)	10. (A)
11. (B)	12. (C)	13. (D)	14. (A)	15. (A)
16. (C)	17. (A)	18. (C)	19. (D)	20. (D)

1. 레이네 시스템에서는 고객에게 컴퓨터 관련 문제를 도와줄 전문가 3명을 채용했다.

해설 빈칸 앞에서 주어, 동사, 목적어를 갖춘 완벽한 문장이 완성되었음을 고려할 때, 빈칸은 수식어구를 만들어주는 자리이므로 to부정사 (D)가 정답이다.

어휘 recruit 채용하다 | expert 전문가 | customer 고객 | computer-related 컴퓨터에 관련된 | issue 문제

2. 이사회 회의의 목적은 은퇴하는 리오 홍 회장의 후계자를 선출하는 것이다.

해설 '회의의 목적은 ~을 고르는 것이다'라는 의미가 되어야 한다. 따라서 보어 역할을 하는 to부정사의 명사적 용법으로 쓰인 (B) is to choose가 정답이다. 문장의 주어로 goal/purpose/aim/objective

등이 나오면 동사는 「be동사 + to부정사」가 나온다는 것을 알아두도록 한다.

어휘 successor 후계자 | retire 은퇴하다

3. 악천후 때문에 비행기가 3시간 이상 지체되었다.

해설 cause라는 동사는 대표적인 5형식 동사로 목적격 보어로 to부정사를 취한다. delay는 타동사로 뒤에 목적어가 없으므로 수동태로 쓰인 (D) to be delayed가 정답이 된다.

어휘 inclement weather condition 악천후 | cause 야기시키다 | delay 지연시키다, 지체시키다

4. 서울 책 박람회에 보낼 책들이 수요일까지 준비가 될 수 있도록 해야 한다.

해설 that 이하에서 주어는 the books이며 동사는 are이다. 빈칸에는 명사인, 주어 the books를 수식할 수 있는 형용사절(관계대명사절)이 올 수도, 형용사구가 올 수도 있다. which[that] will be 또는 to부정사를 이용한 to be로 쓰일 수 있다. 따라서 답은 (A) to be이다.

어휘 make sure that 반드시 ~하도록 하다 | book fair 책 박람회

5. 책 출판에서 선두 자리를 유지하기 위해서, 카슨 인쇄는 경쟁업체 중에서 두 곳을 사들였다.

해설 maintain이라는 동사 앞에 들어가며 목적(~하기 위하여)을 나타내기 위해서는 to부정사의 to가 들어가야 한다. 정답은 (B) In order to가 된다.

어휘 maintain 유지하다 | buy out 사들이다 | competitor 경쟁업체 | in order to ~하기 위하여

6. 메첸 씨는 그의 비서에게 월요일 기자 회견이 있기 훨씬 전에 요약 보고서를 타이핑하라고 요구했다.

해설 urge는 5형식 동사로 목적격 보어로 to부정사를 취하므로 정답은 (D) to type이 된다.

어휘 urge 촉구하다 | summary 요약 | well in advance 훨씬 전에 | press release 기자 회견, 보도 자료

7. 다음 약속 일정에 관해서 홀트 씨가 연락할 수 있도록, 그는 당신의 전화번호가 필요할 것이다.

해설 목적(~하기 위해)을 나타내는 표현 중 in order to가 있다. to contact 앞에 의미상의 주어 Mr. Holt가 있으므로 빈칸에는 의미상 주어 앞의 전치사 (C) for가 들어가야 한다.

어휘 contact 연락하다 | regarding ~에 관하여 | appointment 일정

8. 월터스 박사는 라스베이거스에서 열리는 제10회 글로벌 파트너십 시상식에 초청되어 연설을 하게 되었다.

해설 invite는 목적격 보어로 to부정사를 취하는 동사이므로, 수동태일 때는 「be invited + to부정사」의 형태를 취한다. 따라서 정답은 (C) to speak이 된다.

어휘 invite 초청하다, 초대하다 | speak 연설하다

9. 새로운 정책에 따르면, 웹사이트 관리자들은 회원들의 동의 없이 그들의 사진을 게시할 수 없다.

해설 해석상 '~할 수 없다'라는 be unable to를 찾는 문제이므로 정답은 (C) to post가 된다.

어휘 administrator 관리자 | be unable to ~할 수 없다 | without consent 동의 없이 | post 게시하다

10. 공동의 목표를 향해 어떻게 일해야 하는지 설명하는 것은 잠재 고객들과 관계를 쌓는 훌륭한 방법이다.

해설 문장에 본동사 is가 이미 있으므로 동사 (B), (C), (D)를 모두 제외시킬 수 있다. a way는 to부정사를 이끄는 명사이므로 (A) to build가 정답이다.

어휘 mutual 서로 간의, 공동의 | rapport 관계 | prospective 장래의

11. 직원 대상 조사에 따르면, 회사 워크숍은 직원들이 업무 관계를 강화시키는 데 도움을 준다.

해설 help는 목적격 보어로 to부정사나 동사원형을 취하므로 정답은 (B) strengthen이 된다.

어휘 employee survey 직원 설문 조사 | working relationship 업무 관계 | strengthen 강화하다

12. 우리 식당은 넓은 식당에서 지속적으로 공기를 걸러낼 수 있는 장치가 필요요.

해설 빈칸에 들어갈 알맞은 말은 '~할 능력'이다. 따라서 정답은 (C) ability가 된다. to부정사가 명사를 수식하는 형용사적 용법으로 쓰였다.

어휘 device 장치, 기기 | filter 여과하다, 거르다 | continuously 지속적으로 | dining room 식당 | opportunity 기회 | sense 감각 | ability 능력 | permission 허락, 허가

13. 바다 생물 유산 협회는 고래 섬들의 자연환경을 보호하는 데 전념하고 있다.

해설 be dedicated to는 '~에 전념하다'라는 의미로 쓰이는 숙어이다. to는 전치사로 뒤에 명사나 동명사가 나오는데, 빈칸 뒤에는 목적어가 있으므로 동명사인 (D) preserving이 정답이 된다.

어휘 heritage 유산 | be dedicated to ~에 헌신하다[전념하다] | natural 자연의 | island 섬 | preserve 보존하다

14. 새로운 온라인 경쟁자들의 출현을 고려할 때, 전통적인 금융 서비스 회사들은 경쟁력을 유지하기 위해 노력할 필요가 있다.

해설 strive는 목적어로 to부정사를 취하는 동사로 '고군분투하다'라는 의미로 쓰이므로 정답은 (A) strive이다.

어휘 considering ~을 고려하면 | emergence 출현, 부상 | rival 경쟁자, 경쟁 상대 | traditional 전통적인 | financial service 금융서비스 | remain 계속 ~이다 | competitive 경쟁력 있는, 뒤지지 않는 | strive 몹시 애쓰다, 고군분투하다 | advise 권고하다

15. 일의 중복을 막기 위한 노력으로, 사무 절차를 철저하게 검토하고 단순화할 것이다.

해설 '~하기 위한 노력으로'라는 뜻으로 「in an effort + to부정사」가 되어

야 하므로 정답은 (A) to prevent가 된다.

어휘 duplication 중복, 복사 | office procedure 사무 절차 | thoroughly 철저하게 | simplified 단순화된 | in an effort to ~하기 위한 노력

16. 벨라포 패션의 이사회는 서유럽에서의 소매 판매를 중단하기로 한 결정을 설명하기 위해 수입의 지속적인 감소를 지적했다.

해설 문장에 동사 pointed가 이미 있으므로 동사 (A), (B), (D)를 모두 제외시킨다. decision은 to부정사를 이끄는 명사이므로 (C) to suspend가 정답이다.

어휘 board of directors 이사회 | point to ~을 시사하다[지적하다] | continued 지속적인 | decline in ~의 감소 | revenue 수입 | retail sales 소매 판매 | suspend 중단하다, 유보하다

17. 휴대용 난방기는 충전식 배터리를 사용하여 필요한 전기를 공급한다.

해설 battery를 꾸며줄 수 있는 형용사 역할을 하는 것을 고른다. 동사 supply의 목적어(the required electricity)가 있으므로 정답은 (A) to supply가 된다.

어휘 portable 휴대용의, 휴대가 쉬운 | heater 난방기 | rechargeable battery 충전식 배터리 | require 필요로 하다 | electricity 전기 | supply 공급하다

18. 엄격한 보안 정책은 때때로 문제가 될 수 있지만, 회사와 고객 모두를 보호하기 위한 것이다.

해설 intend는 5형식 동사로 to부정사를 목적격 보어로 취하고, 수동태는 be intended to가 되므로 정답은 (C), (D) 중에 있는데, 뒤에 목적어가 있으므로 수동태인 (D)는 탈락이 되어서, 정답은 (C) to protect가 된다.

어휘 even though 비록 ~일지라도 | strict 엄격한 | security policy 보안 정책 | troublesome 고질적인, 골칫거리인 | at times 때때로, 가끔씩 | intend 의도하다 | protect 보호하다

19. 면접을 준비하는 사람들은 자신이 입사하고 싶은 회사에 대해 조사를 해보는 것이 좋다.

해설 해석상 '~하도록 권고 받다'라는 의미의 「be advised + to부정사」가 들어가야 하므로 정답은 (D) advised가 된다.

어휘 those who ~하는 사람들 | prepare for ~을 준비하다 | be advised to ~하도록 권고되다 | do research 조사를 하다 | criticize 비난하다, 비평하다 | inquire 문의하다 | accept 수용하다 | advise 권고하다

20. 사장은 다음 달에 은퇴하는 제이슨 씨의 뒤를 이을 편집장으로 마이어 씨를 임명하는 것을 고려해 왔다.

해설 consider는 동명사를 목적어로 취하는 동사이므로 정답은 (D) appointing이 된다.

어휘 chief editor 편집장 | succeed 뒤를 잇다 | retire 은퇴하다 | consider -ing ~을 고려하다 | appoint 임명하다

PART 5 GRAMMAR **39**

PART 5 UNIT 12

UNIT 13. 동명사

1. + check   1. (C)   2. (A)   3. (D)   본서 p.114

1. 생산비를 낮추는 데 집중함에도 불구하고, 증가하는 원자재와 임금 가격이 그것을 어렵게 했다.

해설 전치사 on 뒤에 나오는 빈칸에는 명사나 동명사를 써야 하는데, manufacturing costs를 목적어로 취하는 동사가 필요하므로 (C) lowering이 정답이다.

어휘 manufacturing 제조 | raw materials 원자재 | labor 노동 | lower ~을 낮추다

2. 우리 신제품은 시장에 출시되기 전에 검사자 모둠이 사용해 보고 그들의 반응에 따라서 수정되었다.

해설 빈칸 뒤에 동명사를 취하는 전치사가 필요하므로 (A) before가 정답이다.

어휘 modify ~을 수정하다 | according to ~에 따라서 | response 반응 | place on the market 시장에 내놓다 | initial 초기에 | ahead 앞에

3. 도서관 주차 허가증을 얻는 것은 많은 서류 작업이 필요한 어려운 일이었다.

해설 이미 was라는 동사가 있으므로 나머지 보기들은 탈락이고, (D) Obtaining이 정답이다.

어휘 parking permit 주차 허가증 | paperwork 서류 작업 | obtain 얻다

2. + check   1. (C)   2. (D)   3. (B)   본서 p.115

1. 이 미각 테스트에서, 소비자들은 우리의 새로운 커피 브랜드를 몇 개의 다른 브랜드들과 함께 선호도 순으로 평가하도록 요구된다.

해설 전치사 of 뒤에는 명사 혹은 동명사가 나오는 것이 적합하고, 뒤에 목적어를 동반하지 않으므로 (C) preference가 정답이다.

어휘 taste test 미각 테스트 | rank 순위를 매기다, 평가하다 | in order of ~의 순서로 | preference 선호도 | preferential 우선권의, 특혜의

2. 혁신과 성장을 적극적으로 추구함으로써, 로웨나 호텔 그룹은 호텔 산업의 선도자가 되는 것을 목표로 하고 있다.

해설 전치사 by 뒤에 동명사 pursuing이 나왔고, 동명사는 부사가 수식하므로 (D) actively가 정답이다.

어휘 by -ing ~함으로써 | pursue 추구하다 | innovation 혁신 | growth 성장 | hospitality industry 환대산업(관광산업 또는 호텔산업)

3. 행사 일정 조정과 관련된 문의는 212-555-5309로 연락주세요.

해설 빈칸 앞 pertaining to는 전치사로 뒤에 명사나 동명사가 나온다. 빈칸 뒤의 명사 events를 목적어 취할 수 있는 동명사 (B) rescheduling이 정답이다.

어휘 inquiry 문의, 조회 | pertaining to ~에 관련된 | contact 연락하다 | reschedule 일정을 변경하다

3. + check   1. (C)   2. (B)   3. (C)   본서 p.116

1. 연구 보조의 직무는 실험 절차를 촉진시키기 위한 효율적인 방법을 찾는 것을 포함한다.

해설 include는 동명사나 명사를 목적어로 취하는 동사이므로 (C) searching이 정답이다.

어휘 efficient 효율적인 | facilitate 촉진시키다 | experiment 실험 | search for ~을 찾다

2. 기획부는 번화가와 멀리 떨어진 거주 지역에 새 지점을 세우는 것을 추천했다.

해설 빈칸 앞 recommend는 동명사를 취하는 동사이므로 (B) locating 이 정답이다.

어휘 recommend 추천하다 | branch 지점 | residential area 거주 지역 | locate (특정 위치에) 두다, 설치하다

3. 팍스마타 의류의 대표는 내년에 밴쿠버에 또 다른 공장을 건설하는 것을 고려하고 있다.

해설 consider는 동명사를 목적어로 취하는 동사이므로 (C) building이 정답이다. 뒤에 목적어가 나오므로 수동태 (D)는 답이 될 수 없다.

어휘 consider 고려하다, 숙고하다 | another 또 하나의 | build 건설하다, 건물을 짓다

4. + check   1. (D)   2. (B)   3. (B)   본서 p.117

1. 직원들은 내부 서류를 양면 인쇄함으로써 종이를 절약하도록 권장받는다.

해설 빈칸 뒤에 printing이라는 동명사를 취하는 전치사가 필요하므로 (D) by가 정답이다.

어휘 encourage 권장하다 | internal 내부의

2. 입증된 경험과 전문성을 갖춘 슈프림 여행사는 최고 수준의 고객 서비스를 제공하고자 헌신합니다.

해설 빈칸 뒤에 to providing을 힌트로 (B) committed가 정답이며 be committed to -ing는 '~에 헌신하다'라는 뜻의 동명사 관용표현이다.

어휘 proven 입증된 | professionalism 전문성

3. 클레멘츠 씨는 언어 기술의 부족 때문에 중국어로 고객들과 계약을 협상하는 데 늘 어려움을 겪는다.

해설 동명사 관용표현 「have difficulty -ing」로 (B) negotiating이 정답이다.

어휘 lack 결핍, 부족 | have difficulty -ing ~하느라 어려움을 겪다 | negotiate a contract 계약을 협상하다

Practice   본서 p.118

1. (C)	2. (C)	3. (C)	4. (B)	5. (B)
6. (C)	7. (C)	8. (B)	9. (B)	10. (B)
11. (C)	12. (A)	13. (B)	14. (C)	15. (D)
16. (B)	17. (B)	18. (C)	19. (C)	20. (D)

1. 멘티스 출판사의 최고경영자는 내일 회의에서 올해 회사 목표에 대한 개요를 이야기할 예정이다.

해설 전치사 on 뒤에 목적어로 명사나 동명사가 올 수 있다. the company's goals for this year를 목적어로 받기 위해서는 동명사

가 와야 하므로 답은 (C) outlining이 된다.

어휘 plan on -ing ～을 할 계획이다[예정이다] | outline 개요를 말하다

2. 완도사 호텔에서는 여름 동안 6주 이상 전에 미리 방을 예약하는 것을 강력히 추천합니다.

해설 recommend는 동명사를 목적어로 취하므로 정답은 (C) booking이 된다.

어휘 strongly recommend 강력하게 추천하다 | in advance 미리 | during summer 여름 동안에

3. 우리 타랍 섬유 산업은 우리 제조업이 환경에 미치는 영향을 줄이려는 우리의 헌신에 대해 진지하게 생각하고 있습니다.

해설 commitment to -ing는 '～에 대한 약속[전념]'을 의미한다. 따라서 빈칸에는 동명사가 와야 하므로 (C) reducing이 정답이다.

어휘 textiles 섬유 산업 | commitment to ～에의 헌신 | environmental 환경의, 환경과 관련된 | impact 영향 | manufacturing 제조업

4. 3년 전 국립 문화예술 센터에서 공연한 이래로, 클래식 피아노 연주자인 조은빈은 계속해서 자신의 경력을 발전시켰다.

해설 빈칸은 전치사 Since의 목적어 자리이고 '3년 전 공연한 이래로 계속해서 경력을 발전시켜 왔다'라는 의미가 되어야 자연스러우므로 동명사 (B) performing이 정답이다.

어휘 classical pianist 클래식 피아노 연주자 | continue 계속하다 | develop 개발하다, 발전하다 | career 경력 | perform 공연하다

5. 롤렌트 사는 지역에 신제품을 효과적으로 광고함으로써 여러 잠재적 구매자들을 끌어들일 수 있었다.

해설 동명사 advertising은 부사가 수식한다. 따라서 정답은 (B) effectively가 된다.

어휘 attract 끌어모으다 | potential 잠재성 있는 | buyer 구매자 | by -ing ～함으로써 | locally 국부적으로, 그 고장에서 | effective 효과적인

6. 슬리스탁 컨설팅은 호주의 기존 고객들을 유지하는 것 외에도, 향후 10년 안에 동남아시아에 새로운 고객 기반을 설립하기를 바라고 있다.

해설 in addition to는 '～외에도'를 의미하는 전치사구이다. 따라서 빈칸에는 명사 혹은 동명사가 들어가야 한다. 뒤에 the existing clientele이라는 목적어가 있으므로 동명사인 (C) retaining이 정답이 된다.

어휘 in addition to ～외에도 | existing 기존의 | clientele (모든) 고객들, 고객층 | establish 설립하다 | client base 고객 기반 | decade 10년 | retain 유지하다, 보유하다 | retention 유지, 보유

7. 케이티 철도는 승객들에게 미리 공지하지 않고 모든 기차의 출발 시각을 변경할 수 있습니다.

해설 전치사 뒤에는 명사 또는 동명사가 나올 수 있는데 빈칸 뒤에 passengers라는 목적어가 나오므로 정답은 동명사인 (C) notifying이 된다.

어휘 departure time 출발 시각 | in advance 미리, 앞서서 | notify 알리다, 통보하다

8. 도시 개발 위원회의 완전한 승인을 받기 전에는 착공하지 못할 것이다.

해설 빈칸은 동명사 obtaining의 목적어인 명사 자리이므로 (B)가 정답이다.

어휘 construction 건설, 공사 | break ground 착공하다 | obtain 얻다 | full 완전한 | development 개발 | board 위원회

9. 전 직원은 중장비를 다루는 안전 수칙을 알아야 한다.

해설 빈칸은 전치사 for의 목적어인 동명사 자리이며 '전 직원은 중장비를 다루는 안전 수칙을 알아야 한다'는 의미가 되어야 자연스러우므로 (B) handling이 정답이다.

어휘 safety rule 안전 수칙 | heavy machinery 중장비

10. 롬케이 그룹은 파드하스 사와 함께 식음료 업계에서 그 회사의 현 입지를 확보하기 위해 협상할 것을 기대하고 있다.

해설 look forward to -ing는 '～을 고대하다'란 의미이다. 따라서 정답은 (B) negotiating이 된다.

어휘 secure a position 입지를 확보하다 | look forward to -ing ～을 고대하다 | negotiate 협상하다

11. 마샬의 일상 업무에는 비정상적인 거래에 대한 고객 계정 활동을 검토하는 것이 포함된다.

해설 include는 동명사를 목적어로 취하는 동사이므로 답은 (C) reviewing이 된다.

어휘 daily routine 일상 업무 | include 포함하다 | account 계정, 계좌 | unusual 특이한, 흔치 않은 | transaction 거래 | review 검토하다

12. 새로 고용된 건축 디자이너는 그녀의 혁신적인 아이디어로 우리가 빡빡한 프로젝트의 마감 시간을 맞추는 데 도움을 줄 것으로 예상한다.

해설 「be expected + to부정사」는 '～할 것으로 예상하다'라는 의미로 쓰인다. 따라서 정답은 (A) help가 된다.

어휘 hire 고용하다 | be expected + to ～할 것으로 예상하다 | meet a deadline 마감 시간을 맞추다 | tight 빡빡한 | innovative 혁신적인

13. 파클리 리조트의 지역 여행 책자에는 낮 시간동안 숲을 거니는 것을 제안한다.

해설 의미상 '제안'에 해당하는 동사 offers와 suggests 중 하나를 골라야 한다. 동명사를 목적어로 취하는 동사는 (C) suggests이다. (A) offers는 to부정사를 목적어 취하므로 답이 될 수 없다.

어휘 brochure 책자 | during the daytime 낮 동안에 | refuse 거부하다

14. 굿윌 마트는 모든 직원이 고객들의 불만을 정중하고 전문적인 태도로 응대하기를 기대한다.

해설 expect는 to부정사를 목적격 보어로 취하는 동사이므로 정답은 (C) to respond가 된다.

어휘 customer complaint 고객 불만 | in a courteous and professional manner 정중하고 전문적인 태도로

15. 업계 보고서에 따르면, 최근에 설립된 많은 회사가 미디어 사업에 투자 확장을 고려 중이다.

해설 목적어로 동명사구 expanding investment ～ 가 나오고 be동사 are와 함께 쓰여야 하므로 (D) considering이 정답이다.

어휘 according to ～에 의하면 | recently 최근에 | founded 설립된 | expand 확장하다 | investment 투자 | considerable 상당한 | considerate 사려 깊은

16. 이러한 간단한 규칙들을 준수함으로써, 여러분은 사무실 바깥에 있을 때도 보안을 유지할 수 있습니다.

해설 by -ing는 '～함으로써'의 의미로 (B) observing이 정답이 된다.

어휘 ensure 보장하다, 반드시 ～하게 하다 | security 보안 | outside 바깥에 | observe 준수하다

17. 마케팅 매니저는 회사의 이미지를 개선하기 위해 로고를 바꿀 것을 제안했다.

해설 suggest는 동명사를 목적어로 취하는 동사이므로 정답은 (B) changing이 된다.

어휘 enhance 향상시키다, 올리다

18. 신중한 계획 덕분에, 새 경기장 건설이 이 지역에 아주 작은 불편함도 거의 초래하지 않을 것이다.

해설 한정사(관사)가 없고 형용사 careful의 수식을 받으므로 빈칸에는 불가산 명사가 들어가야 한다. (A)와 (B)는 가산 명사이다. 불가산 명사인 (C) planning이 답으로 알맞다.

어휘 construction 건설 | very little 아주 작은 | inconvenience 불편함 | plan 계획 | planner 계획자, 입안자

19. 록스 산업은 재능 있는 지역 학생들을 지도하는 데 헌신하는 자선 재단을 만들었다.

해설 빈칸 뒤의 to mentoring으로 보아 전치사 to와 함께 쓰일 수 있는 동사를 찾아야 한다. 해석을 해보면 '～에 헌신하는 재단'이라는 의미가 적합하므로 정답은 (C) dedicated가 된다.

어휘 charitable 자선의 | foundation 재단 | mentor (멘토가) 지도하다 | talented 재능 있는 | agreeable 기분 좋은, 선뜻 동의하는 | dedicated 헌신적인, 전념하는 | capable 유능한, ～을 할 수 있는

20. 찰튼에 있는 아파트 구매를 결정하기 전에, 러셀 씨는 그 지역에 관해서 동료와 상의했다.

해설 전치사 before 뒤에 명사 혹은 동명사가 오는데 (B)는 앞에 관사가 없으므로 탈락시킨다. 뒤에 to부정사를 목적어로 취하는 동사 형태가 들어가야 하므로 정답은 (D) deciding이 된다.

어휘 consult 상의하다, 상담하다 | decide to ～하는 것을 결정하다

UNIT 14. 분사

1. **+ check** 1. (D) 2. (B) 3. (A) 본서 p.120

1. 환불이나 교환을 위해 물건을 돌려보내시기 전에 동봉된 서류들을 자세히 살펴보십시오.

해설 빈칸은 명사 documents를 수식하는 형용사 또는 분사 자리로 서류는 '동봉되는' 것이므로 (D) enclosed가 정답이다.

어휘 consult 참조하다 | refund 환불 | replacement 교체, 교환 | enclose 동봉하다

2. 학생들은 대학교 입학을 확인하는 신분증을 보여주기 위해 준비되어 있어야 한다.

해설 이미 동사 should be prepared가 나와 있으므로 (C)는 탈락이 되며, 해석상 명사 identification을 수식하는 형용사/분사가 필요하므로 (B) confirming이 정답이다.

어휘 identification 신분증 | enrollment 등록, 입학 | confirm 확인해주다 | confirmation 확인

3. 스마일 어게인 서비스의 설립자인 마이어스 씨는 회사가 고객들을 계속해서 만족시키는 것을 최우선 순위로 두어야 한다고 항상 강조한다.

해설 keep은 5형식 동사로 쓰일 때 목적어 뒤에 보어를 써야 하며, 해석상 고객들은 '만족하게 되는' 것이므로 수동의 과거분사 (A) satisfied가 정답이다.

어휘 founder 설립자 | emphasize 강조하다 | top priority 최우선 순위

2. **+ check** 1. (D) 2. (A) 3. (C) 본서 p.122

1. 전자레인지에서 뜨거운 음식을 꺼낼 때는, 손이 데는 것을 방지하기 위해 주방용 장갑을 꼭 이용하세요.

해설 접속사 When 뒤에는 주어, 동사가 와야 하지만, 분사 구문이 되어 -ing/p.p.도 올 수 있다. 빈칸 뒤에 목적어 hot food가 나오고 해석상 '～할 때'의 의미가 적합하므로 when -ing가 들어가도록 (D) removing이 정답이다.

어휘 microwave 전자레인지 | make sure to 반드시 ～하다 | avoid -ing ～하는 것을 피하다 | burn 화상을 입다

2. 지점 재정에 대한 회계 감사에서 몇 가지 불일치가 발견되어, 추가 조사가 필요했다.

해설 완전한 문장 뒤에, 즉 「S + V, -ing[p.p.]」를 가지는 분사 구문으로 빈칸 뒤에 목적어를 취하는 현재분사 (A) requiring이 정답이다.

어휘 audit 회계 감사 | branch 지점, 지사 | finance 재정, 재무 | reveal 드러내다, 밝히다 | inconsistency 불일치 | further 더 이상의, 추가의 | investigation 조사 | require 필요로 하다

3. 논의한 바와 같이, 당신의 급여는 인센티브와 회사 주식과 함께 연간 62,000달러가 될 것입니다.

해설 「As it is discussed, S + V」의 원래 문장에서 주절 전체를 가리키는 대명사 주어 it과 be동사 is가 생략된 분사구문이므로 (C) discussed가 정답이다.

어휘 as discussed 논의된 대로 | salary 급여 | incentive 인센티브 | stock share 주식

3. +check 1. (B) 2. (C) 3. (C) 본서 p.123

1. 회계부장인 마크 블랙모어의 검토를 위해 업데이트된 지출 보고서를 오늘 제출해 주세요.

해설 명사 expense report를 수식하는 형용사 또는 분사 문제로 '업데이트가 된' 것이므로 (B) updated가 정답이다.

어휘 expense report 지출 보고서 | accounting 회계

2. 기존 건물들의 개조를 포함하여, 어떠한 구조 변경도 건설 위원회의 승인을 받아야 한다.

해설 buildings라는 명사를 수식하는 형용사 또는 분사 문제로, 비록 수동의 의미로 해석한다고 할지라도 자동사는 과거분사가 아닌 현재분사로 사용되므로 (C) existing이 정답이다.

어휘 structural 구조적인 | renovation 개조 | approve 승인하다 | committee 위원회 | existence 존재 | existing 존재하는, 기존의

3. 시상식은 상공회의소 연례 박람회의 정점을 이루는 행사이다.

해설 빈칸은 명사 event를 수식하는 형용사 또는 분사 자리로 '절정에 달하는'이라는 의미의 (C) culminating이 정답이다.

어휘 banquet 연회 | culminating 절정에 달하는, 궁극의

Practice

본서 p.124

1. (C)	**2.** (C)	**3.** (D)	**4.** (A)	**5.** (C)
6. (C)	**7.** (B)	**8.** (C)	**9.** (B)	**10.** (D)
11. (B)	**12.** (D)	**13.** (C)	**14.** (C)	**15.** (A)
16. (C)	**17.** (B)	**18.** (B)	**19.** (C)	**20.** (B)

1. 동봉된 브로슈어는 호락스 배송에서 제공되는 서비스를 명시화해 놓은 것이며, 귀하께서 문의하신 것들은 녹색으로 강조 표시를 했습니다.

해설 이미 문장의 동사가 specifies로 나와 있으므로, (A), (D)는 정답이 될 수 없다. 빈칸에는 services를 뒤에서 수식하는 분사가 와야 하며, '제공되는 서비스'라는 수동의 의미가 적합하므로 과거분사인 (C) provided가 답이 된다.

어휘 enclosed 동봉된 | specify 명시화하다 | highlight 강조 표시를 하다 | inquire 문의하다

2. 마 씨는 중요한 고객과 약속을 하기 위해 늦어도 오늘 오후까지 그녀 여행 일정의 수정본을 받아야 한다.

해설 명사 copy를 수식하는 형용사 또는 분사를 찾는 문제로 '수정된 사본'의 의미인 수동의 의미가 들어가야 하므로 과거분사인 (C) revised가 답이 된다.

어휘 itinerary 여행 일정표 | at the latest 늦어도 | revised 수정된, 개정된

3. 퍼라 피트니스의 멤버십 계약에 따라, 48시간 이상 사물함에서 제거하지 않은 소지품은 폐기될 수 있다.

해설 belongings와 not 사이에 「주격 관계대명사 + be동사」 which are가 생략된 문장으로 문맥상 '48시간 이상 사물함에서 치워지지 않은 소지품'이라는 의미가 자연스러우므로 수동태 be p.p.를 완성하는 과거분사 (D) removed가 정답이다.

어휘 as per ~에 따라 | agreement 계약(서) | belongings 재산, 소유물 | locker 사물함, 개인 물품 보관함 | throw away ~을 버리다

4. 고용주들은 부상을 예방하기 위해서 업무 현장을 안전하게 하는 데 전념해야 한다.

해설 조동사(must) 다음에는 동사원형이 온다. be committed to -ing는 '~에 헌신하다[전념하다]'라는 의미이다. 이때 be동사는 대표적인 2형식 동사이므로 같은 계열(be/become/remain 등)의 동사를 찾으면 된다. 따라서 정답은 (A) remain이 된다.

어휘 employer 고용주 | workplace 업무 현장 | prevent 예방하다 | injury 부상 | be committed to -ing ~하는 데 헌신하다[전념하다]

5. 9시 이후에 사무실에서 일하는 직원들은 안내 데스크에 있는 경비원에게 알려야만 한다.

해설 Employees가 주어이고 are required to가 동사이므로, 동사인 (A), (B)는 탈락이 된다. 여기서 Employees라는 명사를 수식하는 분사는 현재분사와 과거분사가 있는데, 뒤에 in이라는 전치사가 동반된다고 해서 과거분사인 (D)를 고르지 않도록 조심한다. 왜냐하면, work는 자동사이므로 과거분사가 아닌 현재분사 형태로 나와야 한다. 따라서 정답은 (C) working이다.

어휘 inform 알리다 | security guard 경비원

6. 살세도 목장 견학은 온 가족이 즐길 수 있는 즐거운 활동이 많기 때문에 지루하지 않다.

해설 be동사 뒤 보어 자리이므로 형용사 역할이 가능한 분사 자리이다. '살세도 목장 견학은 즐거운 활동이 많아서 지루하지 않다'는 의미가 적절하며, bore는 '지루하게 하다'라는 뜻의 감정 동사로 서술하는 대상이 사물(A trip to Salcedo Ranch)이므로 현재분사 (C) boring이 정답이다.

어휘 ranch 목장 | seldom 좀처럼 ~않는 | since ~ 때문에 | plenty of 많은 | activity (취미 등의) 활동 | whole 전체의

7. 데프토 모터스에서 시장 조사원으로 인상적인 경력을 가진 유누스는 이제 경영에서 도전적인 역할을 하기 위해 고급 학위를 받을 계획이다.

해설 빈칸은 명사 role을 꾸며주는 형용사/분사 자리로, '도전적인 역할'이라는 의미를 만드는 (B) challenging이 정답이다.

어휘 follow (시간, 순서상) 뒤를 잇다, (결과가) 뒤따르다 | impressive 인상적인 | career 경력, 사회생활 | plan to ~할 계획이다 | seek 찾다, 구하다 | advanced degree (석사, 박사 등의) 고급 학위, 상위 학위 | in preparation for ~에 대비하여 | role 역할 | management 경영(진) | challenge 도전; 도전하다 | challenging 도전적인, 힘든

8. 레스터 로빈슨은 몇 분 동안만 영화에 출연했지만, 그의 극적인 연기는 영화 팬들에게 지속적인 영향을 끼쳤다.

해설 빈칸은 명사 impact를 수식하는 형용사/분사 자리로, endure는 '견디다, 참다'라는 뜻으로 쓰일 때는 타동사이지만, '오래가다, 지속되다'라는 뜻으로 쓰일 때는 자동사이다. 이 문제에서는 의미상 자동사의

분사 형태가 적절하므로 (C) enduring이 정답이다.

어휘 appear 출연하다 | dramatic 극적인 | acting 연기 | impact 영향 | moviegoer 영화 팬 | endure 오래가다, 지속되다 | enduring 오래가는

9. 서울에서 부산까지 급행열차 이동 시간은 두 번의 예정된 5분간의 정차를 포함해 세 시간이 채 걸리지 않는다.

해설 빈칸은 명사구 5-minute stops를 수식하는 자리이다. '예정된 5분의 정차'라는 의미가 되어야 문맥상 자연스러우므로 과거분사 (B) scheduled가 정답이다.

어휘 express train 급행열차 | ride 타기, 타고 있는 시간 | stop 멈춤, 정차, 정지

10. 교차로에 접근할 때는, 속도를 줄여서 모든 방향에서 오는 차를 잘 살펴봐야 한다.

해설 주어가 생략된 「접속사 + 분사」 구문이다. 목적어 an intersection이 있으므로 현재분사형으로 쓰이는 (D) approaching이 정답이다.

어휘 intersection 교차로 | slow down 속도를 늦추다 | watch for ~을 가만히 기다리다 | direction 방향 | approach 접근하다

11. 주주총회 중에 의견을 내고자 하는 사람은 매닝 씨에게 먼저 문의해야 한다.

해설 빈칸은 문장의 주어인 Anyone을 수식하는 분사 자리이며 빈칸 뒤 동사 wish의 목적어에 해당하는 to부정사가 있으므로 현재분사 (B) wishing이 정답이다.

어휘 confer 주다 | comment 의견 | shareholder meeting 주주총회 | refer to ~에게 문의하다

12. 체리돔 대학은 지난주에 학교 웹사이트에 접근할 수 없었던 학생들에게 연장된 마감을 허용할 것이다.

해설 명사 deadline을 수식하는 형용사 또는 분사가 들어가야 한다. 보통은 형용사가 답이 될 수 있지만 extensive는 '광범위한'이라는 뜻이라 의미상 맞지 않고 '연장된 마감'이 적합하므로 정답은 분사형 형용사인 (D) extended가 된다.

어휘 grant 승인하다, 수여하다 | be unable to ~할 수 없다 | access 접근하다 | extensive 광범위한 | extend 넓히다 | extended 연장된

13. 별다른 언급 사항이 없으면, 25일까지 모든 월간 보고서를 제출해야 합니다.

해설 unless라는 접속사 뒤에는 「주어 + 동사」가 나와야 하는데, 그렇지 않은 경우 분사 구문을 물어보는 문제이다. 뒤에 목적어가 없으므로 과거분사인 (C) instructed가 정답이 된다. 혹은 unless instructed otherwise라고 해서 '별다른 지시 사항이 없으면'이라고 암기해도 좋다.

어휘 submit 제출하다 | monthly report 월간 보고서 | unless instructed otherwise 별다른 지시 사항이 없으면

14. 고객들과 주주들의 높은 기대에 부응했기 때문에, 케빈은 연례 검토 후 많은 급여 인상을 받았다.

해설 '기대에 부응했기 때문'이라는 '이유'의 의미가 되어야 하므로 목적(~하기 위하여)을 나타내는 to부정사구는 답이 될 수 없다. As he had met에서 「접속사 + 주어」가 생략되고, 주절의 시제(was given)보다 먼저 일어난 일이기 때문에 「Having + 과거분사(met)」으로 쓰여야 하므로 (C) Having이 정답이다.

어휘 meet (요구 등을) 충족시키다 | expectation 기대 | shareholder 주주 | salary raise 급여 인상 | annual 연례의 | review 검토, 논평

15. 방문객들은 어퍼 캠퍼스 주차장의 지정된 구역에 차량을 주차해야만 한다.

해설 빈칸에는 area라는 명사를 수식하는 형용사 또는 분사가 필요하다. 해석을 하면 '지정된 구역'이라는 내용이 적합하므로 정답은 (A) designated가 된다.

어휘 parking lot 주차장 | designated 지정된

16. 산제브는 회사의 3년간의 주니어 분석 프로그램을 완료하여, 투자 은행가로 고용될 수 있는 자격을 얻었다.

해설 becoming ~ 분사 구문으로 주절의 completed와 함께 행해지는 것을 의미한다. 해석상 '~함으로써, ~하면서'의 의미가 가장 자연스러우므로 정답은 (C) thereby가 된다.

어휘 complete 완료하다 | analyst 분석 | eligible for ~에 자격이 있는 | hire 고용 | investment 투자 | banker 은행가

17. 굿트립 관광은 최근에 새로운 여행 상품을 도입했으며 판촉 활동으로 할인된 가격에 판매하고 있다.

해설 '할인된 가격'이라는 의미가 되어야 하므로 정답은 과거분사인 (B) reduced가 된다.

어휘 introduce 소개하다, 도입하다 | promotional 홍보의, 판촉의 | at a reduced rate 할인된 가격에

18. 합격자는 높은 급여와 업계에서 가장 최고의 복지 혜택을 받을 것이다.

해설 해석에만 의존해 '만족된 급여'라고 해서 (A) satisfied를 고르지 않도록 한다. satisfied는 감정의 주체인 사람이 나올 때 쓸 수 있는 단어인데, salary는 감정의 주체(사람)가 아니므로, 정답은 '경쟁적인 급여, 높은 급여'의 의미가 되는 (B) competitive가 정답이 된다.

어휘 successful candidate 합격자 | benefits package 복지 혜택 | competitive salary 높은 연봉 | preventable 막을 수 있는, 예방할 수 있는

19. 직무 기술서에 언급된 바와 같이, 모든 신입 사원은 이곳에서 일을 시작한 후 3개월 이내에 면허 시험에 합격해야 한다.

해설 해석상 직무 기술서에 '언급된 대로'라는 의미는 분사 구문인 As mentioned로 표현하므로 접속사 (C) As가 정답이 된다.

어휘 job description 직무 기술서 | pass 합격하다, 통과하다 | licensing exam 면허 시험 | as mentioned 언급된 바와 같이

20. 많은 사람들은 석유 공급량이 작년에 보았던 다시 활기를 띤 성장세를 지속하면서 반등할 수 있다고 믿는다.

해설 뒤 문장의 생략된 주어 oil supply가 이러한 성장세를 '지속하는' 것이
므로 능동의 뜻을 가진 현재분사가 빈칸에 적절하다. 콤마 뒤에 목적
어 the trend를 동반하면서 콤마 앞뒤의 내용을 이어주는 역할을 하
려면 동사의 분사형인 (B) continuing이 필요하다.

어휘 oil supply 석유 공급 | rebound 다시 튀어 오르다, 반등하다 |
trend 동향, 추세 | reinvigorate 새로운 활기를 불어넣다 | growth
성장, 증가 | continual 거듭되는, 반복되는

UNIT 15. 비교·가정법·도치

1. + check   1. (C)   2. (B)   3. (B)   본서 p.127

1. 회사 역사상 가장 높은 매출 증가로 인해, 전문경영인은 전 직원들이
작년보다 훨씬 더 많은 보너스를 받을 거라고 발표했다.

해설 빈칸 뒤에 비교급 larger가 쓰였으므로 '훨씬 더'라는 의미로 비교급
을 강조해주는 부사 (C) even이 정답이다.

어휘 owing to ~으로 인해

2. 폴란스키 신발은 이탈리아의 모든 제조업체 중에서 최고의 수제 가
죽 신발을 만든다.

해설 빈칸은 정관사와 명사 사이에서 명사를 수식할 형용사를 쓸 자리이며,
'모든 제조업체 중에서'라는 의미인 of any manufacturer가 비교 대
상을 셋 이상 제시하고 있으므로 최상급인 (B) finest가 정답이다.

어휘 handmade 수제의 | manufacturer 생산자, 제조업체

3. 시내에 아파트를 임차하는 것보다는, 가까운 교외에 집을 사는 것을
고려해야 한다.

해설 해석을 해보면 '~보다 (오히려)'의 의미가 적합하므로 (B) Rather
than이 정답이다.

어휘 rent 세내다, 임차하다, 세 놓다, 임대하다 | downtown 시내에 |
nearby 인근의, 가까운 곳의 | suburb 교외 | considering
how 얼마나 ~인가를 고려하면 | rather than ~보다는, ~대신에 |
assuming that ~이라 가정하여 | much less 하물며 ~은
아니다

2. + check   1. (C)   2. (D)   3. (D)   본서 p.128

1. 온라인으로 회원 등록을 하시면, 다가올 행사와 할인 판매 정보가 담
긴 월간 소식지를 받게 됩니다.

해설 if라고 해서 다 같은 if가 아니라, 조건 아니면 가정법으로 사용할 수
있다. 이 문장의 if는 조건의 접속사로 주절의 시제가 미래일 때, 종속
절은 현재 시제를 쓴다. 그러므로 (C) will be sent가 정답이다.

어휘 sign up for ~을 신청하다 | newsletter 소식지, 회보

2. 호프만 씨가 일찍 건축 디자인을 수정했더라면, 그는 3월 말 전에
프로젝트를 시작할 수 있었을 것이다.

해설 if절에 들어가는 접속사로 뒤에 could have p.p.가 나오는 가정법
과거 완료가 적합하다. if절에는 과거 완료가 들어가야 하므로 (D)
had revised가 정답이다.

어휘 revise 수정하다

3. 알바레즈 씨가 사무실이 2주 동안 리모델링될 것이라고 통보를 받았
더라면, 그 시간 동안 휴가를 신청했을 것이다.

해설 if절의 동사가 가정법 과거 완료의 형태인 had been이므로, 빈칸
에는 「조동사의 과거형 + have p.p.」 형태가 와야 한다. 정답은 (D)
could have put이 된다.

어휘 notify 알리다 | put in a request 신청하다

3. + check   1. (B)   2. (D)   3. (C)   본서 p.129

1. 라모로의 투자자들은 회사의 재정 안정성에 자신감을 가지고 있기
때문에 합병 소식은 회사의 주가에 조금도 불리하게 악영향을 미치
지 않았다.

해설 문두에 쓰인 부정의 부사구 In no way '조금도 ~않다' 때문에 도치
구문을 써야 하므로 주어 the news 앞에 did가 쓰였다. 조동사 did
뒤에는 동사원형을 써야 하므로 (B) affect가 정답이다.

어휘 merger 합병 | adversely 불리하게, 반대로 | stock price 주가 |
have confidence in ~을 신뢰하다 | financial stability 재정
안정성

2. 최근에서야 공장 매니저들은 1,000개 이상의 새 마이크가 결함이 발
견되었음을 확인했다.

해설 Only recently가 문두에 쓰이면 도치 구문을 써야 하므로, 동사
have가 주어 앞으로 도치된 구문으로 빈칸에는 have와 함께 쓰이
는 과거분사 (D) confirmed가 정답이다.

어휘 defective 결함 있는 | confirm ~을 확인하다

3. 마이클 민이 디자인한 피완 타워는 그의 다른 건축 프로젝트들과 마
찬가지로 걸출한 작품이다.

해설 「as are + 주어」의 도치 구문을 쓰면 '~하듯이'라는 의미의 접속사
as의 관용 용법이다. 그러므로 (C) as are가 정답이다.

어휘 outstanding 뛰어난, 걸출한 | architectural 건축의

Practice   본서 p.130

1. (C)	2. (B)	3. (C)	4. (D)	5. (A)
6. (B)	7. (A)	8. (C)	9. (B)	10. (B)
11. (B)	12. (B)	13. (A)	14. (C)	15. (D)
16. (C)	17. (B)	18. (D)	19. (A)	20. (B)

1. 제이에이치지 장비 사의 최신 복사기는 생생한 컬러의 사진들을 만
들어내고 만 3년의 품질보증이 딸려 있다.

해설 명사 photocopiers 앞에 들어가는 형용사 자리로 빈칸 앞에 소유격
's가 나오므로 최상급이 들어가야 한다. 그러므로 형용사의 최상급인
(C) latest가 답이 된다.

어휘 photocopier 복사기 | vivid 생생한, 선명한 | warranty 품질보증
서 | late 늦은; 늦게 | lately 최근에 | later 나중에

2. 오스쿠리얀카 식당은 모든 요리에 시중에서 가장 신선한 해산물만을
사용합니다.

해설 관사와 명사 사이에 들어가는 형용사 자리이다. 해석을 해보면 '가장
신선한 해산물'이라는 의미의 최상급이 필요한데 뒤의 명사를 수식하

는 형용사의 최상급이 필요하므로 정답은 (B) freshest가 된다.

어휘 available 이용할 수 있는 | dish 요리

3. 완전히 기재해서 7일 이내에 내야 할 지원서가 편지와 함께 첨부되어 있다.

해설 주어가 길어서 문장의 균형을 위해 도치가 사용되었다. 원래 문장은 An application form ～ is attached along ～. 가 된다. 그러므로 정답은 (C) Attached가 된다. 「Enclosed[Attached] ～ be동사 + 주어」가 도치 구문에 잘 쓰이므로 기억해 두도록 한다.

어휘 along with ～과 함께 | application form 지원서, 신청서 | fill out 기재하다 | attached 첨부된

4. 곤잘레스 씨가 나에게 회의 때문에 뉴욕에 방문하고 있었다는 것을 알렸다면, 내가 공항으로 그를 마중 나갔을 것이다.

해설 if절의 시제가 과거 완료 had informed이므로 가정법 과거 완료 구문이다. 주절은 「조동사의 과거형 + have + p.p.」 형태가 되어야 하므로 (D) would have picked가 정답이 된다.

어휘 inform 알리다 | pick up ～을 태우러 가다

5. 칼스턴 수출은 고장 난 기계를 교체하는 것이 수리하는 것보다 훨씬 더 저렴하다고 결론 내렸다.

해설 비교급을 수식할 수 있는 강조 부사에는 still, even, much, far, a lot 등이 있다. 따라서 (A) much가 정답이다.

어휘 replace 교체하다 | broken equipment 고장 난 기계 | fix 고치다

6. 마샬 씨는 다음 달에 상해로 거처를 옮김에도 불구하고, 바로 최근에서야 중국어 공부를 시작했다.

해설 Only recently가 문두에 나오면서 동사와 주어가 도치되었다. recently는 과거 완료 또는 현재 완료 시제와 잘 사용되고 이미 has 라는 동사가 나왔으므로 빈칸에는 과거분사인 (B) started가 들어가야 한다. Mr. Marshall has only recently started studying Chinese에서 only recently가 강조를 위해 문두로 나온 문장이다.

어휘 only recently 바로 최근에 | even though 심지어 ～에도 불구하고 | move to ～로 거처를 옮기다

7. 흡연 여성의 일상생활은 남성의 것보다 더 악영향을 받는다.

해설 than이 나오므로 비교급의 형태를 묻는 문제이다. 동사인 are affected를 수식하는 부사의 비교급을 찾아야 하므로 정답은 (A) more adversely가 된다.

어휘 daily life 일상생활 | counterpart 상대방 | adversely affect 악영향을 미치다

8. 호텔을 좀 더 일찍 예약했더라면, 참가자들을 한 호텔에 모두 수용할 수 있었을 것이다.

해설 주절의 시제가 「조동사의 과거형(might) + have + 과거분사(been)」 가 나오는 가정법 과거완료 구문이다. 주절은 「If + 주어 + 과거 완료 (had + p.p.)」의 형태이어야 하는데 If가 생략되어 주어와 동사가 도치 되어 있다. '예약되었다'라는 수동의 의미가 들어가야 하므로 정답은

(C) been made이다.

어휘 reservation 예약 | accommodate 수용하다 | participant 참가자

9. 그 지역에 위치한 편의점 중에서, 에프앤씨 상점이 사무실에서 가장 쉽게 갈 수 있는 곳이다.

해설 비교 범위를 나타내는 부사구 Among ～ area가 강조를 위해 문두로 나왔다. 빈칸에는 '가장 ～한'이라는 의미의 be동사의 보어 역할을 하 는 형용사의 최상급이 필요하므로 정답은 (B) easiest가 된다. F&C Store is the easiest (store) ～ among the convenience stores ～. 의 문장에서 뒤의 among 이하가 강조를 위해 문두로 온 것이다.

어휘 convenience store 편의점 | locate 위치시키다 | easy to get to ～에 가기 쉬운

10. 실버 박물관을 방문하는 여행객들의 숫자가 증가함에 따라, 관광 안내인의 필요성도 증가한다.

해설 동사 does 다음에 주어(the need ～ guides)가 나온 도치 구문이다. so가 문두에 올 경우 주어와 동사의 도치가 일어난다. 따라서 (B) so가 정답이다. so, neither, nor로 시작하는 문장이나 절의 경우 주어와 동사의 도치가 일어난다.

어휘 as ～함에 따라 | tour guide 관광 안내인

11. 몇 개의 추가적인 옵션들이 있기는 하지만, 새 에스엑스500 모델은 예전 것과 거의 같은 특징들을 갖고 있다.

해설 'B와 같은 A'라는 의미가 들어가도록 the same A as B가 되어야 하므로 정답은 (B) as가 된다.

어휘 feature 특징, 특색 | previous 이전의 | the same A as B B와 같은 A

12. 린 씨는 그녀 자신에 대해 가장 신랄한 비평가이기 때문에 자기의 그림에 대해 만족하지 못했다.

해설 critic이라는 명사를 수식하는 형용사로 (B)와 (D)가 정답이 될 수 있다. 앞에 소유격이 나오며, 소유격 뒤에는 최상급이 들어가야 하므로 정답은 (D) harshest이다.

어휘 be satisfied with ～에 만족하다 | critic 비평가, 평론가 | harsh 가혹한, 냉혹한

13. 두 품목의 판매 수치를 비교해 볼 때, 에미 캠프파이어의 하이킹복은 그것의 하이킹 장화만큼 인기가 있다.

해설 「as + 형용사/부사 + as」 구문이다. are의 보어로 형용사가 와야 하므로 정답은 (A) popular가 된다.

어휘 compare 비교하다 | sales figures 판매 수치 | outfit 옷, 의복

14. 엔리케 씨는 회사 사무실을 위해 가장 밝은 조명을 주문했다.

해설 '가장 ～한/하게'의 뜻을 가진 「the + 형용사/부사의 최상급 + possible」이 들어가야 하므로 정답은 (C) brightest가 된다.

어휘 the brightest possible 가장 밝은

15. 인사팀에서 인터뷰한 모든 후보자들 중에서, 레이첼이 가장 높은 자격을 갖춘 사람으로 눈에 띄었다.

해설 주절에 the most highly qualified라는 최상급이 있다. 최상급은 보통 비교 범위로 같이 사용되며 '인사팀이 인터뷰한 모든 후보자들 중에서'라는 의미로는 전치사 of가 적합하므로 정답은 (D) Of가 된다.

어휘 candidate 후보자, 지원자 I interview 면접을 보다 I stand out 눈에 띄다, 빼어나다 I highly qualified 뛰어난 자격을 갖춘

16. 모든 지원자는 늦어도 5월 15일까지 반드시 서류를 제출해야 한다.

해설 해석을 해보면 '늦어도 5월 15일까지'라는 의미가 되어야 하므로 (C) no later than이 들어가야 한다.

어휘 applicant 지원자 I submit 제출하다 I more than ~이상 I rather than ~이라기 보다는 I no later than 늦어도 ~까지 I no longer than 더 이상 ~아닌

17. 피어센트 신문의 새로운 전문경영인은 그의 전임자보다 그것의 재정적인 어려움을 극복하기 위한 훨씬 더 대담한 조치들을 고려하고 있다.

해설 빈칸 앞에 비교급 강조 부사 much가 나오고 빈칸 뒤에 than이 나오므로 정답은 비교급 (B) bolder이다.

어휘 overcome 극복하다 I financial difficulty 재정적 어려움 I predecessor 전임자 I bold 용감한, 대담한

18. 주요 한국 회사들의 연간 수입은 한국의 국내 총생산에 훨씬 더 강한 영향을 미친다.

해설 명사 influence 앞에 들어가는 형용사 문제이다. 앞에 even이라는 비교급 강조 부사가 있으므로 정답은 비교급 (D) stronger가 된다.

어휘 annual 매년의 I revenue 수입 I influence 영향 I gross domestic product 국내 총생산

19. 모리스 씨는 인터뷰 일정을 조정하는 것뿐만 아니라 사무용품을 주문하는 일도 책임지게 될 것이다.

해설 Not only ~ but also 구문이다. 부정어가 문장 앞으로 나왔으므로 주어 Ms. Morris와 동사 will이 도치되어 있다. 정답은 (A) Not only가 된다.

어휘 arrange 준비하다, 조정하다 I be responsible for ~을 책임지다 I office supplies 사무용품 I not only A but also B A뿐만 아니라 B도 I so as to ~하기 위해서 I in spite of ~에도 불구하고

20. 리스 기간이 종료된 후 차량 손상이 발견될 경우 수리 비용을 부담해야 할 수 있습니다.

해설 가정법 구문으로 if damage to the vehicle should be discovered ~ 이하에서 if가 생략되어서 should damage to the vehicle be discovered로 도치가 된 형태이다. 따라서 정답은 (B) should가 된다.

어휘 cover 돈을 대다, 부담하다 I repair fee 수리 비용 I damage 손상, 파손

REVIEW TEST 04
본서 p.132

1. (C)	**2.** (A)	**3.** (D)	**4.** (D)	**5.** (B)
6. (D)	**7.** (C)	**8.** (C)	**9.** (D)	**10.** (C)
11. (D)	**12.** (C)	**13.** (C)	**14.** (C)	**15.** (B)
16. (D)	**17.** (D)	**18.** (C)	**19.** (A)	**20.** (A)

1. 반품된 모든 제품들은 고객의 이유를 설명하는 메모와 함께 데이터베이스에 기록되어야 한다.

해설 빈칸은 명사 products를 수식하는 형용사 자리이므로 동사 return(반품하다)의 과거분사인 (C) returned가 정답이다.

어휘 record 기록하다 I return 반품하다

2. 우리는 선루프와 같은 불필요한 옵션을 선택하지 않기로 결정했기 때문에, 우리가 구매한 새 차는 예상보다 훨씬 더 저렴했다.

해설 빈칸 뒤에 than이라는 비교급이 나왔으므로 빈칸에는 비교급을 강조하는 부사가 들어가야 한다. 따라서 정답은 (A) much이다.

어휘 unnecessary 불필요한 I option (자동차의) 옵션 I sunroof 선루프(자동차의 개폐식 지붕) I expect 예상하다

3. 루크 하이메이아는 그의 회사에서 특별히 능력 있는 프로그래머이자 디자이너로 인정받아 왔다.

해설 빈칸은 형용사 skilled를 수식하는 부사나 명사 programmer를 수식하는 형용사 자리로 판단할 수 있는데, 의미상 '특별히 능력 있는 프로그래머'라는 의미가 자연스러우므로 부사 (D) exceptionally가 정답이다.

어휘 recognize (공로를) 인정하다 I skilled 숙련된, 노련한 I exceptional 이례적일 정도로 우수한, 극히 예외적인

4. 부서 간 협력을 도모하기 위해, 저희가 주간 리뷰 회의를 마련했습니다.

해설 빈칸은 명사구와 주절을 연결하는 자리이므로 빈칸 뒤 명사구를 목적어로 삼아 to부정사구를 만들어 주절과 연결해 주는 (D) To facilitate가 정답이다.

어휘 cooperation 협력, 협조 I department 부서 I set up 마련하다, 설치하다 I weekly 주간의 I review 재검토, 리뷰 I facilitate 가능하게 하다

5. 대중의 요구에 부응하여, 산마르코 마트는 평일 시간을 연장하고 일요일에도 문을 열기로 합의했다.

해설 빈칸은 명사 자리로써, 「in + 명사 + to」의 형태로 쓰이는 명사는 보기 중 (B) response뿐이다. '대중의 요구에 ~하여, 일요일에도 문을 열기로 했다'는 의미이므로, '~에 부응하여[대응하여]'라는 뜻의 in response to가 되어야 하므로 정답은 (B) response가 된다.

어휘 popular demand 대중의 요구 I extend 연장하다 I weekday 평일 I counter 계산대, 반작용, 반대 I response 부응, 반응 I cooperation 협력

6. 계약서에 명시된 대로, 물건은 매달 10일에 배송되어야만 한다.

해설 as는 주로 접속사로 사용되며, 접속사 뒤에는 「주어 + 동사」가 나와야 하지만 그렇지 않은 경우는 분사구문이 되어서 뒤에 -ing 또는 p.p.가 온다. 뒤에 목적어 없이 전치사가 나오므로 정답은 과거분사인 (D) indicated가 된다. as indicated를 '명시된 대로'라는 하나의 굳어진 표현으로 암기해 두면 좋다.

어휘 indicative ~을 나타내는 | indication 암시, 조짐 | as indicated 명시된 대로

7. 우리 투자 관계 부서는 올해 우리 회사 자체 스마트폰 제품군을 출시할 계획이라는 보도 자료를 웹사이트에 게시했다.

해설 빈칸은 to부정사를 목적어로 취하므로 (C) intend가 정답이다. intend to는 '~할 예정이다[의도이다]'라는 의미이다. consider는 뒤에 동명사가 나와야 하므로 답이 될 수 없다.

어휘 post 게시하다 | press release 보도 자료, 언론 발표 | state 말하다 | launch 출시하다 | foresee 예상하다 | intend 의도하다 | consider 고려하다

8. 벤자민 마르티네즈는 그의 인상적인 이력서 때문에 수석 연구원직을 제안받을 가능성이 크다.

해설 빈칸은 명사 résumé를 수식하는 형용사 자리이다. (A) qualified '자격 요건을 갖춘'와 (B) skillful '숙련된'이 함정으로 나와 있는데 이 어휘들은 의미상 사람을 수식하는 형용사이므로 오답이다. 정답은 résumé를 의미상 적절하게 수식할 수 있는 (C) impressive가 된다.

어휘 senior researcher 수석 연구원직 | on account of ~때문에, ~으로 | résumé 이력서 | qualified 자격이 있는 | skillful 숙련된, 능숙한 | impressive 인상적인 | informed 잘 아는, 많이 아는

9. 에이미 플라워 사는 수선화뿐만 아니라, 매우 다양한 여름꽃들을 국내 전역의 유통업자들에게 공급합니다.

해설 빈칸은 전치사 to의 목적어 자리이므로 명사가 와야 한다. 문맥상 '다양한 여름꽃들을 국내 전역의 유통업자들에게 공급한다'는 의미가 되어야 하므로 빈칸에는 '유통업자들'이라는 의미의 명사가 와야 한다. 따라서 (D) distributors가 정답이다.

어휘 in addition to ~에 더해서, ~뿐만 아니라 | daffodil 수선화 | supply 공급하다, 제공하다 | a wide range of 다양한, 광범위한 | distribute 배포하다, 유통시키다 | distribution 배포, 유통 | distributor 유통업자

10. 전화로 귀하의 제품에 대해 도움을 받으시려면 프론티어 사의 고객 서비스 센터에 전화하십시오.

해설 동사원형 Call로 시작하는 명령문 구조로 동사 (A), (B)는 제외시키며, '도움을 받기 위해 고객 서비스 센터에 전화하라'는 의미이므로 to부정사의 부사적 용법으로 쓰여 목적을 나타내는 (C) to receive가 정답이다.

어휘 customer service center 고객 서비스 센터 | assistance 도움

11. 케이티씨지 사는 현재 B구역이 공사 중이기 때문에 K구역에 차량을 주차하도록 직원들에게 권하고 있다.

해설 빈칸은 be동사의 보어 자리로서, 빈칸 뒤에 있는 under construction 「전치사 + 명사」가 이미 형용사로 보어 역할을 하고 있으므로 형용사

를 수식하는 부사가 와야 한다. 따라서 정답은 (D) currently이다.

어휘 encourage 권장하다, 장려하다 | under construction 공사 중인 | current 현재의 | currently 현재

12. 직원들은 무급 휴가를 신청할 수 있는데, 그것은 그들의 관리자의 승인을 받아야 한다.

해설 빈칸은 전치사 to의 목적어 자리이므로 명사가 와야 한다. 따라서 (C) approval이 정답이다.

어휘 request 신청하다, 요청하다 | unpaid leave of absence 무급 휴가 | be subject to ~의 대상이다 | supervisor 관리자, 감독관 | approve 승인하다 | approval 승인 | approvingly 찬성하여

13. 엑스티엠 스포츠웨어의 연구개발팀은 극한의 기후 상태에 견딜 수 있는 새로운 직물을 개발하는 작업을 해왔다.

해설 「전치사 + 동명사」 문제이다. 전치사 뒤에 빈칸이 쓰였으며 빈칸 뒤에 목적어가 쓰였으므로 동명사인 (C) developing이 정답이다. (B)는 명사를 수식하는 과거분사로 보면 '개발된 새로운 직물에 대해 작업했다'로 해석되어 어색하므로 정답이 될 수 없다.

어휘 fabric 직물 | withstand ~을 견디다 | extreme 극한의, 극심한

14. 현재의 전자 상거래 사업 상황이 낙관적인 만큼, 미래는 훨씬 더 유망해 보인다.

해설 빈칸은 looks의 보어 자리로 more와 함께 비교급을 완성하는 형용사가 와야 하며, 문맥상 '촉망되는, 유망한'이 적합하므로 정답은 (C) promising이 된다.

어휘 positive 긍정적인, 낙관적인 | current state 현황 | e-commerce 전자 상거래 | promising 유망한

15. 이전 회의에서 논의된 바와 같이, 회사는 계약서의 세부사항을 밝히지 않을 것입니다.

해설 빈칸은 분사 구문을 만드는 동사 자리로써, 뒤에 목적어가 없으므로 과거분사인 (B) discussed가 정답이다.

어휘 previous 이전의 | disclose 밝히다, 폭로하다 | detail 세부사항 | contract 계약(서)

16. 고객님의 정보를 받으면 고객 담당자가 3일 이내에 고객님의 할인 내역을 확정해 드리겠습니다.

해설 빈칸은 앞뒤 문장을 연결하는 접속사 자리이다. 문맥상 '고객의 정보를 받은 후 3일 이내에 할인 내역을 확정해 주겠다'는 의미가 되어야 하므로 빈칸에는 '일단 ~하면'이라는 의미의 접속사가 와야 한다. 따라서 (D) once가 정답이다.

어휘 confirm 확정하다, 사실임을 보여주다 | discount 할인

17. 하이임베르크 가구의 회장인 하인리히 니센은 직원 노동조합 설립 제안을 지지하지도, 반대하지도 않는다.

해설 빈칸 뒤에 nor를 보고 상관접속사 neither A nor B 'A도, B도 아닌' 구문을 떠올릴 수 있어야 한다. 따라서 (D) neither가 정답이다.

어휘 support 지지하다 | oppose 반대하다 | proposal 제안 | labor union 노동조합

18. 매우 기대를 모은 기자회견에서, 청 씨는 자사의 최신 태양열 페인트 제품라인을 선보였다.

해설 빈칸은 과거분사 anticipated를 수식하는 부사 자리이다. '매우 기대를 모은 기자회견에서 최신 제품을 선보였다'는 의미가 되어야 자연스러우므로 (C) highly가 정답이다. 부사 highly와 짝을 이뤄 자주 출제되는 표현인 highly recommended '매우 추천되는', highly anticipated '매우 기대되는', highly qualified '매우 자격을 갖춘, 자격이 아주 뛰어난'를 기억해 두자.

어휘 anticipate 기대하다 ᛁ press conference 기자회견 ᛁ present 제시하다 ᛁ latest 최신의 ᛁ line (상품의) 종류 ᛁ solar paint 태양열 페인트(태양열을 흡수해 에너지를 만들 수 있도록 개발된 페인트) ᛁ customarily 관례상 ᛁ effectually 효과적으로, 완전하게, 적절하게, 실제로 ᛁ highly 매우 ᛁ promptly 지체 없이

19. 계절에 따른 수요로 인해, 주문 처리가 평소보다 하루 더 오래 걸릴 수 있습니다.

해설 빈칸 뒤에 than이 있으므로 비교급 문장구조를 완성하는 부사의 비교급 (A) longer가 정답이다.

어휘 seasonal 계절의 ᛁ demand 수요 ᛁ process 처리하다 ᛁ order 주문 ᛁ than usual 평소보다

20. 그리폰 경비는 회사 웹사이트를 통해 제출되는 모든 고객 불만사항에 하루 안에 답변할 것이다.

해설 빈칸은 명사구 customer complaints를 후치수식하는 분사 자리이다. '고객 불만은 웹사이트를 통해 제출되는' 것이므로 수동 의미관계를 완성하는 과거분사 (A) filed가 정답이다.

어휘 reply 답변하다 ᛁ within ~이내에 ᛁ complaint 불만사항 ᛁ file 제출하다

VOCA

UNIT 01. 동사 어휘 1

본서 p.137

Practice

1. (D)	2. (D)	3. (D)	4. (D)	5. (B)
6. (B)	7. (C)	8. (D)	9. (B)	10. (C)

1. 해외 관리자들은 임금과 근로 조건에 관한 모든 국내법을 준수해야 한다.

해설 빈칸 뒤에 전치사 with가 나오며 '국내 법을 지키다[준수하다]'의 의미가 들어가야 하므로 (D) comply가 정답이다. 만약 with가 뒤에 없다면 (A)가 답이 될 수 있다.

어휘 overseas 해외의 ᛁ regarding ~에 관하여 ᛁ wage 임금 ᛁ working conditions 근로 조건 ᛁ observe 준수하다 ᛁ concern 관련되다, 걱정스럽게 하다 ᛁ accommodate 수용하다 ᛁ comply with 따르다, 준수하다

2. 직원들은 제조 장비 문제를 신속하게 처리해야 한다.

해설 빈칸 뒤에 목적어 issues가 나오는 타동사로 '~을 처리하다'의 개념이 들어가야 하므로 (D) address가 정답이다.

어휘 manufacture 제조하다 ᛁ in a prompt manner 신속한 방법으로 ᛁ inform 알리다 ᛁ address 처리하다

3. 아이유 솔루션즈는 유럽에서의 회사 성장에 맞추기 위해 버밍햄에 새 지사를 열 것이다.

해설 회사의 성장을 수용하기 위해 버밍햄에 새 지사를 열 거라는 의미가 적절하므로 (D) accommodate가 정답이다.

어휘 regional office 지사 ᛁ insulate 보호하다, 격려하다 ᛁ participate 참가하다 ᛁ designate 지정하다, 지명하다 ᛁ accommodate 맞추다, 수용하다

4. 스마트 스토리즈가 브릴리언트 북스를 9월에 인수하면, 두 출판사의 겹치는 부서는 재편성될 것이다.

해설 회사를 '인수하다, 합병하다'라는 의미가 적합한데 merge는 자동사로 merge with로 쓰이므로 타동사인 (D) acquires가 정답이다.

어휘 overlap 겹치다 ᛁ restructure 구조 조정하다, 재편성하다 ᛁ merge 합병하다 ᛁ anticipate 기대하다 ᛁ acquire 인수하다

5. 기자 회견에서, 전문경영인은 데니스 씨가 4월에 새 마케팅 부장직을 떠맡을 것이라고 발표했다.

해설 빈칸 뒤에 position을 목적어로 취하므로 '떠맡다'의 의미인 (B) assume이 정답이다. assume the position[title]이라고 해서 '직책을 떠맡다'로 같이 암기해 두면 좋다.

어휘 press conference 기자 회견 ᛁ engage 종사하다 ᛁ assume(= take on) 떠맡다 ᛁ evolve 진화하다 ᛁ promote 홍보하다

6. 시티 쇼어 유틸리티스의 배관담당자가 수도관을 점검하기 위해서 오후 1시에 패럿 건물을 방문할 것입니다.

해설 배관공이 오는 것은 문제를 점검하기 위해서 오는 것이므로 해석상 가장 자연스러운 (B) assess가 정답이다.

어휘 plumber 배관공 | utility (수도·전기·가스 같은) 공익사업 | premises 부지, 건물 | assess 평가하다 | proceed 진행하다

7. 개별 접속 코드들은 그 시설에서 일하도록 허가받은 직원들에게 주어질 것이다.

해설 허가받은 직원들에게 개별 접속 코드가 주어질 거라는 의미가 적합하므로 (C) authorized가 정답이다.

어휘 individual 개개의, 각각의 | access code 접속 코드 | personnel 직원 | facility 시설 | accrue 누적되다, 누적하다 | adapt 맞추다, 적응하다 | authorize 재가하다, 권한을 부여하다 | adjust 조절하다, 바로잡다

8. 탄도 사는 지금까지 1년 차 직원에게 이렇게 큰 보너스를 지급한 적이 없다.

해설 해석상 '주다'의 의미가 적합하므로 (D) awarded가 정답이다.

어휘 access 접근하다, 접속하다 | accept 수용하다 | assume (직책, 업무 등을) 떠맡다 | award 수여하다, 지급하다

9. 스카이 에어웨이즈는 사이안 콘티넨털과의 합병으로 많은 혜택을 얻었다.

해설 뒤에 전치사 from을 동반하는 자동사로 '혜택을 얻다'라는 benefit가 들어가야 하므로 (B) benefited가 정답이다.

어휘 merger with ~와의 합병 | account 간주하다, 여기다 | benefit from ~으로 혜택을 얻다

10. 세계적으로 유명한 디자이너 소피 펜은 그 회사를 위한 혁신적인 광고를 만들기 위해 트루 아트 사의 직원들과 공동으로 작업했다.

해설 뒤에 전치사 with를 동반하는 자동사 문제로 '~와 협력하다'라는 의미의 (C) collaborated가 정답이다.

어휘 world-renowned 세계적으로 유명한 | innovative 혁신적인 | recall 회상하다 | collaborate with ~와 협력하다 | employ 고용하다, 쓰다[이용하다]

UNIT 02. 동사 어휘 2

Practice

본서 p.139

1. (A) 2. (A) 3. (D) 4. (D) 5. (A)
6. (A) 7. (B) 8. (A) 9. (D) 10. (C)

1. 모레노 박사가 이끄는 연구팀은 이번 달 소비자 설문 조사를 할 예정이다.

해설 빈칸 뒤 목적어 surveys와 잘 쓰이는 동사인 (A) conduct가 정답이다. 평소에 conduct the survey로 같이 암기해 두면 좋다.

어휘 conduct a survey 설문 조사를 하다 | detain 구금하다, 억류하다 | foresee 예견하다 | associate 관련 짓다

2. 마케팅 부서는 우리 제품에 대한 관심도를 측정하기 위해 소비자 조사를 실시할 계획이다.

해설 해석상 '측정하다'의 의미가 적합하므로 (A) gauge가 정답이다.

어휘 conduct 수행하다 | consumer survey 소비자 조사 | in order to ~하기 위하여 | gauge 측정하다, 판단하다

3. 외부 고용 정책에 대한 자세한 내용은 직원 설명서를 참조하십시오.

해설 뒤에 목적어를 동반하는 타동사 문제로, 해석에만 의존해서 전치사 to가 필요한 자동사 (A)를 고르지 않도록 주의하자. '직원 설명서를 참조하다'의 의미가 적합하므로 타동사 (D) consult가 정답이다.

어휘 kindly (특별한 의미 없이 공식 요청을 하기 위해 사용되는 표현) | employee manual 직원 설명서 | details 정보, 세부사항 | employment policy 고용 정책 | consult 참조하다

4. 토니 비보는 최근 네팔 여행에서 만난 사람으로부터 그의 최신 서스펜스 스릴러인 〈비하인드 더 씬〉의 주인공을 착상했다.

해설 '주인공을 (마음속에) 떠올리다'의 의미가 들어가야 하므로 (D) conceived가 정답이다.

어휘 main character 주인공 | latest 최신의 | encounter 맞닥뜨리다 | convince 설득하다 | conceive 마음속으로 하다

5. 직원 매뉴얼은 여러분이 고객과 부딪힐 수 있는 문제들에 대한 해결책들을 포함하고 있습니다.

해설 해석상 '고객과 부딪힐 수 있는 문제들'이라는 의미가 적합하므로 (A) encounter가 정답이다.

어휘 employee manual 직원 수칙 | solution 해결(책) | encounter 맞닥뜨리다, 부딪히다 | comprise 구성되다 | reside 살다, 거주하다 | qualify 자격을 얻다

6. 배우인 지미 크루즈는 제냐 화장품의 새 제품을 홍보하는 것에 동의하여 TV 광고에 출연할 것이다.

해설 해석상 유명인이 특정 상품을 '홍보하다'의 의미가 적합하므로 (A) endorse가 정답이다.

어휘 endorse 지지하다, (유명인이 광고에 나와 특정 상품을) 보증하다, 홍보하다 | persuade 설득하다 | thrive 번성하다

7. 밍 씨는 베라자노 상사에서 제안한 자리를 정중히 거절했다.

해설 해석상 '자리를 정중히 거절했다'는 의미가 적합하므로 (B) declined가 정답이다. 평소에 decline the position으로 같이 암기해두면 좋다.

어휘 courteously 정중하게 | position 자리, 직위 | offer 제공하다 | import 수입 | convert 전환시키다 | lessen 줄다

8. 이달 런던에서 개최하는 크리에이티브 가드닝 박람회는 세계 곳곳의 식물과 꽃을 특징으로 하고 있다.

해설 해석상 '특징을 갖고 있다'라는 의미의 (A) features가 정답이다. 보통 feature가 답이 되는 경우는 주로 전시회, 회의, 행사 등이 나와서 뒤에 그 세부적인 특징을 설명하는 내용이 언급된다.

어휘 plant 식물, 공장 | all over the world 전 세계에 | feature 특징을 갖고 있다 | observe 준수하다

9. 조립이 완료된 후 모든 장치를 검사하여 제대로 작동하는지 확인해야 합니다.

해설 해석상 '모든 장치가 점검되어야 한다'는 의미가 적합하므로 (D) inspected가 정답이다.

어휘 device 기기, 장치 | assembly 조립 | complete 완료된 | confirm 확인해주다 | function 작동하다, 기능하다 | properly 제대로, 적절히 | assign 배정하다 | deliver 배달하다 | market (시장에) 상품을 내놓다 | inspect 점검하다

10. 지난달, 출입국 관리사무소는 외국인 방문객들에게 7천 건의 입국 허가증을 발행했다.

해설 해석상 '입국 허가증을 발행했다'는 의미가 적합하므로 (C) issued가 정답이다.

어휘 immigration office 출입국 관리사무소 | entry 출입, 입국 | permit 허가증 | foreign 외국의 | construct 구성하다

UNIT 03. 동사 어휘 3

Practice
본서 p.141

1. (C)	2. (B)	3. (D)	4. (B)	5. (A)
6. (C)	7. (C)	8. (D)	9. (B)	10. (A)

1. 지방 자치체 직원들은 종이를 사용하지 않는 사무실 만들기 정책을 시행하는 것이 비용을 줄일 것으로 생각하고 있다.

해설 빈칸 뒤에 전치사 to를 동반하는 자동사이면서, '결과를 초래하다, 이끌다'의 의미가 들어가는 (C) lead가 정답이다.

어휘 municipal 시의 | implement 시행하다 | paperless office 종이를 쓰지 않는 사무실 | expense 비용 | lead to 이끌다, 결과를 초래하다 | intend ~할 의도이다

2. 건설 프로젝트를 계획할 때 모든 산업 규정을 반드시 준수하라.

해설 빈칸 뒤에 목적어를 동반하는 타동사 문제로, '~을 준수하다'의 의미가 들어가야 하므로 (B) observe가 정답이다. (D)는 자동사로 adhere to로 사용되어야 한다.

어휘 be sure to 반드시 ~하다 | regulation 규정 | construction 건설 | observe 준수하다 | adhere to ~을 고수하다

3. 새 정책이 매우 창의적이지만, 지금 현재 회사로서 그것을 진행하기에는 큰 비용이 든다.

해설 뒤에 with 전치사를 동반하는 자동사로 해석상 '~을 진행하다'의 의미가 적합하므로 (D) proceed가 정답이다.

어휘 cost a fortune 큰 비용이 들다 | at the moment(= now) 바로 지금 | examine 검토하다 | treat 대우하다, 치료하다 | urge 충고하다 | proceed 진행하다

4. 이상적인 창고 부지를 찾는 일은 예상보다 더 어려운 일임이 드러나고 있다.

해설 형용사를 보어로 취하는 형용사 자리이므로 (B) proving이 정답이다. 주로 사용되는 2형식 동사에는 be, become, remain, stay, seem, appear, prove 등이 있다.

어휘 locate ~의 정확한 위치를 찾아내다 | ideal 이상적인 | site 부지, 장소 | warehouse 창고 | more difficult than expected 예상보다 더 어려운 | prove 입증하다

5. 비용을 절감할 수 있는 기회임에도 불구하고, 론존스 베이커리는 최고의 품질 기준을 유지하기 위해 노력해야 한다.

해설 빈칸 뒤에 to부정사를 취하는 동사로, '고군분투하다'의 의미가 적합하므로 (A) strive가 정답이다.

어휘 cut 줄이다, 삭감하다 | maintain 유지하다 | standard 기준, 표준 | strive 고군분투하다

6. 제퍼슨 씨의 부사장 승진은 생화학 부문에서 선두주자의 하나로 노비스 사의 입지를 공고히 할 것이다.

해설 해석상 '입지[존재]를 굳히다'의 의미가 적합하므로 (C) solidify가 정답이다.

어휘 promotion 승진 | vice president 부사장 | presence 존재, 입지 | incline ~쪽으로 기울다 | solidify 굳히다, 확고히 하다

7. 룸피니 칠리소스의 제조는 필수 재료 부족으로 인해 중단되어야 했다.

해설 해석상 '제조를 중단하다'의 의미가 들어가야 하므로 (C) suspended가 정답이다. (B) expired는 자동사로, 수동태로 사용할 수 없기 때문에 오답이다.

어휘 manufacturing 제조 | shortage 부족 | key 가장 중요한, 필수적인 | ingredient 재료 | direct 지휘하다 | expire 만료되다 | suspend 중단하다 | foretell 예언하다

8. 수석 편집장인 타냐 매디슨은 로슨 언론사의 홍보부에게 모든 국내 케이블 네트워크에 루크 테이어의 최신 소설을 홍보해달라고 요청했다.

해설 빈칸은 to부정사를 목적격 보어로 취하는 5형식 동사 자리이므로 (D) urged가 정답이다.

어휘 public relations division 홍보부 I latest 최신의 I national 국내의 I allege 혐의를 제기하다 I vow 맹세하다 I pursue 추구하다 I urge 촉구하다

9. 국제 제본 연합은 전 세계 출판사의 이익을 대변한다.

해설 '이익을 대변하다'라는 의미가 들어가야 하므로 (B) represents가 정답이다. 평소에 represent the interests of로 같이 암기해 두면 좋다.

어휘 binder 제본 I confederation 연합, 연맹 I interest 흥미, 이익 I publisher 출판사 I worldwide 전 세계적인

10. 새로운 운영 감독인 황 씨는 지난 분기 때 일부 배송 지연을 초래한 일정 충돌 몇 건을 해결했다.

해설 해석상 '일정상의 충돌을 해결했다'는 의미가 적합하므로 (A) resolved가 정답이다.

어휘 scheduling conflict 일정상의 충돌 I lead to ~로 이어지다 I resolve 해결하다

REVIEW TEST 01
본서 p.142

1. (D)	2. (A)	3. (D)	4. (B)	5. (A)
6. (B)	7. (B)	8. (C)	9. (C)	10. (A)
11. (A)	12. (D)	13. (B)	14. (C)	15. (D)
16. (B)	17. (D)	18. (A)	19. (B)	20. (C)

1. 우리는 일선 직원들이 긍정적이든 부정적이든 모든 고객 피드백을 알려주기를 권장합니다.

해설 빈칸은 동사 encourage의 목적격 보어인 to부정사구의 동사 자리이다. 빈칸 뒤에 전치사 of가 있으며 문맥상 '우리에게 모든 고객 피드백을 알리기를 권장한다'는 의미가 되어야 자연스러우므로, inform A(사람) of B(사물) 'A에게 B를 알리다'의 「동사 + 전치사」 관용표현을 완성하는 (D) inform이 정답이다.

어휘 encourage 권장하다 I front-line 일선의, 최전방의 I indicate 나타내다

2. 이번 주 금요일 반짝 세일 때, 선라이즈 애슬리츠 등산화를 구입하시고, 두 번째 신발은 반값에 가져가세요.

해설 빈칸은 명사구 a pair of hiking boots를 목적어로 하는 동사 자리이다. 등위접속사 and로 연결된 문장의 내용을 고려할 때, '등산화 한 켤레를 구입하면 두 번째 신발은 반값에 살 수 있다'는 의미가 되어야 자연스러우므로 (A) buy가 정답이다.

어휘 flash sale 반짝 세일 I hiking boots 등산화 I additional 추가의 I pair 한 쌍[켤레]

3. 7월에 있을 여름 판매 행사에 대한 준비로, 맨드락 백화점은 계절 근로자 몇 명을 채용해야 할 것이다.

해설 전치사구와 주절의 관계를 고려할 때, '행사 준비를 위해 근로자를 더 채용해야 할 것'이라는 의미가 자연스러우므로 (D) hire가 정답이다.

어휘 in preparation for ~의 준비로 I seasonal worker 계절 근로자

4. 호손 산업은 각 직원에게 항상 사원증을 지니고 다니도록 요구한다.

해설 빈칸은 목적어와 to부정사구를 목적격 보어로 취하는 5형식 동사 자리이다. 문맥상 '직원들에게 사원증을 지닐 것을 요구한다'는 의미가 자연스러우므로 (B) requires가 정답이다.

어휘 carry 지니고 다니다 I identification badge 사원증 I at all times 항상 I verify 확인하다, 입증하다

5. 시장이 계획을 승인하자마자 도네갈 시청사의 보수 작업은 시작될 것이다.

해설 문맥상 '계획을 승인하자마자 보수가 시작될 것'이라는 의미가 되어야 자연스러우므로 (A) approved가 정답이다.

어휘 renovation 보수 I commence 시작되다 I mayor 시장 I plan 계획 I approve 승인하다 I presume 추정하다 I designate 지정하다 I fabricate 날조하다, 제작하다

6. 기업 재무를 전문으로 하는 몇몇 변호사들이 카요이드 사의 연락을 받았다.

해설 빈칸 앞에 동사 specializing이 있으므로 specialize in '~을 전문적으로 다루다'라는 「동사 + 전치사」 관용표현을 완성하는 (B) in이 정답이다.

어휘 corporate 기업의; 기업 I finance 재정, 재무 I contact 연락을 하다 I specialize in ~을 전문으로 다루다

7. 이도 의사는 병원 개조작업의 모든 상황을 감독할 인테리어 디자이너를 고용했다.

해설 빈칸은 명사 an interior designer를 수식할 to부정사 자리이다. 문맥상 '병원 개조작업의 모든 상황을 감독할 디자이너'라는 의미가 자연스러우므로 (B) oversee가 정답이다.

어휘 employ 채용하다 I aspect 상황, 양상 I renovation 개조 I strive 고군분투하다 I oversee 감독하다 I urge 강력히 권고하다

8. 만화가 유키토 시로의 홈페이지는 매달 20,000명 이상의 방문객들을 끌어들인다.

해설 빈칸은 주어와 목적어 사이의 동사 자리이다. 문맥상 '방문객들을 끌어들인다'는 의미가 자연스러우므로 (C) attracts가 정답이다.

어휘 comic artist 만화가 I visitor 방문객 I feature 특징으로 하다 I proceed 진행하다

9. 공원 경비원은 야생에서 살아남는 법을 설명할 수 있어야 한다.

해설 빈칸은 조동사 뒤 문장의 동사 자리로, '공원 경비원은 야생에서 살아남는 법을 설명할 수 있어야 한다'는 의미가 되어야 자연스러우므로 (C) demonstrate가 정답이다.

어휘 park ranger 공원 경비원 | survive 살아남다 | wilderness 황야, 야생

10. 이 앱을 사용하면, 당신은 동료들이 어디에 있든지 그들과 연락할 수 있습니다.

해설 빈칸 뒤에 목적어가 없으므로 자동사 자리이다. 빈칸 뒤에 전치사 with가 있으므로 communicate with '~와 연락하다'라는 「동사 + 전치사」 관용표현을 완성하는 (A) communicate가 정답이다.

어휘 application 응용 프로그램, 앱 | coworker 동료 | notify 알리다

11. 피지디 그룹은 외국어 교육 분야의 선두 기관으로 떠올랐다.

해설 빈칸은 문장의 동사 자리이다. 빈칸 뒤 전치사 as와 함께 emerge as '~으로 부상하다[부각되다]'라는 「동사 + 전치사」 관용표현을 완성하는 (A) emerged가 정답이다.

어휘 leading 선두적인, 가장 중요한 | institute 기관, 협회 | field 분야 | foreign language 외국어 | assign 할당하다

12. 우리 회사는 교육 기회 제공에 중점을 둔 지역 자선 단체에 기부하는 것을 항상 방침으로 삼아 왔다.

해설 해석상 '지역 자선 단체에 기부하는 것을 방침으로 삼다'는 의미가 되어야 자연스러우므로 (D) donate가 정답이다.

어휘 firm 회사 | policy 정책, 방침 | charity 자선 단체 | focus on ~에 중점을 두다 | donate 기부하다

13. 전문경영인의 발표에 이어 현직 전 직원을 대상으로 경영진과의 질의 응답이 이어졌다.

해설 문맥상 '전문경영인의 발표 이후에 경영진과의 질의응답이 있었다'는 의미가 자연스러우므로 A be followed by B 'B가 A의 뒤를 잇다'의 구조를 완성하는 (B) followed가 정답이다.

어휘 announcement 발표 | question-and-answer session 질의응답 시간 | management 경영(진) | current 현재의 | conduct 하다

14. 아란데일에서는, 모든 직원들이 존중할 만한 근무 환경을 누릴 자격이 있다고 생각합니다.

해설 빈칸은 that 명사절 내의 동사 자리이다. 문맥상 '직원들이 존중할 만한 근무 환경을 누릴 자격이 있다'는 의미가 자연스러우므로 '받을만한 자격이 되다'라는 의미의 (C) deserve가 정답이다.

어휘 respectful 존중할 만한, 존경심을 보이는 | working environment 근무 환경 | deserve ~을 받을 만하다 | fulfill 다하다, 이행하다

15. 오랫동안 기다려 온 매크로 엔비포 노트북 컴퓨터가 상해 전자제품 박람회에서 마침내 공개될 것이다.

해설 빈칸은 미래시제 수동태 구문의 동사 자리이다. 문맥상 '오랫동안 기다려온 컴퓨터가 마침내 공개될 것'이라는 의미가 자연스러우므로 '공개되다'라는 의미의 (D) unveiled가 정답이다.

어휘 long-awaited 사람들이 오래 기다려온 | tradeshow 무역 박람회 | unveil 공개하다

16. 오후 3시 이후에 도착하는 참석자는 콘퍼런스에 입장 허가를 받으려면 자동화 기기에서 체크인해야 한다.

해설 빈칸은 to부정사의 수동태 구조(to be p.p.)를 완성하는 과거분사 자리이다. '입장을 허가받으려면'이라는 의미가 되어야 자연스러우므로 (B) admitted가 정답이다.

어휘 attendee 참석자 | check in 체크인하다 | automated 자동화된 | kiosk 키오스크 | dismiss 떨쳐 버리다 | redeem ~을 되찾다

17. 슈퍼리어 인스트러멘테이션 주식회사는 호주와 뉴질랜드에서 당사의 최신 제품을 출시할 지역 마케팅 책임자를 찾고 있다.

해설 빈칸은 명사 a regional marketing director를 수식하는 to부정사 구의 동사 자리이다. 빈칸 뒤에 명사구가 있으므로 목적어를 취하는 타동사 자리이며, 문맥상 '최신 제품을 출시할 지역 마케팅 책임자'라는 의미가 자연스러우므로 '출시하다'라는 의미의 (D) launch가 정답이다.

어휘 look for ~을 찾다 | regional 지역의 | latest 최신의 | investigate 조사하다 | convince 확신시키다 | launch 출시하다

18. 오래된 스완스빌 공장은 새 시설이 생산을 시작하면 창고로 개조될 것이다.

해설 빈칸은 수동태 구문의 동사와 명사구 사이의 전치사 자리이다. 문맥상 '공장이 창고로 개조될 것'이라는 의미가 되어야 자연스러우므로 convert A into B 'A를 B로 전환시키다[개조시키다]'라는 「동사 + 전치사」 관용표현의 수동태 구문(A be converted into B)을 완성하는 (A) into가 정답이다.

어휘 plant 공장 | convert 개조하다 | warehouse 창고 | facility 시설, 설비 | production 생산

19. 부마자 씨는 라자 전자의 수익을 크게 향상시킨 여러 판촉 활동들을 개시한 공로를 인정받는다.

해설 빈칸은 수동태 문장의 동사 자리이다. 빈칸 뒤에 전치사 with가 있으므로 credit A with B 'B를 A의 공으로 믿다'라는 「동사 + 전치사」 관용표현의 수동태 구문(A is credited with B)을 완성하는 (B) credited가 정답이다.

어휘 launch 시작하다, 착수하다, 개시하다 | promotion 판촉 | improve 향상시키다, 개선하다 | credit A with B[B to A] B를 A의 공으로 믿다

20. 인사 변동에 관한 모든 결정은 1월 1일로 예정된 합병이 완료될 때까지 연기될 것이다.

해설 빈칸은 미래시제 수동태 구문 내의 동사 자리이다. 문맥상 '합병이 완료될 때까지 모든 결정이 연기될 것'이라는 의미가 자연스러우므로 '미루다, 연기하다'라는 의미의 (C) deferred가 정답이다.

어휘 personnel change 인사 변동 | merger 합병 | completion 완료, 완성 | schedule 예정하다 | defer 연기하다 | compile 엮다, 편집하다

UNIT 04. 명사 어휘 1

본서 p.145

Practice

| 1. (A) | 2. (A) | 3. (B) | 4. (C) | 5. (B) |
| 6. (C) | 7. (C) | 8. (D) | 9. (D) | 10. (D) |

1. 〈아이덴 글로벌 저널〉 웹사이트의 특별 접근 권한을 반드시 이용하시기 바랍니다.

해설 '웹사이트로의 접속 권한'이라는 의미가 적합하므로 (A) access가 정답이다. access는 뒤에 전치사 to와 함께 쓰인다는 것도 기억해 두어야 한다.

어휘 be sure to 확실히 ~하다 | take advantage of (이점을) 이용하다 | access 접근, 접근 권한 | routine 일상 | advance 진보, 발전

2. 직원들은 그 회사를 위해 여러 성공적인 주요 투자 영업 거래를 기획하고 조직한 그들의 부사장, 마컴버 씨에 대해 존경을 표했다.

해설 '~에 대한 존경'이라는 의미로 admiration for가 적합하므로 (A) admiration이 정답이다.

어휘 express 표현하다 | organize 조직하다 | investment 투자 | transaction 거래 | admiration 존경 | persistence 고집, 지속됨

3. 오프랑 씨는 기업 간 선의의 경쟁은 혁신적인 아이디어와 방법을 자극한다고 굳게 믿는다.

해설 빈칸은 that 명사절 내의 주어 자리이다. 빈칸 앞, 뒤로 각각 형용사 friendly와 between 전치사구의 수식을 받고 있어, '선의의 경쟁이 혁신적인 아이디어와 방법을 자극한다'는 의미가 되어야 자연스러우므로 (B) competition이 정답이다.

어휘 firmly 단호히, 확고히 | friendly 우호적인 | corporation 기업, 회사 | spur 원동력이 되다, 자극하다 | innovative 혁신적인 | process 방법, 절차 | condemnation 비난 | condescension 우월감 | congregation 신자[신도]들

4. 모리슨 시는 시 창립기념일을 축하하는 새 조각상을 세우려는 계획에 대한 시민의 의견을 구하고 있다.

해설 '~에 대한 의견'이라는 의미의 comment on이 적합하므로 (C) comment가 정답이다.

어휘 invite (정식으로) 요청하다, 청하다 | erect 세우다, 건설하다 | sculpture 조각 | arrangement 준비, 방식, 합의

5. 키스톤 리미티드에서는, 최고 수익을 내는 지점이 다음해에 최고 마케팅 예산을 받게 될 것이다.

해설 빈칸은 the largest marketing의 수식을 받는 명사 자리이다. '다음 해에 최고 마케팅 예산을 받는다'는 의미가 되어야 자연스러우므로 (B) budget이 정답이다.

어휘 branch 지점 | profit 수익 | award 주다, 수여하다 | upcoming 다가오는 | collections 수집 | capacity 수용력, 능력, 지위

6. 에어론 섬유는 지난 분기에 걸쳐 생산에 있어 빠른 가속도를 경험했다.

해설 빈칸 앞에 속도를 나타내는 rapid와 함께 사용할 수 있는 (C) acceleration이 정답이다.

어휘 quarter 분기 | sector 분야 | adequacy 적절, 타당성 | acceleration 가속도 | inclusion 포함

7. 우리 회사의 새 전자레인지는 사용하기 쉬운 매뉴얼과 저렴한 가격으로 좋은 평가를 받았다.

해설 해석상 '저렴한 가격'이라는 의미가 적절하므로 (C) affordability가 정답이다.

어휘 microwave 전자레인지 | user-friendly 사용하기 쉬운 | manual 매뉴얼, 설명서 | appliance 기기 | affordability 저렴한 가격, 감당할 수 있는 비용 | awareness 의식

8. 경쟁 관계에 있는 두 회사는 환경 문제에 대한 협력으로 칭찬을 받았다.

해설 빈칸 뒤에 on이라는 전치사를 동반하며 해석상 '~에 대한 협력'이 적합하므로 (D) collaboration이 정답이다.

어휘 competing firm 경쟁 회사 | praise 칭찬하다 | environmental issue 환경 문제 | manufacturing 제조 | collaboration 협력

9. 심슨 씨는 지난 월요일 홍보 행사 기간 동안 사업 협상에 전념하고자 함을 밝혔다.

해설 '~에 대한 전념'이라고 해서 full commitment to가 적합하므로 (D) commitment가 정답이다.

어휘 PR(public relations) 홍보 | assessment 평가 | reference 추천 | selection 선발 | commitment 전념

10. 새로운 지불 시스템으로, 시내버스가 더 이상 정확한 잔돈을 요구하지 않을 것이다.

해설 coin은 가산 명사이므로 관사가 들어가야 하며 '정확한 금액[잔돈]'을 의미하는 (D) change가 정답이다.

어휘 payment 지불 | coin 동전 | amount 양 | exact change 정확한 금액[잔돈]

UNIT 05. 명사 어휘 2

본서 p.147

Practice

| 1. (A) | 2. (C) | 3. (D) | 4. (D) | 5. (A) |
| 6. (D) | 7. (D) | 8. (A) | 9. (C) | 10. (D) |

1. 새 환경 규정을 준수하여, 환기 시스템을 설치해야 한다.

해설 '~을 준수하여'의 의미인 in compliance with가 적합하므로 (A) compliance가 정답이다.

어휘 environmental regulation 환경 규정 | set up 설치하다 | air ventilation system 환기 시스템 | in compliance with ~을 준수하여 | competence 능숙함 | arrangement 정리, 준비 | advancement 진보

2. 모든 공장 직원들은 비상 상황에서 무엇을 해야 하는지를 알기 위해서 안전 비상사태 계획을 검토해야 한다.

해설 '비상사태 계획'이라는 복합명사인 contingency plan이 적합하므로 (C) contingency가 정답이다.

어휘 emergency 비상 | termination 종료 | discharge 방출 | contingency 비상사태 | prevention 예방

3. 쿼터메인 솔루션의 대리인인 탈리아 굴랄 씨는 보다 엄격한 품질기준을 위한 회사의 지원을 강조했다.

해설 '~에 대한 지원[지지]'라는 의미로 support for가 적합하므로 (D) support가 정답이다.

어휘 representative 대표자, 대리인 | emphasize 강조하다 | strict 엄격한 | quality 품질 | standard 기준

4. 업무의 위임은 상사의 업무량을 줄이고 다른 직원들이 새로운 임무를 시도하는 것을 가능케 한다.

해설 해석상 '업무의 위임은 업무량을 줄여준다'는 의미가 적합하므로 (D) Delegation이 정답이다.

어휘 duty 업무 | reduce 줄이다 | workload 작업량 | enable 가능하게 하다 | assignment 배정, 임무 | permission 허락 | reputation 평판 | qualification 자격 | delegation 위임, 대표단

5. 에이시티 사는 온라인 네트워크 중단에 대해서 진심으로 사과드립니다.

해설 사과하는 내용이 빈칸에 들어가야 하므로 '네트워크가 잘 안 된다'라는 의미인 (A) disruption이 정답이다.

어휘 sincerely 진심으로 | apologize for ~에 대해 사과하다 | disruption 중단 | precaution 예방

6. 다시 페인트칠하는 것에 대한 견적을 제시하기 전에, 델라노 씨는 각 방의 치수를 결정하기 위해 측정을 해야 한다.

해설 '각 방의 치수를 결정하기 위해 측정을 해야 한다'는 의미이므로 (D) dimensions가 정답이다.

어휘 present 제시하다 | estimate 견적 | measurement 측정 | determine 결정하다, 결론을 내리다 | appearance 외양 | objectives 목적, 목표 | dimensions 면적

7. 탑프로 연구소의 수석 연구원들은 최근 결과물을 비공개로 해야 한다.

해설 해석상 '밝히는 것을 피하다'의 의미가 적합하므로 (D) disclosure가 정답이다.

어휘 permission 허락, 허가 | confession 자백 | allowance 허용, 용돈 | disclosure 폭로, 공개

8. 한 씨는 하청업체로부터 견적을 받을 것이고 그중에서 가장 저렴한 가격을 선택할 것이다.

해설 해석상 '견적(서)'이 적합하므로 (A) estimates가 정답이다.

어휘 subcontractor 하청업체 | estimate 견적(서) | relocation 재배치, 이전

9. 디에고 씨의 웅변력과 단정한 외모 덕택에, 그는 회사 대변인으로 선출되었다.

해설 대변인으로 선택되었다는 것은 말을 잘한다는 내용이 들어가야 하므로 (C) eloquence가 정답이다.

어휘 neat 단정한 | spokesperson 대변인 | prevalence 널리 퍼짐, 유행 | allowance 수당, 용돈 | eloquence 웅변, 능변 | abundance 풍부

10. 투자를 하기 전에, 우리는 시의 그 구역에 집을 지을 수 있는 실행 가능성을 결정할 필요가 있다.

해설 해석상 '실행 가능성'이 들어가야 하므로 (D) feasibility가 정답이다.

어휘 investment 투자 | determine 결정하다, 결론을 내리다 | employment 고용 | fascination 매력 | feasibility 실현 가능성

UNIT 06. 명사 어휘 3

Practice 본서 p.149

1. (D)	2. (B)	3. (B)	4. (D)	5. (A)
6. (C)	7. (C)	8. (D)	9. (D)	10. (D)

1. 직원 신분증에는 홍보 기획의 일환으로 회사 비전과 임무를 포함하고 있을 것이다.

해설 해석상 '기획, 계획'이란 의미가 적합하므로 (D) initiative가 정답이다.

어휘 identification card 신분증 | public relations 홍보 | evaluation 평가 | asset 자산 | initiative 기획, 계획

2. 창고에서 발송된 모든 소포에는 내용물의 원산지뿐만 아니라 거기에 들어 있는 항목을 나열한 송장이 들어 있어야 한다.

해설 해석상 '내용물의 원산지와 목록을 나열한 송장'이라는 의미가 적합하므로 '원산지'라는 의미의 place of origin에서 (B) origin이 정답이다.

어휘 package 소포 | ship 배송하다 | warehouse 창고 | invoice 청구서 | content 내용물 | foundation 설립

3. 스타 배송은 10만 톤의 철강을 예상보다 2개월 일찍 계약상의 의무를 이행하면서 그린데일 사에 보냈다.

해설 앞에 contractual과 잘 쓰이는 명사로 '계약상 의무'를 나타내는 (B) obligation이 정답이다.

어휘 fulfill 이행하다 | surplus 과잉 | contractual obligation 계약상 의무 | forecast 예측하다 | indication 암시

4. 박 씨는 사우버 지엠비에이치와의 파트너십 계약의 범위를 평가하고 있다.

해설 해석상 '파트너십 계약의 범위'라는 의미가 적합하므로 (D) scope이 정답이다.

어휘 evaluate 평가하다 | partnership 파트너십 | agreement 계약, 협정 | grip 꽉 붙잡은 | turn 회전, 방향 전환, 변화 | scope 범위

5. 켄싱턴 호텔은 여러 관광 명소와의 접근성 때문에 거의 항상 꽉 찬다.

해설 해석상 '위치가 좋기 때문에 꽉 찬다'라는 의미인 '접근성'이 적합하므로 (A) proximity가 정답이다.

어휘 capacity 수용 능력 | proximity 접근성 | vacancy 공석 | efficiency 효율성 | availability 이용 가능성

6. 정기 점검으로 금요일 오후 3시에 이 지역 전기 서비스가 잠시 중단될 예정이다.

해설 빈칸은 형용사 brief의 수식을 받는 명사 자리로, '정기 점검으로 이 지역 전기 서비스가 잠시 중단될 예정이다'라는 의미가 되어야 자연스러우므로 (C) interruption이 정답이다.

어휘 brief 잠시 동안의 | electricity 전기 | regular maintenance 정기 점검 | statement 진술 | outline 개요

7. 프로바이오는 자동 보고 시스템으로 완벽하게 성공적으로 전환했다.

해설 '~으로 전환하다'라는 의미로 make a transition to가 들어가는 (C) transition이 정답이다.

어휘 completely 완전히 | automated 자동화된 | cooperation 협력 | transition 전환, 변화 | suspension 중지

8. 나는 그 새 기기를 구매한 것이 그들이 내린 최고의 결정이라고 말한 사용자들의 모든 추천글을 보고 그것을 사용해 볼 것을 확신했다.

해설 해석상 '사용자들의 추천글'이라는 의미가 적절하므로 (D) testimonials가 정답이다.

어휘 convince 확신시키다, 납득시키다 | device 기기, 장치 | contradiction 모순, 반박 | specification 설명서, 사양 | comparison 비교 | testimonial 추천의 글, 추천서

9. 헤이워즈 바베큐는 모든 고객들에게 건물에서 외부 음식이나 음료 섭취를 자제할 것을 당부한다.

해설 '부지[건물] 내에서'의 의미인 on the premises가 적합하므로 (D) premises가 정답이다.

어휘 refrain from ~을 삼가다 | consume 소비하다 | on the premises 부지[건물] 내에서

10. 이곳 마타자노스 제조사는 근로자의 건강과 행복이 최우선 과제입니다.

해설 '최우선 순위'를 나타내는 highest priority가 와야 하므로 (D) priority가 정답이다.

어휘 occasion 기회, 경우, 행사 | priority 우선순위

REVIEW TEST 02
본서 p.150

1. (C)	2. (A)	3. (B)	4. (B)	5. (D)
6. (C)	7. (B)	8. (A)	9. (B)	10. (A)
11. (A)	12. (A)	13. (C)	14. (C)	15. (A)
16. (B)	17. (C)	18. (B)	19. (C)	20. (B)

1. 리베로 타워의 사무실들은 오후 6시까지만 개방하지만, 유효한 인가를 받은 직원들은 개방 시간 이후에도 들어갈 수 있다.

해설 빈칸은 명사 personnel을 수식하는 전치사 with의 목적어 자리이다. 접속사 but으로 연결된 두 문장의 관계를 고려할 때, 문맥상 '유효한 인가를 받은 직원들은 개방 시간 이후, 즉 오후 6시 이후에도 사무실에 출입할 수 있다'는 의미가 되어야 자연스러우므로 (C) authorization이 정답이다.

어휘 personnel 인원, 직원들 | valid 유효한 | hours 업무 시간, 개방 시간 | consolidation 합병, 통합 | capability 능력, 역량 | authorization 권한 | attendance 출석

2. 레슈마트 주식회사는 매일 오전 5시부터 11시까지 산 호세 지점에서 일할 계산원이 필요하다.

해설 빈칸은 San Jose와 복합명사를 이루는 명사 자리이다. 문맥상 '산 호세 지점에서 일할 계산원이 필요하다'는 의미가 자연스러우므로 (A) branch가 정답이다.

어휘 cashier 계산원, 출납원 | branch 지점, 지사 | cover 덮개, 표지 | shift 교대근무 | duty 임무, 직무

3. 편리한 대중교통 체계와 최근에 건설된 두 개의 호텔을 가진, 메이저 케이가 관광지로 광고되고 있다.

해설 빈칸은 명사 tourist와 복합명사를 이루는 명사 자리이다. 주어가 메이저 케이이므로 '관광지'라는 의미를 완성하는 (B) destination이 정답이다.

어휘 convenient 편리한 | public transit 대중교통 | recently 최근에 | construct 건설하다, 짓다 | advertise 광고하다 | tourist 관광객 | destination 목적지 | intention 의도 | commitment 약속, 전념

4. 그 슈퍼마켓은 우리 신용카드 결제 기기에 확인되지 않은 문제로 인해 일시적으로 현금만 받고 있다.

해설 빈칸은 문장의 목적어 자리이다. because of 전치사구와 주절의 관계를 고려할 때, 문맥상 '신용카드 결제 기기의 문제로 인해 일시적으로 현금만 받고 있다'는 의미가 자연스러우므로 (B) cash가 정답이다.

어휘 temporarily 일시적으로 | accept 받다, 받아들이다 | undetermined 미확인의 | issue 문제, 사안 | credit card reader 신용카드 결제 기기

5. 트리오즈 전자의 신임 회장인 지아 웡은 회사의 마케팅 전략의 점검을 요구하였다.

해설 빈칸은 구동사 call for의 목적어 자리이다. 명사를 수식하는 of 전치사구의 내용을 고려할 때, '마케팅 전략의 점검을 요구했다'는 의미

가 자연스러우므로 '철저한 점검'이라는 의미의 (D) overhaul이 정답이다.

어휘 call for 공식적으로 요구하다 | strategy 전략 | inaccuracy 부정확함 | enterprise 기업, 산업 | overhaul 점검

6. 제조공장은 결함이 있는 기계가 수리될 수 있게 오늘 아침 생산을 중단했다.

해설 빈칸은 동사 stopped의 목적어인 명사 자리로, '기계가 수리될 수 있도록 공장에서 생산을 중단했다'는 의미가 되어야 자연스러우므로 (C) production이 정답이다.

어휘 manufacturing plant 제조 공장 | defective 결함이 있는 | machinery 기계(류) | fix 고치다 | fabrication 조작, 날조 | construction 건설, 공사

7. 바린 사는 고객의 기밀정보 보호를 확실히 하기 위해 최상의 품질 보안 조치를 활용한다.

해설 빈칸은 명사 security와 복합명사를 이루는 명사 자리이다. 문맥상 '고객정보 보호를 위해 최상의 보안조치를 고수한다'는 의미가 자연스러우므로 (B) measures가 정답이다.

어휘 utilize 활용하다 | security measure 보안조치 | ensure 확실히 하다 | confidential 기밀의, 비밀의 | consent 동의, 합의 | measures 조치, 방법

8. 확정된 베카 밸리의 복원 노력이 이 지역에 대한 관광객들의 관심을 높이는 데 도움을 주었다.

해설 빈칸은 restoration과 복합명사를 이루는 문장의 주어 자리이다. 문맥상 '복원 노력이 그 지역에 대한 관광객의 관심을 높여주었다'는 의미가 되어야 자연스러우므로 (A) efforts가 정답이다.

어휘 determine 확정하다, 결정하다 | restoration 복원, 복구 | share 몫, 할당량

9. 박물관 보수 비용은 지역사회의 기부에 의해 충당되었다.

해설 빈칸은 문장의 주어 자리이다. 빈칸을 수식하는 of 전치사구의 내용을 고려할 때, '박물관 보수 비용은 기부금으로 충당되었다'는 의미가 자연스러우므로 (B) cost가 정답이다.

어휘 renovation 보수 | cover (자금을) 대다 | donation 기부 | contribution 기여

10. 사용자들은 프로그램을 설치하기 전에 제품 설명서에 있는 계약 조건을 검토해야 한다.

해설 빈칸은 contract와 복합명사를 이루는 문장의 목적어 자리이다. 문맥상 '사용자들은 상품 설명서에 있는 계약 조건을 봐야 한다'는 의미가 자연스러우므로 (A) terms가 정답이다.

어휘 review 검토하다 | contract 계약 | product guide 제품 설명 | install 설치하다

11. 추가 수당은 잠재 고객들에게 현장 시연을 하도록 훈련된 전문가들에게 주어질 것이다.

해설 빈칸은 전치사 to의 목적어 자리이다. 빈칸을 후치 수식하는 과거분사구의 내용을 고려할 때, '현장 시연 교육을 받은 전문가들에게 추가 수

당이 주어질 것'이라는 의미가 되어야 자연스러우므로 (A) specialists가 정답이다.

어휘 additional 추가의 | on-site 현장의 | demonstration 시연 | prospective client 예상 고객 | installment 분할 불입 | account 계좌

12. 드레이븐 광고 회사 입사의 혜택은 뛰어난 실적에 대한 회사의 금전적 보상이다.

해설 빈칸은 be동사 뒤 문장의 주격 보어 자리이다. 문맥상 '입사 혜택은 실적에 대한 금전적 보상(인정)'이라는 의미가 자연스러우므로 (A) recognition이 정답이다.

어휘 benefit 혜택 | agency 대행사, 회사 | monetary 금전상의 | performance 실적, 성과 | recognition 인정 | disregard 무시 | neglect 방치, 소홀

13. 시의회에서는 바르투어의 교외 지역을 연례 가을 축제 장소로 결정했다.

해설 빈칸은 정관사 the의 수식을 받는 명사 자리로, 문맥상 '바르투어의 외곽지역을 연례 가을 축제 장소로 결정했다'는 의미가 되어야 자연스러우므로 (C) location이 정답이다.

어휘 city council 시의회 | decide on ~으로 결정하다 | suburb 교외 | annual 연례의

14. 플라이 하이 전자의 현장 아이티 감독관들은 다양한 범위의 기술에 있어서 풍부한 지식을 갖춘 간부급 직원들이다.

해설 빈칸은 a와 of knowledge 사이의 명사 자리이다. 문맥상 '풍부한 지식을 가진 직원들'이라는 의미가 자연스러우므로 a wealth of '풍부한'이라는 관용표현을 완성하는 (C) wealth가 정답이다.

어휘 on-site 현장의 | supervisor 감독관, 관리자 | a range of 다양한 | a wealth of 풍부한 | respect 존중

15. 앞으로 2년간의 확장 전략이 회의의 중점이 될 것이다.

해설 빈칸은 문장의 보어인 명사 자리로, '확장 전략이 회의의 중점이 될 것'이라는 의미가 되어야 자연스러우므로 (A) focus가 정답이다.

어휘 expansion 확장 | strategy 전략 | scheme 계획

16. 마르가테 건설은 에일러빌 기차역의 복구를 끝냈는데, 이는 박물관으로 재개장할 것이다.

해설 빈칸은 문장의 목적어 자리이다. 빈칸을 수식하는 of 전치사구와 which 관계절을 고려할 때, '기차역의 복구작업이 끝나서 박물관으로 재개장할 것'이라는 의미가 되어야 자연스러우므로 (B) restoration이 정답이다.

어휘 construction 건설 | reopen 재개장하다 | fulfillment 이행, 수행, 성취 | restoration 복구, 복원

17. 삼손 건축가 시상위원회는 환경친화적 자재로 건설된 디자인을 위한 새로운 카테고리를 소개했다.

해설 빈칸은 문장의 목적어 자리이다. 문맥상 '시상위원회에서 친환경 자재 디자인에 수여할 새로운 시상 카테고리를 소개했다'는 의미가 나와야 자연스러우므로 (C) category가 정답이다.

어휘 architect 건축가 | construct 건설하다 | eco-friendly 환경친화적인 | material 재료, 자재 | superiority 우월성, 우세 | recruitment 모집 | engagement 약속

18. 볼로디아 겐리호비치는 다운타운 수리 팀의 리더로서 탁월한 업무로 인정받았다.

해설 해석상 '팀 리더로서 탁월한 업무로 인정받았다'는 의미가 자연스러우므로 (D) work가 정답이다.

어휘 recognize 인정하다 | exceptional 우수한, 특출한 | title 제목, 표제 | appearance 모습, 출현 | work 일, 업무

19. 저희 국립 디시즈 병원에서는 예약된 시간에 환자들을 만나기 위한 최선의 노력을 다합니다.

해설 '제시간에 진찰하기 위해 노력을 한다'는 의미로 정답은 (C) effort이다. effort는 가산 명사라는 것과 뒤에 주로 to부정사의 수식을 받는다는 점도 꼭 기억해야 한다.

어휘 book 예약하다 | output 생산량 | instance 사례 | make an effort 노력하다

20. 지난 몇 달간 강수량의 증가로 인해, 현재 지하수의 축적은 평균보다 훨씬 높다.

해설 빈칸은 문장의 주어 자리이다. Due to 전치사구와 주절의 관계를 고려할 때, '강수량 증가로 지하수의 축적(보유)이 평균 이상치'라는 의미가 되어야 자연스러우므로 축적의 의미인 (B) accumulation이 정답이다.

어휘 amount 양 | rainfall 강수 | groundwater 지하수 | generalization 일반화 | accumulation 축적 | designation 지정

UNIT 07. 형용사 어휘 1

Practice
본서 p.153

1. (D)   **2.** (D)   **3.** (C)   **4.** (A)   **5.** (D)
6. (D)   **7.** (D)   **8.** (B)   **9.** (D)   **10.** (B)

1. 고객 불만이 발생했을 때 관리자가 그것을 인지하는 것이 중요하다.

해설 가주어, 진주어(It ~ that ~) 구문으로 빈칸이 가주어의 보어 자리에 위치해 있으므로 that절 이하의 의미를 확인하면, '고객 불만 발생 시, 관리자가 그 사실을 알고 있는 것이 중요하다'는 의미이므로 (D) critical이 정답이다.

어휘 make aware of ~을 알게 하다 | complaint 불만 | occur 일어나다, 발생하다 | rapid 빠른 | hectic 정신없이 바쁜 | valid 유효한, 타당한 | critical 대단히 중요한, 비판적인

2. 양측은 합병 조건에 동의했고 그것은 지난 수요일에 최종 확정되었다.

해설 해석상 '~에 동의하는, 받아들일 수 있는'의 의미가 적합하므로 (D) agreeable이 정답이다.

어휘 side 측, 쪽 | term (계약) 조건 | merger 합병 | finalize 완결하다, 마무리 짓다 | convinced 확신하는 | focused 집중한 | appreciative 고마워하는 | agreeable 동의하는, 받아들일 수 있는

3. 실론 사의 헌신적인 고객서비스 직원들은 전화를 건 사람들이 필요로 하는 그 어떤 종류의 도움도 제공한다.

해설 해석상 '헌신적인 고객서비스 직원들이 요청받는 어떤 서비스도 제공한다'는 의미가 적합하므로 (C) dedicated가 정답이다.

어휘 personnel 직원들 | assistance 도움, 지원 | require 요구하다 | inevitable 피할 수 없는 | continuous 계속되는 | dedicated 헌신적인 | established 인정받는

4. 모든 주식 시장 투자는 손해를 볼 위험이 있다는 것을 알아야 한다.

해설 숙어적인 표현으로 be aware of[that] '~을 알다'로 암기해 두면 빨리 답을 찾을 수 있다. 그러므로 정답은 (A) aware가 된다.

어휘 stock market 주식 시장 | investing 투자(행위) | involve 수반하다 | risk 위험 | aware 알고 있는, 의식하는 | confirmed 확고부동한 | compensated 보상받은

5. 매년, 시모가모 부도칸은 다양한 뛰어난 무예인들의 시연을 조직한다.

해설 해석상 '뛰어난 무예인들'이라는 의미가 적합하므로 (D) accomplished가 정답이다.

어휘 organize 조직하다, 주최하다 | demonstration 시연 | a variety of 다양한 | martial artist 무예인, 무술가 | concerned 걱정하는, 관심이 있는 | probable 있을 것 같은 | comprehensible 이해할 수 있는 | accomplished 뛰어난

6. 탈로파 씨는 켄 씨가 올해 영업부 부사장으로 승진될 것이라고 확신한다.

해설 '~을 확신하다[자부하다]'라는 뜻의 숙어 표현으로 be confident that인 (D) confident가 정답이다.

어휘 promote 승진시키다 | division 부서 | designated 지정된 | guaranteed 보장된 | be confident that ~을 자부하다[확신하다]

7. 우리 지역은 5주 연속 따뜻한 겨울 날씨를 보였지만, 내일 밤까지는 눈보라가 몰아칠 것으로 예상된다.

해설 해석상 '5주 연속해서'라는 의미가 적합하므로 (D) consecutive가 정답이다.

어휘 region 지역 | blizzard 눈보라 | forecast 예측하다 | consecutive 연이은

8. 코트야드 커뮤니케이션 애플리케이션은 스마트폰을 포함한 모든 주요 컴퓨터 장치와 호환된다.

해설 '~와 호환되다'라는 뜻의 be compatible with라는 관용적인 표현으로 (B) compatible이 정답이다.

어휘 application 응용장치, 애플리케이션 | major 주된, 주요한 | including ~을 포함하여 | derive 끌어내다 | compatible 호환이 되는 | compulsory 강제적인, 필수의

9. 복잡한 교통법규를 설명하는 워크숍이 전일제 운전자에게 무료로 제공된다.

해설 해석상 '복잡한'이라는 의미가 적합하므로 정답은 (D) complicated 가 된다.

어휘 traffic law 교통 법규 | for free 무료로 | full-time 전일제의, 상근의 | extreme 극도의 | complicated 복잡한

10. 10년 이상 이용해 주신 충성스러운 고객들에 감사를 전하고자, 오렌지 여행사는 기꺼이 이번 달 홍콩으로 가는 무료 항공권을 제공합니다.

해설 감사의 표현으로 자연스럽게 이어지는 '무료의'라는 의미의 (B) complimentary가 정답이다.

어휘 in appreciation of ~에 감사하여 | loyal 충성하는 | decade 10년 | be willing to 기꺼이 ~하다 | receptive 수용의 | complimentary 무료의 | approximate 거의 정확한 | experimental 실험적인

UNIT 08. 형용사 어휘 2

Practice
본서 p.155

1. (C)	2. (C)	3. (D)	4. (A)	5. (B)
6. (A)	7. (A)	8. (C)	9. (D)	10. (C)

1. 현재 부동산 시장을 고려해, 크리스토발 투자사는 새로운 부동산을 매입하는 것을 주저하고 있다.

해설 '~하기를 주저하다'라는 뜻의 to부정사 관용표현 be hesitant to의 (C) hesitant가 정답이다.

어휘 given ~을 고려해 볼 때 | present 현재의 | real estate 부동산 | acquire 얻다, 취득하다 | property 부동산, 자산 | delinquent 연체된 | hesitant 망설이는

2. 40대 이상의 전기 차량들로, 스타게이즈 운송은 현재 사우스 햄튼에서 가장 경제적인 택시를 운영하고 있다.

해설 뒤에 taxi fleet과 잘 어울리는 '경제적인'이라는 뜻을 가진 (C) economical이 정답이다.

어휘 electric 전기의 | presently 현재에 | fleet 무리 | internal 내부의 | attentive 주의를 기울이는 | economical 경제적인, 실속 있는 | projected 예상된

3. 입사 10년 이상 된 55세 이상의 직원은 통상 전액 복리후생으로 조기 퇴직의 자격이 된다.

해설 해석상 '입사 10년 이상 된 55세 이상의 직원은 조기 퇴직의 자격이 된다'라는 의미가 적합하므로 (D) eligible이 정답이다. be eligible for 로 같이 암기해 두면 좋다.

어휘 early retirement 조기 퇴직 | benefit 수당, 특전 | optional 선택적인 | suggestible 남의 영향을 받기 쉬운 | eligible ~을 가질 수 있는

4. 우리 채용담당자 입장에서 볼 때, 관련 분야의 안정적인 선행 취업 이력은 학위 보유에 상응한다.

해설 관용적인 표현으로 '~에 상응하다'라는 뜻의 be equivalent to에서 (A) equivalent가 정답이다.

어휘 recruiter 채용담당자 | point of view 관점, 견해 | stable 안정적인 | history 이력 | prior 선행의, 사전의 | field 분야 | possess 보유하다, 소유하다 | degree 학위 | equivalent 동등한

5. 온라인 주문은 특정 주세와 지방세가 면제될 수 있지만, 이를 확인하는 것은 구매자의 책임입니다.

해설 관용적인 표현으로 '~가 면제되다'라는 뜻의 be exempt from이 적절하므로 (B) exempt가 정답이다.

어휘 confirm 확인하다 | exempt 면제되는 | derived 유래된, 파생된

6. 펜테크 대학에서 이번 금요일에 있는 매년 열리는 축제에서 세계적인 피아니스트 마이라 장을 모시게 된 것을 행운으로 생각합니다.

해설 유명한 사람이 나온다는 말과 자연스럽게 어울리는 '~해서 운이 좋다' 라는 뜻의 be fortunate to가 적절하므로 (A) fortunate가 정답이다.

어휘 feature 중요 역할을 하다, ~을 특별 인기거리로 하다 | be fortunate to ~해서 운이 좋다 | admired 칭송받는

7. 모든 문서 기록들을 전자 데이터베이스에 전송하는 것은 만만치 않은 일일 것이다.

해설 해석상 적합한 (A) formidable이 정답으로, 평소에 '만만치 않은 일, 엄청난 도전'의 뜻인 formidable challenge로 같이 암기해 두면 좋다.

어휘 transfer 전송하다 | electronic 전자의 | formidable challenge 만만치 않은 일 | reversible 뒤집을 수 있는 | cohesive 화합하는

8. 월요일 오전의 많은 통화량 때문에, 고객 서비스팀과의 연결이 예상보다 더 오래 걸릴 수 있다.

해설 해석상 '많은 통화량 때문에'라는 의미가 적합하므로 (C) heavy가 정답이다.

어휘 due to ~때문에 | call volume 통화량 | extended 길어진

9. 올해 말에 끝날 것으로 예상되는 식사 공간 리모델링이 지역 당국과의 진행 중인 문제로 지연될 것이다.

해설 issue가 나와서 '해결하다'의 의미인 solve가 들어가는 (A)를 선택하지 않도록 조심하자. dissolved는 '용해된'의 의미로 오답이다. 해석상 '진행 중인 문제'의 뜻으로 적절한 (D) ongoing이 정답이다.

어휘 **authorities** 당국, 관헌 | **dissolved** 용해된 | **considerate** 사려 깊은 | **restrained** 자제하는 | **ongoing** 진행 중인

10. 마케팅 조사 결과처럼 제품 출시 결과가 좋게 나오길 바랍니다.

해설 해석상 '제품 출시 결과가 좋게 나오길 바란다'는 의미가 적절하므로 that절을 목적어로 하는 형용사 (C) hopeful이 정답이다.

어휘 **product launch** 제품 출시 | **favorable** 호의적인, 순조로운 | **suggest** 시사하다, 내비치다 | **be flattered** 으쓱해지다 | **excessive** 지나친, 과도한 | **worrisome** 걱정스러운

UNIT 09. 형용사 어휘 3

Practice
본서 p.157

1. (D)	2. (C)	3. (B)	4. (C)	5. (C)
6. (C)	7. (A)	8. (B)	9. (D)	10. (A)

1. 나무 바닥이 멋지긴 하지만, 여러분은 그것이 물 피해에 매우 취약하다는 것을 인식해야 합니다.

해설 해석상 '물 피해에 취약하다'라는 의미가 적합하므로 '~에 취약하다'라는 뜻의 be vulnerable to에서 (D) vulnerable이 정답이다.

어휘 **wooden floor** 마루 | **attractive** 멋진, 마음을 끄는 | **frequent** 빈번한 | **fond** 좋아하는, 잘하는 | **vulnerable** 취약한

2. 산업 분석가들은 목전에 둔 합병이 다음 주 월요일 제이케이 사에 의해 승인될 것으로 예상한다.

해설 아직 합병이 이루어지지 않았으므로 '임박한'의 의미인 (C) pending이 정답이다.

어휘 **analyst** 분석가 | **merger** 합병 | **pending** 임박한, 미해결의 | **attentive** 주의를 기울이는

3. 우리의 문의에 대한 당신의 빠른 답변에 미리 감사드립니다.

해설 '빠른 답변에 감사드린다'는 의미이므로 '신속한'이란 뜻의 (B) prompt가 정답이다.

어휘 **in advance** 미리, 사전에 | **response** 답변, 응답 | **inquiry** 문의 | **prompt** 신속한 | **obvious** 명확한

4. 노르딕 앵글러는 고객들로 하여금 물품을 구매하는 것에 흥미를 가질 수 있도록 하기 위해 낚시에 열정적인 판매 직원을 채용한다.

해설 해석상 '낚시에 열정적인 판매 직원'이라는 의미가 적절하므로 정답은 (C) enthusiastic이다. '~에 열광적이다'라는 뜻의 be enthusiastic about 표현을 기억해 둔다.

어휘 **hire** 채용하다 | **sales clerk** 판매 직원 | **purchase** 구매하다 | **courteous** 정중한 | **enthusiastic** 열정적인

5. 제이티엘 사의 기업 목표는 신뢰할 만한 직원들 없이는 이룰 수 없다.

해설 '신뢰할 만한 직원들'의 의미로 (C) reliable이 정답이다.

어휘 **objective** 목표, 목적 | **personnel** 직원들 | **content** 만족하는 | **convinced** 확신하는 | **reliable** 신뢰할 만한

6. 7월에, 알버트 박물관에서 유명한 화가 데미안 힐의 30개의 작품을 선보일 것이다.

해설 '유명한 사람의 작품'이라는 의미가 적합하므로 (C) renowned가 정답이다.

어휘 **piece** 조각, 작품 | **estimated** 추정되는 | **founded** 설립된 | **renowned** 저명한 | **allocated** 할당된

7. 커티스 의료 그룹에서 개인 파일에 행하는 정기 업데이트는 전적으로 안전하며, 환자들에게 안전과 기밀을 보장한다.

해설 해석상 '전적으로 안전하다'는 의미가 적합하므로 (A) secure가 정답이다.

어휘 **periodic** 주기적인 | **completely** 완전히, 전적으로 | **ensure** 보장하다 | **patient** 환자 | **safety** 안전 | **confidentiality** 비밀유지 | **authentic** 진짜인 | **dedicated** 전념하는

8. 유목 전문 여행가인 데이빗 무라즈가 쓴 그 이야기는 〈트래블 먼슬리〉의 다음 호에 실릴 예정이다.

해설 해석상 '다음 호'라는 의미가 적절하므로 (B) upcoming이 정답이다.

어휘 **nomad** 유목민 | **feature** 특색으로 하다 | **issue** (잡지의) 호 | **upcoming** 다가오는, 곧 있을 | **ahead** 앞으로, 미리 | **forward** 앞으로; 보내다

9. 트리스톤 도서관은 관내에 방치된 채로 남겨진 개인 소지품을 책임지지 않습니다.

해설 left unattended라고 해서 '방치된 채로'의 의미를 완성하는 (D) unattended가 정답이다.

어휘 **liable** 법적 책임이 있는 | **belongings** 소유물 | **premises** 부지 | **ineligible** 자격이 없는, 부적격의 | **nonreturnable** 반환할 수 없는 | **discontinued** 중지된 | **unattended** 주인이 없는, 방치된

10. 지난 분기의 전례가 없는 수익 증가로 인해, 모든 영업 직원들이 이번 달에 특별 보너스를 받을 것이다.

해설 해석상 '전례가 없는'이라는 의미가 적절하므로 (A) unprecedented가 정답이다.

어휘 **revenue** 수익 | **quarter** 분기 | **be awarded a bonus** 보너스를 받다 | **unprecedented** 전례가 없는 | **imminent** 임박한 | **unsalvageable** 구조될 수 없는 | **extraneous** 관련 없는

60 파고다 토익 고득점 완성 RC

REVIEW TEST 03

본서 p.158

1. (B)	2. (B)	3. (C)	4. (A)	5. (A)
6. (A)	7. (A)	8. (C)	9. (B)	10. (C)
11. (C)	12. (A)	13. (C)	14. (B)	15. (A)
16. (A)	17. (D)	18. (A)	19. (B)	20. (A)

1. 긴급한 주의를 요하는 문제가 아니라면 모든 업무 요청서는 서면으로 제출되어야 한다.

해설 빈칸은 명사 attention을 수식하는 자리이다. 주절과 unless 종속절의 관계를 고려할 때, '긴급하지 않다면, 업무 요청서는 서면으로 제출되어야 한다'는 의미가 자연스러우므로 (B) urgent가 정답이다.

어휘 work request 업무 요청서 | submit 제출하다 | in writing 서면으로 | unless ~이 아닌 한 | issue 문제 | require 요구하다 | attention 주의, 관심

2. 회사 카페테리아 신입사원은 근무 시작 전 필수 건강검진을 통과해야 한다.

해설 빈칸은 명사구 health checkup을 수식하는 형용사 자리이다. '신입사원은 필수 건강검진을 통과해야 한다'는 의미가 적절하므로 (B) mandatory가 정답이다.

어휘 hire 신입사원 | pass 통과하다 | health checkup 건강검진 | employment 고용, 근무 | substantial 상당한 | mandatory 필수의 | prescriptive 지시하는, 권위적인 | ingenious 기발한

3. 지역 꽃집 주인이 시장 취임식용 꽃장식을 준비했다.

해설 빈칸은 명사 florist를 수식하는 형용사 자리이다. '지역 꽃집 주인이 취임식용 꽃장식을 준비했다'는 의미가 되어야 자연스러우므로 (C) local이 정답이다.

어휘 florist 꽃집 (주인), 플로리스트 | arrange 마련하다, 준비하다 | floral decoration 꽃장식 | mayor 시장 | inauguration ceremony 취임식 | dominant 우세한 | prospective 장래의

4. 직원용 새로운 과일 바구니는 퇴근할 때 집으로 가져갈 수 있을 것이다.

해설 빈칸은 be동사 뒤 보어 자리이다. '과일 바구니는 퇴근할 때 집으로 가져갈 수 있을 것'이라는 의미가 나와야 자연스러우므로 (A) available이 정답이다.

어휘 available 이용 가능한 | content 만족하는 | accurate 정확한 | reduced 감소된

5. 오랜 재임 기간 동안, 레이놀즈 교수는 회계 분야에서 광범위한 작업을 수행했으며 새로운 기업 분석 기법을 알아냈다.

해설 빈칸은 명사 work를 수식하는 형용사 자리이다. '오랜 재임 기간 동안 회계 분야에서 광범위한 작업을 수행했다'는 의미가 자연스러우므로 (A) extensive가 정답이다.

어휘 tenure 재임 (기간) | field 분야 | accounting 회계 | analyze 분석하다 | extensive 광범위한 | provisional 임시의 | contiguous 인접한 | simulated 모의의

6. 보수 기간 동안, 직원들은 임시로 화장실을 제한적으로 이용할 수 있게 된다.

해설 빈칸은 명사 access를 수식하는 형용사 자리이다. '보수 기간 동안 임시로 화장실을 제한적으로 이용할 수 있게 된다'는 의미가 자연스러우므로 (A) limited가 정답이다.

어휘 renovation 보수 | temporarily 일시적으로, 임시로 | have access to ~에 접근할 수 있다 | restroom 화장실 | avoidable 막을 수 있는 | managing 처리[경영, 관리]하는, 수뇌의

7. 늦게 떠나는 경우를 대비하여 인증된 입장권을 소지하고 있으면 3시간의 주차요금을 면제받습니다.

해설 빈칸은 명사구 admission ticket을 수식하는 자리이다. 문맥상 '인증된 입장권은 3시간의 주차요금을 공제해 준다'는 의미가 자연스러우므로 (A) validated가 정답이다.

어휘 waive 면제하다 | in case ~인 경우에 대비하여 | validated 인증된

8. 헬싱키 소재의 스타트업 회사인 바호바 금융이 지난 분기에 급속한 성장을 경험했을 때 모든 예측을 뛰어넘었다.

해설 빈칸은 명사 growth를 수식하는 자리이다. 주절과 when 종속절의 관계를 고려할 때, '급속한 성장을 이뤘을 때 모든 예측을 뛰어넘었다'는 의미가 되어야 자연스러우므로 (C) rapid가 정답이다.

어휘 start-up company 스타트업 회사 | surpass 능가하다, 뛰어넘다 | prediction 예상, 예측 | growth 성장 | quarter 분기 | sole 유일한

9. 현재의 직원을 승진시키는 것은 킬케니 사에서 자격을 갖춘 관리자들을 찾는 현실적인 접근법이다.

해설 빈칸은 명사 approach를 수식하는 자리이다. 문맥상 '현 직원을 승진시키는 것이 자격을 갖춘 직원을 찾는 현실적인 접근 방법'이라는 의미가 자연스러우므로 (B) practical이 정답이다.

어휘 promote 승진시키다 | current 현재의 | approach 접근법 | qualified 자격이 되는 | content 만족한

10. 바틀비 저축 대부조합은 고객들에게 다양한 범위의 회사에 투자하라고 권고한다.

해설 빈칸은 명사 range를 수식하는 자리이다. a range of '다양한'은 관용표현이므로, '다양함'의 의미를 가지는 (C) diverse가 정답이다.

어휘 savings and loan 저축 대부조합 | advise 권고하다 | invest 투자하다 | range 범위 | proportionate 비례하는

11. 디더블유-234 프린터의 매출은 신상품 카탈로그에서 독자 섹션을 보장해줄 만큼 충분하지 않았다.

해설 빈칸은 현재 완료 시제의 be동사 뒤 주격 보어 자리이다. 빈칸 뒤 to부정사구를 고려할 때, 문맥상 '카탈로그의 신상품 섹션을 보장해 줄 만큼 매출이 충분하지 않다'는 의미가 나와야 자연스러우므로 enough to V 'V할 만큼 충분한'이라는 형태를 완성하는 (C) enough가 정답이다.

어휘 sales 판매, 매출 | warrant 보장하다, 정당하게 만들다

12. 재정 자문가의 도움 없이 귀사의 자산을 관리하는 것은 힘들고 심지어 위험할 수도 있다.

해설 빈칸은 문장의 주격 보어 자리이다. 등위접속사 and로 연결된 또 다른 주격 보어 hard를 고려할 때, 문맥상 '자산을 관리하는 것은 어렵고 심지어 위험할 수 있다'는 의미가 되어야 자연스러우므로 (A) risky가 정답이다.

어휘 manage 관리하다 | asset 자산 | even 심지어 | financial advisor 재정 자문가 | concentrated 집중된

13. 샘 환 사의 인수는 협상이 긍정적인 방향으로 계속되기만 한다면, 올해 말까지 실현 가능하다.

해설 빈칸은 be동사 뒤의 주격 보어 자리이다. 주절과 as long as 종속절의 관계를 고려할 때, '협상이 잘 진행되는 한, 인수가 연말까지 실현 가능하다'는 의미가 자연스러우므로 (C) feasible이 정답이다.

어휘 acquisition (기업의) 인수 | as long as ~하는 한 | negotiation 협상, 교섭 | blend 섞다 | feasible 실현 가능한 | ultimate 궁극적인

14. 전문가들은 하나 상사가 꾸준한 수익성 기록을 유지해 왔기 때문에 안정적인 회사라 여긴다.

해설 빈칸은 명사 firm을 수식하는 자리이다. 주절과 because 종속절의 관계를 고려할 때, '꾸준한 수익을 기록했기 때문에 안정적인 회사로 여긴다'는 의미가 자연스러우므로 (B) stable이 정답이다.

어휘 firm 회사 | maintain 유지하다 | steady 꾸준한, 변함없는 | profitability 수익성 | distant 거리를 두는

15. 제스퍼 & 해먼드에서는, 정확한 정보를 보장하기 위해 재무제표에 정기적으로 감사가 실시된다.

해설 빈칸은 명사 information을 수식하는 형용사 자리이다. '정확한 정보를 보장하기 위해 재무제표에 정기적으로 감사가 실시된다'는 의미가 자연스러우므로 (A) accurate가 정답이다.

어휘 financial statement 재무제표 | audit 회계를 감사하다 | regularly 정기적으로 | ensure 보장하다 | information 정보 | accurate 정확한 | ample 충분한 | effective 효과적인 | constructive 건설적인

16. 회사가 찾고 있는 자격요건 중 가장 중요한 것은 여러 다른 국가의 직원들을 관리할 수 있는 능력이다.

해설 빈칸은 주어와 보어 간 도치된 문장의 주격 보어 자리이다. 문맥상 '회사가 찾는 자격요건 중 가장 중요한 것은 직원 관리능력'이라는 의미가 자연스러우므로 (A) Primary가 정답이다.

어휘 qualification 자격요건 | seek 찾다 | manage 다루다, 관리하다

17. 우리는 고객들의 비밀을 중요시하기 때문에, 그들의 개인정보를 보호하는 것은 필수적인 일이다.

해설 빈칸은 'It-that' 가주어-진주어 문장의 보어 자리이다. 접속사 so로 연결된 두 문장의 관계를 고려할 때, '고객 정보를 중요시 여기므로, 고객 개인정보의 보호는 필수적'이라는 의미가 되어야 자연스러우므로 (D) imperative가 정답이다.

어휘 confidentiality 비밀, 기밀 | destructive 파괴적인 | remunerative 보수가 많은 | imperative 반드시 해야 하는, 긴요한

18. 킨 씨는 비용 환급 절차를 되도록 투명하게 하기 위하여, 승인된 모든 지출에 대한 자세한 설명을 제공할 것이다.

해설 빈칸은 동사 make의 목적격 보어 자리이다. to부정사구와 주절의 관계를 고려할 때, '비용 환급 절차를 투명하게 하기 위해, 모든 승인된 지출에 대해 자세히 설명할 것'이라는 의미가 되어야 자연스러우므로 '투명한'이라는 의미의 (A) transparent가 정답이다.

어휘 expense 비용 | reimbursement 환급 | procedure 절차 | as ~ as possible 가능한 ~한 | explanation 설명 | approve 승인하다 | spending 지출 | transparent 투명한 | extraordinary 특출난

19. 〈웨스트우드 가이드〉는 근로자들을 더 생산적이 되도록 교육시키는 가장 효과적인 방법들을 제시한다.

해설 빈칸은 명사 methods를 수식하는 자리이다. 문맥상 '직원들을 더 생산적이게 교육하는 가장 효과적인 방법들'이라는 의미가 자연스러우므로 (B) effective가 정답이다.

어휘 present 제시하다, 나타내다 | method 방법, 수단 | train 교육하다 | productive 생산적인 | contained 억제하는 | reluctant 꺼리는

20. 리 씨가 작성한 보고서는 다음 분기에 회사의 브랜드 인지도를 높이는 것에 대한 포괄적인 접근법을 강조했다.

해설 빈칸은 명사 approach를 수식하는 자리이다. 문맥상 '보고서는 포괄적인 접근법을 강조했다'는 의미가 자연스러우므로 (A) comprehensive가 정답이다.

어휘 emphasize 강조하다 | approach 접근법 | raise 높이다, 올리다 | organization 조직, 기관 | brand recognition 브랜드 인지도 | quarter 분기 | comprehensive 포괄적인, 종합적인 | pursue 추구하다 | respective 각각의 | comprising 포함하는

UNIT 10. 부사 어휘 1

Practice
본서 p.161

1. (A)	2. (A)	3. (D)	4. (D)	5. (A)
6. (A)	7. (C)	8. (D)	9. (D)	10. (D)

1. 모든 인구 통계 데이터가 수집되면, 그 구역에 대한 영업 직원들의 숫자가 그에 맞춰 결정될 것이다.

해설 해석상 '부합해서, 알맞게'의 의미가 적합하므로 (A) accordingly가 정답이다.

어휘 demographics 인구 통계 | district 구역 | accordingly 부합해서, 알맞게 | typically 전형적으로 | immeasurably 헤아릴 수 없을

정도로 | **implicitly** 암암리에

2. 많은 센텐셜 은행 직원들은 본문이 너무 흐릿해서 지난 분기 소식지를 거의 읽을 수 없다고 언급했다.

해설 '흐릿해서 거의 읽을 수 없었다'는 부정의 의미가 나오는 것이 적절하므로 (A) barely가 정답이다.

어휘 **text** 본문 | **blurry** 흐릿한 | **barely** 거의 ~아니게 | **nearly** (= almost) 거의

3. 적합한 준비와 신선한 재료는 헤스티아 식당의 요리사들에게 똑같이 중요하다.

해설 해석상 '적절한 준비와 신선한 재료가 똑같이 중요하다'는 의미가 적합하므로 (D) equally가 정답이다.

어휘 **proper** 적절한 | **preparation** 준비 | **ingredient** 재료 | **gradually** 점진적으로 | **equally** 똑같이

4. 기무라 씨의 주문은 8월 9일까지 완전히 배송되지 않았다.

해설 해석상 '배송이 완전히 마무리되지 않았다'는 의미이므로 (D) completely가 정답이다.

어휘 **order** 주문 | **deliver** 배송하다 | **enormously** 엄청나게 | **relatively** 비교적 | **periodically** 주기적으로 | **completely** 완전히

5. 작가 달리아 보른은 10개월마다 새 소설을 써야 할 계약상의 의무가 있다.

해설 동사 obligate와 의미가 맞는 (A), (C)가 답이 될 수 있으나, 뒤에 '10개월마다'라고 해서 구체적으로 표현되어 있으므로 '계약상 의무가 있다'라는 의미를 만드는 (A) contractually가 정답이다.

어휘 **obligate** 의무를 지우다 | **contractually** 계약상으로 | **descriptively** 묘사적으로 | **responsibly** 책임감 있게 | **critically** 비판적으로

6. 지앤비 본사는 뉴 햄튼의 중심부에 편리하게 위치해 있다.

해설 located와 자주 활용되는 부사로 (A) conveniently가 정답이다. 평소에 conveniently located로 암기해 두면 좋다.

어휘 **conveniently locate** 편리하게 위치하다 | **gracefully** 우아하게 | **evenly** 고르게 | **fluently** 유창하게

7. 지난달 꾸준한 좋은 평가 덕택에, 몬타나 로스트가 〈고메 위클리〉에서 '최고의 식당'으로 선정되었다.

해설 최고의 식당으로 선정되었다는 것은 '꾸준하게 호평을 받았다'라는 의미와 같으므로 (C) consistently가 정답이다.

어휘 **owing to** ~때문에 | **good review** 호평 | **select** 고르다, 선정하다 | **practically** 사실상 | **potentially** 가능성 있게 | **consistently** 지속적으로 | **reluctantly** 마지못해

8. 최근의 한 연구는 무료 자전거 임대 프로그램을 제공하는 것이 시내 공기 오염을 급격히 줄여준다는 것을 밝혀냈다.

해설 해석상 '공기 오염을 급격히 줄여준다'는 의미가 적합하므로 (D) drastically가 정답이다.

어휘 **reveal** 밝히다 | **offer** 제공하다 | **reduce** 줄이다

9. 올해, 그린 오토 상은 전기 자동차를 만든 회사들에게 독점적으로 주어질 것이다.

해설 해석상 '독점적으로, 배타적으로'의 의미가 적합하고, 뒤에 전치사구를 수식하는 부사인 (D) exclusively가 정답이다.

어휘 **award** 상을 주다 | **manufacture** 제조하다 | **electronic vehicle** 전기 자동차 | **exceptionally** 뛰어나게 | **routinely** 일상적으로 | **exclusively** 독점적으로

10. 말론 전자의 보증서는 모든 수리 작업이 공인된 기사들에 의해 수행되어야 한다는 것을 명시하고 있다.

해설 궁합으로 암기해 두면 빨리 풀 수 있는 문제로, '명시하다'라는 의미의 (D) explicitly가 정답이다. 평소에 explicitly state로 암기해 두면 좋다.

어휘 **warranty** 보증서 | **repair** 수리 | **authorized** 공인된 | **hardly** 거의 ~않는다 | **cautiously** 주의 깊게 | **indefinitely** 무기한으로 | **explicitly** 명료하게

UNIT 11. 부사 어휘 2

Practice
본서 p.163

| 1. (D) | 2. (C) | 3. (D) | 4. (C) | 5. (C) |
| 6. (D) | 7. (B) | 8. (B) | 9. (C) | 10. (A) |

1. 예전 거주지였던 센터빌은 사무실 단지와 상업 건물들을 수용하기 시작했다.

해설 과거 시제와 쓰이며, '한때, 예전에'의 의미가 적절하므로 (D) formerly가 정답이다.

어휘 **residential area** 거주지 | **accommodate** 수용하다 | **complex** 복합 건물 | **commercial** 상업적인 | **readily** 손쉽게 | **constructively** 건설적으로 | **formerly** 예전에

2. 쳉 박사는 공장의 에너지 수요를 정확하게 기록하기 위해 상세한 차트를 고안했다.

해설 해석상 '정확하게 기록하기 위해서'라는 의미가 적합하므로 (C) precisely가 정답이다.

어휘 **design** 고안하다, 설계하다 | **detailed** 상세한, 자세한 | **record** 기록하다 | **broadly** 넓게 | **relatively** 상대적으로 | **precisely** 정확하게 | **dominantly** 우세하게

3. 우리 제품에 관한 긴급한 모든 요청은 고객 서비스부로 즉시 문의돼야 한다.

해설 urgent라는 형용사와 자연스럽게 이어지는 '즉시'의 의미가 적합하므로 (D) immediately가 정답이다.

어휘 urgent 긴급한 | inquiry 문의 | direct 지시하다, 안내하다 | recently 최근에 | significantly 상당히 | nearly 거의

4. 작년 11월에 디자인된 플릿 풋웨어의 신상 크로스 트레이닝 신발은 마침내 다음 주 생산을 시작할 것이다.

해설 해석상 '마침내'라는 의미가 적절하므로 (C) finally가 정답이다.

어휘 design 디자인하다, 설계하다 | production 생산 | extremely 극도로

5. 벌링턴의 거주자들은 도로에 금이 가 있는 것이 보이기 시작한 이래로 안전에 관해 점차 우려하고 있다.

해설 해석상 '점점'이라는 의미가 적합하므로 (C) increasingly가 정답이다.

어휘 resident 거주민 | worry about ~에 대해 걱정하다 | crack 금 | barely 간신히, 거의 ~않다 | virtually 사실상 | increasingly 점점, 점차

6. 패러웨이 빌더스와 구루 퍼니처 사이의 관계는 상호 이익이 되어 왔다.

해설 '상호 이익이 되는'이라는 의미의 mutually beneficial이 되어야 하므로 (D) mutually가 정답이다.

어휘 beneficial 유익한, 이로운 | commonly 흔히 | dominantly 지배적으로 | exactly 정확히 | mutually 서로, 상호 간에

7. 브라이턴 시립 동물원은 매주 평균적으로 거의 5천여 명의 방문객을 맞이한다.

해설 해석상 '거의 5천 명의 방문객들'의 의미가 적절하며 수사를 수식하는 부사 자리이므로 (B) nearly가 정답이다.

어휘 average 평균 ~이 되다

8. 주간회의에서, 벤틀리 씨는 회계팀이 업무를 더 효율적으로 마무리하는 데 도움이 되는 조언을 자주 제공한다.

해설 해석상 '조언을 자주 제공한다'는 의미가 적합하므로 (B) frequently가 정답이다. 빈도부사는 주로 현재 시제와 함께 온다.

어휘 accounting 회계 (업무) | complete 완료하다, 끝마치다 | task 직무 | efficiently 능률적으로 | neatly 깔끔하게 | frequently 빈번하게 | enormously 엄청나게 | feasibly 실행할 수 있게

9. 그 책자에는 모든 크기의 행사들에 부합할 지역 내 적당한 가격의 광범위한 호텔 목록이 기재되어 있다.

해설 분사 형용사인 priced를 수식하기에 알맞은 부사를 골라야 한다. 지역 내 적당한 가격의 호텔 목록이 있다는 의미이므로 정답은 (C) moderately가 된다.

어휘 brochure 책자 | extensive 광범위한 | listing 명단 | cater to ~을 충족시키다 | rapidly 빨리, 신속히 | relatively 상대적으로 | moderately 적당히, 알맞게 | subsequently 그 뒤에, 나중에

10. 글로벌 마케팅 수석 매니저로서, 타카시마 씨는 종종 한국, 주로 서울을 방문한다.

해설 해석상 '주로'라는 의미가 적합하므로 (A) primarily가 정답이다.

어휘 frequently 종종 | primarily 주로 | relatively 상대적으로 | temporarily 임시적으로

UNIT 12. 부사 어휘 3

Practice

본서 p.165

| 1. (A) | 2. (C) | 3. (C) | 4. (C) | 5. (A) |
| 6. (A) | 7. (C) | 8. (D) | 9. (D) | 10. (A) |

1. 재스퍼 로만의 샘플 작품이 〈갤러리아 갤로어 매거진〉에서 눈에 띄게 다뤄질 것이다.

해설 동사 display를 수식하는 부사로 '눈에 띄게, 현저하게'의 의미가 적절하므로 (A) prominently가 정답이다.

어휘 prominently 눈에 띄게 | critically 비판적으로 | intensely 강렬하게 | mutually 상호적으로

2. 헤론 사는 상업용 제품을 판매하고 개인용 물건은 좀처럼 가지고 있지 않다.

해설 빈칸 앞뒤에 commercial use와 personal use라는 대조적인 단어가 나오므로 부정을 나타내는 (C) rarely가 정답이다.

어휘 commercial 상업의 | stock 재고; 재고를 채우다 | mildly 가볍게 | supremely 극도로 | rarely 드물게

3. 레넥스 자동차의 세단 7의 가격은 다른 타 경쟁 회사에서 만든 차들보다 상대적으로 저렴하다.

해설 비교를 나타내는 문장에서 '상대적으로'라는 의미가 적절하므로 (C) relatively가 정답이다.

어휘 manufacture 제조하다 | competitor 경쟁자 | efficiently 효율적으로 | relatively 상대적으로, 비교적 | gradually 점차

4. 당신의 소포가 발송되었는지 확인하려면, 단지 저희 배송추적 페이지에 방문하셔서 주문번호만 입력하시면 됩니다.

해설 해석상 '단지, 그저 주문번호만 입력하면 된다'는 의미가 적절하므로 (C) simply가 정답이다.

어휘 ship 보내다, 발송하다 | delivery tracking 배송추적

5. 보안 우려 때문에, 서버실 이용이 엄격하게 제한된다.

해설 빈칸은 과거분사 limited를 수식하는 부사 자리이다. '서버실 이용이 엄격하게 제한된다'라는 의미가 적절하므로 (A) strictly가 정답이다.

어휘 security 보안 | concern 걱정, 우려 | access 이용, 접근 |

limited 제한된 | strictly 엄격하게 | barely 간신히, 가까스로 | slightly 조금, 약간 | casually 무심하게, 격식을 차리지 않고

6. 타마라 존스는 엠엔티 실험실에서 나온 연구 보고서를 철저하게 검토하고 몇몇 지역에서 조사가 더 필요함을 지적했다.

해설 동사 reviewed를 수식하는 부사로 '철저하게 검토하다'라는 의미가 적절하므로 (A) thoroughly가 정답이다.

어휘 point out 지적하다 | investigation 조사 | thoroughly 철저하게 | considerably 상당히

7. 영업부장인 소피 힐튼은 온라인으로만 하는 광고는 잠재적인 고객들을 유치할 수 있는 신뢰할 만한 접근 방법이 아니라고 언급했다.

해설 해석상 '오로지, 단지'라는 의미가 적절하므로 (C) solely가 정답이다.

어휘 reliable 신뢰할 만한 | draw 끌다 | prospective 잠재적인 | almost 거의 | closely 면밀하게 | solely 오로지 | otherwise 그렇지 않으면

8. 고객들이 속달 서비스를 선택하지 않는다면, 주문 배송은 명시된 우편 주소로 보통 3일 정도 걸린다.

해설 '보통 얼마 걸린다'라는 의미로 (D) typically가 정답이다.

어휘 unless ~하지 않으면 | express service 속달 서비스 | indicated 명시된 | substantially 상당히 | perpetually 영구히 | familiarly 친근하게 | typically 전형적으로

9. 솔트빌 시의회는 루민 가 도로 보수 공사에 대한 제안을 만장일치로 승인하는 데 투표했다.

해설 보통 문장에서 투표, 회의, 결정과 같은 의미와 잘 쓰이는 단어는 '만장일치로'라는 의미로 (D) unanimously가 정답이다.

어휘 approve 승인하다 | proposal 제안 | disparately 본질적으로 다르게 | numerously 수없이 많이 | separately 별도로 | unanimously 만장일치로

10. 가족 응급 상황으로 인해 델라니 씨는 이번 주 금요일 연례 연회에 유감스럽게도 참석할 수 없다.

해설 해석상 '유감스럽게도 참석을 못 하다'의 의미가 자연스러우므로 (A) regretfully가 정답이다.

어휘 banquet 연회 | emergency 응급 상황 | regretfully 유감스럽게도 | mistakenly 실수로 | forgetfully 잊을 수 없게 | eventually 결국에

REVIEW TEST 04
본서 p.166

1. (A)	2. (A)	3. (C)	4. (C)	5. (C)
6. (A)	7. (B)	8. (A)	9. (B)	10. (B)
11. (A)	12. (C)	13. (D)	14. (B)	15. (A)
16. (A)	17. (A)	18. (A)	19. (C)	20. (D)

1. 일부 직원들, 특히 행사 사진 촬영에 경험이 있는 사람들은 기념행사에서 사진 촬영을 해야 한다.

해설 빈칸은 뒤에 이어지는 those who 명사절을 수식하는 자리이다. 문맥상 '일부 직원 중에서도 특히 행사 사진 촬영 경험이 있는 사람들'이라는 의미가 되어야 자연스러우므로 (A) specifically가 정답이다.

어휘 anniversary celebration 기념행사 | experienced 경험이 많은, 능숙한

2. 무인 자동차를 평가하기 위해, 연구원들은 연료탱크가 빌 때까지 의도적으로 차를 운행시켰다.

해설 빈칸은 주어와 동사 사이에서 동사를 수식하는 자리이다. 문맥상 '연료탱크가 빌 때까지 의도적으로 무인자동차가 운행하도록 두었다'는 의미가 자연스러우므로 (A) intentionally가 정답이다.

어휘 assess 평가하다 | autonomous car 무인 자동차 | intentionally 의도적으로 | forcefully 힘차게, 효과적으로

3. 코루마 디자인은 마리나 씨가 그들의 과거 프로젝트들을 극구 칭찬했기 때문에 새 지점의 내부 장식을 맡도록 고용되었다.

해설 빈칸은 동사와 전치사구 사이에서 부사 so의 수식을 받는 자리이다. 문맥상 '코루마 디자인의 과거 진행 프로젝트들을 매우 칭찬해서, 실내장식에 그 업체를 다시 고용했다'는 의미가 되어야 자연스러우므로 speak highly of '~을 극구 칭찬하다'의 관용표현을 완성하는 (C) highly가 정답이다.

어휘 branch 지사, 지점

4. 여러 번의 안내에도 불구하고, 직원들 중 몇 명은 아직도 소득 신고서를 제출하지 않았다.

해설 빈칸은 주어와 현재완료 구조의 동사 사이의 자리이다. 문맥상 '여러 번의 안내에도 불구하고, 아직도 소득 신고서를 제출하지 않았다'는 의미가 자연스러우므로 still have not p.p. '아직도 ~하지 않았다'의 형태를 완성하는 (C) still이 정답이다.

어휘 reminder 상기시키는 것 | tax return 소득 신고서 | constantly 지속적으로

5. 포리하 시청은 정기적으로 입사지원을 받으므로, 검토가 진행 중인 동안 지원자들에게는 인내력이 요구된다.

해설 빈칸은 주어와 동사 사이에서 동사를 수식하는 자리이다. 접속사 so로 연결된 두 문장의 관계를 고려할 때, '정기적으로 입사지원을 받으므로, 지원자들은 입사지원 검토가 진행되는 동안 인내력이 요구된다'는 의미가 자연스러우므로 (C) regularly가 정답이다.

어휘 job application 입사지원 | candidate 지원자 | underway 진행 중인 | equally 동등하게

6. 관리자의 별다른 공지가 없는 한, 주간 회의는 월요일마다 대회의실에서 열린다.

해설 빈칸은 unless와 announced 사이의 자리이므로 unless otherwise p.p. '별다른 ~가 없는 한'의 관용표현을 완성하는 (A) otherwise가 정답이다.

어휘 announce 발표하다, 알리다 | otherwise 다르게, 달리

7. 새로 생긴 루아르 카페의 주인인 시바 라지는 이전에 파리에서 제빵사로 근무했다.

해설 빈칸은 주어와 동사 사이에서 동사를 수식하는 자리이다. 문맥상 '이전에 제빵사로 일했다'는 의미가 자연스러우므로 (B) previously가 정답이다.

어휘 pastry chef 제빵사 | accordingly 부응해서 | constantly 끊임없이

8. 예약하시려면 적어도 하루 전에 식당으로 전화해 주시기 바랍니다.

해설 빈칸은 문장의 목적어와 부사구 사이의 자리이다. 문맥상 '적어도 하루 전에 미리 예약 전화를 해 달라'는 의미가 되어야 자연스러우므로 부사구 (A) at least가 정답이다.

어휘 in advance 미리, 사전에 | make a reservation 예약하다

9. 아쿨랑의 새 노트북은 경쟁 브랜드보다 거의 2배 빠른 처리 속도를 낸다.

해설 빈칸은 수사를 수식하는 자리이므로 (B) almost가 정답이다.

어휘 laptop 노트북 | achieve 달성하다, 해내다 | processing speed 처리 속도 | competing 경쟁하는 | continually 끊임없이 | further 더 멀리에

10. 업체들은 레이먼 콤플렉스 건설 프로젝트에의 입찰과 관련하여 곧 공지를 받을 것이다.

해설 빈칸은 미래시제 수동태 동사구문과 전치사구 사이의 자리이다. 문맥상 '입찰 결과에 관하여 곧 공지를 받게 될 것'이라는 의미가 되어야 자연스러우므로 (B) soon이 정답이다.

어휘 notify 알리다, 공지하다 | concerning ~에 대해 | bid 응찰, 입찰 | construction 건설

11. 이번 달, 마케팅 부서는 다음 캠페인 준비를 위해 적극적으로 고객 선호도를 조사할 것이다.

해설 빈칸은 현재진행형 동사구문 사이의 자리이다. 문맥상 '적극적으로 고객 선호도를 조사한다'는 의미가 나와야 자연스러우므로 (A) actively가 정답이다.

어휘 preference 선호 | prepare for 준비하다 | excessively 지나치게

12. 머피 씨는 현재 공장 근로자를 대표하는 노동조합의 대표 연사이다.

해설 빈칸은 명사구 전체를 수식하는 부사 자리이다. '현재 노동조합 대표 연사이다'라는 의미가 되어야 자연스러우므로 (C) currently가 정답이다.

어휘 representative 대표하는 | speaker 연사 | union 노동조합 | represent 대표하다 | factory 공장 | formerly 이전에 |

consistently 일관되게, 지속적으로 | currently 현재 | greatly 크게

13. 폰웨어 전자는 온라인 뱅킹에서 잠재적으로 시간을 절약시켜 줄 수 있는 앱의 출시를 발표했다.

해설 빈칸은 형용사를 수식하는 자리이다. 문맥상 '온라인 뱅킹 시 소요되는 시간을 잠정적으로 줄여줄 수 있는 앱의 출시'라는 의미가 자연스러우므로 (D) potentially가 정답이다.

어휘 release 출시 | time-saving 시간을 절약해주는 | app 앱 (application의 약어) | cautiously 신중하게 | potentially 잠재적으로

14. 저희 연구팀은 로봇 공학 세계에 기여하게 되어 대단히 기쁩니다.

해설 빈칸은 pleased를 수식하는 부사 자리이다. '대단히 기쁘다'라는 의미가 되어야 자연스러우므로 (B) extremely가 정답이다.

어휘 research 연구, 조사 | pleased 기뻐하는 | contribution 기여, 이바지 | robotics 로봇 공학 | attentively 조심스럽게, 정중히 | casually 무심하게, 격식을 차리지 않고 | openly 터놓고, 솔직하게

15. 비에프에스 사에서는 여러분이 비용을 더 정확히 추적 관찰하실 수 있도록 특별히 맞춤 제작된 소프트웨어를 제공합니다.

해설 빈칸은 원형부정사 monitor를 수식하는 자리이다. 문맥상 '비용을 더 정확히 추적 관찰할 수 있게 해주는 소프트웨어'라는 의미가 나와야 자연스러우므로 (A) accurately가 정답이다.

어휘 specially 특별히 | customized(= personalized) 특별 주문된, 개개인의 요구에 맞춘 | monitor 추적 관찰하다 | expense 비용 | immensely 엄청나게 | commonly 흔히, 보통

16. 빌더스 트레이드 쇼의 수익은 작년보다 더 낮을 것이라 예상되었으나, 실제로는 훨씬 더 높았다.

해설 빈칸은 be동사와 주격 보어 사이의 자리이다. 접속사 but으로 연결된 두 문장의 관계를 고려할 때, '수익이 내려갈 것으로 예상했지만, 실제로는 훨씬 더 높았다'는 의미로 이어져야 자연스러우므로 (A) actually가 정답이다.

어휘 revenue 수익 | anticipate 예상하다 | broadly 대략

17. 한센 홀딩스는 지점의 운영을 중단한다는 회사의 계획에 고객들이 비판적으로 반응한다는 것을 알게 되어 놀랐다.

해설 빈칸은 동사와 전치사구 사이에서 동사를 수식하는 자리이다. 문맥상 '고객들이 지점 운영 중단에 비판적으로 반응한다는 사실에 놀랐다'는 의미가 되어야 자연스러우므로 (A) unfavorably가 정답이다.

어휘 react 반응하다 | close down 영업을 중단하다 | unfavorably 비판적으로 | unlikely ~일 것 같지 않은 | potentially 잠재적으로

18. 웡 교수의 연구 프로젝트는 그것이 갈수록 시간이 걸리는 일이 되었기 때문에 취소되었다.

해설 빈칸은 주격 보어인 형용사를 수식하는 자리이다. 접속사 because로 연결된 두 문장의 관계를 고려할 때, '프로젝트가 갈수록 시간이 걸리는 작업이 되어서 취소되었다'는 의미가 되어야 자연스러우므로 (A) increasingly가 정답이다.

어휘 research 연구 | time-consuming 시간이 걸리는 | appropriately 적당하게, 알맞게

19. IT 지원 직원은 전 직원의 컴퓨터에 원격으로 접속해 세계 어느 곳에서 발생한 소프트웨어 문제든 고칠 수 있습니다.

해설 빈칸은 앞의 동사구를 수식하는 부사 자리이다. and로 연결된 뒤에 이어지는 내용을 고려할 때 '컴퓨터에 원격으로 접속해 전세계의 소프트웨어 문제를 고칠 수 있다'는 의미가 되어야 문맥상 자연스러우므로 (C)가 정답이다.

어휘 support 지원 | access 접속하다 | employee 직원 | fix 고치다, 해결하다

20. 편집자들은 발행 전에 우리 잡지에 있는 각 기사를 면밀하게 검토한다.

해설 빈칸은 주어와 동사 사이에서 동사를 수식하는 부사 자리이다. '기사를 면밀하게 검토한다'는 의미가 되어야 자연스러우므로 (D) closely가 정답이다.

어휘 editor 편집자 | review 검토하다 | article 기사 | publication 출판, 발행 | utterly 완전히, 순전히 | widely 널리, 폭넓게 | closely 면밀하게

PART 6

UNIT 01. 시제

핵심 문제 유형
본서 p.172

1. (B)

1. [편지]

> 호퍼 자동차 판매
> 11월 1일
>
> 소중한 고객님,
> 기록에 따르면, 고객님의 자동차 보증이 다가오는 12월에 만기가 될 것입니다.
>
> **어휘** valued 소중한 | according to ~에 따르면 | record 기록 | warranty 보증 | coming 다가오는 | expire 만기가 되다

해설 빈칸은 동사 자리이므로 (C)와 (D)는 탈락한다. 이 글을 쓴 날짜는 11월 1일이며 다가오는 12월이 만기임을 밝히고 있으므로 미래 시제인 (B) will expire가 정답이다.

Check
본서 p.173

1. (A)	**2.** (D)	**3.** (A)	**4.** (C)	**5.** (C)
6. (D)	**7.** (D)	**8.** (A)	**9.** (B)	**10.** (D)

1. [편지]

> 브래들리 박사 귀하,
> 귀하도 알다시피, 폰틸로 서비스는 가장 환경친화적인 청소 방법으로 헤이스팅스 전역에 있는 진료소에 서비스를 제공하는 것을 전문으로 하고 있습니다.
>
> **어휘** environmentally responsible 환경을 고려하는 | specialize in ~을 전문으로 하다

해설 폰틸로 서비스라는 회사에 대해서 설명하고 있다. 일반적인 사실을 설명하므로 정답은 현재 시제인 (A) specializes가 된다.

2. [광고]

> 베스트 에이전시 투어는 여행객들의 경험을 쾌적하고 즐겁게 만들어 드립니다. 저희의 각각의 여행 패키지 상품은 입장료, 가이드, 교통 및 점심을 포함합니다.
>
> **어휘** pleasant 쾌적한, 즐거운 | enjoyable 즐거운 | package 패키지 상품 | admission fee 입장료 | transportation 교통

해설 뒤에 목적어가 있고 tour packages가 어떻다는 일반적인 사실을 설명하고 있으므로 능동태 현재 시제를 사용해야 한다. 따라서 정답은 (D) includes이다.

3. [회람]

발신: 러셀 라 살, 조립 관리자
수신: 조립 직원들과 검사관들
날짜: 8월 8일
제목: 엠케이 엑스 20

우리의 신제품인 엠케이 엑스 20 냉장고의 맨 위쪽 칸에 관하여 우리 고객들로부터 몇 통의 이메일을 받았다는 것을 알려드리고자 메모를 씁니다. 이 이메일들의 대부분은 칸이 완전히 닫히지 않아 고객들이 불만을 느꼈다는 것을 보여주고 있습니다.

어휘 inspector 검사관 | alert (위험 등을) 알리다 | regarding ~에 관하여 | drawer 칸, 서랍 | indicate 나타내다 | frustrate 당황하게 하다, 좌절감을 주다 | completely 완전히

해설 빈칸은 동사 자리이다. 회람의 내용은 고객들로부터 이메일을 받았다는 것을 알리기 위함이다. 고객들이 불만을 느끼고 있다는 내용을 통해 이미 이메일들을 받았다는 것을 알 수 있으므로, 빈칸에는 과거나 현재 완료가 와야 하므로 정답은 (A) have received이다.

4. [공지]

제품 개발팀,
이번 주 회의의 안건이 업데이트되었습니다. 이 이메일에 최종 버전을 첨부해 드렸으니 보세요.

어휘 agenda 안건 | attach 첨부하다

해설 두 번째 문장을 보면 첨부된 버전을 보라고 했으니, 최종 버전은 이미 업데이트가 된 상태임을 알 수 있다. 따라서 정답은 현재 완료 시제인 (C) has been updated가 된다.

5. [보도자료]

즉시 보도 요망

2월 2일 – 케이유비 사는 마거릿 이를 최고 경영자로 임명한다는 것을 발표한다. 그녀는 1월에 은퇴한 칼 듀퐁을 대신한다.

이 씨는 도슨 한 자산운용의 인사부에서 경력을 쌓기 시작했다. "마거릿 이의 경험과 리더십은 우리가 다음 단계의 도약으로 진입하는 데 매우 귀중할 것입니다."라고 케이유비의 대변인인 스튜어트 윌시가 말했다.

어휘 immediate 즉시의 | release 보도 | appointment 임명 | CEO(= Chief Executive Officer) 최고 경영인 | replace 대신하다 | retire 은퇴하다 | Human Resources Department 인사부 | invaluable 매우 귀중한 | phase 단계 | spokesperson 대변인

해설 빈칸 앞 문장을 보면 케이유비 사에서 마거릿 이를 최고 경영자로 임명했는데, 그녀의 이전 이력을 다음 문장에서 설명하고 있으므로 정답은 과거 시제인 (C) began이다.

6. [공지]

전 직원은 주목하세요: 새 본사 건물이 완공되었습니다

공사 문제로 인한 몇 번의 지연 끝에, 헤이스팅 페이퍼의 새로운 건물이 이번 주에 마침내 완공되었습니다. 세 개의 별도의 사무실에 있는 모든 직원은 작은 그룹 단위로 새 건물로 이전할 것입니다.

직원들의 개별적인 이전 날짜는 회사 웹사이트를 통해서 알 수 있습니다. 이전은 다음 주에 시작할 예정이며, 모든 직원은 7월 말까지 새 사무실로의 이전을 마무리해야 합니다.

어휘 delay 지연 | due to ~때문에 | corporate 회사의, 기업의 | transition 이행, 이전 | settle 정착하다

해설 새로운 건물이 마침내 완공되어 이전할 것이라는 내용이고, 사무실 이전은 미래의 시점이다. 따라서 미래 시제인 (A) 또는 (D)가 답이 될 수 있다. 미래 완료인 (A)의 경우는 미래 완료 시점인 by next ~, by the end of ~와 같은 시간 어구와 함께 사용되는데, 이 문장에는 그런 것이 없으므로 정답은 단순 미래의 의미인 (D) will be moving이 된다.

7. [기사]

도시 마라톤이 기획되다

베리빌 (4월 1일) – 시장 레지나 파제트는 어제 베리빌 마라톤의 창설을 공지했다. 이 경주는 매년 8월 중순에 개최될 것이다. 첫 번째 마라톤은 올해 8월 16일로 예정되어 있다.

어휘 mayor 시장 | take place 열리다, 벌어지다

해설 베리빌 마라톤의 창설을 공지하는 기사이며, 글을 쓴 날짜는 4월 1일이고 앞으로 매년 8월 중순에 개최된다고 하므로 정답은 미래 시제인 (D) will take place이다.

8. [공지]

채널 9가 9주년을 기념합니다!

10월 10일은 채널 9의 9주년 기념일이었습니다. 근 10년 치의 즐거움을 드리는 프로그램 편성입니다. 이 기간 동안 저희는 시청자 여러분께 생방송 뉴스와 날씨, 그리고 그야말로 최고의 드라마들을 제공해 왔습니다. 이것이 이번 달에 콘테스트 주최를 통해 99명의 행운의 당첨자들을 초대하여 10월 29일 오전 11시부터 오후 7시까지 스튜디오를 방문하도록 할 이유입니다. 선정되면, 스튜디오 문 뒤에서 진행되는 일들을 보고 몇몇 유명 방송인들도 만날 수 있습니다. 이들의 쇼가 어떻게 녹화되는지도 보게 될 것입니다. 콘테스트에 관한 세부 사항 전체를 보시려면, 웹사이트를 방문하시기 바랍니다. 이 놀라운 기회를 놓치지 마세요!

어휘 anniversary 기념일 | decade 10년 | entertaining 즐거움을 주는 | the very best 그야말로 최고의 | personality 유명인

해설 빈칸 앞 문장에서 '거의 10년간 프로그램을 편성해 왔다'라고 했고, 그 시간 동안(During that time) 뉴스, 날씨, 드라마들을 제공해 왔다는 것을 이야기하고 있으므로 정답은 현재 완료 시제인 (A) have provided이다.

9. [기사]

어텀 쿠킹 카니발이 9월 16일 밀타운 남부에서 개최되었다. 지난 10년 동안, 이 유명한 축제는 9월부터 11월까지 주 전역을 순회했다.

올해, 주최자들이 더 넓은 공간을 준비하기로 현명한 결정을 내렸다. 기대했던 대로, 방문객들이 여러 가지 맛있는 음식을 맛보고, 탈 것과 전시품을 즐기고, 음식을 주제로 한 대회에 참여하기 위해서 기록적으로 많이 참가했다.

어휘 carnival 축제 | go on tour 투어를 하다 | show up 나타나다 | record number 기록적인 수 | food-themed 음식을 주제로 한

해설 두 번째 단락을 보면 행사 주최자들이 올해(This year) 결정을 했으며, 현명한 결정이었고(wisely decided), 방문객들이 왔다고(visitors showed up) 시종일관 과거 시제를 쓰고 있으므로, 어텀 쿠킹 카니발이 이미 열렸다는 것을 알 수 있다. 그러므로 정답은 과거 시제인 (B) came이다.

10. [기사]

볼더 사 – 6월 1일

콜로라도 남부에서 고고학 발굴 기간 동안 역사적으로 중요한 꽃병이 발견되었다. 그 물건을 발견했던 고고학자 셀마 바바리아의 말에 따르면, 이것은 믿기 어려운 놀라운 발견이라고 한다. "이 시대의 물건을 여전히 한 점의 아주 좋은 상태로 보기란 드문 일이에요."라고 하면서, "우리는 주로 조각들만을 찾아내죠."라고 말했다.

어휘 archaeological 고고학의 | excavation 발굴 | according to ~에 따르면 | archaeologist 고고학자 | remarkable 놀랄 만한 | discovery 발견 | era 시대 | uncover 알아내다, 찾아내다 | fragment 조각, 파편

해설 빈칸 뒤의 the item이 가리키는 대상은 앞서 언급된 꽃병(vase)이며, 발굴 기간 동안 이 꽃병이 발견되었다고 하여 과거 시제(discovered)로 썼으므로 고고학자가 이 물건을 발견한 시점 역시 과거이다. 따라서 정답은 (D) found가 된다.

Practice

본서 p.176

1. (B)	2. (C)	3. (D)	4. (A)	5. (C)
6. (B)	7. (B)	8. (A)	9. (D)	10. (C)
11. (A)	12. (B)	13. (C)	14. (C)	15. (D)
16. (B)				

[1-4] 다음 공지에 관한 문제입니다.

영업 직원들께,

사무실 내에서 저희는 전자 파일에 대한 가능한 최대한의 보안을 유지하기 위해 노력합니다. 여러분이 고객들을 만나기 위해서 이동할 때도 같아야 할 것입니다. 여러분의 컴퓨터에 있는 모든 업무 관련 파일들을 보호하는 것은 **1** 필수입니다. 만약 여러분이 유에스비에 파일들을 가지고 다닌다면, 유에스비에 있는 자료들을 **2** 보호하기 위해서 유에스비를 항상 소지하십시오. **3** 파일을 암호화하는 것 또한 좋습니다. 마지막으로, 전화로 업무를 논의할 때는, 회사에 관한 자세한 정보에 대해서 가능한 한 논의하는 것을 피하십시오. 이러한 간단한 규칙들을 **4** 준수함으로써, 여러분은 사무실 바깥에 있을 때도 보안이 유지되도록 도울 수 있습니다. 감사합니다.

니키타 바율
정보 기술부장

어휘 maintain ~을 유지하다 | maximum 최대한의 | security 보안 | work-related 업무와 관련된 | protect ~을 보호하다 | transport ~을 옮기다 | memory stick 유에스비 | possession 소유 | at all times 항상 | lastly 마지막으로 | over the phone 전화로 | avoid ~을 피하다 | detailed 자세한 | ensure ~을 보장하다 | conclusive 결정적인 | encrypt 암호화하다 | observe 준수하다

1. 해설 (A) probable은 '가능한', (B) essential은 '필수적인', (C) traditional은 '전통적인', (D) conclusive는 '결정적인'이라는 뜻이며 글 전체에서 회사의 보안을 지키기 위해 필요한 조치들을 설명하고 업무 관련 파일은 반드시 지켜야 하는 것이므로 (B) essential이 정답이다.

2. 해설 동사의 목적어 뒤에 또 다른 동사인 (A) is protecting과 (B) protects는 쓸 수 없으며, 빈칸 뒤에 목적어가 있어 (D)는 과거 동사로 봐야 하므로 역시 쓸 수 없다. 자료를 보호하기 위해 파일들을 항상 가지고 다니는 것이므로 '~하기 위해'라고 해석되는 to부정사 (C) to protect가 정답이다.

3. (A) 전화로 업무에 대해 말하지 않도록 또한 주의하세요.
(B) 사무실 컴퓨터에서 어떠한 업무 관련 파일이라도 삭제하지 마세요.
(C) 직원들은 사무실에서 어떠한 파일도 복사해서는 안 됩니다.
(D) 파일을 암호화하는 것 또한 좋습니다.

해설 앞부분은 모두 전자 파일 보안에 대한 글이고, 빈칸 바로 앞 문장에서 유에스비를 항상 소지하라고 했으므로 유에스비에 있는 파일에 대해 암호화를 하는 것 또한 좋을 것이라는 내용의 (D) It would be best if you encrypt the files as well. 이 적절하다.

4. 해설 전치사와 명사 사이의 빈칸으로 (C) to observe는 쓸 수 없고, 빈칸 뒤에 있는 명사를 목적어로 취해야 하므로 (B) observed도 쓸 수 없다. '이러한 간단한 규칙들을 준수함으로써'라고 해석하며 뒤에 쓰인 명사를 목적어로 취해야 하므로 (A) observing이 정답이다. 전치사의 목적어 자리에 명사를 쓸 수도 있지만 명사는 뒤에 목적어가 올 수 없으므로 (D) observation은 답이 될 수 없다.

메첸 씨 귀하,

최근에 쉴즈 브라더스에서 **5** 구매해 주신 것에 대해서 감사드립니다.

저희의 모든 조명 간판은 비바람을 잘 견디며 5년간 보증됩니다. 만약 그 보증 기간 동안 잘못된 설치나 부품, 혹은 날씨의 손상으로 인한 문제가 생기면, 저희는 그것을 무상으로 수리해 드릴 것입니다. **6** 더 자세한 사항은 첨부된 저희의 보증서를 읽어보시기 바랍니다. 저희 직원이 어떻게 설치할지 **7** 논의하기 위해서 이번 주 목요일에 귀하의 사업체를 방문할 것입니다. **8** 일단 귀하의 간판이 안전하게 설치되면 청구서의 잔금에 대해서 귀하의 계좌에 청구될 것입니다. 저희에게 25%의 표준 보증금을 지불하셨기 때문에, 설치는 무료입니다.

귀사의 광고 필요로 쉴즈 브라더스를 찾아 주신 것에 대해서 다시 한 번 감사드립니다.

진심으로,

앨런 쉴즈

어휘 recent 최근의 | weatherproof 비바람을 견디는 | warranty 보증 | faulty 잘못된 | installation 설치 | part 부품 | at no cost to ~에게 무료로 | representative 직원 | option 선택 | charge ~에게 청구하다 | account 계좌 | remainder 나머지 것 | securely 안전하게 | mount 고정하다 | standard 일반적인, 표준의 | deposit 보증금 | free 무료인

5. 해설 메첸 씨가 쉴즈 브라더스로부터 무언가를 위해 보증금도 지불했으며, 제품에 대해 설명하고 직원이 방문할 것임을 알리고 있으므로 정답은 (C) purchase이다. (A) donation '기부', (B) visit '방문', (D) article '기사'는 모두 문맥상 어울리지 않는다.

6. (A) 귀하께서는 다음 주에 저희 직원 중 한 명으로부터 연락을 받게 될 것입니다.
(B) 더 자세한 사항은 첨부된 저희의 보증서를 읽어보시기 바랍니다.
(C) 수리 작업이 끝나면, 청구서를 받게 될 것입니다.
(D) 귀하를 위해 설치 과정이 순조롭게 진행되길 바랍니다.

해설 품질 보증에 대한 언급이 이전 문장에 열거되어 있으므로 품질 보증에 관한 내용인 (B) Please see the attached copy of our warranty for more details. 가 문맥상 가장 적절하다. 이번 주 목요일에 설치를 위하여 직원이 방문하므로 (A)는 적절하지 않다. 또한, 글의 내용은 수리 작업이 아니라 설치 작업에 관한 내용이므로 (C)도 올바르지 않다. (D)는 문맥상 마지막 부분에 어울린다.

7. 해설 필요한 요소가 모두 갖춰진 문장에서 수식어구 역할을 할 품사가 필요하므로 '논의하기 위해'라는 의미를 갖는 to부정사 형태인 (B) to discuss가 정답이다. 동사가 있기 때문에 동사 (A), (D)는 오답이며, 빈칸 뒤에 목적어 역할을 하는 명사가 쓰였으므로 명사 (C)도 오답이다.

8. 해설 빈칸 뒤에 「주어 + 동사」의 절이 쓰였으므로 접속사인 (A) once '일단 ~하면, ~하자마자'가 정답이다. (B) afterward '후에'는 부사로 접속사 자리에 쓸 수 없고, (C) following '~후에'와 (D) upon '~하자마자'는 전치사로 절 앞에 쓰일 수 없다.

수신: 마치코 노구치 〈nomachi@tokdesmail.com〉
발신: 올리비아 만디그 〈oliviaman@eagdcmail.com〉
날짜: 2월 2일 화요일, 오전 11시 38분
제목: 축하합니다

노구치 씨 귀하,

귀하가 연례 베스트 그래픽 디자이너 어워드에 공식적으로 지명되신 것에 대해서 가장 먼저 축하드리겠습니다. 이미 알고 계시겠지만, 이 상은 전도유망한 그래픽 디자이너에게 매년 **9** 주어집니다. 귀하의 훌륭한 컴퓨터 디자인 작품은 여러 회사에 광고 캠페인을 위한 멋진 그래픽들을 **10** 제공해 왔습니다. 귀하는 귀하의 작품을 작년에 사용했던 하나 또는 그 이상의 회사에 의해 지명되었습니다. **11** 저희는 수상자를 발표할 때 귀하가 저희와 함께하시기를 바랍니다.

이 상은 3월 13일에 마닐라에서 열릴 동아시아 그래픽 디자인 컨퍼런스의 개막식 밤에 수여될 것입니다. 4명의 최종 후보 중 한 명으로서, 귀하는 귀하와 동반 1인을 위한 비행기 표와, 호텔 예약, 그리고 컨벤션 무료입장권을 제공받을 것입니다. 환영식에서 저녁 식사는 **12** 제공될 것이니, 혹시 못 드시는 음식이 있으면 저희에게 알려 주십시오.

귀하께 연락받기를 기대하고 있겠습니다.

진심으로,

올리비아 만디그
이에이지디씨 준비 위원

어휘 congratulate A on B A에게 B에 대해 축하하다 | official 공식적인 | nomination 지명, 추천 | up-and-coming 전도유망한 | incredible 놀라운 | stunning 깜짝 놀랄 만한 | nominate ~을 지명하다[추천하다] | present ~을 주다 | finalist 결승 출전자 | dietary 음식물의 | restriction 제한 | look forward to ~ing ~하는 것을 기대하다 | announce 알리다 | guarantee 보증하다 | postpone 연기하다

9. 해설 수의 일치상 단수 명사가 주어이므로 (A)는 오답이다. 빈칸 뒤에 목적어가 없고, 상은 매년 주어지는 것이므로 수동태인 (D) is given이 정답이다. (B), (C)는 능동태이므로 오답이다.

10. 해설 문장의 동사가 필요한 자리이므로 (D)는 오답이다. 주어인 디자인 작품이 '많은 회사들에게 멋진 그래픽들을 제공했다'로 해석되며 목적어가 뒤에 왔으므로 능동태인 (C) has provided가 정답이다. (A), (B)는 수동태이므로 오답이다.

11. (A) 저희는 수상자를 발표할 때 귀하가 저희와 함께하시기를 바랍니다.
(B) 귀하의 훌륭한 작품이 귀하가 수상자가 되도록 보증해 줄 것입니다.
(C) 불행하게도, 수상식이 가을까지 미뤄졌습니다.

(D) 참가해 주셔서 감사드리고, 다음 기회에 더 좋은 일이 있으시길 바랍니다.

해설 이미 앞 문장에 거론되어 있으므로 (B)는 흐름상 어색하고, (C), (D)는 의미상 전체 글 흐름과 맞지 않다. 뒤 문장에서 수상식이 언제 진행되는지 언급되므로 문맥의 흐름상 가장 올바른 보기는 (A) We hope you can be with us when the winner is announced. 이다.

---

12. 해설 저녁 식사는 '제공된다'는 수동의 해석이 적합하며, 빈칸 뒤에 목적어가 없기 때문에 수동태 (B) be served가 정답이다. (A), (C), (D)는 능동태이므로 오답이다.

[13-16] 다음 공지에 관한 문제입니다.

> 발신: 최고 경영자 해리슨 솔로몬
> 수신: 모든 윔블던 광고 직원들
> 제목: 영업부의 새로운 부서장
> 날짜: 5월 3일
>
> **13** 여러분이 기다리던 소식을 전해드리고자 합니다. 저는 이사진에 의해서 새로운 영업부 부서장이 **14** 임명되었음을 여러분께 알리게 되어 기쁩니다. 이사진은 그 직책에 고려되었던 모든 분께 참고 이해해주신 것에 대해서 감사를 전하고 싶습니다. 5월 19일부터 엘리자베스 쿡 씨가 영업부의 새로운 부서장이 될 것입니다. 쿡 씨는 다른 부서들에서 다양한 역할로 10년 이상 동안 우리와 일했지만, 이 이유만으로 그녀가 **15** 선택된 것은 아닙니다.
>
> 그녀의 통솔력과 수많은 상도 의사 결정 과정에서 중요한 요소들로 언급되었습니다. 그녀가 저희 영업부의 뛰어난 지도자가 **16** 될 것이라고 확신합니다. 기회가 생기면 그녀를 축하해 주십시오.
>
> 해리슨 솔로몬
> 윔블턴 광고 최고 경영자
>
> 어휘 inform A that B A에게 B를 알려주다 | extend one's thanks to ~에게 감사를 전하다 | patience 인내 | effective 효력을 발생하는 | leadership skill 통솔력 | be cited as ~으로 언급되다 | decision-making process 의사 결정 과정 | congratulate ~을 축하해 주다 | regret 유감스럽게 생각하다 | resign 사임하다 | open position 공석 | appoint ~를 임명하다

---

13. (A) 쿡 씨가 사임하였음을 발표하게 되어 유감입니다.
(B) 우리는 여전히 공석을 채우기를 기대하고 있습니다.
(C) 여러분이 아주 기다리던 소식을 전해드리고자 합니다.
(D) 부서장에 지원하는 것에 대해 고려하여 주시기 바랍니다.

해설 글 전체의 내용이 쿡 씨의 부서장 임명 내용이므로 상반된 내용인 나머지 보기들은 정답이 될 수 없고, 자연스러운 문장 흐름을 보이는 (C) I have the news that you have all been waiting for. 가 정답이다.

---

14. 해설 빈칸 뒤에 목적어가 없고 부서장은 '임명된다'고 해석하는 것이 자연스러우므로 능동태 보기인 (A) will appoint와 (B) is appointing 은 쓸 수 없고 수동태 보기인 (C) has been appointed와 (D) will

be appointed 중에 답을 골라야 한다. '고려되었던 모든 분께 참고 이해해 주신 것에 대해서 감사를 전한다'는 빈칸 뒷부분을 단서로 이미 임명된 부서장을 발표하는 내용이므로 완료된 일을 나타내는 현재 완료 시제 (C) has been appointed가 정답이다.

---

15. 해설 '선택되다'라는 수동의 의미가 필요하므로 능동태인 (B)는 오답이다. 나머지는 모두 수동태이므로 앞뒤 문맥을 단서로 시제를 파악해야 한다. 문맥상 새로운 부서장으로 일하게 될 쿡 씨에 관해 소개를 하고 있는 것은 그녀가 이미 선택되었다는 뜻이므로 과거 시제 (D) was chosen이 정답이다.

---

16. 해설 그녀가 앞으로 부서장으로서 좋은 리더가 되어 줄 것임을 확신한다고 말하는 것이므로 미래 시제인 (B) will be가 정답이다.

PART 6 UNIT 02

UNIT 02. 대명사

핵심 문제 유형
본서 p.180

1. (D)

---

1. [회람]

> 수신: 전 직원
> 발신: 브루스 김
> 제목: 새 보안 시스템
> 날짜: 1월 13일, 금요일
>
> 수요일 오전에 새로운 출입 시스템을 설치할 히달고 보안 서비스의 기술자들이 사무실로 올 것입니다. 그날 오후에 모든 직원은 신규 시스템에 개인 식별 코드를 입력하고 지문을 스캔하기 위한 시간을 비워 두는 것이 중요합니다. 두 가지 모두 출근과 퇴근 시에 필요합니다.
>
> 어휘 set up 설치하다 | entry 출입 | set aside 따로 비워 두다 | personal identification 개인 식별 | fingerprint 지문 | depart 떠나다

해설 빈칸은 앞에서 언급된 personal identification codes와 fingerprints 둘을 언급하므로 정답은 (D) Both이다.

Check
본서 p.181

| 1. (A) | 2. (B) | 3. (C) | 4. (C) | 5. (B) |
| 6. (D) | 7. (B) | 8. (B) | 9. (C) | 10. (A) |

1. [회람]

아마도 이미 들으셨다시피, 웬디 장이 셀린 드레스 디자인의 마케팅 팀장으로서 오랜 경력 후에 은퇴를 합니다. 그녀의 회사에 대한 많은 공헌을 기념하고자, 7월 6일 금요일 오후 5시에 파티를 열 것입니다.

어휘 retire 은퇴하다 | in honor of ~을 기념하여 | contribution 공헌

해설 보기가 모두 대명사로 이루어진 대명사 문제이므로 앞에 나오는 명사를 찾으면 된다. 웬디 장을 받는 소유격 대명사 (A) her가 정답이다.

2. [편지]

저희는 귀하에게 새 난방기를 추가 비용 없이 제공하게 된 것을 기쁘게 생각할 것입니다. 하지만 회사 규정에 따라, 귀하는 원본 영수증을 저희에게 보내주셔야 합니다. 일단 저희가 그것을 받으면, 저희 기술자가 방문하는 시간을 정하기 위해 연락을 드릴 것입니다.

어휘 supply 공급하다, 주다 | heater 난방기 | at no extra cost 추가 비용 없이 | original receipt 원본 영수증 | once 일단 ~하면 | technician 기사, 기술자

해설 보기가 모두 대명사로 이루어진 대명사 문제이므로 앞에 나오는 명사를 찾으면 된다. 'original receipt를 받게 되면 연락을 할 것이다'라는 의미이므로, original receipt를 받는 (B) it이 정답이다.

3. [이메일]

네이선 켈로그를 대신하여, 드래곤 힐 인에서의 그의 예약에 관해서 적습니다. 켈로그 씨의 예약은 지난 수요일에 귀사의 웹사이트를 통해 이루어졌습니다. 하지만, 그가 받은 이메일에 있는 세부 예약 확인 정보가 부정확했습니다.

어휘 on behalf of ~을 대표하여[대신하여] | regarding ~에 관하여 | confirmation 확인 | inaccurate 오류가 있는, 부정확한

해설 빈칸은 대명사 문제로, 앞에 나온 네이선 켈로그를 받는 대명사인 (C) his가 적절하다.

4. [광고]

크로포즈 어플라이언스 센터에서, 여러분은 언제나 고품질의 고객 서비스와 최고의 가격을 발견하실 수 있습니다. 한시적으로, 주요 가정용 가전제품을 구매하시면 설치와 무료 배송 서비스가 제공될 것입니다.

이러한 특가 제공을 받으려면 구매하시는 가전제품이 300달러 이상이어야 합니다. 고객 한 분당 오직 한 번의 무료 배송이 제공됩니다. 배송 옵션에 대한 정보를 얻고 싶으시면 고객님 지역의 상점에 연락을 하시거나, 저희의 웹사이트 www.crawfordappliance.com을 방문해 주세요.

어휘 appliance 가전제품 | for a limited time 한시적으로 | installation 설치 | free delivery 무료 배송 | qualify 자격을 갖추다

해설 앞서 나온 you can always find, with your purchase, the appliance you purchase 등을 통해 special offer의 혜택을 받는 사람은 이 광고의 대상인 you라는 것을 알 수 있다. 따라서 (C) your가 정답이다.

5. [안내문]

제10회 연례 멜버른 시티 도서 박람회가 3월 3일 월요일에 시작해서 3월 9일 일요일까지 계속됩니다. 이 행사는 베스트셀러 소설가인 재스민 하룬과 빅토리아 타미미의 출판업계의 최신 경향이라는 주제에 관한 토론으로 월요일 오전 10시에 시작됩니다. 이 두 연사 모두 멜버른 시티 출신들입니다.

어휘 kick off 시작하다 | keynote 기조, 주안점 | novelist 소설가 | publishing industry 출판업계

해설 빈칸은 of these speakers의 수식을 받는데, these speakers는 앞에 나오는 재스민 하룬과 빅토리아 타미미를 의미하므로, 둘을 가리키는 대명사인 (B) Both가 정답이다.

6. [이메일]

흔한 일은 아니지만, 이메일 전송 실패가 잘못된 이메일 주소가 아닌 저희 시스템에 의해 야기되는 가능성도 있습니다. 그러므로, 귀하께서 이메일을 어떤 주소로든 보내실 수 없다면, 도버 메일 고객 지원에 연락 주세요.

어휘 failure 실패 | rather than ~보다는 | incorrect 부정확한

해설 앞선 내용을 보면 시스템의 문제로 인해 이메일 전송이 실패할 수 있다는 내용이 나온다. 따라서 다른(other) 주소가 아니라 어떠한(any) 주소로 이메일을 보내도 문제가 생기면 연락을 달라는 내용이 나와야 자연스러우므로 (D) any가 정답이다.

7. [기사]

다음 달부터 코웬 사는 모든 직원에게 근무 시간에 관한 새로운 정책을 시행할 것입니다. 하지만 몇 가지 규정은 변함이 없습니다. 여느 때와 마찬가지로 직원들은 반드시 업무 시작 시각 10분 전에 건물 안에 있어야 하고 그로부터 5분 후에는 작업실에 있어야 합니다.

어휘 implement 시행하다 | concerning ~에 관하여 | working hours 근무 시간 | prior to ~전에 | work station 작업 장소

해설 빈칸 뒤에 rules라는 복수 명사가 나오므로, 단수에만 쓰이는 (A)와 (C)는 탈락한다. 앞에서 두 가지를 언급한 내용이 없으므로 (D)도 탈락한다. 따라서 일부를 가리킬 때 쓰이는 대명사 (B) some이 정답이다.

8. [이메일]

저는 직원들을 위해서 가장 최신의 연락처 정보를 포함한 새로운 직원 주소록을 만들고 있습니다. 이러한 목적을 위해 여러분의 집 주소와 전화번호를 확인해야 합니다. 첨부된 서류를 검토하시고 둘 중 어느 하나라도 변경 사항이 있으면 연락해 주세요.

어휘 employee directory 직원 주소록 | contact information 연락처 정보 | review 검토하다 | attached 첨부된

해설 빈칸은 주어 자리로, 앞 문장에서 집 주소와 전화번호라는 두 가지 정보가 나왔고, 이 둘 중에서 변경 사항이 있으면 알려달라는 내용이 나와야 적절하므로 정답은 둘 중에 어느 하나를 의미하는 (B) either 이다.

9. [회람]

인사부가 인사 시스템을 업데이트하는 중입니다. 모든 부서가 변경 사항을 안다는 것을 확실히 하기 위해, 직원 근무 시간 추적에 관련된 분들은 우리의 교육 중 하나에 참석하셔야 합니다.

어휘 Human Resources Department 인사부 | in the process of ~하는 중인 | personnel 직원 | be informed of ~을 (잘) 알다 | training session 교육, 연수

해설 빈칸은 문장의 주어 자리로서 involved 이하의 수식을 받아 '~에 관련된 사람들'이라는 의미가 되므로 복수형의 지시대명사인 (C) those 가 정답이다.

10. [편지]

제공된 배송 라벨을 이용해서 원래 상자 안에 원치 않는 상품을 넣어 우편으로 보내세요. 또한, 운반 케이스, 여분의 코드와 렌즈 커버와 같은 비디오 장비와 함께 딸려 온 모든 부품과 액세서리가 포함되어 있는지 확인해 주세요. 만약 이러한 것들이 반납되지 않으면 전액 환불을 받을 수 없을 수도 있습니다. 그렇지 않다면, 귀하가 저희로부터 구매하신 제품을 받은 지 2주 이내에 전액 환불해 드릴 것입니다.

어휘 unwanted 원치 않는 | merchandise 상품 | spare 여분의, 예비의 | full refund 전액 환불

해설 빈칸은 주어 자리로 앞에 나오는 carrying case, spare cords, and lens covers를 포함한 all parts and accessories라는 복수를 받는 대명사가 필요하므로 (A) these가 정답이다.

Practice

본서 p.184

1. (D)	2. (D)	3. (B)	4. (A)	5. (C)
6. (D)	7. (A)	8. (C)	9. (C)	10. (B)
11. (A)	12. (D)	13. (B)	14. (D)	15. (A)
16. (D)				

[1-4] 다음 기사에 관한 문제입니다.

쇼핑센터가 시작됐다

오늘 핼리팩스 가와 서리 가의 모퉁이에 새로운 쇼핑센터 건설이 시작되었다. **①** 한 때 직물 공장이 이 부지의 자리에 위치해 있었다. 완공되면 이 쇼핑센터는 철물점, 세탁소, 두 개의 의류 상점, 스포츠 용품 상점 두 개의 식당을 포함하는 복합 상가가 될 것이다. 주차장도 있을 것이다. 프로젝트는 9개월 **②** 이내에 완성될 것으로 예상된다. 많은 지역 주민은 현재 지역에 상점이 몇 개 없으므로 새로운 쇼핑센터가 그 지역에 환영받는 **③** 보탬이 될 것이라고 말해 왔다. 오늘 아침의 기공식에서, 시장은 이 **④** 와 같은 프로젝트들로 인한 지역 경제의 부양에 대해 개발업자에게 찬사를 보냈다.

어휘 contain ~을 포함하다 | assortment 모음 | hardware store 철물점 | parking garage 주차장 | resident 지역 주민 | neighborhood 근처, 인근 | groundbreaking ceremony 기공식 | praise ~을 칭찬하다 | boost 부양 | go on strike 파업에 들어가다 | viewpoint 관점 | available to ~가 이용 가능한 | textile 직물 | alongside 옆에, 나란히

1. (A) 건설 현장 인부들이 즉각적으로 파업에 돌입했다.
(B) 소비자들은 자신들이 고를 수 있는 선택 사항들에 만족을 표했다.
(C) 그 쇼핑센터는 다음 며칠 안에 문을 열 것이다.
(D) 한때 직물 공장이 이 부지의 자리에 위치해 있었다.

해설 빈칸 앞 문장에서 핼리팩스 가와 서리 가의 모퉁이에서 쇼핑센터 건설을 오늘 시작한다고 언급하였으므로 장소에 대한 설명인 (D) A textile factory once stood on the location of the site. 가 가장 적절하다.

2. **해설** 빈칸 뒤에 기간 명사가 왔고 '공사가 그 기간 내에 완성될 것이다'라는 의미가 적절하므로 (D) within '~이내에'가 정답이다. (A) toward '~을 향해서', (B) between 'A와 B 두 시점 사이에', (C) among '(셋 이상의) 사이에'는 모두 문맥상 어울리지 않는다.

3. **해설** 지역에 새로운 건물이 생기는 것이므로 없던 것이 새롭게 추가되는 것이다. 따라서 (B) addition '추가물'이 정답이다. (A) product '제품', (C) comment '논평', (D) viewpoint '관점'은 모두 문맥상 어울리지 않는다.

4. **해설** 빈칸 뒤에 대명사가 쓰였으므로 전치사 자리이며, 문맥상 this 는 기사에서 다룬 쇼핑센터 건립 프로젝트를 말하는 것이다. 앞에서

말한 내용을 구체적으로 예를 들 때 사용하는 전치사 '～와 같은'을 의미하는 (A) such as가 적절하다.

[5-8] 다음 이메일에 관한 문제입니다.

수신: 윌리엄 델샹 〈willdelchamps@ontmail.com〉
발신: 마이클 도네갈 〈michaeldon@mthcsmail.com〉
날짜: 2월 22일 화요일
제목: 예약 관련

델샹 씨 귀하,

귀하가 언제든지 귀하나 귀하의 동료들의 출장에 관해 저희에게 연락을 주셔서 기쁩니다. 그러나, 안타깝게도, 저희는 귀하가 어제 저희 홈페이지에서 하신 **5** 예약을 처리해 드릴 수가 없었습니다. 분명히, 귀하의 법인 카드의 **6** 유효 기간이 지났습니다.

만약 저희가 귀하를 위해 이 방들을 보류해 두기를 원하시면, 555-9823으로 저에게 전화 주십시오. 만약 아직 귀하의 새로운 신용카드를 받지 못하셨다면, 직접 송금도 **7** 가능한 형태의 지불 방식입니다. **8** 그냥 저에게 연락해 주시면, 어떻게 하는지 알려 드리겠습니다. 감사합니다.

진심으로,

마이클 도네갈
고객 서비스부장
몬트리올 타워 호텔

어휘 **process** 처리하다 | **apparently** 분명히 | **direct** 직접의 | **money transfer** 송금 | **payment** 지불 | **expire** 만료되다 | **acceptable** 받아들여지는 | **capable** 유능한 | **proficient** 능숙한 | **acquainted** 잘 알고 있는 | **wire** 전송하다 | **instruct** 가르치다, 알려 주다

5. 해설 이메일 첫 문장에 쓰인 anytime 단어와 두 번째 단락의 '방을 보류해 두기를 원한다면'의 내용으로 보아 호텔의 단골인 델샹 씨가 이 방을 예약하는 과정에서 문제가 생긴 것임을 알 수 있으므로 (C) reservations '예약'이 정답이다. (A) plans '계획', (B) parts '부품', (D) qualities '특성'은 모두 문맥상 어울리지 않는다.

6. 해설 has 뒤에 명사와 과거분사를 쓸 수 있으므로 (A) expiration과 (D) expired 중에 답을 골라야 하는데, '유효 기간이 지났다'라는 해석이 자연스러우므로 「has + 과거분사」의 형태를 만드는 (D) expired가 정답이다.

7. 해설 어제 예약을 할 때 사용했던 신용카드에 문제가 생겼음을 알리고 직접 송금도 가능한 지불 방법임을 알리는 것이므로 (A) acceptable '받아들여지는'이 정답이다. (B) capable은 사람이 능력이 있다는 뜻의 '유능한'으로, '(실현이) 가능한(possible)'과 혼동하지 않도록 유의한다. (C) proficient '능숙한', (D) acquainted '잘 알고 있는'은 모두 문맥상 어울리지 않는다.

8.
(A) 저희는 더 이상 어떠한 신용카드 지불도 받지 않습니다.
(B) 은행은 귀하가 온라인으로 송금하신 지불금이 도착했음을 확인했습니다.
(C) 그냥 저에게 연락해 주시면, 어떻게 하는지 알려 드리겠습니다.
(D) 저희 호텔에 묵어주셔서 감사합니다.

해설 신용카드 유효 기간 만료로 인해 문제를 겪고 있는 고객에게 대체 지불 방법을 안내하는 글이고, 직접 송금 또한 가능하다고 했기 때문에 (C) Simply contact me, and I can instruct you how to do it. 이 정답이 된다.

[9-12] 다음 편지에 관한 문제입니다.

발렌스 씨 귀하,

귀하가 최근에 **9** 구매한 소니쿠스 스테레오 수신기에 문제가 있다라는 말을 듣게 되어 유감입니다. 귀하께서 이 제품에 연장 보증을 선택하셨기 때문에, 귀하의 제품은 여전히 저희 보증에 의해서 보장을 받습니다. 안타깝게도, 귀하가 선택하셨던 모델은 이제 더 이상 생산되지 않아, 저희는 똑같은 모델을 보내드릴 수는 없습니다. 그렇지만, 저희는 귀하께 새로운 소니쿠스 제품 중에서 **10** 비슷한 제품을 제공해 드릴 수 있습니다. 만약 이것이 수락할 만하면, 이 편지에 들어 있는 양식을 보시기 바랍니다. 귀하께서 받고 싶으신 스테레오를 **11** 나타내는 상자에 표시하셔서, 제공된 봉투에 넣어 저희에게 보내주십시오. **12** 모든 배송비와 처리 비용은 저희가 부담할 것입니다.

진심으로,

브릿 아길라
고객 서비스부
에스브이 전자

어휘 **problem with** ～에 생긴 문제 | **recently** 최근에 | **receiver** 수신기 | **extended** 연장된 | **warranty** 보증 | **option** 선택권 | **unit** (상품의) 한 개 | **cover** ～을 보장하다 | **guarantee** 보증 | **unfortunately** 불행히도 | **no longer** 더 이상 ～하지 않는 | **manufacture** ～을 생산하다[제조하다] | **be unable to** ～할 수 없다 | **acceptable** 수락할 만한 | **envelope** 봉투 | **comparable** 비슷한 | **indicate** ～을 나타내다 | **notify** 알리다

9. 해설 소유격과 명사 사이, 그리고 부사 뒤에서 명사를 수식할 형용사를 쓸 자리이므로 동사인 (A) purchases와 (B) purchase는 쓸 수 없다. 수식을 받는 명사인 스테레오 수신기는 '구매되는' 것이므로 수동의 상태를 표현하는 과거분사 (C) purchased가 정답이다.

10. 해설 제품에 문제가 생긴 고객에게 다른 것으로 교환해 주어야 하는데 단종되었으므로 그에 상응하는 비슷한 물건을 보내주겠다고 제안하는 것이 자연스럽다. 따라서 '비슷한'이라는 의미를 가지고 있는 (B) comparable이 정답이다.

11. 해설 문장에 이미 check이라는 동사가 있기 때문에 동사 자리가 아니며 앞에 있는 명사 the box를 수식하는 분사 자리이므로 (A)와 (D)

중에 선택해야 한다. 받고 싶은 제품을 '나타내는' 상자라는 의미로 능동의 현재분사 (A) indicating이 정답이다.

---

12. (A) 귀하께서는 저희 웹사이트에서 소니쿠스 제품들에 대하여 알아보실 수 있습니다.
(B) 귀하께서 새로운 스테레오 제품으로부터 많은 즐거움을 얻으셨기를 바랍니다.
(C) 다음 주 귀하와의 면접에 대하여 공지를 드릴 것입니다.
(D) 모든 배송비와 처리 비용은 저희가 부담할 것입니다.

해설 문제의 제품이 현재 단종되었으므로 다른 비슷한 제품 목록을 체크해서 보내주면 그 제품으로 보내준다는 내용이다. 따라서 (D) All shipping and handling fees will be covered by us. 가 정답이다. (A), (C)는 문맥상 올바르지 않고, 아직 새로운 제품으로 교환을 받지 않았으므로 (B) 또한 오답이다.

[13-16] 다음 공지에 관한 문제입니다.

전 직원들은 주목하세요.

기술자들이 토요일 새벽 2시에 회사 이메일 시스템의 유지 보수 작업을 할 것입니다. 예정된 보안 개선 작업을 **13** 하는 동안 약 4시간 가량 이메일을 사용할 수 없을 것입니다.

업그레이드 **14** 후에, 직원들은 처음으로 다시 로그인할 때 새로운 비밀번호를 선택하라는 안내를 받을 것입니다. 비밀번호는 7에서 12자리여야 하며 예전 시스템의 비밀번호와 비슷하면 안 됩니다. **15** 다른 사람과 새로운 비밀번호를 공유하지 마십시오.

질문이 있거나 이 문제에 대해서 걱정되는 점이 있으면 내선 번호 4867로 정보 기술팀에 연락하십시오. 귀하의 **16** 안내에 대하여 감사드립니다.

어휘 perform ~을 행하다 I maintenance 유지 access to ~에 대한 접근 I unavailable 이용 불가능한 I approximately 대략 I prompt ~하도록 하다 I for the first time 처음으로 I contain ~을 포함하다 I resemble ~을 닮다 I previous 이전의 I extension 내선 번호 I concern about ~에 대한 걱정 I matter 문제 I clarification 해명

13. **해설** 빈칸 앞뒤에 절이 쓰였으므로 전치사인 (C) during과 (D) along을 제외하고, 접속사인 (A) since '~이후'와 (B) while '~하는 동안' 중에서 답을 골라야 하며, 시스템 점검과 이메일을 사용할 수 없는 것은 동시에 발생하는 상황이므로 정답은 (B) while이다.

14. **해설** 빈칸 뒤에 명사가 쓰였으므로 접속사인 (B) Because와 접속부사인 (C) Moreover를 제외하고 전치사인 (A) After '~후에'와 (D) Except '~을 제외하고' 중에서 답을 고른다. 시스템을 점검한 후에 처음으로 다시 로그인할 때 새로운 비밀번호를 골라야 한다는 것이 문맥상 자연스러우므로 정답은 (A) After이다.

15. **(A) 다른 사람과 새로운 비밀번호를 공유하지 마십시오.**
(B) 예전과 같은 비밀번호를 쓰는 것을 추천합니다.

(C) 시스템은 12시간 정도 다운될 것입니다.
(D) 보안은 우리가 조금 더 생각해야 할 문제입니다.

해설 이전 문장이 예전 비밀번호와 다른 7에서 12자리의 비밀번호를 설정해야 한다는 내용이므로 (B)는 오답이고, 이전 문장과 가장 자연스럽게 연결되는 (A) Do not share your new password with anyone. 이 정답이다.

16. **해설** (A) recommendation '추천', (B) clarification '해명', (C) example '예시', (D) patience '인내' 중에서 시스템 점검 때문에 생기는 불편과 비밀번호 변경 등에 관해서 이야기를 하고 있으므로 이런 모든 것들을 참아 주어서 고맙다고 말하는 것이 자연스럽다. 따라서 (D) patience가 정답이다.

UNIT 03. 연결어

핵심 문제 유형
본서 p.188

1. (D)

1. [이메일]

저희가 광고한 일자리에 대한 귀하의 관심에 감사드립니다. 본 이메일은 우리가 귀하의 이력서와 자기소개서를 받았고 검토했음을 확인시켜 드리기 위한 것입니다. 귀하의 학력과 근무 경력을 바탕으로 보니, 귀하께서 그 자리에 충분한 자격을 가지고 계신 것 같습니다. 그러나, 우리가 계약에 대한 논의를 시작하기에 앞서, 귀하께서 면접을 보러 우리 사무실을 방문해 주셨으면 합니다.

어휘 confirmation 확인 I employment history 근무 경력 I sufficient 충분한 I qualification 자격 I similarly 비슷하게 I rather 다소, 오히려

해설 빈칸은 접속부사 자리이며, 빈칸 앞뒤 문장을 해석해 보면 충분한 자격 요건을 갖췄지만 일단 면접을 봐야 한다는 내용이 나오므로, '그러나'의 의미인 (D) However가 정답이다.

Check
본서 p.189

1. (C)	**2.** (D)	**3.** (D)	**4.** (A)	**5.** (D)
6. (B)	**7.** (A)	**8.** (A)	**9.** (C)	**10.** (B)

1. [공지]

엘스워스 씨에게,

이 안내문은 귀하가 1월 15일 자로 전화 서비스를 취소하기로 선택

한 것을 확인하기 위함입니다. 귀하의 계약서에 나온 정책에 따라, 귀하의 마지막 청구서는 이사를 나가신 날짜 이전 한 달 동안의 비용을 포함하며, 귀하의 새 주소로 발송될 것입니다.

> **어휘** notice 안내문, 공지 | confirm 확인하다 | opt 선택하다 | outline 개요를 서술하다 | contract 계약 | bill 청구서 | in the event of ~할 경우에 | under the circumstances 그러한 사정이므로 | in accordance with ~에 따라 | as a consequence ~의 결과로

해설 콤마 뒤가 완전한 절이므로, 빈칸을 포함한 구는 부사 역할을 해야 한다. 빈칸 뒤에 명사 the policies가 나오므로 빈칸은 전치사로 끝나야 한다. 일단 「전치사 + 명사」 형태인 (B)와 (D)는 탈락하고, 해석상 '정책에 따라서'라는 말이 적합하므로 정답은 (C) In accordance with 이다.

2. [기사]

> 호주, 시드니, 7월 19일 – 호주에서 가장 큰 목재 회사 중 하나인 히나다 산업은 전에 자사의 헤이스팅스 지역의 영업부장으로 일했던 셔먼 파크스턴 씨의 국제 영업부장 임명을 발표했다.
>
> 파크스턴 씨는 히나다 산업이 새로운 수출 시장을 설립하게 될 것이라고 말한다. 특히, 그는 북미와 아시아가 히나다 산업 제품의 시장으로 떠오를 것으로 기대한다.

> **어휘** previously 이전에 | global 세계적인 | export 수출 | emerge 떠오르다, 드러나다 | nevertheless 그럼에도 불구하고 | rather 오히려, 차라리 | as requested 요청받은 대로 | in particular 특히

해설 빈칸 뒤로 「콤마(,) 주어 + 동사」가 이어지므로 빈칸은 접속부사 자리이다. 앞에서 새로운 수출 시장이라는 말이 나오고, 뒤에 구체적으로 북미와 아시아가 나오므로 정답은 구체적인 표현을 나타내는 '특히'라는 뜻의 (D) In particular이다.

3. [이메일]

> 로드리게즈 씨에게,
>
> 귀하의 〈해밀턴 매거진〉의 구독이 8월 31일로 만료됩니다. 한 달에 15달러 할인된 가격으로 조기에 구독을 갱신하세요. 게다가, 지금 갱신하시게 되면 골딩 폭스 출판사에서 나온 〈프로그레시브 디자인〉과 〈패셔너블 데이〉를 포함한 다른 잡지들도 할인된 가격으로 받아 보실 수 있는 자격을 갖춥니다.

> **어휘** subscription 구독 | expire 만료되다 | renew 갱신하다 | reduced rate 할인된 가격 | entitle A to B A에게 B를 주다 | consequently 따라서, 그 결과로 | additionally 또한, 추가적으로

해설 빈칸 뒤에 「콤마(,) 주어 + 동사」가 이어지므로, 빈칸은 접속부사 자리이다. 해석을 해보면 앞에서 할인된 가격을 주는데 뒤에서 또 다른 할

인 혜택이 나오므로, 추가적인 의미를 나타내는 부사가 필요하다. 따라서 정답은 (D) Additionally이다.

4. [공지]

> 주목: 전 직원
>
> 우리의 모든 사무실이 7월 5일 금요일에 공휴일을 준수하여 문을 닫는다는 것을 아시기 바랍니다. 그러므로, 여행 경비 상환에 관한 모든 요청서는 7월 3일 수요일까지 제출되어야 합니다.
>
> 그 날짜 이후에 제출된 건은 7월 8일이 있는 주에 처리될 것입니다.

> **어휘** in observance of ~을 준수하여 | reimbursement 상환 | submit 제출하다 | submission 제출 | process 처리하다

해설 앞에서 휴일로 인해 회사 문을 닫는다고 하고 이에 대한 대안을 말하고 있으므로, 순접의 접속부사가 나와야 한다. 따라서 정답은 (A) Therefore가 된다.

5. [편지]

> 린 씨에게,
>
> 고객 서비스부는 고객님이 지난달에 구매하신 정수 장치 교체에 대한 요청서를 받았습니다. 불편을 끼쳐드려 죄송합니다.
>
> 저희는 기꺼이 무상으로 새것을 제공해 드리도록 하겠습니다. 하지만, 보증서 약관에 따라, 고객님은 먼저 저희에게 원본 영수증을 보내주셔야 합니다. 저희가 영수증을 받으면, 교체품의 즉시 배송 일정을 잡기 위해 연락드리겠습니다.

> **어휘** replacement 교체 | purifier 정화 장치 | inconvenience 불편 | free of charge 무료로 | terms (계약의) 조건 | warranty 품질 보증 | original receipt 원본 영수증 | namely 즉, 다시 말해

해설 빈칸은 접속부사 자리로 일단 전치사 역할을 하는 (B) Instead of는 탈락한다. 해석을 해보면 '무료로 제공하지만 영수증을 보내야 한다'라는 내용이 나오므로 역접을 뜻하는 접속부사가 나와야 한다. 따라서 정답은 (D) However이다.

6. [설명서]

> 지엑스-720 토스터를 구매해 주셔서 감사합니다. 귀하의 안전을 위해서, 기기를 사용하기 전에 사용 설명서를 꼼꼼하게 읽어주십시오. 추가로, 이 같은 기본 예방 조치를 따라 주세요.
>
> * 지엑스-720 내부에 포크나 그 밖의 다른 금속 도구를 넣으려고 하지 마세요.
> * 토스터를 청소하기 전에, 그것을 완전히 식혀 주세요.

> **어휘** safety 안전 | thoroughly 철저히 | appliance 가전제품 | precaution 예방 조치 | utensil 기구 | on the other hand 반면에 | in addition 추가로, 게다가 | as a result of ~의 결과로 | in comparison 비교해 보면

해설 빈칸은 접속부사 자리로, 일단 전치사 역할을 하는 (C) As a result of 는 탈락한다. 해석을 해보면 빈칸 앞에서 설명서를 읽어 보라고 했고, 뒤에는 예방 수칙을 따르라고 했기 때문에, 정답은 '추가로'라는 의미인 (B) In addition이다.

7. [공지]

주목: 모든 주민

지난달 세입자 회의에서 논의했다시피, 우리 거주자들의 편의를 위해 두 번째 세탁 시설을 추가하기로 결정했습니다. 4월 5일부터, 지하실의 일부가 보수될 것입니다. 건물의 이 구역에서 공사가 진행되는 동안에 세입자들은 정문을 사용할 수 없다는 것을 명심해 주십시오. 대신에, 후문을 사용해야 합니다.

어휘 tenant 세입자 | laundry 세탁 | facility 시설 | benefit 혜택, 이익 | basement 지하(실) | renovate 보수하다 | front entrance 현관

해설 공사 때문에 정문을 사용하지 못하니, '대신에 후문을 사용해야 한다'는 말이 적합하다. 그러므로 정답은 (A) Instead이다.

8. [광고]

크라운 신발은 이제 고객들에게 어떤 온라인 소매점보다 더 많은 종류의 유명 회사 제품의 신발을 제공합니다. 저희는 또한 크라운 신발 클럽 회원에게는 심지어 더 많은 혜택을 드리고 있습니다! 배송비를 낼 필요가 없을 뿐 아니라, 클럽 회원은 12월 3일까지 4켤레 이상의 신발을 구매하시면 20% 할인을 받으실 수 있습니다.

어휘 brand-name 유명 회사 제품의 | retailer 소매업자 | shipping fee 배송비

해설 빈칸 뒤에 동명사가 이어지므로, 빈칸에는 전치사가 나와야 한다. 해석을 해보면 '~하는 것 이외에도'라는 의미가 적합하므로 정답은 (A) In addition to가 된다. (B), (C), (D)는 접속부사이다.

9. [이메일]

6월 20일에 엑스제이 스토어는 고객들에게 저희 상점에서 구매된 사용하지 않은 물건에 대한 전액 환불을 보장하는 정책을 시행할 것을 알려드립니다. 물건은 사용되었거나 손상된 흔적이 없다면, 구매한 지 1개월 이내에 반송되어야 합니다.

어휘 implement 시행하다 | full refund 전액 환불 | unused 사용하지 않은 | sign of wear 사용한 흔적 | whereas 그런데, ~에 반해서 | provided (that) ~한다면

해설 빈칸 뒤에 「주어 + 동사」가 있으므로 접속사가 필요하다. 빈칸 뒤에 콤마가 없으므로 접속사가 아닌 접속부사인 (B)와 (D)는 탈락한다. 해석을 해보면 '~한 흔적이 없다면'이라는 조건의 의미가 적합하므로 '~한다면'이라는 의미의 접속사 provided (that)가 적합하다. 그러므로 정답은 (C) provided이다.

10. [전단]

우리 지역에서 당신의 재능을 다른 사람들에게 보여주는 데 관심이 있나요? 그렇다면, 3월 3일 휴밍턴 아트 페어에 당신의 작품을 전시할 기회에 지원해 보세요. 지원서는 www.humintonartfair.org에서 온라인으로 구할 수 있습니다.

어휘 apply for 지원하다 | nevertheless 그럼에도 불구하고 | if so 그렇다면

해설 빈칸은 접속부사 자리이다. 앞 문장을 해석해 보면, '~하는 것에 관심이 있는가?'라는 내용이므로, 빈칸에는 '그렇다면'이라는 의미가 들어가야 자연스럽다. 따라서 정답은 (B) If so이다.

Practice

본서 p.192

1. (C)	2. (B)	3. (B)	4. (B)	5. (B)
6. (C)	7. (D)	8. (B)	9. (D)	10. (C)
11. (A)	12. (C)	13. (B)	14. (B)	15. (D)
16. (C)				

[1-4] 다음 회람에 관한 문제입니다.

수신: 마케팅팀 팀원들
발신: 미나 김, 부장
날짜: 11월 8일
회신: 피터 첸의 은퇴

11월 12일 금요일, 오후 3시 30분에 콘퍼런스룸 C에서 피터 첸을 위한 은퇴 기념 파티가 있을 것입니다. 제 비서 지나가 파티에서 피터에게 ①을 선물을 구매하는 데 사용될 기부금을 모으고 있습니다. ② 저희는 여러분 모두가 모금에 참여해 주시길 희망합니다. 발렌시아 델리에서 다과를 제공할 것입니다.

귀하가 참석할 것 ③ 인지 아닌지를 11월 10일 오후 5시 전에 지나에게 알려주십시오. 저는 모든 사람이 이 행사에 참석해서 피터의 15년 근속을 축하할 수 있기 ④ 를 바랍니다. 피터가 회사에서 마지막으로 근무하는 날은 11월 30일 화요일이 될 것입니다.

어휘 retirement 은퇴 | collect ~을 모으다 | donation 기부(금) | refreshment 다과 | attend ~에 참석하다 | celebrate ~을 축하하다 | sendoff 송별

1. 해설 (A) place '~을 놓다', (B) inspect '~을 검사하다', (C) present '~을 주다', (D) state '~을 말하다'라는 뜻으로, 회사를 은퇴하는 사람을 위해서 모금하는 것은 선물을 '주기' 위한 것이라고 해석하는 것이 자연스러우므로 (C) present가 정답이다.

2. (A) 파티에 참석해 주셔서 정말 감사드립니다.
   (B) 저희는 여러분 모두가 모금에 참여해 주시길 희망합니다.
   (C) 선물이 어떻게 생겼는지 그녀에게 보여달라고 요청하세요.
   (D) 피터는 저희가 송별해 준 것을 정말 감사하고 있습니다.

해설 이전 문장에 기부금을 모으고 있다고 언급하고 있으므로 문맥상 기부에 동참해달라는 내용인 (B) We hope everyone will contribute to the fund. 가 이어지는 것이 가장 적절하다. 아직 파티 이전으로 선물 구매를 하지 않은 상황이기 때문에 다른 선택지들은 정답이 될 수 없다.

3. 해설 타동사 know의 목적어 역할을 하려면 명사절을 이끄는 접속사가 필요한데 문장 끝에 or not이 쓰였으므로 '~인지 아닌지'의 의미인 (B) whether가 정답이다.

4. 해설 빈칸 뒤에 「주어 + 동사」 구조의 완전한 절로 빈칸에는 접속사가 필요하므로 (B) that이 정답이다. (A) 대명사, (C) 전치사, (D) 부사는 절을 연결하는 접속 기능이 없기 때문에 오답이다.

[5-8] 다음 회람에 관한 문제입니다.

수신: 전 직원
발신: 알리사 칼, 급여 코디네이터
날짜: 3월 1일
제목: 휴일 근무 시간 시간표

내셔널 은행은 국경일을 준수해서 3월 15일에 개점하지 않을 것입니다. 이 때문에, 직원들은 평소보다 하루 **5** 이른 3월 14일 목요일에 근무 시간표를 제출해야 합니다. 이것은 모든 지점 직원들과 근무 시간표를 컴퓨터로 제출 **6** 하는 외근 직원들에게 해당될 것입니다. 계약직 직원들은 이 예정된 **7** 휴점이 그들에게 어떤 영향을 미칠지에 대해 결론 내리기 위해 상관들과 상의해야 합니다.

만약 여러분이 3월 14일 오후 5시까지 근무 시간표를 작성할 수 없다면, 대체안을 조정하기 위해서 급여 사무실로 연락해 주십시오. **8** 내선 번호 704로 전화를 걸어서 연락할 수 있습니다. 협조해 주셔서 감사합니다.

어휘 time sheet 근무 시간표 | in observance of ~을 준수해서 | apply to ~에 적용되다 | off-site 외근의 | electronically 전자적으로, 컴퓨터로 | consult ~와 상담하다 | affect ~에게 영향을 미치다 | be unable to ~할 수 없다 | fill out ~을 채우다[작성하다] | alternative 대안이 되는 | arrangement 조정 | cooperation 협력 | paycheck 급료 | day off 쉬는 날

5. 해설 은행이 공휴일에 문을 열지 않을 예정이므로 원래 내던 것보다 하루 일찍 근무 시간표를 제출하라는 공지를 하고 있으므로 (B) earlier '(시간상으로) 더 이른'이 정답이다. (A) faster '(속도가) 더 빠른', (C) previous '(순서상으로) 이전의', (D) advanced '진보된'은 모두 문맥상 어울리지 않는다.

6. 해설 사람 명사 employees '직원들'을 뒤에서 수식하는 주어가 없는 불완전한 구조의 절을 이끌면서 주어와 접속사의 역할을 겸하는 주격 관계대명사를 쓸 자리이므로 (C) who가 정답이다. (A) what과 (D) whoever 모두 불완전한 구조의 절을 이끌지만 선행 명사와 함께 쓰지 못하며, (B) where는 완전한 절을 이끌기 때문에 오답이다.

7. 해설 국경일에 은행이 문을 닫을 것이라는 글이므로, 계약직 직원들에게 은행이 문을 닫는 것이 어떤 영향을 미칠지 알아보라는 뜻이다. 따라서 (D) closure '휴점'이 정답이다. (A) training '훈련', (B) payment '지불', (C) increase '증가'는 모두 문맥상 어울리지 않는다.

8. (A) 임금은 14일에 보내질 것입니다.
(B) 내선 번호 704로 전화를 걸어서 연락할 수 있습니다.
(C) 모든 근무 시간표는 오늘 저녁까지 제 책상에 있어야 합니다.
(D) 모두가 휴일을 즐기셨기를 바랍니다.

해설 이전 문장이 근무 시간표를 작성할 수 없다면, 조정을 위하여 급여 사무실로 연락을 달라는 내용이므로 자연스럽게 구체적인 방법을 이야기하는 (B) It can be reached by dialing extension 704. 가 가장 적합하다.

[9-12] 다음 보고서에 관한 문제입니다.

에이치에이엘 테크놀로지 주가의 급격한 **9** 상승은 최근에 출시된 음성 인식 소프트웨어의 덕분이라고 여겨진다. 그 프로그램의 정확성은 전례가 없는 것이며, 그것의 논리적인 알고리즘은 지금까지 가장 진보된 것이다. **10** 비평가들이 만장일치로 제품에 대한 칭찬을 아끼지 않는다. 그것이 3주 전에 상점에 도착한 이후로 50만 개 **11** 이상의 제품이 팔렸으며, 소프트웨어를 사러 많은 상점에 긴 줄이 만들어졌다. 전문가들은 에이치에이엘 테크놀로지가 연말이면 현재의 시장 선두주자인 다비다 전자보다 **12** 훨씬 더 많은 시장 점유율을 가질 것이라고 예상한다.

어휘 dramatic 극적인 | attribute A to B A를 B의 덕택으로 돌리다 | recognition 인식 | accuracy 정확성 | unprecedented 전례가 없는 | logic 논리적인 | to date 지금까지 | expert 전문가 | predict ~을 예측하다 | market share 시장 점유율 | current 현재의 | decline 감소 | hold 보류 | resemble 닮다, 유사하다 | release 출시하다 | critic 비평가 | unanimous 만장일치의

9. 해설 뒷부분에 새로운 제품의 인기에 관해서 이야기하는 것과 연관해 볼 때 주가는 상승했다고 보는 것이 적당하므로 (D) rise가 정답이다. (A) decline '감소', (B) hold '보류', (C) interest '흥미'는 모두 문맥상 어울리지 않는다.

10. (A) 현재 판매량이 기대한 것만큼 높지 않다.
(B) 그 프로그램은 몇 달 전에 출시되었던 어떤 소프트웨어와 유사하다.
(C) 비평가들이 만장일치로 제품에 대한 칭찬을 아끼지 않는다.
(D) 몇몇 사용자들이 프로그램의 정확성에 대한 오류를 보고한다.

해설 전체적으로 에이치에이엘 테크놀로지의 뛰어난 소프트웨어로 인한 주가 상승을 언급하고 있으므로 (C) Critics are unanimous in their praise of the product. 가 가장 적합하다. 부정적인 의미인 나머지 보기들은 답이 될 수 없다.

11. 해설 over와 still은 부사이고, along과 within은 전치사이다. 빈칸은 부사가 와야 할 자리이다. 빈칸 뒤에 숫자와 함께 쓰여 '~이상'이라는 의미가 되는 (A) Over가 정답이다. (B) Along '~을 따라서', (C)

Still '아직도', (D) Within '~이내에'는 모두 문맥상 어울리지 않는다.

12. **해설** 빈칸 뒤에 비교급 larger이 쓰였으므로 '훨씬'이라는 의미로 비교급을 강조하는 부사 (C) even이 정답이다.

[13-16] 다음 편지에 관한 문제입니다.

> 6월 8일
> 카렌 히로타
> 855 다이조 가
> 시부야쿠, 도쿄, 150-0043, 일본
>
> 히로타 씨 귀하,
>
> 귀하의 지원에 감사드립니다. 귀하께서 저희와 함께 근무하는 것을 고려해 주신 점을 고맙게 생각합니다. 안타깝게도, 공고된 임원 비서 **13** 자리는 채워졌습니다.
>
> **14** 그렇기는 하지만, 저희 인사팀은 귀하의 학력과 업무 경력에 깊은 인상을 받았습니다. 귀하와 같이 훌륭한 지원자들은 찾기 힘듭니다. **15** 앞으로 날 자리를 위해 저희가 귀하의 정보를 보관해 두겠습니다. **16** 한 자리가 나면 연락받으실 겁니다.
>
> 그동안, 앞으로 귀하의 노고에 행운이 깃들기를 바랍니다.
>
> 진심으로,
>
> 버니 해밍스
> 인사 관리자
> 미야기 투자 그룹
>
> **어휘** application 지원(서) | appreciate 고맙게 여기다 | post 게시하다, 공고하다 | executive assistant 비서 | notify 알리다, 통지하다 | in the meantime 그동안, 그 사이에 | wish ~ best of luck ~에게 행운을 빌다 | endeavor 노고, 노력 | openness 솔직함 | enclosed 동봉된

13. **해설** 빈칸은 문장의 주어 자리로 비서 자리가 채워졌다는 내용이므로 '공석, 빈자리'를 의미하는 (B) opening이 정답이다. (A) open은 명사로 '옥외', (D) openness는 '솔직함'을 뜻한다.

14. **해설** 보기를 보고 접속부사 문제로 파악되면 빈칸 앞뒤 문장을 가장 먼저 확인해야 한다. 빈칸 앞의 Unfortunately로 시작하는 문장은 지원한 자리가 이미 채워졌음을 알리는 내용이고, 빈칸 뒤 문장은 지원자의 학력과 경력에 인상을 받았다는 내용이다. 이 두 상반되는 문장을 연결하는 (B) Nonetheless '그렇더라도, 그렇기는 하지만'이 정답이다.

15. (A) 동봉된 서식에 당신의 선택을 확정해 주세요.
(B) 당신은 우리의 새로운 지점에서 일하도록 뽑혔습니다.
(C) 곧 당신의 인터뷰 일정이 잡힐 것입니다.
(D) 앞으로 날 자리를 위해 저희가 귀하의 정보를 보관해 두겠습니다.
해설 빈칸 앞 문장에서 지원자의 학력이나 경력이 인상적이고, 이런 지원자를 찾기가 힘들다고 했고, 뒤 문장에서 자리가 나면 연락

을 받을 것이라고 했으므로 보기 중 '앞으로 날 자리를 위해 지원자의 정보를 보관하겠다'는 내용이 나와야 자연스럽다. 따라서 (D) We will keep your information on file for future positions. 가 정답이다.

16. **해설** 빈칸 앞 문장은 지원자의 학력과 경력이 좋기 때문에, 미래에 날 자리들을 위해 지원자의 정보를 보관해 두겠다는 내용이므로, positions를 가리켜 한 자리가 나면 알려주겠다는 내용으로 연결되어야 적절하다. 따라서 반복을 피하기 위해 앞에 언급된 명사 positions 중에 하나를 받는 (C) one이 정답이다.

UNIT 04. 어휘 선택

핵심 문제 유형

본서 p.196

1. (D)

1. [기사]

> 샌프란시스코 (5월 2일) – 세계적인 화장품 회사인 룩수리아가 최신 미용 제품 혁신을 선보이며 연례 메이크업 컬렉션을 출시했습니다. 매년 출시되는 이 제품은 고객에게 새롭고 흥미로운 제품을 제공하기 위해 설계되었으며, 개발된 많은 품목들이 일반적인 미용 문제와 새로운 트렌드를 파악하기 위한 설문 조사의 피드백을 기반으로 하였습니다.
>
> **어휘** cosmetics 화장품 | launch 출시하다 | annual 연례의 | showcase 선보이다 | release 개봉, 출시 | aim to ~을 목표로 하다 | identify 발견하다 | common 일반적인 | emerging 최근 생겨난

(A) 매일
(B) 매주
(C) 매월
(D) 매년

해설 빈칸은 앞에서 언급한 매년마다 개최하는 행사(its annual Makeup Collection)를 가리키므로 annual을 바꿔 쓴 (D) yearly가 정답이다.

Check

본서 p.197

1. (C)	2. (D)	3. (B)	4. (C)	5. (C)
6. (B)	7. (B)	8. (D)	9. (A)	10. (B)

1. [이메일]

수신인: jessica.smith@mail.net
보낸 사람: FitnessNation@lilmail.com
날짜: 5월 2일
제목: 회신: 회원 수 변화

회원님께:

우리 체육관은 올해 회원 수가 작년에 비해 두 배로 증가하는 등 회원 수가 크게 증가했음을 알리게 되어 기쁩니다. 모든 분들의 체육관 경험을 향상시키기 위해, 우리는 장비와 시설을 업그레이드하고 요가, 복싱과 같은 그룹 피트니스 수업을 추가하고, 더 많은 트레이너를 고용하여 개인에 맞춘 관심과 지원을 제공할 것입니다. 귀하의 피드백은 저희에게 소중하며, 저희는 가능한 한 최고의 체육관 경험을 제공하기 위해 최선을 다하고 있습니다.

어휘 significant 의미 있는, 커다란 | membership 회원, 회원 수 | double 두 배가 되다 | compared to ~와 비교하여 | improve 개선하다 | such as ~와 같은 | personalized 개인의 필요에 맞추어진 | attention 관심, 흥미 | support 지원 | valuable 소중한 | be committed to ~에 전념하다

(A) 관심, 흥미
(B) 요청(사항)
(C) 증가, 인상
(D) 호의, 친절

해설 빈칸 뒤에서 회원 수가 작년에 비해 두 배가 되었다는 내용으로 미루어 보아 빈칸에도 올해 회원 수가 크게 증가했다는 의미가 나오는 것이 적절하다. 따라서 '증가'를 의미하는 (C) increase가 정답이다.

2. [기사]

샌프란시스코 (5월 6일) – 거대 기술 기업인 사비에르 사는 오늘 중 강현실(에이알) 소프트웨어 개발을 전문으로 하는 스타트업 회사인 옐로필드 사의 인수를 완료했습니다. 이번 매입을 통해 사비에르 사는 옐로필드 사의 최첨단 에이알 기술을 보유하게 되었으며, 이는 사비에르 사의 에이알 제품 개발에 박차를 가할 것으로 예상됩니다. 이 거래는 사비에르 사의 혁신에 대한 약속과 고객에게 최첨단 기술을 제공하기 위한 헌신을 보여줍니다.

어휘 giant 거대 기업 | specialize in ~을 전문으로 하다 | Augmented Reality(AR) 증강 현실 | purchase 구매, 매입 | ownership 소유(권) | cutting-edge 최첨단의 | accelerate 가속화하다 | progress 진척, 전진 | deal 거래 | demonstrate 보여주다, 입증하다 | commitment 약속, 전념 | innovation 혁신 | dedication 헌신

(A) 출시, 공개
(B) 협력
(C) 네트워크, 망
(D) 인수

해설 빈칸 뒤 문장에서 이 구매를 통해 사비에르 사가 옐로필드 사의 에이알 기술을 보유하게 되었다고 했으므로 앞 문장은 사비에르 사가

옐로필드 사의 인수를 완료했다는 내용이 나와야 적절하다. 따라서 purchase와 비슷한 의미의 '인수'를 뜻하는 (D) acquisition이 정답이다.

3. [이메일]

수신인: 로드리게스 씨 〈jrodriguez@zoommail.com〉
발신인: 스카이루트 항공 〈srresearch@srairlines.com〉
날짜: 6월 7일
제목: 개선할 수 있도록 도와주세요!

로드리게스 씨께,

이 이메일이 고객님께 잘 도착했기를 바랍니다. 당사의 기록에 따르면 고객님께서는 과거에 스카이루트 항공사를 이용하신 적이 있으며, 저희는 고객님의 의견을 소중히 여깁니다. 전체적인 경험에 대한 고객님의 생각을 공유해주시기 위해 잠시 시간을 내어 간단한 온라인 설문조사를 완료해 주시기를 정중히 요청드립니다. 설문조사는 4개의 질문으로 구성되어 있으며, 가능한 한 솔직하게 답변해주시면 감사하겠습니다. 고객님의 피드백은 당사 서비스 개선 도움에 필수적이며, 고객님의 시간과 의견에 감사드립니다.

어휘 indicate 가리키다, 나타내다 | fly (비행기를) 타다 | value 소중히 여기다 | brief 간단한, 짧은 | share 공유하다 | overall 전체적인 | be composed of ~으로 구성되다 | grateful 고마워하는, 감사히 여기는 | candidly 솔직히, 숨김없이 | aid 돕다 | enhance 향상시키다 | appreciate 감사하게 생각하다 | input 조언

(A) 노력
(B) 피드백
(C) 창의력
(D) 예약

해설 "우리가 개선할 수 있도록 도와달라"는 글의 제목과 함께 빈칸 앞이 이 항공사를 이용한 고객의 의견을 소중히 여기므로, 고객의 생각을 공유해 줄 온라인 설문에 응해달라는 내용이므로 서비스 개선을 위해 필수적인 대상이 고객의 피드백임을 알 수 있다. 따라서 (B) feedback이 정답이다.

4. [웹 페이지]

이스트사이드 메디컬 센터의 웹사이트에 최근 추가된 기능은 "헬스커넥트"로, 환자가 자신의 의료 정보를 보고 의료 기관과 연결할 수 있습니다. 이 기능을 사용하려는 환자는 먼저 몇 가지 간단한 단계를 수행하여 계정을 만들어야 합니다. 시작하려면, register@eastsidehealth.com으로 이메일을 보내거나 555-1212로 "등록" 문자를 보내십시오. 활성화 코드를 받으면, 웹사이트를 방문하여 "헬스커넥트" 탭을 선택하여 컴퓨터, 태블릿 또는 스마트폰을 사용하여 설정 과정을 완료할 수 있습니다.

활성화 코드는 72시간 동안만 유효하므로, 해당 시간 내에 사용해야 합니다. 등록 과정에서 문제가 발생할 경우 support@eastsidehealth.com 또는 555-9876으로 전화하여 기술 지원팀에 문의할 수 있습니다.

…

어휘 latest 최근의, 최신의 | addition 추가(된 것) | feature 기능 | allow ~을 가능하게 하다 | healthcare provider 의료기관 | create an account 계정을 만들다 | activation code 활성화 코드 | setup 설정 | valid 유효한 | time frame 시간, 기간 | encounter 맞닥뜨리다, 부딪히다 | registration 등록, 신청 | technical support 기술 지원(부)

(A) 발상, 생각
(B) 요청
(C) 어려움
(D) 의무

해설 앞 단락에서 환자가 의료 정보 이용을 위해 계정을 개설하는 방법에 대해 안내하고 있으며, 빈칸 앞의 동사 encounter가 뜻밖의 상황, 원치 않는 상황에 '부딪히다, 직면하다'라는 뜻이므로 어떤 문제나 어려운 상황에 직면할 경우 기술 지원팀에 연락하라는 의미로 연결되어야 적절하다. 따라서 '문제, 어려움'을 뜻하는 (C) difficulties가 정답이다.

5. [광고]

당사의 새로운 식사 배달 서비스인 저스트핏을 사용해 보는 데 관심이 있으시다면, 30일간의 평가판 사용 기간 덕분에 아무런 위험 없이 이용하실 수 있습니다. 이 기간 동안에는, 요금이 부과되지 않으며 어떤 종류의 장기 계약에도 얽매이지 않습니다. 평가판에 등록하려면, 귀하의 연락처와 결제 방법을 보관해야 하지만 평가판 사용 기간이 지난 후에도 저스트핏을 계속 사용하지 않으면 요금이 부과되지 않습니다. 만약 당신이 이 서비스가 당신을 위한 것이 아니라고 결정한다면, 그저 우리의 웹사이트 www.justfit.com을 방문하고 "멤버십" 페이지로 이동하기만 하면 됩니다. 여기서 몇 가지 기본 정보를 제공하여 구독을 취소할 수 있습니다. 정말 쉽습니다!

어휘 try out 시험 삼아 해보다 | thanks to ~덕분에 | trial period 시험 기간 | charge 청구하다 | be locked into (곤경 등에) 걸려들다 | enroll 등록하다 | trial 시험(판) | subscription 구독

(A) 결국
(B) 자주
(C) 그저
(D) 주로

해설 문맥상 서비스가 당신에게 맞지 않다면(if), 그저 웹사이트 멤버십 페이지로 가서 구독을 취소하면 된다는 의미가 적절하므로 어떤 일이 얼마나 간단한지를 강조하기 위해 사용되는 (C) simply가 정답이다. 보통 토익에서 if, when, in order to ~가 나오고 뒤에는 simply/just 명령문 구조가 종종 출제가 되므로 굳이 해석하지 않더라도 앞에 if를 보면서 문법적인 궁합으로 simply를 쉽게 찾을 수 있다.

6. [이메일]

받는 사람: 존 데이비스 ⟨johndavis@email.com⟩
보낸 사람: 메리 스미스 ⟨marys@researchco.com⟩
날짜: 6월 2일

제목: 연구

데이비스 씨께,

우리는 현재 선도적인 기술 회사의 새로운 모바일 애플리케이션과 관련된 사용자 참여 패턴에 대한 통찰력을 얻기 위해 연구를 수행하고 있습니다. 이 앱의 소중한 사용자로서 10개 질문에 대한 간단한 설문조사에 참여해 주시면 정말 감사하겠습니다. 귀하의 피드백은 사용자 참여 전략을 개선하는 방법에 대한 귀중한 통찰력을 제공할 것입니다. 귀하의 답변은 극비리에 처리되며 연구 목적으로만 사용됩니다. 감사의 표시로, 주요 소매점에서 교환할 수 있는 15파운드의 기프트 카드를 받으실 수 있습니다. 참여하려면, 이 이메일에 회신해 주십시오. 설문조사 링크를 제공해 드리겠습니다.

본 연구에 시간을 할애해 주셔서 감사합니다.

진심으로,

메리 스미스
평가 조정자

어휘 conduct 수행하다 | gather 모으다, 수집하다 | insight 통찰력 | user engagement 사용자 참여 | leading 선두적인 | valued 소중한 | participation 참여 | appreciate 고마워하다 | invaluable 매우 유용한, 귀중한 | treat 다루다, 처리하다 | with utmost confidentiality 극비리에 | as a token of appreciation 감사의 표시로 | redeem (현금이나 상품으로) 바꾸다, 교환하다 | retailer 소매점 | contribution 기여

(A) 잠깐 동안
(B) 현재
(C) 익명으로
(D) 점점 더

해설 빈칸에 현재진행시제(are conducting)가 쓰였다는 점에서 현재 연구를 수행하고 있다는 의미가 적절하므로 (B) presently가 정답이다. 보통 currently, presently 등은 현재 혹은 현재진행형과 잘 사용되므로 문법적인 궁합을 따져서 쉽게 답을 고를 수 있다.

7. [기사]

(뉴욕 – 10월 15일) 뉴욕에 본사를 둔 지속 가능한 농업 회사인 녹색 성장 벤처 기업에서는 실내 농업 운영을 확장하기 위해 5백만 달러의 투자를 확보했다고 발표했습니다. 이 자금은 새로운 최첨단 시설을 건설하고 현지에서 재배된 신선한 농산물의 생산량을 늘리는 데 사용될 것입니다.

"저는 이 투자가 우리 지역 사회에 지속 가능하고 건강한 음식을 제공하는 우리의 임무를 계속할 수 있게 해줄 것이라고 확신합니다,"라고 녹색 성장 벤처 기업의 전문경영인인, 마리아 로저스가 말했습니다. 우리의 "실내 농업 기술은 전통적인 농업 방식보다 물과 땅을 훨씬 적게 사용하여 연중 내내 농산물을 재배할 수 있습니다. 이는 환경에 도움이 될 뿐만 아니라 고객들이 가능한 한 가장 신선하고 영양이 풍부한 농산물을 받을 수 있도록 보장합니다."

어휘 sustainable 지속 가능한 | agriculture 농업 | based in ~에 본사를 둔, ~에 기반을 둔 | secure 확보하다 | investment 투자 | indoor 실내의 | farming 영농, 농사 | operation 운영 | funding 자금 | state-of-the-art 최신 기술의 | produce 농산물 | year-round 연중 계속 | benefit ~에 혜택을 주다 | ensure 반드시 ~하게 하다, 보장하다 | nutritious 영양이 풍부한

(A) 예상되는
(B) 확신하는
(C) 명백한
(D) ~을 할 수 있는

해설 주어가 I이며, 문맥상 that 이하를 확신한다는 의미가 나와야 적절하므로 (B) confident가 정답이다. (A)나 (C)가 that절을 이끌 때는 보통 가주어 It을 쓰며, (D)는 보통 전치사 of를 동반한다.

8. [안내문]

에이비씨 사는 자사의 최신 제품 라인의 출시를 발표하게 되어 자랑스럽습니다. 이 새로운 컬렉션은 고객의 경험을 향상시키기 위해 최신 기술과 최첨단 디자인을 선보입니다. 출시 행사는 6월 15일에 열릴 것이며, 고객들과 업계 리더들은 신제품을 미리 볼 수 있는 기회를 가질 것입니다. 다과는 오전 10시부터 제공되며, 상품 쇼케이스는 오전 11시 정각에 시작됩니다. 참석자들은 행사가 오후 1시에 끝날 때까지 머물면서 네트워크를 쌓도록 권장됩니다.

어휘 launch 출시, 개시 | showcase 선보이다 | latest 최신의 | cutting-edge 최첨단의 | enhance 높이다, 향상시키다 | take place 일어나다, 발생하다 | preview 미리 보다 | refreshments 다과 | promptly 정각에 | attendee 참석자 | encourage 권장하다 | network 네트워크를 형성하다 | conclude 끝나다

(A) 친숙한
(B) 기쁘게 하는
(C) 필수적인
(D) 자랑스러운

해설 to부정사를 취하는 형용사가 들어갈 자리로, 문맥상 에이비씨 사가 최신 제품 출시를 발표하게 되어 자랑스럽다는 내용이 나와야 적절하므로 (D) proud가 정답이다. (A)는 전치사 with를 동반하며, (B)는 '기쁨을 유발하는'이라는 뜻에서 문맥상 어색하다. (C)는 It is essential to do ~의 패턴을 취하여 '~하는 것이 매우 중요하다'라는 의미를 갖는다.

9. [편지]

랜던 잔디 서비스
그린필드 로 23
써니베일, 캘리포니아 94086.

소중한 고객님께,

이 자리를 빌려 저희 잔디 서비스를 지속적으로 후원해 주신 데 대해 감사의 뜻을 표합니다. 저희는 최선의 관리와 세심한 주의를 기울여 여러분의 잔디밭과 정원을 관리하는 것을 자랑스럽게 생각합니다. 유감스럽게도, 6월 1일부터 잔디 관리 가격을 7% 인상할 것임을 알려드립니다. 장비, 연료, 인건비 상승으로 인해 가격 조정이 필요하게 되었습니다. 가격 인상에도 불구하고 저희의 서비스는 경쟁사에 비해 큰 가치를 유지하고 있다고 생각합니다. 고객님의 이해와 지원에 감사드립니다. 우리는 앞으로 수년간 고객님을 위해 봉사하기를 기대합니다.

진심으로,

랜던 존슨, 소유주

어휘 valued 소중한 | express gratitude 감사를 표하다 | patronage 애용, 후원 | take pride in ~을 자랑하다 | utmost 최고의, 극도의 | attention to detail 세심한 주의 | labor 노동, 작업 | adjust 조정하다 | competition 경쟁(업체) | for many years to come 앞으로도 오랫동안

(A) 효과적인, 시행되는
(B) 서두의, 소개용의
(C) 다가오는, 곧 있을
(D) 분명한

해설 빈칸이 있는 문장은 '6월 1일부터 잔디 관리 가격을 7% 인상할 것이다'라는 의미로 '시점'을 동반하여 그 시점부터 시행된다는 의미를 나타내는 (A) effective가 정답이다. 「effective (from / starting / beginning / as of) + 시점, effective immediately」 표현을 기억해 두자.

10. [이메일]

받는 사람: 아니카 파텔 〈apatel@abcinc.com〉
보낸 사람: 존 스미스 〈jsmith@defcorporation.com〉
날짜: 5월 15일
제목: 월간 주문 업데이트

이 이메일이 잘 도착했기를 바랍니다. 앞으로 몇 달 동안 우리의 고정 주문을 업데이트하기 위해 연락을 드렸습니다. 기억하시겠지만, 저희의 이전 주문에는 비엘 205 펜이 상당수 포함되어 있었습니다. 하지만 팀원들 사이에서 이 펜들에 대한 수요가 감소하고 있다는 것을 알게 되었습니다. 따라서 다음 달부터 비엘 205 펜의 주문을 월 10개로 줄이고 싶습니다. 이 펜 대신 지앤 301 마커를 월 16개로 늘리고 싶습니다.

현시점에서 비엘 205 펜을 완전히 폐기하는 것은 아니지만, 주문에 추가적인 변경 사항이 있다면 꼭 알려드리겠습니다. 덧붙여, 저희에게 이러한 변경 사항을 반영하여 갱신한 월간 청구서와 함께 명세서를 보내주실 것을 요청 드립니다. 저희 재무팀이 기록을 위해 이 정보를 요구해서요.

이 문제에 관심을 가져주셔서 감사드리며, 궁금한 점이나 우려되는 점이 있으면 말씀해주시기 바랍니다.

어휘 reach out 연락을 취하다 | recall 기억해 내다, 상기하다 | decrease 감소 | demand 수요 | in place of ~대신에 | phase out 단계적으로 폐지하다 | entirely 전적으로, 완전히 | statement 명세서 | bill 청구서

(A) 가능한, 가능성 있는

(B) 고정적인, 지속적인

(C) 기한이 지난

(D) 반대의

해설 이메일의 제목이 '월간 주문서 업데이트'인 점에서, 정기적으로 주문해 왔던 것을 변경하겠다는 의미를 품고 있으며, 빈칸 뒤에서 기존의 주문과 앞으로의 주문을 비교하며 변경할 주문량과 수량에 관한 정보를 전달하고 있으므로 빈칸 문장에서도 기존에 고정적으로 해왔던 주문을 업데이트하겠다고 해야 자연스럽게 연결된다. 따라서 '고정 주문'이라는 뜻의 standing order라는 표현을 완성하는 (B) standing이 정답이다.

Practice

본서 p.202

1. (D)	2. (B)	3. (B)	4. (A)	5. (D)
6. (B)	7. (C)	8. (A)	9. (B)	10. (D)
11. (A)	12. (D)	13. (A)	14. (A)	15. (D)
16. (C)				

[1-4] 다음 안내문에 관한 문제입니다.

에피쿠라 디바이스에서는 구매 시점에 당사 웹사이트에 구입 가능하다고 나와 있 **1** 는 물품의 재고가 없는 경우가 생길 수 있습니다. **2** 안타깝게도, 많은 주문량으로 인해 이는 불가피한 문제입니다. 품절된 물품에 대해 결제가 이미 진행된 경우, 바로 환불 처리될 것입니다. 대신에, 대기 명단에 올려달라고 요청하실 수도 있습니다. 이렇게 하면 저희의 다음 **3** 한 회 분에서 물건 수령을 보장받게 됩니다. 추가 요금이 부과되지는 않지만, 주문 처리에 수 주 소요될 수 있습니다.

에피쿠라 디바이스는 싱가포르에 지점 세 개를 보유한 성장 기업입니다. 저희는 고객을 생각하는 기업으로서, 항시 서비스 개선 방법을 물색합니다. **4** 의견이 있으시면, 저희에게 연락해 주시기 바랍니다.

어휘 occasionally 때때로 | inventory 물품 목록 | item 물품 | list 목록에 포함하다 | available 이용 가능한 | purchase 구매 | due to ~으로 인해 | volume 양 | order 주문 | unavoidable 불가피한 | issue 문제 | payment 결제 | go through (절차 등을) 거치다 | sell out 다 팔다 | refund 환불하다 | immediately 즉시, 바로 | alternatively 그 대신에 | request 요청하다 | waitlist 대기자 명단 | ensure 보장하다 | incur 초래하다, 발생시키다 | fulfill 이행하다, 처리하다 | constantly 지속적으로 | promotion 홍보[판촉] | batch 한 회분 | estimate 추정, 견적서 | get in touch 연락하다 | invoice 송장 | supplier 공급자

1. 해설 빈칸은 명사와 동사 사이의 자리이다. 문장의 동사(may lack)가 이미 존재한다는 점을 고려할 때, 빈칸은 뒤에 이어지는 동사구를 명사 items를 수식하는 형용사절로 만들어 주는 관계대명사 (D) that이 정답이다.

2. 해설 빈칸은 앞 문장과 뒤에 이어지는 문장을 연결하는 접속부사 자리이다. 빈칸 앞 문장의 '물품의 재고가 없는 경우가 생길 수 있다'는 내용과 뒤에 이어지는 '주문량이 많아 불가피한 문제'라는 내용을 고려할 때, '안타깝게도, 유감스럽게도'와 같은 내용이 들어가야 문맥상 연결이 자연스러우므로 (B) Regrettably가 정답이다.

3. 해설 빈칸은 our next의 수식을 받는 명사 자리이다. 빈칸 앞부분의 '품절된 물품의 결제가 이미 진행된 경우, 바로 환불받거나 대기자 명단에 올려놓을 수 있다'는 내용을 고려할 때, '대기자 명단에 올려놓으면 다음번 입고되는 물품에서 확실히 수령 가능하다'는 의미가 되어야 문맥상 자연스러우므로 한 회분을 의미하는 (B) batch가 정답이다.

4. **(A) 의견이 있으시면, 저희에게 연락해 주시기 바랍니다.**

(B) 자주 다시 확인하시길 바랍니다.

(C) 최종 송장이 곧 발송될 것입니다.

(D) 저희는 새로운 공급자와 계약을 맺었습니다.

해설 빈칸 앞 문장의 '고객을 생각하는 기업으로서 항시 서비스 개선 방법을 물색한다'는 내용을 고려할 때, '어떤 의견이든 있다면 연락해 달라'는 내용으로 이어져야 문맥상 연결이 자연스러우므로 (A) If you have any comments, please get in touch. 가 정답이다.

[5-8] 다음 기사에 관한 문제입니다.

큐베로 시립 동물원에 새로운 활력을 불어넣다

큐베로 시립 동물원이 다음 달 대중에 다시 문을 연다. 작년 개조 공사로 폐쇄된 이후 새롭게 만들어진 박물관을 대중이 보게 되는 것은 이번이 처음이다.

개조 공사에서 중점을 둔 목표 중 하나는 가족 친화적인 경험을 만들어주는 것이었다. 박물관 방문객은 **5** 곧 보다 많은 관람 플랫폼, 식당, 모든 동물에 관한 유익한 안내판을 누리게 될 것이다.

또한 방문객은 증가된 동물원의 지속 가능성을 위한 노력을 보게 될 것이다. **6** 이를테면, 동물원의 전등 및 안내판 대부분은 태양열로 가동될 것이다. 또한, 실내 전시에는 사용되는 전력량을 낮추는 보다 더 **7** 효율적인 냉난방 시스템을 이용할 것이다.

동물원의 모든 구역이 다음 달에 개방되지는 않을 것이다. 동물원을 시간이 지나며 구역별로 서서히 재개할 계획이다. **8** 전체 일정은 동물원 웹사이트에서 확인할 수 있다.

어휘 breathe 불어넣다 | reopen 다시 문을 열다 | newly 새롭게 | design 설계하다, 만들다 | close off 폐쇄시키다 | renovation 개조, 보수 | focus on ~에 중점을 두다 | family-friendly 가족 친화적인 | informative 정보를 주는 | sign 표지판 | notice 통지하다, 알리다 | sustainability 지속 가능성 | solar-powered 태양열 동력의 | additionally

PART 6 UNIT 04

PART 6 **83**

5. 해설 빈칸은 동사를 수식하는 부사 자리이다. 동사의 시제가 미래이므로 미래 시제와 어울리는 (D) soon이 정답이다.

---

6. 해설 빈칸 뒤에 콤마가 있으므로 빈칸은 앞 문장과 문맥상 자연스럽게 연결해 주는 접속부사 자리이다. 빈칸 앞 문장의 '방문객이 동물원의 지속 가능성을 위한 노력을 보게 될 것'이라는 내용과 빈칸 뒤의 '전등과 안내판이 태양열로 가동될 것'이라는 내용을 고려할 때, 지속 가능성을 위한 노력의 구체적인 예를 들어주고 있음을 알 수 있으므로 (B) For instance가 정답이다.

---

7. 해설 빈칸은 복합 명사 air conditioning systems를 수식하는 형용사 자리이므로 (C) efficient가 정답이다.

---

8. **(A) 전체 일정은 동물원 웹사이트에서 확인할 수 있다.**
(B) 새 프로젝트에 추가 작업자가 필요할 수 있다.
(C) 에어컨 시스템은 추가 시험이 필요할 것이다.
(D) 건강검진이 실시될 예정이다.

해설 빈칸 앞부분의 '동물원의 모든 구역이 한번에 개방되지는 않을 것'이라는 내용을 고려할 때, 동물원을 대중에 개방하는 일정에 관한 내용으로 이어져야 문맥상 연결이 자연스러우므로 (A) A full schedule can be found on the zoo's website. 가 정답이다.

[9-12] 다음 웹 페이지에 관한 문제입니다.

자동 조절 전구

지난 몇 년간 조명 기술은 **9** 상당히 변화했습니다. 떠오르는 기술 중 하나는 자동으로 조절되는 전구인데, 일반 가정용 전구의 **10** 현대적인 대체재입니다. 이 전구는 태양의 자연광 밝기 변화뿐만 아니라 낮 시간을 계산하여 당신의 집에 안정적인 수준의 밝기를 제공합니다.

전구를 시험 사용해 본 지역 사업체 몇 곳의 피드백은 지금까지 아주 긍정적입니다. **11** 그들은 사용의 편의성과 용이성을 높이 평가했습니다. 추가 이점으로, 이 전구는 기존 전구보다 에너지를 덜 소비해 비용을 절약하게 됩니다. 전구들이 올바르게 설치된다면, 훨씬 더 오래 **12** 지속될 것이며, 보다 환경을 의식하는 옵션을 선사할 것입니다.

어휘 auto-adjusting 자동 조정되는 | lightbulb 전구 | light 조명 | emerging 떠오르는, 부상하는 | automatically 자동으로 | alternative 대안 | regular 보통의, 일반적인 | household 가정 | take into account ~을 고려하다, 계산에 넣다 | natural 자연의 | shift 변화 | brightness 밝음 | feedback 피드백, 의견 | test out ~을 시험해 보다 | so far 지금까지 | extra 추가적인 | benefit 이득, 혜택 | end up

9. 해설 빈칸은 동사를 수식하는 부사 자리이다. 빈칸 뒤 문장의 '부상하는 기술 중 하나로 자동 조정 전구를 소개하는 내용을 고려할 때, '상당히 많이 변화했다'는 의미가 되어야 문맥상 연결이 자연스러우므로 (B) substantially가 정답이다.

---

10. 해설 빈칸은 명사 alternatives를 수식하는 형용사 자리이다. 관계대명사로 연결된 문장의 앞부분의 '지난 몇 년간 조명 기술이 상당히 변화했다'는 내용을 고려할 때, '떠오르는 기술인 자동 조정 전구는 일반 가정용 전구의 현대적인 대체재'라는 의미가 되어야 문맥상 연결이 자연스러우므로 (D) modern이 정답이다.

---

11. **(A) 그들은 사용의 편의성과 용이성을 높이 평가했습니다.**
(B) 그것들은 다양한 색상으로 이용될 수 있습니다.
(C) 그들은 관심 있는 모든 지원자들을 받아들입니다.
(D) 그들은 다음 달부터 판매에 들어갈 것입니다.

해설 빈칸 앞 문장의 '전구를 시험 사용해 본 지역 사업체 몇 곳의 피드백은 지금까지 아주 긍정적'이라는 내용을 고려할 때, 긍정적으로 평가한 부분에 대한 내용으로 이어져야 문맥상 연결이 자연스러우므로 (A) They have praised the comfort and ease of use. 가 정답이다.

---

12. 해설 빈칸은 주어 the lightbulbs에 대한 동사 자리이다. 빈칸 앞 문장의 '기존 전구보다 에너지를 덜 소비해 비용을 절약하게 된다'는 내용과 문맥상 '전구들이 올바르게 설치되면 더 오래 지속될 것이다'라는 미래 시제가 되어야 연결이 자연스러우므로 (D) will last가 정답이다.

[13-16] 다음 공고에 관한 문제입니다.

연구 프로젝트 자금 지원 제안서가 현재 그레이슨 시의회 연구소에서 **13** 접수되고 있습니다. 보다 많은 신생 기업을 육성한다는 시의회의 목표에 부합하는 제안서에 보조금이 수여될 것입니다. 저희는 건강, 교통, 컴퓨터 사용과 같은 수익성 좋은 분야에 상업적으로 성공 가능한 **14** 적용성을 보유한 획기적인 방안을 물색하고 있습니다. **15** 자금은 설계도를 바탕으로 한 시제품 제작, 제품을 시장에 내놓을 노련한 직원 채용, 특허 출원처럼 적절한 방식으로 사용될 수 있습니다. 당신의 프로젝트가 저희 기준을 충족한다고 생각되면, 간략한 설명문을 키플링 포인트 21번지, 그레이슨 시의회 연구소, 그레이슨 앞으로 보내주세요. **16** 모든 제출 마감일은 9월 15일입니다.

어휘 proposal 제안 | finance 자금을 대다 | city council 시의회 | research institute 연구소 | grant 보조금 | award 수여하다 | align with ~에 부합하다 | foster 육성하다, 조

성하다 | **start-up** 신생 기업, 스타트업 | **commercially** 상
업적으로 | **viable** 성공할 수 있는 | **lucrative** 수익성이 좋
은 | **computing** 컴퓨터 사용 | **appropriate** 적절한 |
prototype 시제품 | **based on** ~을 바탕으로, 근거하여 |
recruit 채용하다 | **apply for** ~에 지원하다 | **patent** 특
허 | **meet** 충족하다 | **criteria** 기준 | **description** 설
명 | **commence** 시작하다 | **invoice** 청구서를 보내다 |
application 적용 | **applicable** 해당[적용]되는 |
applicably 적절히

13. 해설 빈칸은 현재진행 수동형 동사 구문(be being p.p.)을 완성하는
    과거분사 자리이다. 빈칸 뒤 문장의 '보조금은 보다 많은 신생 기업을
    육성한다는 시의회의 목표에 부합하는 제안서에 수여될 것'이라는 내
    용을 고려할 때, '연구 프로젝트 자금 지원 제안서가 접수되고 있다'는
    의미가 되어야 문맥상 자연스러우므로 (A) accepted가 정답이다.

14. 해설 빈칸은 commercially viable의 수식을 받는 명사 자리이므로
    (A) applications가 정답이다.

15. 해설 빈칸은 문장의 주어 자리이다. 빈칸 앞부분에 '보조금이 수여될
    것'이라는 내용을 고려할 때, '자금은 적절한 방식으로 사용될 수 있다'
    는 의미가 되어야 문맥상 연결이 자연스러우므로 (D) funds가 정답이
    다.

16. (A) 그 연구소는 올해로 6년째를 맞고 있습니다.
    (B) 그레이슨은 현재 많은 신생 기업들의 본거지입니다.
    (C) 모든 제출 마감일은 9월 15일입니다.
    (D) 잘 설계된 웹사이트가 매우 도움이 될 것입니다.

    해설 빈칸 앞 문장의 '당신의 프로젝트가 저희 기준을 충족한다고 생
    각되면, 간략한 설명문을 보내달라'는 내용을 고려할 때, 설명문 제출
    과 관련된 내용으로 이어져야 문맥상 연결이 자연스러우므로 (C) The
    deadline for all submissions is September 15. 가 정답이다.

UNIT 05. 문장 선택

핵심 문제 유형

1. (C)

1. [책자]

3월 20일 토요일 오후 2시부터 5시까지 열리는 제5회 연례 벨몬트
부동산과 재무 세미나에 함께 하세요. 저희 세미나의 목표는 여러분

께 주택 소유를 준비하는 데 필요한 정보를 제공해 드리는 것입니다.

국내 최고의 재무 상담사가 이끄는 이 세 시간짜리 설명회는 여러분
께 주택 구매와 관련된 비용들을 검토하시고 미래의 재정에 관해
식견 있는 결정을 내리시는 데 도움을 드릴 것입니다. 저희는 여러
분께 자신의 수입을 평가하고, 수익성 있는 투자 결정을 내리며, 자
산을 보호하는 방법을 가르쳐 드릴 것입니다. 세미나가 끝날 때 질
의응답 시간이 있을 것입니다. 이 기회를 놓치지 마세요. 등록하시려
면 www.belmontrealtyfinance.com/marchseminar를 방문하세
요.

어휘 **annual** 연례의 | **ownership** 소유 | **associated with**
~와 관련된 | **knowledgeable** 식견 있는 | **evaluate**
평가하다 | **income** 수입 | **profitable** 수익성 있는 |
investment 투자 | **capital** 자산 | **register** 등록하다 |
rewarding 보람 있는

(A) 저희는 당신이 새로운 집을 즐기길 바랍니다.
(B) 여러분은 본인의 회원 자격이 매우 보람 있다는 것을 알게 될 것입
    니다.
(C) 이 기회를 놓치지 마세요.
(D) 지금 바로 커뮤니케이션 기술을 향상시키세요.

해설 빈칸 앞에서는 설명회의 특징에 대해 기술하고 있고, 빈칸 뒤 문장에
    서 등록을 위해 해당 사이트를 방문하라고 했으므로 보기 중 '이 기회
    를 놓치지 마세요.'라고 한 문장이 들어가야 자연스럽게 이어질 수 있
    다. 따라서 (C) Don't miss out on this opportunity. 가 정답이다.

Check

1. (B)	2. (C)	3. (B)	4. (B)	5. (D)
6. (B)	7. (B)	8. (A)	9. (D)	10. (C)

1. [회람]

수신: 전 직원
발신: 가브리엘 펀스턴
날짜: 2월 5일
제목: 웹사이트 개편

모두 안녕하세요.

미러 스튜디오의 IT 팀은 현재 회사의 웹사이트 개편을 진행하고 있
습니다. 그들이 최근에 첫 번째 단계를 완료했습니다. 이 단계는 우
리 고객들이 페이지들을 더 사용하기 쉽게 만드는 데 중점을 두었습
니다.

대중들이 새로운 웹페이지를 이용하기 전에, 작업이 만족스럽게 되
었는지 확인하기 위해 먼저 직원들이 그것들을 시험해 보았으면 좋
겠습니다. 모두가 이 일을 도와줄 것을 정중히 요청합니다. 새 웹사
이트에 관한 설문지가 이메일로 발송될 것입니다. 시간을 내서 모든
질문에 신중하게 답해 주세요. 여러분의 피드백은 우리에게 소중합
니다.

PART 6 UNIT 05

감사합니다.

가브리엘 펀스턴
시스템 관리자

어휘 renovate 개조하다, 새롭게 하다 | focus on ~에 중점을 두다 | user-friendly 사용하기 쉬운 | test ~ out ~을 시험해 보다 | questionnaire 설문지 | concerning ~에 관하여 | take (the) time 시간을 내다 | valuable 소중한, 가치가 큰 | help out 도와주다

(A) 또한 첨부된 문서를 꼭 검토해 보시기 바랍니다.

(B) 모두가 이 일을 도와줄 것을 정중히 요청합니다.

(C) 그러므로 귀하의 예상 마감일을 말씀해 주셔야 합니다.

(D) 누락된 정보를 공란에 설명해 주십시오.

해설 빈칸 앞에서는 새로운 웹페이지를 대중들에게 공개하기 전에 직원들이 먼저 시험해 보도록 할 계획이라고 했고, 빈칸 뒤 문장은 새 웹사이트에 관한 설문지가 이메일로 발송될 것이라고 했으므로 보기 중 '모두가 이 일을 도와줄 것을 정중히 요청한다'는 문장이 들어가야 자연스럽게 이어질 수 있다. 따라서 (B) We respectfully request that everyone help out with this.가 정답이다.

2. [회람]

수신: 전 직원
발신: 엘튼 로스키
회신: 교육
날짜: 9월 20일

도서관 데이터베이스 시스템은 기술 부서에 의해 업데이트되고 있습니다. 관련된 모든 도서관 직원들이 변경 사항들을 숙지하는 것을 확실히 하기 위해, 책과 미디어 자료들을 추적하는 일과 연관된 분들은 우리가 개최할 연수회 중 하나에 참석해야 합니다. 이 연수회들은 10월 8일, 9일, 10일 오후 1시부터 2시로 일정이 잡혀 있습니다.

tech@forestlakelibrary.org로 이메일을 보내서 등록하시고 여러분에게 가장 편한 날짜를 꼭 표시해 주십시오. 이 날짜들에 시간을 낼 수 없다면 eroski@forestlakelibrary.org로 제게 직접 연락해 주시면, 개별 교육을 제공해 드리겠습니다.

어휘 make sure 확실히 하다, 확인하다 | relevant 관련 있는, 적절한 | involved in ~에 연관된 | track 추적하다 | register 등록하다 | indicate 표시하다 | individual 개인의, 개별적인 | open house 공개일 | extend 연장하다

(A) 여러분 모두가 알다시피, 다음 주에 도서관 공개 행사가 열릴 예정입니다.

(B) 포레스트 레이크 도서관은 지역 사회에 좋은 서비스를 제공하는 데 최선을 다하고 있습니다.

(C) 도서관 데이터베이스 시스템은 기술 부서에 의해 업데이트되고 있습니다.

(D) 다음 달부터, 도서관 운영 시간을 연장할 것입니다.

해설 빈칸 뒤에서 관련된 모든 도서관 직원들이 변경 사항을 숙지하도록 하

기 위해 연수회를 개최할 것이니 책과 미디어 자료 추적하는 일을 하는 직원들은 참석하라는 내용이 이어지므로, 보기 중 '도서관 데이터베이스 시스템은 기술 부서에 의해 업데이트되고 있다'는 문장이 들어가야 자연스럽다. 따라서 (C) The library database system is being updated by the Technology Department.가 정답이다.

3. [기사]

11월 10일, 투손 레이크 – 롤로 장난감이 이번에 페더 가 500번지의 클라우드 쇼핑센터 안에 세 번째 지점을 열었다. 업주인 아서 맥과이어는 그의 사업을 더 확장시킬 수 있는 기회를 놓칠 수 없었다고 말했다. "그 쇼핑몰에 소매점 자리가 났다는 사실을 알자마자, 저는 즉시 그곳을 임차했습니다."

맥과이어 씨는 또 페더 가의 상점이 이미 운영될 준비가 되어 있지만, 공식적인 개장식은 11월 15일 일요일 오전 11시에 특별 리본 커팅 행사와 복권 추첨 행사와 함께 열릴 것이라고 말했다. 이 행사는 대중에게 개방된다. 롤로는 최신 어린이용 장난감과 게임, 그리고 풍선과 현수막, 생일 모자를 포함한 다양한 파티용품을 판매한다. 추가 정보를 얻으려면 310-555-5462로 전화하거나 www.rolotoys.com으로 접속하면 된다.

어휘 pass up (기회를) 포기하다 | comment 논평하다, 견해를 밝히다 | operational 가동할 준비가 갖춰진 | opening 개점, 개관 | ribbon-cutting ceremony 리본 커팅 행사 | raffle drawing 복권 추첨 | banner 현수막, 플래카드

(A) 임대료가 너무 비싸서 다른 장소를 알아봐야 했습니다.

(B) 그 쇼핑몰에 소매점 자리가 났다는 사실을 알자마자, 저는 즉시 그곳을 임차했습니다.

(C) 판매 감소로, 가게를 닫을 수밖에 없었습니다.

(D) 내년에 새로운 쇼핑몰을 세운다는 소식에 매우 흥분됩니다.

해설 빈칸 앞에서 롤로 장난감이 세 번째 지점을 열었다고 하면서 업주인 아서 맥과이어의 인터뷰 내용이 언급되었는데, 그가 사업을 더 확장시킬 수 있는 기회를 놓칠 수 없었다고 했으므로 보기 중 '그 쇼핑몰에 소매점 자리가 났다는 사실을 알자마자, 즉시 그곳을 임차했다.'는 문장이 들어가야 자연스럽게 이어질 수 있다. 따라서 (B) Once I found out that retail space was available in the mall, I leased it immediately. 가 정답이다.

4. [이메일]

수신: 스테판 윤 ⟨syoon@macvoylibrary.org⟩
발신: 제사 톰슨 ⟨jthompson@hantechsystems.com⟩
제목: 업데이트
날짜: 1월 4일

윤 씨에게,

맥보이 도서관에 있는 모든 컴퓨터에 대한 위즈 터보 소프트웨어 설치와 관련한 지난주 논의에 덧붙여 말씀드리고자 이 이메일을 드립니다. 제가 말씀드렸던 것처럼, 이 시스템은 도서관 자료들을 추적하는 데 걸리는 시간을 거의 35%나 단축시켜 준다는 것이 증명되었습니다.

예상치 못한 상황이 발생하지 않는다는 가정하에, 설치는 약 한 시간이 소요될 예정입니다. 저희는 당신이 결과에 만족하실 거라 확신합니다. 프로젝트를 계속 진행하길 원하신다면, 되도록 빨리 확답을 주시기 바랍니다.

감사합니다.

제사 톰슨, 소프트웨어 기술자
한텍 시스템

어휘 follow up on ~에 대한 추가 조치를 취하다 | regarding ~에 관하여 | installation 설치 | unforeseen 예상치 못한 | circumstance 상황 | arise 발생하다 | at one's earliest convenience 형편이 닿는 대로 빨리 | proceed 계속 진행하다 | confirmation 확정

(A) 조기에 확정해 주신 데 대해 다시 한번 감사드립니다.
(B) 저희는 당신이 결과에 만족하실 거라 확신합니다.
(C) 그 당시에는 기술적인 문제에 대해서 예상하지 못했습니다.
(D) 당신이 원하신다면 도서관에 대해 더 많은 정보를 드리도록 하겠습니다.

해설 첫 번째 단락에서는 위즈 터보 소프트웨어를 도서관 컴퓨터에 설치하면 어떤 이점이 있는지 언급했다. 빈칸 앞 문장은 위즈 터보 소프트웨어의 설치 시간을 언급했고, 빈칸 뒤는 이 설치 작업을 할 거라면 빨리 확답을 달라는 내용이므로 보기 중 '소프트웨어 설치에 확실히 만족할 것이다'라는 내용의 (B) We are confident that you will be satisfied with the results. 가 정답이다.

5. [회람]

수신: 전 직원
발신: 로렌조 코랄레스
날짜: 2월 17일
제목: 알브이엠-3

우리가 알브이엠-3 이메일 프로그램으로 전환하게 될 것임을 모든 분들께 상기시켜 드리고자 합니다. 오늘 오후 4시 30분 부로, 여러분은 현재의 이메일 시스템인 트랙시스에 접속할 수 없을 것입니다. 따라서, 트랙시스에 보관된 모든 중요한 메시지들은 이 시간 전에 백업해 두는 것이 대단히 중요합니다. 트랙시스 시스템이 제거되면, 저장되지 않은 메시지들은 모두 영구적으로 삭제될 것임을 명심해 주세요.

새로운 프로그램에 관해 더 많은 정보를 얻으시려면, 그 특징들을 모두 기술한 알브이엠-3 데모 비디오를 다운로드하세요: www.rvm.com/rvm3_video. 그 사이트에는 출력할 수 있는 사용자 매뉴얼도 있습니다. 질문이 더 있으시면, supportcenter@encro.com으로 연락 바랍니다.

어휘 remind 상기시키다 | transition 전환하다 | access 접속하다 | crucial 중대한 | back up (파일이나 프로그램 등을) 백업하다 | keep in mind 염두에 두다 | permanently 영구적으로 | demo (샘플 테이프나 음반) 데모 | further 더 이상의, 추가의 | transfer 옮기다

(A) 그때는 고객들이 소프트웨어를 구매할 수 있습니다.
(B) 그렇게 함으로써, 여러분들이 일한 시간을 입력할 수 있습니다.
(C) 그러므로, 모든 중요한 파일은 옮겨 놓아야 합니다.
(D) 그 사이트에는 출력할 수 있는 사용자 매뉴얼도 있습니다.

해설 빈칸 앞 문장에서 특정 사이트 주소를 알려주며 더 많은 정보를 알고 싶으면 데모 비디오를 다운로드하라는 내용이 나오므로, 보기 중 '그 사이트에는 출력할 수 있는 사용자 매뉴얼도 있다'는 내용이 자연스럽게 이어질 수 있다. 따라서 (D) There is also a printable user manual available on the site. 가 정답이다.

6. [기사]

6월 1일, 홍콩 – 엑스이디 자동차의 최고 경영자인 루벤 시린은 오늘 오후 기자 회견에서, 회사가 새로운 고효율 전기 자동차를 이달 말 출시할 계획이라고 발표했다.

시린 씨에 따르면, 이 차량은 두 개의 전기 모터와 진보된 정속 주행 장치 그리고 최신식 지피에스 장치를 특징으로 한다.

자동차 업계 전문가들은 이 최신 차량이 엑스이디 사의 최신 소형차 라인에 훨씬 더 많은 관심을 불러 모을 것이라고 예상한다. 그들은 지속적으로 강세를 보인 영업 성과를 자동차 기술을 끊임없이 개선해 온 회사의 능력 덕분으로 여기고 있다. 엑스이디는 이미 이번 분기 매출 목표를 넘어섰다.

어휘 press conference 기자 회견 | release 출시하다 | energy-efficient 연비가 좋은 | advanced 진보된, 발전된 | cruise control system 정속 주행 장치 | state-of-the-art 최신식의 | device 장치 | bring attention to ~에 관심을 불러모으다 | compact 소형의 | attribute A to B A를 B의 덕분으로 여기다 | consistently 지속적으로 | performance 성과, 업적 | exceed 넘어서다 | discontinue 중단하다 | compensation 보상

(A) 엑스이디는 작년에 처음으로 국제 모터쇼에 자동차를 선보였다.
(B) 엑스이디는 이미 이번 분기 매출 목표를 넘어섰다.
(C) 엑스이디는 자동차 생산 라인 중 하나를 중지할 계획이다.
(D) 엑스이디는 고객들에게 금전적인 보상을 하려고 한다.

해설 앞 문장이 '자동차 기술을 거듭 개선시킨 탓에 엑스이디 사의 영업 성과가 지속적으로 강세를 보였다'는 내용이므로, 보기 중 엑스이디의 영업 성과에 대한 실례를 보여준 문장이 어울린다. 따라서 (B) XED has already exceeded its sales goals for this quarter. 가 정답이다.

7. [이메일]

수신: 신디 윌헴 〈cwilhem@zoommail.com〉
발신: 딜런 로빈스 〈drobins@johanauto.net〉
날짜: 11월 7일
제목: 수리 요청

윌헴 씨에게,

저희 온라인 시스템을 통해 11월 5일에 받았던 고객님의 수리 요청(고객 번호 7695)에 대한 답변을 드립니다. 고객님께서 제공해 주신 정보에 따르면, 고객님은 서비스를 받으려 차를 가져오실 필요가 없

습니다. 저희는 그 문제가 고객님께서 직접 해결 가능하신 부분이라고 생각합니다. 고객님은 차량이 정차했을 때 차량 문이 자동으로 닫힌다고 얘기했습니다. 이것을 비활성화시키기 위해서, 먼저 계기판의 왼쪽에 "자동 잠금"이라고 표시된 스위치를 찾으세요. 그다음, 스위치 바로 옆에 있는 "리셋" 버튼을 누르기 전에 그냥 스위치를 "꺼짐"으로 돌려주시면 됩니다. 만약 이것이 작동하지 않는다면, 555-5735번으로 제게 연락해 주세요.

진심으로,

딜런 로빈스, 서비스 관리자
요한 오토

어휘 via ~을 통하여 | deactivate 비활성화시키다 | locate ~의 위치를 찾다 | marked 표시된 | dashboard 계기판 | flip 탁 돌리다 | reset 다시 맞추다 | right next to ~의 바로 옆에 있는 | fail to work 작동하지 않다

(A) 기술자가 24시간 이내에 차를 정비해 놓을 것입니다.
(B) 저희는 그 문제가 고객님께서 직접 해결 가능하신 부분이라고 생각합니다.
(C) 우리 상점은 구형 모델을 포함해서 모든 차량을 서비스합니다.
(D) 고객님의 이메일에 문제점에 대한 간단한 설명을 포함시켜 주십시오.

해설 빈칸 앞 문장은 서비스를 받으러 차량을 가지고 올 필요가 없다는 내용인데, 빈칸 뒤에 이어지는 문장들을 보면 정차 상태에서 차량 문이 자동으로 잠기는 현상에 대해 해결하는 방법을 설명해 주고 있으므로, 보기 중 '그 문제를 직접 해결할 수 있다고 생각한다'는 내용의 문장이 들어가야 자연스럽다. 따라서 (B) We believe the issue can be resolved by you on your own. 이 정답이다.

8. [기사]

7월 3일 – 9월부터, 동부 학군은 모든 영문학 교재와 강의 교재에 있어 오로지 클리프톤 교육 출판사의 것만 사용할 것이다. 과거에 클리프톤은 그러한 콘텐츠를 제공하는 두 개의 선호되는 공급업체들 중 하나였다. 하지만 9월 1일부로 교육 위원회는 다른 업체와의 계약을 중단할 것이다. 이 결정은 교사들과 다른 교육 관계자들에 의한 투표로 이루어졌는데, 그들은 클리프톤 제품의 품질을 칭찬했다. 클리프톤 교과서들의 가격이 상대적으로 높기는 하지만, 교사용 지도서와 학생용 워크북 같은 보충 교재들은 다른 출판사들의 것보다 덜 비싸다. 이것은 그 학군이 예산 내에서 비용을 유지할 수 있게 해줄 것이다.

어휘 depend on ~에 의존하다 | solely 오직 | text 교재 | teaching material 강의 교재 | supplier 공급업체 | as of ~일자로 | board of education 교육 위원회 | based on ~을 기반으로 하여 | vote 투표; 투표하다 | praise 칭찬하다 | relatively 상대적으로 | supplementary material 보충 교재

(A) 이것은 그 학군이 예산 내에서 비용을 유지할 수 있게 해줄 것이다.
(B) 이것은 제한된 기간 동안 무료로 제공될 것이다.
(C) 이것은 선생님들이 학생들과 더 많은 시간을 보낼 수 있게 해줄 것이다.

(D) 이것은 효과적인 커리큘럼을 만들 수 있게 해줄 것이다.

해설 빈칸 앞 문장을 보면 클리프톤 교과서의 가격이 상대적으로 높기는 하지만, 보충 교재들은 다른 업체들보다 저렴하다고 했으므로 보기 중 '비용이 예산을 넘지 않게 해줄 것'이라는 내용이 자연스럽게 이어질 수 있다. 따라서 (A) This will enable the district to keep expenses within budget. 이 정답이다.

9. [이메일]

수신: 에벌린 패터슨 〈epatterson@focaladvertising.com〉
발신: 채스 무노즈 〈cmunoz@exposportsauthority.com〉
날짜: 8월 12일
제목: 마케팅 캠페인
첨부 파일: 사진

안녕하세요 에벌린,

엑스포 스포츠 협회는 곧 가을 물품 목록을 받게 됩니다. 그에 맞춰, 저는 이번 시즌의 신상품을 홍보하기 위해 또 다른 광고 캠페인을 시작할 계획입니다. 특히, 저는 친환경 재료들로 만든 로드 블레이저 등산용 제품에 주의를 환기시키고 싶습니다. 엑스포 스포츠 협회는 지역에서 이 제품 라인을 제공하는 몇 안 되는 소매업체들 중 하나여서, 우리의 모든 광고에서 그 부분이 강조되었으면 합니다. 첨부된 것은 몇 장의 등산용 제품 사진들입니다. 광고를 제작하실 때 이것들을 당신이 원하는 방식대로 사용하세요.

감사합니다.

채스 무노즈
엑스포 스포츠 협회, 영업 이사

어휘 inventory 재고, 물품 목록 | promote 홍보하다 | in particular 특히 | call attention to ~에 주의를 환기하다 | gear 장비 | be made of ~으로 만들어지다 | eco-friendly 친환경적인 | retailer 소매업체 | estimate 견적서 | display 전시하다

(A) 예산안이 내일까지 귀하의 이메일로 보내질 것입니다.
(B) 귀사의 제품 샘플들을 요청하고 싶습니다.
(C) 광고들은 시내 전역의 영업점에 전시될 것입니다.
(D) 첨부된 것은 몇 장의 등산용 제품 사진들입니다.

해설 빈칸 앞 문장에서는 모든 광고에 친환경 등산용 제품이 강조되기를 원한다고 했고, 뒤 문장은 광고를 제작할 때 이것들을 사용하라는 내용이므로, 보기 중 '등산용 제품 사진들이 첨부되어 있다'고 한 문장이 들어가야 의미가 통한다. 따라서 (D) Attached are some photos of the hiking gear. 가 정답이다.

10. [편지]

6월 23일

그레고리 발렌시아
1150 스펙터클 가
몬트리올, 퀘백 H3A 1J7

발렌시아 씨에게,

지난 6월 20일 금요일에 우리가 논의한 바에 따라, 피네스 오디오 홈시어터 시스템의 배송과 설치에 대한 아래의 견적서를 검토해 주세요. 총 489.99달러로, 구매 가격과 판매세, 인건비를 포함합니다. 이것을 단지 추정치로 이해해 주세요. 정확한 설치 비용은 각 거주지에 따라 조금씩 다를 수 있습니다.

계속 진행하고 싶으시면, 귀하에게 편리한 시간을 정할 수 있도록 555-9483으로 제게 연락 부탁드립니다.

감사드리며,

타이론 브라운
피네스 오디오 시스템, 영업부장

어휘 review 검토하다, 평가하다 | quote 견적서 | installation 설치 | home theater system 홈시어터 시스템 | as per ~에 따라 | come to (합계가) ~이 되다 | sales tax 판매세 | labor cost 인건비 | merely 단지, 그저 | proceed 계속 진행하다 | inventory 물품 목록 | in stock 재고로 | residence 거주

(A) 지난주 금요일의 논의를 이어갔으면 합니다.
(B) 그 제품이 재고가 있는지 제품 목록을 확인하겠습니다.
(C) 정확한 설치 비용은 각 거주지에 따라 조금씩 다를 수 있습니다.
(D) 이번 주 말까지 요금을 지불해야 한다는 것을 기억해 주십시오.

해설 앞에서 견적액이 489.99달러이고 이 금액을 추정치로만 이해해 달라고 했으므로, 보기 중 '정확한 설치 비용은 각 거주지에 따라 조금씩 달라질 수 있다'는 문장이 이어져야 자연스럽다. 따라서 (C) Exact installation cost will vary slightly for each residence. 가 정답이다.

Practice

본서 p.212

1. (C)	**2.** (A)	**3.** (C)	**4.** (C)	**5.** (B)
6. (B)	**7.** (A)	**8.** (A)	**9.** (B)	**10.** (B)
11. (D)	**12.** (C)	**13.** (D)	**14.** (B)	**15.** (C)
16. (B)				

[1-4] 다음 이메일에 관한 문제입니다.

수신: 케이코 후카와 〈keikofu@sapmail.com〉
발신: netoffice.com
날짜: 10월 21일 화요일 오후 2시 38분
제목: 주문

저희에게 주문해 주셔서 감사드립니다. 오늘 오후 2시 34분, 저희는 귀하로부터 품번 893-씨에이치인 체리 빛 접뚜껑이 달린 컴퓨터 책상 주문서를 받았습니다. **1** 이 물품은 특별 가격인 125.99달러에 판매됩니다. 저희가 현재 하고 있는 특별 행사의 일환으로, 귀하는 추가 비용 없이 책상에 어울리는 의자도 받으실 것입니다. 두 물건 모두 수작업된 재료들을 **2** 특징으로 하고 저희의 기본적인 품질 보증을 받습니다. 의자는 약간의 **3** 조립이 요구될 것입니다.

만약 저희가 확인 내역을 잘못 받았다면, 저희 **4** 직원들 중 한 명에게 customerservice@netoffice.com으로 즉시 연락을 주십시오. 그렇지 않으면, 귀하가 주문하신 물건은 영업일 이틀 이내에 선적될 것입니다.

어휘 place an order 주문하다 | stained 얼룩진 | roll-top 뚜껑을 접어서 올릴 수 있는 | currently 현재에 | matching 어울리는 | at no extra charge 추가 비용 없이 | standard 일반적인, 표준 규격에 맞춘 | warranty 품질 보증 | confirmation 확인 | in error 잘못해서 | immediately 즉시 | otherwise 그렇지 않으면 | ship 운송하다 | business day 영업일, 평일 | retail for ~의 값으로 소매되다 | feature 특징으로 하다 | assemble ~을 모으다 | assembly 조립, 집회 | demonstrator 시위 참가자

1.
(A) 이 물품은 현재 주문이 불가능합니다.
(B) 물품에 대한 보증이 불가능합니다.
(C) 이 물품은 특별 가격인 125.99달러에 판매됩니다.
(D) 귀하께서 물품을 구매하시길 희망합니다.

해설 빈칸 다음 문장에서 '특별 행사의 일환으로, 귀하는 추가 비용 없이 책상에 어울리는 의자도 받으실 것입니다'로 특별 행사의 또 다른 혜택을 이야기하고 있으므로 특별 행사의 혜택을 말하고 있는 (C) This item retails for a special price of $125.99. 가 정답이다.

2. 해설 (A) feature '~을 특징으로 하다', (B) contain '~을 포함하다', (C) measure '~을 재다', (D) seek '~을 찾다'라는 뜻으로, 제품을 설명하면서 어떤 특징을 가지고 있는지를 설명하고 있으므로 (A) feature가 정답이다. (B)는 연설이나 책 등에 어떤 내용이 포함되어 있다거나 어떤 물질의 일부로 함유되어 있는 경우에 쓰기 때문에 답이 될 수 없다.

3. 해설 some 뒤에 쓰여서 문장의 주어 역할을 하는 자리이므로 명사 (C) assembly가 정답이다.

4. 해설 (A) producers '생산자들', (B) demonstrators '시연자들', (C) representatives '직원들', (D) applicants '지원자들'이라는 뜻으로, 물건을 주문한 고객에게 주문 확인을 하면서 주문에 문제가 있으면 '직원들'에게 연락을 하라고 말하는 것이 자연스러우므로 (C) representatives가 정답이다.

[5-8] 다음 이메일에 관한 문제입니다.

수신: 혜림 배 〈hyerimbae@gsmmail.com〉
발신: 패트리샤 손 〈pattythorne@gsaccmail.com〉
날짜: 3월 21일 오전 11시 31분
제목: 변경 사항

배 씨에게,

당신의 부서에 채용될 새로운 직원을 수용하기 위해, 당신의 사무실은 3층 전체로 확장될 예정입니다. 안타깝게도, 이것은 당신의 팀이

향후 몇 달간 불편을 감수해야만 할 것이라는 사실을 의미합니다. 당신의 사무실은 **5** 임시로 5층에 있는 2개의 회의실로 이동될 것입니다. 이 상황이 얼마나 지속될지는 아직 말씀드릴 수는 없지만, 보수 공사가 얼마나 **6** 확장되어야 할지에 대한 견적서를 주기 위해 계약자가 다음 주에 옵니다.

회의실은 다소 비좁아서, 더 융통성 있는 업무 일정을 짜는 게 허용될 겁니다. 직원들은 일주일에 이틀은 재택근무가 허락될 것입니다. 그러나 재택 **7** 근무하는 직원들은 집에 휴대전화와 빠른 속도의 인터넷이 있어야만 합니다. **8** 귀하의 직원들이 두 개의 필수 사항을 반드시 알도록 해 주시기 바랍니다. 보수 공사에 관한 질문이나 요청 사항이 있다면, 알려주시기 바랍니다.

진심으로,

패트리샤 손

어휘 accommodate 수용하다 | expand 확장하다 | take up ~을 차지하다 | entire 전체의 | inconvenience 불편 | relocate 이전하다 | last 지속하다 | estimate 견적(서) | renovation 보수 공사 | somewhat 다소 | cramped 비좁은 | flexible 융통성 있는 | work from home 재택 근무 | generally 일반적으로 | temporarily 일시적으로 | permanently 영구적으로 | belatedly 뒤늦게 | extensive 대규모의 | extensively 널리, 광범위하게 | extent 정도, 규모 | workable 실행 가능한 | workably 실행 가능하게 | requirement 필수 사항 | extension 내선 번호 | settle 해결하다 | be up for discussion 논의에 오르다

5. **해설** 문맥상 가장 어울리는 부사 어휘를 선택하는 문제이다. 빈칸 이전 문장에서 '이것은 당신의 팀이 향후 몇 달간 불편을 감수해야만 할 것이라는 사실을 의미합니다'라고 했으므로 사무실이 영구적으로 이전되는 것이 아니라는 사실을 알 수 있다. 따라서 빈칸에 들어갈 부사는 (C) permanently '영구적으로'가 아닌 (B) temporarily '임시로'임을 알 수 있다.

6. **해설** 빈칸 앞에 how가 있고, 빈칸 뒤에 「주어 + be동사」가 나오므로 빈칸에는 how와 함께 쓰이며 동시에 be동사의 보어가 될 수 있는 형용사가 필요하다. 따라서 정답은 형용사인 (B) extensive이다.

7. **해설** personnel이라는 명사를 뒤에서 수식하여 '집에서 근무하는 직원들'의 의미를 만드는 현재분사 (A) working이 정답이다.

8. **(A) 귀하의 직원들이 두 개의 필수 사항을 반드시 알도록 해 주시기 바랍니다.**
   (B) 문의 사항이 있으시면 내선 46번으로 더그 피터슨에게 연락하실 수 있습니다.
   (C) 이 물품들은 아무 때나 제 사무실로 연락하면 얻으실 수 있습니다.
   (D) 이 문제는 해결된 것으로 간주해야 하며 차후 논의에 오르지 않도록 해야 됩니다.

   해설 빈칸 뒤에서 질문이나 문제가 있으면 연락하라는 말이 있으므

로 중복이 되는 (B)는 어색하다. 또한, 앞 문장에서 재택근무에 대한 이야기를 하였고, 빠른 속도의 인터넷과 휴대전화가 필요하다고 나와 있으므로 (C)는 문맥상 어색하다. 또한, 문제에 대한 해결 요구 글이 아니므로 (D)도 정답이 될 수 없다. 재택근무의 두 가지 필수 요건으로 빠른 인터넷과 휴대전화가 있어야 한다고 말했으므로 그 두 가지 필수 사항(these two requirements)을 직원들에게 알리라고 하는 (A) Be sure to make your staff aware of these two requirements. 가 정답이다.

[9-12] 다음 회람에 관한 문제입니다.

수신: 모든 인사부 직원
발신: 인사부 부장, 자밀라 린깃
날짜: 5월 4일, 화요일
회신: 회의

많은 분이 이미 알고 계시듯이, 저는 주말 동안 시카고에서 열린 인사 관리 세미나에 참석했습니다. 제가 거기에 있는 동안, 회사의 전체적인 근로 조건을 향상시키는 데 도움을 줄 것으로 생각되는 많은 기법을 배웠습니다. **9** 제가 배운 지식을 여러분 모두와 공유하고 싶습니다. 내일 아침, 우리는 그 기법들에 대해 논의하기 위해 10시에 회의를 할 것입니다. 그런 다음, 저는 여러분이 목요일에 만날 각각의 부서를 **10** 직접 할당할 것입니다. 회의에서 당신은 그들이 가진 모든 불편과 불평에 대해 논의할 것입니다. 그 부서의 직원들이 다른 사람들 앞에서 논의하기 불편한 문제를 당신에게 **11** 개별적으로 가져오도록 장려 해주시기를 원합니다. 직원들이 **12** 손쉽게 서로서로 협력하는 환경을 만드는 일이 저희의 책무입니다. 다음 월요일에는, 여러분들이 배운 것을 공유하기 위해 다시 만날 예정입니다.

어휘 human resources 인력 자원부 | technique 기법, 기술 | overall 전반적인 | work condition 업무 조건 | assign 배정하다, 부과하다 | complaint 불평, 불만 | comfortable 편안한 | personnel 전 직원; 인사의, 직원의 | collaborate 협력하다 | upcoming 곧 있을 | take advantage of ~을 이용하다 | personality 성격, 개성 | evidently 분명히 | readily 손쉽게 | readiness 준비가 되어 있음

9. (A) 제가 직원회의에서 알게 된 것은 믿어지지 않을 정도였습니다.
   (B) 제가 배운 지식을 여러분 모두와 공유하고 싶습니다.
   (C) 당신이 곧 있을 세미나에 참석하고 싶으면 알려주시기 바랍니다.
   (D) 이것은 모두가 활용할 수 있는 기회가 될 것입니다.

   해설 빈칸 이전 문장에서 '전체적인 근로 조건을 향상시키는 데 도움을 줄 것으로 생각되는 많은 기법을 배웠습니다'라고 언급했고 뒤 문장에서 '내일 아침 10시에 그 기법에 대해 의논하기 위하여 회의를 한다'고 했기 때문에 지식에 대한 공유 내용인 (B) I'd like to share the knowledge that I learned with you all. 이 문맥의 흐름상 가장 적절하다. (A)는 직원회의가 아닌 세미나로 바뀌어야 정답이 될 수 있고, (C)에서 언급되는 세미나는 예정된 게 없으므로 오답이다.

10. **해설** 조동사와 동사원형 사이는 부사 자리이므로 부사형 어미 -ly가 붙은 (B) personally가 정답이다.

11. 해설 문맥상 가장 어울리는 부사 어휘를 선택하는 문제이다. 빈칸 뒷부분의 '다른 사람들 앞에서 논의하기 불편한 문제'라는 단서를 통하여 문맥상 가장 적절한 부사는 '개별적으로'라는 뜻의 (D) individually임을 알 수 있다.

12. 해설 자동사와 전치사 사이에 오는 부사를 묻는 문제이므로 정답은 부사인 (C) readily이다.

[13-16] 다음 공지에 관한 문제입니다.

공지

13 지난달에 공지했듯이, 건물에 약간의 보수 공사가 곧 시작될 것입니다. 다음 주에 시작할 로비 보수 공사 때문에, 일상적인 지각 **14** 정책이 보류될 것입니다. 이 건물에서 두 개의 계단과 세 개의 엘리베이터만이 **15** 우리 층에 도착합니다. 작업이 완성될 때까지, 어떤 시간대에는 그 길들 중에서 **16** 모든 경로를 사용할 수 없을 수도 있기 때문에 양해가 필요합니다. 그러므로, 직원들은 6시 퇴근 시간 이후에 업무 시간을 메꿀 수 있다면 늦어도 10시까지는 도착해도 됩니다. 감사합니다.

카티아 보로즈니
인사과 부장

어휘 renovation 개조, 보수 | commence 시작하다 | lateness 지각 | suspend ~을 보류하다 | stairwell 계단통 | reach ~에 도착하다 | accessible 접근할 수 있는 | concession 양해 | make up ~을 보충하다 | projection 예상 | grant 허가

13. (A) 우리는 한 달 후에 로비에서 약간의 보수 작업을 할 것을 고려하고 있습니다.
(B) 1층에서의 보수 공사가 막 완료되었습니다.
(C) 건물의 수리 공사 기간 동안 여러분의 양해에 감사드립니다.
(D) 지난달에 공지했듯이, 건물에 약간의 보수 공사가 곧 시작될 것입니다.

해설 빈칸 다음 문장부터 로비의 보수 공사가 시작되고, 그로 인해 지각에 대한 회사 정책이 바뀐다는 내용이므로 공사가 시작됨을 알리는 (D) As announced last month, some construction work on the building will start soon. 이 정답이다. 다음 주부터 공사가 시작되므로 (A), (B), (C)는 오답이다.

14. 해설 (A) projection '예상', (B) policy '정책', (C) grant '허가', (D) ranking '등급'이라는 뜻으로 건물에 공사를 하는 동안 지각에 관련된 '정책'이 어떻게 바뀌는지를 설명하고 있으므로 (B) policy가 정답이다. 늦어도 된다는 '허가'가 보류되는 것이 아니라 당분간은 늦어도 된다는 것이니 (C)는 답이 될 수 없다.

15. 해설 건물에 있는 계단이나 엘리베이터는 공지하는 사람과 받는 사람들이 일하고 있는 층으로 그들을 데려다주는 것이므로, 공지를 하는 사람이 포함된 '우리 층'에 오는 계단과 엘리베이터라고 말해야 한다. 따라서 (C) our가 정답이다.

16. 해설 문장의 주어 역할을 할 부정대명사가 필요한 자리이므로 (B) all과 (D) none 중에 답을 골라야 하며, 문맥상 '모든 경로를 사용할 수 없을 수도 있기 때문에'라는 내용이 자연스러우므로 (B) all이 정답이다.

REVIEW TEST

본서 p.216

1. (D)	**2.** (A)	**3.** (A)	**4.** (C)	**5.** (A)
6. (D)	**7.** (B)	**8.** (A)	**9.** (D)	**10.** (B)
11. (C)	**12.** (D)	**13.** (C)	**14.** (C)	**15.** (C)
16. (D)				

[1-4] 다음 편지에 관한 문제입니다.

챔버스 씨 귀하,

5월 7일 고객님께서 받으신 300개의 정찬용 접시 중 20개를 **1** 거절하신 것에 관해 편지합니다. 마에스트로 포터리에서, 저희는 모든 상품의 품질에 상당한 주의를 기울입니다. 제품에 있는 어떠한 결함도 받아들일 수 없는 것으로 **2** 여겨집니다.

고객님의 소매점은 저희의 최고 단골 고객 중 한 곳입니다. **3** 그러므로, 저희는 결함이 있는 접시의 총액을 고객님의 계좌로 환불해 드리도록 하겠습니다.

4 고객님이 가장 편한 시간에 언제든 그 물품들을 보내주시길 바랍니다. 이에 관해서, 또는 그 밖의 다른 염려하시는 사항이나 문제들에 관해서 망설이지 말고 제게 연락해 주시길 바랍니다.

진심으로,

해롤드 신
영업 이사
마에스트로 포터리

어휘 concerning ~에 대해 | pay attention to ~에 주의를 기울이다 | quality 품질 | merchandise 물품, 상품 | defect 결함 | unacceptable 받아들일 수 없는, 수용할 수 없는 | retail outlet 소매점 | loyal client 단골 고객 | refund 환불해 주다 | defective 결함이 있는 | account 계좌 | hesitate 망설이다, 주저하다 | regarding ~에 관하여 | concern 걱정거리 | issue 문제, 사안 | coordination 합동, 조화 | disposal 처리 | proceed 진행하다 | estimate 견적서 | convenient 편리한 | sign up 신청하다

1. 해설 빈칸 뒤에 이어지는 내용에서 이 업체는 모든 상품의 품질에 주의를 기울이고 있으며 그 어떤 결함도 용인하지 않고 결함이 있는 상품의 총액을 환불해 주겠다고 했으므로, 300개의 정찬용 접시 중 20개를 거절한 것에 관해 편지를 썼다는 의미가 적절하다. 따라서 (D) rejection이 정답이다.

2. 해설 문장 구조가 「주어 + 동사 + ~ + 보어」이므로 be동사 뒤에 올 수 없는 선택지 (B) considers를 소거한다. 문맥상 '그 어떤 제품의

결함도 받아들일 수 없는 것으로 간주된다'는 의미가 적절하므로 수동태인 (A) considered가 정답이다. 참고로 consider는 「consider + 목적어 + 목적격 보어」의 패턴을 취할 수 있는데, 이 문장은 We consider any defects in our products unacceptable. 이 수동태 문장으로 바뀐 형태로 볼 수 있다.

----

3. **해설** 고객님의 소매점이 최고 단골 고객 중 하나라는 빈칸 앞의 문장과 결함이 있는 상품의 총액을 환불해 줄 것이라는 뒤 문장은 인과 관계로 연결되는 것이 자연스러우므로, 결과를 나타내는 (A) Therefore가 정답이다.

----

4. (A) 고객님이 이 배송을 진행하기를 원하는지 확정해 주시기 바랍니다.
(B) 다음 주까지 제게 견적서를 보내주세요.
(C) 고객님이 가장 편한 시간에 언제든 그 물품들을 보내 주십시오.
(D) 신청하려면 저희 웹사이트에 방문하세요.

해설 빈칸 앞 문장은 결함 있는 접시들을 환불해 주겠다는 것이고 빈칸 뒤 문장은 궁금한 사항은 언제든 연락을 달라는 것으로, 보기 중 '결함 있는 물건들을 돌려보내 달라'는 내용이 나와야 자연스럽다. 따라서 (C) Please return the items whenever it is most convenient for you. 가 정답이다.

[5-8] 다음 편지에 관한 문제입니다.

저스틴 험프리
2050 라파엘 가
애틀랜타 조지아 30301
11월 5일

험프리 씨 귀하,

락스코 글로벌 사의 영업 관리자직에 지원해 주셔서 고맙습니다. 당신의 자격요건 평가 **5** 에 근거하여, 우리는 당신을 그 자리에 적합한 지원자로 결정하였습니다. **6** 채용 과정의 다음 단계는 대면 면접입니다. 인사부 직원이 회의 일정을 잡기 위해 11월 12일 수요일에 당신께 연락을 드릴 것입니다.

면접이 진행되는 동안, 당신은 과거 업무 경험에 대해 상세히 이야기할 것을 **7** 요청받게 될 것입니다. 면접 다음 날, 직원이 그 자리에 당신이 채용되었는지의 여부를 알려드릴 것입니다. 만약 당신이 이번에 채용되지 못한다면, 저희는 당신에 대한 정보를 9개월간 보관해 두었다가 다른 자리가 났을 때 **8** 당신을 고려할 것입니다.

당신을 만나기를 고대합니다.

진심으로,

노라 크루즈, 인사부 관리자
락스코 글로벌 사

어휘 application 지원(서) | position 일자리, 직위 | assessment 평가 | qualification 자격 | suitable 알맞은, 적합한 | candidate 후보자, 응시자, 지원자 | Human Resources 인사부 | arrange 정하다 | in detail 자세히 | inform 알리다 | consequently 그 결과 | enclose 동봉하다 | consideration 사려 | recruitment 채용 | in-person interview 개인 인터뷰

5. **해설** 빈칸은 명사구인 our assessment 이하를 받아 그 뒤의 절과 연결시키는 전치사 자리이며, 보기 중 전치사는 '~에 근거하여'를 뜻하는 (A) Based on과 '~하기 위하여'를 뜻하는 (C) In order to인데, in order to 뒤에는 동사원형이 이어져야 하므로 (A) Based on이 정답이다.

----

6. (A) 방문할 시간을 정하기 위해 오늘 저희 사무실에 전화 주시기 바랍니다.
(B) 저희는 당신에게 그 직위를 제안합니다.
(C) 저의 이력서를 동봉하였고, 귀하의 사려에 미리 감사드립니다.
(D) 채용 과정의 다음 단계는 대면 면접입니다.

해설 빈칸 앞 문장은 험프리 씨가 그 자리에 적합한 지원자로 결정되었다는 것이고, 뒤 문장은 인사부에서 면접 일정을 위해 연락을 할 거라는 내용이므로, 보기 중 '채용 절차의 다음 단계는 대면 면접이다'라는 문장이 들어가야 자연스럽다. 따라서 (D) The next step in the recruitment process is an in-person interview. 가 정답이다.

----

7. **해설** 빈칸 앞 문장에서 면접 일정을 잡기 위해 연락할 것이라는 내용으로 미루어 보아 인터뷰하는 동안(During the interview) 요구되는 행위가 아직 발생하지 않은 미래의 일이며, 과거 경험에 관해 얘기할 것을 '요구하는' 것이 아니라 '요구받는' 것이므로 미래 시제 수동이 적절하다. 따라서 (B) will be asked가 정답이다.

----

8. **해설** 빈칸 앞 문장은 '선발이 안 된다면, 당신의 정보를 9개월간 보관하겠다'는 내용인데 뒤에 이어지는 내용이 자리가 났을 때 고려 대상이 누구인지를 얘기하는 것이므로 (A) you가 정답이다.

[9-12] 다음 회람에 관한 문제입니다.

수신: 에버클리어 아파트 단지 세입자
발신: 에프엠피 관리 회사
날짜: 4월 2일
제목: 수도관 공사

5월 19일, 오전 10시부터 오후 2시까지 에프엠피 관리 회사는 에버클리어 아파트 단지의 일부 수도관을 **9** 교체할 것이니 참고 바랍니다. 저희 작업반이 새 파이프를 설치하는 동안, 급수 서비스가 일시적으로 중단될 것입니다.

10 그에 따라, 에버클리어 아파트 단지의 모든 세입자분들은 이 시간 동안 수도꼭지를 틀지 않도록 **11** 요구됩니다. 급수 서비스가 재개되면, 몇 분간 수도꼭지를 틀어 놓으세요. **12** 이것은 물을 사용하기에 안전하다는 것을 보장할 것입니다. 질문이나 우려 사항이 있으시면 건물 관리자에게 연락해 주세요.

불편함을 드려 미리 사과드립니다.

어휘 apartment complex 아파트 단지 | tenant 세입자 | maintenance 유지보수 | water pipe 수도관 | crew members 작업반 | install 설치하다 | temporarily 일시적으로 | interrupt 중단하다 | water faucet 수도꼭지 | resume 재개하다, 다시 시작하다 | apologize 사과하다 | in advance 미리 | unload 내리다 | installation 설치

9. 해설   빈칸 뒤 문장을 보면 작업반이 새 파이프를 설치하는 동안 급수가 중단될 거라는 내용을 토대로 수도관이 교체될 것임을 알 수 있다. 따라서 '교체하다'를 뜻하는 (D) replacing이 정답이다.

10. 해설   빈칸 앞 문장에서 작업반이 새 파이프를 설치하는 동안 급수가 중단된다고 했으며, 뒤 문장은 모든 세입자가 그 기간 동안 수도를 사용해서는 안 된다는 내용이므로 인과 관계를 나타내는 접속부사가 필요하다. 따라서 '그에 따라, 그런 이유로'를 뜻하는 (B) Accordingly가 정답이다.

11. 해설   동사 ask의 알맞은 형태를 골라야 하는 문제다. 빈칸이 be동사 뒤에 위치해 있어 수동태를 완성하는 과거분사 (C) asked나 능동진행형을 완성하는 현재분사 (A) asking이 정답으로 유력하다. 둘 중 의미를 고려해 보면, 세입자들(tenants)이 수도꼭지를 틀지 않도록 요구를 받는 대상이므로 (C) asked가 정답이다.

12. (A) 설치 지시사항을 먼저 읽어보도록 하세요.
(B) 저희는 귀하의 다음 공공요금 청구서에 비용을 포함할 것입니다.
(C) 만료되기 전에 임대를 갱신하는 것을 기억하세요.
(D) 이것은 물을 사용하기에 안전하다는 것을 보장할 것입니다.

해설   앞에서 수도관 교체에 관해 얘기하고 있으며, 빈칸 앞 문장은 급수 서비스가 재개되면, 몇 분간 물을 틀어 놓으라는 것이어서 보기 중 '이것이 물을 사용하기에 안전하다는 것을 보장할 것이다'라는 내용으로 이어져야 자연스럽다. 따라서 (D) This will ensure that the water is safe to use. 가 정답이다.

[13-16] 다음 기사에 관한 문제입니다.

8월 10일 – 칼즈배드 시의회는 새 프로젝트를 위하여 바드마예프 건설과 계약을 맺기로 한 결정을 발표했다. 약정에 따라, 바드마예프 사는 78번 고속도로 북쪽에 있는 300야드의 해변 구간을 **13** 개조할 것이다. 시장 미구엘 세르벤테스는 개조된 시설에서 제공되는 **14** 여가활동이 이곳을 가족들에게 인기 있는 곳으로 만들어 줄 것이라고 기대한다. "아이들은 수영과 서핑, 안전한 물놀이 등을 배울 곳이 필요하죠." 세르벤테스 씨가 말했다. "이것이 바로 우리 지역 공동체가 필요로 하는 것입니다." **15** 그러나, 좀 더 안전한 환경이라 할지라도 바다 근처에서의 활동에 위험이 전혀 없을 수는 없다. 바드마예프 대변인 조 마쉬는 이 구역에 진료소와 전문 인명구조요원이 있을 것이라고 강조하기도 하지만 모든 사고를 예방하는 것은 불가능하다는 점도 지적한다. "당연히, 저희는 모든 **16** 노력을 다 하겠지만, 해변의 모든 잠재적인 위험을 제거할 방법은 없습니다."

13. 해설   문맥상 알맞은 시제를 결정해야 한다. 앞 문장에서 시의회가 건설 계약을 발표한 시점이 과거(announced)이긴 하지만, 뒤 문장을 보면 시장이 개조된 시설에서 제공되는 활동들이 이곳을 가족들에게 인기 있는 장소로 만들어 줄 것으로 기대한다고 했으므로 300야드 구간을 앞으로 개조할 것이라고 해야 적절하다. 따라서 미래 시제인 (C) will upgrade가 정답이다.

14. 해설   가족들에게 인기 있는 장소가 되기 위해 그곳에서 여가 활동이 제공된다고 해야 의미가 통하므로 (C) recreational이 정답이다.

15. (A) 반면에, 시 당국은 건설 회사에 관한 결정을 아직 내리지 못했다.
(B) 최근에, 많은 주민이 해변가의 쓰레기에 대해서 불평을 했다.
(C) 그러나, 좀 더 안전한 환경이라 할지라도 바다 근처에서의 활동에 위험이 전혀 없을 수는 없다.
(D) 당분간, 그 프로젝트는 예산 제한으로 승인될 수 없다.

해설   빈칸 앞에서 아이들이 수영, 서핑 등을 배울 수 있는 장소가 필요하다고 했는데, 빈칸 뒤로는 이곳에 진료소와 전문 인명 구조요원이 있으나 모든 사고를 예방하는 것은 불가하다는 내용이 이어지고 있으므로 '그러나 좀 더 안전한 환경이라 할지라도 바다 근처에서의 활동에 위험이 전혀 없을 수는 없다.'는 문장이 들어가야 문맥이 통한다. 따라서 (C) However, even with a more secure environment, activities near the ocean can never be completely risk-free. 가 정답이다.

16. 해설   모든 '노력'은 다하겠지만, 해변에서의 잠재적 위험을 완전히 제거할 방법은 없다는 내용이 나와야 적절하므로 (D) effort가 정답이다.

PART 7

UNIT 01. 문자 대화문과 화자 의도

핵심 문제 유형

1. (A) 2. (A) 3. (A) 4. (C) 5. (D) 6. (B)

[1-2] 다음 문자 대화문에 관한 문제입니다.

> **아일린 조**
> **1** 램버그 씨, 제가 몸 상태가 안 좋아서요. 오늘 저의 식당 교대근무를 대신해 줄 수 있는 사람이 있으면 하루 쉴 수 있을까요?   오전 9:52

> **제임스 램버그**
> 무슨 일 있어요?   오전 9:54

> **아일린 조**
> 두통이 정말 심해서요.   오전 9:55

> **제임스 램버그**
> 알았어요. 마틴이 시간이 되는지 알아볼게요.   오전 9:59

> **아일린 조**
> 사실, 그는 지금 휴가 중인데요.   오전 10:01

> **제임스 램버그**
> **2** 그렇네요. 제가 그걸 깜빡했네요.   오전 10:10

> **제임스 램버그**
> 그럼, 다른 사람에게 알아볼게요.   오전 10:11

> **아일린 조**
> 고맙습니다. 갑자기 알려 드려서 죄송해요.   오전 10:12

어휘 take the day off 하루 쉬다 | shift 교대근무 | headache 두통 | available 시간이 있는, 이용할 수 있는 | on vacation 휴가 중인 | notice 통지, 통보 | confirm 확인해주다 | acknowledge 인정하다

1. 조 씨에 관해 암시된 것은 무엇인가?
(A) 램버그 씨 밑에서 일한다.
(B) 야간 교대근무를 선호한다.
(C) 현재 휴가 중이다.
(D) 최근에 병원을 방문했다.

해설 맨 처음 조 씨의 메시지에서 자신이 몸이 안 좋다며 휴가를 낼 수 있냐고 한 질문을 볼 때 상사에게 허가를 구하는 상황이므로 (A) She works under Mr. Lamburgh. 가 정답이다.

2. 오전 10시 10분에, 램버그 씨가 "그렇네요"라고 쓴 것은 무슨 의미인가?
(A) 어떤 직원이 시간이 안 되는 것이 기억난다.
(B) 어떤 문제에 관하여 그의 상사와 얘기했다.
(C) 조 씨를 위해 어떤 정보를 확인해 줄 것이다.
(D) 그가 실수했다는 것을 인정하지 않는다.

해설 램버그 씨가 대체 근무로 마틴이 시간이 되는지 알아보겠다고 하자, 조 씨는 그가 지금 휴가 중이라고 했고, 이에 대해 램버그 씨가 '그렇네요. 제가 깜빡했네요.'라고 응답한 것이므로, 그는 마틴이 휴가간 것을 잠시 잊고 있었음을 알 수 있다. 따라서 (A) He remembers that an employee is not available. 이 정답이다.

[3-6] 다음 온라인 채팅 대화문에 관한 문제입니다.

> **그웬 린 [오전 10:02]:**
> 안녕하세요. **3** 두 사람은 케빈 브런스윅의 〈잠 못 이루는 행복〉 표지 디자인들을 살펴봤어요?

> **맷 할퍼트 [오전 10:03]:**
> 네 개 중에서, 저는 첫 번째 옵션이 심플하지만 세련되어서 제일 좋은 것 같습니다. 두 번째와 세 번째 옵션은 많이 복잡하고, **3** 마지막 것은 브런스윅 씨의 최근 소설 표지와 너무 비슷합니다.

> **휴이 박 [오전 10:03]:**
> 네. **4** 첫 번째 것이 나머지 것들보다 두드러져 보입니다. 그리고, 앞 표지 이미지가 제목과 정말 잘 어울리네요.

> **그웬 린 [오전 10:04]:**
> **5** 모두 같은 생각이어서 기뻐요. 저는 특히 그 디자인과 배경색이 서로 보완이 아주 잘 돼서 좋네요. 그 밖에 다른 의견이나 제안이 있는 분 있어요?

> **휴이 박 [오전 10:07]:**
> 한 가지 있습니다. 브런스윅 씨의 이름이 제목 바로 밑에 보이게 하는 대신에, 그 문구를 표지 맨 아래에 위치시키는 게 좋을 것 같습니다.

> **맷 할퍼트 [오전 10:08]:**
> 맞아요. 그렇게 하면, 삽화가 더 잘 보일 수 있죠.

> **그웬 린 [오전 10:09]:**
> 브런스윅 씨는 자기 이름의 배치에 매우 분명한 입장이었어요. 하지만, 내일 회의 때 그와 얘기해 볼게요. 다른 건요?

> **맷 할퍼트 [오전 10:10]:**
> 네. 톰 패터슨이 아까 당신이 자리에 안 계실 때 전화했습니다. **6** 당신이 우리 부서의 공석을 채울 후보자들을 결정했는지 알고 싶어 했어요.

> **그웬 린 [오전 10:12]:**
> 알려줘서 고마워요. 지금 가서 톰과 얘기할게요.

어휘 look over 살펴보다 | bliss 더없는 행복 | option 선택권 | complicated 복잡한 | similar to ~와 비슷한 | stand out from the rest 나머지보다 두드러지다 | in addition 게다가, 또한 | suit 걸맞다 | be on the same page 의견이 같다 |

94 파고다 토익 고득점 완성 RC

3. 린 씨는 어느 업종에서 일하겠는가?

(A) 출판사

(B) 실내 디자인 회사

(C) 미술관

(D) 의류 소매 업체

해설 채팅을 시작한 린 씨의 첫 질문이 케빈 브런스윅의 작품인 〈잠 못 이루는 행복〉의 표지 디자인들을 검토해 봤는지에 대한 것이었고, 그다음에 이어진 할퍼트 씨의 의견에서 마지막 것이 브런스윅 씨의 최근 소설 표지와 너무 비슷하다고 한 내용을 토대로 린 씨가 출판업에 종사하고 있음을 알 수 있다. 따라서 (A) A publishing firm이 정답이다.

---

4. 첫 번째 디자인에 관해 언급된 것은 무엇인가?

(A) 어떠한 문구도 들어가 있지 않다.

(B) 복잡하면서도 매력적이다.

(C) 다른 디자인들보다 눈에 더 잘 띈다.

(D) 현재보다 더 많은 색깔이 필요하다.

해설 박 씨가 첫 번째 것이 나머지 것들보다 두드러져 보인다고 했으므로 (C) It is more noticeable than the other designs. 가 정답이다. stand out from the rest가 more noticeable than the other designs로 바꾸어 표현되었다.

---

5. 오전 10시 4분에, 린 씨가 "모두 같은 생각이어서 기뻐요"라고 쓴 것은 무슨 의미인가?

(A) 기한을 맞춰 줘서 기쁘다.

(B) 어떤 프로젝트의 제안을 승인한다.

(C) 최근의 매출액에 만족한다.

(D) 동료들의 견해에 동의한다.

해설 표지 디자인에 대한 의견에서 할퍼트 씨도 첫 번째 시안을 선택했고, 박 씨도 첫 번째가 가장 낫다고 하자, 린 씨가 말한 것으로 다들 같은 디자인 시안을 선택해서 기쁘다는 의미로 쓰였음을 알 수 있다. 따라서 (D) She agrees with the opinions of her coworkers. 가 정답이다. be on the same page는 '합심하다, 의견이 같다'라는 뜻의 관용표현으로, be all on the same page가 agrees with the opinions of her coworkers로 바꾸어 표현되었다.

---

6. 할퍼트 씨의 팀에 관해 암시된 것은 무엇인가?

(A) 새 사무실로 이전할 것이다.

(B) 신입 직원을 고용할 계획이다.

(C) 멤버들 중 한 명이 은퇴할 것이다.

(D) 직원 모두가 교육을 받을 것이다.

해설 할퍼트 씨가 린 씨에게 톰 패터슨으로부터 전화가 왔고 그가 우리 부서의 공석을 채울 후보자들을 결정했는지 알고 싶어 한다고 말했으므로 할퍼트 씨의 부서에 신입 직원이 채용될 것임을 알 수 있다. 따라서 (B) It is planning to hire a new employee. 가 정답이다.

Practice

본서 p.228

1. (B)	2. (A)	3. (D)	4. (A)	5. (B)
6. (D)	7. (C)	8. (B)	9. (B)	10. (D)
11. (D)	12. (C)	13. (A)		

[1-2] 다음 문자 대화문에 관한 문제입니다.

릭 콜린스

오늘 밤 콘서트에 가려면 언제 만나는 게 좋을까요?　오후 2:21

앤지 베이커

오후 2:23　 **1 2** 날씨 때문에 연기될지도 모른대요.

릭 콜린스

정말요? 지금은 그렇게 나빠 보이지 않는데요.　오후 2:25

앤지 베이커

오후 2:30　 **1 2** 근데 오늘 밤늦게 비가 내린대요. 그렇게 되면, 밴드가 악기 연주를 못 할 거예요.

릭 콜린스

2 이해가 되네요. 그럼 어떻게 할까요?　오후 2:33

앤지 베이커

오후 2:35　제가 웹사이트에 들어가서 콘서트 상황을 알아볼게요.

릭 콜린스

좋은 생각이에요.　오후 2:36

어휘 get postponed 연기되다 | due to ~때문에, ~으로 인해 | be supposed to ~하기로 되어 있다 | instrument 악기 | make sense 이해가 되다, 의미가 통하다 | status 상황, 현황 | feature 출연시키다, ~을 특징으로 하다 | free of charge 무료로 | annual 연례의

---

1. 콘서트에 관하여 암시된 것은 무엇인가?

(A) 지역 예술가들을 출연시킬 것이다.

(B) 야외에서 열릴 것이다.

(C) 무료이다.

(D) 연례행사이다.

해설 콘서트에 언제 갈 거냐는 콜린스 씨의 질문에 베이커 씨는 날씨 때문에 연기될 수도 있다고 했고, 비가 오게 되면 연주를 할 수 없게 될 거라는 말을 토대로 공연이 야외에서 열릴 것임을 짐작할 수 있다. 따라서 (B) It will be held outdoors. 가 정답이다.

---

2. 오후 2시 33분에, 콜린스 씨가 "이해가 되네요"라고 쓴 것은 무슨 의미인가?

(A) 공연 일정이 왜 변경될 수도 있는지 이해한다.
(B) 웹사이트가 왜 작동하지 않는지 안다.
(C) 베이커 씨가 왜 늦을 것인지 안다.
(D) 콘서트가 왜 비싼지 알게 되었다.

해설 베이커 씨가 날씨 때문에 연기될 수도 있다고 하면서 비가 오게 되면 연주를 할 수 없게 될 것이라고 한 말에 대해 '이해가 되네요.'라고 응답한 것이므로, 콜린스 씨는 행사 일정이 변경될 수도 있는 이유를 알게 된 것이다. 따라서 (A) He sees why a show might be rescheduled. 가 정답이다.

[3-5] 다음 문자 대화문에 관한 문제입니다.

민디 패리스
안녕하세요, 비샬. 마케팅의 민디예요. 지금 바쁘세요? 오전 9:10

비샬 샤르마
아니요, 무슨 일이세요? 오전 9:12

민디 패리스
3 제 이메일 때문에요. 어떤 파일도 첨부가 되지 않아요. 오늘 오전에 고객에게 중요한 서류를 보내야 하거든요. 오전 9:14

비샬 샤르마
아마 설정이 조정될 필요가 있을 거예요. 오전 9:17

민디 패리스
4 당신 팀의 빌이 제게 똑같이 말했어요. 어젯밤에 그분이랑 연락했고, 그가 오늘 아침 업무를 시작하기 전에 들르기로 했었거든요. 오전 9:20

비샬 샤르마
5 그런데 그걸 봐주지 않았다는 거죠? 오전 9:21

민디 패리스
5 확실히 아닌 것 같아요. 당신이 좀 봐줄 수 있어요? 오전 9:22

비샬 샤르마
물론이죠, 바로 그쪽으로 올라갈게요. 오전 9:23

어휘 attach 첨부하다, 부착하다 | client 고객 | setting 설정 | adjust 조정하다 | come by 들르다 | take care of ~을 처리하다[돌보다] | apparently 분명히, 보아하니 | in a minute 당장, 즉각 | reserve 예약하다

3. 샤르마 씨는 어느 부서에서 일하겠는가?
(A) 회계
(B) 마케팅
(C) 인사

(D) 정보 기술

해설 패리스 씨가 샤르마 씨에게 이메일에 파일 첨부가 되지 않는 문제를 제기하고 있으므로 샤르마 씨는 IT 관련 부서에서 일하는 사람임을 유추할 수 있다. 따라서 (D) Information Technology가 정답이다.

4. 패리스 씨에 관하여 암시된 것은 무엇인가?

(A) 어제 샤르마 씨의 팀원과 얘기를 나눴다.
(B) 출장을 가야 한다.
(C) 샤르마 씨가 일하는 건물과 다른 건물에서 일한다.
(D) 중요한 서류를 찾을 수 없다.

해설 샤르마 씨가 이메일이 첨부되지 않는 문제에 대해 설정을 조정할 필요가 있을 거라고 하자, 패리스 씨는 당신과 같은 팀의 빌도 같은 얘기를 했다면서 어젯밤 그와 연락했다고 했으므로 패리스 씨가 샤르마 씨의 팀원과 어제 얘기했다는 것을 알 수 있다. 따라서 (A) She spoke to Mr. Sharma's team member yesterday. 가 정답이다. Bill from your team이 Mr. Sharma's team member로, contacted가 spoke to로, last night가 yesterday로 바뀌어 표현되었다.

5. 오전 9시 22분에, 패리스 씨가 "확실히 아닌 것 같아요"라고 쓴 것은 무슨 의미인가?
(A) 고객이 연락을 받지 못했다.
(B) 기술적인 문제가 해결되지 않았다.
(C) 프로젝트가 완료되지 않았다.
(D) 회의실이 예약되지 않았다.

해설 패리스 씨가 처음에 이메일에 파일 첨부가 안 되는 문제를 제기하면서, 샤르마 씨의 팀원인 빌이 오전 업무 시작 전에 오기로 했다고 한 데 대해 샤르마 씨가 그런데도 해결이 안 되었느냐는 질문에 '확실히 아닌 것 같다'고 대답하며, 봐줄 수 있는지 되물은 것이므로 (B) A technical issue has not been resolved. 가 정답이다.

[6-9] 다음 온라인 채팅 대화문에 관한 문제입니다.

월터스, 데이비드 [오전 9:20]:
안녕하세요. 다음 주 목요일이 사무엘 타이슨의 바이넥스 마케팅에서의 마지막 날이라서, 그의 송별회를 어디서 열지 의견을 듣고 싶어요. **6** 회계 팀장이 제게 한 사람당 20달러로 제한된다고 얘기했으니 꼭 기억하세요.

추, 마티나 [오전 9:21]:
지난주에 차카스 인디언 키친에 갔는데, 음식이 훌륭하더라고요. **7** 그곳 총괄 주방장인 슈루티 샤가 멕시코 전역을 돌아다니며 지역 음식들을 맛보고 익히면서, 자신의 카레 메뉴에 다양한 재료들을 포함시켰다는 것을 읽었어요.

월터스, 데이비드 [오전 9:21]:
그게 좋은 생각인지 모르겠네요. 사무엘이 매운 음식을 못 먹어서요.

추, 마티나 [오전 9:22]:
깜빡했네요. 레슬리, 당신이 사무엘 바로 옆에 앉잖아요. 그가 어디서 점심 먹는 걸 좋아하는지 알아요?

밍고, 레슬리 [오전 9:24]:
그는 보통 집에서 음식을 싸 와요. 하지만 국수를 자주 먹는 건 알고
있어요. 길 건너편에 새로 생긴 중국집은 어때요?

추, 마티나 [오전 9:26]:
자오 차오 메인을 얘기하시는 거예요? 그곳에 대한 좋은 얘기들을
들었어요.

월터스, 데이비드 [오전 9:31]:
8 제가 지금 자오의 웹사이트에서 추천하는 글들을 보고 있는데,
서빙하는 사람들이 정말 공손하고 능숙하다고 많이들 얘기하네요.
그리고, 가격도 아주 괜찮고요. 모두가 괜찮다고 하면, **9** 가서 다음
주 월요일 오후 6시로 자오에 예약해 둘게요.

밍고, 레슬리 [오전 9:32]:
9 실은, 제가 그날 출장 때문에 자리에 없을 거예요. 하지만 그 다
음 날은 돼요.

추, 마티나 [오전 9:32]:
저도요.

월터스, 데이비드 [오전 9:33]:
9 네, 그럼 그날 저녁으로 예약할게요. 혹시 그 전에 다른 일이 생
기면 제게 말해 주세요.

어휘 suggestion 제안 | farewell dinner 환송 만찬 | limited
to ~으로 제한된 | keep something in mind ~을 명심
하다 | chef 요리사 | incorporate ~을 섞다[포함시키다] |
ingredient 재료 | handle 다루다, 처리하다 | spicy 매운 |
next to ~옆에 | notice 알아차리다 | frequently 자
주, 빈번히 | noodle 면, 국수 | testimonial 추천의 글 |
courteous 공손한 | professional 전문적인; 전문가 |
server 서빙하는 사람, 웨이터 | affordable 가격이 알맞은 |
progress 진척, 진도 | budget 예산 | colleague 동료 |
regularly 주기적으로, 정기적으로

6. 오전 9시 20분에, 월터스 씨가 "꼭 기억하세요"라고 쓴 것은 무슨 의
   미인가?
   (A) 직원들이 회의에 참석할 것을 상기시키고 있다.
   (B) 식사 선택에 대한 아이디어를 원한다.
   (C) 프로젝트의 진행 정도를 보고하고 있다.
   (D) 직원들이 예산을 알고 있기를 원한다.

해설 처음에 월터스 씨가 어떤 동료의 송별회에 대한 다른 동료들의 의견
   을 묻고 나서, 회계 팀장이 일 인당 20달러로 비용이 제한되어 있다고
   말했으니 그것을 기억하라고 한 것이므로, 이는 송별회 비용을 일인
   당 20달러 이내에서 써야 한다는 것을 강조한 것이다. 따라서 (D) He
   wants staff members to be aware of the budget. 이 정답이다.

7. 대화에 따르면, 샤 씨에 관하여 사실인 것은 무엇인가?
   (A) 매운 음식을 먹을 수 없다.
   (B) 최근에 차카스 인디언 키친에 고용되었다.
   (C) 다른 나라에서 온 재료들을 이용한다.
   (D) 추 씨의 동료이다.

해설 샤 씨를 언급한 추 씨의 말을 확인해 보면, 차카스 인디언 키친의 음

식이 맛있다고 하면서, 총괄 주방장인 샤 씨가 멕시코를 여행하면서
알게 된 다양한 재료들을 그녀의 카레 요리에 사용했다고 했으므로
(C) She uses ingredients from a different country. 가 정답이다.

8. 자오 차오 메인에 관하여 암시된 것은 무엇인가?
   (A) 직원 숫자를 늘렸다.
   (B) 고객들의 평가를 온라인에 게시한다.
   (C) 그곳의 광고 캠페인은 바이넥스 마케팅에서 만들어졌다.
   (D) 메뉴들이 정기적으로 바뀐다.

해설 월터스 씨가 지금 식당 웹사이트에 올라온 추천 글을 읽어보고 있다
   고 했으므로 자오 차오 메인이 온라인에 고객 평가를 게시하고 있음을
   알 수 있다. 따라서 (B) It posts reviews by customers online. 이
   정답이다. testimonials가 reviews by customers로, website가
   online으로 바뀌어 표현되었다.

9. 저녁 식사는 언제 이루어지겠는가?
   (A) 월요일에
   (B) 화요일에
   (C) 수요일에
   (D) 목요일에

해설 월터스 씨가 다음 주 월요일에 자오 식당을 예약하겠다고 했는데, 밍
   고 씨가 월요일은 안 되고 그 다음 날은 시간이 된다고 하자 그럼 그날
   저녁으로 예약하겠다고 했으므로 저녁 식사는 월요일 다음 날인 화요
   일에 할 것임을 알 수 있다. 따라서 (B) On Tuesday가 정답이다.

[10-13] 다음 온라인 채팅 대화문에 관한 문제입니다.

데이빗 킬데이 [오후 3:24]
테레사, 전문경영인이 쓰실 브이비34에이 모델 완성됐어요? **11** 당
신에게 그것을 엑스피에스-83과 주문 제작하라고 하셨잖아요.

테레사 폴 [오후 3:26]
10 그 새 마이크 말이죠? 그건 보통 주문에서 설치까지 이틀 정도
걸려요.

데이빗 킬데이 [오후 3:27]
그건 너무 늦어요. 전문경영인이 이곳 공장에서 수요일에 있을 제품
시연회 전에 그걸 원한다고 하셨어요.

테레사 폴 [오후 3:28]
알았어요. 더 빨리할 수 있는지 알아볼게요. 생산 담당 매니저에게
지금 바로 연락하죠.

테레사 폴 [오후 3:29]
12 케빈, 당신 팀은 새 마이크(엑스피에스-83)를 내일까지 입수해서
설치할 수 있나요? 브이비34에이에 그걸 결합시킬 거예요.

케빈 사토 [오후 3:31]
할 수 있을 거예요. **13** 내일 오후까지 해도 되나요?

데이빗 킬데이 [오후 3:32]
네, **13** 그러면 될 거예요. 정말 고마워요.

어휘 customize 주문 제작하다 | incorporate (일부로) 포함하다 |
   appreciate 감사히 여기다 | ceramics 도자기류

10. 공장에서 어떤 유형의 제품을 만드는 것 같은가?

    (A) 자동차

    (B) 도자기

    (C) 가구

    (D) 전자 제품

해설　첫 번째 킬데이 씨가 폴 씨에게 특정 모델에 관해서 묻자 폴 씨가 새 마이크를 이야기하느냐고 했으므로, 정답은 (D) Electronics이다.

---

11. 전문경영인은 무엇을 하길 원하는가?

    (A) 발표 날짜를 옮긴다

    (B) 비용을 줄인다

    (C) 어떤 판매상에게 전화한다

    (D) 어떤 제품을 변형한다

해설　전문경영인은 원하는 것을 물어봤는데, 오후 3시 24분에 전문경영인이 원하는 것은 브이비34에이 모델을 엑스피에스-83과 함께 맞춤화하는 것을 원하는 것이므로 (D) Modify a product가 정답이다.

---

12. 폴 씨는 왜 사토 씨에게 연락했는가?

    (A) 휴가 날짜에 관한 변경 사항을 알려주기 위해

    (B) 운송 상황을 확인하기 위해

    (C) 제안된 마감 기한을 받아들일 수 있는지 알아보기 위해

    (D) 회의 결과를 보고하기 위해

해설　오후 3시 29분에 폴 씨가 사토 씨에게 업무가 내일까지 가능하겠냐고 물어봤으므로 정답은 (C) To see if a proposed deadline is acceptable이다.

---

13. 오후 3시 32분에, 킬데이 씨가 "그러면 될 거예요"라고 쓴 것은 무슨 의미인가?

    (A) 일을 내일까지 완료한다면 CEO가 만족할 것이다.

    (B) 완제품의 외관에 만족한다.

    (C) 생산팀은 새 근무조를 괜찮아할 것이다.

    (D) 몇몇 새 장비의 구매를 승인한다.

해설　앞 문장을 읽어보면, 사토 씨가 내일 오후까지 하면 괜찮겠냐고 물어보자 that should be fine이라고 괜찮다고 했으므로 정답은 (A) The CEO will be pleased if a task is done by tomorrow. 가 된다.

UNIT 02. 편지·이메일·문장 삽입

핵심 문제 유형 본서 p.233

1. (C)　　**2.** (C)

[1-2] 다음 이메일에 관한 문제입니다.

> 발신: ⟨t.harrison@almometas.com⟩
> 수신: ⟨ptroung@transfreelance.com⟩
> 제목: 귀하의 작업
> 날짜: 9월 20일
> 첨부: 번역 업무
>
> 트롱 씨에게,
>
> 우리는 지난주에 귀하가 우리를 위해 해주신 기술 설명서의 번역본을 받았습니다. 귀하의 작업은 훌륭했고, 우리는 귀하가 앞으로도 우리의 번역 업무를 해주시기를 바랍니다.
>
> 저는 두어 가지 이유 때문에 이 이메일을 보냅니다. **2** 먼저, 제가 귀하에게 보냈던 원본 설명서를 받지 못했습니다. 그것들을 아직 갖고 계신다면 제게 돌려줄 수 있나요? **1** 그리고 제가 이 이메일에 첨부한 또 다른 문서의 추정 견적 비용을 알려주십시오. 그것을 가급적 빨리 보내 주시면 좋겠습니다.
>
> 진심으로,
>
> 티모시 해리슨
>
> 어휘　translation 번역 | technical 기술의, 기술적인 | instruction (사용) 설명서, 지시 | take care of ~을 처리하다 | a couple of 두어 가지의 | original 원래의 | estimate 견적서, 추정 | additional 추가적인 | attach 첨부하다

---

1. 해리슨 씨는 트롱 씨에게 무엇을 요청했는가?

    (A) 이메일 주소

    (B) 마케팅 계획

    (C) 견적서

    (D) 최신 이력서

해설　두 번째 단락에서 이메일에 첨부한 문서를 번역하는 견적 비용을 알려달라고 하므로 estimate가 paraphrasing된 (C) A price quote가 정답이다.

---

2. [1], [2], [3], [4]로 표시된 곳 중에서 다음 문장이 들어가기에 가장 적절한 곳은 어디인가?

    "그것들을 아직 갖고 계신다면 제게 돌려줄 수 있나요?"

    (A) [1]

    (B) [2]

    (C) [3]

    (D) [4]

해설　주어진 문장은 대명사 them이 가리키는 대상이 나오는 문장 뒤에 와야 한다. [3] 앞에 상대방에게 보냈던 원본 설명서를 받지 못했다는 내용이 나오므로 주어진 문장이 들어갈 위치는 (C) [3]이 적절하다.

Practice

본서 p.234

1. (D)	2. (A)	3. (C)	4. (C)	5. (B)
6. (B)	7. (C)	8. (B)	9. (C)	10. (C)
11. (B)	12. (C)	13. (D)	14. (C)	15. (C)
16. (B)	17. (A)	18. (B)	19. (B)	20. (B)
21. (D)	22. (B)	23. (A)	24. (A)	

[1-3] 다음 편지에 관한 문제입니다.

더스틴 링겐
탑쇼 사
3484 톨미 가
밴쿠버, BC V6B 6LB
2월 29일

링겐 씨에게,

이 편지는 탑쇼 사의 **2** 홍보 매니저 엘리자베스 앳킨스를 대신하여 요청한 사항에 응하고자 쓰여졌습니다. **1** 요청사항은 사운즈 오브 더 밸리 뮤직 페스티벌에서 공연할 아티스트 프랭크 포르투갈을 위한 공식 사진과 로고를 사용하는 것이었습니다.

1 심사숙고 끝에, 포르투갈 씨는 허락해 주기로 결정했습니다. xctalent.com/webbox로 가셔서, 비밀번호 SVMF229를 입력하시면 요청하신 자료에 접속하실 수 있습니다.

3 프랭크 포르투갈의 사진이나 로고를 사용한 모든 포스터와 전단지는 공개 전에 검토를 위해 반드시 저희 에이전시로 보내주셔야 한다는 점을 당부드립니다. 앞에 언급했던 마케팅 자료의 사용에 대한 조건을 설명하는 문서는 동봉된 문서에서 확인하실 수 있습니다.

자료 승인이나 다른 궁금증이 있으시면 저에게 ziggya@xctalent.com으로 이메일을 통해 연락 주십시오.

진심으로,

Ziggy Akinola

지기 아키놀라, 탤런트 매니저
엑스씨 탤런트 에이전시

첨부서류 있음

어휘 in response to ~에 응하여 | on behalf of ~을 대신하여[대표하여] | grant permission 허가해 주다 | make public 공표하다, 세상에 알리다 | terms 조건

1. 아키놀라 씨가 이 편지를 쓴 이유는 무엇인가?
(A) 웹사이트의 비밀번호를 얻기 위해
(B) 음악 축제의 티켓에 대해 문의하기 위해
(C) 광고용 사진을 요청하기 위해
(D) 시각 자료 사용을 승인하기 위해

해설 글의 목적은 지문 전반에 주로 위치하고 있으며, 두 번째 단락의 첫 문장까지 읽어보면 프랭크 포르투갈의 사진과 로고 사용에 대한 요청을 받고 그것을 허가해 주는 편지임을 알 수 있다. 그러므로 정답은 (D)

To approve the use of graphics이다.

2. 링겐 씨는 누구이겠는가?
(A) 앳킨스 씨의 비서
(B) 음악 제작자
(C) 포르투갈 씨의 밴드 멤버
(D) 로고 디자인 아티스트

해설 링겐 씨는 이 편지를 받는 사람이며, 첫 문장에서 엘리자베스 앳킨스를 대신하여 요청했다고 했으므로 링겐 씨는 앳킨스 씨의 비서라고 유추할 수 있다. 그러므로 정답은 (A) Ms. Atkins' assistant이다.

3. 엑스씨 탤런트 에이전시에 보내야 하는 것은 무엇인가?
(A) 오디오 샘플
(B) 서명한 계약서
(C) 홍보 자료
(D) 공연 일정

해설 문제에 must be sent to the XC Talent Agency라는 키워드가 있으므로 지문을 훑어봐서 이 키워드를 찾아낸다. 세 번째 단락에서 posters or flyers를 대신할 수 있는 (C) Promotional material이 정답이다.

[4-7] 다음 이메일에 관한 문제입니다.

수신: 바이퍼벨트 전 직원
발신: 셰리 윌커슨
날짜: 11월 17일
제목: 바이퍼벨트 도서관

동료 여러분께,

바이퍼벨트 그룹의 직원은 사내 도서관을 모두 이용하실 수 있습니다. **4** 도서관에서 제공하는 서비스에 대해 아직 못 들어 보셨다면, 도서관은 단지 책과 문서만을 위한 공간 그 이상입니다. 수년간 직원들이 개인 소장품에서 수천 권의 책을 기부했습니다. **4** 게다가, 저희는 아주 다양한 종류의 잡지를 구독하고 있으며, 심지어 아주 우수한 자율 학습 프로그램 자격도 보유하고 있습니다. 직원들 사이에 유명한 프로그램은 음악 학습 프로그램입니다! 또한, 현재 도서관에서 소장하고 있지 않는 것을 찾으시는 경우, 신청해 주시면 됩니다. 원하시는 것과 시기만 알려주시면, 저희가 다른 도서관에 연락해 책을 찾아 드립니다.

5 **7** 마지막으로 저희가 새롭게 작업하고 있는 것은 신규 앱으로, 이제 공식적으로 이용 가능합니다. 2년 동안 개발 단계에 있었습니다. **5** 앱을 통해 전자책과 전자 학습 자료를 핸드폰이나 태블릿으로 다운받을 수 있습니다. 버스를 타고 있든 집에서 쉬고 있든, 어디서든 도서관 자료를 이용할 수 있게 된다는 뜻입니다. **6** 최근 규모가 커진 도서관 팀이 여러분에게 도움을 드리기 위해 항상 상주하고 있으니, 저희에게 library@viperbelt.co.uk로 이메일을 보내 연락주세요.

셰리 윌커슨
바이퍼벨트 도서관장

4. 이메일에 따르면, 도서관에서 제공하는 서비스는 무엇인가?

(A) 자매 도서관 회원권

(B) 회의실

(C) 자율 학습 프로그램 이용

(D) 연구 관련 업무 지원

해설 첫 번째 단락에서 도서관은 책과 문서뿐만 아니라 아주 다양한 종류의 잡지를 구독하고 있고 우수한 자율 학습 프로그램 자격도 보유하고 있다고 했으므로 (C) Access to self-learning programs가 정답이다.

5. 윌커슨 씨는 왜 도서관 앱을 언급하는가?

(A) 향후 개발을 위한 기부를 요청하기 위해

(B) 최신 프로젝트의 출시를 알리기 위해

(C) 직원들에게 스마트폰 구입을 장려하기 위해

(D) 회원 요금의 이행을 정당화하기 위해

해설 두 번째 단락에서 새롭게 작업하고 있는 신규 앱을 이제 공식적으로 이용 가능하다고 하면서 전자책과 전자 학습 자료를 다운받을 수 있다고 했으므로 (B) To announce the launching of a recent project 가 정답이다.

6. 윌커슨 씨는 도서관에 대해서 무엇을 언급하는가?

(A) 격주로 주말에 문을 닫는다.

(B) 최근 더 많은 사서를 채용했다.

(C) 직원에게 연체료를 면제해 줄 것이다.

(D) 최근 개조되었다.

해설 두 번째 단락에서 최근 규모가 커진 도서관 팀에 대한 말이 언급되므로 (B) It has recently hired more librarians. 가 정답이다.

7. [1], [2], [3], [4]로 표시된 곳 중에서 다음 문장이 들어가기에 가장 적절한 곳은 어디인가?

"2년 동안 개발 단계에 있었습니다."

(A) [1]

(B) [2]

(C) [3]

(D) [4]

해설 주어진 문장은 개발과 연관되는 내용이라고 볼 수 있는데, 빈칸 [3]의 앞 문장이 새롭게 작업하고 있는 신규 앱에 관한 내용이다. 이곳에 주어진 문장을 넣으면 문맥이 자연스러우므로 정답은 (C) [3]이다.

[8-11] 다음 이메일에 관한 문제입니다.

8. 이메일의 목적은 무엇인가?

(A) 소프트웨어 설치 과정을 설명하기 위해

(B) 신입 직원들에게 정보를 주기 위해

(C) 주차 요금 인상을 발표하기 위해

(D) 관리자들에게 사무용품 신청 양식을 보내라고 요청하기 위해

해설 지문의 주제나 목적은 항상 도입부에서 알아낼 수 있다. 첫 문장에서 신입 직원들에게 환영 인사를 하면서 이어지는 문장에서는 건물 내에서 필수적으로 준수해야 하는 사항들을 알려주겠다고 말하고 있으므로 (B) To give information to newly recruited employees가 정답이다. requirements가 information으로 paraphrasing 되었다.

---

9. 첫 번째 문단, 첫 번째 줄의 단어 "growing"에 의미상 가장 가까운 것은
(A) 생산하는
(B) 펼쳐지는
(C) 확장하는
(D) 증가하는

해설 growing firm은 '성장하고 있는 회사'라는 뜻인데, 회사가 성장하고 있다는 것은 앞으로 번창할 것으로 보인다는 의미이므로 문맥상 growing과 의미상 가장 가까운 것은 (C) expanding이라고 볼 수 있다.

10. 직원들은 어디서 다과를 구매할 수 있는가?
(A) 지하에서
(B) 로비에서
(C) 4층에서
(D) 9층에서

해설 purchase refreshments가 이 문제의 키워드이므로 지문에서 이 부분을 찾아야 한다. 4번째 단락에서 4층 휴게실에 작은 카페가 있다고 말했다. 다과는 카페에서 구매할 수 있으므로 정답은 (C) On the fourth floor이다.

11. 이메일에 따르면, 무엇이 무료로 제공되는가?
(A) 식사
(B) 체육관 회원권
(C) 주차권
(D) 개인 노트북 컴퓨터

해설 문제의 키워드 provided for free가 바꾸어 표현된 available for all employees at no charge가 들어있는 문장에서 정답을 찾아내야 한다. 레크리에이션 센터를 무료로 이용할 수 있다고 했는데, 레크리에이션 센터는 주로 운동 시설이므로 정답은 (B) Gym membership이다.

[12-14] 다음 편지에 관한 문제입니다.

7월 21일

섀넌 브라이스
3475 E. 로렐 가
노스 세인트 메리스
뉴사우스웨일스 2760
호주

브라이스 씨에게,

🔟 이 편지는 시드니 항공기술학교(SIAT)에 성공적으로 등록되었음을 알려 드리기 위함입니다. 첫 납입금 495달러가 처리되었으며 여기에는 첫 3개월간의 수업과 수업자료, 시험 응시료가 포함됩니다. 온라인 계정에 로그인하면, 등록 가능한 수업을 보실 수 있습니다. 각 수업은 이론과 디자인, 응용기법 등으로 이루어져 있습니다.

🔟 등록비에는 식권이 포함되지 않음을 유의하시기 바랍니다. 식권 신청에 대해 알아보고 싶으시면 저에게 말씀해 주세요. 완전한 가격 목록을 보려면 저희 구내식당 웹사이트를 방문하라고 하세요.

수업 방침이 상세히 적혀 있는 계약서와 필요할 수도 있는 기타 용품의 신청 양식을 동봉했습니다. 🔟 계약서는 서명하여 첫 수업 최소 일주일 전에 돌려보내 주시면 고맙겠습니다.

성취감을 가져다줄 경력의 첫걸음을 내디디신 것을 환영합니다.

진심을 담아,

Anna Cornwall
애나 콘월
SIAT 학생처장

첨부서류 있음

어휘 **initial** 처음의, 초기의 | **cover** (무엇을 하기에 충분한 돈을) 대다 | **account** 계정 | **theory** 이론 | **application** 적용, 응용 | **component** 요소 | **meal plan** 식권 | **enclose** 동봉하다 | **detail** 상세히 알리다 | **supplies** 필수품, 용품 | **fulfilling** 성취감을 주는 | **transcript** 성적증명서

12. 콘월 씨는 왜 편지를 썼는가?
(A) 새 강좌를 광고하기 위해
(B) 성적증명서를 요청하기 위해
(C) 대금 지불을 확인해 주기 위해
(D) 요금 인상을 발표하기 위해

해설 지문의 주제나 목적을 묻는 문제는 거의 대부분 도입부에서 정답을 알 수 있다. 첫 문장에서 495달러의 등록금이 접수되었고, 이에 따라 등록이 완료되었다는 내용이므로 이 편지는 등록생에게 비용의 납입을 확인시켜 주기 위한 것이라는 것을 파악할 수 있어 정답은 (C) To confirm a payment가 된다.

13. 브라이스 씨는 무엇을 미리 제출하라고 요청받는가?
(A) 신청서
(B) 청구서
(C) 인턴 지원서
(D) 계약서

해설 지문에서 문제의 키워드 submit in advance를 찾아내야 한다. 키워드는 지문에서 return the agreement at least a week before the first day of classes로 paraphrasing되어 있으므로 agreement의 동의어가 될 수 있는 (D) A contract가 정답이다.

14. [1], [2], [3], [4]로 표시된 곳 중에서 다음 문장이 들어가기에 가장 적절한 곳은 어디인가?

"완전한 가격 목록을 보려면, 저희 구내식당 웹사이트를 방문하세요."

(A) [1]
(B) [2]
(C) [3]
(D) [4]

해설 주어진 문장에서 가격 목록을 보려면 웹사이트를 방문하라고 했으며, 빈칸 [3]의 앞 두 문장이 식권 구매에 관한 내용이므로 여기에 주어진 문장을 넣으면 식권 종류에 따른 가격을 구내식당 웹사이트에서 확

인할 수 있다는 내용이 되어서 문맥이 자연스럽다. 따라서 정답은 (C) [3]이다.

[15-19] 다음 웹페이지와 이메일에 관한 문제입니다.

www.nationalweldersasso.org/content

전국 용접 기사 연합(엔더블유에이)
콘텐츠 기고

15 지난 몇 회의 이메일 회보에서, 저희는 회원 여러분에게 〈먼슬리 웰더〉를 개선할 방법에 대한 피드백과 제안을 달라고 요청했습니다. 훌륭한 아이디어에 매우 깊은 인상을 받았으며 그중 하나를 바로 다음 회보에 싣겠습니다. 다음 달부터, 회보에는 리얼 웰더스라는 새 페이지가 생깁니다. 이 섹션은 동영상과 사진, 그 밖의 회원 여러분이 만든 내용을 선보입니다. 임원들과 고위 의사 결정권자들은 모두 이것이 회원들로 하여금 엔더블유에이나 동료 회원들에 대한 더 큰 유대감을 느끼게 하는 훌륭한 방식이 될 것이라는 점에 동의합니다.

여러분 중 상당수는 이미 용접 학회나 엔더블유에이 지부 회의, 기타 관련 행사에서 찍은 동영상과 사진을 갖고 계십니다. 특히 알래스카의 429 지부와 같이 **17** 멀리 떨어져 있는 지부에 계신 분들이 콘텐츠를 제출하셔서 여러분이 하는 일에 대해 더 알게 해 주시기를 바랍니다.

이 링크를 통해 샘플 동영상 몇 개를 확인하실 수 있습니다. 다른 분들과 공유하고자 하는 것이 있으시다면, 간단한 설명과 함께 jackd54@natwelder.com으로 잭 데커에게 이메일을 보내기 바랍니다. **18** 10월 15일까지 보내주신 것들은 다음 회보에 실릴 수 있습니다.

마지막으로, 이것은 저희가 〈먼슬리 웰더〉에 대해 하고자 계획하고 있는 많은 개선사항 중 첫 번째에 불과합니다. **16** 몇 주 후 11월 호의 새로운 지면 배치와 몇몇 추가적인 언어 옵션을 공개할 때 이 웹사이트를 다시 방문하세요!

어휘 welder 용접공, 용접 기사 | contribution 기고 | board member 임원 | division 지부 | wrap up 매듭짓다

수신: 메간 헤임〈mhame@iceliners.com〉
발신: 케빈 비숍〈kb@nwa.org〉
날짜: 10월 22일
제목: 요청

헤임 씨에게,

18 당신과 당신의 429 지부 동료들이 10월 12일에 보내주신 동영상에 감사드립니다. 저희는 모두 이 동영상을, 특히 동영상 마지막에 포함해 주신 혹한에서 근무하는 요령을 다른 회원들과 공유할 수 있어서 기쁩니다. 또, 그렇게 많은 용접 기사가 북부 극지방에서 근무하고 있다는 것을 알고 놀랐으며, 더 많은 분이 장차 엔더블유에이 가입을 고려해 주길 희망합니다.

19 한 가지만 더 말씀드리자면, 파일을 조금 잘라내서 2분을 넘지 않게 해주시면 좋겠습니다. 일부 회원들은 인터넷 접속 요금이 매우 비싸기 때문에, 이분들을 위해 다운로드를 되도록 빠르게 해드리고 싶습니다. 이렇게 해주실 수 있는지 알려주시기 바랍니다.

진심을 담아,

케빈 비숍
〈먼슬리 웰더〉 수석 편집장

어휘 tips and tricks 유용한 정보, 요령

15. 웹페이지 정보는 누구를 대상으로 하는 것이겠는가?
(A) 잡지 편집자들
(B) 용접 학교 학생들
(C) 엔더블유에이 회원들
(D) 웹사이트 디자이너들

해설 지문의 주제, 목적, 대상 등은 대부분 도입부에서 알아낼 수 있다. 잡지를 개선하기 위한 제안을 회원들에게 요청했다는 첫 문장에 이어 여러분의 훌륭한 아이디어에 감명받았다는 말이 나오고 있으므로 지문은 엔더블유에이 회원들을 대상으로 쓰여졌다는 것을 알아낼 수 있다. 따라서 정답은 (C) NWA members이다.

16. 웹페이지에 따르면, 회보에 관하여 사실인 것은 무엇인가?
(A) 몇몇 섹션이 변경될 것이다.
(B) 여러 언어로 출간될 것이다.
(C) 알래스카의 다양한 지역을 중점적으로 다룬다.
(D) 인쇄판으로 이용할 수 있다.

해설 마지막 문장에서 몇 주 후 웹사이트에 다시 들어오면 새 언어 옵션을 확인할 수 있다고 말하는 것으로 미루어 보아 이 회보는 여러 언어로 출간된다는 것을 알 수 있다. 그러므로 정답은 (B) It will be published in different languages. 이다.

17. 웹페이지 두 번째 문단, 두 번째 줄의 단어 "remote"에 의미상 가장 가까운 것은
(A) 먼
(B) 관련 없는
(C) 접근할 수 없는
(D) 약간의

해설 remote의 사전적인 의미는 '외딴, 먼'과 '(가능성이) 희박한'이 있기 때문에 문맥에 따라 보기에 있는 네 개의 형용사는 모두 동의어가 될 수 있다. 그러나 문장에서 remote의 수식을 받는 부분이 '알래스카의 429 지부와 같은 지부'이므로 문맥상 remote는 '외딴곳에 멀리'의 의미이다. 따라서 정답은 (A) far이다.

18. 헤임 씨의 제출물에 관해 암시된 것은 무엇인가?
(A) 엔더블유에이 회원들을 위한 수정된 설명 지침이 들어있다.
(B) 회보의 다음 호에 실릴 것이다.
(C) 비숍 씨가 10월 15일에 받았다.
(D) 컴퓨터 시스템과 호환되지 않는다.

해설 두 지문을 연계해서 풀어야 하는 문제로, 웹페이지에서 회원들에게 동영상이나 사진 등의 제출을 장려하면서 10월 15일까지 접수된 제출물을 다음 회보에 싣겠다고 했다. 그리고 이메일을 보면 10월 12일에 보낸 동영상에 대해 고맙다는 내용으로 시작하고 있으므로 헤임 씨가 보

낸 동영상은 다음 회보에 실릴 것으로 유추할 수 있다. 그러므로 정답은 (B) It will be included in the newsletter's next issue. 이다.

19. 헤임 씨은 무엇을 하라고 요청받는가?

(A) 추가적인 팁을 제공한다

(B) 내용을 편집한다

(C) 〈먼슬리 웰더〉를 친구들에게 추천한다

(D) 연락처를 갱신한다

해설 이메일을 받는 사람이 요청을 받는 것은 보내는 사람이 요청하는 것이므로 지문 후반부에 보통 나오며, 동영상의 길이가 2분을 넘지 않도록 파일을 잘라달라고 요청하고 있다. 그러므로 이 부분을 paraphrasing한 (B) Edit her content가 정답이다.

[20-24] 다음 기사와 편지, 이메일에 관한 문제입니다.

그리어튼 **21** (11월 18일) – 그리어튼 시 의회는 상당한 개선이 필요한 오래된 산책로로 어텀 가와 관련하여 어떤 조치를 취해야 할지 논의하기 시작했다. 가장 큰 딜레마는 수리 작업이 역사적으로 중요한 몇몇 건물을 위험에 처하게 할 수 있다는 점이다.

"산책로의 건물들의 수준을 현대적인 기준에 맞게 끌어올리는 것은 단기적으로 약간의 경제적인 부담을 유발할 것입니다." **21** 도시 설계가 카일리 김이 말했다. "몇 채의 건물을 철거하는 것이 복원하는 것보다 비용이 덜 들 것이라고 결론을 내렸습니다."

비용 요인 외에, 일부 낡은 건물들은 건강에 위협을 제기한다는 우려도 있다. **20** "식당들에 적용되는 새 식품 안전 규정이 연말에 발효됩니다." 시 검열관 브라이언 굴드가 설명한다. "어텀 가의 많은 구조물들은 더 엄격해진 기준에 완전히 부합되지 못할 겁니다. 그래서, 제 생각에는 그곳에 새 건물을 짓는 게 최상의 선택입니다."

24 더 알아보거나 의견을 피력하고자 하는 지역 주민들에게는 다음 주 토요일 오후 4시 그리어튼 시청에서 있을 지역 주민 토론회 참여를 권장한다.

어휘 significant 상당한 | endanger 위태롭게 만들다 | landmark (반드시 보존해야 할) 역사적인 건물 | bring up to ~까지 올리다 | short-term 단기적인 | economic stress 경제적 압박 | urban planner 도시 설계자 | tear down (건물·담 등을) 허물다 | restore 복원하다 | factor 요인, 인자 | pose (위협·문제 등을) 제기하다 | regulation 규정 | go into effect 효력이 발생되다 | structure 구조물, 건축물 | comply with 순응하다, 부합하다 | local 주민 | forum 토론회

---

21 11월 19일

편집장님 귀하:

21 이 편지는 어텀 가 공사와 관련하여 어제 발간된 기사에 관한 것입니다. **21** 이 거리의 옛 건물들은 그리어튼에서 중요한 장소이며 철거해서는 안 됩니다. **21** 이 역사적으로 중요한 지점은 상당수의 관광객을 지역으로 끌어들이기 때문에 많은 사업체도 또한 여기서 이익을 얻습니다. 그러므로 이러한 역사적인 건물들의 파괴는 상당한 경제적 손실을 유발할 것입니다.

진심을 담아,

웨스 스미스
그리어튼 보존 연합(지피에이) 부의장

어휘 in regard to ~에 대한 | site 위치 | benefit from ~으로부터 이익을 얻다 | quite a few 상당수 | destruction 파괴 | preservation 보존 | alliance 연합, 협회

수신: all@gpa.org
발신: kate-adalja@gpa.org
날짜: 11월 25일
제목: 어텀 가 최신 정보

지피에이 회원 여러분, 고맙습니다.

23 우리가 해냈습니다! 시 공무원들에게 편지를 쓰느라 보냈던 **22** 수많은 시간과 토요일 시청 회의의 많은 참석자 수가 **23** 어텀 가의 건물 철거 계획을 중단시켰습니다. 시장은 자금을 옛 건물들을 개조하는 데 사용하겠다고 발표했습니다. 또한, 도로 양쪽에 동시에 공사를 할 수 없도록 제한하는 기획안이 만장일치로 승인되었습니다. 공사 기간 중 관련 사업체들은 위플 가의 이용 가능한 공간으로 임시 이전할 것입니다.

지역 역사를 보존하는 것은 후대에 선물을 주는 것이며, **24** 여러분은 지난주 토요일 목소리를 냄으로써 이것을 가능하게 했습니다.

고맙습니다.

케이트 아달자

어휘 update 최신화 | official (고위) 공무원 | turnout 참가자의 수 | demolish (건물을) 철거하다 | unanimously 만장일치로 | relevant 관련된 | preserve 보존하다

---

20. 기사에 따르면, 그리어튼에 관하여 무엇이 언급되었는가?

(A) 가이드가 안내하는 버스투어를 시작할 것이다.

(B) 몇몇 지역 법을 개정할 것이다.

(C) 몇몇 건물의 임대료를 낮출 것이다.

(D) 기업들에게 안전 규정 위반에 대한 벌금을 부과할 것이다.

해설 기사의 세 번째 단락에서 식당에 대한 음식과 안전에 관한 새로운 규정이 연말에 실행될 것이라는 내용을 paraphrasing한 (B) It will revise some local laws. 가 정답이다.

---

21. 스미스 씨에 관하여 시사되지 않은 점은 무엇인가?

(A) 11월 18일에 신문 기사를 읽었다.

(B) 김 씨에게 동의하지 않는다.

(C) 어떤 건물들이 시의 경제를 증진시킨다고 생각한다.

(D) 굴드 씨의 동료이다.

해설 첫 번째 기사글과 두 번째 지문을 연계해서 푸는 문제로, (A)는 첫 번째 기사는 11월 18일 날짜이며, 두 번째 지문은 11월 19일 편지로 어제 나온 기사를 읽고 나서 글을 쓴 것이므로 맞다. (B)는 첫 번째 기사에서 카일리 김이 몇 개의 건물을 허무는 것이 복원하는 것보다 저렴하

다고 말한 것이 나와있고, 편지에서는 그와 반대로 허물지 않고 그대로 두는 것이 좋다라고 나와 있으므로 맞다. (C)는 편지에서 많은 지역 업체들이 관광으로 인해 혜택을 얻을 수 있다고 했고 언급되지 않은 (D) He is a colleague of Mr. Gould. 가 정답이다.

22. 이메일 첫 번째 문단, 첫 번째 줄의 단어 "endless"에 의미상 가장 가까운 것은
(A) 제한된
(B) 많은
(C) 최종적인
(D) 완성된

해설 endless는 '무한한, 한없는, 끝없는'의 의미로 이 문장에서는 많은 시간을 보냈다는 의미가 적합하므로 정답은 (B) many이다.

23. 아달자 씨는 지피에이 회원들에게 왜 고마워하는가?
(A) 시의 결정을 확정하도록 도움을 주었다.
(B) 뉴스 보도에서 언급되었다.
(C) 최근 한 행사에서 상을 받았다.
(D) 다가오는 프로젝트를 위한 돈을 모금했다.

해설 아달자 씨는 마지막 지문인 이메일을 쓴 사람으로, 건물을 허물지 않기로 한 노력이 결실을 이루었다는 말이 언급되므로 지피에이 회원들이 큰 역할을 했다는 내용의 (A) They helped determine a town's decision. 이 정답이다.

24. 지피에이 회원들에 관하여 무엇이 언급되는가?
(A) 일부는 그리어튼 시청에 갔다.
(B) 매주 토요일에 회의를 한다.
(C) 일부는 어텀 가에 사업체를 소유하고 있다.
(D) 어떤 개조 작업을 도와주었다.

해설 연계 지문 문제로, 첫 번째 지문 마지막 단락에서 의견을 피력하고 싶은 분들은 다음 주 토요일에 그리어튼 시청에서 개최되는 포럼에 참석하라고 나와 있으며 세 번째 지문 마지막 단락에서 지난 토요일에 의견을 내주셨다고 했으므로 (A) Some of them went to Grierton Town Hall. 이 정답이다.

UNIT 03. 광고

핵심 문제 유형

1. (A)   2. (B)

[1-2] 다음 광고에 관한 문제입니다.

카우보이 짐스

국내의 선도적인 스테이크 음식점인 카우보이 짐스가 우리의 전 지점에서 웨이터를 채용합니다. **1** 우리 팀에 합류해서 직원들을 어떻게 대하는지 아는 회사에서 근무하세요. 우리는 많은 복리후생과 쾌적한 근무 환경을 제공합니다. 전국적으로 200개가 넘는 지점을 갖춘 우리는 다양한 일자리를 보유하고 있습니다.

자격 요건:
* 최소 2년의 웨이터 경력
* 식당업에 대한 지식
* **2** 좋은 대인관계 기술과 긍정적인 자세

우리 팀에 합류하는 것에 관심이 있다면 이력서를 humanresources @cowboyjims.com으로 보내거나 303-555-6228로 팩스를 보내세요.

어휘 leading 선도적인 | hire 고용하다, 채용하다 | treat 대하다, 다루다 | numerous 수많은 | working environment 근무 환경 | nationwide 전국적으로 | plenty of 많은 | available 이용할 수 있는, 구할 수 있는 | requirement 자격 요건 | minimum 최저의, 최소한의 | interpersonal 대인관계의

1. 카우보이 짐스 광고가 시사하는 것은 무엇인가?
(A) 직원들이 행복하다.
(B) 새 주방장을 찾고 있다.
(C) 2년 전에 설립되었다.
(D) 다른 나라에서도 운영된다.

해설 첫 번째 단락에서 직원들을 어떻게 대하는지 안다고 자신 있게 말하며 많은 복리후생과 유쾌한 근무 환경을 제공한다는 것으로 보아 (A) It has happy workers. 를 추론할 수 있다.

2. 일자리에 대해 언급된 자격 요건은 무엇인가?
(A) 회사의 역사에 대한 많은 지식
(B) 다른 사람들과 함께 일을 잘할 수 있는 능력
(C) 해외를 여행하려는 의지
(D) 몇 년간의 관리 경력

해설 자격 요건 중 '대인관계 기술' 즉, 다른 사람들과 일하는 능력이 필요함을 알 수 있다. 따라서 (B) Ability to work well with others가 정답이다.

Practice

본서 p.244

1. (C)	**2.** (B)	**3.** (B)	**4.** (A)	**5.** (C)
6. (D)	**7.** (D)	**8.** (A)	**9.** (B)	**10.** (A)
11. (D)	**12.** (C)	**13.** (A)	**14.** (B)	**15.** (C)
16. (B)	**17.** (A)	**18.** (B)	**19.** (B)	**20.** (C)

[1-2] 다음 광고에 관한 문제입니다.

게시물: 에스지 락트레일 8 산악자전거
금액: 1,300달러
위치: 메트로 애틀랜타

제품 설명:
- **1** 1년 전 재판매업자에게서 거의 새 제품을 구매했음. 1,900달러에 구매함.
- 6개월 제조사 품질 보증서와 같이 있음.
- **1** 구매자가 금이 간 핸들을 교체해야 함.
- 보통 정도의 마모 상태. (현재 사진 없음.)

1 1,300달러 혹은 제시받은 가격의 최고가.

2 도시권에서는 운송 가능.

연락: 선착순 (404) 555-2794

어휘 mountain bike 산악자전거 | reseller 재판매업자 | manufacturer 제조사 | warranty 품질 보증서 | responsible for ~에 책임이 있는 | cracked 금이 간, 갈라진 | moderate 중간의, 보통의 | wear and tear 마모 | metro area 수도권 | first come, first serve 선착순

1. 자전거에 대해 알려지지 않은 것은 무엇인가?
(A) 망가진 부분이 있다.
(B) 가격은 조정 가능하다.
(C) 연장된 품질 보증서가 포함되어 있다.
(D) 몇 명의 주인을 거쳤다.

해설 제품 설명의 첫 문장에서 1년 전 재판매자에게서 구매했다고 나오므로 이 자전거는 지금까지 최소 두 명의 소유자가 있었음을 유추할 수 있다. 따라서 (D)는 지문에 언급된 내용이 된다. 또한, 구매자가 직접 금이 간 핸들을 교체해야 한다고 했으므로 망가진 부분이 있다는 내용인 (A)도 언급된 것이다. 그리고 판매가로 1,300달러 혹은 가장 높은 제안가를 제시했으므로 가격은 고정되어 있는 것이 아니라고 말하는 (B)도 언급된 것이다. 따라서 지문에 언급되지 않은 (C) It includes an extended warranty. 가 정답이다.

2. 판매자는 무엇을 해줄 수 있는가?
(A) 제품 사진을 제공한다
(B) 도시 내에서 이동한다
(C) 제조사에 연락한다
(D) 구매자를 위해 제품을 예약한다

해설 Will deliver within the metro area. 는 도시 내에서 배달해 주겠다는 의미이므로 (B) Travel within the city가 정답이다.

[3-4] 다음 광고에 관한 문제입니다.

아스펜의 지씨 사에서 회사 전속으로 **3** 병원용으로 개발되는 기기의 매뉴얼을 작성해 줄 경력 기술작가를 구합니다.

4 지원자는 이전에 각종 병원이나 임상 환경에서 일해본 경력이 있어야 합니다.

4 입사 후보는 프로젝트 매니저나 엔지니어들과 원활히 소통하고 조화를 이룰 수 있어야 합니다.

4 집필물 목록이 방대한 이에게는 심사의 우선권이 주어집니다.

모든 지원자는 영어, 언론 혹은 정보통신 분야의 학사 학위를 소지해야 합니다. 더불어, 최소 3년의 기술 작가 경력도 필요합니다.

어휘 in-house (회사·조직) 내부의 | previously 이전에 | clinical setting 임상 현장 | coordinate 조화되다 | smoothly 원활하게 | extensive 방대한 | preferential 우선권을 주는 | bachelor's degree 학사 학위 | communications 정보 통신 | specialized 전문적인 | well-regarded 높게 평가받는

3. 지씨 사에 관하여 무엇이 언급되어 있는가?
(A) 최근 아스펜 지역으로 확장했다.
(B) 전문 장비를 생산한다.
(C) 높게 평가받는 회사다.
(D) 프리랜서 직원을 찾고 있다.

해설 병원용 기기를 개발하는 회사라고 소개하고 있으므로 이 부분을 paraphrasing한 (B) It produces specialized equipment. 가 정답이다.

4. 작가 자리의 자격 요건으로 언급되지 않은 것은 무엇인가?
(A) 2개 언어의 능통함
(B) 의학 분야의 경력
(C) 다른 이들과 협력하는 능력
(D) 작업 견본 모음집의 소지

해설 병원이나 임상 환경에서 근무해 본 경력과 다른 이들과의 의사소통 및 조화의 능력, 집필물 포트폴리오가 자격요건으로 언급되었고, 지문에서 언급하지 않은 내용은 (A) Proficiency in two languages이다.

[5-7] 다음 광고에 관한 문제입니다.

왓포드 비즈니스 온라인   11월 17일

왓포드 상업지구의 7층짜리 베이크웰 건물 1층에 위치한 200 평방미터의 매력적인 임대용 점포. 11월 20일부터 이용 가능. 월 1750파운드

- 최근에 설치한 배관시설
- 건물 뒤편의 주차장 및 하역장
- 로비의 공중화장실

PART 7

UNIT 03

- 벽 금고가 설치되어 있는 매장 뒤편 사무실
- **6** 감시 카메라가 하루 24시간, 일주일 내내 감시함
- **5 6** 관리비는 1층부터 3층까지의 회사끼리 분담
- **6** 공과금 불포함
- 리모델링 시 허가 필요

7 계약 체결 시 손해보험증서 필요

부동산 관리인 존 애드먼슨에게 020 7946 0457로 연락하세요.

어휘 **storefront** 가게 앞에 딸린 공간 I **ground floor** 1층 I **business district** 상업 지역 I **plumbing** 배관 I **loading area** 하역장 I **built-in** 붙박이의 I **wall safe** 벽금고 I **surveillance camera** 감시 카메라 I **expense** 비용 I **property insurance** 손해보험 I **property manager** 부동산 관리인 I **tenant** 세입자

---

5. 베이크웰 건물에 관하여 무엇이 언급되는가?
(A) 새 상업지구에 위치해 있다.
(B) 1층 아래에 주차장이 있다.
(C) 일부 세입자가 관리비를 공동 부담한다.
(D) 이번 달에 일부 주민이 이사 나간다.

해설 건물에 관한 설명 중 7층짜리 건물에서 1층부터 3층까지의 입주 회사들이 관리비를 나누어 낸다는 내용을 paraphrasing한 (C) Some of its tenants share maintenance fees. 가 정답이다.

---

6. 월세에는 무엇이 포함되는가?
(A) 무선 인터넷
(B) 공과금
(C) 시설관리 서비스
(D) 보안 시스템

해설 우선 무선 인터넷에 대해서는 전혀 언급이 없고, 공과금은 임대료에 포함되지 않는다고 했으므로 (A)와 (B)는 정답이 아니다. 또한, 관리비는 일부 세입자들이 나누어 따로 낸다고 했으므로 Maintenance service를 paraphrasing한 (C) Housekeeping services도 월세에 포함되지 않는 것이다. 감시 카메라가 항상 감시한다고 했으므로 (D) Security systems가 정답이다.

---

7. 광고에 따르면, 임차인에게 요구하는 것은 무엇인가?
(A) 장기 임대 계약에 동의한다
(B) 보험 전문가와 만난다
(C) 안전 교육에 참석한다
(D) 어떤 서류를 제출한다

해설 임차인에게 요구되는 것을 물어보는 문제로 요청하는 내용은 주로 지문 후반부에 있다. 계약 체결 시 손해보험증서가 필요하다고 했으므로 Proof of property insurance를 documents로 paraphrasing한 (D) Provide some documents가 정답이다.

[8-10] 다음 광고에 관한 문제입니다.

산책하며 예술도 즐기세요!

1981년에 설립된 샤이엔 미술협회(씨에이오)는 관심 있는 수집가들에게 미술가와 화랑을 적극적으로 홍보하려고 애쓰는 위원회입니다. 이달 주말 저녁마다, 가이드와 함께 루파인 가를 따라 화랑과 스튜디오들을 둘러보는 산책에 여러분을 초대합니다. 참가하는 모든 장소는 유명한 〈스튜디오 가이드〉를 연 2회 발간하는 샤이엔 미술공동체의 일원입니다.

미술관 산책에서 여러분은:

● 샤이엔의 미술 문화를 경험할 수 있습니다
● **8** 지역의 저명한 미술가들의 최근 작품을 특별 할인가로 구매할 수 있습니다
● 저녁 7시부터 카페 보아에서 씨에이오가 후원하는 모임을 통해 몇몇 미술가들을 만나고 라이브 음악도 즐길 수 있습니다

미술관 산책은 무료이지만, 스튜디오 측에서 월 운영비에 사용할 약간의 찬조금을 요청할 수 있습니다. 산책은 오후 5시에 시작해서 7까지 이어집니다. 참가자 수는 회당 15명으로 제한됩니다. 산책의 속도는 느긋하겠지만, **9** 앉을 수 있는 기회는 많지 않을 것이라는 점 유의하시기 바랍니다.

10 구매 가능한 독점 품목 등 화랑들에 관한 더 많은 것들을 알아보시려면, www.cheyennearts.org를 방문하세요.

어휘 **take a stroll** 산책하다 I **commission** 위원회 I **seek to** ~하도록 시도하다[추구하다] I **venue** 장소 I **collective** 공동 사업(체) I **renowned** 저명한 I **gathering** 모임 I **pace** 속도 I **relaxed** 느긋한, 여유 있는 I **exclusive** 독점적인, 전용의 I **subscription** 구독

---

8. 무엇을 광고하고 있는가?
(A) 예술작품을 살 수 있는 기회
(B) 유명한 화가
(C) 잡지 구독
(D) 대학교 수업

해설 지문 상단의 제목을 통해서 알 수 있듯이 산책하며 미술관을 둘러보는 것으로, 참가자가 작품을 구매할 수 있다고 나오므로 정답은 (A) A chance to buy artwork이다.

---

9. 참가자들이 무엇을 하도록 기대하겠는가?
(A) 15분 일찍 도착한다
(B) 대부분 시간을 서 있는다
(C) 설문 조사를 작성한다
(D) 포트폴리오를 제출한다

해설 행사가 진행되는 동안 앉을 기회가 많지 않을 것이라고 안내했으므로 참가자는 대부분 시간을 서서 보내게 될 것이라고 예상할 수 있다. 따라서 정답은 (B) Stand most of the time이다.

10. 씨에이오에 관하여 무엇이 언급되는가?

(A) 온라인으로 상품을 보여준다.

(B) 박물관 가이드들을 교육한다.

(C) 매달 음악회를 준비한다.

(D) 여러 도시에 지점이 있다.

해설 마지막 문장에서 웹사이트에 들어가면 화랑들에 관한 추가 정보를 얻을 수 있는데, 여기에는 구매 가능한 독점 상품이 포함된다고 했으므로 웹사이트에서 물건을 보여주고 있다고 유추할 수 있다. 따라서 정답은 (A) It displays merchandise online. 이다.

[11-15] 다음 광고와 이메일에 관한 문제입니다.

http://www.topadproductions.com

탑 에드 프로덕션즈

당신의 사업을 위한 TV 광고를 만들어 고객층을 넓혀보세요

탑 에드 프로덕션즈에서는 비용 효율이 높은 텔레비전 광고를 만들어서 당신이 새로운 고객에게 다가갈 수 있도록 도와드립니다. 저희는 단 몇 주 만에, 고급의 맞춤 제작된 광고를 만드는 것을 전문으로 하고 있습니다.

서비스:

- ☛ **맞춤형 아이덴티티** – 저희의 그래픽 디자이너들이 광고에 등장할 당신의 사업체의 로고를 매력적으로 만들어 드립니다.

- ✎ **전문 배우** – 다양한 연예기획사와 협력하여 당신이 타깃으로 하는 시청자와 회사 이미지를 나타낼 노련한 연기자를 찾아드립니다. **¹¹** www.topadproductions.com에서 저희의 샘플 클립 영상을 보고 어떤 배우가 당신의 광고에 가장 잘 맞을지 확인해 보시기 바랍니다.

- 🎬 **대본** – 저희의 재능 있는 작가들이 당신의 사업체에 딱 맞춘 창의적인 원고와 고객에게 전달하고자 하는 메시지를 써 드립니다.

- ♫ **음악 제작** – 저희는 전문 제작자들과 함께 당신의 메시지 어조에 맞는 배경음악을 제작해 드립니다.

¹⁵ 귀하의 전화번호와 필요하신 내용을 간단히 적어서 info@topadproductions.com으로 보내주십시오. 다음 날 직원이 전화를 드려 원하시는 광고에 대해 더 알아보고 제작 과정에 대한 세부 사항을 알려 드리겠습니다.

어휘 **customer base** 고객층 ǀ **cost-effective** 비용 효율이 높은 ǀ **commercial** 광고 ǀ **customized** 주문 제작된 ǀ **eye-catching** 눈길을 끄는 ǀ **coordinate with** ~와 협력하다 ǀ **represent** 대표하다, 표현하다 ǀ **talented** 재능이 있는 ǀ **imaginative** 창의적인 ǀ **convey** 전달하다 ǀ **tone** 어조, 말투

수신자: info@topadproductions.com

발신자: dstapleton@stapletonlegal.com

¹⁵ 날짜: 10월 10일

제목: 문의

¹² 저는 귀사의 게시물을 〈스톡턴 헤럴드〉에서 보았고, **¹³** 제 법률 사무소로 의뢰인을 끌어모으기 위해 귀사의 서비스를 이용하고 싶습니다. **¹⁴** 저는 전문적인 음악과 로고가 들어간 진지한 어조의 광고를 만들 생각입니다. 컨셉에 대해 말하자면, **¹⁴** 잠재 고객들이 제

회사를 신뢰할 만하다고 느낄 수 있도록 해줄 대본을 쓰는 데 도움을 받고 싶습니다. 제 휴대전화로 오전 8시에서 오후 6시 사이 아무 때나 연락을 주십시오. 연락 기다리겠습니다.

안부를 전하며,

데이빗 스테이플튼

스테이플튼 리걸

704-555-1265 (휴대전화)

2484 콩코드 가

매튜스, 노스캐롤라이나 28105

어휘 **clientele** 모든 의뢰인들 ǀ **law firm** 법률 사무소 ǀ **as for** ~에 대해 말하자면 ǀ **potential** 잠재적인 ǀ **get in touch with** ~와 연락하고 지내다 ǀ **look forward to** ~을 기대하다

---

11. 광고에 따르면, 고객들이 회사 웹사이트를 방문하도록 권장받는 이유는 무엇인가?

(A) 고객 피드백을 검토하기 위해

(B) 예약을 하기 위해

(C) 가는 길을 알아보기 위해

(D) 비디오 영상을 보기 위해

해설 문제에서 키워드가 website로 나오므로 지문에서 웹사이트 주소가 들어간 문장에서 Check our sample clips를 paraphrasing한 (D) To watch some videos가 정답이다.

---

12. 탑 에드 프로덕션즈에 대해 알 수 있는 것은 무엇인가?

(A) 법률 상담을 제공한다.

(B) 평일에만 운영한다.

(C) 신문에 광고를 낸다.

(D) 최근 상을 받았다.

해설 이메일의 첫 문장에서 정답을 알 수 있다. 고객이 〈스톡턴 헤럴드〉에서 광고를 보고 이 회사에 대해 알게 되었으므로 (C) It places advertisements in the newspaper. 가 정답이다.

---

13. 스테이플튼 씨에 대해 사실인 것은 무엇이겠는가?

(A) 사업체를 소유하고 있다.

(B) 배우이다.

(C) 로고를 제작한다.

(D) 영화를 제작한다.

해설 이메일 첫 문장에서 스테이플튼 씨는 법률 회사(law firm)를 운영한다는 것을 알 수 있다. 따라서 정답은 (A) He owns a business. 이다.

---

14. 스테이플튼 씨가 탑 애드 프로덕션즈에게 요청한 서비스 내용이 아닌 것은 무엇인가?

(A) 맞춤형 아이덴티티

(B) 전문 배우

(C) 대본

(D) 음악 제작

해설 서비스 내용이 아닌 것을 물어보는 문제로, 하나씩 소거해 나가보면

(A) 맞춤형 아이덴티티와 (D) 음악 제작은 이메일의 두 번째 줄에 나와 있으며, (C) 대본 같은 경우는 지문에서 a script that would make potential clients feel like they can trust my firm이라고 나와 있으므로 정답은 (B) Professional actors이다.

---

15. 스테이플튼 씨가 10월 11일에 할 일은 무엇이겠는가?
 (A) 광고를 촬영한다
 (B) 그래픽을 디자인한다
 (C) 에이전트와 통화한다
 (D) 음악을 듣는다

해설 이중/삼중 지문의 마지막 문제이거나 날짜가 나오면 거의 연계 지문 문제로, 먼저 문제에서 주어진 날짜 10월 11일에 해당하는 부분을 찾아 보면 이메일을 쓴 날짜가 10월 10일이다. 광고 지문 마지막 단락에서 다음 날 직원이 전화를 준다고 했으므로, 이메일을 보낸 다음 날, 즉 10월 11일에 탑 에드 프로덕션즈가 스테이플튼 씨에게 전화할 것이라고 유추할 수 있다. 그러므로 정답은 (C) Talk to an agent이다.

[16-20] 다음 광고와 이메일, 문자 메시지에 관한 문제입니다.

시티 파크 극장
1029 엘리엇 가, 칼더데일
www.lloydfosterproductions.co.uk

도시를 벗어나지 않고도 외딴곳에서 여름밤을 보내세요! **16** 시티 파크 야외무대로 18세기부터 현대까지의 유명한 작품을 보러오세요. 티켓은 시티 파크 매표소나, 전화 1-800-555-8649에서 구입하실 수 있습니다. **20** 극장 회원권을 소지한 고객은 공연 전날까지 추가 티켓을 구매할 경우 25퍼센트 할인받을 수 있습니다.

- 〈캔디드 드리머〉: 6월 1-24일 이 고전 작품과 사랑에 빠지세요
- **18** 〈피셔맨스 저니〉: 6월 27일-7월 25일 극적인 반전을 즐기세요
- 〈라이프 오브 어 비즈니스맨〉: 7월 26-27일 오직 주말 동안만 상연하는 마크 브라운의 명작
- 〈필즈 오브 위트〉: 7월 28일-8월 25일까지의 상연으로 시즌을 마감하세요

어휘 faraway 멀리 떨어진 | production 작품, (영화·연극 등의) 제작 | era 시대 | patron 고객 | off 할인하여 | classic 고전, 명작 | plot twist 반전 | wrap up 마무리짓다 | showing 상연

수신: 제이에시 파텔
발신: 데비 파울러
참조: 메러디스 아스카니
제목: 다가오는 클라크 사 발표
날짜: 6월 29일

17 **18** 이 이메일은 새 시제품의 시연회가 7월 25일과 26일로 확정되었음을 확인시켜 드리기 위함입니다. 회사의 보안상의 이유로 알앤디 회의실을 예약했습니다. 회의실은 노트북 컴퓨터와 프린터, 비디오 장비를 갖추고 있습니다. 그밖에 필요한 것이 있으시면 되도록 일찍 알려주시기 바랍니다.

매러디스 아스카니 마케팅 부사장이 발표 후의 질의응답 시간에 도움을 주시기 위하여 두 번 모두 참석하실 것입니다. 그리고 첫날 회의 후에, 다른 부서장들을 몇 명과 당신을 회식과 그 후에 있는 야외극장 공연에 데리고 나가고 싶어 하십니다.

어휘 cc 참조 | prototype 시제품 | corporate 회사의 | be equipped with ~을 갖추고 있다 | take ~ out ~를 데리고 나가 대접하다

수신: 데비 파울러

발신: 메러디스 아스카니
시간: 오전 8:43

파텔 씨로부터 런던에서 방금 전화가 왔어요. 그의 비행편이 세 시간 지연되었답니다. 이것 때문에 오늘 발표 일정에 영향이 있지는 않겠지만, **20** 파텔 씨가 첫날 저녁 공연 관람은 하루 연기해달라고 요청했어요. 연기하고도 할인율을 적용받을 수 있게 즉시 내일 공연 티켓을 예약할게요. **19** 다른 간부들에게도 계획 변경에 관하여 알려주세요.

어휘 put off 미루다 | book 예약하다 | senior staff 간부 직원

---

16. 시티 파크 극장에 관해 무엇이 시사되어 있는가?
 (A) 최근 시설을 확장했다.
 (B) 다양한 역사적인 시대의 연극을 상연한다.
 (C) 다가오는 시즌을 위해 새 배우들을 모집하고 있다.
 (D) 현재 런던에 위치해 있다.

해설 광고에서 18세기부터 현대에 이르기까지의 유명 작품들을 볼 수 있다고 했으므로 여러 역사적인 시대의 연극을 상연하는 곳임을 파악할 수 있다. 따라서 정답은 (B) It features plays from various historical periods. 이다.

---

17. 파텔 씨는 출장 동안 무엇을 할 것인가?
 (A) 어떤 제품의 작동 방법을 설명한다
 (B) 보안 소프트웨어를 설치한다
 (C) 클라크 사의 역사를 논한다
 (D) 비디오 장비를 고친다

해설 이메일의 작성 목적이 파텔 씨의 제품 시연회 일정을 확인시켜 주는 것이라고 했으므로 여기서 파텔 씨가 출장에서 할 일을 알 수 있다. 그러므로 demonstration을 설명한 보기 (A) Explain how a product works가 정답이다.

---

18. 파텔 씨는 당초 어느 작품을 볼 예정이었는가?
 (A) 〈캔디드 드리머〉
 (B) 〈피셔맨스 저니〉
 (C) 〈라이프 오브 어 비즈니스맨〉
 (D) 〈필즈 오브 위트〉

해설 이메일을 보면 파텔 씨의 시연회 날짜는 7월 25일과 26일이고 첫날 야외극장 공연을 볼 예정이므로 7월 25일에 공연을 보러 갈 것이다. 그

리고 광고를 보면 7월 25일에 있는 공연은 〈피셔맨스 저니〉이다. 그러므로 정답은 (B) Fisherman's Journey이다.

─────────────

19. 파울러 씨는 이후에 무엇을 하겠는가?
(A) 식사 예약을 변경한다
(B) 몇몇 동료에게 연락한다
(C) 어떤 발표를 검토한다
(D) 새 비행편을 예약한다

해설 파울러 씨가 이후에 할 것을 물어보는 문제로, 앞으로 할 일은 지문 후반부에 위치하며 문자 메시지의 마지막 문장에 다른 간부들에게 변경 사항을 알려주라는 지시를 받았으므로 정답은 (B) Contact some colleagues이다.

20. 아스카니 씨는 왜 즉시 새 티켓을 사려고 계획하겠는가?
(A) 파텔 씨가 공연을 좋아할지 확실하지 않다.
(B) 어떤 공연이 갑자기 취소되었다.
(C) 시티 파크 극장 회원이다.
(D) 파텔 씨가 하루 늦게 도착할 것이다.

해설 이 문제는 연계 지문 문제로써, 첫 광고에서 회원은 공연 하루 전날까지 티켓을 구매할 경우 25퍼센트 할인을 받을 수 있다고 나오며, 마지막 문자 메시지에서 첫날 공연을 하루 연기해달라고 했다면서 할인율을 적용받을 수 있게 내일 티켓을 즉시 사야겠다고 말하는 것으로 보아 회원임을 유추할 수 있으므로 정답은 (C) She is a City Park Theater member. 이다.

UNIT 04. 공지·회람

핵심 문제 유형
본서 p.253

1. (B)   **2.** (A)

[1-2] 다음 회람에 관한 문제입니다.

티볼리 커뮤니티 센터
수신: 조지 코넬
발신: 돈 마틴
날짜: 8월 30일
회신: 예산 승인

목요일의 우리 회의는 정말 생산적이었던 것 같습니다. **1** 우리가 논의했던 예산 절감에 관한 모든 아이디어 중에서, 일주일에 하루 시설의 문을 닫는 계획이 가장 효과적일 것 같습니다. 제 추정으로는 우리가 하루에 1천 달러를 절약할 것 같고, **2** 존스 회장님이 다음 월요일 회의에서 이 아이디어를 승인하실 것으로 자신합니다. 그때 봐요!

돈 마틴
과장

─────────────

어휘 budget 예산 | approval 승인 | productive 생산적인 | facility 시설 | effective 효과적인 | estimate 추정하다, 추산하다 | confident 자신 있는

1. 회람에 무엇이 언급되어 있는가?
(A) 예산이 증가되어야 한다.
(B) 커뮤니티 센터는 비용을 절감하고 싶어 한다.
(C) 코넬 씨의 발표가 성공적이었다.
(D) 마틴 씨가 보고서를 준비할 것이다.

해설 두 번째 문장에서 티볼리 커뮤니티 센터는 비용을 절감하는 방안을 모색 중임을 알 수 있다. 따라서 (B) The community center wants to cut costs. 가 정답이다. reducing the budget이 cut costs로 paraphrasing되었다.

2. 월요일에 무슨 일이 일어날 것인가?
(A) 임원이 회의에 참석할 것이다.
(B) 건설 공사가 시작될 것이다.
(C) 시설 방문이 제공될 것이다.
(D) 연설이 있을 것이다.

해설 회람 끝부분에서 월요일 회의에 회장이 참석할 것임을 알 수 있다. 따라서 (A) An executive will attend a meeting. 이 정답이다.

Practice
본서 p.254

1. (D)	**2.** (A)	**3.** (C)	**4.** (C)	**5.** (C)
6. (B)	**7.** (A)	**8.** (B)	**9.** (C)	**10.** (C)
11. (C)	**12.** (D)	**13.** (D)	**14.** (A)	**15.** (A)
16. (C)	**17.** (A)	**18.** (C)	**19.** (C)	**20.** (C)
21. (A)	**22.** (D)			

[1-2] 다음 공지에 관한 문제입니다.

1 그린 테이블 고객님들께,

1 저희 운영진은 오늘 손님들께 따뜻한 음식을 대접해 드리지 못하는 것에 대해 사과드립니다. **1 2** 저희는 이번 주말에 오븐과 스토브를 업그레이드하고 있으며 월요일에 정상 영업을 재개하겠습니다. 새 구성은 저희로 하여금 고객의 미각을 만족시켜 줄 훨씬 더 다양한 식단을 만들어 내게 할 것입니다.

이것이 오늘의 메뉴에 나오는 요리의 개수나 품질을 떨어뜨리지는 않을 것이니 안심하셔도 좋습니다. 고객님께서 더 좋은 경험을 하시도록 해드리기 위해 저희가 할 수 있는 일이 있다면 주저하지 말고 저희 직원 중 한 명에게 말씀하시기 바랍니다.

어휘 diner 식사하는 사람 | management 경영진 | resume 다시 시작하다 | operation 사업, 영업 | setup 구성, 장치 | taste bud 미뢰 | please be assured that ~이니 안심하시기 바랍니다

1. 공지는 어디에서 볼 수 있겠는가?
(A) 창고 뒤편에서
(B) 슈퍼마켓 뒤편에서
(C) 백화점 앞에서
(D) 식당 앞에서

해설 지문 도입부에서 Dear Green Table Diners에서 diner는 식당 손님을 뜻하므로 이것만 봐도 식당 앞에 붙어있을 만한 공지라는 것을 알 수 있다. 게다가 첫 두 문장에서 식당의 조리용 기계들을 교체하는 작업 때문에 따뜻한 음식을 제공할 수 없다는 말까지 하고 있으므로 정답은 (D) At the front of a restaurant이다.

2. 무엇이 변경되는가?
(A) 장비
(B) 초대 손님 명단
(C) 컴퓨터 네트워크
(D) 테이블 배치

해설 지문에서 오븐과 스토브에 변화가 있을 것이라고 말하므로 정답은 (A) Some equipment이다.

[3-5] 다음 회람에 관한 문제입니다.

> **공지**
>
> 날짜: 9월 4일
>
> 건물 내 모든 휴게실의 블라스트 팝 자판기들은 이번 주말에 철거될 것입니다. **4** 회사는 자판기 공급사와의 계약을 갱신하지 않기로 결정했습니다. 블라스트 팝과의 5년 계약은 회사 직원이 겨우 10명이었을 때 체결되었습니다. 회사가 성장함에 따라, 우리 직원들의 건강에 대한 경영진의 비전 및 투자 여력도 바뀌었습니다. 따라서, **3** 2달 전, 한나 콜린스는 회사의 모든 금융거래 책임자이기 때문에 보다 적절한 판매상을 찾는 업무를 부여받았습니다. 많은 조사 후에, 콜린스 씨는 완벽한 공급 업체를 찾아냈습니다.
>
> 오늘, 우리는 뉴트릴리셔스와의 독점계약 발표를 기쁘게 생각하며, 이들은 다음 주 월요일에 새 자판기를 설치할 것입니다. **5** 자판기는 신선하고 다양한 과일, 저지방 유제품 그리고 몸에 좋은 주스를 공급할 예정이고 모든 제품의 가격은 1달러 이하입니다. **5** 또한, 뉴트릴리셔스는 감사의 표시로 각 직원에게 무료 종합 견과 세트를 배포할 것입니다. 변경 사항에 대해 질문 있으시면, 콜린스 씨에게 연락 바랍니다.
>
> 어휘 vending machine 자판기 | remove 제거하다 | renew 갱신하다 | vendor 상인 | suitable 적절한 | corporate 회사의 | financial transaction 금융거래 | exclusive 독점의 | low-fat 저지방 | dairy 유제품의 | complimentary 무료의 | assorted 여러 가지의 | appreciation 감사

3. 콜린스 씨는 어느 부서에서 일하겠는가?
(A) 마케팅
(B) 연구
(C) 회계
(D) 관리

해설 문제에 등장한 콜린스 씨를 지문에서 찾아보면 회사의 금융거래를 담당하는 사람이라고 했으므로 정답은 (C) Accounting이다.

4. 회사는 블라스트 팝 자판기를 몇 년 동안 사용하였는가?
(A) 1
(B) 4
(C) 5
(D) 10

해설 만료될 블라스트 팝과의 계약을 갱신하지 않기로 결정했다고 했는데, 이것은 5년짜리 계약이었으므로 자판기를 5년 동안 사용한 것이다. 따라서 정답은 (C) 5이다.

5. 새로운 자판기에 포함되지 않을 것은 무엇인가?
(A) 과일
(B) 주스
(C) 견과
(D) 우유

해설 지문을 훑어서 문제의 키워드 included in the new vending machines를 찾아내면 어렵지 않게 해결할 수 있다. 두 번째 단락 The vending machines provide로 시작하는 문장을 읽어보면 과일, 유제품, 그리고 주스를 판매한다고 했고, 견과는 뉴트릴리셔스가 감사의 표시로 직원들에게 무료로 나눠주는 것이지 자판기에서 판매하는 제품이 아니므로 (C) Nuts가 정답이다.

[6-8] 다음 회람에 관한 문제입니다.

> **조비안 가구 카로빌 지점 선공개 행사**
> 조비안 가구가 카로빌 쇼핑몰 내의 새 지점을 미리 둘러보도록 전 직원 여러분을 초대합니다. **6** 궂은 날씨로 인해 당초 잡혀있던 기념행사 일정이 연기되기는 했지만, 마침내 여러분 모두를 맞이할 준비가 되었습니다. 행사는 12월 5일 오후 5시부터 8시까지이며 음식은 링스 다이너에서 제공합니다.
>
> **7** 본사에서 카로빌 쇼핑몰까지의 길 안내
> **7** 라이트 가를 타고 북쪽 방향으로 출발해서 메인 가로 우회전하세요. 메인 가와 피프스 가 교차로에서, 우회전 후 남쪽으로 팜 가까지 가시면 됩니다. 쇼핑센터는 북동쪽 모퉁이에 있습니다. 매장은 3층 에스컬레이터 옆입니다.
>
> **카로빌 쇼핑몰 주차**
> **8** 행사에 참석하는 모든 직원은 조비안 사원증을 보여주면 당일 주차 요금을 낼 필요 없습니다. 단, A 주차장에 주차하는 걸 명심하세요. 대중교통을 이용하실 분들은, 인사부의 마가렛에게 말씀하세요.
>
> 어휘 branch 지점 | postpone 연기하다 | inclement (날씨가) 궂은 | cater 음식을 공급하다 | intersection 교차로 | as long as ~하는 한

6. 행사와 관련하여 무엇이 변경되었는가?
(A) 손님 수
(B) 날짜
(C) 장소
(D) 음식 선택권

해설 changed가 문제의 키워드인데, 지문을 훑어보면 originally scheduled에서 처음에 잡아 두었던 일정이 연기되었다는 내용이므로 정답은 (B) The date이다.

---

7. 본사는 어디에 위치해 있는가?

(A) 라이트 가에
(B) 메인 가에
(C) 피프스 가에
(D) 팜 가에

해설 문제의 키워드 headquarters가 등장하는 본사에서 쇼핑몰까지 가는 길 안내를 보면 본사에서 라이트 가를 타고 출발하라고 했으므로 (A) On Wright Avenue가 정답이다.

---

8. 카로빌 쇼핑몰과 관련하여 무엇이 시사되어 있는가?

(A) 대중교통 시설 근처에 있다.
(B) 보통 주차 요금을 징수한다.
(C) 링 다이너로부터 길 건너편에 있다.
(D) 오후 8시에 문을 닫는다.

해설 행사에 참석하는 직원들이 사원증을 보여주고 A 주차장을 이용한다는 조건 하에 주차 요금을 면제해 준다는 내용이 나오므로 카로빌 쇼핑몰은 원래 차량에 주차요금을 부과하는 곳이라는 것을 유추할 수 있다. 따라서 정답은 (B) It normally charges for parking. 이다.

[9-12] 다음 공지에 관한 문제입니다.

봄의 즐거움!

9 마운트 버논에서 이 대단한 행사들과 함께 봄을 기념하세요:

마운트 버논 세계 음악 축제 (4월 20일)
마운트 버논 문화센터에서 아프리카, 아시아, 남아메리카 그리고 유럽에서 온 연주자들과 함께 음악 탐험을 떠나 보세요.

10 **마운트 버논 연극 공연 (4월 21일)**
〈이지 스트릿〉, 〈메이커스 하우스〉, 〈티 위드 베티〉와 같은 연극을 보러 오세요. 마운트 버논 문화센터에서 마운트 버논 극단이 공연합니다.

11 **마운트 버논 도서 박람회 (4월 27일)**
30명이 넘는 미국 작가들의 작품을 소개하는 책 읽기 및 토론. 마운트 버논 지역의 다양한 도서관 및 서점에서 열립니다.

10 **마운트 버논 예술 경연 (4월 28일)**
지역 예술가들이 명망 높은 베이커 상을 놓고 경쟁합니다. 이 대회는 마운트 버논 현대 예술 박물관에서 버지니아 대학교 미술학부의 교수님들이 심사할 것입니다.

마운트 버논 주민 회관 개장식 (5월 4일)
많은 기대를 받은 주민 회관이 드디어 개장합니다. **10** **12** 마운트 버논 주민 회관에서 스미스 바비큐가 제공하는 무료 점심을 즐기고, 스탠 크로커와 리틀 캣의 음악을 들어보세요.

이 행사들에 대한 세부 사항을 보시려면 www.mtvernon.org/springevents를 방문하세요.

어휘 exploration 탐험 | book fair 도서 박람회 | showcase 소개하다 | prestigious 명망 있는 | much-anticipated 상당한 기대를 모은 | cater 음식을 제공하다 | take place 열리다, 일어나다 | in case of ~의 경우에 | multiple 복수의 | venue 장소

---

9. 모든 행사에 관해 암시된 것은 무엇인가?

(A) 대중에게 공개되지 않는다.
(B) 여름까지 연기될지 모른다.
(C) 마운트 버논 지역에서 열릴 것이다.
(D) 우천 시 일정이 변경되지 않을 것이다.

해설 첫 문장에서 마운트 버논에서 이 다양한 행사들과 함께 봄을 기념하라고 했으므로 행사들은 마운트 버논 지역에서 열린다는 것을 알 수 있다. 정답은 (C) They will take place in the Mt. Vernon area. 이다.

---

10. 행사 중의 하나로 열거되지 않은 것은 무엇인가?

(A) 예술 대회
(B) 무료 점심
(C) 노래자랑 대회
(D) 연극 공연

해설 두 번째와 네 번째 행사명에서 연극 공연과 예술 대회가 있음을 알 수 있고, 마지막 행사인 마운트 버논 주민회관 개장식 소개 내용에서 무료 점심이 제공됨을 알 수 있다. 따라서 행사 내용이 아닌 것은 (C) A singing competition이다.

---

11. 어떤 행사가 여러 장소에서 열릴 것인가?

(A) 마운트 버논 세계 음악 축제
(B) 마운트 버논 연극 공연
(C) 마운트 버논 도서 박람회
(D) 마운트 버논 예술 경연

해설 세 번째 행사인 마운트 버논 도서 박람회에서 장소는 마운트 버논 지역의 다양한 도서관 및 서점이라고 했으므로 정답은 (C) The Mt. Vernon Book Fair이다.

---

12. 크로커 씨에 대해 무엇이라고 나타나 있는가?

(A) 대회를 심사할 것이다.
(B) 지역 요리사이다.
(C) 행사를 준비했다.
(D) 새로운 장소에서 연주할 것이다.

해설 마지막 부분에서 마운트 버논 주민회관 개장식에서 많은 기대를 받은 주민 회관이 개장한다고 하며 스탠 크로커와 리틀 캣의 음악을 들어보라고 소개했다. 따라서 크로커 씨는 새 주민 회관에서 연주할 것임을 알 수 있다. 정답은 (D) He will play at a new venue. 이다.

[13-17] 다음 회람과 양식에 관한 문제입니다.

발신: 브라이언 바버, 인사부장
수신: 모든 인사부 직원
날짜: 1월 2일
제목: 재고 기록표
첨부: officeinvent_list.doc

연간 사무용품 재고 기록표를 이달 안에 제출할 것을 당부합니다. 매년, 경리부에서 회사 사무실에서 사용하는 장비에 대한 감사를 **14** 실시합니다. 수집된 정보는 올해 구매 예산을 결정하는 데 도움이 될 것입니다.

여러분의 부서에서 사용된, 스캐너와 노트북과 같은 모든 장비를 기입할 양식을 첨부해 두었습니다. **13** 그 장비의 현 상태부터, 연식까지 여러분들께서 아는 최대한 명시해 주십시오. **13 17** 연식이 4년 이상 된 복사기와 프린터는 교체될 예정입니다. **15** 양식을 잃어버렸을 때는, 미카 사토(msato@dmsat.com)에게 연락해서 한 장 더 받기 바랍니다.

1월 31일 예산 회의 전에 이 목록들이 확정되어야 하기 때문에, **16** 직원 여러분은 1월 19일까지 라이언 델랩에게 이메일 ryandelap@dmsat.com으로 목록을 보내기 바랍니다. 또한 반드시 다른 팀원들과 조정하여 각 품목이 양식에 중복되지 않게 기재될 수 있도록 확인 바랍니다. 이 일과 관련하여 여러분이 내주신 시간과 도움에 대해 미리 감사드립니다.

어휘 yearly 매년 있는 | submit 제출하다 | audit 회계 감사 | budget 예산 | indicate 명시하다 | replace 교체하다 | misplace 제자리에 두지 않다, (제자리에 없어서) 찾지 못하다 | finalize 완결하다

요청자 성명: **14** 다니엘라 모랄레스
요청자 소속 부서: 영업부
요청자 부서장: 로날드 해밀턴
빌딩/층: C/19층
제출일: 1월 16일

품목	모델명	상태	연식
스캐너	CT3400	좋음 보통 나쁨	3년
17 복사기	XZR650	좋음 보통 나쁨	5년
프린터	HG8000	좋음 보통 나쁨	3년
		좋음 보통 나쁨	
		좋음 보통 나쁨	

13. 직원들은 왜 서식을 작성하도록 요청받는가?
(A) 어떤 장비를 수리해야 하는지 확인하기 위해
(B) 사무실 점검을 위한 날짜를 배정하기 위해
(C) 사무실 상태를 감독관에게 보고하기 위해
(D) 어떤 장비를 교체해야 할지 결정하기 위해

해설 회람의 두 번째 단락에서 양식을 되도록 자세히 작성해 달라고 말한 다음 4년 이상된 복사기와 프린터가 교체될 거라고 했으므로 양식을 작성하는 목적에는 어느 장비를 교체할 필요가 있는지를 판단

하는 데 있다고 볼 수 있다. 그러므로 정답은 (D) To decide what equipment needs to be replaced이다.

14. 회람의 첫 번째 단락, 두 번째 줄의 단어 "conducts"에 의미상 가장 가까운 것은
(A) 완료하다
(B) 지시하다
(C) 안내하다
(D) 만들다

해설 conduct an audit은 '감사를 실시하다'라는 의미이므로 동사를 바꿨을 때 가장 의미가 가까운 것은 '감사를 완료하다'이다. 따라서 정답은 (A) completes이다. (D) drives는 어떤 대상이 특정한 행위를 하거나 특정한 상태가 되도록 만든다는 의미이므로 여기서는 문맥상 맞지 않다.

15. 직원들이 추가 서식을 받으려면 누구에게 연락해야 하는가?
(A) 미카 사토
(B) 로날드 해밀턴
(C) 라이언 델랩
(D) 브라이언 바버

해설 연락 방법은 주로 지문 후반부나 이메일 주소를 보면 된다. 회람의 두 번째 단락에서 키워드 form이 있는 문장을 보면 정답이 (A) 미카 사토임을 알 수 있다.

16. 직원들이 서식을 제출해야 하는 날짜는 언제인가?
(A) 1월 2일까지
(B) 1월 16일까지
(C) 1월 19일까지
(D) 1월 31일까지

해설 문제에 있는 submit the form라는 키워드가 날짜와 함께 등장하는 문장을 찾아보면 된다. 회람 세 번째 단락에 키워드를 email the list로 paraphrasing된 문장을 통해 정답은 (C) By January 19임을 알 수 있다.

17. 모랄레스 씨에 대해 유추할 수 있는 것은 무엇인가?
(A) 새로운 복사기를 받게 될 것이다.
(B) 지난달에 스캐너를 새로 구매했다.
(C) 최근에 영업팀으로 전근했다.
(D) 델랩 씨의 부서장이다.

해설 모랄레스 씨가 작성한 양식의 표를 보면 사무실의 복사기가 5년이 되었음을 알 수 있다. 회람 두 번째 단락에서 연식이 4년 이상된 복사기와 프린터는 교체될 예정이라고 했으므로 정답은 (A) She will receive a new photocopier. 이다.

[18-22] 다음 공지와 지시사항, 이메일에 관한 문제입니다.

시식회 참가자 구인

유니피크 홍보 대행사는 이번 주 토요일 포트 웨인 시내 큐 호텔 대연회장에서 있을 특별 시식 행사에 참가할 19세에서 55세까지의 성인들을 찾습니다. 참가자들은 선샤인 버거의 여름 메뉴로 기획된 다

양한 추가 품목들을 맛보고 진행자들에게 의견을 제시해 주면 됩니다. **18** 시식 참가자들에게 보수는 주어지지 않지만, 모든 음식이 무료이며, 저녁 시간 동안 많은 상품이 무료로 제공됩니다. **18** 전화 1-800-555-2301, 내선 번호 44번으로 유니피크 홍보 대행사에 전화하여 간단한 설문 조사에 참여하면, 참가자로 선발될 경우 등록을 마무리하는 방법에 관한 안내가 나옵니다.

어휘　PR(public relations) 홍보 | ballroom 대연회장 | addition 첨가 | panel 전문 위원회 | moderator 관리자 | compensate 보상하다 | give away 거저 주다 | over the course of ~동안 | directions 안내, 지시, 명령 | finalize 완결 짓다 | registration 등록

데이비드에게,

시식 행사를 **19** 진행하겠다고 해줘서 고마워요. 세부 사항 여기 있습니다. 의뢰인 측에서 자신들의 타겟 시장의 성향이 잘 나타나게 하기 위해 **18** 일주일에 최소 세 번은 패스트푸드점에서 식사를 하는 120명의 사람을 찾아달라고 요청했어요. 각 그룹은 각각 다른 메뉴 품목의 조합을 제공받게 될 겁니다.

시식단	시간
1	오후 5:30
2	오후 6:30
3	오후 7:30
4	오후 8:30

20 당신은 식사가 제공될 때 30명으로 이루어진 각 그룹에게 요리를 소개할 것입니다. 그리고, 식사가 끝나면, 패널들과 되도록 많은 의견을 공유하도록 독려해 주세요. 모든 식사는 다음 네 개의 카테고리에서 각각 한 품목씩을 포함합니다.

A: 감자튀김, 오크라튀김, 고구마튀김
B: 하와이안 버거, 비비큐 포크 번, 피시 샌드위치
C: 애플 슬라이스, 파인애플 쿠키, 당근 스틱
22 D: 무화과 스무디, 아이스티, 캐러멜 라테

21 피드백 시간에 반드시 참가자들의 이름을 일지에 기록하셔서 나중에 우리가 누구 얘기를 하고 있는 건지 알도록 해주세요. 질문 있으시면 알려주세요.

패트릭 스콧

어휘　facilitate 쉽게 하다, 용이하게 하다 | represent 나타내다, 대표하다 | locate 찾아내다 | distinct 별개의 | sweet potato 고구마 | fig 무화과 | logbook 일지 | phase 단계

수신: b.lazsco@sunshineburger.com
발신: patricks@unifiquepr.com
날짜: 11월 19일
제목: 6번 사례
첨부파일: 6번 사례 결과

라즈스코 씨에게,

선샤인 버거의 메뉴 변경에 관한 대중 논평이 완료되었음을 확인해 드립니다. 첨부파일에서 보시다시피, 한 특정 카테고리가 네 개의 포커스그룹 각각으로부터 좋은 평가를 많이 받았습니다. **22** 이 피드백에 근거하여, 새 음료수 제품에 대한 반응이 매우 긍정적일 것으로 기대합니다. 수집한 데이터를 검토할 시간이 언제 있으신지 알려주세요. 손으로 쓴 일지와 비디오 파일을 맞춰서 보는 방법을 설명해 드리겠습니다.

고맙습니다.

패트릭 스콧
유니피크 홍보 대행사 조사 감독

어휘　attachment 첨부파일 | alteration 변경 | focus group (테스트할 상품에 대해서 토의하는) 소비자 그룹 | anticipate 예상하다 | offering 팔 물건 | log 일지

---

18. 시식 참가자들에 관해 시사되지 않은 것은 무엇인가?
(A) 정기적으로 패스트푸드를 먹는다.
(B) 보수를 지급받지 않을 것이다.
(C) 호텔 직원들이다.
(D) 전화로 의견을 제시했다.

해설　일치하지 않는 것을 찾는 문제로 소거법을 이용해 풀어보면, (A)는 지시사항 지문에서 일주일에 적어도 세 번 패스트푸드를 먹는 사람들이라고 언급되고 있고 (B)는 공지 지문에 무보수라고 나오며, (D)도 역시나 공지 지문에서 전화 통화를 통해 설문 조사하는 내용이 나오므로 정답은 (C) They are hotel employees. 이다.

---

19. 지시사항 첫 번째 문단, 첫 번째 줄의 단어 "facilitate"에 의미상 가장 가까운 것은
(A) 전달하다
(B) 속도를 올리다
(C) 감독하다
(D) (단계별로 차례차례) ~에게 …을 보여 주다

해설　facilitate는 원래 '쉽게 하다, 용이하게 하다'의 뜻이며, 지시 사항의 전체 내용으로 보아 데이비드는 시식 행사를 진행하는 사람임을 알 수 있다. 따라서 '시식 행사를 감독하다'의 의미가 가장 잘 어울리므로 정답은 (C) oversee이다.

---

20. 6번 사례에 관해 무엇이 언급되었는가?
(A) 그룹들이 옵션에 관한 정보를 받지 않았다.
(B) 선샤인 버거 본사에서 열렸다.
(C) 각 그룹은 같은 수의 구성원으로 이루어졌다.
(D) 식음료 산업의 전문가들만 참가할 수 있었다.

해설　지시사항 지문에서, 각각 30명으로 구성된 그룹이라는 문장을 통해서 정답은 (C) Every group had an equal number of members. 임을 알 수 있다.

21. 이메일에 따르면, 일지는 왜 사용되었는가?

   (A) 참가자들을 식별할 수 있도록 한다.

   (B) 조사 시간을 기록할 수 있도록 한다.

   (C) 나중에 참가자들에게 연락할 수 있도록 한다.

   (D) 연구원들의 근무 시간을 알아낼 수 있도록 한다.

해설　문제의 키워드 logbook이 나오는 지시사항 지문에서 참가자들의 이름을 일지에 기록하는 것을 확실히 하고, 이는 나중에 누구인지를 알기 위해서라고 나와 있으므로 정답은 (A) So participants could be identified. 이다.

---

22. 연구 결과에 근거하여, 어느 카테고리가 가장 인기 있었는가?

   (A) A

   (B) B

   (C) C

   (D) D

해설　문제의 키워드 study's results는 이메일 지문에서 찾을 수 있으며, 제품 종류가 보기로 나올 때는 거의 연계 지문이다. 이메일 지문에서 설문 조사에 따르면, 새 음료에 대해서 가장 좋은 피드백을 예상한다고 나와 있고, 지시사항 지문에서 음료 종류가 나와 있는 것을 찾으면 정답은 (D) D이다.

UNIT 05. 기사

핵심 문제 유형

본서 p.263

1. (D)　　**2.** (A)

[1-2] 다음 기사에 관한 문제입니다.

야마타 전자가 완전히 자동화된 공장을 만들다

① 야마타 전자는 최근에 자사의 후쿠시마 공장이 완전히 자동화되어 가동 중이라고 발표했다. 최첨단 로봇 기술을 사용하여, 공장은 제품 생산 과정에서 사람의 인력을 투입할 필요성을 제거했다. 사실, 공장에서 근무하는 유일한 사람들은 자동 생산 관리팀의 일원들이다. 팀은 엔지니어들, 소프트웨어 전문가들, 그리고 기계 디자이너들로 이루어져 있다. 이 전문가들은 로봇들을 유지하고, 자동화된 생산 라인이 원활하고 효율적으로 가동되도록 필요한 변경을 한다.

야마타는 공장 전체를 자동화함으로써 생산 경비를 반으로 줄였다고 주장한다. "이것은 회사의 가치에 엄청난 영향을 미쳤어요. **②** 투자자들이 우리의 계획을 알고 난 후로 우리 주가는 꾸준히 오르고 있죠."라고 야마타 전자의 기획실장인 이치로 다나카가 말했다.

야마타 전자는 완전 자동화에 필요한 모든 기계를 만드느라 엄청난 투자를 해야 했지만, 장기적으로는 회사는 이 조치로부터 이득을 볼 것이 분명하다.

어휘　automated 자동화된 | plant 공장 | operational 가동하는, 운영하는 | state-of-the-art 최첨단의 | robotic technology 로봇 기술 | eliminate 제거하다, 없애다 | input 투입 | consist of ～으로 구성되다 | expert 전문가 | smoothly 원활히 | efficiently 효율적으로 | stock price 주가 | steadily 꾸준히 | investor 투자자 | make an investment in ～에 투자하다 | automation 자동화 | in the long run 장기적으로

1. 기사는 주로 무엇을 논의하고 있는가?

   (A) 전자 대회

   (B) 환경 정책

   (C) 회사 매출 하락

   (D) 공장의 변화

해설　첫 단락의 첫 문장에서 야마타 전자가 공장을 완전히 자동화해서 가동한다고 발표했다는 내용이 나오므로 기사는 공장의 변화에 관한 내용이다. 따라서 (D) A change at a factory가 정답이다.

---

2. 야마타 전자에 관해 암시된 것은 무엇인가?

   (A) 투자자들이 더 많아지고 있다.

   (B) 최근에 이전했다.

   (C) 신상품을 출시했다.

   (D) 더 많은 노동자들을 고용했다.

해설　두 번째 단락에서 투자자들이 야마타 전자의 계획을 알고 주가가 꾸준히 오른다고 하였으므로 (A) It is attracting more investors. 가 정답이다.

Practice

본서 p.264

1. (A)	**2.** (C)	**3.** (D)	**4.** (D)	**5.** (B)
6. (B)	**7.** (D)	**8.** (C)	**9.** (B)	**10.** (D)
11. (C)	**12.** (D)	**13.** (B)	**14.** (C)	**15.** (B)
16. (A)	**17.** (B)	**18.** (D)	**19.** (A)	**20.** (B)
21. (C)	**22.** (B)	**23.** (B)	**24.** (C)	

[1-3] 다음 기사에 관한 문제입니다.

어제 기자회견에서, 테일러 스테이셔너리는 대규모 사무용품 판매 체인점인 이도 오피스 월드에 인수될 예정이라고 밝혔다. 테일러 스테이셔너리의 창립자 셰릴 테일러는 애초에 이 일을 성사시키려고 하지 않았다. **①** 하지만, 충분한 숙고 끝에, 이도의 매입 제안을 받아들이기로 결정했다. 대학 시절, 테일러 씨는 친구와 가족을 위해 장식이 된 카드와 봉투를 만들었다. 졸업 후에는, **②** 자신의 고향 팜 스프링스에서 테일러 스테이셔너리의 첫 매장을 시작했다. **③** 몇 년 후, 그녀는 슐라 비스타, 엘 카종, 라 호야로 사업을 확장했으며, 35년 만에 전국에 60개 지점을 설립해 냈다.

1. 테일러 씨에 관해 암시된 것은 무엇인가?

   (A) 이도 오피스 월드가 자신의 사업을 인수하도록 허락했다.

   (B) 이도 오피스 월드가 자신의 매장에 용품을 공급하도록 계약을 맺었다.

   (C) 최근 이도 오피스 월드의 전문경영인으로 임명되었다.

   (D) 이도 오피스 월드의 최신 지점을 관리하도록 선출되었다.

해설 매입 제안을 받아들이기로 했다고 했으므로 자기 사업을 팔기로 했다는 (A) She has allowed Edo Office World to buy her business. 가 정답이다.

2. 기사에 따르면, 테일러 씨는 어디 출신인가?

   (A) 슐라 비스타

   (B) 산디에고

   (C) 팜 스프링스

   (D) 라 호야

해설 지문에서 그녀의 고향이 팜 스프링스라고 했으므로 (C) Palm Springs 가 정답이다.

3. 테일러 스테이셔너리에 대해 언급된 것은 무엇인가?

   (A) 최근에 수익성이 없었다.

   (B) 다른 나라에도 지점을 갖고 있다.

   (C) 이제 막 새로운 시장으로 확장했다.

   (D) 최소 35년간 운영했다.

해설 사업을 시작한 지 35년 만에 60개 지점을 가진 회사가 되었다고 했으므로 이 회사는 최소 35년은 넘게 운영되어 온 회사이다. 그러므로 정답은 (D) It has been operating for at least 35 years. 이다.

[4-6] 다음 기사에 관한 문제입니다.

(1월 2일) **4** 메트로 와이어리스의 대변인 데이트리히 랭은 다음 달 매디슨에 있는 휴대전화 판매업체 일렉트리컬을 시작으로 향후 1년에 걸쳐 경쟁업체 네 곳을 인수하겠다고 한다. 저렴한 요금으로 알려져 있는 메트로 와이어리스는 다음으로 4월에 그래디턴 근처에 있는 네트워크 릴레이를 인수할 것이다. **6** 다비빌에 있는 또한 군데의 매장 폰콜 익스프레스를 8월 하순에 인수할 것이다. 매각될 마지막 회사에 대한 세부 사항은 아직 공개되지 않았다.

메트로 와이어리스는 지난 몇 년 동안 주 전체에 걸쳐 지점을 열어왔다. 이 매장들은 다양한 전화기와 친절한 직원, **5** 그리고 값싼 데이터 요금제에 힘입어 고객 수가 많이 증가했다. 메트로 와이어리스의 대표인 마리앤 클라우의 말에 따르면, 이 마지막 이유야말로 정말 회사의 인기 성장을 이끌어가고 있다고 한다. "요즘 많은 휴대전화 사용자들이 다양한 콘텐츠를 다운로드하고 싶어 하지만 다른 회사들의 비싼 요금을 감당할 수가 없죠."라고 클라우는 말한다. 작년에, 메트로 와이어리스는 브렌트 스미스를 마케팅 담당 이사로 고용했고 몇 달 후 지금은 유명한 "모두를 위한 데이터" 기획을 발표했다.

4. 기사는 주로 무엇에 관한 것인가?

   (A) 요금제에 만족하지 못하는 고객들

   (B) 다른 도시로 이전하는 매장

   (C) 비용을 절감하는 휴대전화 판매업체들

   (D) 경쟁 업체들을 인수하는 한 회사

해설 지문의 주제는 주로 도입부에 있으며, 첫 문장에서 회사가 경쟁업체 네 군데를 인수할 계획이라고 알려주고 있으므로 acquire four of its competitors를 paraphrasing한 (D) A company purchasing rival businesses가 정답이다.

5. 클라우 씨는 고객들이 메트로 와이어리스에 관하여 가장 좋아하는 점이 무엇이라고 말하는가?

   (A) 전화기 디자인

   (B) 경쟁력 있는 가격 책정

   (C) 독특한 광고

   (D) 편리한 위치

해설 클라우 씨는 값싼 데이터 요금제를 회사의 인기 성장의 진짜 이유라고 생각한다고 했기 때문에 정답은 (B) Its competitive pricing이다.

6. [1], [2], [3], [4]로 표시된 곳 중에서 다음 문장이 들어가기에 가장 적절한 곳은 어디인가?

   "다비빌에 있는 또 한 군데의 매장 폰콜 익스프레스를 8월 하순에 인수할 것이다."

   (A) [1]

   (B) [2]

   (C) [3]

   (D) [4]

해설 [2]의 앞부분에서 메트로 와이어리스가 인수할 네 곳의 회사 중 두 군데(일렉트리컬, 네트워크 릴레이)를 알려주고 있고, 뒤 문장에서 마지막 회사에 대해서는 밝혀진 바가 없다고 말하고 있으므로 인수할 세 번째 회사가 폰콜 익스프레스라는 것을 알려주는 위치 (B) [2]가 정답이다.

[7-10] 다음 기사에 관한 문제입니다.

7 더블린(5월 10일) 메리 크레이버는 27년 만에 자신의 유명한 카페 더 라이트 로스트의 열쇠를 넘겨주게 되었다.

이곳은 원래 남편 대릴이 운영하던 작은 식당이었다. **8** 그러나, 크레이버 씨가 인수했을 때, 식사 제공을 중단하고 대신 최고 품질의 음료와 디저트를 만드는 데 집중했다. 카페는 최고급 납품업체들로부터 들여온 커피 원두와 코코아, 우유만 사용함으로써 우수성에 대한 명성을 얻었으며, 메리에게는 "커피의 여왕"이라는 별명이 붙었다. **9** 도쿄나 요하네스버그와 같이 멀리 떨어진 지역의 사람들까지 이 가게의 성공 이야기를 읽고, 매우 큰 수익을 남기고 있는 메리의 사업에 관해 더 알아보기 위해 방문했다.

카페 주인 자리는 크레이버 씨의 조카 루이 래스트가 이어받을 것이다. 래스트 씨는 이전과 다름없이 사업을 계속해 나갈 계획이지만 새 지점을 여는 것을 고려하고 있다. 두 번째 지점의 가능성에 관한 질문에 관해, 래스트 씨는 "일이 별 탈 없이 진행된다면 내년쯤 가능합니다."라고 대답했다. **10** "현재로는, 전국의 라이트 로스트 팬들은 더 자세한 발표를 기다리는 수밖에 없습니다."

한편, 크레이버 씨는 여전히 이따금 카페에 들러 여느 때와 다름이 없는지 확인하기야 하겠지만, 그래도 은퇴 생활을 기대하고 있다. 향후 몇 달 동안은, 고객들이 크레이버 씨에게 작별을 고하고 래스트 씨를 환영할 수 있는 여러 특별 행사들이 있을 것이다.

어휘 hand over 넘겨주다 | diner 작은 식당 | run 운영하다 | reputation 명성, 평판 | high-end 고급의 | profitable 수익성이 있는 | carry on with ~을 계속하다 | all goes well (일이) 만사태평하다 | meanwhile 한편 | from time to time 가끔 | as usual 여느 때와 다름없이 | patron 고객 | bid farewell 작별을 고하다 | transition 전환 | for now 현재로는, 당분간은

---

7. 기사는 왜 쓰였는가?
   (A) 지역 어느 식당의 폐업을 발표하기 위해
   (B) 새 음료수 제품군을 홍보하기 위해
   (C) 어떤 회사의 이전을 설명하기 위해
   (D) 사업체 소유권의 전환을 보도하기 위해

해설 기사의 목적을 물어보는 문제로, 첫 문장의 '카페의 열쇠를 넘겨준다'에서 사업체의 주인이 바뀐다는 내용의 기사임을 알 수 있으므로 (D) To report on a transition of business ownership이 정답이다.

---

8. 크레이버 씨는 더 라이트 로스트를 어떤 식으로 변화시켰는가?
   (A) 더 좋은 장비를 사용했다.
   (B) 더 많은 고객이 들어오도록 공간을 확장했다.
   (C) 메뉴의 선택 사항을 변경했다.
   (D) 매장 인테리어를 다시 장식했다.

해설 남편으로부터 사업을 물려받은 후 식사 제공은 중단하고 음료와 디저트에 주력했다는 내용이 있으므로 이 부분을 paraphrasing한 (C) She changed the menu options. 가 정답이다.

---

9. 더 라이트 로스트에 관하여 무엇이 언급되었는가?
   (A) 오직 한 납품업체만 이용한다.
   (B) 국제적으로 알려져 있다.
   (C) 최근 할인 판매를 했다.
   (D) 이름을 변경할 것이다.

해설 더블린에 있는 사업체임에도 불구하고 도쿄나 요하네스버그와 같은 외국 도시에도 알려져 있으므로 이 업체는 국제적으로 유명한 곳이다. 따라서 정답은 (B) It is known internationally. 이다.

---

10. [1], [2], [3], [4]로 표시된 곳 중에서 다음 문장이 들어가기에 가장 적절한 곳은 어디인가?

   "현재로는, 전국의 라이트 로스트 팬들은 더 자세한 발표를 기다리는 수밖에 없습니다."

   (A) [1]
   (B) [2]
   (C) [3]
   (D) [4]

해설 주어진 문장은 불확실한 계획과 연관되는 내용이라고 볼 수 있는데, 빈칸 [4]의 앞 문장이 아직 확정되지 않은 새 지점 개업에 관한 내용이다. 이곳에 주어진 문장을 넣으면 문맥이 자연스러우므로 정답은 (D) [4]이다.

[11-14] 다음 기사에 관한 문제입니다.

신설 사업이 포틀랜드에 활기를 불어넣다

1월 30일 – 스카일락 사가 다음 주에 첫 소매점을 개점한다. **11** 저비용의 태양 전지판을 제공하고자 하는 스카일락의 사명에는 앞으로 3년간 3개의 소매점을 개점하는 것이 포함되어 있다. **12** 오리건주 포틀랜드에 있는 상점은 스카일락의 가장 큰 매장이 될 것이며 올해 회사 판매의 거의 40퍼센트를 차지할 것으로 예상된다.

본사 옆에 위치해 있는 스카일락의 첫 번째 매장은 매우 다양한 가정용 및 상업용 제품들을 제공할 것이다. 벌써, 150명이 넘는 계약자들이 회사의 우대 고객 약정에 가입했다.

스카일락의 전문경영인 브라이언 카샤니에 의하면 이렇게 놀라운 출발은 당사뿐만 아니라 산업 전체를 위해서도 중요한 사건임을 보여 준다. "이 회사를 설립하는 데 있어서, 우리는 많은 시간, 자본 그리고 많은 노력이 요구되리라는 것을 알고 있었습니다." **14** "우리는 건설 업체들과 지방 정부로부터 받은 도움에 감사하게 생각합니다." 이곳 포틀랜드에 있는 우리가 사용할 수 있는 자원들 덕분에, 우리는 단지 주거 지역 구매자들뿐만 아니라 지역 건설 산업을 위해서도 많은 기회를 창출할 수 있었습니다."하고 카샤니 씨는 설명했다. **13** "캘리포니아에 위치할 우리의 다음 매장은 일사분기 말에 개점합니다. 샌디에이고 매장은 현재 건설 중이며, 우리의 매장을 맡는 데 관심이 있는 도시들에서 벌써 연락이 오고 있습니다."

다른 소매점들은 몬태나주와 콜로라도주에서 개점한다. 이 매장들은 포틀랜드 분점보다는 규모가 작지만, 앞으로 성장해서 그들의 지역 사회에 기여할 것으로 기대된다.

어휘 startup 신설 사업 | energize 활기를 불어넣다 | retail 소매 | mission 사명, 임무 | low-cost 저비용의 | solar panel 태양 전지판 | project 예측하다 | make up 차지하다, 구성하다 | commercial 상업용의 | contractor 계약자, 용역업체 | preferred-customer 우대 고객 | plan 약정 | represent ~을 보여 주다[나타내다] | milestone 중대 시점, 이정표 | resource (주로 복수로) 자원 | residential 주택지의 | host (사업 등을) 맡아서 돌보다 | branch 분점, 지사 | serve a community 지역 사회에 기여하다 | grateful 감사히 여기는

---

11. 스카일락 사에 관하여 사실인 것은 무엇인가?

    (A) 최근에 인수되었다.

    (B) 주로 주택 보유자들과 거래를 한다.

    (C) 적당한 가격의 에너지 제품들을 판매한다.

    (D) 본사를 이전할 것이다.

해설 본문에서 스카일락 사에서 저가의 태양 전지판을 제공한다고 나와있으므로 '저가의'라는 말을 paraphrasing한 (C) It sells affordable energy products. 가 정답이다.

---

12. 포틀랜드에 있는 매장에 관하여 언급된 것은 무엇인가?

    (A) 건설 중인 유일한 매장이다.

    (B) 다른 분점들보다 수입이 적다.

    (C) 태양열로 운영된다.

    (D) 회사에서 제일 큰 매장이다.

해설 질문의 키워드인 포틀랜드를 지문에서 찾아보면 가장 클 것이라고 나와 있으므로 정답은 (D) It is the company's largest store. 이다.

---

13. 다음 스카일락 매장은 어디에 지어질 것인가?

    (A) 오리건에

    (B) 캘리포니아에

    (C) 몬태나에

    (D) 콜로라도에

해설 지문의 세 번째 단락에서 캘리포니아가 다음으로 지어질 곳이라고 나와 있으므로 정답은 (B) In California이다.

---

14. [1], [2], [3], [4]로 표시된 곳 중에서 다음 문장이 들어가기에 가장 적절한 곳은 어디인가?

    "우리는 건설 업체들과 지방 정부로부터 받은 도움에 감사하게 생각합니다."

    (A) [1]

    (B) [2]

    (C) [3]

    (D) [4]

해설 주어진 문장에서 건설회사나 지방 정부에서 받은 도움에 감사하다고 하므로, 앞뒤에 도움을 받은 구체적인 내용이 나와 있는 곳을 찾아보면 되는데, 빈칸 [3] 뒤에 Thanks to로 시작하면서 주어진 자원의 덕택으로 지역 산업에 영향을 미칠 수 있었다는 구체적 내용이 나오므로 정답은 (C) [3]이다.

[15-19] 다음 편지와 기사에 관한 문제입니다.

듀클랜드 전자

12월 5일

투자자 여러분께:

저희 회사가 공기업으로 출범한 지 햇수로 2년이 되어가며, 그동안 커다란 진전을 이뤄냈습니다. **15** 이제 저희는 온라인 전용 소매점에서 멜버른에 오프라인 매장을 내는 방향으로 사업을 확장할 예정입니다.

상당한 기간 동안 다음과 같은 변화를 준비해 왔습니다.

· 4월에는, 위럴 빌라즈 복합 건물에 저희의 첫 번째 플래그십 매장을 위한 소매점 공간을 확보했습니다.

· 6월에는, 쿠빙 시공사와 계약을 체결하고 매장을 건설하기 시작했습니다.

· 10월에는, 제이피 가정용품 및 디프로브 가전과 제휴를 맺고 해당 업체 제품을 저희 매장에 도입했습니다.

내년에는 성공적인 매장 개장을 중점으로 활동할 예정입니다. 저희의 계획은 다음과 같습니다.

· **16** 3월부터 고객이 매장에서 보고 싶은 것에 관해 설문 조사를 실시한다.

· 5월에는 포커스 그룹을 매장으로 초대해 매장 이용 경험에 관한 피드백을 수집한다.

· **18** 7월 17일에는 매장 개장 행사를 개최한다.

다가올 계획에 대해 저희만큼이나 기뻐하시길 바랍니다. 조만간 더 많은 소식으로 찾아뵙겠습니다.

진심으로,

일레인 타운센드, 전문경영인

어휘 investor 투자자 | approach 다가가다 | stride 진전 | expand 확장하다 | solely 오로지, 단독으로 | retail 소매점 | include 포함하다 | brick-and-mortar store 오프라인 매장 | move (행동의) 변화, 움직임 | in the works 논의[진행]되고 있는 | secure 확보하다 | flagship store 대표 매장 | complex 복합 건물, 건물 단지 | partner with ~와 제휴를 맺다 | homeware 가정용품 | appliance 가정용 기기 | poll 여론 조사를 하다 | invite 초대하다 | focus group 포커스 그룹 | gather 수집하다, 모으다 | in-store 매장 내의 | host 주최하다

18 멜버른(8월 12일) — 주말 동안 위럴 빌라즈 복합 건물에 듀클랜드 전자가 입점했다. **17** 전자제품 매장은 2년 전 복합 건물이 문을 열었을 때부터 개장한 최초의 매장 중 하나인 카이버 홀에 합류하게 된다. 이번 주에, 스노엘프 스포츠라는 또 다른 매장이 추가로 문을 열 것이다.

위럴 빌라즈의 운영팀은 서관을 추가 매장들에 개방할 계획이다. 복합 건물에의 사업 수요가 급등하면서, 소매점 공간을 놓고 경쟁이 아주 치열해질 전망이다. 위럴 빌라즈의 대변인인 티나 고든은 회사가 나아가는 **19** 방향에 대해 팀에서 아주 흡족해하고 있다고 언급했다.

어휘 additional 추가의 | management 운영, 관리 | intend 의도하다 | open up 가능하게 하다, 문을 열다 | spike 급등, 급증 | expectation 기대, 예상 | fight 싸움 | highly 매우 | competitive 경쟁을 하는 | spokesperson 대변인 | comment 견해를 밝히다

15. 편지의 하나의 목적은 무엇인가?

    (A) 구인 공고를 내기 위해

    (B) 계획에 대한 최신 정보를 제공하기 위해

(C) 제품에 대한 관심을 알아내기 위해

(D) 프로젝트에 대한 협력 관계를 모색하기 위해

해설   편지 지문의 도입부에서 오프라인 매장을 내는 사업을 확장하는 내용을 설명하고 있으므로 (B) To provide updates on a plan이 정답이다.

---

16. 편지에 따르면, 고객들은 언제 설문조사를 받겠는가?

(A) 3월에

(B) 6월에

(C) 7월에

(D) 10월에

해설   편지 지문에서 3월부터 고객 대상으로 설문 조사를 실시할 것으로 나와 있으므로 (A) In March가 정답이다. poll이 survey로 paraphrasing되었다.

---

17. 기사는 카이버 홀에 관하여 어떤 점을 시사하는가?

(A) 멜버른 지역 도처에 여러 매장이 있다.

(B) 최소 2년째 복합 건물에 입점해 있었다.

(C) 최근 매장을 개조했다.

(D) 위럴 빌라즈 복합 건물 내 최대 규모의 매장이다.

해설   기사 지문 첫 번째 단락에서 카이버 홀이 2년 전 복합 건물이 문을 열었을 때부터 개장한 최초의 매장이라고 나와 있으므로 (B) It has been in the complex for at least two years. 가 정답이다.

---

18. 듀클랜드 전자 매장에 관하여 알 수 있는 것은?

(A) 제이피 가정용품에서 소유한다.

(B) 복합 건물의 서관에 위치한다.

(C) 자사 제품에 대해 무료 배송을 제공한다.

(D) 개장일을 미뤄야 했다.

해설   편지 지문 세 번째 단락을 보면 개장 행사를 7월 17일에 개최하는 것으로 나와 있는데 기사 지문 첫 번째 단락에서 개장이 8월로 미뤄졌음을 알 수 있으므로 (D) It had to delay its grand opening. 이 정답이다.

---

19. 기사 두 번째 문단, 여덟 번째 줄의 단어 "direction"에 의미상 가장 가까운 것은

(A) 방향

(B) 순서

(C) 범위

(D) 책임

해설   direction은 '방향'의 의미이며 이 문장에서는 회사가 나아가는 방향을 말하므로 같은 의미를 갖는 (A) path가 정답이다.

[20-24] 다음 기사와 광고, 평론에 관한 문제입니다.

재스퍼 사 브랜드 이미지를 쇄신하다

20 포틀랜드 (10월 22일) 시애틀의 프레쉬 디쉬 다이렉트가 6개의 지역 건강 식당을 운영하는 회사 재스퍼 사를 인수하는 작업이 완료되었다. 프레쉬 디쉬 다이렉트는 재스퍼 사의 식당들을 합치며 이제 포틀랜드와 주변 지역에 17개의 식당을 운영하게 되었다.

22 프레쉬 디쉬 다이렉트는 이 체인 사업체를 매입하기 전, 이미 가격을 의식하는 고객들을 겨냥한 알맞은 가격의 메뉴로 잘 알려져 있었다. 반면, 재스퍼 사의 여섯 지점은 특별한 분위기와 최고 품질의 재료에 돈을 좀 더 쓰기 원하는 사람들의 취향에 부합한다. 1935년에 설립된 고전적인 스타일의 식당 로 슬라이스와 하트 그레인은 시내에서 가장 높은 평가를 받는 채식주의 식당들로, 현재 프레쉬 디쉬 다이렉트가 운영하고 있다.

"재스퍼 사의 식당들은 프레쉬 디쉬 다이렉트의 포트폴리오를 완성시켜줍니다." 프레쉬 디쉬 다이렉트 홍보 담당 이사 토니 알론조가 말했다. **20** "이들이 고객들과 비평가들로부터 얻은 인기는 새 사업 분야에서 우리를 강력한 경쟁 업체로 만들어 줄 것이며, 반면 재스퍼 사는 이제 대기업 재정 자원의 혜택을 볼 수 있습니다."

어휘   rebrand 브랜드 이미지를 새롭게 하다 | health-conscious 건강을 고려한 | property 건물 | affordable (가격이) 알맞은 | meanwhile 한편 | cater to ~의 구미에 맞추다 | atmosphere 분위기 | bistro 작은 식당 | complement 보완하다 | PR(public relations) 홍보 | critic 비평가 | benefit from ~으로부터 이익을 얻다

---

21 다운타운 포틀랜드

외식하신다고요? 예산이 한정되어 있는, 비평가들이 극찬해 마지않는 곳을 찾고 싶든 프레쉬 디쉬 다이렉트는 포틀랜드에 모든 이들에게 알맞은 식당들을 갖추고 있습니다. **21** 다음번 시내에 나오실 때, 다음 식당 중 한 군데에 꼭 들러보세요.

클라우드 나인

클라우드 나인은 낮에는 카페로 밤에는 고급 식당으로, 가장 신선한 재료만을 사용하여 대표 샐러드와 파스타를 전문으로 만듭니다. 인테리어의 우아함은 시내에서 비길 데가 없습니다.

22 테리 멜리

간단한 그릴 치즈 샌드위치를 먹고 싶든, 푸짐한 쇠고기 수프를 원하든, 이 동네 식당은 적당한 가격 때문에 매력적입니다.

탑 셸프

지중해 요리를 전문으로 하는 탑 셸프는 연중무휴로 맛있으면서 건강에 좋고 신선한 요리를 제공합니다. 호화로운 분위기와 요리에 관하여 잘 아는 웨이터들이 이곳을 주목할 만한 식당으로 만들어줍니다.

콜드워터 가든

강변에서 5성급 식사를 경험해 보세요. 다양한 음료와 함께 훌륭한 식사를 즐기세요. **23** 이제는 최근 완공된 윌리어멧 강을 내려다보는 데크에서 야외 좌석도 이용하실 수 있습니다. 드레스코드는 정장이며, 예약은 필수입니다.

저희 웹사이트 www.freshdishdirect.com/locations에서 포틀랜드 지역의 저희의 다른 유명 식당들도 둘러보세요.

어휘 **on a budget** 한정된 예산으로 | **rave** 격찬하다, 극찬하다 | **suit** (~에게) 알맞다, 편리하다 | **eatery** 음식점, 식당 | **fine dining** 고급 식당 | **unrivaled** 타의 추종을 불허하는 | **in the mood for** ~할 기분이 나서 | **hearty** 푸짐한 | **establishment** 기관, 시설 | **appealing** 매력적인 | **cuisine** 요리 | **flavorful** 맛좋은 | **year-round** 1년 내내 | **knowledgeable** 박식한 | **remarkable** 주목할 만한 | **luxurious** 호화로운 | **waterfront** 물가 | **overlooking** 내려다보는 | **dress code** 복장 규정

---

23 콜드워터 가든
★★★★☆

이 식당은 정말 기대 이상이었습니다. 올리브와 치즈 애피타이저는 매우 친절한 웨이트리스가 추천해 준 음료수와 멋지게 조화를 이루었습니다. 랍스터는 딱 알맞게 요리되어 나왔고 더할 나위 없이 신선했습니다! **24** 그러나, 발레파킹 직원은 차를 가져오는 게 느려서, 거의 30분이나 추운 날씨에 서 있어야 했습니다. 이 점 외에는, 이 식당에서 식사하는 것을 강력히 추천합니다.

23 24 사무엘 오르테즈
스페인, 바르셀로나

어휘 **exceed** 초과하다 | **pair** 짝을 짓다 | **attendant** 종업원 | **retrieve** 되찾아오다 | **other than** ~외에

---

20. 프레쉬 디쉬 다이렉트에 관하여 무엇이 시사되어 있는가?
(A) 고급 식당 경영 경험이 많다.
(B) 더 다양한 손님들의 취향을 맞출 계획이다.
(C) 포틀랜드에 새 본사가 있다.
(D) 단골손님에게 할인을 제공한다.

해설 기사 지문에서 프레쉬 디쉬 다이렉트가 재스퍼 사를 인수를 한다는 내용이 나오면서, 좀 더 경쟁력 있는 위치에 놓이게 된다는 말이 나오므로 종합해 보면 폭넓은 종류의 서비스를 제공할 수 있다는 (B) It plans to cater to a wider range of diners. 가 정답이다.

---

21. 광고에 나온 네 식당에 관하여 무엇이 언급되어 있는가?
(A) 모두 1930년대에 설립되었다.
(B) 모두 상을 받았다.
(C) 모두 포틀랜드 시내에 근거지를 두고 있다.
(D) 모두 예약이 필요하다.

해설 광고 지문에서 답을 찾아보면, 제일 상단에 다운타운 포틀랜드가 있으며, 프레쉬 디쉬 다이렉트가 포틀랜드에 식당이 여러 개가 있으며, 다음에 방문할 기회가 있으면 들르라고 했기 때문에 정답은 (C) They are all based in downtown Portland. 이다.

---

22. 재스퍼 사의 지점이 아닌 식당은 어디겠는가?
(A) 클라우드 나인
(B) 테리스 델리
(C) 탑 셸프
(D) 콜드워터 가든

해설 연계 지문 문제로 첫 번째 지문 기사 두 번째 단락에서 재스퍼 사의 식당들은 특별한 분위기와 최고 품질에 돈을 좀 더 쓰기 원하는 고객들에 부합한다고 하였으므로, 두 번째 지문 광고에서 저렴한 가격의 (B) Terry's Deli는 재스퍼 사의 고급 식당 지점이 아니다.

---

23. 오르테즈 씨가 식사한 식당에 관하여 어떤 정보가 주어지는가?
(A) 샌드위치로 유명하다.
(B) 일주일 내내 문을 연다.
(C) 최근 새 직원들을 채용했다.
(D) 추가적인 좌석 공간을 마련했다.

해설 연계 지문 문제로, 세 번째 평론 지문에서 오르테즈 씨가 콜드워터 가든에 대해서 평가하고 있음을 알 수 있고, 두 번째 광고 지문에서 이 식당을 보면, 최근에 야외 좌석도 있다고 설명되어 있으므로 정답은 (D) It has added another seating area. 이다.

---

24. 오르테즈 씨는 경험의 무엇이 실망스러웠는가?
(A) 부정확한 주문
(B) 비싼 청구 금액
(C) 서비스의 지연
(D) 질 낮은 음식

해설 오르테즈 씨가 실망한 부분은 마지막 지문에서 답을 찾을 수가 있으며, 발레파킹 직원의 서비스 문제로 30분을 기다렸다는 내용이 나오므로 정답은 (C) A delay in a service이다.

UNIT 06. 양식

핵심 문제 유형
본서 p.273

1. (A)   2. (D)

[1-2] 다음 청구서에 관한 문제입니다.

웨스트우드 포토 앤 비디오
날짜: 10월 22일
구매자: 제프 키처너
우편 주소: 제프 키처너
2425 킹 가, 시애틀, 워싱턴 89807

청구지 주소: 제프 키처너
7876 콘웰 가, 터코마, 워싱턴 88745

고객 계정 번호: 8823142

배송 추적 번호: DVL-33978

지불 방법: 신용 카드 (8872-0797-XXXX)

❷ 구매 품목	가격
펜탁스 옵티마 카메라	349.00달러
64기가바이트 메모리 카드	46.00달러
텐바 카메라 가방	25.00달러

❶ 배송비: 0.00달러

합계: 420달러

❶ *저희와 10년 이상 거래한 고객은 무료 배송 자격이 주어집니다.

웨스트우드 포토 앤 비디오와 거래해 주셔서 감사합니다. 귀하의 주문은 영업일 기준으로 3일 후에 도착할 것입니다. 주문과 관련하여 질문이 있으면, 1-800-555-9654로 소비자 상담실에 수신자 부담 전화를 하세요. 감사합니다.

어휘 mailing address 우편 주소 | billing 청구서 발부 | account 계정 | shipping tracking 배송 추적 | method of payment 지불 방법 | item 물품, 품목 | eligible for ~의 자격이 있는 | business day 영업일 | regarding ~에 관해 | toll free 수신자 부담으로

1. 키쳐너 씨에 관해 암시된 것은 무엇인가?

(A) 오래된 고객이다.

(B) 특급 배송을 선택하였다.

(C) 전문 사진가이다.

(D) 최근에 터코마로 이사했다.

해설 배송료가 0달러임을 확인하고, 10년 이상 거래한 고객은 배송비가 무료라고 하였으므로 (A) He is a long-time customer. 이다.

- -

2. 고객이 주문하지 않은 물품은 무엇인가?

(A) 메모리 카드

(B) 가방

(C) 카메라

(D) 삼각대

해설 표의 Items purchased의 항목을 찾아보면 주문한 물품 목록에 삼각대는 없으므로 정답은 (D) A tripod이다.

- -

Practice

본서 p.274

1. (D)	**2.** (B)	**3.** (C)	**4.** (B)	**5.** (C)
6. (A)	**7.** (D)	**8.** (B)	**9.** (A)	**10.** (A)
11. (A)	**12.** (C)	**13.** (C)	**14.** (C)	**15.** (C)
16. (C)	**17.** (D)	**18.** (C)	**19.** (C)	**20.** (A)

[1-2] 다음 영수증에 관한 문제입니다.

브라이트 센터

13 W. 피치트리 가

애틀랜타, 조지아 30309

(404) 258-3921

브라이트 센터에서 쇼핑해 주셔서 감사합니다!

#72934	❶ 광택지 2팩	9.98달러
#32948	화첩	6.00달러
#92843	폼브러시	1.99달러
#09232	그래픽펜	4.95달러
	소계	22.92달러
	세금(8%)	1.83달러
	총계	24.75달러

지불 현금: 24.75달러

사용하지 않은 상품은 구매 15일 이내에 영수증을 지참할 경우 교환이나 환불받을 수 있습니다.

안내데스크에 가시거나 관리자에게 매장 환불 및 교환 정책에 관하여 문의하세요.

❷ 평가 카드를 작성해서 계산 직원에게 제출하시고, 다음 구매 시 20%를 할인받으세요 (최대 50달러)!

어휘 glossy paper 광택지 | drawing pad 화첩 | subtotal 소계 | tender 지불하다

1. 브라이트 센터는 어떠한 유형의 사업체이겠는가?

(A) 컴퓨터 수리점

(B) 슈퍼마켓

(C) 인쇄소

(D) 미술용품점

해설 영수증에 나와 있는 품목이 화첩, 폼브러시, 그래픽펜 등으로 미술용품을 판매하는 곳이라는 것을 유추할 수 있다. 따라서 정답은 (D) An art supply store이다.

- -

2. 영수증에 따르면, 고객은 어떻게 할인을 받을 수 있는가?

(A) 50달러 이상 구매함으로써

(B) 피드백을 제공함으로써

(C) 매장 관리자에게 말함으로써

(D) 안내데스크에 전화함으로써

해설 평가서를 작성해서 제출하면 20%를 할인받을 수 있다고 나와 있으므로 이 부분을 paraphrasing한 (B) By providing some feedback이 정답이다.

[3-4] 다음 문서에 관한 문제입니다.

3 카본 카피어스

주문 번호: 피에이4501엘

연락처: 매들린 던
애로우코프 사
m.dunn@arrowcorp.ca
555-7874

요청 내용: 연례 마케팅 보고서
스프링 제본 500부, 329 페이지(A4)
무늬 없는 백지

3 프로젝트 담당자: 잭 슈프

주문 일자: 11월 7일

4 완성 일자: 11월 10일

특별 요청 사항: 익일배송으로 보내주세요; 우편요금은 선불로 결제됨.

어휘 annual 매년, 연례의 | spiral-bound 스프링 제본된 |
plain 무늬가 없는 | designate 지정하다 | via ~을 통해 |
overnight 밤새 | stationery 문구류 | eligible for ~의 자
격이 있는

---

3. 슈프 씨는 어디에서 주로 일하겠는가?
(A) 애로우코프 사에서
(B) 우체국에서
(C) 카본 카피어스에서
(D) 문구점에서

해설 지문이 서류 제본 주문서인데, 슈프 씨가 이 제본 업무의 담당자이므
로 이 사람은 주문을 받은 카본 카피어스 인쇄소의 직원이라는 것을
알 수 있다. 따라서 정답은 (C) At Carbon Copiers이다.

---

4. 문서에서 던 씨에 대해 암시하는 것은 무엇인가?
(A) 특별 컬러 종이를 요청했다.
(B) 그녀의 주문은 11월 11일에 배송될 것이다.
(C) 11월 7일에 카본 카피어스에 들를 것이다.
(D) 그녀가 한 구매는 할인 대상이다.

해설 서류 제본 완성 일자가 11월 10일인데 특별 요청 사항을 보면 익일배
송을 요청했으므로 완성된 물건은 11월 11일에 던 씨에게 전달될 것
이라는 걸 유추할 수 있다. 그러므로 정답은 (B) Her order will be
delivered on November 11. 이다.

[5-7] 다음 서식에 관한 문제입니다.

미국 수면 장애 협회
회원 가입 신청서

6 30여 년간, 미국 수면 장애 협회(에스디에이에이)는 더 나은 치
료법을 찾기 위한 연구의 자금을 대 왔으며 **전문가와 도움이 필요한
이들을 연결시켜 주는 일을** 해왔습니다. 내과 의사부터 임상 연구원
까지, 저희 회원들은 다양한 분야를 전문으로 하고 있습니다.

에스디에이에이 회원은 다음과 같은 혜택을 받습니다:

6 • 연례 세미나 무료입장
5 • 웹사이트에서 구매한 모든 물품에 대한 30% 할인
6 • 에스디에이에이 월간 소식지 무료
• 연구 기록 보관소의 이용 권한

오늘 신청하세요!

이름: _____
기관: _____
주소: _____
이메일: _____
전화: _____

연회비
☐ 의료 전문가 - 125달러
☐ 연구원 - 80달러
☐ **7** 수면 장애가 있는 개인 - 무료

지불정보
신용 카드 번호: _____
만료일: _____

에스디에이에이
미국 수면 장애 협회

어휘 disorder 장애 | association 협회 | fund 자금을 대다 |
treatment 치료 | specialist 전문가 | physician
의사, 내과의사 | specialize in ~을 전문으로 하다 |
complimentary 무료의 | access to ~에 대한 접근 |
archive 기록 보관소 | expiration 만료 | consultation 상
담 | host 개최하다

---

5. 할인된 가격으로 제공되는 것은 무엇인가?
(A) 잡지 구독권
(B) 연구 자료 이용 권한
(C) 온라인으로 판매되는 제품
(D) 의료 상담

해설 문제에 '할인된 가격'을 키워드로 보고, 지문에서 회원 혜택의 두 번째
항목의 30 percent off를 찾을 수 있다. '웹사이트에서 구매한 모든
물품을 paraphrasing한 (C) Products sold online이 정답이다.

---

6. 에스디에이에이에 대해 알 수 있는 것이 아닌 것은 무엇인가?
(A) 여러 진료소를 운영한다.
(B) 연간 행사를 개최한다.
(C) 30여 년 전에 설립되었다.
(D) 소식지를 발행한다.

해설 지문의 첫 번째 문장에서 보기 (C)의 내용을 유추해 낼 수 있으며, 회
원 혜택의 첫 번째 항목에 있는 our annual seminars라는 말을 통
해 (B)도 유추할 수 있다. 또한, 회원 혜택의 세 번째 항목에서 (D)의
내용도 알 수 있으므로 지문에 언급되지 않은 내용인 (A) It manages
several clinics. 가 정답이다.

7. 에스디에이에이에서 무료로 혜택을 받을 수 있는 사람은 누구인가?

    (A) 의사

    (B) 연구원

    (C) 대학생

    (D) 환자

해설   문제에 for free라는 키워드의 동의어를 찾아보면, 연회비 부분의 세 번째 항목에 보이는 no charge이고, 수면 장애가 있는 개인은 무료로 회원이 될 수 있음을 알 수 있다. 그러므로 Individuals with sleep disorders의 동의어인 (D) Patients가 정답이다.

[8-10] 다음 양식에 관한 문제입니다.

브리즈 호텔

브리즈를 이용해 주셔서 고맙습니다! 🔟 고객님의 투숙 경험이 어 떠했는지 의견을 말씀해 주셔서, 저희가 고객들에게 더 나은 경험을 제공하도록 도와주시기 바랍니다. 편하실 때, 이 설문 조사를 작성하 여 체크아웃할 때 제출해 주시면 유용한 지역 사업체들의 쿠폰북을 받으실 수 있습니다.

날짜: 8월 4일

고객명: 제이미 보헴

연락처: (307) 555-7942

투숙날짜 / 지점

8월 1일–3일 / 뉴올리언스 브리즈 호텔

비고: 스탠다드룸으로 예약했으나 스위트룸으로 옮김

4를 '최고'로 했을 때, 1부터 4까지의 범위 내에서 각 영역을 어떻게 등급을 매기시겠습니까?

· 투숙객 서비스

전문성	1	2	③	4
예약 시스템	1	②	3	4

· 객실

정돈 / 청결	1	2	3	④
🔟 안락함	1	2	3	④

저희 호텔에 다시 투숙하시겠습니까?	네	아니오	불확실함
타인에게 투숙을 권하시겠습니까?	네	아니오	불확실함

고객 의견:

저는 출장 갈 때마다 브리즈 호텔을 이용하고 있고 항상 만족해왔습 니다. 그런데, 최근, 제가 뉴올리언스 지점에 도착했을 때, 예약이 취 소되었다는 것을 알게 되었습니다. 제 비행편이 연착되었고 제가 예 정보다 훨씬 늦게 체크인한 것은 사실이지만, 안내데스크에서 이렇 게 하기 전에 전화를 해주거나 이메일이라도 한번 보냈어야 합니다. 🔟 저는 직원에게 더 비싼 방이라도 이용하게 해달라고 할 수밖에 없었습니다.

어휘   **clientele** 고객들 | **at your convenience** 편하실 때 | **complete** 기입하다 | **present** 제출하다 | **scale** 규모 | **rate** 등급을 매기다 | **neatness** 깔끔, 정돈 | **comfort** 안 락, 편안 | **have no choice but to** ~할 수밖에 없다 | **measure** 측정하다 | **performance** 업무 실적

---

8. 브리즈 호텔은 양식에서 수집한 데이터를 어떻게 사용하겠는가?

    (A) 직원 업무 실적을 평가한다

    (B) 고객 만족도를 향상시킨다

    (C) 더 나은 체크인 시스템을 설계한다

    (D) 일부 영역의 비용을 절감한다

해설   지문 초반에 고객들의 투숙 기간의 의견을 말씀해 주시면, 더 나은 경 험을 제공하겠다고 나와 있으므로 provide a better experience for our clientele을 paraphrasing한 (B) Improve customer satisfaction이 정답이다.

---

9. 보헴 씨는 호텔 객실에 관하여 어떤 점을 시사하는가?

    (A) 꽤 편안했다.

    (B) 매우 불결했다.

    (C) 가격이 할인되었다.

    (D) 애초에 스위트룸으로 예약되었다.

해설   설문 조사 표의 객실(Room) 평가에서 안락함(Comfort) 부문에서 최 고(4) 점수를 주었으므로 보헴 씨는 호텔 객실을 편안한 곳으로 느꼈다 는 것을 알 수 있다. 그러므로 (A) It was quite comfortable. 이 정 답이다.

---

10. 보헴 씨는 자신이 경험한 서비스에 관하여 어떤 점을 시사하는가?

    (A) 호텔이 예상보다 비용을 더 부과했다.

    (B) 예약 시스템이 사용하기 수월했다.

    (C) 안내데스크가 너무 일찍 문을 닫았다.

    (D) 취소 때문에 비행편이 연착했다.

해설   보헴 씨가 경험한 것에 대해 구체적으로 물어보므로 지문 하단에 있는 고객 의견을 읽어보면, 예약이 취소되는 바람에 어쩔 수 없이 더 비싼 방을 이용해야 했다고 말하고 있으므로 (A) The hotel charged her more than expected. 가 정답이다.

[11-15] 다음 이메일과 문서에 관한 문제입니다.

발신: 다부 버마 〈diyav@xmail.com〉

수신: 고객 지원 센터 〈help@federalrent.com〉

🔟 제목: 계약 문의

🔟 날짜: 4월 9일

저는 귀사 월 임대 프로그램의 장기 회원입니다. 그러나, 세인트 루 이스로 곧 돌아갈 것이라서, 서비스가 더 이상 필요하지 않게 됐습 니다. 🔟 제 계약(#에프알216)은 🔟 자동으로 갱신되므로, 자동 갱 신이 있기 전에 차를 반납하고 싶습니다. 그렇게 하면, 다음 달 요금 이 청구되지 않을 테니까요.

🔟 4월 30일에 떠날 것인데 항공권은 아직 구매하지 않았습니다. 🔟 차를 최소 4월 29일까지는 사용하고 싶습니다. 그러나, 계약 갱 신이 그 전에 일어난다면, 이번 달 계약의 마지막 날에 차를 반납하 겠습니다.

적절한 준비를 할 수 있도록 정확히 어느 날짜에 다음번 갱신이 있 는지 회신 주시기 바랍니다.

안부를 전하며,

다부 버마

페더럴 렌트			
현재 월 임대 계약			
월 임대의 마지막 날짜	월 요금	차종	계약 번호
3	250달러	보칸트	에프알752
30	310달러	마르와리	에프알413
29	285달러	색슨	에프알398
14 28	**13** 305달러	프레이시안	에프알216

* **15** 계약 종료 시, 임차인은 계약서에 명시된 날짜 오후 5시 전에 차량을 반납해야 한다. 이것이 이루어지지 않을 경우 자동차 계약의 자동 갱신이 발생한다.

11. 이메일의 목적은 무엇인가?

(A) 계약 세부 사항을 요청하기 위해

(B) 서비스 비용에 대해 문의하기 위해

(C) 임대 상품을 홍보하기 위해

(D) 티켓 구매를 확인하기 위해

해설 대부분 이메일의 목적은 지문 전반에 있거나, 이메일 제목만 봐도 잘 알 수 있다. 제목이 '계약 문의'이므로 (A) To ask for contract details가 정답이다.

12. 버마 씨에 대한 무엇이 사실이겠는가?

(A) 페더럴 렌트에서 일한다.

(B) 세인트 루이스에 가족이 살고 있다.

(C) 곧 비행편을 예약할 것이다.

(D) 주중에만 차를 사용한다.

해설 이메일을 보낸 날짜가 4월 9일인데, 떠나는 날짜는 4월 30일이고 아직 항공권은 구매하지 않았다고 했다. 여기서 곧 비행편을 예약할 것이라고 유추할 수 있으므로 (C) He will book a flight soon. 이 정답이다.

13. 버마 씨의 월 요금은 얼마인가?

(A) 250달러

(B) 285달러

(C) 305달러

(D) 310달러

해설 숫자에 관련된 문제는 거의 연계 지문인데, 이 문제 역시 첫 번째 지문에서 계약번호가 #에프알216이라고 했으며, 두 번째 지문의 도표에 월 요금을 찾아보면 (C) $305가 정답이다.

14. 버마 씨는 어느 날짜에 차를 반납해야 하는가?

(A) 4월 3일

(B) 4월 28일

(C) 4월 29일

(D) 4월 30일

해설 역시나 날짜가 나오는 연계 지문 문제로, 첫 번째 이메일에서 버마 씨는 계약이 자동으로 갱신되기 전에 차를 반납하고자 하며 최소 4월 29일까지는 차를 사용하고 싶지만, 계약이 그전에 갱신된다면 계약 마지막 날에 차를 반납하겠다고 말했다. 이메일에 나와 있는 버마 씨의 계약번호 #에프알216을 임대 계약 목록에서 찾아보면 만료 날짜가 4월 28일이라고 나와 있으므로 정답은 (B) April 28이다.

15. 월간 계약에 대해 사실인 것은 무엇인가?

(A) 매월 말일에 만료된다.

(B) 무료 운행 유도 시스템을 포함한다.

(C) 계약 마지막 날짜 오후 5시 이후에 연장된다.

(D) 6개월 단위로만 제공된다.

해설 임대 계약 목록 아래에 늦어도 계약서에 명시된 마지막 날짜 오후 5시까지 차를 반납하지 않으면 계약이 자동 갱신된다고 나와 있으므로 정답은 (C) It is extended after 5 P.M. on the last contract date. 이다.

[16-20] 다음 양식과 이메일, 편지에 관한 문제입니다.

www.sabatierauctions.com/SAC_form

사바티에 경매 카탈로그 응답 양식

16 이름: 호르헤 페레즈

직책: 인수 이사

이메일: jperez@zgsca23.com

전화번호: 415-555-3323

사바티에 경매 카탈로그(에스에이씨)가 우편으로만 수신되기 때문에, 다양한 갤러리를 대표하는 입찰자들이 때때로 부정적인 영향을 받고 있습니다. 저희의 경우, 카탈로그가 사바티에의 월례 경매 하루 전날이 되어서야 도착하는 일이 있습니다. 지난 1년간 다섯 번이나 늦게 도착하는 우편으로 인해 저의 갤러리 징크가 경매에서 고객들을 위해 입찰을 하지 못하고 수수료를 잃는 상황이 발생했습니다. **16** 비슷한 문제를 방지하기 위해, 에스에이씨가 귀사의 웹사이트에도 업로드되어야 한다고 생각합니다. 이 방법은 기존의 인쇄판 카탈로그와 함께 구독자들에게 매우 큰 가치가 있을 것입니다.

지금 제출   취소

수신: 에스에이씨 직원들
발신: 바나비 웨스트
날짜: 3월 7일, 화요일
제목: 어제 회의

18 3월 6일에 있었던 관리자 회의의 요약을 주의 깊게 읽어 주시기 바랍니다. 늦춰지는 우편배달 시간에 대한 부분적인 문제 해결을 위해, 우리 회사의 편집장인 **19** 르네 마틴이 에스에이씨를 올해 9월부터 한 달에 한 번이 아니라 2주마다 한 번씩 출간하겠다고 말했습니다. 그리고, 그녀는 한 구독자가 출판물의 전자 버전 제작을 제안했다고 말했습니다. 그녀가 이사회에 이번 주 말까지 제안서를 제출할 것입니다. 매달 발행하는 카탈로그 콘텐츠를 새해부터 나누는 문제 역시 논의했습니다. 이제 각 호에는 세 개의 정기 기사만이 실릴 것입니다. **17** 전기문, 예술 동향 칼럼, 그리고 지정된 경매 물품의 역사입니다. 이를 맡게 될 전속 기자들은 각각 휴, 바네사, 그리고 카일리입니다. **18** 프리랜서 기자인 모하메드와 알리자는 기존처럼 기고할 것입니다. 이분들의 기사는 회의 당시 여전히 진행 중이었습니다.

어휘 summary 요약 | partial 부분적인 | chief editor 편집장 | publish 출간하다 | electronic 전자의 | publication 출판물 | submit 제출하다 | proposal 제안서 | board of directors 이사회 | divide 나누다 | regular 정규의 | biography 전기 | assigned 할당된, 부여된 | respectively 각자, 각각 | freelance 프리랜서로 일하는 | contribute 기여하다 | pending 보류하는, 매달려 있는

사바티에 경매 카탈로그 11월 호 · 27호 · 11번

전문경영인의 메시지:

16 이번 달, 에스에이씨에서 인쇄판 카탈로그를 보완할 온라인 구독 서비스를 선보이게 되어 기쁩니다(더 자세한 정보는 30페이지에 있습니다). 그리고, **20** 12월에는, 사바티에의 새로운 애플리케이션인 옥션 패들이 대중에게 무료로 이용 가능하게 됩니다. 이 어플리케이션은 사용자들로 하여금 각 품목의 정보를 볼 수 있도록 해주고, 실시간으로 입찰을 추적할 수 있도록 할 뿐만 아니라 그들이 실제로 경매장에 있는 것처럼 온라인으로 입찰을 할 수도 있게 해줍니다. **19** 내년 2월부터는, 에스에이씨가 격주 단위로 인쇄판과 온라인 버전 둘 다 제공됩니다.

진심으로,

아드리안 메르시에
사바티에 경매장, 전문경영인

어휘 present 보여주다; 참석한 | complement 보완하다 | free of charge 무료로 | application 어플리케이션 | lot (경매용) 품목 | track 추적하다 | bid 입찰, 가격 제시 | in real time 실시간으로, 동시에 | biweekly 격주의 | basis 기준, 단위

---

16. 페레즈 씨에 대해 사실인 것은 무엇인가?
(A) 12개월 전에 에스에이씨 구독자가 되었다.
(B) 에스에이씨에서 면접을 볼 것이다.
(C) 그의 제안이 실제로 진행될 것이다.
(D) 사업상 해외로 예술품을 판매한다.

해설 양식에서 페레즈 씨는 카탈로그를 웹사이트에도 업로드하기를 제안했다. 그리고 편지를 보면 첫 문장에서 새로운 서비스를 소개하고 있다. 두 문장을 종합해 보면 사바티에가 페레즈 씨의 제안을 실행에 옮긴 것으로 정답은 (C) His suggestion will be put into action. 이다.

17. 경매 품목의 배경에 관해 기사를 쓰게 될 사람은 누구인가?
(A) 르네
(B) 바네사
(C) 휴
(D) 카일리

해설 문제의 키워드인 background of an auction item은 이메일에서 the history of a selected auction item의 동의어이다. 이 부분을 읽어보면 '전기문, 예술 동향 칼럼, 그리고 지정된 경매 물품의 역사는 각각 휴와 바네사, 카일리가 맡는다'라고 나와 있으므로 경매 품목의 역사를 다룰 직원은 (D) Kylie이다.

18. 알리자에 관해 암시된 것은 무엇인가?
(A) 3월에 관리자 회의에 참석했다.
(B) 그녀의 사무실은 다른 도시에 있다.
(C) 3월 6일 자 회의에 그녀의 기사가 제출되지 않았다.
(D) 모하메드와 함께 책을 공저했다.

해설 문제에 나와 있는 알리자를 찾아보면, 이메일에서 두 프리랜서 작가는 평소대로 기고할 것이지만, 회의 당시 아직 미완료 상태라고 말했고 첫 문장에서 회의는 3월 6일에 있었음을 알 수 있다. 3월 6일에 기사는 제출되지 않은 상태였으므로 (C) Her article was not submitted by the March 6 meeting. 이 정답이다.

19. 에스에이씨에 관해 암시된 것은 무엇인가?
(A) 총 30페이지이다.
(B) 독자층이 늘어나고 있다.
(C) 한 달에 두 번 발행하겠다는 계획을 미뤘다.
(D) 징크의 고객층을 위해 독점 출판된다.

해설 이메일에서는 '9월부터' 카탈로그를 2주에 한 번 발행하겠다고 발표했는데, 편지에는 '내년 2월부터' 격주간으로 이용할 수 있다는 내용이 나온다. 두 문장을 통해 사바티에 사의 계획이 연기되었음을 유추할 수 있으므로 정답은 (C) It postponed a plan to print two issues a month. 이다.

20. 옥션 패들에 대해 언급된 것은 무엇인가?
(A) 12월에 개시된다.
(B) 여러 언어를 제공한다.
(C) 에스에이씨 독자들만 사용할 수 있다.
(D) 에스에이씨 기사를 읽는 데 사용될 수 있다.

해설 문제의 키워드 Auction Paddle을 마지막 편지에서 찾아낼 수 있는데, 12월에 사바티에의 새로운 앱 옥션 패들을 일반 대중에게 공개한다고 했으므로 (A) It will be launched in December. 가 정답이다.

UNIT 07. 이중 지문

핵심 문제 유형

본서 p.284

1. (C)　　2. (B)　　3. (A)　　4. (B)　　5. (A)

[1-5] 다음 광고와 이메일에 관한 문제입니다.

에즐리 스포츠용품 (이에스이)

이에스이는 영국에서 가장 큰 스포츠용품 소매점 중 하나이며, **1** 우리 맨체스터 지점의 아르바이트 자리를 충원해야 합니다.

의류 부서: 계산원 경험 필요. 금요일부터 일요일까지 근무 가능해야 함. 주당 10-20시간.

용품 부서: **2** 이전 판매 경험은 필요하지 않지만, 스포츠에 대한 깊은 지식이 필요함. **4** 월요일부터 목요일까지 근무 가능해야 함. 주당 25-40시간.

재고 전문가: 연말에 2주간 근무하는 특별한 직책. 우리 창고 관리자가 재고를 파악하는 것을 돕게 됨. 토요일과 일요일 밤에 근무해야 함. 합계 50시간.

판촉 보조: 매장 내부의 진열과 물품 디자인과 배열을 보조함. 토요일과 일요일 저녁에 시간을 내야 함. 주당 10-15시간.

어떤 일자리에든 지원하시려면, brandon@esemail.com으로 브랜든 에즐리에게 연락하세요.

어휘　retailer 소매점 | opening 공석 | prior 이전의 | in-depth 깊은 | inventory 재고 | warehouse 창고 | stock 재고 | arrangement 정리, 배열 | merchandise 상품

수신: 브랜든 에즐리 〈brandon@esemail.com〉
발신: 스티븐 마이크로프트 〈stevemy@balmail.edu〉
보낸 일자: 11월 23일 금요일 오전 11:33
제목: 취업

에즐리 씨 귀하,

5 저는 발리올 대학교의 학생이고, 곧 겨울 방학이 시작됩니다. **3** 그 기간 동안, 저는 일을 해서 돈을 벌고 싶습니다. **4** 저는 많은 클럽 활동을 주말에 하기 때문에, 주중 일자리를 찾기를 원합니다.

5 저는 학교에서 야구팀 소속이고, 테니스와 배드민턴 같은 많은 스포츠를 해왔습니다. 따라서, 많은 다양한 종류의 스포츠용품을 다루는 법을 압니다. **5** 저도 귀사의 상점을 자주 찾는 단골인데, 귀하의 서비스와 제품에 항상 깊은 인상을 받습니다.

귀사의 아르바이트 일자리 중 하나를 채우는 것에 관해 귀하와 얘기를 나눌 수 있는 기회를 가졌으면 좋겠습니다. 감사합니다.

진심을 담아,

스티븐 마이크로프트

어휘　frequent 빈번한 | impressed 감명받은

---

1. 광고된 자리에 대해 무엇이 언급되어 있는가?
   (A) 관련된 업무 경력을 필요로 하지 않는다.
   (B) 모두 주말 시간을 포함한다.
   (C) 아르바이트 자리들이다.
   (D) 여러 곳의 매장 지점에서 일하는 것을 필요로 한다.

   해설　광고 지문의 첫 문장을 통해 파트타임 직원을 구하는 광고임을 알 수 있다. 따라서 정답은 (C) They are part-time positions.이다.

---

2. 광고 세 번째 문단 첫 번째 줄의 단어 단어 "prior"에 의미상 가장 가까운 것은
   (A) 현재의
   (B) 더 이전의
   (C) 직접적인
   (D) 개인적인

   해설　prior sales experience는 '이전의 판매 경험'이라는 뜻으로서, prior는 '이전에'라는 의미를 갖는다. 따라서 보기 중에서 '더 이전의'라는 의미를 가진 (B) earlier가 정답이다.

---

3. 이메일의 목적은 무엇인가?
   (A) 일자리 공석에 대해 문의하기 위해
   (B) 에즐리 씨의 연락처 정보를 요청하기 위해
   (C) 일자리에 동료를 추천하기 위해
   (D) 근무 시간 축소를 요청하기 위해

   해설　이메일의 첫 번째 단락에서 스티븐 마이크로프트는 일자리를 찾고 있으며, 일자리에 대해 문의하기 위해 이메일을 보낸다는 사실을 알 수 있다. 따라서 정답은 (A) To inquire about a job opening이다.

---

4. 마이크로프트 씨에게 가장 잘 맞는 일자리는 무엇인가?
   (A) 의류 판매 보조
   (B) 용품 판매 보조
   (C) 물품 목록 전문가
   (D) 판촉 보조

   해설　이메일의 첫 번째 단락에서 스티븐 마이크로프트는 주말에는 일할 의사가 없다는 사실을 알 수 있다. 광고에 게시된 4개의 채용 분야 중에서 주말에 일하지 않는 분야는 근무 조건이 '월요일에서 목요일'인 Equipment Department '용품 부서'뿐이다. 따라서 정답은 (B) Equipment sales associate이다.

---

5. 마이크로프트 씨에 관해 언급되지 않은 사실은 무엇인가?
   (A) 예전에 소매업에서 일했다.
   (B) 대학생이다.
   (C) 많은 종류의 스포츠를 즐긴다.
   (D) 종종 에즐리 스포츠용품에서 쇼핑한다.

   해설　이메일을 보면 스티븐 마이크로프트는 다양한 스포츠를 즐기는 대학생이며 에즐리의 단골손님임을 알 수 있다. 하지만 소매업 경력은 언급되지 않았으므로 (A) He worked in the retail industry before.가 정답이다.

Practice

1. (B)	**2.** (D)	**3.** (D)	**4.** (C)	**5.** (A)
6. (B)	**7.** (D)	**8.** (D)	**9.** (C)	**10.** (B)
11. (D)	**12.** (C)	**13.** (B)	**14.** (D)	**15.** (A)

[1-5] 다음 웹페이지와 이메일에 관한 문제입니다.

www.madelinesattic.com

매들린스 애틱
파리의 일부를 집으로 가져가세요!

저희 매장은 파리 전역에서 온 수천 점의 기념품을 보유하고 있습니다. **1** 매들린스 애틱은 파리의 낭만과 세련됨, 역사를 자랑하는 물건들을 가지고 있습니다.

1 당신의 취미가 우표 수집이든 거리 표지판 수집이든, 저희에게는 모든 이들을 만족시킬 수 있는 것들이 있습니다. **1** 다양한 19, 20세기의 흥미로운 물건과 사진을 찾을 수 있습니다.

아래에서 기념품 유형을 선택하고 저희 웹사이트 매장 페이지에서 구매 가능한 것들을 알아보세요.

포스터와 지도, 엽서: 5달러부터
장식용 조각상과 수집품: 15달러부터
안내 책자와 영화, 음악 씨디: 8달러부터
유명 랜드마크 복제품: 20달러부터
3 사진과 그림: 40달러부터

2 모서리나 끝이 뾰족한 상품들은 배송해 드릴 수 없으며 오프라인 매장에서만 구매할 수 있습니다. 각 유형의 상품에 대한 추가 정보를 이용하려면 bstevens@madelinesattic.fr로 브릿지 스티븐스에게 이메일을 보내기를 바랍니다.

어휘   **sophisticated** 세련된, 정교한 | **figurine** 작은 조각상 | **replica** 복제품 | **ship** 배송하다

발신: afleury@doldeantiques.com
수신: bstevens@madelinesattic.fr
제목: 바르도의 작품
날짜: 12월 21일

스티븐스 씨에게,

4 저희 골동품 매장을 재정비하다, 유럽의 유명 경매인 산드라 레인이 저에게 준 파리 거리의 놀라운 소묘 작품을 발견했습니다. **3** 직원 중 한 명이 당신의 매장에서 아마 이것을 사서 재판매하고 싶어할 것이라고 하길래, 당신에게 연락하기로 했습니다.

4 이 소묘 작품은 당초 1960년대에 유명했던 인상주의 화가 진 바르도가 산드라의 아버지에게 그려준 것입니다. 그의 작품은 세계 곳곳의 박물관에 전시되어 있습니다. 산드라는 5년 전 제 가게의 10주년 선물로 이 작품을 주었죠.

---

5 당신의 구매 절차와 대금 지불이 이루어지는 방식에 대한 정보를 보내주시면 고맙겠습니다. 감사합니다.

진심을 담아,

아서 플루어리
더블린 올드 앤티크스

어휘   **antique shop** 골동품 상점 | **auctioneer** 경매인 | **resell** 되팔다 | **payment** 지불

---

1. 매들린스 애틱에 관해 암시되지 않은 것은 무엇인가?
(A) 상품들이 제작된 시대가 다양하다.
(B) 매달 예술 작품의 할인을 제공한다.
(C) 상품이 다양한 흥미를 가진 사람들을 만족시킨다.
(D) 프랑스 문화와 관련된 상품을 판다.

해설   웹사이트 지문에서 상품이 파리의 낭만과 세련됨, 역사를 보여주는 것이라는 문장은 (D), 모든 이들을 만족시킬 수 있는 상품이 있다는 것은 (C), 19, 20세기의 물품이 있다는 것은 (A)로 paraphrasing 되었다. (B) It offers monthly discounts on artwork. 는 언급되지 않았으므로 정답이다.

---

2. 매들린스 애틱에 대해 무엇이 나타나 있는가?
(A) 몇몇 유럽 국가에 지점이 있다.
(B) 모든 상품이 파리에서 제작된다.
(C) 1960년대에 설립되었다.
(D) 일부 상품은 온라인으로 이용할 수 없다.

해설   웹페이지에 모서리나 끝이 뾰족한 물건은 오프라인 매장으로 가야 구매할 수 있다고 했으므로 일부 상품을 온라인으로 살 수 없다고 나와 있는 (D) Some of its products are not available online. 이 정답이다.

---

3. 플루어리 씨의 상품이 매들린스 애틱에서 팔릴 수 있는 가장 낮은 가격은 얼마인가?
(A) 5달러
(B) 15달러
(C) 20달러
(D) 40달러

해설   이메일을 보면 플루어리 씨가 자신의 매장에서 sketch 작품을 발견했고, 매들린스 애틱에 이 작품을 팔 수 있다는 말을 듣고 연락을 취했다. 즉, 플루어리 씨가 팔고자 하는 작품은 그림인데, 웹페이지에 그림 가격은 40달러부터 시작한다고 하였으므로 (D) $40가 정답이다.

---

4. 플루어리 씨에 관해 암시된 것은 무엇인가?
(A) 매들린스 애틱의 전 직원이다.
(B) 더블린에서 레인 씨를 만날 것이다.
(C) 바르도 씨가 만든 상품을 소유하고 있다.
(D) 유럽에서 열리는 경매에 정기적으로 참석한다.

해설   이메일에서 플루어리 씨는 판매장에서 산드라 레인이 자신에게 준 소묘 작품을 발견했는데 이것은 진 바르도가 그린 것이라고 했으므로

126   파고다 토익 고득점 완성 RC

(C) He owns a product made by Mr. Bardot. 이 정답이다.

---

5. 플루어리 씨는 무엇에 대해 물어보는가?

(A) 매들린스 애틱에 상품을 파는 절차

(B) 가게에서 본 사진의 가격

(C) 인터뷰할 예술가의 이력

(D) 박물관에 작품을 전시하는 절차

해설 이메일 마지막 부분에서 플루어리 씨는 매들린스 애틱이 골동품을 구매하는 절차에 대해 묻고 있으므로 이것을 paraphrasing한 (A) The procedure for selling merchandise to Madeline's Attic이 정답이다.

[6-10] 다음 이메일과 보고서에 관한 문제입니다.

수신: 품질 관리팀
발신: 파블로 에반스
날짜: 9월 13일
제목: 성능 테스트

직원 여러분, 안녕하십니까:

아마 들으셨겠지만, **8** 우리 회사는 최근 뉴스 보도에서 많은 비판의 대상이 되었습니다. 우리 모델들이 명시된 기준 성능을 충족시키지 못하고 있다는 **7** 주장이 있습니다. **6** **9** 무엇보다도 걱정스러운 것은 공교롭게도 우리의 가장 많이 판매되는 모델인 "미니" 모델 다섯 종의 연비가 광고에 나온 것만큼 높지 않다는 주장입니다. **8** 우리는 이러한 부정적인 시선이 우리의 신뢰성에 손상을 주어서, 당연하지만, 판매량의 감소를 야기하는 것을 우려하고 있습니다.

8 우리 하이다 자동차는, 우리가 판매하는 차량에 대해 자부심을 갖고 있으며 각 차량이 고객들이 지난 40년에 걸쳐 진가를 인정해 온 것과 동일한 수상 경력에 빛나는 품질을 제공하기를 기대합니다. **6** 그래서, 업계에서 공인된 방식을 사용하여 이 차량들의 연비를 측정하기 위해 컨설팅 회사 글릭 사를 고용했습니다. 모델 중 하나라도 제 성능을 발휘하지 못한다는 점이 밝혀진다면, 즉각적인 조치를 취해 라벨 표시와 광고를 수정할 것입니다.

지금의 상황은 우리로 하여금 현재의 방식을 재평가하여 우리 차량들의 최고의 품질임을 보장하게 해줄 것입니다.

파블로 에반스

최고 운영 책임자

어휘 assurance 보증, 보장 | performance (기계의) 성능 | come in for ~의 대상이 되다 | criticism 비평 | stated 명백히 규정된 | allegation 주장 | gas mileage 연비 | happen to 공교롭게 ~하다 | efficient 효율적인 | credibility 신뢰성 | appreciate 진가를 알아보다 | reveal 밝히다 | underperform (예상보다) 기량 발휘를 못하다 | reevaluate 재평가하다 | ensure 보장하다 | Chief Operations Officer(COO) 최고 운영 책임자

연비 성능 테스트 결과
하이다 자동차 귀하
글릭 사 시행

모델명	도로 주행 연비*	소비자 보고 연비*
타르타 미니	38	35
코스모스 미니	32	34
10 엑스토마 미니	22	23
브라보소 미니	28	26
히말라야 미니	24	29

* 1갤런당 마일(mpg)

9 가장 크게 우려되는 모델들에 대한 성능 테스트가 글릭 사 시설과 공용 도로에서 실시되었습니다. 소비자들에게도 일상생활에서 사용할 때의 연비를 알려달라고 요청하였습니다. 차후 이 수치를 광고된 연비와 비교하였습니다.

어휘 concern 우려 | conduct 수행하다 | facility 시설 | compared to ~와 비교하여

---

6. 이메일은 왜 보내졌는가?

(A) 새 자동차 제품군을 발표하기 위해

(B) 어떤 문제점에 대한 해결책을 제시하기 위해

(C) 글릭 사와의 제휴 가능성을 논하기 위해

(D) 회사 행사를 홍보하기 위해

해설 이메일 전체의 내용을 읽어보고 후반부에서 정답을 알아낼 수 있다. 판매 중인 자동차가 광고에 나온 만큼의 연비 성능을 내지 못하여 언론으로부터 부정적인 평가를 받자, 신뢰성의 위축과 판매량 감소를 우려한 회사 측에서 한 컨설팅 회사에 연비 측정을 의뢰해 그 결과에 따른 조치를 취하기로 했다는 내용의 이메일이다. 따라서 이메일의 목적은 문제점에 대한 해결책 제시라고 할 수 있으므로 정답은 (B) To propose a solution to a problem이다.

---

7. 이메일 첫 번째 문단, 두 번째 줄의 단어 "claims"에 의미상 가장 가까운 것은

(A) 수요

(B) 소유권

(C) 흥미

(D) 비난

해설 명사 claim은 '주장'이라는 뜻인데, 주어진 단어가 들어있는 문장을 보면 제품이 명시된 기준에 미치지 못하는 성능을 내고 있다는 부정적인 주장이므로 문맥상 의미가 가장 가까운 것은 '비난'이라는 뜻의 (D) accusations가 정답이다.

---

8. 하이다 자동차에 관하여 언급되지 않은 것은 무엇인가?

(A) 뉴스에 등장했다.

(B) 수십 년 동안 영업을 해왔다.

(C) 제품의 품질로 인정받아 왔다.

(D) 최근 판매 수치가 하락하고 있다.

해설 지문과 보기를 대조해서 언급된 것들을 제거하여 정답을 찾아야 한다.

우선 이메일 지문에서 회사가 최근 뉴스 보도에서 많은 비판의 대상이 되었다는 문장을 보고 (A)를 제거한다. 그리고 두 번째 문단 첫 번째 문장에서 40년 동안 회사를 운영해 왔다는 점과 품질로 고객들의 인정을 받아왔다는 점을 알 수 있으므로 (B)와 (C)도 제거한다. 첫 번째 문단 마지막에서 판매량이 떨어질까 봐 우려한다는 내용이지 이미 그렇게 되었다는 것은 아니므로 정답은 (D) Its sales numbers have been decreasing recently. 이다.

9. 조사에 사용된 차량에 관해 암시된 것은 무엇인가?
(A) 여러 제조업체가 만들었다.
(B) 올해 출시되었다.
(C) 회사의 가장 인기 있는 모델들이다.
(D) 고속도로에서만 테스트 됐다.

해설 이메일에서 가장 큰 우려를 자아내는 것은 회사의 가장 인기 있는 모델이 비판을 받고 있다는 점이라는 것을 파악해야 한다. 그리고 보고서에서 가장 큰 우려의 대상인 모델에 대해 성능 테스트를 했다는 문장을 읽으면 양쪽을 종합해서 회사의 가장 인기 있는 모델에 대한 연비 테스트가 있었다는 것을 간파할 수 있다. 따라서 정답은 (C) They are the company's most popular models. 이다.

10. 보고서에 따르면, 어느 차량이 연비 성능이 가장 안 좋았는가?
(A) 타르타 미니
(B) 엑스토마 미니
(C) 브라보소 미니
(D) 히말라야 미니

해설 표에 적혀있는 수치를 비교해 보면 쉽게 정답을 알 수 있다. 가장 낮은 수치가 적혀있는 모델 (B) 엑스토마 미니가 정답이다.

[11-15] 다음 편지와 이메일에 관한 문제입니다.

7월 12일

제프리 해링턴 씨
에스엠이 세무 컨설팅
80 W. 필버트 가
버논, 비씨

해링턴 씨에게,

11 저는 켈로나에 세무사무소 개업을 생각하고 있는 사람입니다.

지난 17년 동안 버논에 있는 클라인-보갈 세무사무소에서 근무했습니다. 그동안 얻은 지식과 지역 내 많은 사람과 맺은 **11 12** 유대관계가 **11** 이 사업을 성공으로 이끌어 줄 것이라고 믿습니다. 또한 제 아내가 켈로나에서 카페를 운영하고 있는데, 저는 이곳에서 여러 해 동안 많은 주민을 사귀어 왔습니다.

15 귀사의 프랜차이즈 회원으로 개업하면, 소규모 사업체들이 처음 시작할 때 맞닥뜨리게 되는 여러 문제를 피해 갈 수 있을 것이라고 생각합니다. 직접 상담이 가능한지의 여부와 어떤 서류를 가지고 가야 하는지 알려주시기를 바랍니다.

답장 기다리겠습니다.

진심을 담아,

공인회계사 벤자민 C. 슈레이더

어휘 **tax preparation business** 세무대리업 | **tie** 유대 관계 | **venture** 신규 개발 사업 | **run** 운영하다, 경영하다, 관리하다 | **resident** 주민 | **face** 직면하다 | **start up** 시작되다 | **in-person** 직접의 | **CPA(Certified Public Accountant)** 공인회계사

수신: 〈켈로나 에스엠이 세무 컨설팅 고객 목록〉
발신: 벤 슈레이더
14 날짜: 9월 19일
제목: 기념합니다!

소중한 고객님,

14 작년 9월 19일에 회사 문을 열었을 때, **13** 저와 제 동료들은 켈로나 주민들이 자금을 절약하고 번창하도록 도움을 드리는 세무 상담을 제공함으로써 영향을 미치게 될 것이라는 걸 알고 있었습니다. **14** 1주년을 기념하면서, 우리 고객님들께 훌륭한 서비스를 계속 제공해 드리길 소망합니다.

저희는 사람들에게 더 나은 삶을 만들어 주겠다는 확고한 결의를 보였기 때문에 **13** 개업 몇 달도 지나지 않아 이미 탄탄한 고객층을 확보했습니다. 중년의 한 부부는 모아놓은 돈이 충분하지 않아 자녀의 대학 등록을 감당할 수 없을까 봐 걱정하고 있었습니다. 저희의 재무설계 서비스는 추가적으로 은퇴자금까지 만들어 드리는 계획을 짜드렸습니다. 알스 컴퓨팅이라는 또 다른 고객사는 운영 10년 만에 가장 적은 금액을 세금으로 낸 후 감사의 편지를 써주셨습니다.

점점 더 많은 사람이 저희 서비스를 선택하시는 이유는 바로 이렇게 만족하신 고객님들입니다. **15** 또한 네트워크에 들어오도록 저희를 환영해 주고 지금까지의 모든 과정에 도움을 주신 에스엠이 세무 컨설팅 그룹에도 매우 큰 "감사"의 인사를 드려야 합니다. 켈로나에서 사업을 하고 에스엠이 가족의 일원이 된 것은 저의 영광입니다.

공인회계사 벤자민 C. 슈레이더

어휘 **make a difference** (~에) 영향이 있다, 차별을 두다 | **prosper** 번영하다 | **mark** 기념하다 | **solid** 탄탄한, 확실한 | **client base** 고객층 | **firm** 굳은, 단단한, 견고한 | **resolve** 결심 | **middle-aged** 중년의 | **savings** 저축한 돈 | **afford** (~을 살 금전적[시간적]) 여유가 되다 | **tuition** 수업료 | **retirement** 은퇴 | **decade** 10년 | **operation** 사업, 영업 | **owe ~ to ...** ~을 …에게 신세지다

11. 편지의 목적은 무엇인가?
(A) 추가 자금을 요청하기 위해
(B) 신청서를 요구하기 위해
(C) 신제품을 홍보하기 위해
(D) 경력을 설명하기 위해

해설 도입부에 자기 사업을 시작하겠다는 계획을 말하면서 오랫동안 세무사무소에서 근무하면서 쌓은 지식과 인맥이 운영에 도움을 줄 것이라는 생각을 밝히고 있으므로 사업 시작의 승인을 받기 위해 경력을 설

명하는 것이 편지의 목적이라는 것을 알 수 있다. 따라서 정답은 (D) To describe job experience이다.

---

12. 편지 두 번째 문단, 두 번째 줄의 단어 "ties"에 의미상 가장 가까운 것은
(A) 의류
(B) 범위
(C) 연줄이 있는 사람
(D) 매듭

해설 tie는 의류의 일종이기도 하고 동사로 '묶다'라는 뜻도 있기 때문에 문맥에 따라 (A)와 (B), (D)도 모두 동의어가 될 수 있지만, 편지의 ties는 '지역 주민들과 맺고 있는 유대관계'라는 의미이다. 따라서 '인맥'이라는 뜻이 있는 (C) connections가 정답이다.

---

13. 슈레이더 씨는 왜 이메일을 보냈는가?
(A) 은퇴자금 마련 계획을 설명하기 위해
(B) 회사의 성공을 강조하기 위해
(C) 지역의 어떤 프로그램에 대한 지지를 보이기 위해
(D) 기념행사에 초대하기 위해

해설 첫 문단에서 사업을 시작할 때부터 지역사회에 영향을 미칠 것이라는 걸 알고 있었고 지금까지 제공하던 훌륭한 서비스를 지속하겠다고 말하고 있으므로 자신의 사업이 성공적으로 영위되고 있음을 암시하고 있다. 또한 두 번째 문단에서 사업 초기부터 탄탄한 고객층을 확보했다는 말을 하고 있고, 성공적으로 서비스를 제공한 사례 두 가지까지 전해주고 있으므로 이 편지의 목적은 사업에 성공을 거두고 있다는 점을 강조하므로 정답은 (B) To highlight a company's success이다.

---

14. 켈로나 에스엠이 세무 컨설팅에 관하여 무엇이 언급되어 있는가?
(A) 새 컴퓨터를 구매할 계획이다.
(B) 가족을 위한 새로운 서비스가 있다.
(C) 영업시간을 연장할 것이다.
(D) 1년 동안 운영해 왔다.

해설 이메일을 보낸 날짜가 9월 19일인데, 작년 같은 날짜에 사업체의 문을 열었다는 문장이 있고, 1주년을 기념하고 있다고 했으므로 켈로나 세무사무소는 문을 연 지 정확히 1년 된 곳이라는 것을 파악할 수 있다. 따라서 정답은 (D) It has been operating for a year. 이다.

---

15. 슈레이더 씨에 관해 암시된 것은 무엇인가?
(A) 그의 제안이 받아들여졌다.
(B) 아내의 카페에서 10년 동안 일했다.
(C) 17년 전에 버논으로 이사 갔다.
(D) 사업을 해외로 확장할 것이다.

해설 에스엠이 세무 컨설팅에 보낸 편지에서 프랜차이즈 회원으로 사업을 시작하게 해달라는 요청을 하고 있다. 그리고 이메일에서는 에스엠이의 회원사가 된 것에 대한 감사를 표하고 있다. 두 부분을 종합하면 프랜차이즈 회원이 되겠다는 슈레이더 씨의 제안을 에스엠이 측에서 받아들였다는 사실을 유추할 수 있으므로 (A) His proposal was accepted. 가 정답이다.

UNIT 08. 삼중 지문

핵심 문제 유형　　　　　　　본서 p.294

1. (C)　　**2.** (C)　　**3.** (B)　　**4.** (C)　　**5.** (A)

[1-5] 다음 웹페이지와 이메일들에 관한 문제입니다.

www.reaveportgc.com/membership

홈	회사 정보	회원권	예약

리브포트 골프 클럽 회원권 정보

회비:
– **③** 1회 등록비 70달러 (노령자는 면제됨)
– **④** 리브포트 주민들의 월 이용료는 110달러, 비거주자는 150달러

혜택은 다음을 포함합니다:
– 개인 지도와 장비 대여에 대해 30% 할인
– 클럽 파티에서 다른 회원들과 어울릴 기회
– 골프 경기 시간의 우선 예약

질문이 있으시면, 회원권 관리자인 벤자민 린에게 blin@reaveportgc. com으로 **①** 보내주세요.

어휘 **membership** 회원권 | **registration fee** 등록비 | **waive** 면제해주다 | **senior citizen** 노령자, 정년 퇴직자 | **equipment rental** 장비 대여 | **socialize with** ~와 어울리다[교제하다] | **priority booking** 우선 예약

수신: 〈blin@reaveportgc.com〉
발신: 〈mbeauregard@txpo.net〉
날짜: 4월 29일
제목: 회원권

린 씨에게,

저는 최근에 회원권 신청 방법을 보려고 귀사의 웹사이트를 방문했습니다. 하지만, 제가 어느 항목에 해당하는지 잘 모르겠네요. **③** 저는 노령자로, 한 해의 첫 일곱 달은 웰셔의 퇴직자 전용 주택에서 거주하고, **④** 8월부터 12월까지는 리브포트에서 삽니다.

② 제가 두 곳에서 지내기 때문에, 귀사의 거주자 회원 요금을 적용받을 자격이 되는지 모르겠네요. 제가 주민으로서 자격이 되는지의 여부를 확인해 주시겠어요? 제가 오랫동안 여가로 골프를 쳐왔기 때문에, 귀하의 클럽에 가입하는 데 관심이 정말 많습니다.

당신의 도움에 매우 감사드립니다.

진심을 담아,

미셸 보레가드

어휘 **apply for** 신청하다, 지원하다 | **category** 목록, 범주 | **fall under** ~에 해당되다 | **retirement home** 퇴직자 전용 아파트 | **qualify for** ~의 자격을 얻다 | **recreational** 여가의, 오락의

수신: 〈mbeauregard@txpo.net〉
발신: 〈blin@reaveportgc.com〉
날짜: 4월 30일
제목: 회신: 회원권

보레가드 씨에게,

저희 골프 클럽에 대한 귀하의 관심에 감사드립니다. **4** 저희는 리브포트에서 최소 5개월간 살고 계신 분이라면 누구든 거주자로 간주해서, 귀하께서는 당연히 저희 거주자 회원 요금의 자격을 갖추고 계십니다. **5** 저희 회원권은 보통 7월에 모두 차로 되도록 빨리 신청해 주실 것을 권해 드립니다. 문의 사항이 더 있다면 제게 전화해 주세요.

진심을 담아,

벤자민 린
리브포트 골프 클럽, 회원권 관리자 이사

어휘 at least 적어도, 최소한 | certainly 틀림없이, 분명히 | fill up 가득 차다 | further 그 이상의 | inquiry 문의

---

1. 웹페이지 세 번째 단락, 첫 번째 줄의 단어 "direct"와 의미상 가장 가까운 것은
(A) 관리하다
(B) 가르치다
(C) 전달하다
(D) 수행하다

해설 어떤 질문이든 회원권 관리자에게 보내라는 내용이므로 이 문장에서 direct는 '보내다'의 의미로 쓰였다. 따라서 '전달하다, 보내다'를 뜻하는 (C) forward가 정답이다.

---

2. 보레가드 씨가 첫 번째 이메일을 쓴 이유는 무엇인가?
(A) 서비스를 취소하기 위해
(B) 회원권을 갱신하기 위해
(C) 더 많은 정보를 요청하기 위해
(D) 새 주소를 제공하기 위해

해설 첫 번째 이메일 지문의 두 번째 단락에서 자신의 상황이 특별하기 때문에 거주자 회원 요금을 낼 자격이 되는지 확인해 달라고 요청하고 있으므로 (C) To request more information이 정답이다.

---

3. 보레가드 씨에 관해 암시된 것은 무엇인가?
(A) 전문 골프 선수이다.
(B) 등록비를 지불할 필요가 없다.
(C) 작년에 리브포트로 이사했다.
(D) 린 씨를 전에 만난 적이 있다.

해설 보레가드 씨가 쓴 이메일을 보면, 자신을 노령자로 밝히고 있는데, 웹페이지의 회비 관련 내용을 확인하면 노령자는 등록비가 면제된다고 했으므로 (B) She does not have to pay a registration fee. 가 정답이다.

---

4. 보레가드 씨의 월 회비는 얼마인가?
(A) 30달러
(B) 70달러
(C) 110달러
(D) 150달러

해설 월 회비와 관련된 첫 번째 단서는 웹페이지의 회비(Dues) 부분에 나온다. 리브포트 거주자는 110달러, 비거주자는 150달러이다. 보레가드 씨가 쓴 이메일을 보면 자신이 리브포트에 8월부터 12월(5개월)까지 사는데 거주자 요금 혜택이 있는지 물었고, 회신 이메일인 두 번째 이메일에서 최소 5개월간 거주자로 리브포트에 살고 있다면 거주자 회원 요금을 적용받을 수 있다고 했으므로 (C) $110가 정답이다.

---

5. 리브포트 골프 클럽에 관하여 무엇이 사실이겠는가?
(A) 회원권 신청이 많다.
(B) 리브포트 주민들에게만 개방된다.
(C) 최근에 수리되었다.
(D) 여러 지점이 있다.

해설 리브포트 골프 클럽에서 보낸 두 번째 회신 이메일을 보면, 이곳 회원권이 보통 7월이면 모두 차기 때문에 되도록 빨리 신청할 것을 권하고 있으므로 이곳에 회원권을 신청하는 사람이 많다는 것을 알 수 있다. 따라서 (A) It receives many membership applications. 가 정답이다.

Practice
본서 p.296

1. (B)	2. (B)	3. (B)	4. (D)	5. (D)
6. (B)	7. (B)	8. (C)	9. (B)	10. (C)
11. (D)	12. (D)	13. (A)	14. (D)	15. (A)

[1-5] 다음 이메일들과 일지에 관한 문제입니다.

발신: m_leonard@tagetdata.com
수신: billing@nationwidewater.com
날짜: 11월 4일
제목: 고객 번호 #235923의 청구서

안녕하세요,

1 최근 귀사로부터 받은 청구서와 관련하여 말씀드리려고 합니다. 10월 저희 사무실 수도 사용료 총액이 1050.20달러까지 나왔는데, 이것은 지난 몇 달보다 훨씬 더 많은 금액입니다.

계약에 따라, 완납을 하긴 했습니다. 하지만, 내년의 물 낭비를 줄일 계획을 세우기 위해, 수도 사용료가 증가한 이유에 관한 증빙 서류의 제공을 요청하는 바입니다. 만약 실수에 의해 작성된 것이라면, 저에게 직접 연락해주시기를 바랍니다.

2 저희 시설관리 부장님이 이 문제는 지하 수도관의 결함에 의해 유발되었을 수도 있다고 의견을 말씀하셨고 저도 동의합니다. 그러므로, 저희 영업시간 중에 사무실로 직원을 보내셔서 혹시 문제가 있는지 확인해 주시면 좋겠습니다.

진심을 담아,

미나 레너드, 타겟 데이타

어휘 account 단골, 고객 | in regard to ~과 관련하여 | in keeping with ~와 일치하여 | set up ~을 세우다 | documentation (무엇에 요구되는, 또는 무엇을 입증할) 서류 | utility cost (전기·가스·수도 등의) 에너지 비용 | maintenance (건물·기계 등을 정기적으로 점검, 보수하는) 유지 | supervisor 감독, 상관 | faulty 결함이 있는 | representative 직원

서비스 일지			
③ 11월 12일			
직원명	**장소**	**도착 시간**	**작업 내역**
데이비드 노벨로	1920 페어레인 가	오후 1:15	수도관 교체
③ 나디아 앤더슨	9932 바이어스 가	오후 1:20	수도관 수리
앤드리아 킴	1244 센트럴 가	오후 3:20	수도관 교체
토냐 가르시아	1029 웨슬리언 가	오후 3:45	수도관 수리

어휘 description 설명 | replace 교체하다 | fix 고치다

발신: dana_meyer@nationwidewater.com
수신: m_leonard@tagetdata.com
날짜: 11월 13일
제목: 회신: 고객 번호 #235923의 청구서

레너드 씨에게,

저희 네이션와이드 수도는 고객님의 연락에 감사드립니다. ③ 바이어스 가에서의 문제에 관하여 결과를 말씀드리고자 하는데, ② 저희 직원이 지하 수도관의 누수로 인해 문제가 발생했다고 판단했습니다. 그것이 계량기가 귀사 건물의 수도 사용량을 잘못 ④ 측정한 원인입니다. 수도관은 수리됐으며, 앞으로는 이러한 일이 발생하지 않을 것이라고 약속드립니다.

⑤ 다음 달 청구 금액에서 220달러가 공제될 것입니다.

추가로 도움이 필요하실 경우, 언제든 연락해 주시기를 바랍니다.

진심을 담아,

다나 마이어
네이션와이드 수도 청구서 발송과

어휘 get in touch with ~와 연락하다 | leak (액체·기체가) 새다 | meter (전기·가스·수도 등의) 계량기 | word 약속 | credit 입금하다

---

1. 레너드 씨는 왜 이메일을 보냈는가?
(A) 계약을 검토하기 위해
(B) 요금에 관해 논하기 위해
(C) 할인율에 관해 묻기 위해
(D) 월 정기구독을 신청하기 위해

해설 첫 번째 이메일의 첫 번째 줄에 보면 지난 몇 달간보다 물 사용량이 너무 많이 나온 것에 대해 글을 쓴다고 나와 있으므로 정답은 (B) To discuss a charge가 된다.

---

2. 레너드 씨에 관해 암시된 것은 무엇인가?
(A) 더 이상 네이션와이드 수도의 서비스를 이용하지 않을 것이다.
(B) 문제의 원인을 올바르게 추측했다.
(C) 최근 다른 지사로 전근했다.
(D) 마이어 씨에게 처음으로 연락하고 있다.

해설 연계 지문 문제로 첫 번째 이메일 지문에서 추측건대 문제가 지하 수도관이 잘못된 것 같다고 언급했으며, 두 번째 이메일 지문에서 수도관 누수라고 했으므로 두 문장을 연결해 보면 문제의 원인을 올바르게 추측했음을 알 수 있다. 따라서 정답은 (B) She correctly guessed the cause of a problem. 이다.

---

3. 11월 12일에 누가 타겟 데이타 사무실을 방문했는가?
(A) 데이비드 노벨로
(B) 나디아 앤더슨
(C) 앤드리아 킴
(D) 토냐 가르시아

해설 연계 지문 문제로 두 번째 이메일 지문에서 Byers Drive location에 관련된 문제에 대해 이메일을 보낸다고 하였고, 11월 12일에 작성된 두 번째 일지에서 그 주소를 찾아보면 나디아 앤더슨이 나오므로 정답은 (B) Nadia Anderson이다.

---

4. 두 번째 이메일 첫 번째 문단, 네 번째 줄의 단어 "read"와 의미상 가장 가까운 것은
(A) 감지했다
(B) 보았다
(C) 훑어보았다
(D) 측정했다

해설 뒤에 목적어로 물 사용량을 '읽었다'는 이야기는 '측정했다'라는 말과 가장 유사하므로 정답은 (D) measured이다.

---

5. 마이어 씨는 이메일에서 무엇을 언급하는가?
(A) 추가 요금이 부과될 것이다.
(B) 만족도 설문 조사가 발송될 것이다.
(C) 새 수도관이 곧 설치될 것이다.
(D) 청구 금액에서 일부가 공제될 것이다.

해설 마이어 씨의 이메일은 마지막 지문이므로, 마지막 문장에 다음 달 청구 금액에서 220달러가 공제될 것이라고 했으므로 정답은 (D) A portion of the bill will be deducted. 이다.

로드업 운송 차량 임대 서비스(엘티알에스)

다른 도시로 이동하든 다른 나라로 가든, 엘티알에스에 오늘 전화하세요. **6** 모든 차량이 운송용 상자와 가위나 테이프, 버블랩 같은 유용한 물품들을 충분히 갖추고 있습니다. 요청하면 냉장 장치도 이용할 수 있습니다. 차량 인수는 캘리포니아 전역에서 이루어질 수 있으며, 또는 전문 운전기사가 계신 곳으로 가져다드릴 수도 있습니다.

이용 가능한 차량:

유형	**6** 적재 수단	길이 (m)	바닥 넓이 (m²)	**6** 내부 용적 (m³)
유형 A	램프	5.5m	13.75m²	55m³
9 유형 B	전기 리프트	9.0m	22.5m²	90m³
유형 C	전기 리프트	12.5m	31.25m²	125m³
유형 D	전기 리프트	15.0m	37.5m²	150m³

연락하여 저희 물류관리 전문가와 예약을 잡으면 어느 유형의 차량이 잘 맞추는지 판별해 드립니다. 가격 정보는, 웹사이트 www.loaduprental.com에서 확인하세요.

어휘 be equipped with ~을 갖추고 있다 | crate (물품 운송용 대형 나무) 상자 | refrigerated 냉장한 | upon request 요청 시에 | ramp 경사로, 램프 | logistics 물류 관리

---

www.loaduprental.com/requestform

차량에 관한 정보를 요청하려면 양식을 작성해 주세요:

이름: 아론 디아즈	**8** 업체명: 디아즈 클리너스
이메일: aaron@dzclean.com	날짜: 1월 27일

7 최근 다른 도시로 이사하면서 당신의 서비스를 이용했던 동료 알리사 벨의 추천을 받고 연락드립니다. **8** 제 회사도 매우 빠르게 성장하고 있어서 이전이 필요합니다. 그래서, 주말 동안 트럭을 임대하고 싶습니다. 대형 청소 장비가 있기 때문에, 트럭 뒤편에 전기 리프트와 모든 물건을 실을 수 있을 만큼 충분히 큰 트레일러 공간이 필요할 것입니다. 또한, 기계의 손상을 예방하기 위해 차량 내부에 충전재가 있다면 유용할 것입니다.

어휘 fill out 작성하다 | associate 동료 | relocate 이전하다 | padding 충전재

---

www.loaduprental.com/feedback

홈페이지	가격	연락처	고객 반응

사용 후기:

최근 엘티알에스의 차량을 이용하고, 매우 감명받았습니다. 추가적인 혜택으로 엘티알에스 고객 소개 프로그램으로 저는 20% 할인을, **7** 제 친구는 선물 상품권을 받았습니다. **9** 처음에는 125 입방 미

터 차량이 필요할 것으로 생각했는데, 엘티알에스 직원의 **9** **10** 말이 맞았고, 한 사이즈 작은 걸로도 충분하더군요. 그 상담이 비용을 절약하게 해주었고, 이사는 원활하게 진행되었습니다. 이사를 위해 차량을 빌려야 한다면 엘티알에스가 최고입니다.

디아즈 클리너 사장, 아론 디아즈

어휘 referral 소개 | voucher 상품권 | turn out ~인 것으로 드러나다 | representative 직원

---

6. 광고에 엘티알에스에 관한 어떤 정보가 언급되지 않는가?
(A) 적재 방식의 선택권
(B) 트럭의 연료 소비율
(C) 제공되는 운송용 장비
(D) 내부 공간의 정도

해설 광고에서 운송용 장비가 제공된다는 것을 알 수 있으며, 표에서 적재 수단과 내부 용적을 알아낼 수 있다. 트럭의 연료 소비율은 광고에 언급되지 않으므로 (B) The mileage rates for its trucks가 정답이다.

---

7. 벨 씨에 관하여 무엇이 사실이겠는가?
(A) 디아즈 씨의 부하 직원이다.
(B) 쿠폰을 받았다.
(C) 다른 나라로 이전할 계획이다.
(D) 청소 회사에 장비를 공급한다.

해설 온라인 양식에서 디아즈 씨는 벨 씨의 소개로 이 차량 임대 회사를 알았다고 했고 마지막 사용 후기에서 고객 소개 프로그램 덕분에 자신은 할인을 받고, 친구는 선물 상품권을 받았다고 진술하고 있으므로 voucher를 coupon으로 paraphrasing한 (B) She was given a coupon. 이 정답이다.

---

8. 디아즈 클리너에 관해 무엇이 암시되어 있는가?
(A) 벨 씨의 사업장 근처로 이사했다.
(B) 환경친화적인 제품을 사용한다.
(C) 잘되고 있다.
(D) 몇 개의 지점이 있다.

해설 온라인 양식에 회사의 급속한 성장으로 이전이 필요해졌다는 내용의 문장이 있으므로 (C) It is doing well. 이 정답이다.

---

9. 디아즈 씨는 어느 차량을 이용했는가?
(A) 유형 A
(B) 유형 B
(C) 유형 C
(D) 유형 D

해설 사용 후기에 당초 이용하려고 했던 차량은 내부 용적 125 입방 미터짜리였지만 직원의 조언으로 한 치수 작은 것을 사용했더니 적절했다는 내용이 있다. 광고의 표에서 125 입방 미터짜리보다 한 치수 작은 차량은 Class B라는 것을 알 수 있으므로 (B) Class B가 정답이다.

---

10. 사용 후기 첫 번째 단락 세 번째 줄의 구 "turned out"에 의미상 가장 가까운 것은

(A) 끝났다

(B) 참석했다

(C) 뜻밖에 ~이었다

(D) 뒤집었다

해설 이 문장에서 turned out은 '드러났다'라는 의미로, it happened that '~이 뜻밖에 ~이었다'라는 뜻이 있으므로 turned out에 의미상 가장 가까운 (C) happened가 정답이다.

[11-15] 다음 편지들과 청구서에 관한 문제입니다.

윙필즈 이탈리아 골동품점
75 W. 그랜드 가
세인트 루이스, 미주리 63112

윙필드 씨에게,

제가 기억하는 한 윙필즈 이탈리아 골동품점은 항상 저희 동네와 함께 해왔습니다. 저는 귀하의 가게를 자주 둘러보았으며 진열되어 있는 상품들의 좋은 품질에 감탄했습니다. 최근에, 저는 귀사의 웹사이트에 광고된 여러 유리 골동품들을 제 개인 수집품들에 추가하려고 마음먹었습니다. 저는 완벽의 상태에 가까운 수집품들만 구입하기 때문에, 그 골동품들을 주문하기 전에 각 품목의 명세를 자세히 읽는 것을 소홀히 하지 않았습니다.

11 12 그러나, 주문한 상품을 받아 보니, 아우렐리아노 토소 물건이 반으로 깨져 있고 형편없이 붙여 놓은 것을 볼 수 있었습니다.

이 문제를 해결하기 위해 가능한 한 빨리 응답해 주시면 감사하겠습니다.

진심으로,

Lanie Dalton
라니 달튼

어휘 antique 골동품 | as long as I can remember 내가 기억하는 한 | browse (가게 안의 물건들을) 둘러보다 | admire 감탄하다, 높이 평가하다 | collection 수집품, 소장품 | description 명세, 서술 | poorly 형편없이, 서툴게 | resolve (문제 등을) 해결하다

윙필즈 이탈리아 골동품점
75 W. 그랜드 가
세인트 루이스, 미주리 63112

무라노 베니니 　유리 컵받침	212.00달러
살비에티 다르떼 　호박 면이 있는 유리 접시	90.00달러
세네디스 　**15** 유니콘 유리 조각상	55.00달러
무라노 솜머소 　하늘빛 유리 꽃병	120.00달러
아우렐리아노 토소 　**12** 대리석 무늬의 유리 물 주전자	325.00달러
합계	802.00달러

***13** 비고: 윙필즈 골동품점에서의 모든 판매는 교환 및 반품이 불가능함.

어휘 saucer 컵받침 | amber (광물) 호박 | faceted (깎인) 면이 있는 | platter (큰 서빙용) 접시 | figurine 작은 조각상 | azure 하늘빛의 | marbled 대리석 무늬의 | pitcher 물 주전자 | final 변경할 수 없는, 교환 및 환불이 안 되는

윙필드 이탈리아 골동품점
75 W. 그랜드 가
세인트 루이스, 미주리 63112

라니 달튼
1022 미노우 가
세인트 루이스, 미주리 63105

달튼 씨에게,

저희의 모든 유리 제품들은 판매용으로 광고되기 전에 꼼꼼히 점검된다는 것을 알려 드립니다. 고객님께서 말씀하시는 물품을 기억하는데, **14** 그 물품은 저희에게 도착했을 때도 꼼꼼히 살펴보았고, 고객님 댁에 배송 드리기 전에도 다시 살펴보았음을 확인해 드립니다. 골동품 중개 상인을 오랫동안 해온 사람으로서, 저는 이 골동품이 100여 년 전에 원래의 공예가가 다시 붙여 놓은 거라고 생각합니다. 따라서, 이 상품은 사실 원상태입니다.

고객님께서 언짢으실 수도 있다고 생각되어서, **15** 세네디스 유니콘에 대한 값을 환불해 드리고자 하니 제가 드리는 선물로 간직해 주십시오.

다른 궁금한 것이 있으시면 연락해 주십시오.

안부를 전하며,

Esther Wingfield
에스더 윙필드

어휘 glassware 유리 제품 | inspect 점검하다 | assure 보장하다 | dealer 중개 상인 | craftsman 공예가, 장인 | original condition 원상태 | refund the charge for ~의 값을 환불하다

11. 달튼 씨가 쓴 편지의 목적은 무엇인가?

(A) 반송 우편 주소를 요청하기 위해

(B) 몇몇 상품들의 구매 가능성을 확인하기 위해

(C) 배송 지연에 대해 문의하기 위해

(D) 제품 상태에 대해 불만을 표하기 위해

해설 첫 번째 편지 지문의 목적을 물어보는 문제로, 주문을 받자마자 주문한 상품의 상태가 좋지 않음을 알려주는 내용이므로 정답은 (D) To express dissatisfaction with the condition of a product이다.

---

12. 달튼 씨가 걱정스러워하는 골동품은 무엇인가?

(A) 유리 컵받침

(B) 호박 면이 있는 유리 접시

(C) 하늘빛 유리 꽃병

(D) 대리석 무늬의 유리 물 주전자

해설 달튼 씨가 언급한 제품은 아우렐리아노 토소로 청구서 지문에서 Marbled glass pitcher로 나와 있으므로 정답은 (D) The marbled glass pitcher이다.

---

13. 윙필드 이탈리아 골동품점에 관하여 알 수 있는 것은 무엇인가?

(A) 반품을 허용하지 않는다.

(B) 희귀한 골동품을 온라인으로 판매하지 않는다.

(C) 지역 주민에게 할인을 제공한다.

(D) 유명한 미술품 수집가가 운영한다.

해설 청구서 하단의 Note를 보면 윙필드 골동품점에서 판매하는 모든 제품은 교환 및 환불이 안 됨을 알 수 있으므로 정답은 (A) It does not accept returns. 이다.

---

14. 두 번째 편지에서 언급된 것은 무엇인가?

(A) 달튼 씨의 배송품이 아직 도착하지 않았다.

(B) 윙필드 씨는 서류 몇 개를 제출할 것이다.

(C) 달튼 씨는 주문에 상품을 추가할 것이다.

(D) 윙필드 씨는 상품을 직접 점검했다.

해설 두 번째 편지에서 글을 쓴 윙필드 씨가 배송하기 전에 직접 꼼꼼하게 살펴봤다고 했으므로 정답은 (D) Ms. Wingfield examined an item herself. 이다.

---

15. 달튼 씨는 얼마를 환불받을 것인가?

(A) 55달러

(B) 90달러

(C) 120달러

(D) 212달러

해설 세 번째 지문에서 세네디스 유니콘에 대한 것에 환불을 해준다고 했으며, 두 번째 청구서에서 그 금액을 찾으면 55달러이므로 정답은 (A) $55이다.

REVIEW TEST

본서 p.302

1. (A)	2. (C)	3. (C)	4. (C)	5. (C)
6. (B)	7. (C)	8. (B)	9. (A)	10. (A)
11. (D)	12. (A)	13. (A)	14. (D)	15. (D)
16. (A)	17. (C)	18. (C)	19. (B)	20. (A)
21. (A)	22. (C)	23. (A)	24. (A)	25. (C)
26. (D)	27. (D)	28. (C)	29. (A)	30. (B)
31. (A)	32. (D)	33. (D)	34. (B)	35. (B)
36. (C)	37. (D)	38. (C)	39. (B)	40. (C)
41. (D)	42. (C)	43. (A)	44. (C)	45. (C)
46. (A)	47. (C)	48. (C)	49. (B)	50. (D)
51. (C)	52. (C)	53. (A)	54. (C)	

[1-2] 다음 제품 후기에 관한 문제입니다.

스캔텍 디비40-에스엘 휴대용 선풍기는 환상적입니다. 작은 크기 덕분에 어떤 바지나 재킷 주머니에도 들어갑니다. **1** 제가 어딜 가든 디비40-에스엘을 들고 다니고, 이 선풍기는 출퇴근길의 더운 지하철 이동 중에 아주 쓸모 있습니다. 한 가지 불만 사항이 있긴 합니다: **2** 선풍기가 언제 전원이 나갈지 전혀 알 길이 없다는 것입니다. 배터리를 언제 재충전해야 할지 경고하는 표시등 같은 것이 달린 새 버전이 나오면 좋을 것 같습니다. 저는 심지어 업그레이드된 버전 구매를 고려해 볼 겁니다.

-로버트 한나

어휘 portable 휴대용의 | fan 선풍기 | fantastic 환상적인 | compact 소형의 | fit into ~에 맞는 | come in handy 쓸모가 있다 | complaint 불만, 불평 | indicator 지표, 표시 | warn 경고하다 | recharge 재충전하다 | consider 고려하다

---

1. 한나 씨에 관해 암시된 것은 무엇인가?

(A) 대중교통을 자주 이용한다.

(B) 몇 개의 휴대용 선풍기를 사용해 보았다.

(C) 최근 새로운 일을 시작했다.

(D) 사무실에서 멀리 떨어진 곳에 산다.

해설 두 번째 줄에서 선풍기는 출퇴근길의 더운 지하철 이동 중에 아주 쓸모 있다고 했으므로 (A) He uses public transportation often. 이 정답이다.

---

2. 한나 씨에 따르면, 스캔텍 디비40-에스엘은 어떻게 향상될 수 있는가?

(A) 더 작아질 수 있다.

(B) 추가 배터리가 포함될 수 있다.

(C) 경고등이 추가될 수 있다.

(D) 손에 쥐기 더 편해질 수 있다.

해설 네 번째 줄에서 선풍기가 언제 전원이 나갈지 전혀 알 길이 없어 배터리를 언제 재충전해야 할지 경고하는 표시등 같은 것이 달린 새 버전이 나오면 좋을 것 같다고 했으므로 (C) A warning light could be added. 가 정답이다.

[3-4] 다음 공지에 관한 문제입니다.

〈루벡스 레지스터〉 구독자 귀하,

3 인쇄 비용의 증가로 인해, 〈루벡스 레지스터〉가 일간지의 분량을 축소할 예정임을 참고해 주십시오. 따라서, 다음 달부터 의견란이 인쇄되지 않는 대신, 저희 웹사이트 www.roubaixregister.com에 등장할 것입니다.

의견란의 견본이 다음 주에 온라인으로 게시될 것입니다. 게시가 되면, 구독자 여러분 모두 이것을 확인해 볼 것을 권장해 드립니다. **4** 만약 형식이나 스타일에 변화가 있어야 한다고 생각하신다면, 저에게 ttyrell@roubaixregister.com으로 이메일을 보내 주시면 바로 살펴보겠습니다.

감사합니다,

토드 타이렐
편집장

어휘 subscriber 구독자 | note ~에 주의하다[주목하다] | cut down 줄이다, 축소하다 | length 길이 | print edition 인쇄판 | consequently 결과적으로, 따라서 | section 분야, 구역 | appear 등장하다, 나타나다 | sample 샘플, 견본 | opinion 의견 | encourage 격려하다, 권장하다 | check out 확인하다, 점검하다 | format 포맷, 형식 | look into 조사하다, 살펴보다

3. 〈루벡스 레지스터〉는 무엇을 바꿀 것인가?
(A) 편집자를 교체할 예정이다.
(B) 새로운 섹션을 추가할 예정이다.
(C) 일부 내용을 온라인으로 옮길 것이다.
(D) 더 이상 매일 이용할 수 없을 것이다.

해설 첫 번째 단락에서 인쇄 비용의 증가로 인해, 〈루벡스 레지스터〉가 일간지의 분량을 축소할 예정이라서 다음 달부터 의견란이 인쇄되지 않는 대신, 웹사이트 www.roubaixregister.com에 등장할 것이라고 했으므로 (C) It will move some content online. 이 정답이다.

4. 공지에 따르면, 구독자들은 왜 타이렐 씨에게 연락할지도 모르는가?
(A) 서비스 연장하기 위해
(B) 환불을 요청하기 위해
(C) 제안을 하기 위해
(D) 기사를 제출하기 위해

해설 두 번째 단락에서 형식이나 스타일에 변화가 있어야 한다고 생각하신다면, ttyrell@roubaixregister.com으로 이메일을 보내 주시면 바로 살펴보겠다고 했으므로 (C) To provide some suggestions가 정답이다.

[5-6] 다음 문자 대화문에 관한 문제입니다.

제나 브로드스키 [오후 4:46]:
버켓 씨, **5** 계약서 신규 조항을 방금 전송했습니다. 받으셨나요?

루카스 버켓 [오후 4:59]:
받았습니다. **5** 계약 조건을 업데이트해 주셔서 정말 감사합니다.

제나 브로드스키 [오후 5:00]:
5 천만에요. 타당한 지적을 하셨어요. **6** 이제 계약서에 우리 아파트 단지의 테라스를 짓는 것에 대해 저희가 당신에게 4,500유로가 아닌 5,000유로를 지불한다고 명시되었습니다.

루카스 버켓 [오후 5:06]:
좋습니다. 제가 한 번 더 검토해 보고 나서, 서명해서 이메일로 회신드릴게요.

제나 브로드스키 [오후 5:10]:
좋아요. **6** 귀사에 대해 좋은 이야기들을 들었습니다. 테라스가 어떻게 나올지 보게 되어 신이 나네요.

어휘 send over 전송하다 | terms (합의·계약 등의) 조건 | agreement 합의, 계약 | appreciate 감사하다 | update 가장 최근의 정보를 알려주다[덧붙이다] | condition 조건, 상태 | bring up (화제를) 꺼내다 | fair 공정한, 타당한 | point 지적, 요점 | indicate 나타내다, 명시하다 | apartment complex 아파트 단지 | patio 파티오, 테라스 | review 검토하다, 평가하다 | turn out 모습을 드러내다, 나타나다

5. 오후 5시에, 제나 브로드스키가 "천만에요"라고 쓴 것은 무슨 의미인가?
(A) 이미 지시 사항을 알고 있다.
(B) 문제를 처리하길 원한다.
(C) 업무를 완료해서 기뻤다.
(D) 주제에 대해 논의하고 싶어 하지 않는다.

해설 오후 4시 46분 ~ 5시 대화에서 제나 브로드스키가 계약서 신규 조항을 방금 전송했는데 받았는지 묻자 루카스 버켓이 계약 조건을 업데이트해 주셔서 정말 감사하다고 했고, 제나 브로드스키가 천만에요라고 대답한 것이므로 (C) She was glad to complete a task. 가 정답이다.

6. 버켓 씨는 어디에서 일하겠는가?
(A) 회계 회사
(B) 건설 회사
(C) 부동산 사무실
(D) 법률 사무소

해설 오후 5시, 제나 브로드스키의 메시지에서 계약서에 우리 아파트 단지의 테라스를 짓는 것에 대해 저희가 당신에게 4,500유로가 아닌 5,000유로를 지불한다고 명시되었다고 했고, 오후 5시 10분, 제나 브로드스키의 메시지에서 귀사에 대해 좋은 이야기들을 들어 왔고, 테라스가 어떻게 나올지 볼 수 있다니 신이 난다고 했으므로 (B) A construction firm이 정답이다.

[7-8] 다음 계약서에 관한 문제입니다.

작업 변경서

조경 도급자: 플로렌스 로잘레스, 그린썸 가드너스, 475 아처 가, 샌디에이고, 캘리포니아
부동산 관리인: 윌리엄 야마모토, 7534 위버 가, 샌디에이고, 캘리포니아

프로젝트 개시일: 4월 4일
8 프로젝트 완료일: 4월 10일

도급자는 이에 원 계약에 대한 다음 변경 사항을 검토하여 실시하도록 지시받는다.

변경 세부 사항:
7 이제 고객이 종자와 토양, 화초를 제공할 것이다. 그 결과, 프로젝트의 총비용은 인건비만을 포함하도록 조정된다.

원 계약 금액: 1,223달러
주문 변경에 의한 조정액: -546달러
주문 변경에 의한 수정 총액: 677달러

조정 지불 일정:
수정 총액의 25%(169달러)는 계약 체결 시 지급하며, 150달러를 프로젝트 개시일에 지급한다. **8** 잔액(358달러)은 프로젝트 완료일에 지급한다.

도급자: 플로렌스 로잘레스
부동산 관리인: 윌리엄 야마모토

어휘 landscape 조경술 | contractor 도급(업)자 | property 부동산 | hereby 이에 의하여, 이로써 | direct 지시하다 | initial 처음의, 초기의 | adjust 조정하다, 조절하다 | collect 수금하다, 징수하다 | remainder 나머지

---

7. 프로젝트의 비용은 왜 조정되었는가?
(A) 도급자가 용품의 가격을 너무 적게 추산했다.
(B) 도급자가 잘못된 종류의 종자를 심었다.
(C) 고객이 모든 자재를 공급할 것이다.
(D) 고객이 인건비를 협상하고 싶어 한다.

해설 Details of the Change에서 이제 고객이 종자와 토양, 화초를 제공할 것이고 그 결과, 프로젝트의 총비용은 인건비만을 포함하도록 조정된다고 했으므로 (C) The client will supply all the materials. 가 정답이다.

---

8. 4월 10일에 야마모토 씨는 로잘레스 씨에게 얼마의 돈을 주겠는가?
(A) 169달러
(B) 358달러
(C) 546달러
(D) 677달러

해설 Last Day of Project(프로젝트 완료일)가 April 10(4월 10일)이라고 했고, The New Payment Schedule(조정 지불 일정)에서 잔액(358달러)은 프로젝트 완료일에 지급한다고 했으므로 (B) $358이 정답이다.

[9-11] 다음 구인 광고에 관한 문제입니다.

www.calientejobs.org/listing201

더블유티 헬스에서 일하세요!

대부분의 회사가 영업 직원들에게 고객이 정말 필요하지 않은 제품을 강요하고 판매하라고 요구하지만, 저희 팀은 모든 고객에게 정직하고 솔직하단 것에 자긍심을 갖습니다. 공격적이 되는 것 대신,

---

더블유티 헬스는 지역 주민들에게 저희가 가진 기술의 이점에 대해 가르쳐주려 노력하고 있습니다. **9** 저희 수수료는 당신이 데려오는 고객들의 수를 기반으로 하는 것이 아니라, 당신의 제품 시연에 참석하는 참가자들의 수를 기반으로 합니다.

10 3주간의 교육 과정을 수강하면서 돈을 버세요. 합격하여 공인 영업 담당자가 된다면, 당신은 저희 팀의 정규직이 될 자격을 갖추게 될 것입니다.

대학 학위와 의학 기술 분야에 경력은 가점이 되지만, 저희는 열정적이고 조리 있게 말을 잘하는 사람의 지원을 고려할 것입니다. 저희 고객들은 다양한 지역에 위치하고 있기 때문에, 본사에서 최대 100킬로미터까지 외근하라는 요청을 받을 수도 있지만, 이 과정에서 발생하는 모든 비용에 대해서는 환급을 받을 것입니다.

이 직무에 지원하려면, 칼리엔테 잡스 계정에 로그인하여 이력서와 자기소개서를 제출해 주십시오. 전화번호를 포함하는 것을 잊지 마세요. 저희는 문자 메시지로 연락하는 것을 선호합니다. 질문이 있으시면, 919-555-2333으로 메시지를 보내주세요. **11** 대부분의 합격자들은 면접을 보러 오기 전에 저희 상품에 대해 익히는 시간을 갖습니다. 그렇게 하시려면, www.wthealth.com을 방문해 주세요.

어휘 sales force 판매 인력 | pushy 지나치게 밀어붙이는, 강요하려 드는 | pride oneself on ~을 자랑하다, 자긍심을 갖다 | straightforward 솔직한, 간단한 | aggressive 공격적인, 적극적인 | strive 노력하다, 분투하다 | commission 커미션, 수수료 | bring in 들여오다, 참여하게 하다 | demonstration 시연, 입증, 설명 | certified 보증된, 공인의, 자격증을 갖춘 | eligible for ~에 대한 자격이 있는 | passionate 열정적인 | articulate (생각을) 잘 표현하는, 똑똑히 말을 잘하는 | reimburse 변제하다, 배상하다 | incur (비용을) 발생시키다 | correspond 통신하다, 서신 왕래하다; 일치하다 | familiarize oneself with ~을 익히다[정통하다]

---

9. 광고에 따르면, 명시된 직무는 무엇인가?
(A) 회사 제품을 소개하는 것
(B) 의료 총회에 참석하는 것
(C) 신기술을 개발하는 것
(D) 주간 판매 수수료 목표를 달성하는 것

해설 첫 번째 단락에서 수수료는 당신이 데려오는 고객들의 수를 기반으로 하는 것이 아니라, 제품 시연에 참석하는 참가자들의 수를 기반으로 한다고 했으므로 (A) Presenting company products가 정답이다.

---

10. 정규직을 얻기 위한 요건은 무엇인가?
(A) 영업사원 자격증
(B) 전 고용주로부터의 추천
(C) 의료기술 관련 경험
(D) 대학 학위

해설 두 번째 단락에서 3주간의 교육 과정을 수강하고 합격하여 공인 영업 담당자가 된다면, 팀의 정규직이 될 자격을 갖추게 될 것이라고 했으므로 (A) A sales associate certificate가 정답이다.

---

11. 광고에 따르면, 지원자는 왜 더블유티 헬스의 웹사이트를 방문해야 하는가?

(A) 입사지원서를 제출하기 위해

(B) 보건 콘퍼런스에 등록하기 위해

(C) 사무실 가는 방법을 알기 위해

(D) 일부 상품에 관해 읽어보기 위해

해설　네 번째 단락에서 대부분의 합격자들은 면접을 보러 오기 전에 상품에 대해 익히는 시간을 갖는데 그렇게 하려면, www.wthealth.com을 방문하라고 했으므로 (D) To read about some merchandise가 정답이다.

[12-14] 다음 회람에 관한 문제입니다.

수신: 아이알엠 기술사업부 직원들

발신: 팻 자오, 전문경영인

날짜: 12월 2일

제목: 중요 공지 사항

12 13 여러분 대부분이 지금쯤 아시겠지만, 우리의 기술 담당 최고 책임자 탬 프라데시가 이번 분기 말에 은퇴하십니다. **13** 12월 21일 저녁 6시 30분에 크리스탈 호텔에서 그분에게 경의를 표하며 회사 만찬을 가질 예정입니다. 여러분 모두의 참석을 환영합니다.

12 14 이참에, 프라데시 씨의 후임자도 발표하겠습니다. **14** 제이미 헤이스가 12월 26일부터 저희와 함께합니다. 헤이스 씨는 사이-렌더 전자에서 소프트웨어 개발 담당 부사장이었고 시큐리키 사의 최고 기술 경영자로 근무하면서 개선된 바이러스 예방 프로그램을 개발한 팀을 지도하고 이끌면서 명성을 얻었습니다. 이분이 우리 조직의 일원이 되는 것이 기대됩니다.

헤이스 씨의 소개는 12월 30일 오전 10시에 있을 1/4분기 주주총회에서 있을 것이며, 웹사이트에서 볼 수 있을 것입니다. 총회에서는, 그녀와 재무 이사 샬럿 위즈너가 아이알엠 사의 내년 계획에 대해 논의할 것입니다. 이 행사 참석은 사원들에게는 선택사항이지만, 부서장들은 의무적으로 참석해야 합니다.

어휘　company-wide 회사 전반의 | in one's honor ~에게 경의를 표하여, ~을 축하하여 | replacement 대신할 사람 | accolade 포상, 칭찬 | shareholder's meeting 주주총회 | viewable 볼 수 있는 | CFO(chief financial officer) 재무 담당 최고 책임자 | optional 선택적인 | mandatory 의무적인 | head (단체·조직의) 책임자

---

12. 회람은 무엇을 발표하고 있는가?

(A) 인사 변동

(B) 신제품을 위한 언론 보도자료

(C) 회의 일정 변경

(D) 직원 승진

해설　첫 번째 단락에서 기술 담당 최고 책임자 탬 프라데시가 이번 분기 말에 은퇴한다고 했고, 이참에 프라데시 씨의 후임자도 발표하겠다고 했으므로 (A) A personnel change가 정답이다.

---

13. 회람에 따르면, 12월 21일에는 무슨 일이 일어날 것인가?

(A) 프라데시 씨가 만찬에 참석할 것이다.

(B) 자오 씨가 투자자들에게 연설할 것이다.

(C) 헤이스 씨가 교육 세미나를 실시할 것이다.

(D) 위즈너 씨가 상을 나눠줄 것이다.

해설　첫 번째 단락에서 우리의 기술 담당 최고 책임자 탬 프라데시가 이번 분기 말에 은퇴하므로 12월 21일 저녁 6시 30분에 크리스탈 호텔에서 그분에게 경의를 표하며 회사 만찬을 가질 예정이라고 했으므로 (A) Mr. Pradesh will attend a dinner. 가 정답이다.

---

14. 헤이스 씨는 누구인가?

(A) 호텔 매니저

(B) 재무 전문가

(C) 입사 지원자

(D) 최근 영입된 간부

해설　두 번째 단락에서 프라데시 씨의 후임자인 제이미 헤이스가 12월 26일부터 저희와 함께할 거라고 했으므로 (D) A recently hired executive가 정답이다.

[15-18] 다음 기사에 관한 문제입니다.

구이 요리, 서울을 사로잡다

서울 (11월 12일) — **15** 맥신 이는 6년째 대한민국에 살고 있다. 그 기간 동안, 그녀는 자신이 가장 좋아하는 음식인 전통 선데이 구이를 파는 식당을 한 번도 보지 못했다. 고기, 감자, 당근 위에 그레이비 소스가 얹혀진 선데이 구이는 이 씨가 어렸을 때 뉴질랜드에서 주로 먹던 음식이었다.

한국에 있는 다른 뉴질랜드인들과 이야기를 나눠본 후, 이 씨는 자신의 직접 구이 요리를 전문으로 제공하는 식당 허티 딜라이츠를 차리기로 결심했다. 최초의 식당은 아주 좁은 주방에, 10명 정도 간신히 앉을 정도의 크기였다. 현지인들이 구이 요리에 익숙하지 않다 보니 초기엔 반응이 미적지근했다. 하지만, 금세 소문을 타기 시작하면서, 문밖으로 줄이 생겼다.

"현지인이 많이 보이기 시작하면서 깜짝 놀랐어요."라고 이 씨가 말했다. **16** "확실히, 국내에서 식자재를 조달하는 게 힘들었습니다. 예를 들면, 양고기는 구하기가 힘들어요. 그런 경우엔, 해외에서 식재료를 구입하는 데 의지해야 했어요. 하지만 이곳 농민을 지원하기 위해 현지에서 조달하려고 최선을 다했습니다."

17 이 씨는 뉴질랜드 국제 무역(엔지아이티)에서 제공한 보조금으로 자신의 식당을 차렸는데, 이곳에서는 뉴질랜드 문화를 널리 전파하고 싶어 한다. **18** 최근에는 아시아에 주목해 왔다. "그분들 아니었으면 해내지 못했을 거예요. 대단한 분들이세요."라고 그녀가 말했다.

이 씨는 11월 26일에 더 큰 규모로 두 번째 매장을 열 예정이다. 서울 중심부인 강남구에 위치하는 새로운 건물은 100석을 수용할 것이다. 더불어, 허티 딜라이츠에서는 웹사이트를 통해 주문 및 수령 서비스를 제공하기 시작할 것이다. 더 자세한 내용은 www.heartydelights.co.kr/order에서 확인하면 된다.

어휘 roast 구이 요리 | hit 대인기 | serve (식당 등에서 음식을) 제공하다 | favorite 가장 좋아하는 | meal 식사 | traditional 전통적인 | consist of ~으로 구성되다 | drizzle (액체를) 조금 붓다 | gravy 그레이비(고기를 익힐 때 나온 육즙에 밀가루 등을 넣어 만든 소스) | staple 주요 식품 | childhood 어린 시절 | specialize in ~을 전문으로 하다 | tiny 아주 작은 | barely 간신히, 가까스로 | initial 처음의, 초기의 | local 현지인 | unfamiliar with ~에 익숙하지 않은 | spread 퍼져 나가다 | admittedly 인정하건대 | source 조달하다 | hard to come by 구하기 어려운 | resort to ~에 의지하다, 기대다 | overseas 해외에 | grant 보조금 | in the heart of ~의 중심부에 | district 구역, 지역 | premises 부지, 구내 | capacity 수용력 | additionally 또한

15. 이 씨에 대해 무엇을 알 수 있는가?
(A) 사업을 물려받았다.
(B) 원래 회계사 교육을 받았다.
(C) 업무상 자주 이사한다.
(D) 서울 토박이가 아니다.

해설 첫 번째 단락에서 맥신 이는 6년째 대한민국에 살고 있으며 그 기간 동안 그녀는 자신이 가장 좋아하는 음식인 전통 선데이 구이를 파는 식당을 한 번도 보지 못했다고 했으므로 (D) She is not a Seoul native. 가 정답이다.

16. 이 씨가 구이 요리에 관해서 말하는 것은 무엇인가?
(A) 수입 재료를 포함한다.
(B) 전통적인 가정식 조리법을 따른다.
(C) 시즌에 따라 달라진다.
(D) 준비하는 데 엄청난 시간이 소요된다.

해설 세 번째 단락에서 국내에서 식자재를 조달하는 게 힘들었고 예를 들어, 양고기는 구하기가 힘들다고 했으므로 (A) They include imported ingredients. 가 정답이다.

17. 엔지아이티에 관하여 무엇이 나타나 있는가?
(A) 서울에서 구이 요리를 광고하는 데 도움을 줬다.
(B) 이 씨에게 업계 연락망을 공유해 줬다.
(C) 새로운 식당의 위치를 제안했다.
(D) 이 씨의 식당에 자본을 제공했다.

해설 네 번째 단락에서 이 씨는 뉴질랜드 국제 무역(엔지아이티)에서 제공한 보조금으로 자신의 식당을 차렸는데, 이곳에서 뉴질랜드 문화를 널리 전파하고 싶어 한다고 했으므로 (D) It provided capital for Ms. Lee's restaurant. 가 정답이다. a grant가 capital로 바꿔 표현되었다.

18. [1], [2], [3], [4]로 표시된 곳 중에서 다음 문장이 들어갈 위치로 가장 적절한 곳은 어디인가?
"최근에는 아시아에 주목해 왔다."
(A) [1]

(B) [2]
(C) [3]
(D) [4]

해설 네 번째 단락에서 이 씨는 뉴질랜드 국제 무역(엔지아이티)에서 제공한 보조금으로 자신의 식당을 차렸는데, 이곳에서 뉴질랜드 문화를 널리 전파하고 싶어 한다고 하여 주어진 문장이 이어지기에 자연스러우므로 (C)가 정답이다.

[19-21] 다음 안건에 관한 문제입니다.

밥 로버츠 발표:
〈감춰진 잠재력을 드러내세요〉
21 5월 27일(오후 1-6시)
21 세미나 티켓 99달러부터

오후 1시: 어디로 가고 싶으세요?
자기 계발을 증진시키기 위해서는, 무엇을 개선해야 하는지 알아야 합니다. **19 20** 이 시간은 갓 졸업한 학생들이 성취 가능한 목표를 세우고 좋은 직업을 얻을 기회를 늘리는 데 도움이 될 것입니다.

오후 2시: 누구에게 기댈 수 있을까요?
강력하고 도움이 되는 관계를 구축하고, 여러분의 성공을 방해하는 관계들을 버리는 법을 배우세요.

오후 3시: 당신의 연료는 무엇인가요?
참가자들은 신체 건강과 영양의 중요성 또한 배울 것입니다. **21** 저희 총주방장이 조리법과 팁을 공유하고, 맛있는 무료 샘플을 제공할 것입니다.

오후 4시: 단체 연습
참석자들은 자신들의 개인적 여정에 관한 이야기를 나누고, 행동 계획에 관한 솔직한 피드백과 확인을 받습니다.

오후 5시: 진행 상황 점검
당신의 건강과 직업에 대한 향상을 계속 파악하세요. 여러분이 얼마나 멀리 왔는지 그리고 다음으로 무엇에 집중할 것인지를 객관적으로 평가하는 것을 배우세요.

어휘 potential 잠재성 | advance 증진시키다, 나아가다 | count on 기대하다, 기대다 | discard 버리다, 폐기하다 | get in the way of ~을 방해하다 | affirmation 확인, 확언 | keep track of ~을 기록하다, ~에 대해 계속 파악하다 | objectively 객관적으로 | evaluate 평가하다

19. 세미나는 누구를 대상으로 하겠는가?
(A) 채용 담당자
(B) 최근 졸업생
(C) 피트니스 강사
(D) 의대생

해설 1:00 P.M.: Where Do You Want to Go? 에서 이 시간은 갓 졸업한 학생들이 성취 가능한 목표를 세우고 좋은 직업을 얻을 기회를 늘리는 데 도움이 될 것이라고 했으므로 (B) Recent graduates가 정답이다.

20. 어떤 섹션이 목표 설정을 포함하는가?

(A) 어디로 가고 싶으세요?

(B) 누구에게 기댈 수 있을까요?

(C) 단체 연습

(D) 진행 상황 점검

해설 1:00 P.M.: Where Do you Want to Go? 에서 이 시간은 갓 졸업한 학생들이 성취 가능한 목표를 세우고 좋은 직업을 얻을 기회를 늘리는 데 도움이 될 것이라고 했으므로 (A) Where Do You Want to Go? 가 정답이다.

---

21. 세미나에 관하여 언급되지 않은 것은?

(A) 이력서 상담을 제공할 것이다.

(B) 하루 동안 열린다.

(C) 참석하는 데 비용이 든다.

(D) 무료 음식을 제공한다.

해설 지문의 단서와 보기를 매칭시키면, 지문 앞부분에서 세미나가 5월 27일 하루 열리며 티켓이 99달러이므로 (B), (C)를 제거한다. 세 번째 문단에서 무료 음식 샘플을 준다고 하므로 (D)도 제거하고, 이력서 상담을 제공한다는 내용은 언급된 바 없으므로 (A) It will provide résumé consultations. 가 정답이다.

[22-25] 다음 온라인 채팅 대화문에 관한 문제입니다.

> **칼 르뮤 [오후 1:04]**
> 제닝스 그룹과 좀 더 오래 있을 것 같네요. 월요일에 있을 전문경영인 방문을 위한 준비가 모두 잘 될까요?
>
> **에이프릴 포인덱스터 [오후 1:04]**
> 그럴 것 같아요. 방문 준비를 위해 주말에 전체 바닥 청소를 진행할 예정이에요.
>
> **아니카 마투 [오후 1:06]**
> 22 23 몇 주 전 기계들을 업그레이드해서, 올해 트럭 모델 생산이 큰 문제 없이 순조롭게 진행되고 있어요. 하지만 24 조만간 직원 안전 세미나 일정을 다시 잡아야 해요.
>
> **칼 르뮤 [오후 1:07]**
> 올해 초에 한 번 하지 않았나요?
>
> **아니카 마투 [오후 1:07]**
> 24 그 뒤로 신입 직원이 많이 들어왔으니까요.
>
> **칼 르뮤 [오후 1:09]**
> 24 좋은 지적이에요. 세미나를 언제로 잡을까요?
>
> **에이프릴 포인덱스터 [오후 1:10]**
> 그리고, 아니카와 제가 퇴근 전에 돌아가면서 매일 조립 라인을 점검하고 있어요.
>
> **아니카 마투 [오후 1:10]**
> 아마 다음 주 화요일이요. 제가 오늘 오후에 일정을 잡을 수 있습니다.
>
> **칼 르뮤 [오후 1:11]**
> 고마워요, 여러분. 25 사실, 아니카, 그건 나중에 논의하도록 합시다. 우리는 오늘 있는 직원 감사 파티 준비가 모두 잘되었는지 확인해야 해요. 30분 후에 가서 도와드릴게요.

어휘 entire 전체의 | smoothly 순조롭게 | incident 일, 사건 | arrange 주선하다 | inspect 조사하다 | assembly line 조립 라인 | appreciation 감사 | assist 돕다

22. 글쓴이들은 어디에서 일하겠는가?

(A) 자동차 정비소에서

(B) 자동차 대여점에서

(C) 자동차 제조사에서

(D) 운송회사에서

해설 오후 1시 6분, 아니카 마투의 메시지에서 몇 주 전 기계들을 업그레이드해서, 올해 트럭 모델 생산이 큰 문제 없이 순조롭게 진행되고 있다고 말했으므로 (C) At a vehicle manufacturer가 정답이다.

---

23. 최근 무슨 일이 있었는가?

(A) 장비 몇 대가 업데이트되었다.

(B) 박람회가 열렸다.

(C) 일부 직원들이 은퇴했다.

(D) 과태료를 물었다.

해설 오후 1시 6분, 아니카 마투의 메시지에서 몇 주 전 기계들을 업그레이드해서, 올해 트럭 모델 생산이 큰 문제 없이 순조롭게 진행되고 있다고 말했으므로 (A) Some equipment was updated. 가 정답이다.

---

24. 오후 1시 9분에, 르뮤 씨가 "좋은 지적이에요"라고 쓴 것은 무슨 의미이겠는가?

(A) 어떤 교육이 제공되어야 한다.

(B) 마감 기한이 연장되어야 한다.

(C) 채용 가이드라인 일부가 수정되어야 한다.

(D) 제품 특징이 추가되어야 한다.

해설 오후 1시 6분 ~ 1시 9분 대화에서 아니카 마투가 조만간 직원 안전 세미나 일정을 다시 잡아야 한다고 했고, 오후 1시 7분에 그녀가 다시 그 뒤로 신입 직원이 많이 들어왔다고 말한 것에 대해 오후 1시 9분, 칼 르뮤가 좋은 지적이라며 세미나를 언제로 잡을지 물으므로 (A) Some training needs to be provided. 가 정답이다.

---

25. 마투 씨는 다음으로 무엇을 하겠는가?

(A) 기계를 고친다

(B) 소포를 찾으러 간다

(C) 행사를 준비한다

(D) 임원과 만난다

해설 오후 1시 11분, 칼 르뮤의 메시지에서 나중에 논의하자며, 우리는 오늘 있는 직원 감사 파티 준비가 모두 잘되었는지 확인해야 하니 30분 후에 가서 도와주겠다고 했으므로 (C) Get ready for an event가 정답이다.

팔레 로열의 새로운 시대

찰스튼 (8월 2일) — 유명한 팔레 로열은 오랫동안 콜팩스 가의 명소였지만, 곧 중대한 변화를 겪게 될 것이다. 지난주에 뉴브런즈윅에 본사를 둔 토마스 사가 오랜 주인에게 125년 된 시설을 매입하면서 대연회장은 최근에 소유권이 바뀌었다. **26** 회사 대표 에보니 살렘은 작업반이 시설의 원래 목조 부분을 복원하고 현재의 천장 조명을 옛날식 상들리에로 교체하는 작업을 하는 올겨울 동안 대연회장을 폐쇄할 계획이라고 말한다. **29** 전통 벽지 또한 추가될 것이다.

"하지만, 우리는 건물의 현대 음향 시스템을 유지할 것이므로, 공간은 여전히 라이브 콘서트와 다른 사교 행사들에 사용될 수 있습니다."라고 살렘 씨는 덧붙였다.

최근 몇 년간, 팔레 로열은 한정된 수의 행사를 주최해 왔다. 전 소유주인 제시카 그래슬리는 1970년대 이전처럼 이 대연회장을 시민 생활의 중심지로 만들려고 수년 동안 노력했다. **27** "이것은 저에게 열정을 담은 프로젝트였습니다."라고 그래슬리는 말했다. "그래서 힘들었습니다. 저는 팔레 로열을 포기하고 싶지 않았지만, 결국에는 토마스 사가 이 오래된 대연회장에 새로운 활기를 줄 것이라 생각합니다."

이 새로운 소유 그룹은 이 대연회장이 더 많은 결혼식, 학교 무도회, 그리고 고수익의 기업 행사들을 끌어들일 수 있기를 희망하고 있다. **28** 팔레 로열은 또한 연례 자선행사를 계속 주최할 것이다. 올해의 모임은 4월 11일에 열릴 것이다. 이 행사는 언제나처럼 일반대중에게 공개될 것이지만, 올해는, 모든 참가자에게 정장 착용이 요구된다. **28** 또한, 그것은 더 이상 팔레 자선 운동으로 알려지지 않을 것이다. 대신, 그것은 홍보 자선 행사라고 불릴 것이다.

어휘 era 시대 | undergo 겪다 | transformation 변화, 변신 | ballroom 무도회장, 대연회장 | shut down 폐쇄하다, 문을 닫다 | chandelier 상들리에 | civic 시민의, 시의 | passion 열정 | spark 불꽃, 활기 | big-ticket 돈이 많이 드는 | charity 자선, 자선 행사 | gathering 모임 | as always 언제나처럼 | be open to ~에게 공개되다 | formal attire 정장 | drive (조직적인) 운동

26. 팔레 로열에 관해 암시된 것은 무엇인가?
(A) 1970년대에 개장했다.
(B) 입장료를 인상할 것이다.
(C) 이전에 가족경영 시설이었다.
(D) 곧 개조될 것이다.

해설 첫 번째 단락에서 회사 대표 에보니 살렘은 작업반이 시설의 원래 목조 부분을 복원하고 현재의 천장 조명을 옛날식 상들리에로 교체하는 작업을 하는 올겨울 동안 대연회장을 폐쇄할 계획이라고 말했으므로 (D) It will be renovated soon. 이 정답이다.

27. 기사에 따르면, 그래슬리 씨에게 무엇이 힘들었는가?
(A) 대연회장을 팔기로 결정한 것
(B) 좋은 직원을 계속 유지하려고 애쓴 것
(C) 적절한 디자인을 선정하는 것
(D) 관심 있는 구매자를 찾는 것

해설 세 번째 단락에서 그래슬리가 열정을 담은 프로젝트였어서 힘들었고 팔레 로열을 포기하고 싶지 않았지만, 결국에는 토마스 사가 이 오래된 대연회장에 새로운 활기를 줄 것이라 생각한다고 했으므로 (A) Deciding to sell the ballroom이 정답이다.

28. 다시 이름 지어진 것은 무엇인가?
(A) 자선 행사
(B) 직책
(C) 지역 사업체
(D) 도시 거리

해설 네 번째 단락에서 팔레 로열은 연례 자선행사를 계속 주최할 것이고 홍보 자선 행사라고 불릴 것이라고 했으므로 (A) A charity event가 정답이다.

29. [1], [2], [3], [4]로 표시된 곳 중에서 다음 문장이 들어가기에 가장 적절한 곳은 어디인가?

"전통 벽지 또한 추가될 것이다."

(A) [1]
(B) [2]
(C) [3]
(D) [4]

해설 첫 번째 단락에서 회사 대표 에보니 살렘은 작업반이 시설의 원래 목조 부분을 복원하고 현재의 천장 조명을 옛날식 상들리에로 교체하는 작업을 하는 올겨울 동안 대연회장을 폐쇄할 계획이라고 말하므로 주어진 문장이 이어지기에 자연스러운 (A)가 정답이다.

라운드 더 베이스 경주

라운드 더 베이스 경주가 올해 다시 돌아와, 3월 14일로 날짜가 확정되었습니다. 매년 그렇듯이, 경로에는 절벽 전망뿐만 아니라 아름다운 바다 전망이 포함합니다. **30** 올해, 저희는 라인업에 새로 추가된 마타우리 베이를 통과해 달려 다양성을 선보일 예정입니다. **31** **33** 본 행사는 21킬로미터에 걸쳐 펼쳐집니다. 하지만, 보다 가볍게 달리는 분들을 위해 10킬로미터(10K) 달리기와 5킬로미터(5K) 달리기도 제공합니다.

참가자 전원은 경주용 번호판과 개별 물병을 받습니다. 물품 발송에는 영업일 7일이 소요되기에, 등록과 납부 마감일은 3월 4일입니다. 추가 등록도 가능하지만, 물품을 행사 당일에 수령해야 합니다.

www.roundthebays.com/register로 가셔서 오늘 등록하세요. **33** 본 경주는 50달러이며, 10K는 30달러, 5K는 20달러입니다. **32** 모든 수익금은 아름다운 해변을 청소하는 일에 사용됩니다. 문의 사항은 에릭 차베즈에게 e.chavez@roundthebays.com으로 이메일을 보내주세요.

어휘 clifftop 절벽 꼭대기 | variety 다양성, 변화 | addition 추가된 것 | lineup (행사 등의) 전체 예정표, 라인업 | stretch (어떤 지역에 걸쳐) 펼쳐지다, 이어지다 | participant 참가자 | personalized 개인 맞춤형의 | bib (스포츠 경기 때 몸에 다는) 번호판 | mail out 발송하다 | business day 영업일

수신: e.chavez@roundthebays.com
발신: dbuchanan@magmail.com
제목: 라운드 더 베이
날짜: 3월 9일

차베즈 씨에게,

33 저는 도라 뷰캐넌이고, 본 행사에서 달리는 걸로 등록했습니다. 제 카드 명세서를 확인해 보니, 전액 결제되었습니다. 그런데, 아직 제 물품을 받지 못했습니다. **34** 제 결제가 처리되었는지 확인해 주시겠어요? 제 명의 신용카드로 3월 2일에 행사 신청 및 결제를 했습니다.

제 물품을 발송하기 너무 늦었다면, 그 대신 제가 행사 때 수령하는 게 더 수월할까요?

진심으로,

도라 뷰캐넌

어휘 **credit card statement** 신용카드 명세서 | **full payment** 전액 지불[납입] | **go through** 성사[통과]되다 | **pay for** 지불[결제]하다

30. 라운드 더 베이 경주의 경로에 관해 암시된 것은 무엇인가?
(A) 매년 바뀐다.
(B) 올해는 새로운 경로다.
(C) 단축되었다.
(D) 국립공원에서 끝난다.

해설 첫 번째 공지 지문의 첫 번째 단락에서 올해, 라인업에 새로 추가된 마타우리 베이를 통과해 달려 다양성을 선보일 예정이라고 했으므로 (B) It is a new route this year. 가 정답이다.

31. 공지에서 첫 번째 단락, 네 번째 줄의 단어, "stretch"와 의미상 가장 가까운 것은
(A) (어떤 지역에) 걸치다
(B) 발달시키다
(C) 긴장시키다
(D) 만들어내다

해설 공지 첫 번째 단락에서 본 행사는 21킬로미터에 걸쳐 펼쳐집니다에서의 stretch는 '(어떤 지역에 걸쳐) 펼쳐지다'라는 의미로 쓰였으므로 보기 중 '(어떤 지역에) 걸치다'라는 의미를 가진 (A) cover가 정답이다.

32. 3월 14일에 열리는 다양한 경주에 관하여 사실인 것은 무엇인가?
(A) 경주 별 연령 요건이 다양하다.
(B) 경주 별 최대 참가자 수가 있다.
(C) 우승자에게는 상을 수여한다.
(D) 대의를 위한 돈을 마련하기 위한 것이다.

해설 공지 세 번째 단락에서 모든 수익금은 아름다운 해변을 청소하는 일에 사용된다고 했으므로 (D) They are intended to raise money for a cause. 가 정답이다.

---

33. 뷰캐넌 씨에 관하여 알 수 있는 것은?
(A) 매년 경주에 참가한다.
(B) 행사에 늦게 등록했다.
(C) 경로 설계를 도왔다.
(D) 50달러를 결제했다.

해설 첫 번째 공지 지문, 첫 번째 단락에서 본 행사는 21킬로미터에 걸쳐 펼쳐진다고 했고, 세 번째 단락에서 본 경주는 50달러이며, 10K는 30달러, 5K는 20달러라고 했는데, 두 번째 지문[이메일], 첫 번째 단락에서 저는 도라 뷰캐넌이고 본 행사에서 달리는 걸로 등록했고 제 카드 명세서를 확인해 보니, 전액 결제되었다고 했으므로 (D) She made a payment of $50. 가 정답이다.

---

34. 뷰캐넌 씨의 이메일의 목적은 무엇인가?
(A) 조건을 변경하기 위해
(B) 결제를 확인하기 위해
(C) 제안하기 위해
(D) 장소를 확인하기 위해

해설 두 번째 이메일 지문, 첫 번째 단락에서 결제 처리를 확인해 달라며 본인 명의의 신용카드로 3월 2일에 행사 신청 및 결제를 했다고 했으므로 (B) To verify a payment가 정답이다.

[35-39] 다음 경비 보고서와 이메일에 관한 문제입니다.

신 컬렉션즈 월간 경비 보고서

월	7월
제출일	8월 9일
제출자	**35 36** 코트니 플라워스
사무소장	**36** 태미 프렌치
지점명	**36** 캘리포니아

품목	날짜	비용	내용
1	7월 3일	60.51달러	**35** 클라이언트 점심 회의
2	7월 7일	201.23달러	학회 참석용 네바다행 왕복항공권
3	7월 12일	40.84달러	콜로라도행 소포
39 4	7월 18일	130.11달러	**39** 직원 생일기념 저녁 식사
5	7월 25일	52.75달러	사무용품
총액		485.44달러	

본사 선지급 수표	500.00달러
본사 지불 경비	
본사 귀속 잔액	14.56달러

어휘 **monthly** 매월의 | **expense** 경비, 비용 | **submission** 제출 | **submit** 제출하다 | **head** 책임자 | **branch** 지점 | **amount** 액수, 총액 | **return flights** 왕복항공권 | **employee** 직원 | **office supplies** 사무용품 | **advance** 사전의 | **check** 수표 | **HQ** 본사, 본부 (headquarters의 약어) | **expense** 비용 | **pay** 지불하다 | **balance due** 잔금

발신: 태미 프렌치 〈tfrench@xincollections.com〉
수신: 코트니 플라워즈 〈cflowers@xincollections.com〉
날짜: 8월 13일
제목: 경비보고서 수정 사항

코트니께,

보내주신 월간 경비 보고서를 검토했습니다. 다음 수정 사항을 요청 드립니다. 일반적으로, 저희 오하이오 본사에서는 이러한 보고서를 매월 초에 수령하는 것을 선호합니다. **38** 관리자로의 새로운 책무에 아직 적응 중이신 걸로 알고 있습니다. 하지만, 훌륭한 관리자가 되는 중요한 부분은 필수 문서 업무를 항상 잘 파악하고 있는 능력입니다.

39 그리고, 보고서에서 4번 항목을 삭제해 주시겠어요? **37** 이 비용은 본사에서 부담합니다. 지금까지 수년째 그래왔습니다. '본사 지불 경비' 항목으로 보고하시면 됩니다. 그렇게 하면, '본사 선지급 수표' 와 '본사 귀속 잔액' 총액이 바뀌게 되니, 수치를 새로 계산하셔서 새로운 금액으로 수표를 발행해 주시기를 바랍니다.

진심으로,

태미 프렌치

어휘 adjustment 수정 | look over 검토하다 | as a general rule 일반적으로, 보통 | situate 자리를 잡다 | responsibilities 책무 | stay on top of ~을 항상 잘 알고 있다 | additionally 또한, 게다가 | result in 결과가 ~가 되다 | calculate 계산하다 | figure 수치

35. 경비 보고서에 따르면, 플라워즈 씨는 7월에 무엇을 했겠는가?
(A) 사무실 수리를 했다
(B) 업무 회의에 참석했다
(C) 책을 반품했다
(D) 설문조사를 실시했다

해설 첫 번째 지문 경비 보고서 두 번째 표[품목 1]에 Client lunch meeting(클라이언트 점심 회의)이 나와 있으므로 업무 회의를 했음을 알 수 있으므로 (B) Attended a business meeting이 정답이다.

36. 플라워즈 씨와 프렌치 씨는 어디에서 일하는가?
(A) 콜로라도에서
(B) 보스턴에서
(C) 캘리포니아에서
(D) 오하이오에서

해설 첫 번째 지문 경비 보고서 첫 번째 표[지점명]에 캘리포니아라고 나와 있으므로 (C) In California가 정답이다.

37. 이메일에서 두 번째 단락, 두 번째 줄의 단어, "case"와 의미상 가장 가까운 것은
(A) 개요
(B) 약속
(C) 불만
(D) 정책

해설 두 번째 지문 이메일 두 번째 단락에서 비용은 본사에서 부담하며 지금까지 수년째 그래왔다고 하는데 여기서 case는 '실정, 사실'이라는 의미로 쓰였으므로 보기 중 '정책, 방침'을 뜻하는 (D) policy가 정답이다.

38. 이메일에 따르면, 플라워즈 씨에 관하여 사실인 것은 무엇이겠는가?
(A) 충분한 교육을 받지 못했다.
(B) 7월에 주어진 예산을 초과했다.
(C) 최근 해당 직책으로 승진했다.
(D) 서류를 늦게 제출하는 경우가 잦다.

해설 두 번째 지문 이메일 첫 번째 단락에서 관리자로의 새로운 업무에 아직 적응 중이신 걸로 알고 있지만 훌륭한 관리자가 되는 중요한 부분은 필수 문서 업무를 항상 잘 파악하고 있는 능력이라고 하여 플라워즈 씨가 최근 관리자가 되었음을 알 수 있으므로 (C) She was recently promoted to her position. 이 정답이다.

39. 이메일에 따르면, 플라워즈 씨가 보고서에 잘못 작성한 항목은 무엇인가?
(A) 배송 서비스
(B) 기념행사
(C) 항공권
(D) 사무용품

해설 첫 번째 지문 경비 보고서 두 번째 표[품목 4]에 Employee birthday dinner(직원 생일기념 저녁 식사)가 있는데, 이메일 지문 두 번째 단락에서 그리고, 보고서에서 4번 항목을 삭제해 달라고 했으므로 (B) Celebration event가 정답이다.

[40-44] 다음 공지와 문자 메시지, 이메일에 관한 문제입니다.

일정 변경 규정

40 저희 안데스 레일은 고객님이 최대한 순조로운 여행을 하실 수 있도록 돕기 위해 최선을 다합니다. 고객님의 편의를 위해, 일정은 7일 전 저희 웹사이트에 공지됩니다. 그러나, 날씨나 일정에 없던 정비와 같은 예기치 못한 상황으로 지연이나 취소가 될 수 있습니다.

일정 변경 정보를 보는 방법

41 모든 최신 기차 시각이 안데스 레일 애플리케이션에 게시되어 있으며 변경이 발생할 때마다 업데이트됩니다. 안데스 레일에서 직접 티켓을 구매하실 경우, 변경이 일어나자마자 고객님이 선택하신 연락 수단으로 즉시 알림도 보내드립니다. **42** 만약 제3의 판매자를 통해 티켓을 구매하셨을 경우, 해당 업체는 모든 변경에 대해 고객님에게 4시간 이내 업데이트를 제공하도록 연락할 의무를 가집니다.

지연이 일정 충돌을 야기할 경우
대부분의 일정 변경은 고객님의 원래 도착 시각보다 한 시간 이내로 영향을 미칩니다. 하지만, 심각한 지연이 발생하거나, 원래 예약하신 대로 여행을 완료하는 것이 불가능한 경우, 저희 고객 서비스팀에게 customerservice@andesrail.com으로 이메일을 보내주시기를 바랍니다.

환불을 받을 수 있는 경우
아주 드물지만, 저희가 고객님에게 다른 기차 편을 제공하지 못할 수

도 있습니다. 그러한 경우, 고객님께서는 전액 환불을 받으실 수 있지만, 전액 환불을 받으시려면, 고객님의 일정 변경이 다음 조건들을 충족해야 합니다:

- 고객님의 원래 도착 혹은 출발 시각이 적어도 3시간 이상 변경되었다.
  또는
- 일정 변경으로 인해 기차를 놓쳤다.

어휘 policy 규정 | convenience 편의 | unforeseen 예측하지 못한, 뜻밖의 | circumstance 환경, 상황 | delay 지연 | cancellation 취소 | immediate 즉각적인 | notification 공지 | vendor 판매자 | obligated 의무인 | excessive 지나친, 과도한 | eligible 자격이 있는 | reimbursement 환불 | accommodate 수용하다

수신: 니콜라이 클라트카스키
발신: 555-9657 (5월 9일, 오후 10:47)

42 귀하의 우앙카요행 기차가 2시간 30분 지연될 거라고 안데스 레일에서 저희에게 알렸습니다. 업데이트된 일정표는 다음과 같습니다.

출발일: 5월 10일
출발역: 리마
도착역: 우앙카요
출발 예정 시각: 오전 6:00
*신규 출발 시각: 오전 8:30
도착 예정 시각: 오후 1:45
43 ***신규 도착 시각:** 오후 4:15

어휘 itinerary 여행 일정표

발신: 니콜라이 클라트카스키
수신: 빈스 레임즈
날짜: 5월 9일
제목: 계획 변경
첨부: 분기 예상

빈스께,

우앙카요행 아침 기차가 지연될 예정이에요. **43** 그리썸 그룹 회의 진행을 맡아주실 수 있나요? 그 시간에 저는 아직 가는 중일 거예요. 저희 분기별 수익 예상 슬라이드쇼를 첨부해 드려요. **44** 그쪽 팀이 투자 성과에 대해 우려하고 있지만, 우리 회사의 신규 노트북과 스마트폰이 해외 시장에서 얼마나 성공적이었는지를 보면 만족할 거라고 생각합니다.

인사를 드리며,

니콜라이

어휘 quarterly 분기별의 | projection 예상, 예측 | en route 도중에 | attach 첨부하다 | revenue 수익, 세입 | concerned 우려하는 | performance 성과 | investment 투자 | successful 성공적인 | overseas 해외의

---

40. 안데스 레일에 관해 사실인 것은 무엇인가?
(A) 최근 새로운 웹사이트를 열었다.
(B) 열차가 자주 늦는다.
(C) 일정을 일주일 전 게시한다.
(D) 선로가 정기 점검을 받고 있다.

해설 첫 번째 지문 공지의 첫 번째 단락에서 안데스 레일은 고객님의 편의를 위해 일정을 7일 전 웹사이트에 공지한다고 하였으므로 (C) It posts schedules one week in advance. 가 정답이다.

---

41. 공지에 따르면, 안데스 레일 승객은 최신 열차 정보를 어떻게 받을 수 있는가?
(A) 약간의 요금을 지불함으로써
(B) 안데스 레일 매표소에 방문함으로써
(C) 안데스 레일 관리자에게 이야기함으로써
(D) 애플리케이션을 확인함으로써

해설 첫 번째 지문 공지의 두 번째 단락에서 모든 최신 기차 시각이 안데스 레일 애플리케이션에 게시되어 있으며 변경이 발생할 때마다 업데이트된다고 하였으므로 (D) By checking an application이 정답이다.

---

42. 클라트카스키 씨에 관해 암시된 것은 무엇인가?
(A) 환승 열차를 놓칠 것이다.
(B) 전액 환불을 받을 것이다.
(C) 안데스 레일에서 직접 티켓을 구매하지 않았다.
(D) 여행을 갈 때 안데스 레일을 자주 이용한다.

해설 첫 번째 공지 지문의 두 번째 단락에서 제3의 판매자를 통해 티켓을 구매하셨을 경우, 해당 업체는 모든 변경에 대해 고객님에게 4시간 이내에 업데이트를 제공하도록 연락할 의무를 가진다고 하였고, 두 번째 문자 메시지에서 귀하의 우앙카요행 기차가 2시간 30분 지연될 거라고 안데스 레일에서 저희에게 알렸다고 하였으므로 클라트카스키 씨가 제3의 판매자를 통해 티켓을 구매했음을 알 수 있으므로 (C) He did not purchase his ticket from Andes Rail directly. 가 정답이다.

---

43. 그리썸 그룹 회의에 관하여 무엇이 사실이겠는가?
(A) 오후 4시 15분 전에 시작할 것이다.
(B) 클라트카스키 씨가 진행할 것이다.
(C) 리마에서 열릴 것이다.
(D) 연기될 것이다.

해설 두 번째 문자 메시지 지문에서 New Arrival Time(신규 도착 시간)이 오후 4시 15분이라고 하였는데, 세 번째 이메일 지문에서 그리썸 그룹 회의 진행을 맡아주실 수 있을지, 그 시간에 아직 가는 중일 거라고 하였으므로, 회의가 기차 도착 시각 전에 시작할 것임을 알 수 있으므로 (A) It will start before 4:15 P.M. 이 정답이다.

---

44. 클라트카스키 씨는 어떤 사업에 종사하겠는가?
(A) 여행사
(B) 투자회사
(C) 전자기기 제조사
(D) 철도회사

해설 세 번째 이메일 지문에서 그쪽 팀이 투자성과에 대해 우려하고 있지만, 우리 회사의 신규 노트북과 스마트폰이 해외 시장에서 얼마나 성공적이었는지를 보면 만족할 거라고 생각한다고 하였으므로 (C) An electronics maker가 정답이다.

[45-49] 다음 광고와 이메일, 웹페이지 피드백에 관한 문제입니다.

빈센조 드림 투어
로마, 이탈리아

47 빈센조 드림 투어는 모든 이용 가능 투어에 대해 여름 마무리 20% 할인을 제공함을 알려 드리게 되어 기쁩니다. 이 할인은 8월 1일 전에 완료한 예약에만 유효하므로, 서두르세요. **45** 저희가 왜 〈로마 레저 매거진〉에서 이탈리아 최고의 투어 회사로 뽑혔는지 경험해 보세요.

저희의 가장 인기 있는 투어는 다음과 같습니다:

- **캄파니아 지역 (2일 투어):** 고대 도시 폼페이를 거닐며 로마 제국의 삶은 어땠는지 느껴보세요. 그러고 나서, 베수비오산에 올라 이 도시를 파괴한 화산을 가까이에서 살펴보십시오. 다음에는, 아말피 해안의 좁은 절벽 길을 따라 드라이브를 하며 숨이 막힐 정도로 아름다운 경관을 즐겨보세요.

- **가르가노와 트레미티섬 (3일 투어):** 이 투어는 자연을 사랑하는 사람들을 위한 투어입니다. 가르가노반도에는 모래사장과 낭만적인 자연 오솔길, 그리고 우거진 초목이 있습니다. 이 투어에서 포레스타 움브라로 저녁 하이킹을, 트레미티섬 주변에서 보트 타기와 수영을, 그리고 유네스코 세계 유산인 몬테 산탄젤로로의 방문을 즐겨보세요.

- **바티칸 시티 (1일 투어):** 성 베드로 광장과 시스틴 성당, 바티칸 박물관에서 세계적인 예술, 건축 걸작품들을 만나보세요. 저녁 투어도 가능합니다.

46 단체인원이 있는 조직의 요청 시, 개별 패키지 또한 가능합니다.

어휘 valid 유효한 | operator (특정 사업을 하는) 회사 | ancient 고대의 | empire 제국 | up-close 바로 가까이에서 | destroy 파괴하다 | breathtaking 숨이 막힐 듯한 | cliff 절벽 | peninsula 반도 | feature ~을 특징으로 하다 | lush 무성한, 우거진 | vegetation 초목 | artistic 예술적인 | architectural 건축의 | masterpiece 걸작 | private 개인의

수신: tlorenz@hotspot.com
발신: info@vincenzosdream.com
47 제목: 예약 영수증
48 날짜: 7월 25일

로렌츠 씨에게,

귀하의 투어 패키지를 위한 영수증입니다. 모든 정보가 정확한지 다시 한번 확인해 주십시오.

---

49 투어 패키지: 캄파니아 지역	
시작일 및 시간:	8월 7일 오전 8시
종료일 및 시간:	8월 8일 오후 8시
총액:	215유로

실수가 있거나 질문이 있으실 경우, 저희 고객 서비스 상담원들이 귀하를 도와드릴 수 있습니다. cs@vincenzosdream.com으로 이메일을 보내시거나 +39 (06) 5555 8294번으로 전화해 주십시오.

저희 회사를 이용해 주셔서 감사드리며 곧 뵙길 기대합니다!

어휘 appreciate 감사하다

투어 후기

역사를 좋아하는 사람으로서 저는 이탈리아에 가고 싶었습니다. **48** 이 투어는 저의 모든 기대를 충족했어요. **49** 저희 투어가이드였던 잔 리치는 아주 준비가 잘 되어 있었고 호감 가는 분이었습니다. 그는 이 지역에서 자랐기 때문에, 대부분의 방문객이 알지 못하는 곳으로 데려가 주셨죠. 매우 박식하셨고 이 지역의 건축과 전통, 문화에 관련된 저의 모든 질문에 정확하게 답변해 주셨습니다. 이 투어를 모두에게 추천하겠습니다.

태미 로렌츠의 후기

어휘 expectation 기대, 예상 | engaging 호감이 가는, 매력적인 | knowledgeable 아는 것이 많은 | respond 반응하다 | accurately 정확하게

---

45. 빈센조 드림 투어에 관해 알 수 있는 것은 무엇인가?
(A) 목적지를 더 추가했다.
(B) 여름에만 운영한다.
(C) 높은 평가를 받는 회사이다.
(D) 다른 유럽 도시들에도 지점을 열 것이다.

해설 첫 번째 광고 지문 첫 번째 단락에서 저희가 왜 〈로마 레저 매거진〉에서 이탈리아 최고의 투어 회사로 뽑혔는지 경험해 보라고 하였으므로 (C) It is a highly rated business. 가 정답이다.

---

46. 광고에 따르면, 빈센조 드림 투어는 고객들에게 무엇을 제공할 수 있는가?
(A) 회원이 많은 단체 대상의 독점 투어
(B) 첫 고객들을 위한 특별 할인
(C) 기념품점에서 제공하는 무료 선물
(D) 현지 공항에서의 교통 서비스

해설 첫 번째 광고 지문 여섯 번째 단락에서 단체인원이 있는 조직의 요청 시, 개별 패키지 또한 가능하다고 했으므로 (A) Exclusive tours for groups with many members가 정답이다.

---

47. 로렌츠 씨의 투어에 관해 암시된 것은 무엇인가?
(A) 3일간 지속될 것이다.
(B) 매일의 식사가 포함된다.

(C) 더 싼 가격에 예약되었다.

(D) 가족을 위해 특별히 설계되었다.

해설 첫 번째 광고 지문 첫 번째 단락에서 빈센조 드림 투어는 모든 이용 가능 투어에 대해 여름 마무리 20% 할인을 제공함을 알려드리게 되어 기쁘며, 이 할인은 8월 1일 전에 완료한 예약에만 유효하므로 서두르라고 하였고, 두 번째 이메일 지문의 Subject와 Date에서 7월 25일 투어 예약을 했으므로, 할인된 가격에 투어 예약을 했음을 알 수 있다. 따라서, (C) It was booked at a lower rate. 가 정답이다.

---

48. 웹페이지 피드백에서, 첫 번째 줄의 단어 "met"와 의미상 가장 가까운 것은

(A) 준수했다

(B) 합류했다

(C) 만족했다

(D) 행했다

해설 세 번째 웹페이지 피드백 지문 첫 번째 줄에서 이 투어는 저의 모든 기대를 충족했다고 하는데 여기서 met은 '충족했다'는 의미로 쓰였으므로 보기 중 같은 의미를 갖는 (C) satisfied가 정답이다.

---

49. 리치 씨에 관해 암시된 것은 무엇인가?

(A) 지역 잡지사에서 일한다.

(B) 캄파니아 출신이다.

(C) 대학생이다.

(D) 다수의 언어를 구사한다.

해설 두 번째 이메일 지문 표의 첫 번째 항목 투어 패키지에서 여행 지역이 캄파니아 지역이라는 것을 알 수 있고, 세 번째 웹페이지 지문 세 번째 문장에서 저희 투어가이드였던 잔 리치는 아주 준비가 잘 되어 있었고 호감 가는 분이었고 이 지역에서 자랐다고 했으므로 (B) He is a native of Campania. 가 정답이다.

[50-54] 다음 매장 행사와 이메일들에 관한 문제입니다.

뷔르펠 공급회사

저희는 여러분이 필요로 하는 모든 일회용 컵, 빨대와 뚜껑을 보유한 바타타운 최고의 도매업체입니다.

오늘 주문하고 돈을 절약하세요

특별 할인 행사의 일부로, **50** 신규 고객은 아래 열거된 할인을 받으실 수 있습니다.

● 50달러 이상 구매 시 5달러 할인

● 150달러 이상 구매 시 15달러 할인

● **52** 250달러 이상 구매 시 30달러 할인

● 300달러 이상 구매 시 50달러 할인

250달러 이상 구매 시 배송비도 면제됩니다.

할인을 받으시려면, 이 페이지 하단에 있는 코드를 이용하세요. 혜택은 7월 31일까지 유효합니다.

46EUEEEE

*한 번만 사용할 수 있는 코드입니다. 일부 제한이 있을 수 있습니다.

어휘 wholesale 도매의, 대량의 | disposable 일회용의 | straw 빨대 | lid 뚜껑 | promotion 할인 행사 | eligible for ~할 자격이 되는 | waive 면제하다 | single-use 한 번만 사용할 수 있는 | restriction 제한 | apply 적용하다

수신: customerservice@wuerfelsupplyco.nz

발신: nbrie@dawsoncatering.com.nz

날짜: 7월 19일

제목: 주문번호 37991

관계자분께,

저는 며칠 전 500ml 커피 컵과 빨대 한 상자를 주문했습니다. **51** 행사에서 안내한 대로, 프로모션 코드(46EUEEEE)를 입력했습니다. **51 52** 그리고 배송비는 면제되었지만, 광고하신 30달러 할인은 받지 못했습니다. **51** 저희 회사 계좌로 그 금액을 송금해 주실 수 있나요?

이 문제를 제외하면, 사무실 모두가 컵의 품질, 특히 컵의 내부 내열 처리가 뛰어나서 매우 좋아했습니다. 어쨌든, 환불을 받고 나면, 또 주문을 할 계획입니다. 성장하는 케이터링 업체로서, 저희는 자주 이 물품들을 보충해야 할 것입니다. 귀하의 웹사이트에서 월간 배송을 제공한다는 것을 봤습니다. **54** 매달 첫 화요일이나 목요일이 저희에게는 이상적입니다. 이 날짜가 일정에 맞으시나요?

인사를 드리며,

노라 브리

도슨 케이터링 운영팀

어휘 enter 입력하다 | direct 지시하다, 안내하다 | advertise 광고하다 | wire 송금하다 | appreciate 인정하다, 감사하다 | heatproof 내열의 | lining 내벽, 안감 | reimbursement 변제, 상환 | catering 케이터링(행사·연회 등을 대상으로 하는) 음식 공급, 음식 공급업 | restock 다시 채우다, 보충하다 | frequently 자주 | ideal 이상적인

수신: nbrie@dawsoncatering.com.nz

발신: mmaron@wuerfelsupplyco.nz

날짜: 7월 19일

제목: 회신: 주문번호 37991

브리 씨에게,

시간을 내어 이 문제를 저희에게 알려주셔서 감사드립니다. 귀하의 구매에 할인을 적용해 드리지 못해 죄송합니다. 이미 환불 처리를 해드렸습니다. **53** 보상의 의미로, 커피 컵과 빨대 추가 한 세트도 무료로 보내드릴 것입니다. 소포는 이번 주 내로 받아보실 수 있을 겁니다.

그리고 정기 배송 일정을 정하는 것도 도와드릴 수 있습니다. **54** 저희 배송기사들이 이미 매달 첫 수, 목, 금요일에 귀하의 지역으로 배달을 하고 있으므로, 귀하를 저희 배송 일정에 포함해 드릴 수 있습니다. 원하신다면 바로 다음 달부터 시작 가능합니다.

최근의 부주의에 다시 한번 사과드리며, 계속 거래해 주셔서 감사드립니다. 귀하의 미래 필요 사항에도 저희가 부응할 수 있기를 기대합니다.

인사를 드리며,

마커스 마론, 고객서비스팀

어휘　attention 주의, 관심 | apologize 사과하다 |
compensation 보상 | arrange 주선하다 | regular 정기
적인 | route 노선 | recent 최근의 | oversight 실수, 간과

---

50. 혜택에 관해 알 수 있는 것은 무엇인가?
(A) 7월 31일 전에 만료된다.
(B) 한 가지 제품에만 유효하다.
(C) 소규모 기업에는 해당하지 않는다.
(D) 신규 고객을 위한 것이다.

해설　첫 번째 매장 행사 지문에서 신규 고객은 아래 열거된 할인을 받으실 수 있다고 했으므로 (D) It is for first-time customers. 가 정답이다.

---

51. 첫 번째 이메일은 왜 발송되었는가?
(A) 주문 수량을 수정하기 위해
(B) 손상을 지적하기 위해
(C) 요금 청구 실수를 알리기 위해
(D) 건물에 찾아가는 방법을 물어보기 위해

해설　두 번째 이메일 지문 첫 번째 단락의 행사에서 안내한 대로, 프로모션 코드(46EUEEEE)를 입력했고 배송비는 면제되었지만, 광고하신 30달러 할인은 받지 못했는데 저희 회사 계좌로 그 금액을 송금해 주실 수 있을지 물으므로 (C) To bring attention to a billing mistake가 정답이다.

---

52. 브리 씨는 뷔르펠 공급회사에 얼마를 지불했는가?
(A) 50달러 이상
(B) 150달러 이상
(C) 250달러 이상
(D) 500달러 이상

해설　두 번째 이메일 지문 첫 번째 단락에서 배송비는 면제되었지만, 광고하신 30달러 할인은 받지 못했다고 하였고, 첫 번째 매장 행사 지문에서 $30 off purchases over $250(250달러 이상 구매 시 30달러 할인)에 미루어 브리 씨가 30달러 할인을 받을 수 있는 기준 금액인 250달러 이상을 지불했음을 알 수 있으므로 (C) Over $250이 정답이다.

---

53. 두 번째 이메일에서, 마론 씨는 브리 씨에게 무엇을 제공하는가?
(A) 무료 제품
(B) 속달 배송
(C) 할인 쿠폰
(D) 회원 카드

해설　세 번째 이메일 지문 첫 번째 단락에서 보상의 의미로, 커피 컵과 빨대 추가 한 세트도 무료로 보내드릴 것이라고 하였으므로 (A) Complimentary items가 정답이다.

---

54. 뷔르펠 공급회사는 도슨 케이터링에 언제 배달을 하겠는가?
(A) 매달 첫 번째 화요일
(B) 매달 첫 번째 수요일
(C) 매달 첫 번째 목요일
(D) 매달 첫 번째 금요일

해설　두 번째 지문인 이메일 두 번째 단락에서 매달 첫 화요일이나 목요일이 저희에게는 이상적인데 이 날짜가 일정에 맞는지 물었고, 세 번째 지문 두 번째 단락에서 저희 배송기사들이 이미 매달 첫 수, 목, 금요일에 귀하의 지역으로 배달하고 있으므로, 귀하를 저희 배송 일정에 포함해 드릴 수 있다고 했으므로, 도슨 케이터링이 배송을 원하는 화, 목요일 중 뷔르펠 공급회사가 해당 지역으로 배송할 수 있는 요일은 목요일임을 알 수 있다. 따라서, (C) The first Thursday of the month가 정답이다.

MEMO

MEMO